THE GEOGRAPHY OF TOURISM AND RECREATION

Environment, Place and Space

Second edition

C. Michael Hall and Stephen J. Page

London and New York

First published 1999
by Routledge
11 New Fetter Lane, London EC4P 4EE

Simultaneously published in the USA and Canada
by Routledge
29 West 35th Street, New York, NY 10001

Second edition 2002

Routledge is an imprint of the Taylor & Francis Group

Typeset in Sabon by Keystroke, Jacaranda Lodge, Wolverhampton
Printed and bound in Great Britain by Bell & Bain Ltd, Glasgow

British Library Cataloguing in Publication Data
A catalogue record for this book is available from the British Library

Library of Congress Cataloging in Publication Data
Hall, Colin Michael
The geography of tourism and recreation : environment, place and space / C.M. Hall and
S.J. Page.—2nd ed.
p. cm.
Includes bibliographical references (p.).
1. Tourism. 2. Recreation. 3. Recreation areas. I. Title: Geography of tourism and
recreation. II. Page, Stephen. III. Title.
G155.A1 H343 2001
338.4′791—dc21
2001052026

ISBN 0–415–25080–3 (hbk)
ISBN 0–415–25081–1 (pbk)

THE GEOGRAPHY OF TOURISM AND RECREATION

The fully updated second edition of *The Geography of Tourism and Recreation* continues to be a comprehensive and accessible introduction to tourism, leisure and recreation. It not only introduces landmark studies and recent contributions to geographers' expanding interest in how people spend their leisure time, but also seeks to illustrate how recreation and tourism phenomena are seemingly separate and yet integrated aspects of the wider leisure phenomenon. Each chapter offers a distinctive series of insights into how the geographer has approached the analysis of tourism and recreation. New perspectives from human geography are considered, such as the new cultural geographies and gender studies, and this collaboration with other disciplines gives different aspects to explanations of the tourism and recreation phenomena. A range of chapters explore:

- the demand for recreation and tourism;
- the supply of recreation and tourism;
- the impacts of recreation and tourism;
- recreation and tourism in urban, rural and coastal environments;
- recreation and tourism in wilderness areas and national parks;
- recreation and tourism policy and planning;
- the future of recreation and tourism and the role of geography in applied research.

The Geography of Tourism and Recreation remains the only book in the field systematically to compare and contrast tourism and recreation, in relation to the use of leisure time in a spatial context. The second edition has been substantially revised and updated, with new case study material to reflect the new research agendas being engaged in by geographers and non-geographers concerned with space. Summary points and questions are included to encourage discussion among readers. The text is well illustrated with plates, maps and diagrams to highlight international examples that address key concepts and issues in tourism and recreation research in Australasia, Europe, North America and Asia-Pacific.

C. Michael Hall is Professor of Tourism in the Department of Tourism, University of Otago, New Zealand.
Stephen J. Page is Scottish Enterprise Forth Valley Chair in Tourism at the University of Stirling, Scotland.

CONTENTS

PLATES

FIGURES

TABLES

ACKNOWLEDGEMENTS

The purpose of this book is to provide an account of the growth, development and changes that are occurring within the geography of tourism and recreation. A purpose made all the more interesting because it is written by two geographers who, at the time this manuscript was completed, did not work in geography departments. While the book covers a lot of material, the authors acknowledge that there are a number of significant areas which have not been fully covered, and could not be unless the book was almost twice its size and more encyclopaedic than some of the reviewers of the first edition noted!

To a great extent this book concentrates on the developed world. However, it is not a discussion solely of Anglo-North American geography, as this would neglect the substantial contribution of geographers from Australia, New Zealand and the South Pacific; rather it deals with the literature on the geography of tourism and recreation in English. This is not to deny the substantial research base that European geographers have in tourism and recreation (see Chapter 1). But, with a small number of significant exceptions, such as Doug Pearce in New Zealand who has introduced much of the European literature to North America and Australasia (e.g. Pearce 1989), the majority of English-speaking geographers have developed most of their work in tourism and recreation in isolation from the European experience.

This book therefore serves to identify many of the major concerns and interests of geographers in the fields of tourism and recreation. There is clearly a substantial body of work in the subdiscipline. However, as the book also notes, the field is not seen as seriously as perhaps it should be; a conclusion with substantial implications not only for the further development of the subdiscipline but also for the growth of Tourism Studies as a separate field of academic endeavour. Indeed, the book observes that we are in a time of transformation and change in terms of a better positioning of tourism and recreation issues within the contemporary concerns of social theory and human geography, while simultaneously also having increased demands to be more 'applied' with respect to industry and tourism education. The second edition has been thoroughly revised, updated and expanded within the very tight constraints of space. At a time of rapid growth in tourism- and recreation-related literature by geographers, this was more than a challenge. For that reason, many of the seminal and leading studies which have been incorporated where space permits are reflected in the expanded bibliography.

Stephen Page would like to acknowledge a number of people who made this book possible. Massey University's very helpful and congenial library staff and the enormous number of journal articles and books they supplied have helped make this second edition a more reflective and integrated text which is hopefully able to accommodate some of the debates and issues which colleagues and researchers have raised. A number of people have also contributed ideas and the time to discuss themes and offer hospitality including: Martin Oppermann, Simon Milne, Charles Johnston, Pip Forer, Doug Pearce, Tom Hinch, Graham and Frances Busby, and Kevin Woo. Tim Bentley and Michael Barker, both former Postdoctoral Researchers in Tourism at Massey University, provided a welcome source of intellectual stimulation and focus for research-oriented issues. Roy Wood at the Scottish Hotel School also provided his usual hospitality and critical perspective on tourism and hospitality research which was invaluable. Of course no mention would be complete without Rosemary, who let me drag her around all those tourist and recreational sites in 1996, 1998 and 1999. She always knew geographers were odd! Also, thanks to Stephen Williams, Staffordshire University for engendering my early interest in the geography of leisure and recreation and for permission to reproduce material from his *Recreation and the Urban Environment* text.

Other people who have had a very formative effect for both authors are Professor Tony Vitalis, Robin Smith and the Department of Management Systems at Massey University at Palmerston North; and the Faculty of Commerce and Administration at Victoria University of Wellington.

Michael would like to thank Bill Bramwell, Dimitrios Buhalis, Dick Butler, Cate Clark, Chris Cooper, Nicola Costley, Dave Crag, Ross Dowling, Ian Dutton, Thor Flognfeldt, Atsuko Hashimoto, James Higham, Tom Hinch, John Jenkins, Linda Kell, Neil Leiper, Alan Lew, Niki Macionis, Steve Mark, Simon McArthur, Richard Mitchell, Dieter Müeller, Meiko Muramaya, Peter Murphy, John Pigram, Greg Richards, Chris Ryan, John Selwood, Liz Sharples, Valene Smith, John Swarbrooke, David Telfer, Dallen Timothy, Lesley Tipping, Geoff Wall, Jim Walmesley, Allan Williams and Bernie Walsh, who have all contributed in various ways to some of the ideas contained within, although the interpretation of their thoughts is, of course, my own.

Gavin Bryars, Jeff Buckley, Nick Cave, Bruce Cockburn, Elvis Costello, Stephen Cummings, The Sundays, Ed Kuepper, Neil and Tim Finn, Sarah McLachlan and David Sylvian also helped ensure that the book was completed. Frances Cadogan and the administrative staff of the Department of Tourism also proved extremely helpful in assisting this book to completion along with the kind assistance of Donna Keen and Angela Smith. Ingrid Van Aalst, Chris Daly, John Jenkins, Simon McArthur, Carleen and Richard Mitchell, Jacqui Pinkava, David Press, and especially Jody Cowper, provided much appreciated moral support which, as usual, will be repaid with food, wine and services rendered. Finally, he would like to thank Jody for coping with yet another book and having yet more tourism experiences damaged by analysis. He hopes that the amount of leisure time will increase in the future as opposed to its analysis although, with the current state of higher education, he is not entirely certain of this prospect.

Finally, the authors would like to express their appreciation to Andrew Mould and Ann Michael at Routledge for their continued interest in the project.

C. Michael Hall   Stephen J. Page
City Rise   Stirling

PERMISSIONS

A number of organisations and bodies have provided the authors with permission to reproduce material in the book and they wish to express their thanks to them. Plates 5.3, 5.4 and 5.5 provided by the former London Docklands Development Corporation are reproduced with permission from English Partnerships. The Office for National Statistics has been particularly helpful and willing to allow permission to reproduce a number of tables and figures from *Social Trends* (2000) and *Regional Trends* for the years 1996, 1999 and 2000 which certainly convey the statistical elements of recreational and tourism demand within the UK and remain an invaluable source for researchers. The material is reproduced in Tables 2.4, 2.5, 2.6, 2.7, 2.8, 2.9, 2.10 and Figure 2.5. The Geographical Association provided permission to redraw Figure 2.8 (although it is a pity they feel the need to charge such high copyright fees when much of the work of the GA relies on goodwill and contributions from geographers who receive no payment); Routledge kindly agreed to allow Stephen J. Page to reproduce material from his *Urban Tourism* book for the first edition of this publication. Likewise, the authors are grateful to Routledge for permission to reproduce other material from their publications including Pacione's *Applied Geography: Principles and Practice* (particularly Figure 10.1 and Table 9.2) and Pigram and Jenkins' *Outdoor Recreation Management*. Routledge also gave permission to reproduce Figures 2.1, 2.10 and 2.12. Carolyn Harrison for permission to reproduce the map of leisure and recreation provision in the London Borough of Havering on behalf of the TML Partnership publishing house (Figure 3.2).

Channel View Publications, the publishers of the *Journal of Sustainable Tourism* consented to the use of tables from Bahaire and Elliott-White's article on geographical information systems in sustainable tourism planning (Tables 10.2 and 10.3); The Countryside Agency provided the source for the spatial distribution of protected areas in the UK (Figure 9.1) and the help of Lisa Hooper is greatly appreciated.

The Planner kindly agreed to the use of Figure 2.9; Addison Wesley Longman (now Pearson Education) for permission to reproduce material from numerous sources, including Figures 2.11 and 5.8 and Tables 3.1, 3.2 and 3.3. The National Recreation Park Association in the USA provided permission to reproduce Table 2.1 from the *Journal of Leisure Research*; Taylor & Francis gave permission to use Figure 2.3 from Crawford, Jackson and Godbey's 'Hierarchical model of leisure' published in *Leisure Sciences*; John Wiley & Sons for Tables 2.2, 3.5 and Figure 2.13; David Fulton Publishers for Figure 5.6; International Thomson Business Publishing (now Thomson Learning) for Figures 6.4 and 6.5 and Tables 5.1, 5.2 and 5.3; Travel and Tourism Intelligence for the use of Figure 6.3 which is duly acknowledged. E & FN Spon for Table 2.3; The Johns Hopkins University Press for the use of Table 3.3. The Royal Dutch Geographical Society for permission to reproduce Madge's map from *Tijdscrift voor Economische en Sociale Geografie* (Figure 5.3) courtesy of Blackwell. Similarly, Blackwell allowed permission to reproduce Table 3.4; Elsevier Science provided permission to reproduce Tables 10.5 and 10.6 and Figure 3.5.

Leicester City Council's Legal Services Department also consented to the use of Figure 5.2. The London Borough of Newham allowed use of the Unitary Development Plan, adopted 9 June 1997, to compile the maps of urban space provision in the borough (Figure 5.4). Macmillan Press Ltd (now Palgrave) consented to the use of materials from I. Henry's *Management and Planning in the Leisure Industries*. Finally, thanks are due to James Higham, Centre for Tourism, University of Otago for permission to use Tables 7.6 and 7.7 from his Ph.D. thesis and Simon McArthur for permission to use Tables 4.3 and 4.4.

If any unintentional use of copyright material has been made in this book, the authors would be grateful if copyright owners could contact them via the publishers. Every effort has been made to trace the owners of copyright material.

1

INTRODUCTION
Tourism Matters!

> Geographical knowledge is more important than ever in an increasingly global and interconnected world. How can a graduate claim to be a learned scholar without any understanding of geography?
> (Susan Cutter, President of the Association of American Geographers (2000: 2))

Tourism is widely recognised as the world's largest industry. The figures on the size and significance of tourism are staggering. For example, according to the World Tourism Organisation (WTO 1996), in 1995:

- World tourist arrivals reached 567 million.
- More than 360 million passengers were carried on international air services, an increase of 5 per cent over the preceding year.
- International tourism receipts (excluding international transport) increased by 7.2 per cent between 1994 and 1995 to US$372 billion. International fare receipts in 1995 were estimated at US$60 billion.
- Tourism receipts represented more than 8 per cent of the world merchandise exports and one-third of world trade in services.

Five years on the figures were even more incredible (WTO 2001):

- World tourism arrivals were estimated to have reached 698.3 million.
- World tourism grew by an estimated 7.4 per cent – its highest growth rate in nearly a decade and almost double the increase of 1999.
- Receipts from international tourism climbed to

US$476 billion, an increase of 4.5 per cent over the previous year.

However, tourism, tourists and their impacts, are clearly not evenly distributed. Substantial differentiation occurs at a variety of international, regional and local scales. For example, to continue the snapshot from 2000 (WTO 2001):

- All regions of the world hosted more tourists in 2000, although the fastest developing area continued to be East Asia and the Pacific with a growth rate of 14.5 per cent and some 14 million more tourists than in 1999.
- Europe, which accounts for 58 per cent of international tourism, grew by 6.2 per cent to 403 million arrivals, nearly 25 million more trips than one year earlier.
- Despite the strong dollar, the United States achieved a growth rate of 8.7 per cent in international tourism arrivals.
- Africa increased its international arrivals by 1.5 per cent – its poorest growth rate ever. While Kenya, Zambia, Mauritius, Morocco, Tunisia and Algeria all enjoyed strong growth, international arrivals to South Africa and Zimbabwe, two of Africa's biggest destinations, stagnated.

Yet tourism is also highly dynamic and is strongly influenced by economic, political, social, environmental and technological change. For example, following the dramatic downturn in a number of South-East Asian economies in the second half of 1997 and early 1998, the WTO revised its outbound figures for intraregional travel in the East Asia Pacific (EAP) region from a previous estimate for 1998 of 8 per cent growth to a revised estimate of there being no growth, while in terms of travel from EAP countries to outside the region the change was from an original estimate of 6.3 per cent growth to a fall of 2 per cent. In addition, of great significance in terms of outbound tourism and the overall competitiveness of some international tourism destinations is the extent to which the devaluation of some Asian currencies has served to attract tourists (WTO 1998; Hall and Page 2000).

At a global level the World Travel and Tourism Council (WTTC 2000), using a tourism satellite accounting system, have measured that, directly and indirectly, the travel and tourism industry constitutes: 11 per cent of global GDP (US$3,575 billion); supports 200 million jobs worldwide; 8 per cent of total employment or 1 in every 12.4 jobs. By 2010, the travel and tourism economic contribution is estimated to grow to 11.6 per cent (US$6,591 billion) of global GDP and will support 250 million jobs, 9 per cent of total employment or 1 in every 11 jobs. More recently, the WTTC (2001a) estimated that by 2011, the travel and tourism economy will constitute: 11.0 per cent of global GDP; support 260,417,000 jobs worldwide, 9 per cent of total employment or 1 in 11.2 jobs.

The immediate economic significance of such figures is to be seen not only in tourist destination and tourist generating areas but also in those destinations from which tourists switch their travel in order to take advantage of cheap prices. However, changes in the international tourism market will also be related to domestic holiday travel, as consumers can switch their travel plans not only between international destinations but also between domestic and international destinations. Tourism, as with other forms of economic activity, therefore reflects the increasing interconnectedness of the international economy. Indeed, by its very nature in terms of connections between generating areas, destinations and travel routes or paths, tourism is perhaps a phenomenon which depends more than

most not only on transport, service and trading networks but also on social, political and environmental relationships between the consumers and producers of the tourist experience. Such issues are clearly of interest to geographers. For example, according to Mitchell (1979: 237), in his discussion of the contributions that geography can make to the investigation of tourism:

> The geographer's point-of-view is a trilogy of biases pertaining to place, environment and relationships. . . . In a conceptual vein the geographer has traditionally claimed the spatial and chorographic aspects as his realm. . . . The geographer, therefore, is concerned about earth space in general and about place and places in particular. The description, appreciation, and understanding of places is paramount to his thinking although two other perspectives (i.e. environment and relationships) modify and extend the primary bias of place.

Yet despite the global significance of tourism and the potential contribution that geography can make to the analysis and understanding of tourism, the position of tourism and recreation studies within geography is not strong. However, within the fields of tourism and recreation studies outside mainstream academic geography, geographers have made enormous contributions to the understanding of tourism and recreation phenomena. It is therefore within this somewhat paradoxical situation that this book is being written, while the contribution of geography and geographers is widely acknowledged and represented in tourism and recreation departments and journals, relatively little recognition is given to the significance of tourism and recreation in geography departments, journals, non-tourism and recreation-specific geography texts, and within other geography subdisciplines. This book therefore seeks to explain how this situation has developed, indicate the breadth and depth of geographical research on tourism and recreation, and suggest ways in which the overall standing of research and scholarship by geographers on tourism and recreation may be improved.

This first chapter is divided into several sections. First, it examines the relationship between tourism and recreation. Second, it provides an overview of the development of various approaches to the study of tourism and recreation within geography. Finally, it outlines the approach of this book towards the geography of tourism and recreation.

THE RELATIONSHIP BETWEEN TOURISM AND RECREATION

Tourism, recreation and leisure are generally seen as a set of interrelated and overlapping concepts. While there are many important concepts, definitions of leisure, recreation and tourism remain contested in terms of how, where, when and why they are used. In a review of the meaning of leisure, Stockdale (1985) identified three main ways in which the concept of leisure is used:

1 as a period of time, activity or state of mind in which choice is the dominant feature; in this sense leisure is a form of 'free time' for an individual;
2 an objective view in which leisure is perceived as the opposite of work and is defined as non-work or residual time;
3 a subjective view which emphasises leisure as a qualitative concept in which leisure activities take on a meaning only within the context of individual perceptions and belief systems and can therefore occur at any time in any setting.

According to Herbert (1988), leisure is therefore best seen as time over which an individual exercises choice and undertakes activities in a free, voluntary way.

Leisure activities are of considerable interest to geographers (e.g. Lavery 1975; Patmore 1977, 1978, 1979, 1980; Coppock 1982; Herbert 1987). Traditional approaches to the study of leisure by geographers focused on leisure in terms of activities. In contrast, Glyptis (1981a) argued for the adoption of the concept of leisure lifestyles which emphasised the importance of individual perceptions of leisure.

> This allows the totality of an individual's leisure experiences to be considered and is a subjective approach which shifts the emphasis from activity to

people, from aggregate to individual and from expressed activities to the functions which these fulfill for the participant and the social and locational circumstances in which he or she undertakes them.
> (Herbert 1988: 243)

Such an experiential approach towards leisure has been extremely influential. For example, Featherstone (1987: 115) argued that 'The significance and meaning of a particular set of leisure choices . . . can only be made intelligible by inscribing them on a map of the class-defined social field of leisure and lifestyle practices in which their meaning and significance is relationally defined with reference to structured oppositions and differences'. Similarly, such an experiential definition of leisure was used by Shaw and Williams (1994) in their critical examination of tourism from a geographical perspective.

However, while such a phenomenological approach to defining leisure, and therefore tourism and recreation, is valuable in highlighting the social context in which leisure is both defined and occurs, such an approach will clearly be at odds with 'objective', technical approaches towards definitions which can be applied in a variety of situations and circumstances (see Chapter 2). Yet it should be emphasised that such definitions are being used for different purposes. A universally accepted definition of leisure, tourism and recreation is an impossibility. Definitions will change according to their purpose and context. They are setting the 'rules of the game' or 'engagement' for discussion, argument and research. By defining terms we give meaning to what we are doing.

Even given the subjective nature of leisure, however, at a larger scale it may still be possible to aggregate individual perceptions and activities to provide a collective or commonly held impression of the relationship between leisure, tourism and recreation. In this sense, tourism and recreation are generally regarded as subsets of the wider concept of leisure (Coppock 1982; Murphy 1985; Herbert 1988). In the wider context of geography, Johnston (1985a: 10) argued that 'Academic disciplines exist to maintain, further and promote knowledge', and this is certainly the case in tourism and recreational geography.

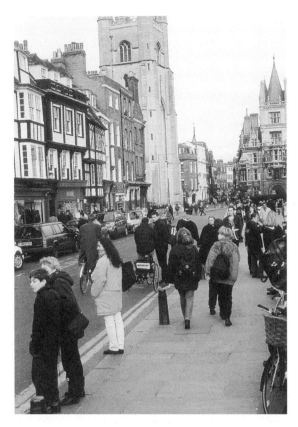

Plate 1.1: Which of the people in this Cambridge High Street scene are tourists or recreationalists? Researchers need to carefully differentiate between recreationalists and tourists.

Figure 1.1 illustrates the relationship between leisure, recreation and tourism. As Parker (1999: 21) eloquently explained, 'It is through studying leisure as a whole that the most powerful explanations are developed. This is because society is not divided into sports players, television viewers, tourists and so on. It is the same people who do all these things.' This indicates the value of viewing tourism and recreation as part of a wider concept of leisure. Broken lines are used to illustrate that the boundaries between the concepts are 'soft'. Work is differentiated from leisure with there being two main realms of overlap: first, business travel, which is seen as a work-oriented form of tourism in order to differentiate it from leisure-based travel;

second, serious leisure, which refers to the breakdown between leisure and work pursuits and the development of leisure career paths with respect to their hobbies and interests (Stebbins 1979). As Stebbins (1982: 253) observed:

> leisure in postindustrial society is no longer seen as chiefly a means of recuperating from the travail of the job. . . . If leisure is to become, for many, an improvement over work as a way of finding personal fulfillment, identity enhancement, self-expression, and the like, then people must be careful to adopt those forms with the greatest payoff. The theme here is that we reach this goal through engaging in serious rather than casual or unserious leisure.

Figure 1.1 also indicates the considerable overlap that exists between recreation and tourism. For example, Bodewes (1981) saw tourism as a phenomenon of recreation. Similarly, Pearce (1987a: 1) observed the 'growing recognition that tourism constitutes one end of a broad leisure spectrum'.

Historically, research in outdoor recreation developed independently of tourism research. As Crompton and Richardson (1986: 38) noted: 'Traditionally, tourism has been regarded as a commercial economic phenomenon rooted in the private domain. In contrast, recreation and parks has been viewed as a social and resource concern rooted in the public domain.' Outdoor recreation studies have focused on public-sector (i.e. community and land management agencies) concerns, such as wilderness management, social carrying capacity and non-market valuation of recreation experiences. In contrast, tourism has tended to have a more 'applied orientation' which concentrates on traditional private-sector (i.e. tourism industry) concerns, such as the economic impacts of travel expenditures, travel patterns and tourist demands, and advertising and marketing (Harris *et al.* 1987).

Although the division between public and private activities may have held relatively true from the end of the post-war period through to the early 1980s, in recent years the division between public and private sector activities has been substantially eroded in western countries (Hall and Jenkins 1995). The distinction between tourism and recreation may therefore be regarded as one of

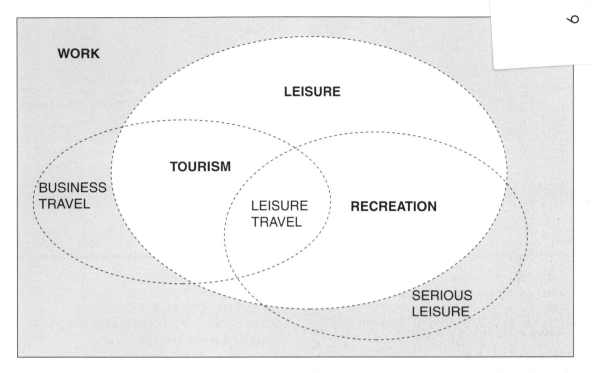

Figure 1.1: Relationships between leisure, recreation and tourism

degree. Tourism primarily relates to leisure and business travel activities which centre around visitors to a particular destination, which will typically involve an infusion of new money from the visitor into the regional economy (Hall 1995). According to Helber (1988: 20), 'In this sense, tourism can be viewed as a primary industry which, through visitor spending, increases job opportunities and tax revenues, and enhances the community's overall economic base'. On the other hand, recreation generally refers to leisure activities which are undertaken by the residents of an immediate region, while their spending patterns will involve 'a recycling of money within the community associated with day, overnight and extended-stay recreation trips' (Helber 1988: 20–1).

Natural settings and outdoor recreation opportunities are clearly a major component of tourism, perhaps especially so since the development of interest in nature-based and ecotourism activities (e.g. Valentine 1984, 1992; Weiler and Hall 1992;

Lindberg and McKercher 1997). Indeed, outdoor recreation and tourist resources should be seen as complementary contexts and resources for leisure experiences (Fedler 1987). Nevertheless, while authors such as Pigram (1985: 184) take the view that 'tourism is carried on within an essentially recreational framework', others such as Murphy (1985) have expressed an opposing view, conceptualising recreation as one component of tourism. However, this argument smacks of something of the 'glass is half-full or half-empty' argument. The reality is that as tourism and recreation studies have grown and borrowed concepts from each other (Ryan 1991), and as society has changed, particularly with respect to the role of government, so the demarcation line between recreation and tourism has rapidly become 'fuzzy and overlap is now the norm' (Crompton and Richardson 1986: 38). As Pigram (1985: 184) argued:

> Little success has been afforded to those attempting to differentiate between recreation and tourism and

Plate 1.2: Recreationalists at Wenderholm Regional Park, Auckland, a natural resource setting.

Plate 1.3: Recreational and tourist use of San Francisco's waterfront on a public holiday. Urban areas can absorb large numbers of visitors if purpose-built areas are designated for tourist use.

such distinctions appear founded on the assumption that outdoor recreation appeals to the rugged, self-reliant element in the population, whereas tourism caters more overtly for those seeking diversion without too much discomfort.

Similarly, in a wider context, Jansen-Verbeke and Dietvorst (1987: 263) argued that 'in the perception of the individual at least, the distinction between recreation and tourism is becoming irrelevant'. As with Shaw and Williams (1994), we would argue that this is not completely the case, particularly with respect to how individuals define their own activities. However, it is readily apparent that there is increasing convergence between the two concepts in terms of theory, activities and impacts, particularly as recreation becomes increasingly commercialised and the boundaries between public and private responsibilities in recreation and leisure change substantially. Indeed, it is interesting to note the inclusion of a same-day travel, 'excursionist' category in official international guidelines for the collection and definition of tourism statistics, thereby making the division between recreation and tourism even more arbitrary (United Nations 1994). Tourism may therefore be interpreted as but one of a range of choices or styles of recreation expressed either through travel or a temporary short-term change of residence. Technical definitions of tourism are examined in more detail in Chapter 2.

THE ISSUE OF SCALE: EMPIRICISM, PARADIGMS AND TRANSFORMATIONS

The geographers' preoccupation with place, space and environment, all of which feature in many of the seminal studies of geography (e.g. Haggett 1979), reveals a preoccupation with one fundamental concept – namely scale (Del Casino and Hanna 2000). For the geographer, it is the scale at which phenomena are studied, analysed and explained which differentiates it from many other areas of social science. The ability to recognise phenomena at different geographical scales ranging from a global, national, regional through to local scale and the interactions of processes and change at each scale have traditionally been the hallmark of a positivist–empiricist geography (see Johnston (1991) for more detail). In many of the classic studies reviewed in the next section, it is clear that Aitchison's (1999) critique of geographical contributions to leisure and recreation research have been overwhelmingly modelled on the empiricist–positivist mode of analysis, where the route to scientific explanation closely follows the positivist models developed in Anglo-American geography in the period 1945 to 1970. The preoccupation with building and testing models in human geography and their application to tourism and recreation (see Pearce (1995a) for a review) has largely mirrored trends in the main discipline, while new developments in behavioural geography, humanistic geography and, more recently, cultural geography have only belatedly begun to permeate the consciousness of tourism and recreation geographers.

What began to develop in the last decade of the twentieth century and has now gathered momentum in tourism and recreation geography is the evolution of new paradigms (i.e. ways of thinking about and conceptualising research problems). As a result, developments in the 'new cultural geography' have begun to permeate, transform and redefine the way in which geographers approach tourism and recreation. Crouch (1999a) conceptualises leisure and tourism as an encounter, in the anthropological tradition, noting the geographers' contribution to this perspective, where the concern is between people, between people and space and the contexts of leisure/tourism. However, what is a fundamental redefinition of the geographers' concern with space, is the manner in which space is viewed and contextualised. Crouch (1999a) argued that space may be something material, concrete, metaphorical or imagined questioning the traditional notion of location and space, where activity is located. This new conceptualisation is reflected in that 'The country and the city, the garden, the beach, the desert island, and the street hold powerful metaphorical attention in significant areas of leisure/tourism' (Crouch 1999a: 4).

This concern with conceptions from cultural geography, where space is something metaphorical, whereby it is something that shapes people's enjoyment of leisure/tourism, derives much of its origins from humanistic geography (Relph 1976, 1981) and cultural studies. For example, Squire (1994) argued that leisure and recreation practices are a reflection of the way in which people make maps of meaning of their everyday word. This concern with the individual or group, the human experience and the symbolic meaning of leisure and tourism in space has opened a wide range of geographical avenues for research in tourism and recreation. For example, Cloke and Perkins (1999)

examined representations of adventure tourism, exploring many of the issues of meaning and symbols.

Williams and Kaltenborn's (1999) analysis of the use and meaning of recreational cottages is significant in this context because it also questioned the traditional notion of geography and tourism, with the focus on tourism as a temporary phenomenon in time and space (see also Williams and Hall 2000). Indeed, they challenged the conventional way of viewing tourism, arguing that tourism and leisure needs to be viewed as a more dynamic phenomenon, where the circulation and movement of people in space is the rule rather than the exception. They argue that it is the movement to tourism and leisure spaces that adds meaning, by allowing people to establish an identity and to connect with place. In other words, tourism and leisure are deeply embedded in everyday lives and the meaning people attach to their lives, since changing work practices and less separation of work, leisure and pleasure has made tourism and recreation more important to people's lives. This is intrinsically linked to the rapidly changing nature of time–space compression (see Page (1999) and Hall and Williams (2001) for more detail), with other mechanisms contributing to people's lives increasingly connected to the concept of a 'global village'. What is clear from the transformation occurring in what one might term the new cultural geographies of leisure and tourism is the lack of a specific frame of reference or guiding research agenda to incorporate these perspectives into mainstream tourism and recreation geography. What appears to be emerging is a social and cultural detachment within the subdiscipline, mirroring other developments in human geography, where two different languages, knowledge bases and modes of analysis are emerging (i.e. the empiricist–positivist and inducture–qualitative culturalists), neither of whom have found a common language to communicate with each other. With these issues in mind, attention now turns to the historical development of the geography of tourism and recreation and a discussion of many of the formative studies.

Plate 1.5: Geyeserland, Rotorua, New Zealand. How do visitors evaluate their enjoyment of this experience?

Plate 1.4: What is the cultural meaning of visiting a man-made attraction such as Universal Studios, Los Angeles? Is it a retreat into a fantasy world?

THE DEVELOPMENT OF THE GEOGRAPHY OF TOURISM AND RECREATION

Tourism and recreation have been the subject of research and scholarship in Anglo-American geography since the 1930s (Cornish 1930, 1934; McMurray 1930; Jones 1933; O'Dell 1934; Selke 1936; Carlson 1938). Brown (1935: 471) offered what he termed 'an invitation to geographers' in the following terms: 'From the geographical point of view the study of tourism offers inviting possibilities for the development of new and ingenious techniques for research, for the discovery of facts of value in their social implications in what

is virtually a virgin field.' However, as Campbell (1966: 85) wryly commented, 'it would appear that this invitation was declined'. As Deasy (1949: 240) observed: 'because of the inadequate attention to the tourist industry by geographers, there exists a concommitant dearth of techniques, adaptable to the collection, analysis, interpretation and cartographic representation of geographical data of the subject.' Yet the period from 1945 to the late 1960s is perhaps not as barren as Campbell would have us believe.

Building on the initial research on tourism and recreation in American economic geography in the 1930s, research was primarily undertaken in the post-war period in the United States on the economic impact of tourism in both a regional destination setting (e.g. Crisler and Hunt 1952; Deasy and Griess 1966) and on travel routes (Eiselen 1945). Although Cooper's (1947) discussion of issues of seasonality and travel motivations foreshadowed some of the geographical research of the 1980s and 1990s, interest in this area of study lay dormant for many years. Nevertheless, the geography of recreation and tourism was at least of a sufficient profile in the discipline to warrant a chapter in an overview text on the state of geography in the United States in the 1950s (McMurray 1954). (See also Meyer-Arendt's (2000) article on tourism as a subject of North American doctoral dissertations and masters theses 1951 to 1998, which expands on the earlier studies by Jafari and Aaser (1988) and Meyer-Arendt and Lew (1999) in the United States.)

In Britain, significant research was undertaken by Gilbert (1939, 1949) on the development of British seaside resorts. However, little further direct research was undertaken on tourism and recreation in the United Kingdom until the 1960s. There was certainly an interest from the generation of geographers studying patterns of tourism and recreation in postcolonial South Asia, as Robinson (1972) noted the contribution of earlier studies by Spencer and Thomas (1948), Withington (1961) and Sopher (1968) published in *The Geograhical Review*. In Canada over the same period substantive geographical research on tourism was primarily focused on one geographer, Roy Wolfe (1964), whose early work on summer cottages in Ontario (1951, 1952), laid the foundation for later research on the geography of second home development (e.g. Coppock 1977a).

While significant work was undertaken on tourism and recreation from the 1930s to the 1950s, it was not really until the 1960s that research started to accelerate with a blossoming of publications on tourism and recreation in the 1970s. During the 1960s several influential reviews were undertaken of the geography of tourism and recreation (Murphy 1963; Winsberg 1966; Wolfe 1967; Mitchell 1969a and b; Mercer 1970), while a substantive contribution to the development of the area also came from regional sciences (e.g. Guthrie 1961; Christaller 1963; Piperoglou 1966). Nevertheless, even as late as 1970, Williams and Zelinsky (1970: 549) were able to comment that 'virtually all the scholarship in the domain of tourism has been confined to intra-national description and analysis'. Indeed, in commenting on the field of tourism research as a whole they observed:

> In view of its great and increasing economic import, the probable significance of tourism in diffusing information and attitudes, and its even greater future potential for modifying patterns of migration, balance of payments, land use, and general socio-economic structure with the introduction of third-generation jet transport and other innovations in travel, it is startling to discover how little attention the circulation of tourists has been accorded by geographers, demographers, and other social scientists.
>
> (Williams and Zelinsky 1970: 549)

Similarly, Mercer (1970: 261) commented: 'Until recently geographers have had surprisingly little to say about the implications of growing leisure time in the affluent countries of the world. Even now, leisure still remains a sadly neglected area of study in geography.'

During the 1970s and early 1980s, a number of influential texts and monographs appeared in the geography literature (e.g. Lavery 1971c; Cosgrove and Jackson 1972; Coppock and Duffield 1975; Matley 1976; Robinson 1976; Coppock 1977a; Pearce 1981, 1987a; Mathieson and Wall 1982; Patmore 1983; Pigram 1983; Smith 1983a), giving the appearance of a healthy area of research. However, despite the growth in publications by geographers on tourism and recreation, concerns were being expressed about the geography of tourism. In the introduction to a special issue of *Annals of Tourism Research* on the geography of tourism, Mitchell (1979: 235) observed that 'the geography of tourism is limited by a dearth of published research in geographical journals, the relatively few individuals who actively participate in the sub-discipline, and the lack of prestige the subject matter specialty has in geography'. In the same issue, Pearce (1979: 246), in an excellent historical review of the field, commented, 'even after half a century, it is difficult to speak of the geography of tourism as a subject with any coherence within the wider discipline of geography or in the general field of tourism studies'. More recently, Pearce (1995a: 3) argued that 'the geography of tourism continues to lack a strong conceptual and theoretical base'; even so, models such as Butler's (1980) cycle of evolution and those reviewed in Pearce (1987a) have assisted to a limited degree in developing a conceptual understanding, while Mitchell (1991: 10) also expressed concern that 'there is no widely accepted paradigm or frame-of-reference that serves as a guide to tourism research'. These comments therefore raise questions about the current status of the geography of tourism and recreation, and it is to these concerns that we now turn.

THE STATUS OF THE GEOGRAPHY OF TOURISM AND RECREATION

The study of the geography of tourism and recreation does not occur in isolation from wider trends in geography and academic discourse, nor of the society of which we are a part. Tourism and recreation geographers are 'a society within a society', academic life 'is not a closed system but rather is open to the influences and commands of the wider society which encompasses it' (Johnston 1991: 1). The study of the development and history of a discipline 'is not simply a chronology of its successes. It is an investigation of the sociology of a community, of its debates, deliberations and decisions as well as its findings' (Johnston 1991: 11). Indeed, Johnston (1985a: 21) highlighted the prevailing criticisms of applied geography where

> Promotion of geography as an applied empirical-analytic science firmly grounds it, according to some, in the political status quo. The problems identified are at the levels of the empirical and the actual and the solutions advanced do not attach the real, the processes that produce the current problems. Symptoms are treated, not causes. Arguments for a more fundamental applied geography, especially applied human geography, seek to distance the discipline from links with governments, public services and commercially oriented enterprises.

The problem in tourism and recreation is that the organisation, management and funding of research is primarily a public and private sector activity. In this sense, it raises moral dilemmas for the geographer since it is increasingly difficult to disengage from the public policy framework or economic/ decision-making context in which research is commissioned or undertaken. Indeed, detachment can lead to valid criticisms of academic 'ivory towers' and a fundamental failure to engage in critical public and private sector policy making.

Tourism geographers are a subcommunity of the geographic community within the wider community of academics, scientists and intellectuals which is itself a subset of wider society; that society has a culture, including a scientific subculture within which the content of geography and tourism is defined. Action is predicated on the structure of society and its knowledge base: research praxis is part of that programme of action, and includes tourism research. The community of tourism academics is therefore an 'institutionalizing social group' (Grano 1981: 26), a context within which individual tourism academics are socialised and which defines the internal goals of their sub-discipline in the context of the external structures within which they operate (after Johnston 1991). The content of the subdiscipline must be linked to its milieu, 'so that disciplinary changes (revolutionary or not) should be associated with significant events in the milieu' (Johnston 1991: 277). Similarly, Stoddart (1981: 1) in his review of the history of geography stated, 'both the ideas and the structure of the subject have developed in response to complex social, economic, ideological and intellectual stimuli'.

'The contents of a discipline at any one time and place reflect the response of the individuals involved to external circumstances and influences, within the context of their intellectual socialization' (Johnston 1983a: 4) see Table 1.1 for categorisations of the main approaches to the geography of tourism and recreation. Grano (1981) developed a model of external influences and internal change in geography that provides a valuable framework within which to examine the geography of tourism and recreation (Figure 1.2). The figure is divided into three interrelated areas:

1 knowledge – the content of the geography of tourism and recreation studies;
2 action – tourism and recreation research within the context of research praxis;
3 culture – academics and students within the context of the research community and the wider society.

Table 1.1: Categorisations of main approaches to the geography of tourism and recreation

Pearce (1979)	Smith and Mitchell (1990)	Mitchell and Murphy (1991)	Pearce (1995a)	Hall and Lew (1998)
spatial patterns of supply	spatial patterns	environmental considerations	tourism models	environmental considerations
spatial patterns of demand	Third World tourism	regional considerations	demand for tourist travel	regional considerations
geography of resorts	evolution of tourism	spatial considerations	international tourism patterns	spatial considerations
tourist movements and flows	impacts of tourism	evolutionary considerations	intra-national travel patterns	evolutionary considerations
impact of tourism	tourism research methods		domestic tourist flows	tourism planning
models of tourist space	planning and development		spatial variations in tourism	urban tourism
	coastal tourism		national and regional structures of tourism	modernisation and development
	tourism accommodation		spatial structure of tourism on islands	gender and identity
	resort cycles		coastal resorts	place marketing and promotion
	tourism concepts		urban areas	globalisation and economic and cultural change
	tourism destinations			sustainable development

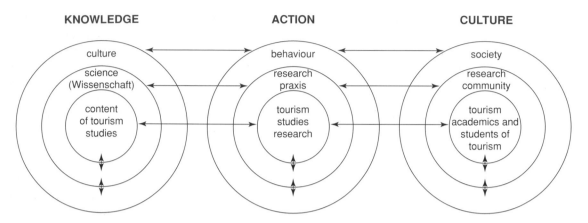

Figure 1.2: The context of tourism studies
Source: After Grano (1981)

KNOWLEDGE

The Dictionary of Human Geography (Johnston *et al.* 1986) defines geography as 'The study of the earth's surface as the space within which the human population lives' (Haggett 1986: 175). Such a concise definition is deceptively simple, and conceals the changing and contested nature of academic geography and, consequently, the geography of tourism and recreation. The development of geography as an academic discipline and its ability to provide specialist educational contributions to knowledge can be dated to the 1870s when geography departments were established in Germany (Taylor 1985). Similar developments were closely followed in the UK and the USA, although the main growth of the discipline came in the twentieth century. James (1972) argued that the establishment of specialised programmes of training marked the evolution of geography from the classical age as it entered the contemporary period. Freeman's (1961) *A Hundred Years of Geography* identified six principal trends within geography. These were:

1 The encyclopaedic trend where new information about the world was collated for the rulers, mercantile classes and residents of western Europe and North America.

2 The educational trend where an academic discipline began to establish its need to generate knowledge, determine relevance and ensure its own reproduction to derive its future. The development of geographical work in schools, colleges and universities characterised this trend.

3 The colonial tradition in the early decades of the twentieth century characterised by a concern with the environment. In the UK, the focus on empire, and its spatial and political organisation from a metropolitan hub, made extensive use of geographical skills.

4 The generalising trend describes the use to which data are put generated through the encyclopaedic and colonial tradition. The methods used to interpret these data formed the basis of the early paradigms of the discipline's development.

5 The political trend was indicative of the way in which contemporary uses of geographical expertise were used for political purposes (e.g. the redrawing of the map of Europe after the First World War).

6 The specialisation trend was the natural corollary of the expansion of knowledge in geography and the inability of one person to be an expert in every field. The expansion of more rigorous research training required geographers to specialise.

Following on from these trends, Johnston (1991: 38) argued that 'some of these trends represent philosophies, some methodologies, and some ideologies with regard to the purpose of academic geography'. However, Johnston regarded three particular paradigms as being especially important in the development of human geography: exploration, environmental determinism and possibilism, and regional studies.

Exploration

Exploration refers to the situation where unknown areas of the world (to those who live outside of them) are explored to collect and classify information. Many of these activities were financed by geographical societies as well as by philanthropists. The Royal Geographical Society of London (RGS) was one such example, and even today the RGS is a major sponsor of expeditions which are reported in its publication – *The Geographical Journal*. The theme of exploration remains significant in tourism geography, particularly as the images of places conveyed by explorers in the metropolitan regions has served to create destination images that remain to the present day. For example, the 'discovery' of the Pacific by Europeans was the crucial point for the imaging of the Pacific as a romantic paradise (Douglas and Douglas 1996).

Environmental determinism and possibilism

Environmental determinism and possibilism were two competing approaches which, according to Johnston (1991), were early attempts at generalisation in the modern period. These approaches sought explanations rather than just descriptions of patterns of human occupation on the earth. The underlying assumption was that human activity was controlled by the elements in the physical environment within which it was located. Environmental determinism can be dated to the research by Darwin and *On the Origin of Species* (published in 1859), where ideas on evolution were used by an American geographer William Morris Davies to develop the model of land form development. The nineteenth century also saw a number of geographers become protagonists of environmental determinism, especially the German geographer Ratzel, and the American geographer Ellen Churchill Semple, whose book *Influences of Geographic Environment* (1891) stated that 'man is the product of the earth's surface'.

The response to determinism was the counter-thesis possibilism. French geographers presented arguments to show that people perceive a range of alternative uses to which the environment could be put. This was, in part, determined by their own cultural traditions and predispositions. The debate on possibilism and determinism continued into the 1960s and has had some influence on tourism geography because of the extent to which concepts such as place, cultural landscape and heritage underlie much debate about tourism's impacts.

The region

Ideas of the region and regional geography dominated British and American geography until the 1950s, based on the principle that generalisations and explanations were best derived from an areal approach. Johnston (1991) points to the role of Herbertson (1905) in dividing the earth into natural regions and the attempt to examine areas at a smaller scale to identify particular characteristics. In North America, the influence of Hartshorne's ongoing research established the focus of geography as a concern for areal differentiation so that the principal purpose of geographical scholarship is synthesis, an integration of relevant characteristics to provide a total description of a place – a region – which is identifiable by its peculiar combination of those characteristics (Johnston 1991: 43). This established regional geography as a powerful focus for the discipline which remained a feature of many school, college and university programmes even in the 1990s. In the new millennium the region has become integrated into what Murphy and Le Heron (1999: 15) describe as the '"new regional geography" which incorporates elements of the earlier regional geography and new elements from political economy, geography, feminist geography and geographic information systems'. The development of regional synthesis required topical specialisms in geography to contribute to the regional paradigm.

Regional concepts continue to play a major role in the geography of tourism and recreation and underlie five main areas of research and scholarship:

1 *Regional tourism geographies*   A number of collections of regional material have been developed by geographers in recent years, in part influenced by the development of regional economic and political blocs, which serve as frameworks for the development of baseline studies of contemporary tourism processes. Major regional reviews of tourism have been undertaken by geographers on western Europe (Williams and Shaw 1988), Canada (Wall 1989), eastern Europe (Hall 1991), Europe (Montanari and Williams 1995), polar regions (Hall and Johnston 1995), Australia (Hall 1995), China (Lew and Wu 1995), the South Pacific (Hall and Page 1996), the Pacific Rim (Hall *et al.* 1997), and South and South-East Asia (Hall and Page 2000).

2 *Destination regions*   Given the importance of the destination as an analytical concept in tourism, significant effort has been given to the ways in which destination regions can be identified, managed, and marketed (see Smith and Brown 1981; Mitchell 1984; Smith 1983a, 1987, 1995; Heath and Wall 1992).

3 *Regional planning and development*   The delineation of political and administrative regions provides a focus for administrative and planning research as well as a focus for the encouragement of development efforts through tourism and recreation. There is a significant body of research in this area, particularly with reference to Europe and the overall focus by government on tourism as a tool for economic development (see e.g. Pearce 1988a, 1992a, 1995a, b; Williams and Shaw 1988; Hall 1991; Heath and Wall 1992; Hall *et al.* 1997; Hall 1999).

4 *Synthesis and integration*   The importance of synthesis and integration within regions has proven to be an important component in the development of approaches to integrated resource management within a regional context (see e.g. Lang 1988; Wight 1993, 1995; Pearce 1995b; Hall 1999).

5 *Reviews of progress*   In the development of the subdiscipline (e.g. Pearce 1979) and specific progress reports for individual countries such as the UK (Duffield 1984), Spain (Bote Gomez 1996), Australasia (Pearce 1999), the Antipodes (Pearce and Mings 1984), Japan (Takeuchi 1984), France (Barbier and Pearce 1984) and the USA (Mitchell 1969a, 1979, 1984; Smith and Mitchell 1990; Mitchell and Murphy 1991).

Johnston (1991) also charts the development of geography as a discipline, focusing on a number of other trends which provided a direction for development. These are:

- the growth of systematic studies and adoption of a scientific method, where methods of investigation are developed;
- the development of a new focus around the spatial variable and the analysis of spatial systems in the 1960s and 1970s where spatial analytical techniques were developed and systems theory was introduced;
- the development of behavioural geography as a response to the spatial science approaches, recognising that human behaviour cannot easily be explained using logical positivist models. Behavioural geography focuses on the processes which underlie human decision-making and spatial behaviour rather than the outcomes which are the focus of much conventional spatial analysis (Gold 1980);
- the rise of humanistic geography with its emphasis on the individual as a decision-maker. The behavioural approach tended to view people as responses to stimuli to show how individuals do not correspond to models built to predict possible human outcomes. In contrast, humanistic geography treats the

individual as someone constantly interacting with the environment that changes both self and milieu (Johnston 1991). It does not use any scientifically defined model of behaviour, with each paradigm recognising appropriate contexts where the respective approaches are valid;

- applied geography, which refers to 'the application of geographical knowledge and skills to the solution of economic and social problems' (Johnston 1986: 17);
- radical approaches to geography, often with a neo-Marxist base (Peet 1977a, b), but which have broadened in the 1980s and 1990s to consider issues of gender, globalisation, localisation, identity, postcolonialism, postmodernism and the role of space in critical social theory (e.g. Harvey 1987, 1988, 1989a, 1989b, 1990, 1993; Soja 1989; Benko and Strohmmayer 1997; Crouch 1999b; Blom 2000).

All of the above approaches to geography have relevance to the study of tourism and recreation. However, their application has been highly variable with the greatest degree of research being conducted in the areas of spatial analysis and applied geography (Table 1.2). It is useful to note that two of the most influential books on the geography of tourism and recreation – Pearce (1987a, 1995a) on tourism and Smith (1983a) on recreation – primarily approach their subjects from a spatial perspective although both give an acknowledgement to the role of behavioural research. In contrast, the text on geographical perspectives on tourism by Shaw and Williams (1994) provides a far more critical approach to the study of tourism with acknowledgement of the crucial role that political economy, production, consumption, globalisation and commodification play in the changing nature of tourism. In one sense, Pearce (1995a) and Shaw and Williams (1994) represent the two most significant strands in present-day tourism and recreation geography. The former, dominant approach represents a more 'traditional' form of spatial analysis and 'applied' geography (in the sense that it may be immediately useful to some

public sector and commercial interests). The latter, emerging approach represents more discursive and reflexive forms of analysis with a broader perspective on what the appropriate focus for the study of tourism and recreation should be. Although arguably the recent edition of Crouch (1999b) represents another reflexive form of analysis that has taken a different direction through its focus on identities, encounters and people as socialised and embodied subjects, but which may act as a bridge for greater communication between tourism and cultural geography.

In many ways Shaw and Williams (1994) represent an explicit response to Britton's (1991) call for a theorisation of geography of tourism and leisure that explicitly recognises, and unveils, tourism as a predominantly capitalistically organised activity driven by the inherent and defining social dynamics of that system, with its attendant production, social and ideological relations. An analysis of how the tourism production system markets and packages people is a lesson in the political economy of the social construction of 'reality' and social construction of place, whether from the point of view of visitors and host communities, tourism capital (and the 'culture industry'), or the state – with its diverse involvement in the system (Britton 1991: 475).

To many students of the geography of tourism and recreation such a call would not seem appropriate, as it would be seen to be taking geography too far from its spatial core interpreting the mapping of decision-making outcomes in space. This should be no surprise though, as the subdiscipline reflects the wider turmoil in the discipline as a whole in terms of competition between various frameworks of analysis. Nevertheless, while conventional spatial science may yield useful information, it does little to promote an understanding of the processes by which outcomes at given points of time are actually reached, nor does it do much to connect the geography of tourism and recreation to wider debates and issues in the social sciences.

One of the great stresses in the geography of tourism and recreation is the extent to which it connects with other components of the discipline.

Table 1.2: Approaches to geography and their relationship to the study of tourism and recreation

Approach	Key concepts	Exemplar publications
Spatial analysis	positivism, locational analysis, maps, systems, networks, morphology	• spatial structure: Fesenmaier and Lieber 1987 • spatial analysis: Smith 1983b; Wall et al. 1985; Hinch 1990; Ashworth and Dietvorst 1995 • tourist flows and travel patterns: Williams and Zelinsky 1970; Corsi and Harvey 1979; Forer and Pearce 1984; Pearce 1987a, 1990a, 1993b, 1995a; Murphy and Keller 1990; Oppermann 1992 • gravity models: Malamud 1973; Bell 1977 • morphology: Pigram 1977 • regional analysis: Smith 1987
Behavioural geography	behaviouralism, behaviourism, environmental perception, diffusion, mental maps, decision-making, action spaces, spatial preference	• mental maps: Walmsley and Jenkins 1992; Jenkins and Walmsley 1993 • environmental cognition: Aldskogius 1977 • tourist spatial behaviour: Carlson 1978; Cooper 1981; Debbage 1991 • tourist behaviour: Murphy and Rosenblood 1974; Arbel and Pizam 1977; Pearce 1988a • environmental perception: Wolfe 1970 • recreational displacement: Anderson and Brown 1984
Humanistic geography	human agency, subjectivity of analysis, hermeneutics, place, landscape, existentialism, phenomenology, ethnography, lifeworld	• placelessness of tourism: Relph 1976 • historical geography: Wall and Marsh 1982; Marsh 1985; Towner 1996
Applied geography	planning, remote sensing, Geographic Information Systems (GIS), public policy, cartography, regional development, carrying capacity	• planning: Murphy 1985; Getz 1986a; Dowling 1993, 1997; Hall et al. 1997; Hall 2000 • regional development: Coppock 1977a, b; Pearce 1988b, 1990a, 1992a • tourism development: Pearce 1981, 1989; Cooke 1982; Lew 1985; Murphy 1985 • indigenous peoples: Mercer 1994; Butler and Hinch 1996; Lew and van Otten 1997 • rural tourism and recreation: Coppock and Duffield 1975; Getz 1981; Glyptis 1991; Page and Getz 1997; Butler et al. 1998 • urban tourism and recreation: Ashworth 1989, 1992b; Law 1991, 1993, 1996; Page 1995a; Hinch 1996; Murphy 1997 • health: Clift and Page 1996 • destination marketing: Dilley 1986; Heath and Wall 1992 • place marketing: Ashworth and Voogd 1988; Madsden 1992; Fretter 1993 • public policy and administration: Cooper 1987; Pearce 1992b; Jenkins 1993; Hall 1994; Hall and Jenkins 1995 • tourism impacts: Pigram 1980; Mathieson and Wall 1982; Edington and Edington 1986; Edwards 1987 • destination life cycle: Butler 1980; Cooper and Jackson 1989; Debbage 1990; Agarwal 1994

attractions: Lew 1987

- second homes: Aldskogius 1968; Coppock 1977; Gartner 1987
- GIS: Kliskey and Kearsley 1993; Elliott-White and Finn 1998
- national parks: Nelson 1973; Olwig and Olwig 1979; Marsh 1983; Calais and Kirkpatrick 1986; Cole et al. 1987; Davies 1987; Hall 1992a; McKercher 1993c
- heritage management: Gale and Jacobs 1987; Lew 1989; Ashworth and Tunbridge 1990, 1996; Hall and McArthur 1996, 1998
- outdoor recreation management: Pigram and Jenkins 1999
- sustainable development: Butler 1990, 1991, 1992, 1998; Pigram 1990; Ashworth 1992b; Cater 1993; Dearden 1993; McKercher 1993a, 1993b; Cater and Lowman 1994; Ding and Pigram 1994; Murphy 1994; Mowforth and Munt 1997; Hall and Lew 1998
- ecotourism: Weiler 1991; Eagles 1992; Cater 1993; Cater and Lowman 1994; Blamey 1995; Weaver 1998; Fennel 1999; Page and Dawling 2001

- political economy: Britton 1982; Ley and Olds 1988
- social theory: Britton 1991; Shaw and Williams 1994
- semiotic analysis: Waitt 1997
- place promotion and commodification: Ashworth and Voogd 1990a, b, 1994; Kearns and Philo 1993; Waitt and McGuirk 1996; Chang et al. 1997; Tunbridge and Ashworth 1997

- cultural identity: Byrne et al. 1993; Squire 1994
- gender: Adler and Brenner 1992; Kinnaird and Hall 1994; Aitchison 1997, 1999, 2000
- 'new cultural studies': Crouch 1999; Aitchison 2000

'Radical' approaches

neo-Marxist analysis, role of the state, gender, globalisation, localisation, identity, postcolonialism, postmodernism role of space

While it is quite easy to agree with Matley's (1976: 5) observation that 'There is scarcely an aspect of tourism which does not have some geographical implications and there are few branches of geography which do not have some contribution to make to the study of the phenomenon of tourism' (see also Mercer 1970), one must also note that the relative influence of these branches has proven to be highly variable over the past 70 years.

One of the great difficulties has been that while tourism and recreation geographers have seen the significance of relationships to other geographical subdisciplines and, indeed, other disciplines, such relationships are not reciprocal. For example, while Mercer (1970) recognised the significance of recreation, tourism and leisure for social geography (see also Williams 1979), textbooks, such as that by Jackson and Smith (1984), do not examine such concepts. Similarly, a text such as Whitehead (1993) on the *Making of the Urban Landscape* failed to note the role of tourism and recreation activities in urban environments. Perhaps the most significant indicator of the way the geography of tourism and recreation is seen by the wider discipline can be found in Johnston's (1991) standard work on post-war Anglo-American geography. Here the terms leisure, recreation and tourism are absent from the index, while the only comment on the subject is three lines in the environmentalism section of the chapter on applied geography: 'A topic of special interest was the study of leisure, of the growing demand for recreation activities on the environment' followed by reference to the work of Patmore (1970, 1983) and Owens (1984) (two of which have the wrong publication dates in the text!). This is not to denigrate Johnston's magnificent work of scholarship. It is probably an appropriate comment on the perception of the standing of tourism and recreation geography in Anglo-American geography, that the only area where tourism and recreation is considered significant is in rural areas where, perhaps, tourists and recreationists are seen as a nuisance! The reasons for this situation are manifold but perhaps lie in the cultural and action dimensions of geographical research.

ACTION: THE DEVELOPMENT OF AN APPLIED GEOGRAPHY OF TOURISM AND RECREATION

Within the literature on geographical research, there was a growing concern for relevance in the 1950s (see Johnson 1991). Part of that concern may have been a function of trying to improve the marketability of the discipline. At the same time, this call for relevance was accompanied by the growth of scientific methods in geography that highlighted the growing systematic focus and concern with applying geographical principles and concepts to real-world problems. One possible interpretation of the post-1945 concern with relevancy and, more belatedly, an applied focus, may be related to the expansion of undergraduate student enrolments in geography departments and the need to secure employment opportunities beyond teaching. The 1960s also saw the development of notable studies (e.g. Stamp 1960) extolling the virtues of the geographer's art and tools in relation to their contribution to society. Yet recreation and tourism received only a passing mention in that seminal study, as geography remained preoccupied with the move towards 'scientific method', 'logical positivism', quantification and a move away from regional description to more systematic forms of spatial analysis. Such developments were crucial, since they provided the training and foundations for the next generation of geographers who were to begin to nurture the recreation–tourism continuum as a legitimate research focus. But one consequence of geography's development in the 1950s and 1960s and the rise of a more 'applied' focus was the increasing move towards narrow specialisation which appears to have reached its natural peak in the 1990s. Johnston (1991) outlines an increasing tension within geography in the 1960s and 1970s over the focus of the discipline, which in part transcended the debate over radical approaches (see Harvey 1974). The basic tension related to how geographers should contribute their skills to the solution of societal problems. This questioned the philosophical basis of geography – who should the geographer benefit with an applied focus?

Both British and American geography conferences in the 1970s saw an increasing debate and awareness of the value of geographers contributing to public policy. Coppock (1974) felt that policy-makers were unaware of the contribution geographers could make to policy-making. But critics questioned the value of advising governments which were the paymasters and already constrained in what geographers could undertake research on. Harvey (1974) raised the vital issue of 'what kind of geography for what kind of public policy?', arguing that individuals involved in policy-making were motivated by 'personal ambition, disciplinary imperialism, social necessity and moral obligation at the level of the whole discipline, on the other hand, geography had been co-opted, through the Universities, by the growing corporate state, and geographers had been given some illusion of power within a decision-making process designed to maintain the status quo' (Johnston 1991: 198). Indeed, Pacione's (1999a) defence of applied geography reiterates many of the inherent conflicts and problems which the 'Purists' in human geography raise, in that

> Applied geography is concerned with the application of geographical knowledge and skills to the resolution of real-world social, economic and environmental problems. The underlying philosophy of relevance of usefulness and problem-orientated goals of applied geography have generated critical opposition from other 'non-applied' members of the geographical community. Particular criticism of the applied geography approach has emanated from Marxist and, more recently, postmodern theorists who reflect the potential of applied geography to address the major problems confronting people and places in the contemporary world.
>
> (Pacione 1999a: 1)

In fact, the recent emergence of the 'new cultural geography' highlights the increasing tensions within the discipline where 'the idea of applied geography or useful research is a chaotic concept which does not fit with the recent "cultural turn" in social geography or the postmodern theorising of recent years' (Pacione 1999a: 3). In fact, Pacione claimed that it was a matter of individual conscience as to what individual geographers study. What is clear

is that some research is more 'useful' than other forms, and the application to tourism and recreation phenomenon is certainly a case in point. Although the 'concept of "useful research" poses the basic questions of useful for whom? Who decides what is useful' (Pacione 1999a: 4) is part of the wider relevance debate which continues in human geography as paradigm shifts, and new ways of theorising and interpreting information question the central role of the discipline. In Taylor's (1985) provocative and thoughtful analysis of 'The value of a geographical perspective', a cyclical function emerged in the development of eras of pure and applied research. What Taylor (1985) observed was that when external pressures are greatest, problem-solving approaches are pursued within the discipline. Conversely, in times of comparative economic prosperity, more pure academic activity is nurtured. Taylor (1985) related these trends to longer-term trends in the world economy, identifying three distinct periods when applied geography was in its ascendance: the late nineteenth century, the inter-war period, and the mid-1980s.

However, Johnston (1991) also points to a liberal contribution to an applied geography which can be dated to Stamp's land use survey of Britain in the 1930s and his involvement in post-war land use planning (Stamp 1948). While much of this early 'applied geography' was set in an empiricalist tradition, Sant's (1982) survey of applied geography traces the use of the term back to the late nineteenth century with the early conferences of the International Geographical Union (IGU). While the title lapsed until the 1960s, the principal interest in applied geography has been promulgated by that organisation and a number of publications have resulted (e.g. Ackerman 1963). Sant's (1982) study concurs with Johnston's (1991) analysis, in that geographers' interest in applied geography between the 1930s and 1950s was based on:

- administrative regionalisation (Gilbert 1951);
- land use surveys (Stamp 1948);
- terrain analysis and air-photointerpretation (Taylor 1951);
- urban and regional planning.

Stamp's (1960) influential book on *Applied Geography* documents his own research activities in geography, and the spirit of the book highlights how a spatial focus could offer so many potential areas for study. Sant (1982: 8) assesses Stamp's contribution as follows:

> There is a deceptive innocence about Stamp's book which stems not from naivety but from confidence in his own judgement and experience. He had achieved much and his credentials commanded attention. Today we live in a less confident age. Perhaps this is because we have a greater propensity to invent complexities. . . . At any rate, the scope and methods of applied geography are more elaborate than they were a generation ago.

Sant (1982) argued that applied geography was not a subdiscipline but had a dependent relationship with academic geography. It has a different *modus operandi*. It is intended to offer prescription, has to engage in dialogue with 'outsiders' not familiar with the discipline, its traditions, problems and internal conservatism, and an ability to overtly criticise developments which are not central to the prevailing paradigm. While the discipline has published a range of journals with an applied focus (e.g. applied geography) and offers a number of applied courses in universities, the term is used loosely. As Sant (1982: 136) argued, 'the crux of applied geography is (at the risk of tautology) fundamentally that it is about geography. That is, it deals with human and physical landscapes.' What is interesting to note in Sant's text is the inclusion of recreation and the contribution of geographers to this area of applied geography, a feature reiterated in the study edited by Kenzer (1989) and the brief mention by Johnston (1991) noted above.

Some commentators, however, feel that the rise of an 'applied focus' has meant the discipline has lost touch with its roots, and thereby compromised the ability of 'explicating the relationship between people, places, cultures and the global/ regional mix of each' (Kenzer 1989: 2). One indication of this, according to critics, is the greater emphasis on techniques and their application to geographical concerns among human geographers and a subsequent decline in real-world, fieldwork-oriented studies. For example, the application of Geographical Information Systems (GIS) in research has meant a move away from traditional fieldwork and more laboratory-based analysis (Van der Knaap 1999), which may be distant from the real world. As Forer (1999: 96) argued, 'New geographic information technology is becoming ubiquitous, and is revolutionising what we measure and how we measure it.' In fact, as Tarrant and Cordell (1999) noted in their examination of outdoor recreation in United States national forest areas, the use of GIS can be an extremely valuable tool in the analysis of environmental justice and equity. The natural corollary of the development of more techniques-based geographical courses, some critics suggest, is the potential loss of the 'core' in human geography if applied studies become dominant, and traditional concepts and the roots of the discipline are no longer taught. It is ironic, therefore, that in many undergraduate geography degrees where the development of geographical thought is taught, the broader context of applied geography often receives limited or poor treatment in contrast to the emphasis now placed on quantification, computer-based analysis and skills-based training.

In contrast, supporters of a more applied focus have argued that despite the apparent splintering and fragmentation of geography in the late 1980s and 1990s as a function of specialisation, it has made a valid contribution to society. Many able geographers have recognised the need to move away from academia in order to make their skills, knowledge and perspective of use to society through a range of contributions while still being capable of reflexive analysis of their actions.

In the case of recreation and tourism, many geographers involved in these areas may no longer be based in geography departments in universities. However, they maintain and extend the value of a geographical analysis and understanding for the training and research in the wider field of recreation and tourism studies. The discipline of geography, in the UK at least, paid very little attention to the growing role of geographers in the educational and research environment of tourism. Only in the 1990s have organisations such as the Institute of British

Geographers acknowledged the significance of recreation and tourism as a serious area of academic study. In contrast, the Association of American Geographers and the Canadian Association of Geographers have been much more active, with their study groups being established since the 1970s. International organisations such as the International Geographical Union (IGU) Study Group on the Geography of Tourism, Leisure and Global Change (lifespan: 2000 to 2004) (formerly the IGU Geography of Sustainable Tourism, 1994 to 2000; and IGU Commission on Tourism and Leisure, 1984 to 1992) provided another forum for research developments and interaction by geographers and non-geographers with similar research interests. Nevertheless, despite such initiatives, the relationship of the geography of tourism and recreation to the broader discipline of geography has suffered two major problems:

- the rise of applied geography within the discipline, and tourism and recreation geography within it, has seen critics view it as rather ephemeral and lacking in substance and rigour;
- in some countries (e.g. the UK), national geographical organisations and geography departments have often failed to recognise the significance of recreation and tourism as a legitimate research area capable of strengthening and supporting the discipline.

One consequence is that many geographers who developed recreational and tourism research interests in the 1980s and 1990s have left the inherent conservatism and ongoing criticism of their research activity to move to fresh pastures where autonomous tourism research centres or departments have eventuated. This does not, however, denigrate the excellent contribution that leading geographers such as Patmore, Coppock, Mercer, Glyptis and Pearce have made to establishing recreation and tourism as serious areas of academic study within the discipline. Nevertheless, a significant number of geographers are now based in business schools or tourism, recreation or leisure departments where their research interests are aligned within a multidisciplinary environment that can cross-fertilise their research and support an applied focus. Indeed, in some respects, history is perhaps repeating itself all over again, where planning emerged as a discipline and split from some of its geographical roots and where the development of environmental studies departments has also led to a departure of geographers to such centres.

In the 1980s and 1990s, many geographers unwilling to have the progress of their careers impeded by views held by peers who did not see tourism and recreation as mainstream spatial research have similarly split from the discipline. For example, in New Zealand, with the exception of one or two notable researchers, all the geographers with a tourism or recreation focus are now located in business schools, departments of tourism and recreation or other non-geographical bases. This situation is not dramatically different to the situation in Australia, where educational expansion in this area has made extensive use of professional geographers to develop and lead such developments (Weiler and Hall 1991). As Janiskee and Mitchell (1989: 159) concluded:

> This is certainly an interesting and exciting time to be a recreation geographer. After a slow start, the sub-discipline has achieved a critical mass and seems destined to enjoy a bright future. . . . There is no question that the application of recreation geography knowledge and expertise to problem solving contexts outside academia offers potential rewards of considerable worth to the sub-discipline: more jobs for recreation geographers, a stimulus to academic research with implications for problem solving, a more clearly defined sense of purpose or social worth, and greater visibility, both within and outside academic circles.

It is interesting to note that Janiskee and Mitchell (1989: 159) also perceive that 'since there is no clear distinction between "basic" and "applied" research, nor any appreciable threat to quality scholarship, there is no simmering argument on the issue of whether applied research is good for recreation geography. Rather, the real question is whether recreation geographers will have the resources and the zeal to move into the problem-solving domain on a much more widespread and consistent basis.'

While this may be true in a North American context, it is certainly not the case in the UK in 2001, and a number of other countries where applied geographical research in recreation and tourism has been viewed as dissipating the value and skills of the geographer for pecuniary reward, or without contributing to the development of the discipline. Ironically, however, the proliferation of 'dabblers' (i.e. people who do not consider themselves recreation geographers, but contribute papers to journals using simplistic notions of tourism and recreation) has grown and still abounds in the geography, and, to a lesser extent, in the recreation and tourism journals. Indeed, tourism and recreation have been 'discovered' by geographers and other social scientists in the late 1980s and 1990s as tourism is utilised by governments to respond to the effects of global economic restructuring and increasing concerns over conserving the environment (Hall and Lew 1998). Such contributions, according to Janniskee and Mitchell (1989: 157), 'although welcome, are not a satisfactory substitute for output of a substantial number of specialists doing scientific–theoretical–nomothetic research which is needed for the area to progress'. Calls for a 'heightened awareness and appreciation of problem solving needs and opportunities outside the traditional bounds of scholarly research' (Janiskee and Mitchell 1989: 159) are vital if academics are to connect with the broad range of stakeholders and interests that impinge upon geography and academia. Geographers with knowledge and skills in the area of tourism and recreation research need to develop a distinctive niche by undertaking basic and applied research to address public and private sector problems, which illustrates the usefulness of a spatial, synthesising and holistic education. Even so, 'the list of research undertaken by applied geographers is impressive, but there are no grounds for complacency . . . [as] . . . the influence of applied geography has been mixed, and arguably less than hoped for. . . . Several reasons may account for this [including] the eclectic and poorly focused nature of the discipline of geography and the fact that "geographical work" is being undertaken by "non- geographers" in other disciplines. This undermines the identity of geography as a subject with something particular to offer' (Pacione 1999a: 10–11). Even so, in Pearce's (1999a) review of tourism geography in New Zealand, many of the geographers' applied contributions appear to have been overlooked in favour of geographical journal publications on tourism. For this reason, it is worth considering the skills and techniques the geographers can harness in tourism and recreation research.

CULTURE

The cultural dimensions of the geography of tourism and recreation – the sociology of knowledge of the subdiscipline – as with that of tourism and recreation studies as a whole, have been little studied. This is extremely unfortunate as it means there is a very incomplete comprehension of where the subdiscipline has been, which must also clearly affect our understanding of where it might go. As Barnes (1982: 102–3) commented: 'Social, technical and economic determinants routinely affect the rate and direction of scientific growth. . . . It is true that much scientific change occurs despite, rather than because of, external direction or financial control. . . . Progress in the disinterested study [of certain] . . . areas has probably occurred just that bit more rapidly because of their relevance to other matters.'

Similarly, Johnston (1991: 24–5) observed:

the study of a discipline must be set in its societal context. It must not necessarily be assumed, however, that members of academic communities fully accept the social context and the directives and impulses that it issues. They may wish to counter it, and use their academic base as a focus for their discontent. But the (potential) limits to that discontent are substantial. Most academic communities are located in universities, many of which are dependent for their existence on public funds disbursed by governments which may use their financial power to influence, if not direct, what is taught and researched. And some universities are dependent on private sources of finance, so they must convince their sponsors that their work is relevant to current societal concerns.

As noted above, research into the geographical dimensions of tourism has received relatively little attention in the wider fields of academic geography. Several related factors can be recognised as accounting for this situation:

- there is only a narrow set of official interest in conducting research into the geography of tourism;
- tourism is not regarded as a serious scholarly subject;
- not only are there substantial unresolved theoretical issues in conducting geographical studies of tourism and recreation but much theorisation is also relatively weak;
- tourism and recreation geographers have had little success in promoting their subdiscipline in the broader geographical context;
- many tourism and recreation geographers are now operating in non-geography departments or in the private sector.

Unlike some areas of tourism research, such as politics and public policy, for example (Hall 1994; Hall and Jenkins 1995), there is some government support for research and consulting on the geography of tourism and recreation. However, such research support tends to be given to the analysis of spatial patterns of tourist flows and issues of infrastructure location rather than areas of applied geographical research in gender and social impacts that may produce unwanted political results. Indeed, even support for research on the environmental impacts on tourism has the potential to produce politically contestable results, particularly if the results are not seen as supportive of industry interests. Therefore, funding for tourism and recreation research will tend to reinforce the more conservative spatial science aspects of the geography of tourism and recreation at the expense of more fundamental analysis which would have a greater capacity to extend the theoretical contributions of the subdiscipline. Despite the apparent lack of interest in studies of the broader dimensions of tourism by government and industry, and the community conflicts that occur in relation to

tourism development, it is important to recognise that such research may be of an extremely practical nature. The results of such research may help facilitate and improve tourism planning through an increased understanding of decision-making processes (e.g. Murphy 1985), and help maintain the long-term viability of tourist destinations.

Despite the extensive growth of research on tourism and recreation in the 1980s and 1990s, many people still do not regard tourism as a serious subject of study, often equating it with booking a holiday at a travel agency or learning how to pour a beer. Indeed, research on tourism is often seen as frivolous. The observation of Matthews (1983: 304) that 'at a typical American university, a political scientist with a scholarly interest in tourism might be looked upon as dabbling in frivolity – not as a serious scholar but as an opportunist looking for a tax-deductible holiday', holds almost universal applicability. Similar to Smith's (1977: 1) observations on the anthropology of tourism in the 1970s, it is a topic that still appears to be thought by many in the discipline as unworthy of consideration by the serious geography scholar. Indeed, Mitchell (1997), a noted scholar within tourism and recreation geography, in a personal communication following a discussion on RTSnet (the interest newsgroup of the recreation, tourism and sport speciality group of the Association of American Geographers) regarding the position of recreation and tourism in American geography, argued that

> Recreation geography, has never been a valued member of the establishment, because, it is believed, it is impossible to be serious about individuals and groups having fun. Note the subtitle of the feminist oriented tourism conference being held in California this month ('Tourism is not about having fun'). In spite of the fact that tourism is the number one economic activity in the world, that recreation (especially passive recreation) takes up a large portion of the population's time, and that sport is almost a religion for many in this country, geographers who study these phenomena are not highly regarded.

There are also substantial methodological, theoretical and geographical problems in conducting geographical research. Problems have arisen because of the multiplicity of potential frameworks for analysis as well as relatively weak theorisation in some quarters. As Ioannides (1996: 221) notes, 'Although tourism geography has long been an established specialization, the weak theoretical grounding associated with this research area relegates it to the discipline's periphery'.

The lack of a clearly articulated or agreed-upon methodological or philosophical approach to geography *per se*, let alone the geography of tourism and recreation, may create an intellectual and perceptual minefield for the researcher, particularly as the value position of the author will have an enormous bearing on the results of any research. Burton (1982: 323–4), for example, argued that leisure and tourism research is plagued by problems of 'lack of intellectual co-ordination and insufficient cross-fertilization of ideas among researchers; an inadequacy of research methodologies and techniques; and a lack of any generally agreed concepts and codes in the field'. However, in contrast, Hall (1994: 7) argued that 'In fact, the debate which marks such concepts should probably be seen as a sign of health and youthful vigour in an emerging area of serious academic study and should be welcomed and encouraged rather than be regarded as a source of embarrassment'.

Another factor which may have influenced the standing of the geography of tourism and recreation is the extent to which the subdiscipline is being promoted to the discipline as a whole. For example, in the American context, Mitchell (1997) argued:

> There is no one individual superstar in the US who has popularized the subject matter through publications and/or personality. From my perspective a lot of good geographic research has been published and the research frontier has been advanced, however, little of this research has appeared in the geographic literature; rather it tends to be found in specialty or multi-disciplinary journals. . . . Lots of publications are produced but they do not engender the kind of interest or reputation that leads to widespread recognition.

In the British context, the publication of *Critical Issues in Tourism* by Shaw and Williams (1994) as part of the Institute of British Geography Studies in Geography Series helped raise the profile of the area. Nevertheless, the situation remains that the key academic audience of the majority of research and publications by tourism and recreation geographers are people within tourism and recreation departments rather than geography. However, there are some signs that this situation may be changing. First, there is the publication of the journal *Tourism Geographies* in 1999 (edited by Alan Lew and published by Routledge) which seeks to promote the subdiscipline both within its immediate audience and beyond. To some extent the emergence of this specialised journal may be regarded as a sign of maturity of the field akin to other specialist geography journals (e.g. *Applied Geography, Journal of Transport Geography*). Second, there are activities of the IGU Study Group on the Geography of Tourism, Leisure and Global Change and its forerunner, the Study Group on the Geography of Sustainable Tourism which has co-hosted a number of conferences and special sessions with other IGU Commissions, such as Sustainable Rural Systems, and with national associations, such as the Association of American Geographers. Third, the increased significance of tourism and recreation in urban and rural environments in contemporary society has led to a greater appreciation of the potential significance of the field. In other words, tourism is now such a significant activity in the cultural landscape that it would be difficult for other geographies to ignore it for much longer. Finally, tourism and recreation geographies are now arguing that they have something to contribute to the wider discipline, particularly in such areas as understanding the service economy, industrialisation and regional development (e.g. Ioannides 1995, 1996; d'Hauteserre 1996), as well as more traditional resource management concerns and sustainability (e.g. Zurick 1992; Hall and Lew 1998).

The final factor influencing the standing of the subdiscipline is the extent to which geographers in the field are increasingly undertaking employment outside geography departments and in tourism, recreation and leisure studies departments, business schools, and environmental studies and planning departments. Across most of the western world tourism has become recognised as a major employer which, in turn, has placed demands on educational institutions to produce graduates with qualifications relevant to the area. Therefore, there has been a substantial growth in the number of universities and colleges that offer undergraduate and graduate qualifications in tourism, recreation and hospitality which provide potential employment for tourism and recreation geographers. The opportunity to develop a career path in tourism and recreation departments which are undergoing substantial student growth, or in a new department, will clearly be attractive to individuals whose career path may be slower within long-established geography departments and who carry the burden of being interested in a subdiscipline often on the outer edge of mainstream geographic endeavour. As Johnston (1991: 281) recognised, 'this reaction to environmental shifts is undertaken by individual scholars, who are seeking not only to defend and promote their own status and careers within it'.

The massive growth of tourism and recreation studies outside geography also means that increasingly many geographers publish in tourism and recreation journals rather than in geography journals. Such publications may be extremely significant for tourism studies but may carry little weight within geography beyond the subdiscipline (e.g. Butler's (1980) hugely influential paper on the destination life cycle). This has therefore meant that the geographers who work in non-geography departments may find themselves being drawn into interdisciplinary studies with only weak linkages to geography. The question that of course arises is: Does this really matter? Disciplines change over time, areas of specialisation come and go depending on intrinsic and extrinsic factors. As Johnston (1991: 9) observes:

> The continuing goal of an academic discipline is the advancement of knowledge. Each discipline pursues that goal with regard to particular areas of study.
>
> Its individual members contribute by conducting research and reporting their findings, by integrating material into the disciplinary corpus, and by pedagogical activities aimed at informing about, promoting and reproducing the discipline: in addition, they may argue the discipline's 'relevance' to society at large. But there is no fixed set of disciplines, nor any one correct division of academic according to subject matter. Those disciplines currently in existence are contained within boundaries established by earlier communities of scholars. The boundaries are porous so that disciplines interact. Occasionally the boundaries are changed, usually through the establishment of a new discipline that occupies an enclave within the pre-existing division of academic space.

However, to borrow the title of a leading geography textbook of the 1980s, *Geography Matters!* (Massey and Allen 1984), it matters because concepts at the heart of geography such as spatiality, place, identity, landscape and region are critical, not only to the geography of tourism and recreation but also to tourism and recreation studies as a whole. In commenting on work undertaken by geographers in the tourism field, Britton (1991: 451) noted that they have 'been reluctant to recognise explicitly the capitalistic nature of the phenomenon they are researching. . . . This problem is of fundamental importance as it has meant an absence of an adequate theoretical foundation for our understanding of the dynamics of the industry and the social activities it involves.' However, such a criticism may be made of tourism and recreation studies overall (Hall 1994).

INSIGHT: The geography of tourism and recreation outside the Anglo-American tradition

While this book concentrates on the geography of tourism and recreation within the English-speaking world, it is important to note that the growing interest of geographers in tourism and recreation is also occuring within other geographical traditions. The internationalisation of the tourism and recreation academic community through such organisations as the IGU Study

Group on Tourism, the growth of student and academic exchanges within the European Union and the use of English as the international language of scholarship has also meant a growing interchange between native English-speaking and English as a second language scholars. Academic journals in English are now increasingly being produced in countries where English is not the native tongue, for example, *Anatolia* in Turkey, and *Tourism Today* in Cyprus. In addition, several tourism geographers, most notably Doug Pearce who undertook his doctoral studies in France, have had the capacity to bring non-English literature to the attention of English-speaking geographers (most significantly his book *Tourism Development* (1981, 1989)).

In examining the tourism and recreation literature of a number of languages and countries, it may be noted that the growth of publishing on tourism and recreation in English is mirrored in these other traditions along with some of the disciplinary differences and issues noted above. For example, a review of *German Geographical Research 1996–1999* edited by the Committee of the Federal Republic of Germany for the IGU (2000) reveals that tourism is now a major subject for publication. Similarly, a recent review of German geographical research in East and South-East Asia also reveals a substantial growth in research on tourism in the region over the past decade (Kraas and Taubmann 2000). Similarly, the excellent review of Spanish tourism geography by Rubio (1998–99) also reveals the very significant expansion in publications on the geography of Spanish tourism, particularly in terms of rural areas, which has gone hand-in-hand with the growth of international visitor arrivals.

French geography also has a strong tradition of research on tourism and recreation that was, arguably, much further advanced in the 1960s and 1970s in terms of both theoretical development and extent of publication than the Anglo-American tradition. One reason for this advanced interest possibly lay in the long recognition of

tourism as a factor in the economic development of French alpine regions and its impact on the cultural and physical landscape (e.g. Knafou 1978). In addition, the growth of tourism on the Mediterranean coast provided a basis for research on coastal resort development (e.g. Burnet 1963; Barbaza 1966) while the significance of second homes for tourism and leisure also has a strong research tradition. More recently, French geographers have written substantive works regarding the impacts of tourism (e.g. Michaud 1983, 1992; Escourrou 1993; Debarbieux 1995), urban tourism (e.g. Lazzarotti 1995; Potier and Cazes 1996, 1998), as well as the social construction of tourism (e.g. Boyer 1996; Deprest 1997). In a review of the geography of tourism and leisure in France, Knafou (2000) notes the diversity of approaches and topics that exist. Indeed, an examination of recent French texts and readings (e.g. Lozato 1985; Clary 1993; Dewailly and Flament 1993; Deprest 1997; Baron-Yellés 1999) suggests that, as in Anglo-American human geography, traditional spatial approaches to studying tourism geography are increasingly under challenge from perspectives strongly influenced by postmodernism (Knafou *et al.* 1997).

Dutch and Scandinavian geographies have been much more influenced by Anglo-American tourism and recreation geography than their French and German counterparts to a great extent because of the role of English as a second language and the publication of much of their research in English. Coastal tourism, rural tourism and regional development are particularly strong themes in Dutch tourism geography (Ashworth and Dietvorst 1995; Dietz and Kwaad 2000), while the work of Greg Ashworth has had a major influence on the fields of urban and heritage tourism (see e.g. Ashworth 1989, 1999; Ashworth and Tunbridge 1996; Ashworth and Ennen 1998) (see also Chapter 5). Scandinavian tourism and recreation geography has had considerable influence in the areas of tourism in peripheral regions and second home development (e.g. Finnveden, 1960; Aldskogius 1968; Jaakson 1986; Halseth and Rosenberg 1995; Kaltenborn 1997, 1998; Müller 1999). Nevertheless, as with Anglo-American tourism geography, a number of significant geographers are not based in departments of geography and are instead located in business schools (e.g. Ettema and Timmermans 1997; Timmermans and Morgansky 1999) or departments of tourism (e.g. Flognfeldt 1998). Asian tourism geographers have also been substantially influenced by Anglo-American publications and research, although unfortunately there is much of the Asian research which is yet to be published in English. For example, recent reviews of Korean human (Kim 2000) and applied (Lee 2000) geography indicate a large body of literature in Korean on event tourism, rural tourism, coastal tourism and resort development. There is also evidence of a growing interest in the geography of tourism in China (e.g. Lew and Wu 1995; Guo *et al.* 2000).

The above discussion is by no means comprehensive of the enormous body of literature of tourism and recreation which exists outside of English. Nevertheless, it does indicate that there appears to be almost universal growth in research on tourism and recreation by geographers regardless of language, and that several of the tensions existing in Anglo-American tourism and recreation geography exist elsewhere. Moreover, there is also increasing cross-over between the different literatures as English continues to expand its academic influence, as indicated by both the growing literature by non-native English speakers in journals published in English and the continued growth in attendance at IGU conferences in which papers are primarily presented in English.

TRANSFORMING THE GEOGRAPHY OF TOURISM AND RECREATION

The situation described in this chapter is that of an area of academic endeavour which is at a critical point in its evolution. Tourism and recreation geography is an applied area of study that is at the periphery of its own discipline but with strong connections to academic research and scholarship outside the area. Dominated by systematic spatial analysis it has a relatively weak theoretical base that has exacerbated its inability to influence wider disciplinary endeavours. Nevertheless, in recent years there appear to be signs of a transformation in its character and fortunes. First, there has been a major growth in the number and quality of publications by tourism and recreation geographers which, although not influencing geography outside the subdiscipline, has had a major impact on the direction of tourism and recreation studies. Second, there is clearly a conscious attempt to provide a stronger theoretical base to tourism and recreation geography which would both be informed by and contribute to contemporary social theory, particu-

larly with respect to such issues as globalisation, localisation, commodification, restructuring and sustainability (e.g. Britton 1991; Hall 1994; Shaw and Williams 1994; Hall and Jenkins 1995; Ioannides 1995, 1996; Montanari and Williams 1995; Hall and Lew 1998). Finally, tourism and recreation geographers are seeking to promote their work more actively in academic and non-academic spheres.

This book reinforces several of the above themes. At one level it seeks to highlight the scope, nature and contribution of geography and geographers to the study of tourism and recreation. However, at another it also aims to provide some insights into the nature of the theoretical transformations which are occurring in the field. Figure 1.3 provides an overall framework for many of the key issues discussed in the book. The figure attempts to illustrate the relationships between some of the foci of the geography of tourism and recreation, including the opportunity spectrum that exists in relation to home-based leisure, recreation and tourism, and corresponding factors of demand and supply. These are themselves influenced and

2

THE DEMAND FOR RECREATION AND TOURISM

Understanding why human beings engage in recreational and tourism activities is an increasingly important and complex area of research for social scientists. Historically, geographers have played only a limited part in developing the literature on the behavioural aspects of recreational and tourists' use of free time (Jackson 1988), tending to have a predisposition towards the analysis of aggregate patterns of demand using quantitative measures and statistical sources. This almost rigid demarcation of research activity has, with a few exceptions (e.g. Goodall 1990; Mansfeld 1992), meant that behavioural research in recreation and tourism has only recently made any impact on the wider research community (see e.g. Walmesley and Lewis (1993) on the geographer's approach to behavioural research), with notable studies (e.g. Walmesley and Jenkins 1992; Jenkins and Walmesley 1993) applying spatial principles to the analysis of recreational and tourism behaviour.

Within the recreational literature, the geographers' contributions have often been subsumed into social science perspectives, such as sociology, psychology and planning, so that the spatiality and placefulness of their contribution has been implicit rather than explicit. For this reason, this chapter discusses some of the key behavioural issues associated with recreation and tourism demand followed by an analysis of the major data sources which researchers use, emphasising how the geographer has used and manipulated them to identify the patterns, processes and implications of such activity.

Within the literature on recreation and tourism, there is a growing unease over the physical separation of the theoretical and conceptual research that isolates behavioural processes and spatial outcomes, and fails to derive generalisations applicable to understanding tourism in totality (see Chapter 1). According to Moore *et al.* (1995: 74) there are common strands in the 'relationships between the various motivating factors applicable to both leisure and tourism'; and as Leiper (1990) argued, tourism represents a valued category of leisure, where there is a degree of commonality between the factors motivating both tourist and recreational activities and many of the needs, such as relaxation or being with friends, can equally be fulfilled in a recreational or tourism context. Although there is some merit in Leiper's (1990) approach, grouping leisure into one amorphous category assumes that there are no undifferentiated attributes which distinguish tourism from leisure. As Pigram and Jenkins (1999: 19) confirm, 'the term recreation demand is generally equated with an individual(s) preferences or desires, whether or not the individual has the economic and other resources necessary for their satisfaction'. In this respect, it is the preference–aspiration–desire level, reflected in behaviour or participation in activities. It is interesting to note that Leiper's (1990) approach has a great deal of validity if one recognises that some tourism motivations may in fact differentiate tourism from leisure experiences, just as the reverse may be true, and that ultimately the particular range of motives associated with a tourism or recreational activity will be unique in each case despite a range of similarities. For this reason, the following discussion examines recreational demand, emphasising many of the explanations commonly advanced in the recreational literature followed by a discussion of the tourism context and the issues raised, bearing in mind the need to compare and contrast each literature base in the light of the arguments advanced by Moore *et al.* (1995) and Leiper (1990).

RECREATIONAL DEMAND

Human activity related to recreation and tourism is a function of an individual's or group's willingness or desire to engage in such pursuits. Yet understanding this dimension in recreation and tourism requires a conceptual approach which can rationalise the complex interaction between the desire to undertake leisure activities, however defined, and the opportunities to partake of them. As Coppock and Duffield (1975: 2) argued: 'the success of any study of outdoor recreation depends on the synthesis of two contrasting elements: the sociological phenomenon of leisure or . . . that part of leisure time which an individual spends on outdoor recreation [and tourism] and . . . the physical resources that are necessary for the particular recreational activities.'

In other words, Coppock and Duffield (1975) acknowledged the need to recognise the interrelationship between human demand as participation or a desire to engage in recreation and tourism, and the supply of resources, facilities and opportunities which enable such demand to be fulfilled. The concepts of demand and supply have largely been developed and applied to conventional market economies, where the individual has a choice related to the consumption of recreation and tourism (see Vendenin (1978); Shaw (1979); Riordan (1982) for a discussion of these issues in the former Soviet Union). According to Smith (1989: 45):

> Recreation geographers use the work [demand] in at least four different ways. The most traditional sense is a neoclassical definition: demand is a schedule of the quantities of some commodity that will be consumed at various prices. . . . A second definition of demand

is that of current consumption . . . [which] is of limited utility to recreation planners because it tells nothing about trends in participation or about current levels of unmet need. Demand is also used to refer to unmet need. This is sometimes referred to as latent demand. . . . Finally, demand is used to describe the desire for a psychological experience.

In contrast, Patmore (1983: 54) acknowledges, 'leisure is far more easily recognised than objectively analysed . . . the difficulties are only in part conceptual: equally important are the nature and limitations of available data', which this section will seek to explain in a recreation context.

According to Pigram (1983) there is a general lack of clarity in the use of the term *demand* in the recreational literature. One can distinguish between demand at a generic level, where it refers to an 'individual's preferences or desires, whether or not the individual has the economic or other resources necessary for their satisfaction' (Pigram 1983: 16) reflecting behavioural traits and preference for certain activities. At another level, there are the specific activities or participation in activities often expressed as visitation rates and measured to reflect the actual observed behaviour. One factor that prevents observed demand equating with participation is the concept of latent demand (the element which is unsatisfied due to a lack of recreational opportunities). Knetsch (1969) identified the mismatch and confusion between participation and demand, arguing that one cannot simply look at what people do and associate it with what people want to do, so ideally any analysis of demand should also consider why people do not participate, and examine ways of overcoming such obstacles by the provision of new resources as well as understanding social and cultural barriers. As Pigram and Jenkins (1999: 20) argued, 'In the real world, recreation demand rarely equals participation. The difference between aggregate demand and actual participation (or expressed, effective, observed, revealed demand) is referred to as latent demand or latent participation – the unsatisfied component of demand that would be converted to participation if conditions of supply of recreation opportunities were brought to ideal levels' (Pigram and Jenkins

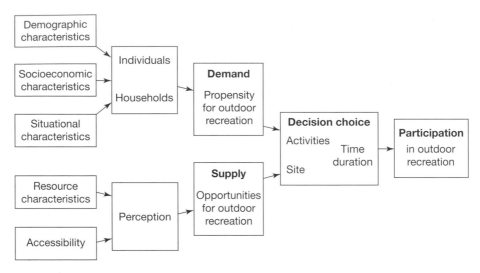

Figure 2.1: The decision-making process in outdoor recreation
Source: Pigram (1983)

1999: 20). Attempting to summarise the factors which influence the decision to participate in recreation led Pigram (1983) to construct Figure 2.1 which highlights the complex range of variables that affect the process.

Most research has examined effective demand which is actual participation rather than latent demand, and the geographers' contribution has largely been related to the spatial and temporal expression of demand in relation to supply (i.e. demand at specific sites). This is very much resource specific, and dates back to the geographical tradition of resource identification, use and analysis which can be traced to at least the 1930s. However, Coppock and Duffield (1975) also distinguish between passive recreation and active recreation, thereby beginning to differentiate between different forms of demand. While passive recreation is by far the most important type numerically, it is difficult to study due to its diffuse and often unorganised nature. Coppock and Duffield (1975: 40) argued that

> Active recreation in the countryside differs from passive recreation in a number of ways. Not only are participants a minority of those visiting the countryside

for outdoor recreation, but they are generally younger and differ in respect of a number of socio-economic characteristics: they often depend on particular (and sometimes scarce) recreational resources in the countryside ... yet as with passive recreation, information about such activities is scanty.

This illustrates the necessity of trying to measure recreational demand together with gauging the types of factors which can facilitate and constrain recreational demand. But what motivates people to engage in recreational activities?

Argyle (1996) argues that part of the reason why people undertake leisure and recreational activities can be found in the process of socialisation and personality traits, where childhood influences such as parents and peers are forms of social influence and learning that affect future activity choice. In fact, nearly half of adult leisure interests are acquired after childhood, and personality factors influence preferences towards specific forms of recreation. However, understanding the broader psychological factors which motivate individuals to undertake forms of recreation is largely the remit of psychologists, being an intrinsic form of motivation (i.e. something one is not paid to undertake).

Table 2.1: Crandall's list of motivations

1	*ENJOYING NATURE, ESCAPING FROM CIVILISATION* To get away from civilisation for a while To be close to nature	10	*RECOGNITION, STATUS* To show others I could do it So others would think highly of me for doing it
2	*ESCAPE FROM ROUTINE AND RESPONSIBILITY* Change from my daily routine To get away from the responsibilities of my everyday life	11	*SOCIAL POWER* To have control over others To be in a position of authority
3	*PHYSICAL EXERCISE* For the exercise To keep in shape	12	*ALTRUISM* To help others
4	*CREATIVITY* To be creative	13	*STIMULUS SEEKING* For the excitement Because of the risks involved
5	*RELAXATION* To relax physically So my mind can slow down for a while	14	*SELF-ACTUALISATION (FEEDBACK, SELF-IMPROVEMENT, ABILITY UTILISATION)* Seeing the results of your efforts Using a variety of skills and talents
6	*SOCIAL CONTACT* So I could do things with my companions To get away from other people	15	*ACHIEVEMENT, CHALLENGE, COMPETITION* To develop my skills and ability Because of the competition To learn what I am capable of
7	*MEETING NEW PEOPLE* To talk to new and varied people To build friendships with new people	16	*KILLING TIME, AVOIDING BOREDOM* To keep busy To avoid boredom
8	*HETEROSEXUAL CONTACT* To be with people of the opposite sex To meet people of the opposite sex	17	*INTELLECTUAL AESTHETICISM* To use my mind To think about my personal values
9	*FAMILY CONTACT* To be away from the family for a while To help bring the family together more		

Source: Crandall (1980)

A simplistic approach to recreational motivation is to ask recreationalists what actually motivates them. Crandall (1980) outlined 17 factors from leisure motivation research (Table 2.1), derived from a synthesis of previous studies in this field, while Kabanoff (1982) identified a similar list of factors (Table 2.2). From Tables 2.1 and 2.2 it is apparent that relaxation, the need for excitement and self-satisfaction are apparent, though Argyle (1996) argues that specific motivations are evident in particular forms of recreation. Torkildsen (1992: 79), however, posits that homeostasis is a fundamental concept associated with human motivation where people have an underlying desire to maintain a state of internal stability. Human needs, which are 'any lack or deficit within the individual either acquired or physiological' (Morgan and King 1966: 776), disturb the state of homeostasis. At a basic level, human needs have to be met where physiological theory maintained that all human behaviour

Table 2.2: Kabanoff's list of leisure needs

Leisure needs scale	Items comprising scales	Item means
1 Autonomy	Organise own projects and activities	2.78
	Do things you find personally meaningful	3.39
2 Relaxation	Relax and take it easy	3.20
	Give mind and body a rest	2.94
3 Family activity	Bring family closer together	2.81
	Enjoy family life	3.30
4 Escape from routine	Get away from responsibilities of everyday life	2.85
	Have a change from daily routine	3.12
5 Interaction	Make new friends	2.35
	Enjoy people's company	2.55
6 Stimulation	To have new and different experiences	2.66
	For excitement and stimulation	2.89
7 Skill utilisation	Use skills and abilities	2.89
	Develop new skills and abilities	2.61
8 Health	Keep physically fit	2.47
	For health reasons	2.46
9 Esteem	Gain respect or admiration of others	2.11
	Show others what you're capable of	2.15
10 Challenge/competition	Be involved in a competition	1.87
	Test yourself in difficult or demanding situations	2.31
11 Leadership/social power	Organise activities of teams, groups, organisations	1.79
	To gain positions of leadership	1.48

Source: Kabanoff (1982)

is motivated. This leads to one of the most commonly cited studies in relation to recreation and tourism motivation – Maslow's hierarchy of human needs.

Maslow's hierarchy model of human needs and recreational and tourist motivation

Within the social psychology literature on recreation and tourism, Maslow's (1954) needs hierarchy remains one of the most commonly cited theories of motivation. It follows the principle of a ranking or hierarchy of individual needs (Figure 2.2), based on the premise that self-actualisation is a level to which people should aspire. Maslow argued that if the lower needs in the hierarchy were not fulfilled then these would dominate human behaviour. Once these were satisfied, the individual would be motivated by the needs of the next level

of the hierarchy. In the motivation sequence, Maslow identified 'deficiency or tension-reducing motives' and 'inductive or arousal-seeking motives' (Cooper *et al.* 1993: 21), arguing that the model could be applied to work and non-work contexts. Despite Maslow's research shaping much of the recreation and tourism demand work, how and why he selected five basic needs remains unclear, though its universal application in recreation and tourism appears to have a relevance with regard to understanding how human action is related to understandable and predictable aspects of action compared to research which argues that human behaviour is essentially irrational and unpredictable.

While Maslow's model is not necessarily ideal, since needs are not hierarchical in reality because some needs may occur simultaneously, it does emphasise the development needs of humans, with individuals striving towards personal growth.

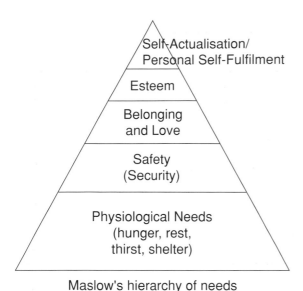

Maslow's hierarchy of needs

Figure 2.2: Maslow's hierarchy of needs

Therefore, Maslow assists in a recreational (and tourism context) in identifying and classifying the types of needs people have. Tillman (1974) summarised some of the broader leisure needs of individuals within which recreational needs occur, and these may include the pursuit of:

- new experiences (i.e. adventure);
- relaxation, escape and fantasy;
- recognition and identity;
- security (freedom from thirst, hunger or pain);
- dominance (to control one's environment);
- response and social interaction (relating and interacting with others);
- mental activity (to perceive and understand);
- creativity;
- a need to be needed;
- physical activity and fitness.

A different perspective is offered by Bradshaw (1972), who argued that social need is a powerful force, explaining need by classifying it as normative, felt, expressed and comparative need. Mercer (1973), Godbey (1976) and McAlvoy (1977) extended Bradshaw's argument within a recreational

context, modifying the four categories of need by adding created, changing and false needs. Normative needs are based on value judgements, often made by professionals who establish that what they feel is appropriate to the wider population. Felt needs, which individuals may have but not necessarily express, are based on what someone wants to do and is a perceived need. Expressed needs relate to those needs and preferences for existing recreational activities which are often measured but can only be a partial view of demand, since new recreational opportunities may release latest demand. Comparative needs are apparent where existing provision for the general population is compared with special groups (e.g. the elderly, ethnic minorities or disabled) to establish if existing provision is not fulfilling the needs of the special group. Created needs may result from policy-makers and planners introducing new services or activities which are then taken up by the population. A false need is one that may be created by individuals or society, and which is not essential and may be marginal to wider recreational needs. Changing needs, however, are a recognition of the dynamic nature of human needs which change through time as individuals develop and their position in the life cycle changes. Thus what is important at one point in the life cycle may change through time as an individual passes through four key stages (Ken and Rapoport 1975):

1 youth (school years);
2 young adulthood;
3 establishment (extended middle-age);
4 final phase (between the end of work and of life).

Other researchers (e.g. Iso-Ahola 1980; Neulinger 1981) prefer to emphasise the importance of perceived freedom from constraints as a major source of motivation. Argyle (1996) synthesises such studies to argue that intrinsic motivation in leisure relates to three underlying principles:

1 social motivation;
2 basic bodily pleasures (e.g. eating, drinking, sex and sport);

3 social learning (how past learning explains a predisposition towards certain activities).

One useful concept which Csikszentmihalyi (1975) introduced to the explanation of motivation was that of flow. Individuals tend to find a sense of intense absorption in recreational activities, when self-awareness declines, and it is their peak experience – a sense of flow – which is the main internal motivation. The flow is explained as a balance resulting from being challenged and skill which can occur in four combinations:

1 where challenge and skill are high and flow results;
2 where the challenge is too great, anxiety results;
3 if the challenge is too easy, boredom may occur;
4 where the challenge and skill level is too low, apathy may result.

But this does not mean that everyone always seeks recreational activities which provide forms of high arousal. Some recreational activities may just fulfil a need to relax, being undemanding and of low arousal. As Ewert and Hollenhurst (1989) reported, those who engaged in outdoor recreational sports with a high-risk factor (i.e. whitewater rafting) viewed the sport as providing a flow experience, and the study predicted that as their skill level improved they would increase the level of participation and risk. Yet even though this occurred the internal motivation of the group remained unchanged, where low and high arousal seem to be juxtaposed. Thus levels of arousal vary from time to time, a factor which can be used by adventure tourism operators to manage the adventure experience and increase the level of satisfaction of participants (Hall and McArthur 1994).

Recreation may also lead to an enhanced self-image, where the identity becomes a basis for motivation because recreational activities can lead to a sense of belonging to a particular and identifiable group. Some activities may also require the development of special skills and enhanced self-esteem. Where recreational activities require a degree of competency, Bandura (1977) proposed that perception of one's ability to perform the skill is a motivator and may result in self-efficacy, a form of self-confidence and judgement of one's ability.

In spite of the significance of motivation, it is apparent that no single theory or even a clear consensus exists in relation to recreation. Instead, 'in theories of motivation need is seen as a force within the individual to gain satisfactions and completeness. There appear to be many levels and types of need, including the important needs of self-actualisation and psychological growth' (Torkildsen 1992: 86). An understanding of needs and intrinsic motivation and some of the ideas implicit in studies of recreational motivation may offer a range of insights into why people engage in recreational activities. But not only is it necessary to understand why people engage in recreation, but also what factors or barriers may inhibit them from participating. Torkildsen (1992) outlines the influences on leisure participation in terms of three categories: personal, social and circumstantial, and opportunity factors. These influences (Table 2.3) are also of value in understanding some of the constraints on recreation.

BARRIERS TO RECREATION

Within the wider literature on recreation and leisure, a specialist research area has developed, focused on constraints, namely those factors, elements or processes which inhibit people from participating in leisure activities. From the diverse range of studies published, two forms of constraint have been identified: intervening constraints, namely those which intervene between a preference and participation, and antecedent constraints, which influence a person's decision not to undertake an activity.

Although the constraints on recreation and leisure literature can be dated to the 1960s, the 1980s saw a range of studies published, a number of which (e.g. Crawford and Godbey 1987; Crawford et al. 1991) have set the research agenda in recent years. In the initial formulation, Crawford

Table 2.3: Influences on leisure participation

Personal	Social and circumstantial	Opportunity factors
Age	Occupation	Resources available
Stage in life cycle	Income	Facilities – type and quality
Gender	Disposable income	Awareness
Marital status	Material wealth and goods	Perception of opportunities
Dependants and ages	Car ownership and mobility	Recreation services
Will and purpose in life	Time available	Distribution of facilities
Personal obligations	Duties and obligations	Access and location
Resourcefulness	Home and social environment	Choice of activities
Leisure perceptions	Friends and peer groups	Transport
Attitudes and motivation	Social roles and contacts	Costs: before, during, after
Interests and preoccupations	Environment factors	Management: policy and support
Skill and ability – physical, social and intellectual	Mass leisure factors	Marketing
Personality and confidence	Education and attainment	Programming
Culture born into	Population factors	Organisation and leadership
Upbringing and background	Cultural factors	Social accessibility
		Political policies

Source: Torkildsen (1992)

and Godbey (1987) proposed that constraints were associated with intrapersonal, interpersonal and structural constraints. In the subsequent reformulation of their thinking, Crawford *et al.* (1991) proposed a hierarchical process model, with their three types of constraint integrated. As a consequence of their model, they proposed Figure 2.3, which indicates that:

- participation in leisure is a negotiation process, where a series of factors became aligned in a sequence;
- the order in which constraints occur leads to a 'hierarchy of importance', where intrapersonal constraints are the most powerful in sequence ending with no structural constraints;
- that social class has a strong influence on participation and non-participation leading to a hierarchy of social privilege, i.e. social stratification is a powerful conditioning factor and may act as a constraint.

This research has provided a framework for further evaluations of constraints (e.g. Samdahl and Jekubovich 1997, and subsequent criticisms by Henderson 1997). In fact, subsequent research by Jackson *et al.* (1993) suggested that the real key to understanding leisure constraints was embedded in the negotiation process: namely how an individual will proceed with experiencing an activity even when constraints are apparent. Ultimately, Pigram's (1983) model helped to frame the context in which participation may occur, and the way that process may be affected by underlying constraints on one's participation. It is against this background that one can appreciate the use of leisure time and leisure space in different cultures (see e.g Horne's (1998) review of Japanese society) and among groups where leisure time in a western conception is inappropriate. For example, in a fascinating review of poor rural women's leisure experiences in Bangladesh by Khan (1997), it is evident that 'the conventional approach to leisure studies which has a myopic view of leisure as free or non-obligatory time' (Khan 1997: 18) is meaningless due to blurring of boundaries between free or non-work time and obligatory activities which are often cumbersome and all-encompassing in everyday life. At an empirical level, a range of notable studies have highlighted the prevailing constraints to recreation. For example, Kay and Jackson's (1991) notable study of 366 British adults' recreational constraints identified:

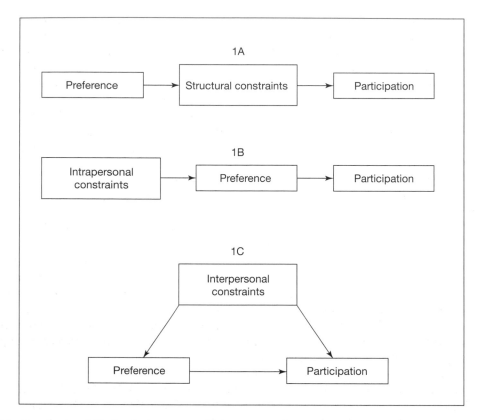

Figure 2.3: Crawford and Godbey's three types of leisure constraints
Source: Crawford *et al.* (1991)

- 53 per cent who cited money as the main constraint;
- 36 per cent who felt lack of time was the main limitation;
- conflicts with family or work, transportation problems and health concerns as other contributory factors.

A study in Alberta which surveyed 1,891 people asked respondents to rate 15 possible barriers to a desired activity, and the results highlighted social isolation, accessibility, personal reasons (lack of confidence or skill), costs, time and facilities as the main constraints. It has been proposed that such constraints have a specific ordering in terms of importance, with the most significant constraints being interpersonal ones, followed by structural ones (e.g. lack of time or money). Yet such arguments have been queried by Shaw *et al.* (1991), who found that in a survey of 14,674 Canadians, of 11 constraints, only lack of energy and ill-health were associated with a lower rate of participation. Therefore, barriers may be negotiable or solvable, as Kay and Jackson (1991) suggest. Patmore (1983) summarises the main physical barriers to recreation in terms of:

- seasonality;
- biological and social constraints;
- money and mobility;
- resources and fashions;

with the availability of time also being a major constraint.

Coppock and Duffield (1975: 8) recognised the principal variations which exist in terms of demand due to variable uses of leisure time budgets by individuals and groups in relation to the day, week and year. Both Coppock and Duffield (1975) and Patmore (1983) use similar data sources (e.g. the UK's Pilot National Recreation Survey (British Travel Association and Univeristy of Keele 1967 and 1969) and sociological studies of family behaviour in the pioneering study by Young and Wilmott (1973)) to examine time budgets, variations in demand and constraining factors. One of the most important distinctions to make is that 'the weekend thus represents a large increase in the time that can be committed to leisure pursuits, which in turn affects the weekend time budget' (Coppock and Duffield 1975: 14). Yet when one looks beyond the day and week to the individuals and groups concerned, a wider range of influences emerge which are important in explaining recreation patterns.

Argyle (1996) highlights the fact that one of the main reasons for examining constraining and facilitating factors is to understand 'how many people engage in different kinds of leisure, how much time they spend on it, and how this varies between men and women, young and old, and other groups' (Argyle 1996: 33). This is because some groups such as 'women, the elderly and unemployed face particular constraints which may affect their ability to engage in leisure and recreational activities which people do because they want to, for their own sake, for fun, entertainment or self-improvement, or for goals of their own choosing, but not for material gain' (Argyle 1996: 33).

SEASONALITY

Patmore (1983: 70) argued that 'one of the most unyielding of constraints is that imposed by climate, most obviously where outdoor activities are concerned. The rhythms of the seasons affect both the hours of daylight available and the extent to which temperatures are conducive to participant comport outdoors.' This is reflected in the seasonality of recreational activity which inevitably leads to peaks in popular seasons and a lull in less favourable conditions. Patmore (1983) identified a continuum

in recreational activities from those which exhibit a high degree of seasonality to those with a limited degree of variation in participation by season. The first type, which is the most seasonal, include outdoor activities often of an informal nature which are weather dependent. The second, an intermediate group, is transitional in the sense that temperature is not necessarily a deterrent since a degree of discomfort may be experienced by the more hardened participants (e.g. when walking and playing sport). The final group is indoor activities which can be formal or informal, and have virtually no seasonality. In addition, the physical constraints of season, climate and weather inhibit demand by curtailing the periods of time over which a particular resource can be used for the activity concerned (Patmore 1983: 72), although resource substitution (e.g. using a man-made ski slope instead of a snow-clad one) may assist in some contexts, but often the man-made resource cannot offer the same degree of excitement or enjoyment.

FINANCIAL RESOURCES AND ACCESS TO RECREATIONAL OPPORTUNITY

Argyle (1996) observed that while many studies emphasised lack of money as a barrier to engaging in recreational activities, Coalter (1993) found that it had little impact on participation in sports. In fact, Kay and Jackson (1991) also acknowledged that money or disposable income was a barrier to undertaking activities which were major consumers of money (drinking and eating socially) whereas it had little impact on sport which was comparatively cheap. Income, occupation and access to a car combined have a significant impact on participation, and as Patmore (1983: 78) succinctly summarised, 'those with more skilled and responsive occupations, with higher incomes, with ready access to private transport and with a longer period spent in full-time education tend to lead a more active and varied leisure life, with less emphasis on passive recreations both within and beyond the home'. It is the car which has provided the greatest degree of personal mobility and access to a wider range of recreational opportunities in time and space since the 1960s in many developed countries (and earlier in some cases such as the USA and Canada). For example, most car-owning households in UK studies have twice the propensity to participate in sport and recreation than non-car-owning households (Hillman and Whalley 1977). Even so, Martin and Mason (1979: 62) observe that 'one of the paradoxes of leisure is that while time and money are complementary in the production of leisure activities, they are competitive in terms of the resources available to the individual. Some leisure time and some money to buy leisure goods and services are both needed before most leisure activities can be pursued.'

GENDER AND SOCIAL CONSTRAINTS

The influence of gender on recreation remains a powerful factor influencing participation, a feature consistently emphasised in national surveys of recreational demand. As Argyle (1996: 44) argues, 'there is an influential theory about this topic, due to a number of feminist writers, that women have very little or no leisure, because of the demands of domestic work and the barriers due to husbands who want them at home . . . [and] that leisure is a concept which applies to men, if it is regarded as a reaction to or contrast with paid work' (see Deem 1986).

Thus women with children appear to have less time for recreation, while those in full- and part-time employment have less time available than their male counterparts (see Argyle (1996) for more discussion of this topic). These general statements find a high degree of support within the recreational literature, with gender differences in part explained by the male free time occurring in larger blocks and in prime time (e.g. evenings and weekends) (Pigram 1983). Even so, studies by Talbot (1979) explore this theme in more detail. Rodgers (1977) documents the wide discrepancy in male:female participation in sport as a form of recreation within a

European context where for every 100 females engaging in sport, there were 188 male participants in Britain, 176 in Spain, 159 in France, 127 in Belgian Flanders, 127 in Norway, 116 in the Netherlands and 111 in former West Germany. While definitions and the variations in data sources may in part explain the variability, the presence of a gender gap is prominent.

Age also exerts a strong influence on participation in recreation, with Hendry *et al.* (1993) describing adolescence as the peak time of leisure needs. Therein lie two key explanations of participation and constraints. Stages in the life cycle present a useful concept to explain why women with young children appear to have fewer opportunities for recreation than adolescents. Likewise, physical vigour and social energy are traditionally explained in terms of a decline in the later stages of adulthood resulting in a decline in active recreation throughout later life. The Greater London Recreation Survey of 1972 (Greater London Council 1976) identified some of these traits in that:

- activities exist where participation markedly declined by age (e.g. energetic sports like football);
- activities occur with sustained participation through the life cycle (e.g. tennis and indoor swimming);
- some activities exist where participation increased as a person got older (e.g. golf and walking).

In fact these results not only illustrate the importance of age (and to a degree gender), but also the need to consider the significance of the life cycle in relation to changes or 'triggers' (Patmore 1983). One such trigger is retirement, and while it is sometimes interpreted as a stressful life event, Long (1987) found that for 58 per cent of male retirees there was no change in their leisure activities, while 8 per cent undertook education, 3 per cent developed an interest in photography and 3 per cent partook of sport. What Argyle (1996: 63) emphasises from studies of retirement are that 'people carry on with the same leisure as before, though they are more passive and more house-bound, and do not take up much new leisure'.

CASE STUDY: The geography of fear in recreation and leisure: gender-based barriers to participation

Since the 1980s there has been a growing interest in the role of fear, personal safety and the spatial implications in the urban environment (e.g. Fyfe and Banister 1996; Koskela and Pain 2000). There has also been an accompanying interest in the gender dimensions of personal safety (Smith 1987; Valentine 1989), which has important implications within an urban environment in relation to the use of public leisure resources such as open space and urban parks. In fact, the concern with such issues may be traced to the changes in the discipline of geography 'and transformative developments both resulting from, and contributing to, a number of new and competing philosophies with the social sciences' (Aitchison 1999: 20). In relation to leisure and recreation geography, this transformation effect can be related to the concern with gender relations and theoretical perspectives associated with the new cultural geography as a mechanism to conceptualise and theorise leisure space. One of the central tenets of this approach is embodied in Green *et al.*'s (1990: 311) comment where 'A significant aspect of the social control of women's leisure is the regulation of their access to public places, and their behaviour in such places'. These critical perspectives have only recently begun to emerge in tourism geography (see Crouch 2000), where empirical, logical–positivist approaches to personal safety have paid little attention to gender and public places.

In conceptual terms, the analysis of the geography of fear, particularly the implications for gender, is a good illustration of the participation issues for particular groups of women. The application of this perspective to recreational and leisure spaces in the city reveals the male domination of public leisure space (Aitchison 1999). The new cultural geographies have seen leisure and recreational geographers move away, albeit slowly, from a positivist paradigm and the model-

building era as new [ ]tualised and theoris[ ] perspectives in leisure[ ] notable development, with the impetus provided by landmark studies by feminist leisure studies (e.g. Talbot 1979; Deem 1986; Green *et al.* 1987).

One of the principal problems with the emergence of a new cultural geography is epitomised in Sharmar-Smith and Hannam's (1994: 13) comments: 'Place is a deceptively simple concept in geographical thought. We want to make it difficult, uneasy.' Herein lie many of the criticisms of the new cultural geography: one must have a sound grounding in social theory, cultural studies and a knowledge of the new tenets underpinning the debates. One consequence is that 'the new cultural geography as it has been referred to since the early 1990s demonstrates that space, place and landscape – including landscapes of leisure and tourism – are not fixed but are in a constant state of transition as a result of continuous, dialectical struggles of power and resistance among and between the diversity of landscape providers, users and mediators'

Plate 2.1: Disneyland is a popular family setting for tourism and recreation. Personal security is a hallmark of its atmosphere.

itchison 1999: 29). This means that the focus is on agency rather than structure, criticising earlier geographical studies of leisure and recreation which did not problematise space or recognise the human element in the landscape. This perspective – and one has to recognise it is only one perspective in geographical research – emphasises the diversity, differences and nuances in cultural phenomena which is the antithesis of logical positivist geographical thought that searches for certainty, coherence and generalisations in relation to patterns, forms and processes of spatial phenomena. As a consequence the new interest in leisure and tourism as cultural phenomena in the 'post-positivist geography [is such] that the new cultural geography has emerged and become merged with sociological and cultural studies analyses which are now combining to investigate the multiplicity of behaviours, meanings, consumption trends and identities constructed in and through leisure and tourism' (Aitchison 1999: 30), and this case study focuses on the sexuality dimension.

Given the growing interest in feminism within the leisure constraints literature (e.g. Henderson 1997), and the concern with constraints to participation (e.g. Jackson 1994), it is timely to focus on the issue of fear, derived from Madge's survey of Leicester's urban park system (Madge 1997).

THE GEOGRAPHY OF FEAR AND RECREATIONAL PARTICIPATION: IMPLICATIONS FOR SOCIAL EXCLUSION

Urban parks are estimated to be used by 40 per cent of the British population (Garner 1996) on a regular basis, but critics argue that urban parks as a recreational resource are being avoided by the general public (Vidal 1994). This is particularly acute for certain groups of the population (e.g. women, children and ethnic groups) (see e.g.

Mowl and Turner 1995), where fear acts as a constraint on use. This adds a new dimension to the recreational constraints literature. Explanations of the growing neglect of urban parks within the UK have been related to a decline in public spending, from 54 per cent of leisure budgets in 1981 to 1982 to 44 per cent in 1991 to 1992, although these statistics need to recognise greater financial efficiencies derived from contracting out park services.

In the 1990s there was growing evidence that urban parks were not perceived as peaceful sanctuaries for recreational and leisure pursuits among the wider population. Burgess et al.'s (1988a) innovative Greenwich Open Space Project documented the dimensions of fear. Dimensions included antisocial behaviour among teenagers and vandalism that reduced local enjoyment and participation. Similar concerns of insecurity, fear and use of parks and open spaces have also been recorded in Australia (Melbourne Parks 1983), and North America (Taylor et al. 1985; Westover 1985; Solecki and Welch 1995). Additional research shows how women, black people, the elderly and the gay community may be excluded from using urban space as freely as other subgroups of the population (Adler and Brenner 1992; Maitland 1992). As Burgess et al. (1988a: 472) remarked in the Greenwich context: 'many people expressed feelings of insecurity and vulnerability in open spaces, reflecting fears of personal attack and injury. Among the Asian community, these feelings are exacerbated by the growth in incidence of racially motivated attacks in public open spaces.' The outcome, as Madge (1997: 238) recognised, was that 'This fear, which reflects structural inequalities in society, is translated into spatial behaviour which usually involves a reluctance to occupy certain public spaces at certain times of the day'. For the geographer, it is the spatial manifestation of that fear and its implications for recreational resource use. Although the evolution and development of Leicester's urban parks are reviewed later in this book in Chapter 5, it is worth observing the socio-demographic context of Madge's study prior to outlining the principal findings.

THE GEOGRAPHY OF FEAR AND URBAN PARK USE IN LEICESTER

Leicester, located in the East Midlands in the UK, is a medium-sized city with a population of 272,000 people. What is notable is its diverse ethnic mix: 72 per cent of the population are white, 24 per cent are Asian, 2 per cent Afro-Caribbean, 2 per cent Chinese and other 'ethnic groups'. Despite the city's urban-industrial development (see Pritchard 1976; Page 1988), it is widely acknowledged that the city has an enviable distribution of open space. By 1994, Leicester City Council was responsible for over 1200 ha of open space, which comprised 20 per cent of the total city area. This is a significant level of provision within an international context, and certainly enhances the city's green and open feel as a British city.

In this context, Madge's (1997) analysis of the geography of fear was timely. The sampling framework, namely face-to-face interviews with Leicester residents at on-street locations sought to derive a sample of city-wide park and open space use, with some 535 respondents inter-viewed. From the survey, ten main constraints emerged which influenced park use. In order of importance these were:

1 Fear
2 Weather
3 Lack of time due to work
4 Family constraints
5 Lack of transport
6 Lack of interest
7 Limited awareness of facilities available
8 Housework
9 Distance of parks/too far away
10 Physically unable to get to the parks.

Some 43 per cent of respondents attributed fear as a 'very important' factor constraining their use of parks. The gender difference was striking with 75 per cent of women compared to 50 per cent of men stating fear was a major constraint on park use. This is in line with Westover's (1985) finding in North America, where 90 per cent of female respondents felt unsafe if alone in parks. Studies of victimisation in Leicester (e.g. Willis 1992) recognise that women have a greater sense of insecurity due to their vulnerability to crime.

When ethnicity was examined, Asian groups expressed higher levels of fear compared with white and Afro-Caribbean groups reflecting victimisation statistics, racial abuse and attacks in the urban environment. In terms of age, those over 45 expressed the greatest levels of fear. As Madge (1997: 241) rightly acknowledged: 'The result of fear of crime is, however, concrete: the elderly are less likely to use public parks for recreation.'

In terms of causes of fear, Madge (1997) observed that the main causes of fear of park use were: anxieties related to actual or potential bodily harm (e.g. mugging, sexual attack, loitering people, gangs of youths, dogs and racial attack). Women's fears were greatest in relation to fear of sexual attack by men. These findings reflected the prevailing levels of fear of sexual violence which women in Leicester harbour, particularly the high level of sexual harassment which was rarely reported (Women's Equality Unit 1993). In fact 77 per cent of female respon-dents were fearful of sexual attacks in parks, a much higher figure than in similar surveys in Edinburgh (Anderson et al. 1990) and Seattle (Warr 1985). Fear of racial attack was also much higher for Afro-Caribbean and Asian groups than for white groups.

The implications of these findings are reflected in the behaviour and use of parks. Women tended to avoid large open spaces, unlit areas and those areas with dense undergrowth and trees. The onset of nightfall also elevated fear of using such places, especially if they were alone. As Madge (1997: 245) suggested, 'Fear is a significant factor structuring the use of public parks in Leicester. The intensity and cause of fear varied with social traits of gender, ethnicity and age and affected spatial behaviour regarding use of parks. The geography of fear is mediated through a set of overlapping social, ideological and structural power relations which become translated into spatial behaviour.'

The findings of Madge's study highlight how a new constraint on leisure behaviour has specific gender, ethnic and social ramifications for recreational resource use. Although Madge (1997) criticises the existing recreational literature for neglecting this issue, fear is a more profound issue in urban environments than has hitherto been the case in recreational research. While Hoyles (1994) argued for a greater feminisation of public space, and Madge (1997) argued for increased informal surveillance to encourage public participation and use of parks and open spaces, creating safer parks is deeply embedded in more complex notions of creating safe cities. Koskela and Pain (2000) point to the problems and failures of designing out fear from the urban environment, given the extent to which fear of crime pervades city spaces. In a review of urban public space in Tokyo and New York, Cybriwsky (1999) recognised the growth in the surveillance of public spaces to improve security which could lead to a return to private spaces and attempts to modify social behaviour in recreational spaces. This is a feature which Giddens (1990: 20) recognised whereby 'surveillance is a means of levering the modern social world away from traditional modes of social activity'. Indeed, Koskela and Pain (2000: 279) argued that 'Geographers and planners should take greater account of the complexity of fear.

... Places have some influence on fear, but perhaps of equal or greater significance is the ways in which fear shapes our understanding, perception and use of space and place.' This is certainly a truism in the case of recreational use of urban parks in Madge's (1997) findings which have a wider application to urban recreational resource use in the developed world. A great deal of progress will need to be made in addressing fear of crime and recreational and leisure spaces in urbanised societies until Koskela and Pain's (2000: 274) analysis that 'Green urban spaces and woodlands are commonly perceived as dangerous places and feelings of insecurity often have a deterrent effect on women's use of them' is no longer a valid assessment.

SUMMARY POINTS

- The geography of fear is an important factor shaping participation by certain social groups in recreational activities.
- The problem of fear affects certain groups' participation patterns (e.g. the elderly and women) more than others.
- The creation of safer recreational open spaces is more problematic since it will involve greater surveillance, monitoring and control of informal leisure spaces.
- The new cultural geography, particularly the geography of gender, provides invaluable insights to explain how women's leisure space is embedded in notions of fear, constraints on the use of urban space and the resultant inequalities.
- A more detailed discussion of the development and use of urban parks can be found in Chapter 5.

RESOURCES AND FASHIONS

While models of participation and obstacles to recreation have attempted to predict the probability of people participating in activities, using variables such as age, sex, marital status and social variables (e.g. housing tenure, income and car ownership), predictions decline in accuracy when attempting to identify individual activities (e.g. golf). What such recreational models often fail to acknowledge is the role of choice and preference given a range of options. In this respect, geographical proximity to recreational resources and access to them is a major determinant. This is demonstrated by Burton (1971), who found that in Britain, people were three times as likely to use a recreational resource if they lived between half and three-quarters of a mile away, a feature emphasised by Patmore (1983) and Page *et al.* (1994) in research on urban parks. Veal (1987) expressed this using classic distance–decay theory reproduced in Figure 2.4. This shows that the proximity to a recreational resource increased the propensity for use at a swimming pool, yet for leisure centres where attendees used cars to visit them, the distance–decay function had a less rapid decline in attendance in relation to distance. Outside urban areas, the occurrence of recreational resources are more varied in their spatial distribution, and recreational opportunities need to be closely examined in relation to demand and supply. To provide a number of detailed insights into the patterns of recreation in different countries, and how demand is influenced and constrained, a number of national recreational patterns are examined followed by a case study of regional demand.

MEASURING RECREATIONAL DEMAND

Most geographers acknowledge the continued lack of suitable data on recreational demand, as Patmore (1983: 55) explains:

> Prior to the 1960s sources were scattered and fragmentary, and lacked any coherent basis. The studies undertaken for the American Outdoor Recreation Resources Review Commission and published in 1962 gave the impetus for work in Britain. Two wide-ranging national surveys were carried out later in the latter part of that decade: the Pilot National Recreation Survey . . . and the Government social survey's Planning for Leisure. . . . These surveys remain unique at national level.

Although such surveys also have a number of limitations – they were 'one-off' studies, the methods of data collection did not allow comparability of the data for each survey, and the results are often dated on publication due to the time required to analyse the results – they were a starting point for analysing demand. Yet since 1972 no major survey specifically focusing on leisure has been undertaken in the UK, although the General Household Survey (GHS), which normally occurs every four years (see Parker 1999), has included a number of questions on leisure.

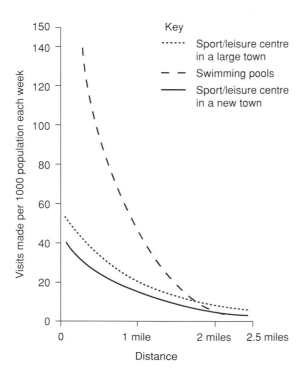

Figure 2.4: The impact of distance and geographical catchment areas on the provision of leisure facilities
Source: Based on Veal (1987)

PROBLEMS AND METHODS OF MEASURING RECREATIONAL DEMAND

When seeking to understand their recreational habits, asking individuals questions about their recreational habits using social survey techniques remains the most widely used approach. A landmark study by Rowntree and Lavers (1951) of *English Life and Leisure* provides a good illustration of the early use of a diverse range of research methods and sources to construct patterns of participation in leisure and recreation in post-war Britain. Even so, researchers recognise that precision is needed to identify participation, non-participation and the frequency of each. For this reason, questions on surveys need to follow the type of format used on the GHS, to provide both a temporal and quantitative measure of demand. Patmore (1983: 57) cites the GHS, which begins by asking respondents: 'What . . . things have you done in your leisure time . . . in the four weeks ending last Sunday?'

Survey data rarely record all the information a researcher seeks (e.g. respondents' recall ability may not accurately record the full pattern), or respondents have a different understanding of a term to that intended by the researcher. As a result, a variety of survey techniques are necessary to derive a range of complementary and yet unique insights into recreation demand.

Within the recreation literature, three techniques have primarily been used:

1 A continuous record of recreation activities of a sample population for a given time period which involves respondents keeping a diary of activities (the time budget approach) (Zuzanek *et al.*'s (1998) cross-national survey of Dutch and Canadian use of time is a good source to consult).
2 Questionnaire surveys which require respondents to recall activities either in the form of an individual case study, which are detailed and sometimes contain both qualitative and quantitative questions and which are inevitably small-scale due to the time involved in in-depth qualitative interviews.
3 Questionnaire surveys which are large scale, enabling subsamples to be drawn which are statistically significant. Such surveys may be derived using simple and unambiguous questions which focus on a specific recreation activity

or one that covers the entire spectrum of leisure activities (e.g. the GHS which surveyed 17,574 people in 1993 in Great Britain aged 16 and over). To illustrate how these techniques have been used and the way such data have been analysed, the time budget approach and national surveys of recreational activities are now examined.

TIME BUDGET SURVEY TECHNIQUES

According to Coppock and Duffield (1975: 5), 'recreation takes place in that portion of people's lives in which they are free (within constraints) to choose their activities, that is, their leisure time, [and] how they spend their time (time-budgets) is of paramount importance in any attempt to establish recreational demand, since it determines where recreational activities are possible'. Therefore, time budget analysis is a vital tool in analysing demand (Anderson 1971). Time budgets provide a systematic record of a person's use of time. They describe the duration, sequence and timing of a person's activities for a given period, usually of between a day and a week. When combined with the recording of the location at which activities occur, the record is referred to as a space time budget. Time budget studies provide for the understanding of spatial and temporal behaviour patterns which may not be directly observable by other research techniques either because of their practicality or their intrusion into individual privacy. Such studies are often undertaken through the use of detailed diaries which are filled in by participants (see Pearce 1988a; Debbage 1991). However, this method has not been widely used in comparison with more traditional survey techniques due to the difficulty for individuals of accurately keeping records. For example, in 1966 and 1974 to 1975 the British Broadcasting Corporation used its Audience Research Department to recruit people to keep a diary for a full week with half-hour entries. Yet even in such a short time span, diarists' willingness to record information accurately declined towards the end of the week (Patmore 1983).

However, pioneering research by Glyptis (1981a) used a diary technique which examined a sample of 595 visitors to the countryside. Respondents kept a diary record spanning three days and five evenings, recording the dominant pursuit in half-hour periods. While respondents identified up to 129 different leisure activities, each cited an average of 11. The value of the study was that through the use of cluster analysis to statistically analyse the sample and to group the population (see Smith (1989) for more detail of this technique), it identified the leisure lifestyles of respondents with distinct groupings, where people of different social classes engaged in similar activities. The value of such research is in the identification of factors beyond simplistic analogies of demand determined by biological, social and economic factors.

NATIONAL EVALUATIONS OF RECREATIONAL DEMAND: INTERNATIONAL PERSPECTIVES

The most useful survey of national surveys of leisure time and the recreational activities undertaken may be found in Cushman *et al.* (1996a) which reviews international data on leisure and the existence of cross-national comparative research. It is also useful since the origins and role of participation surveys are reviewed, a feature subsequently updated by Parker (1999) in the UK context.

The United Kingdom

Since the publication of Patmore's (1983) detailed review of data sources for analysing leisure and recreation patterns in the UK, Veal (1992) updated the situation pointing to the GHS and the role of the Australian Commonwealth government in commissioning the first National Recreation Participation Survey in Australia in 1985 to 1986. This section examines demand at the national level in a number of countries to provide comparisons. Table 2.4 outlines the results from the GHS as a national survey of leisure and recreation habits, with the range of activities included and variations

through time. However the most up-to-date and accessible source which documents these issues in the UK is the Office of Population and Censuses (OPCS) Social Trends. The 1999 edition compiles data from a wide variety of sources and examines:

- Use of time for leisure and other activities showing that men in full-time employment had around two more hours of free time than women in full-time employment.
- Participation in home-based leisure activities in the period 1977 to 1997 indicated that watching television remained the most important pastime, while other activities vary by age and

Table 2.4: Participation in home-based leisure activities: by gender, in Great Britain 1977–97[1]

	1977	1987	1996–97
Males			
Watching TV	97	99	99
Visiting/entertaining friends or relations	89	94	95
Listening to radio	87	89	90
Listening to records/tapes/ CDs	64	76	79
Reading books	52	54	58
DIY	51	58	58
Gardening	49	49	52
Dressmaking/needlework/ knitting	2	3	3
Females			
Watching TV	97	99	99
Visiting/entertaining friends or relations	93	96	97
Listening to radio	87	86	87
Listening to records/tapes/ CDs	60	71	77
Reading books	57	65	71
DIY	22	30	30
Gardening	35	43	45
Dressmaking/needlework/ knitting	51	47	37

Note
[1] Percentage of those aged 16 and over participating in each activity in the four weeks before interview.

Source: General Household Survey, *Social Trends*, Office for National Statistics (2000: 210) © Crown Copyright

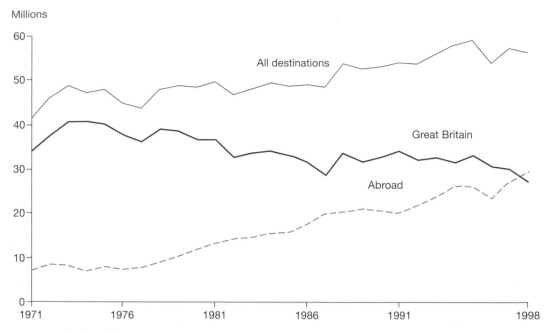

Figure 2.5: Holidays of four nights or more by British residents by number taken per year, 1971–98
Source: British National Travel Survey, British Tourist Authority, *Social Trends*, Office for National Statistics (2000: 209) © Crown Copyright

of consumption of high forms of culture (e.g. visiting museums, exhibitions and concert halls).

More detailed time budget studies have been examined by Olszewska (1989), and Jung (1996) highlighted a number of key global influences upon leisure participation: a growing media influence on mass culture, outbound travel by the Polish population (and inbound tourism), despite the withdrawal of state social subsidies for holiday travel. The electronic mass media also had an impact on leisure consumption. In the post-communist era, problems associated with the commercialisation of leisure and a growing polarisation of wealth, less economic security, rising unemployment and increasing rates of crime provide a new context for leisure participation.

Hungary

Fukaz (1989) examined the Csepel project undertaken in Hungary, which in 1969 sampled 400 blue-collar workers in one of the country's largest metal factories. Further in-depth interviews were undertaken in the period 1969 to 1972, 1975 to 1979 and 1979 to 1982, to collect time budget data as well as in-depth case studies. The longitudinal nature of the survey up to 1982 allows changes to be charted through time, and a simulation sample in 1985 (not using the original 1969 workers) provided a further in-depth case study. While the Csepel project is not representative of the Hungarian population, macro-economic changes in Hungarian society are reflected in the lifestyles of the population and these are reflected in the Csepel sample.

Over the period 1969 to 1985, hours of work in Hungary were reduced from 48 to 40 hours a week, which is often argued by researchers as a precondition for the expansion of leisure. But in Hungary the reduction in official hours of work was accompanied by increases in overtime working and the growth of second jobs. Fukaz (1989: 41) argued that 'as Hungary's economy developed, the prestige of leisure appears to have grown. . . . Only 6.4 per cent in 1976 and 3.9 per cent in 1979 preferred work to leisure on Saturdays'. Yet the evidence from the Csepel study indicates that 'the main obstacles to a growth and enrichment of leisure in Hungary are not rooted in inadequate leisure education, or in a weakening or absence of leisure values. Rather, the barriers have been erected by objective material and financial conditions. The latter have discouraged individuals from using reductions in official work time to enhance their leisure' (Fukaz 1989: 42) preferring to use the time in some cases for pecuniary reward.

In terms of leisure activities undertaken by the Csepel workers, these were largely related to passive forms of recreation. The most popular activities were watching television and just relaxing, though seasonal variations exist, with winter leisure being home-based but urban work patterns tend to dominate leisure in present-day Hungary. The growth of second home ownership (Dingsdale 1986) has also characterised weekend and vacation leisure time for those families with access to such resources.

These three examples of recreational demand show that the patterns of leisure activities for each population exhibit a common range of characteristics, in terms of the predominance of passive activities, and the constraints of urban living which largely structure the time budgets of those in employment due to weekday work commitments. In other words, the patterns of demand highlighted in the three national surveys point to the existence of factors which facilitate and constrain recreational activities in each particular context. Even so, it is important to recognise the current criticisms and concerns with national participation surveys observed by Cushman *et al.* (1996b: 12) as 'Recently surveys have had a "bad press" from academics, particularly in light of the growing popularity – and indeed orthodoxy – of qualitative research methods in the field'. As a result, qualitative researchers point to the shortcomings, limitations and somewhat outmoded approach of quantitative 'positivist' research methods (see Johnston (1991) for a discussion of philosophical perspectives on geography, geographers and research methodologies). However, so far the

discussion of demand has focused on national patterns, and therefore attention now turns to the regional level to examine the contribution the geographer can make to the analysis of demand within a regional geographic framework.

THE REGIONAL DEMAND FOR LEISURE AND RECREATION IN NORTH-WEST ENGLAND

Within the studies of national recreational demand reviewed in the previous section, it is clear that the analyses of geographical patterns of demand were relatively scant, given the tendency for national studies to lack a regional dimension. It is the spatial variations in demand which are of interest to the geographer, and a number of studies have been undertaken which utilise the geographer's spatial analytical approach to examine demand patterns. North-West England is one such area which has seen a significant contribution made to understanding the scale and nature of regional recreational demand including evidence in Rodgers' (1969) insights from the *Pilot National Recreation Survey*, Rodgers' (1977) contribution to leisure in the North-West and Rodgers and Patmore's (1972) *Leisure in the North-West*.

The North-West of England (see Figure 2.6) is an interesting region with a variety of socio-economic contrasts ranging from the urban decline apparent in inner-city areas through to a range of country districts with high levels of prosperity akin to South-East England (see Tables 2.8, 2.9 and 2.10 for a comparison of key socio-economic indicators for North-West England with the situation in the United Kingdom). What Rodgers (1993) explored was the changing political climate for leisure provision at national level, namely the rolling back of the frontiers of the state and changing social philosophy that active and creative leisure pursuits deserved to 'be promoted as widely as possible, with the support of public funding and subsidy, to an increasing emphasis on the concept that the provision of recreation is simply another service industry best left to the operation of the

Figure 2.6: North-West England

Table 2.8: Weekly earnings and hours of work for employees: by gender, April 1998

| | £ Total | £ Overtime | % Earning under | | | | Average weekly hours (total incl. overtime) | Overtime hours |
			£200	£300	£400	£500		
All full-time employees (thousands)								
NW	404.4	28.4	10.5	38.1	62.0	79.2	41.8	3.1
UK	425.6	28.3	9.2	34.6	58.5	75.3	41.7	3.0
Full-time manual male employees								
NW	323.7	44.3	13.2	50.3	76.7	90.9	44.5	5.1
UK	327.2	46.2	12.8	48.6	76.8	90.7	45.0	5.3
Full-time non-manual employees								
NW	480.1	13.6	8.0	26.7	48.3	68.3	39.2	1.2
UK	504.5	13.9	6.4	23.3	43.8	62.9	39.1	1.2
All female employees								
NW	287.1	6.7	26.2	64.1	82.2	93.7	37.6	0.9
UK	308.7	7.2	23.8	58.8	78.2	90.6	37.6	0.8
Full-time manual female employees								
NW	207.3	14.6	53.9	88.2	97.7	99.6	40.4	2.3
UK	209.9	14.1	53.8	88.2	97.1	99.2	40.2	2.0
Full-time non-manual female employees								
NW	303.7	5.1	20.4	59.0	79.0	92.5	37.1	0.6
UK	329.1	5.8	17.5	52.7	74.3	88.9	37.0	0.6

Source: Stationery Office (1999) Regional Trends © Crown Copyright

Table 2.9: Weekly earnings for employees: average gross weekly earnings, 1995

	£ Total	£ Overtime	£170	£220	£300	£400	Average weekly hours	Overtime hours
All full-time employees (thousands)								
NW	354.2	27.6	8.1	21.6	46.6	70.3	42.0	3.4
UK	373.4	26.7	7.7	20.1	43.8	67.7	41.9	3.3
Manual male full-time employees								
NW	290.4	43.3	10.9	28.9	61.4	85.3	44.9	5.6
UK	290.2	43.7	11.0	28.9	60.9	85.0	45.2	5.7
Non-manual male full-time employees								
NW	414.4	12.8	5.5	14.7	32.5	56.2	39.1	1.3
UK	442.4	12.5	5.0	12.8	29.7	53.1	39.0	1.2
All female full-time employees								
NW	254.1	6.6	23.1	48.7	72.8	88.8	37.5	0.9
UK	269.3	6.5	21.4	43.7	68.6	86.2	37.6	0.8
Female manual full-time employees								
NW	187.5	12.3	49.6	74.5	92.5	98.2	40.2	2.0
UK	182.0	11.6	51.8	76.5	93.7	99.1	39.8	1.9
Female non-manual full-time employees								
NW	270.6	5.4	16.5	42.4	68.0	86.4	37.0	0.7
UK	287.7	5.1	15.1	36.7	63.2	83.4	37.0	0.6

Dwelling stock (thousands)	*1981*		*1986*		*1991*		*1994*	
NW	2,466		2,526		2,593		2,637	
UK	21,586		22,601		23,712		24,248	

Source: Stationery Office (1999) *Regional Trends* and other years © Crown Copyright

market for most efficient delivery at least cost' (Rodgers 1993: 118).

This marks a shift in political ideology: that leisure is no longer a significant welfare service to be delivered to all sectors of the population at free or subsidised prices due to the contribution it makes to enhanced quality of life (see Coalter (1998) for a discussion). Thus the move to a market-driven approach (Bennington and White 1988) requires local authorities as the principal planners of community-based leisure provision to recognise the existence of leisure markets which comprise different forms of recreational demand in time and space. Local leisure markets are diverse, where a multitude of factors may affect their composition. For example, those where unemployment, social stress due to environmental factors and low rates of population growth exist may offer little commercial opportunity for the private sector despite real leisure needs. Yet if left to the market, such needs may not be served adequately due to the apparent lack of prosperity or ability of individuals to pay for a resource that poor people view as a luxury item when they cannot always command the financial resources to meet basic needs. Thus, at a regional level, a detailed district-by-district assessment of the market is necessary to show which areas and markets may still require local authority support to avoid gross inequalities in access and provision from developing any further.

Table 2.10: Household income: by source, 1980–81 and 1995–98

Percentage of average gross weekly household income		NW	UK
Wages and salaries	1980–81	72.8	72.9
	1995–98	66.0	66.0
Self-employment	1980–81	6.0	6.1
	1995–98	8.0	8.0
Investments	1980–81	3.1	3.6
	1995–98	4.0	5.0
Annuities and pensions	1980–81	2.7	3.0
	1995–98	6.0	7.0
Social Security benefits[1]	1980–81	14.4	13.2
	1995–98	15.0	13.0
Other income	1980–81	1.0	1.2
	1995–98	1.0	1.0
Average gross weekly household income (£)	1980–81	148.0	150.5
	1995–98	384.0	408.0

Note
[1] These figures cannot directly be compared due to rebates and allowances related to rent/rates/council tax/housing benefit being excluded from gross income calculations after 1994.

Source: Stationery Office (1999) *Regional Trends* and other years © Crown Copyright

Rodgers (1993) used two principles to underpin an analysis of leisure markets:

1 a significant proportion of demand is age-related, and changes through time will affect future needs;
2 socio-economic well-being is a powerful determinant of the volume and pattern of demand in the present and the future.

By combining these factors in an overall assessment, Rodgers (1993) was able to develop a typology of districts and their ability to support a market-based approach to leisure provision. In terms of age-related markets, Rodgers (1993: 119–20) identified four groups:
1 the teenage–young adult, who is active and a major generator of recreational demand, especially active pursuits. Within the North-West, this group exhibits an almost universal decline;
2 the family phase (aged 25 to 44 years), with a distinctive set of leisure interests;
3 a post-family phase (aged 45 to 60 years), where

active recreational interests are in decline but an interest in general leisure activities is strong;
4 the elderly, with a significant range of passive leisure interests.

By analysing forecast population growth in each of these groups, Rodgers (1993: 125) concluded that for planning future leisure provision the following characteristics needed to be incorporated into any geographical assessment of demand:

• A common feature of districts in the region is the absence of growth, except in the family phase. Rates of growth of 4 per cent above the national average are apparent in the age group 25 to 44 years for 1981 to 1991. The opportunities for market-driven provision include fitness training, outdoor pursuits in the countryside, water-sports and ten-pin bowling.
• In the post-family phase, growth rates are less than the national average, with a degree of localised growth in the industrial towns of Greater Manchester, West Lancashire and

Plates 2.2 and 2.3: This coastal area is Wenderholm Regional Park, Auckland. Overuse by recreationalists has eroded the vegetation and these dunes are off limits to visitors to allow the resource to recover.

noted that the 1980s were ripe for behavioural analysis which had been neglected in relation to site surveys. While reviews of site surveys are too numerous to list (see Harrison 1991), novel research methods which examine the behaviour rather than the socio-economic characteristics of recreationalists have remained less common in the published literature, although some reports have probed this area (e.g. Locke 1985). Glyptis' (1981b) analysis of one 242 ha site – Westwood Common, Beverley near Hull (UK) – is one such example. By employing participant observation methods to examine an undulating grassland area of common pasture land 13 km from the urban area of Hull, the spatial distribution of site use by recreationalists was observed and analysed. The main recreational activities observed at the site were sitting, sunbathing, walking, picnicking, informal games and staying inside one's car. On a busy Sunday in summer, up to 2,000 visitors came to the site. Using dispersion maps, observational mapping permitted the visitor distributions to be located in time and space while length of stay (using car registration data) and maps of use for different days and times complemented traditional social survey methods to analyse visitor behaviour. The site features, access points, availability of parking and location of landscape features and facilities permit a more detailed understanding of site use. Glyptis (1981b) used observations on five days in August and

September between 11 a.m. and 6 p.m. to collate data. Visitor arrivals at the site during the weekend occurred between 12 noon and 2 p.m., and peak use occurred at 4.30 p.m., with the majority of visitors spending one to two hours on site. The gradual increase in intensity of use by time of day varied by activity, with informal games and picnicking declining after Sunday lunch and walking increasing throughout the afternoon. Local users also displayed a preference to use the site at off-peak times, with increased patterns of dispersion and clumping through time (Figure 2.8). This reflects access roads, with visitors parking close to (within 15 yards) the site they visited. Visitors were also recorded going to landmarks and facilities (e.g. viewpoints) as well as buying refreshments (e.g. from mobile vans), with the density of use increasing through the day rather than the distribution.

Glyptis (1981c) devised a simple model to explain the dynamics of visitor dispersion (Figure 2.9). Figure 2.9 shows that initial visitors to a site choose a favoured location linked to parking areas, with further inflows of visitors during the early afternoon marking an 'invasion phase' which extends the initial cluster. Thereafter, as the pace of arrivals slows, a degree of infilling and consolidation occurs. Then as people depart, dispersion occurs, with a more irregular pattern of distribution arising, although it may be affected by new arrivals in the afternoon who intensify the pattern. What

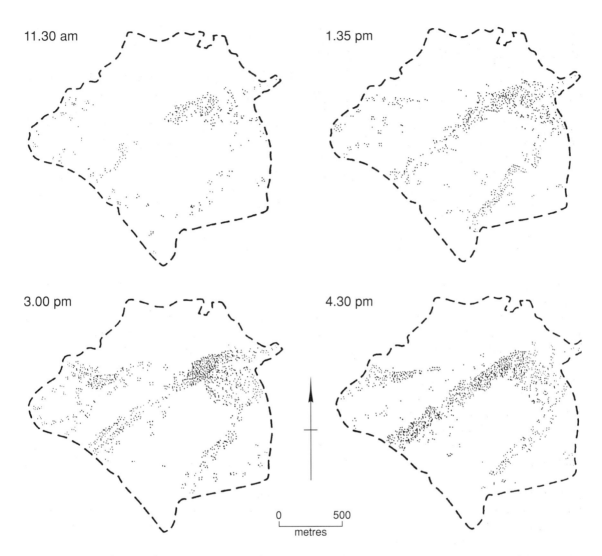

Figure 2.8: Distribution of visitors at Westwood, 3 August 1975
Source: Glyptis (1981b)

Glyptis (1991: 119) recognised was that even though 'sites clearly experience an increase in visitor density, visitor dispersion in a spatial sense remains fairly constant, even with space to spare and no restrictions on public access'. Using nearest neighbour analysis, Glyptis (1981c) was able to measure the distances between groups of visitors, and that comfortable levels of tolerance exist for visitors in terms of proximity to other people, although the amount of personal space which recreationalists require may vary between different cultures. In fact, Glyptis (1991: 119) remarked that 'as levels of use increase on a given day, the percentage occupancy of space actually decreases: visitors only ever use about a fifth of the space available to them, and at times of heaviest use they choose to occupy even less. In other words, site carrying capacity changes continually.' This study also highlighted the significance of recreation sites with multiple uses, where a variety of recreational

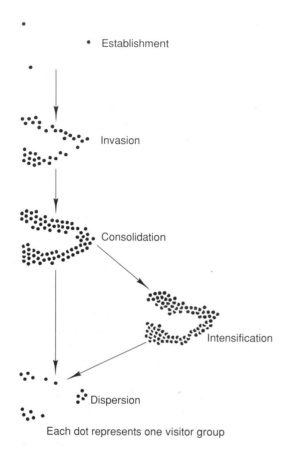

Figure 2.9: Glyptis' model of visitor dispersion at an
informal recreation site
Source: Redrawn from Glyptis (1981c)

needs are capable of being met and, as Burton's
(1974) survey of Cannock Chase, Staffordshire
(UK) found, individual sites cannot be viewed in
isolation: there are relationships between them and
understanding them is vital to site management.
Glyptis (1981c) highlighted a certain degree of
consistency in visitor use of a site, explaining the
patterns as a function of the resource base, visitor
use and behavioural factors. It may be possible to
accommodate or reduce capacity through simple
modifications as 'the geographer is well placed to
examine fundamental aspects of . . . recreation, to
diagnose issues in site management, and to propose
solutions' (Glyptis 1981b: 285). Therefore, having
outlined many of the factors and dimensions of

recreational demand at a variety of spatial scales
from the national, regional and local level, the
discussion now turns to tourism demand.

TOURISM DEMAND

One of the fundamental questions tourism
researchers consistently seek to answer is: Why do
tourists travel? This seemingly simple proposition
remains one of the principal challenges for tourism
research. D.G. Pearce (1995a: 18) expands this
proposition by asking 'What induces them to leave
their home area to visit other areas? What factors
condition their travel behaviour, influencing their
choice of destination, itineraries followed and
activities undertaken?' Such questions underpin not
only issues of spatial interaction, but also lead the
geographer to question:

- why tourists seek to travel;
- where they go;
- when they go and how they get there.

These basic issues have spatial implications in
terms of the patterns of tourism, where tourism
impacts will occur and the nature of management
challenges for destinations which may attract a
'mass market' or be seeking to develop tourism
from a low base. In other words, an understanding
of tourism demand is a starting point for the
analysis of why tourism develops, who patronises
specific destinations and what appeals to the client
market. However, geographers are at a comparative
disadvantage in answering some of the principal
questions associated with tourism demand since
'geographers have not been at the forefront of this
research which has been led by psychologists,
sociologists, marketers and economists. Some of
these researchers have touched on such issues as the
potential significance of variations in motivation on
destination choice' (D.G. Pearce 1995a: 18).
However, tourist behaviour and the analysis of
motivation has not traditionally been the logical
positivist and empirical approach of traditional
forms of spatial analysis on tourism with some

exceptions (e.g. Walmesley and Jenkins 1992). The area of tourist behaviour has a more developed literature within the field of social psychology than geography, and the emphasis in this section is on the way such approaches assist in understanding how tourist behaviour may result in the spatial implications for tourism.

WHAT IS TOURISM DEMAND?

The precise approach one adopts to the analysis of tourism demand is largely dependent upon the disciplinary perspective of the researcher (see Crouch 1994). Geographers view demand in a uniquely spatial manner as 'the total number of persons who travel, or wish to travel, to use tourist facilities and services at places away from their places of work and residence' (Mathieson and Wall 1982: 1), whereas in this context demand 'is seen in terms of the relationship between individuals' motivation [to travel] and their ability to do so' (D.G. Pearce 1995a: 18) with an attendant emphasis on the implications for the spatial impact on the development of domestic and international tourism. In comparison, the economist emphasises 'the schedule of the amount of any product or service which people are willing and able to buy at each specific price in a set of possible prices during a specified period of time. Psychologists view demand from the perspective of motivation and behaviour' (Cooper et al. 1993: 15), while Uysal (1998) reviewed the wider context of tourism demand.

In conceptual terms, there are three principal elements to tourism demand:

1 *Effective or actual demand* comprises the number of people participating in tourism, commonly expressed as the number of travellers. This is most commonly measured by tourism statistics which means that most official sources of data are measures of effective demand.
2 *Suppressed demand* is the population who are unable to travel because of circumstances (e.g. lack of purchasing power or limited holiday

entitlement) which is called potential demand. Potential demand can be converted to effective demand if the circumstances change. There is also deferred demand where constraints (e.g. lack of tourism supply such as a shortage of bedspaces) can also be converted to effective demand if a destination or locality can accommodate the demand.
3 *No demand* is a distinct category for the population who have no desire to travel.

According to Cooper et al. (1993: 16) the demand for tourism may be viewed in other ways using a number of other concepts:

* *substitution of demand* where the demand for a specific activity is substituted by another activity;
* *redirection of demand* where the geographical distribution of tourism is altered due to pricing policies of competing destinations, special events or changing trends and tastes.

Therefore, it is apparent that the analysis of tourism demand as an abstract concept remains firmly within the remit of tourism economics (Witt and Martin 1989, 1992; Bull 1991). Figure 2.10 based on Uysal's (1998) overview of tourism demand summarises the main determinants of demand within a multidisciplinary context. However, the factors which shape the tourist decision-making process to select and participate in specific forms of tourism is largely within the field of consumer behaviour and motivation.

TOURIST MOTIVATION

According to Moutinho (1987: 16), motivation is 'a state of need, a condition that exerts a push on the individual towards certain types of action that are seen as likely to bring satisfaction'. In this respect Cooper et al. (1993: 20) rightly acknowledge that 'demand for tourists at the individual level can be treated as a consumption process which is influenced by a number of factors. These may be

Figure 2.10: Determinants of tourism demand
Source: Uysal (1998)

a combination of needs and desires, availability of time and money, or images, perceptions and attitudes'. Not surprisingly, this is an incredibly complex area of research and it is impossible within a chapter such as this to overview the area in depth. Nevertheless, P. Pearce's (1993) influential work in this field outlined a 'blueprint for tourist motivation', arguing that in an attempt to theorise tourist motivation one must consider the following issues:

- the conceptual place of tourism motivation;
- its task in the specialism of tourism;
- its ownership and users;
- its ease of communication;
- pragmatic measurement concerns;
- adopting a dynamic approach;
- the development of multi-motive perspectives;
- resolving and clarifying intrinsic and extrinsic motivation approaches.

To date no all-embracing theory of tourist motivation has been developed which has been adapted and legitimised by researchers in other contexts. This is largely due to the multidisciplinary nature of the research issues identified above and the problem of simplifying complex psychological factors and behaviour into a set of constructs and ultimately a universally acceptable theory that can be tested and proved in various tourism contexts. As a result, Cooper *et al.* (1993: 20) prefer to view the individual as a central component of tourism demand to understand what motivates the tourist to travel. Their research rightly acknowledges that:

> No two individuals are alike, and differences in attitudes, perceptions and motivation have an important influence on travel decisions [where] attitudes depend on an individual's perception of the world. Perceptions are mental impressions of . . . a place or travel company and are determined by many factors which include childhood, family and work experiences. However, attitudes and perceptions in themselves do not explain why people want to travel. The inner urges which initiate travel demand are called travel motivators.

If one views the tourist as a consumer, then tourism demand is formulated through a consumer decision-making process, and therefore one can discern four elements which initiate demand:

1 *energisers of demand* – factors that promote an individual to decide on a holiday;
2 *filterers of demand* – which means that even though motivation may prevail, constraints on demand may exist in economic, sociological or psychological terms;
3 *affecters* – which are factors that may heighten or suppress the energisers that promote consumer interest or choice in tourism;
4 *roles* – where the family member involved in the purchase of holiday products and the arbiter of group decision-making on choice of destination, product, and the where, when and how of consumption.

These factors underpin the tourist's process of travel decision-making although it does not explain why people choose to travel.

MASLOW'S HIERARCHY MODEL AND TOURIST MOTIVATION

Within the social psychology of tourism there is a growing literature which has built upon Maslow's work (discussed earlier in relation to recreation) to identify specific motivations beyond the concept of needing 'to get away from it all' pioneered by Grinstein (1955), while push factors motivating individuals to seek a holiday exist, and pull factors (e.g. promotion by tourist resorts and tour operators) encourage as attractors. Ryan's (1991: 25–9) analysis of tourist travel motivators (excluding business travel) identifies the following reasons commonly cited to explain why people travel to tourist destinations for holidays, which include:

- a desire to escape from a mundane environment;
- the pursuit of relaxation and recuperation functions;
- an opportunity for play;
- the strengthening of family bonds;

- prestige, since different destinations can enable one to gain social enhancement among peers;
- social interaction;
- educational opportunities;
- wish fulfilment;
- shopping.

From this list, it is evident that while all leisure involves a temporary escape of some kind, 'tourism is unique in that it involves real physical escape reflected in travelling to one or more destination regions where the leisure experience transpires . . . [thus] a holiday trip allows changes that are multidimensional: place, pace, faces, lifestyle, behaviour, attitude. It allows a person temporary withdrawal from many of the environments affecting day to day existence' (Leiper (1984) cited in D.G. Pearce (1995: 19)).

Within most studies of tourist motivations these factors emerge in one form or another, while researchers such as Crompton (1979) emphasise that socio-psychological motives can be located along a continuum, Iso-Ahola (1980) theorised tourist motivation in terms of an escape element complemented by a search component, where the tourist is seeking something. However, Dann's (1981) conceptualisation is probably one of the most useful attempts to simplify the principal elements of tourist motivation into:

- travel as a response to what is lacking yet desired;
- destination pull in response to motivational push;
- motivation as fancy;
- motivation as classified purpose;
- motivation typologies;
- motivation and tourist experiences;
- motivation as definition and meaning.

This was simplified a stage further by McIntosh and Goeldner (1990) into:

- physical motivators;
- cultural motivators;
- interpersonal motivators;
- status and prestige motivators.

On the basis of motivation and using the type of experiences tourists seek, Cohen (1972) distinguished between four types of travellers:

1 The organised mass tourist, on a package holiday, who is highly organised. Their contact with the host community in a destination is minimal.
2 The individual mass tourist, who uses similar facilities to the organised mass tourist but also desires to visit other sights not covered on organised tours in the destination.
3 The explorers, who arrange their travel independently and who wish to experience the social and cultural lifestyle of the destination.
4 The drifter, who does not seek any contact with other tourists or their accommodation, preferring to live with the host community (see V.L. Smith 1992).

Clearly, such a classification is fraught with problems, since it does not take into account the increasing diversity of holidays undertaken and inconsistencies in tourist behaviour (Pearce 1982). Other researchers suggest that one way of overcoming this difficulty is to consider the different destinations tourists choose to visit, and then establish a sliding scale similar to Cohen's (1972) typology, but which does not have such an absolute classification.

In contrast, Plog (1974) devised a classification of the US population into psychographic types, with travellers distributed along a continuum (see Figure 2.11) from psychocentrism to allocentrism. The psychocentrics are the anxious, inhibited and less adventurous travellers while at the other extreme the allocentrics are adventurous, outgoing, seeking new experiences due to their inquisitive personalities and interest in travel and adventure.

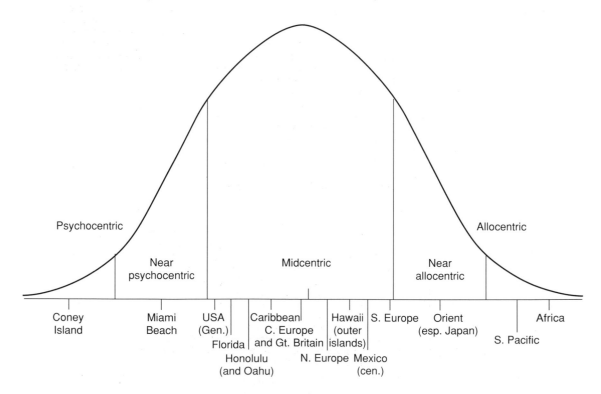

Figure 2.11: Plog's psychographic positions of destinations
Source: Redrawn from Plog (1977)

D.G. Pearce (1995) highlights the spatial implications of such conceptualisations, that each tourist type will seek different destinations which will change through time. However, criticisms by P. Pearce (1993) indicate that Plog's model is difficult to use because it fails to distinguish between extrinsic and intrinsic motivations without incorporating a dynamic element to encompass the changing nature of individual tourists. P. Pearce discounts such models, suggesting that individuals have a 'career' in their travel behaviour where people 'start at different levels, they are likely to change levels during their life-cycle and they can be prevented from moving by money, health and other people. They may also retire from their travel

career or not take holidays at all and therefore not be part of the system' (P. Pearce 1993: 125).

Figure 2.12 outlines Pearce's model based on a leisure ladder, which builds on Maslow's hierarchial system where there are five motivational levels. These are:

1 a concern with biological needs;
2 safety and security needs;
3 relationship development and extension needs;
4 special interest and self-development needs;
5 fulfilment or self-actualisation needs.

Cooper *et al.* (1993: 23) argue that 'the literature on tourism motivation is still in an immature phase of development, it has been shown that motivation

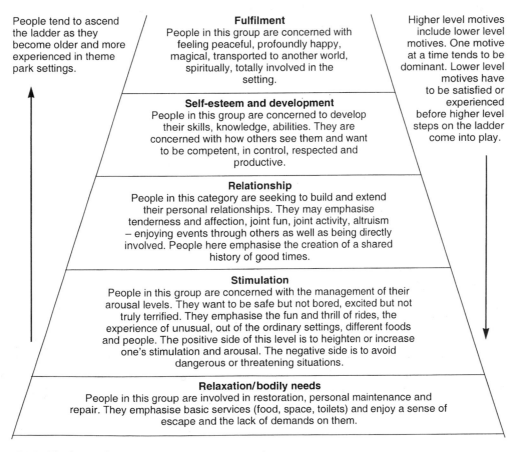

Figure 2.12: The leisure ladder for theme park settings (domestic visitors)
Source: Pearce (1993a)

is an essential concept behind the different patterns of tourism demand'. From the existing literature on tourist motivation, the problems of determining tourist motivation may be summarised as follows:

- Tourism is not one specific product, it is a combination of products and experiences which meet a diverse range of needs.
- Tourists are not always conscious of their deep psychological needs and ideas. Even when they do know what they are, they may not reveal them.
- Tourism motives may be multiple and contradictory (push and pull factors).
- Motives may change over time and be inextricably linked together (e.g. perception, learning, personality and culture are often separated out but they are all bound up together) and dynamic conceptualisations such as P. Pearce's (1993) leisure ladder are crucial to advancing knowledge and understanding in this area.

Having examined some of the issues associated with what motivates tourists to travel, attention now turns to the process of measurement and recording tourist demand using statistical measures.

THE MEASUREMENT OF TOURISM DEMAND: TOURISM STATISTICS

Ritchie (1975, cited in Latham 1989: 55) argued that 'an important part of the maturing process for any science is the development or adaptation of consistent and well-tested measurement techniques and methodologies which are well-suited to the types of problems encountered in practice'. In this context, the measurement of tourists, tourism activity and the effects on the economy and society in different environments is crucial to the development of tourism as an established area of study within the confines of social science. Burkart and Medlik (1981) provide a useful insight into the development of measurements of tourism phenomena by governments during the 1960s and their subsequent development through to the late 1970s.

While it is readily acknowledged by most tourism researchers that statistics are a necessary feature to provide data to enable researchers, managers, planners, decision-makers and public and private sector bodies to gauge the significance and impact of tourism on destination areas, Burkart and Medlik (1981: 74) identify four principal reasons for statistical measurement in tourism:

1 to evaluate the magnitude and significance of tourism to a destination area or region;
2 to quantify the contribution to the economy or society, especially the effect on the balance of payments;
3 to assist in the planning and development of tourism infrastructure and the effect of different volumes of tourists with specific needs;
4 to assist in the evaluation and implementation of marketing and promotion activities where the tourism marketer requires information on the actual and potential markets and their characteristics.

Consequently, tourism statistics are essential to the measurement of the volume, scale, impact and value of tourism at different geographical scales from the global to the country level down to the individual destination. Yet an information gap exists between the types of statistics provided by organisations for and the needs of users. The compilation of tourism statistics provided by organisations associated with the measurement of tourism has established methods and processes to collect, collate and analyse tourism statistics (World Tourism Organisation (WTO) 1996), yet these have been understood by only a small number of researchers and practitioners. Thus this section attempts to demystify the apparent sophistication and complexity associated with the presentation of statistical indicators of tourism and their value to spatial analysis, since geographers have a strong quantified methods tradition (Johnston 1991), which is reflected in the use and reliance upon such indicators to understand spatial variations and patterns of tourism activity. All too often, undergraduate and many postgraduate texts assume a prior knowledge of tourism statistics and they are only dealt with in a limited way by most tourism texts, and where such issues are raised they are usually discussed in over-technical texts aimed at a limited audience (e.g. Frechtling 1996).

A commonly misunderstood feature which is associated with tourism statistics is that they are a complete and authoritative source of information (i.e. they answer all the questions posed by the researcher). Other associated problems are that statistics are recent and relate to the previous year or season, implying that there is no time lag in their generation, analysis, presentation and dissemination to interested parties. In fact, most tourism statistics are 'typically measurements of arrivals, trips, tourist nights and expenditure, and these often appear in total or split into categories such as business or leisure travel' (Latham 1989: 55–76). Furthermore, the majority of published tourism statistics are derived from sample surveys, with the results being weighted or statistically manipulated to derive a measure which is supposedly representative of the real-world situation. In reality, this often means that tourism statistics are subject to significant errors depending on the size of the sample.

The statistical measurement of tourists is far from straightforward, and Latham (1989) identifies a number of distinctive and peculiar problems associated with the tourist population:

- Tourists are a transient and highly mobile population, making statistical sampling procedures difficult when trying to ensure statistical accuracy and rigour in methodological terms.
- Interviewing mobile populations such as tourists is often undertaken in a strange environment, typically at ports or points of departure or arrival where there is background noise which may influence responses.
- Other variables, such as the weather, may affect the responses.

Even where sampling and survey-related problems can be minimised, one has to treat tourism statistics with a degree of caution because of additional methodological issues that can affect the results. For example, tourism research typically comprises:

- pre-travel studies of tourists' intended travel habits and likely choice of destination (intentional studies);
- studies of tourists in transit to provide information on their actual behaviour and plans for the remainder of their holiday or journey (actual and intended studies);
- studies of tourists at the destination or at specific tourist attractions and sites, to provide information on their actual behaviour, levels of satisfaction, impacts and future intentions (actual and intended studies);
- post-travel studies of tourists on their return journey from their destination or on-site experience or once they have returned to their place of residence (post-travel measures).

In an ideal world, where resource constraints are not a limiting factor on the generation of statistics, each of the aforementioned approaches should be used to provide a broad spectrum of research information on tourism and tourist behaviour. In reality, organisations and government agencies select a form of research which meets their own particular needs. In practice, most tourism statistics are generated with practical uses in mind and they may usually, though not exclusively, be categorised as follows:

- measurement of tourist volume, enumerating arrivals, departures and the number of visits and stays;
- expenditure-based surveys which quantify the value of tourist spending at the destination and during the journey;
- the characteristics and features of tourists to construct a profile of the different markets and segments visiting a destination.

However, before any tourism statistics can be derived, it is important to deal with the complex and thorny issue of defining the population – the tourist. Therefore, how does one define and differentiate between the terms *tourism* and *tourist*?

DEFINING TOURISM

The terms *travel* and *tourism* are often interchanged within the published literature on tourism, though they are normally meant to encompass 'the field of research on human and business activities associated with one or more aspects of the temporary movement of persons away from their immediate home communities and daily work environments for business, pleasure and personal reasons' (Chadwick 1994: 65). These two terms tend to be used in differing contexts to mean similar things, although there is a tendency for the United States to continue to use the term 'travel' when in fact they mean tourism. Despite this inherent problem which may be little more than an exercise in semantics, it is widely acknowledged that the two terms are used in isolation or in unison to 'describe' three concepts:

1 the movement of people;
2 a sector of the economy or an industry;
3 a broad system of interacting relationships of people (including their need to travel outside their communities and services that attempt to respond to these needs by supplying products) (Chadwick 1994).

From this initial starting point, one can begin to explore some of the complex issues in arriving at a working definition of the terms *tourism* and *tourist*.

In a historical context, Burkart and Medlik (1981: 41) identify the historical development of the term *tourism*, noting the distinction between the endeavours of researchers to differentiate between the concept and technical definitions of tourism. The concept of tourism refers to the 'broad notional framework, which identifies the essential characteristics, and which distinguishes tourism from the similar, often related, but different phenomena'. In contrast, technical definitions have evolved through time as researchers modify and develop appropriate measures for statistical,

legislative and operational reasons implying that there may be various technical definitions to meet particular purposes. However, the concept of tourism, and its identification for research purposes, is an important consideration in this instance for tourism statistics so that users are familiar with the context of their derivation.

While most tourism books, articles and monographs now assume either a standard definition or interpretation of the concept of tourism, which is usually influenced by the social scientists' perspective (i.e. a geographical, economic, political, sociological approach or other disciplines), Burkart and Medlik's (1981) approach to the concept of tourism continues to offer a valid assessment of the situation where five main characteristics are associated with the concept.

1 Tourism arises from the movement of people to, and their stay in, various destinations.
2 There are two elements in all tourism: the journey to the destination and the stay including activities at the destination.
3 The journey and the stay take place outside the normal place of residence and work, so that tourism gives rise to activities which are distinct from those of the resident and working populations of the places, through which tourists travel and in which they stay.
4 The movement to tourist destinations is of a temporary, short-term character, with the intention of returning home within a few days, weeks or months.
5 Destinations are visited for purposes other than taking up permanent residence or employment remunerated from within the places visited (Burkart and Medlik 1981: 42).

Furthermore, Burkart and Medlik's (1981) definition of tourism as a concept is invaluable because it rightly recognises that much tourism is a leisure activity which involves a discretionary use of time and money, and recreation is often the main purpose for participation in tourism. But this is no reason for restricting the total concept in this way and the essential characteristics of tourism can best be interpreted to embrace a wider concept. All tourism includes some travel but not all travel is tourism, while the temporary and short-term nature of most tourist trips distinguishes it from migration. Therefore, from the broad interpretation of tourism, it is possible to consider the technical definitions of tourism (also see Leiper (1990) for a further discussion, together with Medlik (1993) and Hall (1995) for a concise set of definitions).

TECHNICAL DEFINITIONS OF TOURISM

Technical definitions of tourism are commonly used by organisations seeking to define the population to be measured, and there are three principal features which normally have to be defined (see BarOn (1984) for a detailed discussion):

1 Purpose of travel (e.g. the type of traveller, be it business travel, holiday-makers, visits to friends and relatives or for other reasons).
2 The time dimension involved in the tourism visit, which requires a minimum and a maximum period of time spent away from the home area and the time spent at the destination. In most cases, this would involve a minimum stay of more than 24 hours away from home and less than a year as a maximum.
3 Those situations where tourists may or may not be included as tourists, such as cruise passengers, those tourists in transit at a particular point of embarkation/departure and excursionists who stay less than 24 hours at a destination (e.g. the European duty-free cross-channel day-trip market).

Among the most recent attempts to recommend appropriate definitions of tourism was the World Tourism Organisation (hereafter WTO) International Conference of Travel and Tourism in Ottawa in 1991 which reviewed, expanded and developed technical definitions, where tourism comprises 'the activities of a person travelling outside his or her usual environment for less than a specified period of time and whose main purpose of travel is other than exercise of an activity remunerated from the place visited', where 'usual environment' is intended to exclude trips within the areas of usual residence and also frequent and regular trips between the domicile and the work-place and other community trips of a routine character, where 'less than a specified period of time' is intended to exclude long-term migration, and 'exercise of an activity remunerated from the place visited' is intended to exclude only migration for temporary work. The following definitions were developed by the WTO:

• International tourism: consists of inbound tourism.
• Visits to a country by non-residents and outbound tourism residents of a country visiting another country.
• Internal tourism: residents of a country visiting their own country.
• Domestic tourism: internal tourism plus inbound tourism (the tourism market of accommodation facilities and attractions within a country).
• National tourism: internal tourism plus outbound tourism (the resident tourism market for travel agents and airlines) (WTO, cited in Chadwick 1994: 66).

In order to improve statistical collection and improve understanding of tourism, the United Nations (UN) (1994) and the WTO (1991a) also recommended differentiating between visitors, tourists and excursionists (day trippers). The WTO (1991a) recommended that an international tourist be defined as: 'a visitor who travels to a country other than that in which he/she has his/her usual residence for at least one night but not more than one year, and whose main purpose of visit is other than the exercise of an activity remunerated from within the country visited'; and that an international excursionist (e.g. cruise ship visitors) be defined as 'a visitor residing in a country who travels the same day to a country other than which he/she has his/her usual environment for less than

24 hours without spending the night in the country visited and whose main purpose of visit is other than the exercise of an activity remunerated from within the country visited'. Similar definitions were also developed for domestic tourists, with domestic tourists having a time limit of 'not more than six months' (WTO 1991a; UN 1994).

Interestingly, the inclusion of a same-day travel, 'excursionist' category in UN/WTO technical definitions of tourism makes the division between recreation and tourism even more arbitrary, and there is increasing international agreement that 'tourism' refers to all activities of visitors, including both overnight and same-day visitors (UN 1994: 5). Given improvements in transport technology, same-day travel is becoming increasingly important to some countries, with the UN (1994: 9) observing, 'day visits are important to consumers and to many providers, especially tourist attractions, transport operators and caterers'.

Chadwick (1994) moves the definition of tourists a stage further by offering a typology of travellers (tourists) which highlights the distinction between tourists (travellers) and non-travellers (non-tourists) which is summarised in Figure 2.13. Figure 2.13 is distinctive because it highlights all sections of society which are involved in travel of some kind, but it also looks at the motivation to travel. It is also useful because it illustrates where technical problems may occur in deciding which groups to include in tourism and which to exclude.

From this classification of travellers, the distinction between international and domestic tourism needs to be made. Domestic tourism normally refers to tourists who travel from their normal domicile to other areas within a country. In contrast, international tourism normally involves a tourist leaving their country of origin to cross into another country which involves documentation, administrative formalities and movement to a foreign environment.

DOMESTIC TOURISM STATISTICS

D.G. Pearce (1995a) acknowledges that the scale and volume of domestic tourism worldwide exceeds that of international tourism, though it is often viewed as the poorer partner in the compilation of statistics. For example, most domestic tourism statistics tend to underestimate the scale and volume of flows since certain aspects of domestic tourist movements are sometimes ignored in official sources. The 'visits to friends and relatives, the use of forms of accommodation other than hotels (for example, second homes, camp and caravan sites) and travel by large segments of a population from towns to the countryside are not for the most part included' (Latham 1989: 65). This is supported by the WTO, who argue that 'there are relatively few countries that collect domestic travel and tourism statistics. Moreover some countries rely exclusively on the traditional hotel sector, thereby leaving out of account the many travellers staying in supplementary accommodation establishments or with friends and relatives' (WTO (1984), cited in Latham 1989: 65). Therefore, the collection of domestic tourism statistics requires the use of different data sources aside from the more traditional sources such as hotel records which identify the origin and duration of a visitor's stay.

To assist in the identification of who to include as a domestic tourist, the WTO (1983) suggests the following working definition: 'any person, regardless of nationality, resident in a country and who travels to a place in the same country for not more than one year and whose main purpose of visit is other than following an occupation remunerated from within the place visited.'

Such a definition includes domestic tourists where an overnight stay is involved and domestic excursionists who visit an area for less than 24 hours and do not stay overnight. In fact, Latham (1989: 66) points to the variety of definitions which exist aside from those formulated by WTO and the following issues complicate matters further:

- *Purpose of visit* – all countries using this concept define a domestic tourist as one who travels for a purpose other than to perform a remunerated activity.
- *The length of trip and/or distance travelled* – certain definitions state that travellers should,

(1) 'Tourists' in international technical definitions
(2) 'Excursionists' in international technical definitions
(3) Travellers whose trips are shorter than those which qualify for travel and tourism, e.g. under 50 miles (80 km) from home
(4) Students travelling between home and school only – other travel of students is within scope of travel and tourism
(5) All persons moving to a new place of residence including all one-way travellers such as emigrants, immigrants, refugees, domestic migrants and nomads

Figure 2.13: A classification of travellers
Source: Chadwick (1987)

for example, be involved in an overnight stay and/or travel a prescribed minimum distance.

- *Type of accommodation* – for practical reasons, some countries restrict the concept of domestic tourism to cover only those persons using commercial accommodation facilities (after Latham 1989: 66).

Problems in applying WTO definitions may also reflect an individual country's reasons for generating such statistics, which may not necessarily be to contribute to a better understanding of statistics *per se*. For example, WTO (1981) identified four uses of domestic tourism statistics:

1 To calculate the contribution of tourism to the country's economy, whereby estimates of tourism's value to the Gross Domestic Product is estimated due to the complexity of identifying the scope of tourism's contribution.
2 To assist in the marketing and promotion of tourism, where government-sponsored tourism organisations seek to encourage its population to take domestic holidays rather than to travel overseas (see Hall (1997a) for a discussion of this activity among Pacific Rim countries).
3 To aid the regional development policies of governments which harness tourism as a tool for area development where domestic tourists in congested environments are encouraged to travel to less developed areas and to improve the quality of tourism in different environments.
4 To achieve social objectives, where socially oriented tourism policies may be developed for the underprivileged which requires a detailed understanding of the holiday-taking habits of a country's nationals.

Regional and local tourist organisations also make use of such data to develop and market destinations and different businesses within the tourism sector. But how is domestic tourism measured?

Burkart and Medlik (1981) argue that two principal features need to be measured: first, the volume, value and characteristics of tourism among the population of the country; second, the same data relating to individual destinations within the country. The WTO (1981, cited in Latham 1989) considers the minimum data requirements for the collection of domestic tourism statistics in terms of arrivals and tourist nights in accommodation classified by:

- month;
- type of grade of accommodation establishment;
- location of the accommodation establishment and overall expenditure on domestic tourism.

Latham (1989) argues that it is possible to generate additional data from such variables including length of stay, occupancy rate and average expenditure. Many countries also collate supplementary information beyond the minimum standards identified by WTO, where the socio-economic characteristics of tourists are identified, together with their use of tourist transport and purpose of visit, though the cost of such data collection does mean that the statistical basis of domestic tourism in many less developed countries remains poor.

The methods used to generate domestic tourism statistics are normally based on the estimates of volume, value and scale derived from sample surveys due to the cost of undertaking large-scale surveys of tourist activities. The immediate problem facing the user of such material is the type of errors and degree of accuracy which can be attached to such data. For example, Latham (1989) identifies the following sample surveys which are now used to supplement data derived from hotel records:

- *Household surveys*, where the residents of a country are interviewed in their own home to ascertain information of tourist trips for the purpose of pleasure. A useful example of a pan-European study is the EC Omnibus study. Even so, little progress has been made internationally to collate common data on household surveys since the OECD's attempt in 1967 to outline the types of data which national travel surveys should collect.

- *Destination surveys*, where high levels of tourist activity occur in a region or resort. Such studies frequently compile statistics on accommodation usage, sample surveys of visitors and may be linked to existing knowledge derived from household surveys.
- *En route surveys*, where tourists are surveyed en route to examine the characteristics and features of tourists. Although it is a convenient way to interview a captive audience depending upon the mode of transport used (see Page 1994a, b), the results may not necessarily be as representative without a complete knowledge of the transport flows for the mode of tourist transport being surveyed.

The problem of incomplete questionnaires or non-response may occur where such surveys require a respondent to post the form back to the surveyor (see Hurst (1987) for a review on the use of this survey type).

INTERNATIONAL TOURISM STATISTICS

The two principal organisations which collate data on international tourism are the World Tourism Organisation (WTO) and the Organisation for Economic Cooperation and Development (OECD). In addition, international regional tourism organisations such as the Pacific Asia Travel Association and the ASEAN Tourism Working Group also collect international tourism statistics (Hall 1997a). Page (1994b) reviews the major publications of the first two organisations in relation to international tourism, noting the detailed contents of each. In the case of the WTO, the main source is the *Yearbook of Tourism Statistics*, which contains a summary of the most salient tourism statistics for almost 150 countries and territories. In the case of the OECD, their *Tourism Policy and International Tourism* (referred to as the 'Blue Book') is less comprehensive, covering only 25 countries, but it does contain most of the main generating and receiving areas. While the main thrust of the publication is

government policy and the obstacles to international tourism, it does expand on certain areas not covered in the WTO publication (for a more detailed discussion of data sources see Withyman 1985).

In contrast to domestic tourism, statistics on international tourism are normally collected to assess the impact of tourism on a country's balance of payments, though as Withyman (1985: 69) argued:

> Outward visitors seem to attract less attention from the pollsters and the enumerators. Of course, one country's outward visitor is another country's (perhaps several countries) inward visitor, and a much more welcome sort of visitor, too, being both a source of revenue and an emblem of the destination country's appeal in the international market. This has meant that governments have tended to be generally more keen to measure inward than outward tourism, or at any rate, having done so, to publish the results.

This statement indicates that governments are more concerned with the direct effect of tourism on their balance of payments. Yet such statistics are also utilised by marketing arms of national tourism organisations to base their decisions on who to target in international campaigns. The wider tourism industry also makes use of such data as part of their strategic planning and for more immediate purposes where niche markets exist. Even so, Shackleford (1980) argued that the collection of tourism statistics should be a responsibility of the state to meet international standards for data collection (WTO 1996). However, it is increasingly the case that only when the economic benefits of data collection can be justified will national governments continue to compile tourism statistics. Where resource constraints exist, the collection and compilation of tourism statistics may be impeded. This also raises important methodological issues related to what exactly is being measured. As Withyman (1985: 61) argued: 'In the jungle of international travel and tourism statistics, it behoves the explorer to step warily; on all sides there is luxuriant growth. Not all data sources are what they appear to be – after close scrutiny some show themselves to be inconsistent and often unsuitable for the industry researcher and planner.' The key point Withyman (1985) recognises is the lack of comparability in tourism data in relation to what is measured (e.g. is it visitor days or visitor nights?) and the procedures and methodology used to measure international tourism.

Frechtling (1976) concluded that the approaches taken by national and international agencies associated with international tourism statistics were converging towards common definitions of trip, travel and traveller (see Chadwick (1994) for a fuller discussion). Yet the principal difficulty which continues to be associated with this is whether business travel should be considered as a discrete activity in relation to tourism. Chadwick (1994: 75) notes that 'the consensus of North American opinion seems to be that, despite certain arguments to the contrary . . . business travel should be considered part of travel and tourism'. While BarOn (1984) examines the standard definitions and terminology of international tourism as used by the UN and WTO, research by Ngoh (1985) is useful in that it considers the practical problems posed by such definitions when attempting to measure international tourism and find solutions to the difficulties.

Latham (1989) suggests that the main types of international tourism statistics collated relate to:

- volume of tourists;
- expenditure by tourists;
- the profile of the tourist and their trip characteristics.

As is true of domestic tourism, estimates form the basis for most statistics on international tourism since the method of data collection does not generate exact data. For example, volume statistics are often generated from counts of tourists at entry/exit points (i.e. gateways such as airports and ports) or at accommodation. But such data relate to numbers of trips rather than individual tourists since one tourist may make more than one trip a year and each trip is counted separately. In the case of expenditure statistics, tourist expenditure normally refers to tourist spending within a country

and excludes payments to tourist-transport operators. Yet deriving such statistics is often an indirect measure based on foreign currency estimates derived from bank records, from data provided by tourism service providers or more commonly from social surveys undertaken directly with tourists. Research by White and Walker (1982) and Baretje (1982) directly questions the validity and accuracy of such methods of data collection, examining the main causes of bias and error in such studies.

According to Edwards (1991: 68–9), 'expenditure and receipts data apart, tourist statistics are usually collected in one of the five following ways':

1 Counts of all individuals entering or leaving the country at all recognised frontier crossings, often using arrival/departure cards where high-volume arrivals/departures are the norm. Where particularly large volumes of tourist traffic exist, a 10 per cent sampling framework is normally used (i.e. every tenth arrival/departure card). Countries such as New Zealand actually match the arrival/departure cards, or a sample, to examine the length of stay.
2 Interviews carried out at frontiers with a sample of arriving and/or departing passengers to obtain a more detailed profile of visitors and their activities within the country. This will often require a careful sample design to gain a sufficiently large enough sample with the detail required from visitors on a wide range of tourism data including places visited, expenditure, accommodation usage and related items.
3 Selecting a sample of arrivals and providing them with a self-completion questionnaire to be handed in or posted. This method is used in Canada but it fails to incorporate those visitors travelling via the United States by road.
4 Sample surveys of the entire population of a country including travellers and non-travellers, though the cost of obtaining a representative sample is often prohibitive.
5 Accommodation arrivals and nights spent are recorded by hoteliers and owners of the accommodation types covered. The difficulty with this type of data collection is that accommodation

---

INSIGHT: The United Kingdom's International Passenger Survey

As a government-sponsored survey which began in 1961, the International Passenger Survey now covers all ports of entry/exit to the UK. It is based on a stratified random sample of tourists arriving and departing from the UK by air and sea (see Griffith and Elliot (1988) for further details on the sample design features of IPS). According to Latham (1989: 64), IPS' four principal aims are:

1   To collect data for the travel account (which

acts to compare expenditure by overseas visitors to the UK with expenditure overseas by visitors from the UK) of the balance of payments;
2   To provide detailed information on foreign visitors to the UK, and on outgoing visitors travelling overseas.
3   To provide data on international migration.
4   To provide information on routes used by passengers as an aid to aviation and shipping authorities.

---

owners have no incentive to record accurate details, particularly where the tax regime is based on the turnover of bed-nights (see Page 1989 for a discussion of this problem in the context of London).

The final area of data collection is profile statistics, which examine the characteristics and travel habits of visitors. For example, the UK's International Passenger Survey (IPS) is one survey that incorporates volume, expenditure and profile data on international tourism.

METHODOLOGICAL ISSUES

Latham (1989) reviews the major types of questionnaire/social survey type of data collection used for tourism statistics. He reports that among state-sponsored tourism research in the United States, conversion studies are a popular method to examine and evaluate advertising campaigns and visitor surveys, to assess a sample of visitors to individual states. The use of other methods of data collection are also discussed (e.g. diary questionnaires, participant observation and personal interviews – see Mullins and Heywood 1984; Perdue 1985). Yet few studies consider the issue of sampling, sample design and the sources of error which may arise from such surveys (Aaker and Day

1986; Cannon 1987). In fact the lack of research on the reliability of the estimate from a sample survey (the standard error) is rarely discussed in most tourism surveys (see Latham (1989: 71–2) for a more technical discussion of this point). In many cases, large tourism surveys focus on the logistics of drawing the sample and the bias which may be reflected in the results. Therefore, any tourism survey will need to pay careful attention to the statistical and mathematical accuracy of the survey, especially the survey design and the effect it may have on the results, a feature which is discussed in great detail by Ryan (1995).

Ryan (1995) provides an excellent review of survey design, questionnaire design, sampling and also an insight into the statistical techniques to use for different forms of tourism data. As a result it serves as an important reference point for issues of methodology and the technical issues associated with the statistical analysis of tourism data. Without reiterating the excellent features of Ryan's findings, it is appropriate to consider some of the main accuracy problems associated with the collection of domestic and international tourism statistics.

PROBLEMS OF ACCURACY

Ryan (1995) argues that errors in data collection can lead to errors in data analysis. Among the most frequently cited problems associated with domestic and international tourism statistics are:

- the methods by which the data are collected, which are influenced by administrative, bureaucratic and legislative factors in each country;
- sample sizes which are too small and lead to unacceptable sampling errors and in some instances where the sample design is flawed;
- the procedures for collecting tourism statistics are not adhered to by the agency collecting the data.

In addition, Edwards (1991: 68) argues that a 'fourth potential reason – arithmetic mistakes and data processing errors – only occasionally produce significant errors'. In fact, Edwards (1991: 68) supports the cause of 'tourist statisticians [who] are both knowledgeable and conscientious, but are having to work with tools which they know could produce inaccurate or misleading data', concluding that for any set of tourist data, potential sources of error obviously depend on the method of collection employed. This, in turn, tends to be largely determined by the legislative and administrative framework and by the financial and manpower resources available.

In the case of tourist expenditure and receipts data, organisations such as the International Monetary Fund (IMF) issue guidelines for the compilation of balance of payments statistics. But errors may occur where leakage results from tourist services paid for in overseas bank accounts and in extreme cases, where a black market exists in currency exchange. Edwards (1991) suggests that a regular programme of interviews with departing tourists and returning residents may assist in estimating levels of expenditure.

Despite the apparent problems which may exist with tourism statistics, Edwards (1991: 72) argues that data on arrivals and nights spent for most destinations outside of Europe appear reasonably reliable.

Within Europe, data for both inbound and outbound travel are fairly satisfactory for the UK. Greece, Portugal, Spain and [the former] Yugoslavia all appear to have usable frontier arrivals data. The most serious problems are in core continental European countries such as France, Germany, Italy and the Netherlands for which there are no adequate volumetric measures of travel in either direction.

Accommodation arrivals and nights data are clearly gross understatements for many European countries . . . often expenditure and receipts data appear better indicators. Outside Europe, the major problems are also in relation to high volume land flows, as between Canada and the USA (in both directions), from the USA to Mexico and from Hong Kong to China.

Therefore, in view of these potential constraints, Edwards (1991) advocates that researchers should compile a range of data from different sources which will not only highlight the deficiencies in various sources, but also extend the existing baseline data. Although Edwards (1991) provides guidelines for comparative tourism research using a range of data for different countries (see also Dann (1993) for the limitations of using different tourism indicators such as nationality), trends in tourism data remain one of the main requirements for travel industry organisations. Edwards (1991: 73) lists key issues to consider in examining tourism trends (i.e. Have arrivals or accommodation data been changed in coverage or definition? Have provisional data for earlier years been subsequently revised? Has the reliability of the data changed and how are changing tastes in travel products affecting the statistics?). Even so, the analysis of trends remains the fundamental starting point for most research studies in tourism. Having considered the issues associated with how tourism statistics are generated, attention now turns to the ways in which geographers analyse such statistics, and variations in tourism activity at different scales.

PATTERNS OF TOURISM: INTERNATIONAL PERSPECTIVES

D.G. Pearce's (1995a) seminal study on the geographer's analysis of tourism patterns offers an excellent synthesis reflecting his international contribution to the methodological development of spatial analysis of tourism. By using geographical methodologies and concepts, D.G. Pearce (1995a) uses statistical sources and primary data on tourist activity patterns to analyse the processes and patterns associated with the dynamics of domestic and international tourist activity. This section can only provide a limited evaluation of the geographer's approach to analysis of the presentation of spatially oriented insights on modern-day tourism demand (for more detail consult D.G. Pearce 1995a).

GLOBAL PATTERNS OF TOURISM

The WTO provides the main source of data for international tourism, collated from a survey of major government agencies responsible for data collection. While most international tourists are expressed as 'frontier arrivals' (i.e. arrivals determined by means of a frontier check), arrival/departure cards (where used) offer additional detail to the profile of international tourists, and where they are not used periodic tourism surveys are often employed. WTO statistics are mainly confined to all categories of travellers, and in some cases

geographical disaggregation of the data may be limited by the collecting agency's use of descriptions and categories for aid of simplicity (e.g. rest of the world) rather than listing all categories of arrivals.

In terms of the growth of international travel, Table 2.11 documents the expansion of outbound travel with constant growth in the 1960s in an age of discovery of outbound travel for many developed nations. The late 1960s saw international travel expanded by new technology in air travel (e.g. the introduction of the Boeing 747 jumbo jet and the 737 as well as the DC10) which led to rapid growth until the oil crisis in the early 1970s. Growth rates varied in the 1980s, with 'shock waves' to the upward trend being caused by events such as the Gulf Crisis, but international travel has maintained strong growth rates, often in excess of 5 per cent per annum. In contrast, international receipts from travel have outperformed arrivals, with consistent rates of growth (with the exception of the oil crisis and Gulf Crisis) of 10 to 20 per cent which is indicative of the powerful economic effect of tourism for countries. Table 2.12 outlines the top tourism destinations for 1980 and 1990, where the ranking of France has remained prominent throughout the 14-year period with certain devel-

Table 2.11: International tourist arrivals and tourist receipts, 1950–2000

Year	Arrivals of tourists from abroad (day visitors excluded)		Receipts from international tourism (international transport excluded)	
	Total (thousands)	% change over previous year	Total (US$million)	% change over previous year
1950	25,282	–	2,100	–
1960	69,320	10.61	6,867	12.58
1965	112,863	7.90	11,604	15.20
1970	165,787	15.52	17,900	6.55
1975	222,290	8.08	40,702	20.34
1980	286,249	1.12	105,198	26.23
1985	329,538	3.29	117,374	4.36
1990	459,212	6.56	264,714	21.22
1995	561,027	2.78	380,693	10.17
2000[1]	698,300	7.4	476,000	4.5

Note
[1] 2000 data are preliminary only (WTO 2001).

Source: World Tourism Organisation (WTO) (1996, 2001)

Table 2.12: The world's top fifteen tourism destinations in 2000 and 1980

Country	Ranking 2000[1]	Arrivals (millions)	Ranking 1980	Arrivals (millions)
France	1	74.5	1	30.1
United States	2	52.7	3	22.5
Spain	3	48.5	2	23.4
Italy	4	41.2	4	22.1
China	5	31.2	19	3.5
United Kingdom	6	24.9	7	12.4
Russian Federation	7	22.8	–	–
Canada	8	20.4	6	12.9
Mexico	9	20.0	8	11.9
Germany	10	18.9	9	11.1
Poland	11	18.2	13	5.7
Austria	12	17.8	5	13.9
Hungary	13	15.6	10	9.4
Hong Kong	14	13.1	27	1.7
Greece	15	12.5	17	4.8

Note
[1] 2000 data are preliminary only (WTO 2001).

Source: World Tourism Organisation (1996, 2001)

oping nations such as China recording major growth and, with the exception of the USA and China, Europe still dominates the pattern of arrivals by country with comparatively little change in the ranking of the first seven destinations. However, China is the notable success story in terms of growth in receipts while a number of European destinations (e.g. the Netherlands and Belgium) have retained the volume of arrivals but their ranking of expenditure has dropped.

As the world's largest tourism markets by expenditure, the USA and Germany have retained their prominence in the top two rankings, whereas Japan has increased its importance as an outbound high spending market as have a number of other Pacific Rim nations such as Taiwan, Singapore and South Korea until the 1997 Asian financial crisis (Hall and Page 2000). As a result of the growth of major outbound growth and travel within the Pacific Rim region, a case study of the outbound South Korean market is now examined.

CASE STUDY: Tourism demand in East Asia Pacific: the case of the South Korean outbound market and activity patterns in New Zealand (Kyung-Sik Woo and Stephen J. Page)

Prior to the Asian financial crisis, Korea represented one of the major outbound markets in the Asia-Pacific region (McGahey 1996; Hall 1997a; Hall and Page 1999). Outbound travel grew from 484,000 in 1985 to 725,000 in 1988 to 3.1 million in 1994, which quadrupled in a six-year period up to 1994 (Table 2.13). By 1995, outbound travel had reached 3.8 million, representing 9 per cent of the national population of 45 million. Within New Zealand, inbound Korean arrivals increased consistently between 1989 and 1995 as the fastest growing market and remained the focus of industry attention until the Asian financial crisis (New Zealand Tourism Board 1995), despite any substantive and detailed research to consider the needs, aspirations and impact of this market in New Zealand.

Table 2.13 outlines the motivation for Korean inbound tourists to visit New Zealand. Holiday travel has remained a major reason to visit, while females outnumbered males in holiday travel by 54.4 per cent: 45.66 per cent in 1994 and VFR by 63.5 per cent: 36.5 per cent, highlighting the trend towards housewives comprising the majority of outbound female visitors. Male visitors dominated in the purpose of visiting in relation to business travel (91 per cent), to attend a convention (87.7 per cent) and official travel (91.3 per cent). The age profile of the most common outbound Korean tourist was the 31 to 40 age group followed by the 21 to 30 age group, with a significant proportion of 'honeymooners' and single female office workers. According to the 1994 Nationals Overseas Travel Survey

Table 2.13: Korean departures by purpose of trip, 1985–94

	1985	1986	1987	1988	1989	1990	1991	1992	1993	1994
'000 departures										
Total	484.2	455.0	510.5	752.2	1,213.1	1,563.9	1,856.0	2,043.3	2,419.9	3,154.3
% share										
Pleasure	0.4	0.7	2.5	18.5	37.0	37.8	35.1	35.4	35.0	41.0
Business	27.7	30.8	32.3	31.2	25.9	25.7	26.3	25.7	26.4	24.9
VFR	9.5	9.9	9.1	8.6	10.2	13.0	17.2	18.3	16.0	13.6
Official	1.1	1.2	1.2	1.1	1.0	0.8	0.9	0.9	0.7	0.8
Convention	2.4	2.2	2.1	1.9	1.2	1.1	1.1	1.2	1.0	0.9
Other	59.0	55.3	52.8	38.7	24.8	21.6	19.4	18.6	20.8	19.0

Source: Ministry of Justice, Korea, and Woo (1996)

(McGahey 1996), shopping was a major leisure activity for Korean tourists, with an average spend of US$413 per person on purchases such as cosmetics, alcoholic beverages, electronic goods, clothing and toys. McGahey (1996) observed that 40 per cent of these purchases were for gifts.

THE KOREAN INBOUND MARKET IN NEW ZEALAND

According to New Zealand's International Visitor Survey (New Zealand Tourism Board 1995), the Korean market was estimated to have generated NZ$225 million of spending at 1995 prices, equating to an average spend of NZ$2253 per person of NZ$345 a day, the highest amount for any inbound market. In the 12 months ended March 1996, Koreans comprised 8 per cent of New Zealand's international visitor market, increasing from 2,018 in 1987 to 4,184 visitors in 1990 to 61,583 in 1994. The significance of this market was reflected in the New Zealand Tourist Board's (1995) optimistic forecasts for a further doubling of visitor arrivals over the next five years and a target of 114,000 arrivals. However, the size of the impact of the Asian financial crisis on Korea can be illustrated by the 78 per cent drop in Korean visitors to New Zealand in December 1997 compared with the previous year, with there being an expected 75 per cent drop in arrivals from South Korea in 1998 over the previous year (Coventry 1998; Yoon and Bedford 1999).

In contrast to the age profile of the entire Korean tourist outbound market, the main age group of visitors to New Zealand was dominated by the visitors aged 45 to 64 years, predominately those aged 55 to 64 (New Zealand Tourism Board 1995). Yet among those visitors aged under 24 years, females outnumber males as unmarried office workers or tertiary level students are more likely to travel than their male counterparts, since the former enjoy relatively more leisure time.

Since group travel tends to predominate among the inbound Korean market, the length of stay in New Zealand was conditioned by two key factors. First, it is a medium long-haul destination, and second, Korean holiday entitlement was still limited to under ten paid days a year and is not available in one block. Therefore, the maximum length of stay for most outbound Korean tourists was less than one week. According to research (New Zealand Tourism Board 1995), Korean tourists perceived the main appeal of visiting New Zealand as its unspoiled natural phenomena such as hot springs in Rotorua and volcanic areas such as Mount Tongariro (Figure

Although time budget studies may still be viewed as experimental in tourism research, they do offer great potential to gain a detailed insight into tourist activity patterns.

The survey

During three weeks in July 1996, a time budget survey was developed using the 'yesterday technique' and the time sequencing technique advocated by P.L. Pearce (1981) as part of a more detailed survey of inbound Korean tourists. The complete survey was designed to be completed by Korean tourists during their tour of the North Island of New Zealand and four sites were selected as distribution points for the surveys during the tourists' initial familiarisation point of their tour in Auckland and Rotorua. Two major hotels and two Korean restaurants were selected to provide a degree of close contract with Korean tourists in a familiar environment. Due to the highly organised nature of the Korean itineraries, a one-page diary was distributed at the key sites over a three-week period. One immediate problem facing the use of the budget approach was in soliciting responses. While a Korean researcher approached the respondents on a random basis, it was essential to keep the survey to one A4 page to encourage participation. As a result, only time-budget questions could be included and key demographic data were omitted (a separate survey by the authors was undertaken examining demand issues among Korean tourists which did consider the profile of visitors). However, from participant observation conducted during the data collection, it is apparent that the sample of 78 tourists who were prepared to participate in the time budget exercise were typical of the Korean tourist then visiting New Zealand, being largely aged 31 to 50, being of middle-class status, earning between NZ$40,000 and $60,000 a year and undertaking a multi-destination product.

ACTIVITY PATTERNS OF KOREAN TOURISTS IN AUCKLAND AND ROTORUA

According to D.G. Pearce (1995a), few data are collected to examine circuit tourism which this market is following, since they adhere to a predetermined circuit pattern. Data exist in a New Zealand context (e.g. Oppermann 1993, 1994) on the touring patterns of international tourists which builds on Forer and Pearce's (1984) innovative study of coach tours by nights spent at key nodes and inter-regional flows. Forer and Pearce (1984) established the Auckland to Rotorua and Taupo axis by examining tour group itineraries for package tours. While it is apparent that a great deal of continuity and similarity exists in terms of the Korean tour group itineraries which follow a series of linear routes, activity patterns of the tour groups and their specific time budgets remain largely unresearched.

One immediate feature which emerges from the 78 completed schedules is that the activity patterns of the visitors closely follow the tour itineraries. The respondents were undertaking three commonly used itineraries developed by tour companies which comprised (see Figure 2.14):

- Itinerary 1: Auckland to Rotorua and return to Rotorua (12 tourists).
- Itinerary 2: Auckland to Rotorua and Waitomo Caves and return to Auckland (39 tourists).
- Itinerary 3: Auckland to Rotorua and Waitomo Caves to Taupo and return to Auckland.

Both itinerary 1 and 2 record only a limited amount of free time, being the shortest tour schedules among inbound visitors to New Zealand. The typical itinerary commences at 07:00 and finishes at 18:00 to 19:00 hours, with sightseeing comprising the major activity (30 to

32 per cent), undertaken over two nights and three days. During the 53 to 59-hour period, respondents spent their time:

- sleeping (33 per cent);
- touring (30 per cent);
- free time (14 per cent);
- transfers (12 per cent);
- eating/meals (11 per cent).

On the basis of these results, three types of Korean tourists could be identified based on time budget research by Ashworth and Dietvorst (1995):

1 *Organised sightseeing oriented visitors*, who comprise the large majority of visitors, with a city tour in a chartered coach during the day, interspersed with shopping before or after meals and a limited amount of free time spent walking around attractions and taking photographs. Evenings were spent at the accommodation base to rest after the day's activities.
2 *Shopping and conviviality oriented tourists*, where shopping activities were conducted near to the accommodation base in the morning. The age profile of this group was younger (typically under 40 years of age), in search of specialist markets, tourist attractions and not venturing far from the accommodation base. In the evening, this group spent their leisure time at a wide variety of fun-related facilities (e.g. at a pub, gambling at the Casino in Auckland or at a night-club). In Rotorua, this group spent most of their free time at Korean pubs in the central tourist district.
3 *Health and sports oriented tourists*, comprising the majority of the senior group (aged 50-plus) and a number of business travellers who pursued largely 'private' leisure activities. While no 'typical' activity patterns could be discerned during the day, with some preferring walking or going shopping, the time spent on these activities was much less than the two former groups. In the afternoons, sports activities dominated (e.g. golf and fishing) and in the early evening they frequented health facilities followed by relaxation for the remaining part of the evening.

While the results from the Korean case study indicate that removal of travel restrictions in 1989 has significantly increased outbound travel, there were significant 'pull' factors promoting Korean travel to New Zealand (e.g. immigration policy, no-visas agreement, new air services and 15,000 Korean residents living in Auckland promoting VFR traffic) which can be related to the motivational literature and the unique attractions available in New Zealand. The analysis of tourist activity patterns shows that in urban areas, Korean visitors do not venture far from their accommodation base. This limits the flow and distribution of visitors, with a tendency for bunching and concentration at key nodes around Auckland, Rotorua and Taupo. Concerns over a saturation of tourists at key attraction sites accentuates the problem of managing the geographical patterns of this short and concentrated experience of New Zealand tourism. Many attractions are unable to cope with the arrival of large numbers of tour groups simultaneously, as this highly organised and almost regimented form of tourism is posing significant strains on the visiting infrastructure. In this respect, a spatial analysis of activity patterns and time budgets illustrates not only the shape of existing demand, determined by tour operators and group leaders, but also the geographical interaction and time constraints under which these tourists visit New Zealand have clear spatial implications for the type of tourism experience they require in time and space.

income redistribution on a regional basis. In aggregate, a quarter of all expenditure is on accommodation and just over a quarter is on food. Shopping of all types consumes one-fifth of expenditure, while transport, recreation and alcohol account for about 10 per cent each. Business travel is getting on for three times the cost of other trips per night, and is heavily weighted towards travel and accommodation costs when compared with other sectors, both proportionately and in real terms. VFR travel is slightly more demanding of travel expenditure than are holidays, but accommodation costs, not surprisingly, are considerably less (Forsyte Research 2000; Hall and Kearsley 2002).

CONCLUSIONS

The analysis of behavioural issues in recreational and tourism research indicates that 'in behavioural terms then, there seems little necessity to insist on a major distinction between tourism and leisure phenomena. Therefore, it should follow that a greater commonality between the research efforts in the two areas would be of advantage' (Moore et al. 1995: 75) although different social theoretical approaches exist towards the analysis of recreation and tourism phenomena. As a result, Moore et al. (1995: 79) conclude that 'there is little need, if any, to take a dramatically different approach to the behavioural analysis of tourism and leisure'. One needs to view each activity in the context of the everyday life of the people involved to understand how each is conceived. There is a clear distinction within the literature between what motivates recreationalists and tourists, and comparative studies of similar groups of people and the similarities and differences between these motivations has yet to permeate the research literature. While geographers have focused on recreational and tourist behaviour in relation to demand issues, the analysis has largely been quantitative, site specific, and has not adapted a comparative methodology to examine the recreation–tourism continuum.

QUESTIONS

- What is recreational demand and how have geographers attempted to measure it?
- How far does the use of recreational resources conform with models of leisure and recreational demand?
- What is the role of tourism demand in the analysis of tourism patterns in time and space?
- 'The use of psychological constructs and models of tourist behaviour does not explain why people go on holiday to specific locations.' Discuss.

READING

For recreational demand the following studies are very useful introductions:

Pigram, J.J. and Jenkins, J. (1999) *Outdoor Recreation Management*, London: Routledge.

This is by far the best book on recreational research published to date by geographers. In terms of factors constraining demand see:

Crawford, D., Jackson, E. and Godbey, G. (1991). 'A hierarchical model of leisure constraints', *Leisure Sciences* 13: 309–20.

A good example of the constraints on demand can be found in:

Madge, C. (1997) 'Public parks and the geography of fear', *Tijdschrift Voor Economische en Sociale Geografie*, 88, 237–50.

At a general level, the best overviews of studies of tourism demand are:

Crouch, G. (1994) 'The study of tourism demand: A review of findings', *Journal of Travel Research*, 33(1): 2–21.
Shaw, G., Argawal, S. and Bull, P. (2000) 'Tourism consumption and tourist behaviour: A British perspective', *Tourism Geographies*, 2(3): 264–89.
Uysal, M. (1998) 'The determinants of tourism demand: A theoretical perspective', in D. Ioannides and K. Debbage (eds) *The Economic Geography of the*

Tourist Industry: A Supply-side Analysis, London: Routledge, pp. 79–95.

For tourism demand the following is a useful introduction to the growth of demand in one country:

Barke, M., Towner J. and Newton, M. (eds) (1996) *Tourism in Spain: Critical Issues*, Wallingford: CAB International.

This should be read in conjunction with:

Shaw, G. and Williams, A. (eds) (1997) *The Rise and Fall of British Coastal Resorts: Cultural and Economic Perspectives*, London: Mansell.

3

THE SUPPLY OF RECREATION AND TOURISM

Within the literature on recreation and tourism, there is a paucity of conceptual and theoretical research on the supply component of these activities (Sinclair and Stabler 1992). The geographer has traditionally approached the supply of recreation and tourism from a somewhat traditional spatial analysis perspective reflecting the tendency to apply concepts and models from economic geography and, to a lesser degree, from cognate areas of geography where the underlying concern has been with location and the spatial distribution of recreational and tourism resources which shape the activity patterns and spectrum of opportunity for leisure pursuits.

THE SUPPLY FACTOR IN RECREATION

According to Kreutzwiser (1989: 21), 'supply refers to the recreational resources, both natural and man-made, which provide opportunities for recreation. It is a complex concept influenced by numerous factors and subject to changing interpretations.' As Pigram and Jenkins (1999: 57) recognised, 'In a perfect world, demand for outdoor recreation activities would be matched by an ample supply of attractive and accessible recreation resources. . . . In reality, interaction between demand and supply factors is qualified by spatial, social/institutional/political, psychological, economic and personal impediments.' Recreational supply is also a concept which has prompted much thought in terms of classification and evaluation,

particularly among geographers. Yet Coppock and Duffield (1975: 151) pursue this theme a stage further in a spatial context, claiming that it is the 'spatial interaction between the homes of recreationalists and the resources they use [which] has emerged as a key factor in the demand/supply model' and, arguing for an integrated analysis of such interactions to explain how the activity patterns of recreationalists in terms of their origins and destinations affect the supply variable in terms of where they go, what they do there and how this affects the resource base. For this reason, this section commences with a discussion of the underlying approach used to describe and document the supply of recreational opportunities by geographers, which is followed by an analysis of the spatial interaction of demand and supply to illustrate how the two components are interrelated. This is developed in relation to the three characteristics that geographers have synthesised to analyse recreational activities, namely:

1   the locational characteristics associated with the supply of different forms of recreational resource;
2   the patterns of demand and usage;
3   the spatial interactions which occur between the demand for and supply of the recreational resource, emphasising journey patterns and the patterns of usage of specific resources.

This gives rise to concentrated, dispersed and combinations of each pattern at the site of the resources, which therefore raises questions as to how to evaluate the capacity of such resources to accommodate users and to reconcile conflicts in use and the identification of management and planning issues.

HOW HAS THE GEOGRAPHER APPROACHED THE ANALYSIS OF RECREATIONAL SUPPLY ISSUES?

The geographer's approach is epitomised in many of the classic recreational texts (e.g. Patmore 1970; Lavery 1971c; Simmons 1974; Pigram 1983) where the supply perspective is largely dependent upon the evaluation and assessment of resources for recreation. The concept of a resource may often be taken to include those tangible objects in nature which are of economic value and used for productive purposes. But when looking at leisure and recreation natural resources have an important bearing, particularly those such as water bodies, countryside and open space. The fact that resources have a physical form (i.e. coal and iron ore) does not actually mean they constitute a resource. Such elements only become a resource when society's subjective evaluation of their potential leads to their recognition as a resource to satisfy human wants and needs (O'Riordan 1971).

Yet a resource is far from just a passive element – it has to be used creatively to meet certain socially valued goals. Thus recreational resources are 'an element of the natural or man-modified environment which provides an opportunity to satisfy recreational wants. Implicit is a continuum ranging from biophysical resources to man-made facilities' (Kreutzwiser 1989: 22). However, according to Glyptis (1989a: 135), to 'couple recreational with resources complicates definitions. . . . In a recreational context resources are the natural resources of land, water and landscape, together with man-made resources including sport centres, swimming pools, parks and playing fields', though she also notes that few recreational activities make use of resources solely designed or in existence for recreational purposes.

As Pigram and Jenkins (1999: 59) argued, 'identification and valuation of elements of the environment as recreation resources will depend upon a number of factors (e.g. economics, social attitudes and perceptions, political perspectives and technology'. As a result, Pigram and Jenkins (1999: 59) recognised that outdoor recreational resources may encompass a wide range of settings associated with space, topography and climatic characteristics. This expands upon Hart's (1966) early notion of the 'recreation resource base', which were the natural values of the countryside or respective landscape. Such a notion was clarified in specific terms by Clawson and Knetsch (1966: 7) thus: 'There is nothing in the physical landscape or features of any particular piece of land or body of water that makes it a recreation resource; it is the combination of the natural qualities and the ability and desire of man to use them that makes a resource out of what might otherwise be a more or less meaningless combination of rocks, soil and trees.' However, such resources are not static, since new trends or cultural appraisals can lead to new notions of the environment as a recreational resource.

Recreation in rural contexts (Chapter 6) often occurs alongside agriculture, forestry and water supply functions (Goodall and Whittow 1975). In this respect, the identification of recreational resources needs to recognise the management implications of multiple use, a feature discussed below. While Glyptis (1989a) also outlined the demands of many forms of recreation which have few land needs, this analysis is concerned with recreational forms that have a land use component given the geographers' interest in how human activities and phenomena are interrelated and occur on the earth's surface. Yet even Glyptis' (1989a) review pays little explicit attention to the resource base – the supply dimension – beyond highlighting Patmore's (1983) 'perspective [which] is specifically geographical, but with full recognition of the interplay of social, economic and political factors, and with a wealth of data. . . . The bulk of the text concerns [sic] contemporary patterns of recreational activity and the demands they place on the

Table 3.1: The land use classes of the Canada land inventory

Classes	
1 Very high capability	These lands have natural capability to engender very high total annual use of one or more intensive activities. These lands should be able to generate and sustain a level of use comparable to that evident at an outstanding and large bathing beach or a nationally known ski slope.
2 High capability	These lands have natural capability to engender and sustain high total annual use based on one or more intensive activity.
3 Moderately high capability	These lands have a natural ability to engender and sustain moderately high total annual use based on moderate to intensive or intensive activities.
4 Moderate capability	These lands have natural capability to engender and sustain moderate total annual use based on dispersed activities.
5 Moderately low capability	These lands have natural capability to engender and sustain moderately low total annual use based on dispersed activities.
6 Low capability	These lands lack the natural quality and significant features to rate higher, but have the natural capability to engender and sustain low total annual use based on dispersed activities.
7 Very low capability	These lands have practically no capability for any popular type of recreation activity, but there may be some opportunity for very specialised activities with recreation aspects, or they may simply provide open space.

located, mapped and defined biotic and abiotic resources and human resource patterns at a regional level. Deglomerative studies remain more widely used than the latter. Yet such methods of analyses pay less attention to the importance of human (i.e. subjective) evaluations of resources for recreation (e.g. Coppock and Duffield's (1975) assessment of recreational potential in the countryside).

One of the notable debates in resource studies for recreation in the late 1960s and early 1970s was the evaluation of recreation environments (Duffield and Owen 1970) related to preferential descriptions of recreational resources, namely aesthetic studies which measure human preferences and how they respond to landscape alterations. According to Pigram and Jenkins (1999: 76) the multi-faceted nature of landscape, personal preferences and individual perception make evaluation a highly subjective activity. In the assessment of scenic landscape elements, two fundamental elements exist: the character of the landscape (i.e. the components of the landscape which are visual and part of an inventory such as vegetation, water, human occupation), and quality which is a

comparative–evaluative concept, in part determined by landscape characteristics. Unwin (1976) identified landscape quality as a three-stage process:

1 *Landscape description*, which is the objective inventory of landscape characteristics to classify the landscape type;
2 *Landscape preference*, where visual preference ratings are allocated to specific landscape characteristics. This is largely dependent upon subjective preferences and value judgements;
3 *Landscape evaluation*, where the specific qualities of the landscapes being considered are assessed to examine preferences of specific respondents.

Fines' (1968) influential study in East Sussex epitomises this approach, where a group of people with a background in design work were asked to assign a value to a series of landscape photographs compared to a reference photograph with an indifferent landscape. Once the landscapes were assessed by individuals, a consensus score was assigned and then the people were asked to rank

Table 3.2: Linton's landscape evaluation scale

Landforms	Points	Land uses	Points
Mountains	8	Wild landscapes	6
Bold hills	6	Richly varied farming	5
Hill country	5	Varied forest with moors and farms	4
Plateau uplands	3	Moors	3
Low uplands	2	Treeless farms	1
Lowlands	0	Continuous forest	–2
		Urban and industrial land	–5

Source: Linton (1968)

landscapes viewed around East Sussex. While Linton (1968) disagreed with both the nomenclature and scale used by Fines, he concluded that two key elements existed in the landscape: land use and landforms. These could be mapped and categories established, where a composite score could be devised to reflect the beauty of the landscape (Table 3.2). Linton (1968) developed his study in Scotland, and again, controversy was associated with the almost arbitrary use of a points system, where urban areas were seen as low scoring.

The importance of the geographer's contribution to landscape evaluation (see Cornish (1934) for an early contribution) was summarised by Penning-Rowsell (1975) whereby it could assist in landscape management with direct consequences for outdoor recreation. The four areas of significance were:

1 *Landscape preservation*, so that landscapes worthy of conservation could be identified;
2 *Landscape protection*, where landscapes that are under threat from pressure for development (e.g. economic activity and environmental impacts) can be placed under planning controls;
3 *Recreation policy*, where specific policies and forms of outdoor recreation can be facilitated in valued environments within planning constraints;
4 *Landscape improvement*, where potential negative landscape features (e.g. eyesores) can be remedied to transform the landscape into more attractive recreational purposes. A good example is the transformation of former extractive sites for gravel within urban fringe

locations to provide angling and recreational boating opportunities.

Indeed, the application of such techniques in a wider recreational context is noted by Pigram and Jenkins (1999) in relation to New Zealand. The *1991 Resource Management Act* (see Page and Thorn 1997, 1998; Hall and Kearsley 2002), has seen planning move away from land use zoning methods to ones where the impacts of specific activities are evaluated so that what the environmental outcomes might be are also considered.

Yet urban areas remain important for recreation and tourism (Chapter 5) and it seems naive to dismiss certain resources in such a generalised manner. While a great deal of debate exists in relation to such approaches to landscape evaluation, it does illustrate the importance of human perception, and recognition of what is attractive and valued by different people in relation to recreational time. In terms of descriptive research on travel, it has little immediate relevance to supply unless one is concerned with the impact of demand on the resource base. As a result, the geographer's concern with recreational travel using concepts such as nodes, routes, mode of travel and accessibility of resources for recreationalists has little immediate value.

EXPLANATORY RESEARCH ON LOCATION AND TRAVEL

Moving from purely descriptive to explanatory research illustrates the importance of location as a recreational facility which someone may want to use. Smith (1983a) outlined two concerns regarding the location of such facilities: those factors affecting public and those affecting private location decisions, although the distinction between such issues has blurred where public–private sector involvement, co-operation and management has complicated traditional locational models developed in economic geography, which has separated public and private goods (Hall and Jenkins 1995). For example, Mitchell (1969b) applied central place theory to the location of urban parks as public recreational resources, establishing that a hierarchy existed, but it rather simplified a number of real-world issues by substituting assumptions, while also ignoring influential variables such as land prices, availability and political influences (see Chapter 5). Other studies (e.g. Mitchell and Lovingwood 1976; Haley 1979) adopted empirical measures to examine correlations between variables which might explain locational patterns, where Haley (1979) observed that present-day patterns often reflect the demands of previous generations. Likewise, where new suburban developments did not require developers to provide park facilities, a dearth of parks exist. Communities in such areas have not sought such provision due to local factors (e.g. private recreation sites and access to the urban fringe). The role of private recreation provision was examined by Mitchell and Lovingwood (1976) and Lovingwood and Mitchell (1978), who mapped 172 public and 112 private recreational facilities, using nearest-neighbour analysis to examine the spatial patterns. They concluded that public facilities had a tendency to cluster while private facilities had a regular pattern of distribution for camp sites, country clubs and miscellaneous uses, while water-based facilities and hunting/fishing clubs tended to cluster. The outcome of their analysis was that:

- public facilities are concentrated in areas of population density to meet the wider good and in accessible locations; having no major resource considerations;
- private facilities are located on one of two bases:

either in or near open space, as in the case of campsites and country clubs and are located throughout the region, or conversely, water-based facilities and hunting clubs are closely tied to a land or water location, clustering around the resource.

In contrast, much of the geographical research on private recreational facility development has been based on the approach developed in retail marketing and location studies, where location is seen as the critical success factor, although Bevins *et al.* (1974) observed that this was not necessarily a critical factor for private campsites in North-East USA. Within most studies of recreational location, principal concepts are related to the threshold population, catchment areas or hinterlands and distance to travel to the facility. As Crompton and Van Doren (1976) observed, tram companies in mid-nineteenth-century America built amusement parks at the end of tramlines to attract weekend visitors, illustrating the importance of recreational travel as part of the overall experience.

PREDICTIVE RESEARCH ON LOCATION

The geographer's tradition of model building to predict location of characteristics of private enterprise has been applied to recreational geography in terms of the transfer of location theory and site selection methods. Within the research on location theory, transport cost has played a significant role based on Von Thünen's agricultural land use model, and Vickerman (1975) simplistically applied the model to predict urban recreation businesses. Yet the use of concepts such as locational interdependence, where the potential buyers are not uniformly distributed in space, means that businesses may be able to exercise a degree of control over their clients by their location. Such studies based on the early work of economic geographers such as Christaller (1933), Lösch (1944) and Reilly (1931) developed a number of principles which geographers have used to underpin locational modelling recreational research. While subsequent research by Isard (1956) and Greenhut (1956) can be added to the list, S. Smith (1983a: 106) summarises the contribution of such studies to the analysis of recreational location choices by business:

1　A firm with relatively low transportation costs and a relatively large market area will have a greater chance of success than a firm with high transportation costs and a small market area.

2　Some trade-offs are possible between transportation costs, production costs, land rents and market size.

3　Transportation costs include both the cost of bringing resources to the site of the firm and the costs of distributing the product to the customer. The relative costs of transporting both resources and products determine, in part, where the firm will locate: high resource transportation costs pull a business close to the resource; high product transportation costs pull a business close to the market.

4　Some types of business seek to locate close to each other; some are indifferent to each other; some are repelled by each other.

5　Different locations will be attractive to different types of businesses. Attractiveness is based on resources; market location; transportation services; availability of capital, labour and business services; and personal preferences of the decision-maker.

6　Firms in any given industry will tend to divide up the available market by selecting different locations to control different spatial segments of the market.

7　The size of the market and the number and location of competitors tend to limit the size of the potential development.

These need to be examined in relation to the decision-making of entrepreneurs and individual firms. In terms of site selection methods, feasibility studies have provided a starting point for geographers seeking to assess the most suitable site from a range of alternatives, with the purpose of maximising profit (or wider social benefits in the public sector) though comparatively little research has been published given the scope of such studies (i.e. sources of capital, management issues, design and development issues, market size, population characteristics, economic profile of the potential market and the suitability of the site) and the tendency for such documents to remain commercially sensitive in both the public and private sector. What is evident from the existing research seeking to predict locational characteristics for recreational activities and facilities is the reliance upon economic geography, particularly retail geography with its concomitant concern for marketing.

NORMATIVE RESEARCH ON LOCATION

Within the public sector, the objectives for locational decision-making are distinctly different (or at least traditionally have been different, despite changing political philosophies towards public recreation provision). The characteristics of public sector provision have traditionally been associated with taxes paying for facility provision and its ongoing operation, with a collective use that cannot be withheld, so that access is not knowingly prohibited to anyone. In other words, their contribution to the quality of life and wider social well-being of the affected population underpins public provision that cannot easily be accommodated into conventional locational theory which is market driven. Austin (1974) identifies recreational facilities as 'site preferred' goods, where proximity to their location is often seen as a measure of their use (i.e. its utility function). Thus maximum distances exist as in the case of urban parks (see Chapter 5). The object, therefore, in public facility location for recreation is to balance the 'utility' factor with minimising the distance people have to travel and providing access to as many people as possible; though Cichetti (1971) examined a number of the problems associated with different methods of balancing travel distances, social utility and other approaches to demand maximisation.

Plate 3.3: How would you classify this recreational resource? It is a reservoir in the Waitakere Ranges, Auckland. It has multiple use as a recreational resource.

to take stock of the quantity, quality and extent of the resource base. For this reason, classification schemes have been derived. In the previous section, the preliminary attempt by Clawson *et al.* (1960) to derive a classification system distinguished between recreation areas according to location, activity type, major uses, size of the area and who was responsible for recreation resource management (Table 3.3). One of the problems with this classification scheme was that it neglected urban and near-urban sites and developed a narrow conception of outdoor recreation resources. Even so, this classification was a critical turning point in

recreational thinking, since it spurned numerous adaptations, stimulating new ways of thinking about classifying recreational resources.

Although no definitive scheme exists for classifying recreational resources, the need to distinguish between man-made and natural resources, different resource environments and resource types provides a useful starting point. In this respect, Chubb and Chubb's (1981) classification is valuable since it incorporates much of the thinking in recreational research, building on Clawson *et al.* (1960) where the following classes of recreation resources exist:

- *the undeveloped recreation resources*, where the physical attributes of land, water and vegetation are untouched;
- *private recreation resources*, such as second homes, resources owned by quasi-public organisations (e.g. conservation groups, farm and industrial sites);
- *commercialised private recreation resources*, such as shopping malls, theme parks, museums, gardens, stadia and resorts;
- *publicly owned recreation resources*, including parks, sports and leisure facilities, national parks, forest and tourist sites;
- *cultural resources*, based in both the public and private sector, such as libraries, the Arts and what is increasingly being termed 'the cultural industries' (see Pratt 1998);

Plate 3.4: Dover Castle is a major commercialised tourist resource in Kent.

Plate 3.5: This Spanish cathedral in Toledo, Spain is an important cultural resource for visitors.

- *professional resources*, which may be divided into the administrative functions for recreational provision (organisation, policy-making and financial support systems) and management (e.g. research, planning, development and conservation/programming functions).

Other attempts to classify recreational resources have also recognised that a continuum exists from the home-oriented space through to the neighbourhood (including the street – see Williams 1995) with increasing scale through to community and regional space (Gold 1980). With these issues in mind, attention now turns to the recreational resources that exist in an urban landscape – the urban fringe.

Recreational resources and the urban fringe

The impact of urbanisation on the development of industrial societies and the effects in terms of recreational resource provision is discussed in detail in Chapter 6. Yet the growing consumption of rural land for urban uses has led to increased concerns for the loss of non-urban land, as observed by Abercromby (1938). Pigram (1983: 106) observed that 'every year some 1.2 ha of rural land are converted to urban and built-up uses across America' and the greatest competition over the retention of land for recreational uses is in the city periphery or what is termed the 'urban fringe'. Elson (1993) recognised the considerable potential of the urban fringe as a resource able to accommodate recreation and sport for four reasons:

1 It comprises an area of recreational supply, accessible with good public transport to large populations (though Fitton (1976) and Ferguson and Munton (1978, 1979) recognised the inaccessibility to the most deprived areas of inner London). As the Countryside Commission (1992) noted, one in five informal recreational day trips to the countryside had a return trip of less than 10 miles.

2 It may be an overflow location for recreational and sporting activities displaced from urban areas.
3 It can function as an 'interceptor area', reducing pressure on more fragile and vulnerable rural resources.
4 It may be an area of opportunity as environmental improvements and landscape regeneration (e.g. the reclamation of former quarry sites or gravel extraction) and may generate new forms of recreation including fishing, sailing and informal use.

As Elson (1993) observes, with active recreation the fastest growing sector of countryside recreation in the UK, the urban fringe has the potential to absorb such uses. Thus by altering supply, it is assumed that demand may be directed to new resources. In this sense, the urban fringe is a useful example in which to examine the nature of spatial interactions between demand and supply.

THE GREEN BELT CONCEPT

Within the UK the urban fringe has been a created landscape. In the 1930s the green belt concept was developed in London, along with many other European cities, based on the influential work of Raymond Unwin and the 1933 Green Belt Act. Unwin helped establish the principle of creating a band of open space on the city's periphery in order to compensate for the lack of open space in the built urban environment. These principles were embodied in post-war planning during the 1950s (Ministry of Housing and Local Government 1955). While such designations were intended to limit urban sprawl, recreational provision was never their intended purpose. Elson (1986) shows that planning authorities in the West Midlands, Manchester and Sheffield identified green belt plans (e.g. green wedges, recreation and amenity areas) in their development plans only to find them downgraded or removed through the ministerial assessment of the plans. In fact, Harrison (1991: 32) argued that public authorities adopted a standards approach to provision that was a legacy of the inter-war period with its heavy emphasis on organised sport rather than on a wider range of individual and family pursuits. Moreover, while these standards were based on the number of active members of the population who might be expected to participate . . . even the minimum standard of provision of 2.4 hectares per 1000 head of population could not be met in inner cities.

As a result, the urban fringe and its green belt was seen as the likely location for provision. At a policy level it is interesting to note that in the late 1960s both the Countryside Commission and local authorities used green belts as a mechanism to reduce standards of provision in the inner city (see Harrison (1991) for more discussion of the politics of green belt land and recreational use). Even so, Harrison (1980–81) found that the carrying capacity of many sites could be improved through better resource management, with the Greater London Council (1975) study of London's green belt indicating that organised activities constituted half of the trips to the green belt for recreation. In spatial terms, approved green belts now comprise 3,824,000 acres or 12 per cent of the land of England and it is expected to continue to grow as more cities use this mechanism for urban contain-ment. For example, Elson (1993) reports that the designation of 12 community forests in the UK of between 8,000 and 20,000 ha will add environ-mental improvements and resources for the urban fringe. One notable development which pre-dates much of the early research on the urban fringe is the Countryside Commission's (1974) involvement in the establishment of Country Parks in the urban fringe, following on from a UK government White Paper *Leisure and the Countryside* (1966). The Countryside Commission viewed Country Parks as an area of '25 acres in extent, with basic facilities, for the public to enjoy informal open air recreation' (Harrison 1991: 95). While a number of studies account for the evolution of Country Park policy (Zetter 1971; Slee 1982; Groome and Tarrant 1984), it is clear that the researchers point to the absence of research which indicates whether park provision provides the experiences recreationalists require. Despite growing provision of Country Parks

in the 1970s, disparities existed in their spatial distribution, with large conurbations having only limited provision (Ferguson and Munton 1979).

Thus spatial inequalities in supply simply reinforced existing patterns of provision, though Country Parks have assisted in retaining land for recreation at a time of pressure for development. Fitton (1979), for example, found that while Country Parks comprised 0.13 per cent of the land surface of England and Wales, they accounted for 4.2 per cent of trips, a finding supported by Elson (1979) whose analyses of 31 sites visited in South-East England found that urban fringe sites with a range of facilities were visited more frequently than other recreational destinations, though patterns of use were related to distance–decay functions, distance from individuals' home area, other attractions, individual choice and a range of other factors. As Harrison (1991: 103) suggests, Country Parks 'had not achieved a separate identity but people's experiences of particular sites within [them] . . . contributed to their own separate evaluations of what particular locations offered'. The continual gap between provision and users was evidenced in the Countryside Commission's (1988) study which concluded that while 58 per cent of people had heard of a Country Park, only 26 per cent could name one correctly, reflecting a lack of promotion and general awareness of their existence.

At a national level, Country Parks appear to have only a minor role to play in diverting demand from the countryside, with some parks having catch-ments that are extremely localised. For example, Harrison (1981, 1983) found that 75 per cent of visitors to south London's green belt were car users. Their study discovered that inner city residents never comprised more than 10 per cent of users. Although sites were also accessible to those not having access to a car over short distances, Groome and Tarrant (1984) found public transport to Country Parks effective over a 5–8 km distance (i.e. short distance) for a local population. At an aggregate level, it is clear that Country Parks (and their forerunner – Regional Parks) in the UK play a vital role in locating recreational resources near to demand. The somewhat dated 1981 National

Survey of Countryside Recreation found that 40 per cent of destinations were within the urban area or within 1 km (Sidaway and Duffield 1984), with a further 22 per cent in the countryside around urban areas. Only 16 per cent of destinations were located 10 km from the urban areas.

As Figure 3.1 shows, the spatial distribution of visits to South London's green belt were predominantly within or close to the built environment, and given the rapid expansion of urban fringe use it is not surprising that conflicts arise over its use. The more recent experiments in the urban fringe, including the introduction of Countryside Management to resolve small-scale conflicts (e.g. trespass, vandalism, litter and footpath maintenance) develop a conciliatory approach to problems that fall outside the remit of the planning framework. The example of Havering in Greater London (Figure 3.2) illustrates how the development of a management plan by a project officer acknowledged the problems of multiple use and the legacy of former derelict land.

In the case of Havering, the scale of dereliction and the variety of land agencies involved created problems for the development of recreation provision. While the Countryside Commission (1983) reviewed Havering's scheme and found a legacy of poor public provision in public housing areas and inadequate recognition of rights of way, landscaping schemes also remained a neglected feature. Expecting the London Borough of Havering to set a precedent for landowners to follow has taken a long time to reach fruition. Nevertheless, the approach has brought modest success through environmental improvements establishing attractive recreational facilities by effectively tidying up many sites (Harrison 1991). The success of such projects was also followed by a new initiative in 1985 – the Groundwork Trust, based on a scheme in St Helens' urban fringe (Groundwork Foundation 1986).

Variability in the usage of Country Parks reflects public knowledge of their existence and the attraction of individual locations. The precise location of recreation sites in the urban fringe appears to directly influence usage, with those located near to residential areas which permit residents to walk to them recording highest usage rates. As Harrison (1991: 166) concludes

> the recreational role played by sites in the urban fringe will differ depending upon their ease of access to local people who walk or cycle to them and not necessarily on the preferences of a wider constituency served by car . . . [and] the recreational role of countryside areas embedded in the urban area or abutting it is likely to be very different from that of more distant countryside sites.

What is clear is that the supply of recreational resources alone (e.g. Country Parks) is not sufficient in the urban fringe if the needs and recreational preferences of users are not analysed since these factors directly affect recreational behaviour.

THE MULTIPLE USE OF RECREATIONAL RESOURCES

The example of the urban fringe highlights the diversities of land uses which may occur in a sometimes contested landscape, where a wide range of resource management issues emerge. O'Riordan (1971: 19) described resource management 'as a process of decision-making whereby resources are allocated over space and time according to the needs, aspirations and desires of man'. In this process, it is the ability to accommodate multi-functional resource use in specific recreational spaces that is critical to achieving societal recreation objectives. The key to achieving this lies in the compatibility of specific recreational activities with both the resource base and other users. Although Chapter 9 discusses the role of planning and management in more detail, it is important to recognise at this point that two fundamental concepts need to be explored in managing the supply of recreational resources: *conflict* and *compatibility*.

Many notions of recreational conflict (avoidance of which is one of the goals of planning) are predicated on the concept of the incompatibility of one activity versus another. Jacob and Schreyer (1980: 369) define conflict thus: 'For an individual, conflict is defined as goal interference attributed to

HERTFORDSHIRE

ESSEX

Greater
London
boundary

River Thames

F

C

G

D

A

E

B

⑪

⑩

KENT

⑭

③ ⑦

⑨

①

④ ⑧

⑥

② ⑯

⑬

⑮ ⑫

⑤

South London boroughs

A Bexley
B Kingston upon Thames
C Lambeth
D Lewisham
E Merton
F Southwark
G Wandsworth

SURREY

0   km   10

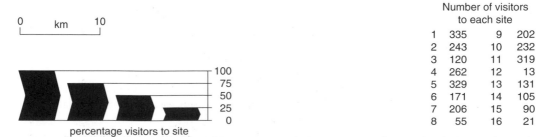

percentage visitors to site

```
100
 75
 50
 25
  0
```

Number of visitors
to each site

1	335	9	202
2	243	10	232
3	120	11	319
4	262	12	13
5	329	13	131
6	171	14	105
7	206	15	90
8	55	16	21

Figure 3.1: Number and origin of visitors to sites in South London's green belt
Source: Modified from Harrison (1981)

Figure 3.2: The London Borough of Havering's urban fringe countryside management area
Source: Based on Countryside Commission (1982) in Harrison (1991)

another's behaviour.' This definition assumes that people recreate to achieve certain outcome goals. Yet they argue that goal interference does not necessarily lead to incompatibility. In understanding the nature of recreation user conflict, the interactions which occur need to be understood in relation to a range of factors:

- the nature of the activity and personal meaning attached to it;
- the significance attached to a specific recreation resource;
- the mode of experience, especially how the natural environment is perceived;
- lifestyle tolerance, namely an individual's willingness to accept or reject lifestyles different from one's own.

These factors provide an interesting framework in which to evaluate conflict, especially for recreational resources with a high degree of conflict potential. As Jacob and Scheyer (1980: 378) assert, 'In failing to recognise the basic causes of conflict, inappropriate resolution techniques and management strategies are likely to be adopted'.

These findings are reflected in the recreational behaviour observed in Illinois by Bristow *et al.* (1995), where a wide variety of activities were incompatible and led to increased travel times to seek recreational sites able to accommodate personal preferences. Not only does this raise important planning issues for recreation site planning and design (see Ravenscroft (1992) and Pigram and Jerkins (1999) for more technical detail), it also raises the importance of recreation resource management to monitor sites to ensure the resource base can continue to accommodate the compatibility of uses.

THE SUPPLY OF TOURISM

Within most conventional texts on tourism, the issue of supply attracts comparatively little attention. According to Sinclair and Stabler (1992: 2), 'past research on the tourism industry can be classified into three main categories: first, descriptions of the industry and its operation, management and marketing; second, the spatial development and interactions which characterise the industry on a local, national and international scale; and third, the effects which result from the development of the industry.' In contrast, Shaw and Williams (1994) prefer to view the issue in relation to two other concepts: production and consumption. Shaw and Williams (1994: 16) acknowledge that the production and consumption of tourism are important approaches to the analysis of tourism since 'production is the method by which a complex array of businesses and industries are involved in the supply of tourism services and products, and how these are delivered to consumers, and consumption is how, where, why and when the tourist actually consumes tourism services and products'. Sessa (1993: 59), however, considers 'tourism supply is the result of all those productive activities that involve the provision of goods and services required to meet tourism demand and which are expressed in tourism consumption' which comprises: resources for tourists, infrastructure, receptive facilities, entertainment, sports venues as well as tourism reception services (Table 3.4). While there is an inevitable degree of overlap in this conceptualisation of tourism supply with leisure and recreational uses, it highlights the scope of productive activities associated with tourism supply.

The feature which makes many of these resources of interest to the geographer is what Urry (1990) describes as 'spatial fixity'. In other words, tourists are mobile consumers and able to consume at a global level. This contrasts with most forms of supply which are fixed at specific locations. Perhaps the exception here are the transnational corporations that are able to relocate capital at a global level to meet shifts in demand. Underlying the concept of spatial fixity is the nature of tourism entrepreneurs who are largely small scale in their operations and less able to access forms of capital to relocate to new sources of demand. Thus supply is often unable to respond geographically to demand beyond a fixed point, and this means that

Table 3.4: Elements of the tourism industry

Tourism resources
- Natural resources
- Human resources

General and tourism infrastructure
- Means of communication and travel
- Social installations
- Basic installations
- Telecommunications

Receptive facilities
- Hotels, guest houses, towns and villages
- Condominiums
- Complementary residences
- Residences for receptive personnel
- Food and beverage installations

Entertainment and sports facilities
- Recreational and cultural facilities
- Sports facilities

Tourism reception services
- Travel agencies
- Hotel and local promotional offices
- Information offices
- Car hire
- Guides, interpreters

Source: Sessa (1993)

peaks and troughs in demand at particular locations need to be managed through differential forms of pricing (Seaton and Bennett 1996) and the use of seasonal labour (Ball 1989).

Law (1993) expands upon these simple notions, arguing that 'in many respects tourism is the geography of consumption outside the home area; it is about how and why people travel to consume. . . . [On] the production side it is concerned to understand where tourism activities develop and on what scale. It is concerned with the process or processes whereby some cities are able to create tourism resources and a tourism industry' (Law 1993: 14). Law emphasises here the way in which scale is a critical concept in understanding supply issues together with the ways in which the tourism industry is organised and geographically distributed through time and space. While production and consumption have been the focus of the more theoretically derived explanations of tourism production (e.g. Mullins 1991), such approaches raise conceptual issues related to how one should view production and consumption in the context of urban tourism. The purpose of this chapter is to address how one can examine the relationship between production and consumption in terms of the supply of products. Both the tourist's consumption (often expressed as the demand – examined in Chapter 2) and the products and services produced for their visit (the supply) form important inputs in the overall system of tourism and the wider development of society. However, prior to examining different facets of production, the geographer's contribution to theoretical analysis in this area is examined.

INSIGHT: The destination life cycle

The notion of a destination product life cycle has been extremely influential in tourism research and probably ranks as one of the most substantial contributions by geographers to the wider tourism literature. Butler's (1980) concept of a tourist area cycle of evolution, based on some of the initial observations of Christaller (1963) and Plog (1974, 1977), has been applied in a number of environments and settings representing the development of a destination through time and space (Cooper and Jackson 1989; Cooper 1992, 1994; Ioannides 1992). Even though, as Graber (1997) argued, identification of the forces behind the life cycle and the key actors responsible is not yet available. Because of its relative simplicity, the concept of a destination product life cycle has emerged as a significant concept for strategic destination marketing and planning and which underpins much of our understanding of urban tourism development.

According to Cooper and Jackson (1989) the two most substantial managerial benefits of the life cycle concept are its use as a descriptive guide for strategic decision-making and its capacity as a forecasting tool. As a descriptive guide the life cycle idea implies that in the early stages of product development the focus will be on building market share while in the later stages the focus will be on maintaining that share (Rink and Swan 1979). However, the utility of the life cycle concept as a forecasting tool relies heavily on the identification of those forces that influence the flow of tourists to a specific destination. As Haywood (1986) recognised, most models work well in their early stages but then fail in their prediction of the latter stages of the model. Haywood (1986) along with other commentators (e.g. Rink and Swan 1979; Cooper 1992; Ioannides 1992) note that there are a variety of different shaped curves with the shape of the curve depending on both supply and demand side factors. Indeed, Haywood (1986: 154) goes so far as to argue that the life cycle approach 'represents the supply side view of the diffusion model', by which consumers adopt a new product.

According to Haywood (1986), there are six operational decisions when using the life cycle concept:

1 unit of analysis;
2 relevant market;
3 pattern and stages of the tourist area life cycle;
4 identification of the area's shape in the life cycle;
5 determination of the unit of measurement;
6 determination of the relevant time unit.

Using Haywood's insights as a basis for undertaking research on the life cycle, Graber (1997) undertook an analysis of the destination life cycles of 43 European cities using the variables of growth data for domestic and international tourism, first-time visitor percentage, length of stay, guest-mix distribution and number of competitors. Only a small number of the variables tested proved to be significant correlates of the life cycle. According to Graber (1997: 69), 'A diminishing rate of first-time visitors is obvious for cities passing through later stages of the cycle'. The implications of these results are significant for destinations, as monitoring of the variables may provide a more strategic approach to tourism marketing and planning (Getz 1992).

TOWARDS A CRITICAL GEOGRAPHY OF TOURISM PRODUCTION

According to Britton (1991: 451), the geography of tourism has suffered from weakly developed theory since 'geographers working in the field have been reluctant to recognise explicitly the capitalistic nature of the phenomenon they are researching'. While Shaw and Williams (1994) review the concepts of production and consumption, it is pertinent to examine critically Britton's (1991) innovative research in this area since it provides a theoretical framework in which to interpret tourism production. Within the tourism production systems are:

- economic activities designed to produce and sell tourism products;
- social groups, cultural and physical elements included in tourism products as attractions;
- agencies associated with the regulation of the production system.

In a theoretical context, Britton (1991: 455) argued that the tourism production system was 'simultaneously a mechanism for the accumulation of capital, the private appropriation of wealth, the extraction of surplus value from labour, and the capturing of (often unearned) rents from cultural and physical phenomena (especially public goods) which are deemed to have both a social and scarcity value'. The production system may be viewed as having a division of labour between its various components (transport, accommodation, tour operators, attractions and ancillary services) as well as markets (the demand and supply of tourist products) and regulatory agencies (e.g. industry associations) as well as industry organisations and structures to assist in the production of the final product. Britton (1991: 456) rightly points out that 'the geography texts on tourism offer little more than a cursory and superficial analysis of how the tourism industry is structured and regulated by the classic imperatives and laws governing capitalist accumulation'.

The tourism industry is made up of a range of separate industry suppliers who offer one or more component of the final product which requires intermediaries to co-ordinate and combine the elements which are sold to the consumer as a discrete package. Both tour operators and travel agents have a vital role to play in this context when one recognises the existence of a supply chain (Figure 3.3). What this emphasises is the variety of linkages which exist and the physical separation of roles and responsibilities to the supply chain (see Page 1994b). While information technology may assist in improving communication and co-ordination between different components associated with the production of tourism, other developments (notably horizontal and vertical integration) assist in addressing the fragmentation of elements within the supply system. Strategic alliances also assist in this regard, since suppliers in one part of the system are dependent on those either upstream or downstream. Therefore, there is pressure on suppliers to exert control over other

Figure 3.3: Four types of tourism transaction chain
Source: After Witt *et al.* (1991: 81) and Page (1994b)

shown with respect to retirement from the UK to southern Europe (Williams and Hall 2000).

Thus to understand some of these components of the tourism production system the geographer is required to appreciate concepts related to capital–labour relations, the interweaving of consumption, the business environment associated with the competitive strategies of enterprises, economic concepts (e.g. transaction analysis), product differentiation, international business as a mode of operation and global markets, along with basic business and marketing concepts. Within a capitalist mode of production this is essential so that one may under-

stand how each component in the tourism production system operates (i.e. how it develops products, generates profits and competes with other businesses) and how social groups and places are incorporated into the production system, so that the production system and the spatial relationships which exist may be fully understood. To illustrate these ideas, the example of international hotel chains is used to examine relationships between the geography of supply, functions, the industrial structure of the business and the social relations which exist.

INSIGHT: Economic globalisation

Globalisation is a complex, chaotic, multiscalar, multitemporal and multicentric series of processes operating in specific structural and spatial contexts (Jessop 1999). Globalisation should be seen as an emergent, evolutionary phenomenon which results from economic, political, socio-cultural and technological processes on many scales rather than a distinctive causal mechanism in its own right. It is both a structural and a structuring phenomenon, the nature of which critically depends on subglobal processes. According to Jessop (1999: 21), 'structurally, globalisation would exist in so far as co-variation of relevant activities becomes more global in extent and/or the speed of that covariation on a global scale increases'. Therefore, global interdependence typically results from processes which operate at various spatial scales, in different functional subsystems, and involve complex and tangled causal hierachies rather than being a simple, unilinear, bottom-up or top-down movement (Jessop 1999). Such an observation clearly suggests that globalisation is developing unevenly across space and time. Indeed, 'a key element in contemporary processes of globalisation is not the impact of "global" processes upon another clearly defined scale, but instead the relativisation of

scale' (Kelly and Olds 1999: 2). Such relativities occur in relation to both 'space–time distantiation' and 'space–time compression'. The former refers to the stretching of social relations over time and space (e.g. through the utilisation of new technology such as the internet), so that they can be co-ordinated or controlled over longer periods of time, greater distances, larger areas and on more scales of activity. The latter involves the intensification of 'discrete' events in real time and/or increased velocity of material and non-material flows over a given distance; again this is related to technological change, including communication technologies and social technologies (Jessop 1999).

The discourse of globalisation therefore goes further than the simple description of contemporary social change; it also carries with it the power to shape material reality via the practical politics of policy formulation and implementation (Gibson-Graham 1996; Kelly and Olds 1999). It can also construct a view of geographical space that implies the deferral of political options from the national to the supranational and global scales, and from the local to the national. In effect, globalisation 'itself has become a political force, helping to create the institutional realities it purportedly merely describes' (Piven 1995: 8), as indicated by the growth of structures such as APEC and NAFTA.

In addition to the 'structural context' of globalisation noted above, authors such as Ohmae (1995), Jessop (1999) and Higgott (1999) point to a more strategic interpretation of globalisation, which refers to individual and institutional actors' attempts to promote the global co-ordination of activities on a continuing basis within different orders or functional systems. For example, interpersonal networking, inter-firm strategic alliances, the creation of international and supranational regimes to govern particular fields of action, and the broader development of modes of international and supranational systems of governance. Therefore, given the multiscale, multitemporal and multicentric nature of globalisation we can recognise that globalisation 'rarely, if ever, involves the full structural integration and strategic coordination across the globe' (Jessop 1999: 22). Instead, processes usually considered under the rubric of 'economic globalisation' include:

- The formation of regional economic and trading blocs – particularly in the triadic regions of North America (North American Free Trade Area (NAFTA)), Europe (European Union (EU)) and East Asia-Pacific (Asia–Pacific Economic Cooperation) – and the development of formal links between those blocs (e.g. the Asia–Europe Meetings). In all of these regions tourism is a major component of economic and social policy (Hall 2001).

- The growth of 'local internationalisation', 'virtual regions', through the development of economic ties between contiguous (e.g. 'border regions'), or non-contiguous local and regional state authorities (e.g. growth regions and triangles) in different national economies which often bypass the level of the nation state but which still retain support at the national level. For example, the Pacific NorthWest Economic Region (PNWER) consisting of the American states of Alaska, Idaho, Montana, Oregon and Washington plus the Canadian provinces of Alberta, British Columbia and Yukon Territory, as well as private sector members, has a tourism working group to promote greater economic development in the region (Hall 2001).
- The widening and deepening of international and supranational regimes which cover economic and economically relevant issues and which may also provide for regional institutionalised governance.
- The internationalisation of national economic spaces through growing penetration (inward flows) and extraversion (outward flows) as with the increasing mobility of tourists and capital.
- The extension and deepening of multinationalisation by multinational firms including hospitality and tourism firms.
- The 'emergence of globalisation proper through the introduction and acceptance of global norms and standards, the development of globally integrated markets together with globally oriented strategies, and "deracinated" firms with no evident national operational base' (Jessop 1999: 23).

INTERNATIONAL HOTEL CHAINS

The hotel industry is arguably a global industry, since it fulfils some of the criteria which distinguish businesses as truly global, whereby it may be one which can create a competitive advantage from its activities on a worldwide basis. Alternatively it may be one in which the strategic positions of competitors in major geographic or national markets are fundamentally affected by their overall global positions (Porter 1980: 175). Much of the debate on the influence of international hotel chains may

Plate 3.6: Hotels on small islands such as Fiji aimed at the luxury end of the market have to import many of the products and materials, adding to the leakage noted by Britton (1991). This picture shows the Sheraton Hotel, Denarau Island, Fiji.

be dated to the research by Dunning and McQueen (1982) on what constitutes a multinational, international and transnational firm. Dunning and McQueen's (1982) use of an international hotel company, which has direct investments and other types of contractual agreements in more than one country, remains a simple but effective definition (see also Shaw and Williams 1994: 120–5).

Gannon and Johnson (1995) provide an interesting and comparatively up-to-date assessment of the principal global hotel company characteristics (recent changes may have changed the precise size of their holdings, but Table 3.5 does illustrate the scale and order of magnitude of global hotels). While Table 3.5 illustrates that Choice Hotels International was the largest group, at the other end of the scale Orient-Express has 12 units, yet operates globally, implying that size of operation is not necessarily a precondition to achieving global status. Go and Pine (1995) examine some of the corporate strategies to explain the differences between the companies according to the countries in which they operate, while in Table 3.5, 'domicile continent' identifies the operating base and likely source of finance, which illustrates that no global companies operate in Africa, Oceania or South America. (See Gannon and Johnson (1995) for more detail on possible explanations for the geographical patterns of operation and strategies for expansion and development by area.)

Britton (1991: 460) analysed the product which hotel chains offered in terms of their competitive strategies as

a package of on-premises' services which provide a certain experience (ambience, lifestyle) based on kinds and qualities of accommodation, on-site recreation and shopping facilities, and catering; the offering of off-premises' services (airport shuttles, local excursions, booking facilities); and a trademark guarantee

Table 3.5: Global hotel company characteristics

Number	Name	Domicile continent	Units worldwide	Countries worldwide	FIM (%)
1	Accor	Europe	2,127	73	65.2
2	Choice Hotels International	North America	2,663	25	16.6
3	Forte	Europe	910	33	63.1
4	Hilton International	Europe	151	48	78.1
5	Holiday Inn World-Wide	Europe	1,772	56	98.8
6	Hyatt International	North America	202	35	42.6
7	Inter-Continental	Asia	106	47	98.1
8	ITT Sheraton	North America	472	63	52.5
9	Marriott	North America	749	21	6.4
10	Meridien	Europe	55	33	94.5
11	Orient-Express	Asia	12	8	100.0
12	Radisson	North America	255	23	60.8
13	Ramada	Asia	158	39	98.7

Source: Gannon and Johnston (1995)

which signals to the customer a predictable quality of service.

The competitive strategies which follow from these features are based on an understanding of the customer (i.e. needs and preferences), where the brand name is able to command a premium price in the market place. Britton (1991: 460) explains the commercial advantage of international chains in terms of:

- the firms' location in the customers' home country;
- experience in understanding demand through operating hotels in the domestic markets;
- managerial expertise and staff training to ensure the elements of the tourists' experience related to the brand name are met through appropriate training and operating manuals.

The key to successful competition is for the hotel company to internalise its firm-specific intellectual property (i.e. training methods and manuals), while ensuring profit levels for shareholders. Unfortunately this is extremely difficult when staff leave and move to competitors, since the intellectual property is essentially 'know-how'. Yet this is often the basis for horizontal integration into overseas markets, with management contracts a preferred mechanism for operation rather than outright ownership to control design, operation, pricing and staffing, though the same companies (e.g. Holiday Inns) prefer to use franchising as a mechanism to control managerial, organisational and professional input.

One notable dimension here is the effect of international hotel and tourism development on less developed countries. For example, in Kenya, 60 per cent of hotel beds were accounted for through equity participation schemes with such hotel groups (Rosemary 1987; Sinclair 1991). The implications are that where international involvement occurs, there is a concomitant loss of central control and leakage of foreign earnings, and where there is concentrated development of enclaves remote from local population this inevitably leads to little benefit for the host country. Despite these problems,

attitudes towards such development among a survey of 22 developing countries (WTO 1985) saw the benefits outweighing the cash. This may lead to dependency relationships, as Britton (1980a) indicated in his innovative study of the distribution of ownership and commercial control by metropolitan tourist markets of less developed world destinations.

Britton's model of tourism development (Figure 3.4) illustrates the nature of tourism dependency, where international tourism organisations (in the absence of strong government control) develop and perpetuate a hierarchical element to tourism development. While dependency theory is useful in explaining how capitalist production leads to the resulting patterns of tourism demand and supply, it is evident that this is only a simplification of the wider geographical dimensions of capital–labour relations in a global context, where political economy perspectives assist in explaining the processes leading to the spatial patterns of tourism development that occur. The economic dynamics of the tourism production system begin to help to develop a more central perspective of tourism which fits into the broader conceptualisation of capitalist accumulation, and the social construction of reality, though marketing and the construction of place may provide new areas for future geographical research. In fact, what one realises from a critical analysis of tourism using political economy perspectives is that it is a constantly changing phenomenon, with an ever-changing spatial organisation. The processes affecting the political economy of production and consumption require a critical awareness of the role and activities of entrepreneurs, the flow of capital and its internationalisation, the impact of industrial and regional restructuring, urban development, changes in the service economy and how the production of tourism results in new landscapes of tourism in a contemporary society. Aside from theoretical analysis, geographers have developed other concepts and methods of analysis, and we now turn to these approaches.

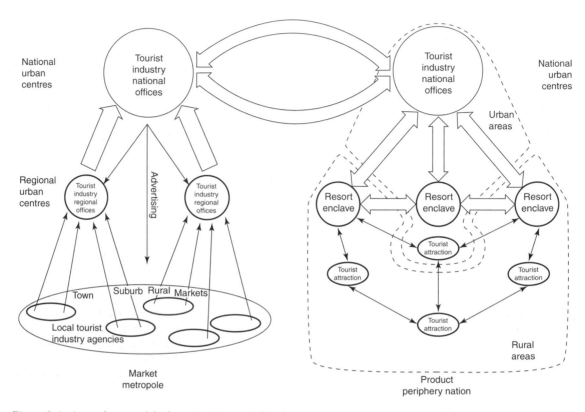

Figure 3.4: An enclave model of tourism in a peripheral economy
Source: Redrawn from Britton (1980a)

THE LEISURE PRODUCT

Within the context of urban tourism, Jansen-Verbeke (1986) viewed the urban area as a 'leisure product' (Figure 3.5) which comprises primary elements including a variety of facilities that may be grouped into:

- an activity place, thereby defining the overall supply features within the city, particularly the main tourist attractions;
- a leisure setting, which includes both the physical elements in the built environment and the socio-cultural characteristics which give a city a distinct image and 'sense of place' (see Walmesley and Jenkins (1992) for a discussion of this concept) for visitors;

and secondary elements which consist of:

- the supporting facilities and services which tourists consume during their visit (e.g. hotel and catering outlets and shopping facilities) which shape the visitor's experience of the services available in the city;
- additional elements which consist of the tourism infrastructure that conditions the visit, such as the availability of car-parking, tourist-transport provision and accessibility and tourist-specific services (e.g. visitor information centres and tourist signposting).

Shaw and Williams (1994: 202) rightly argue that 'while such an approach allows a systematic consideration of the supply side of urban tourism,

PRIMARY ELEMENTS		SECONDARY ELEMENTS
Activity place	**Leisure setting**	
Cultural facilities	**Physical characteristics**	• Hotels and catering facilities
• Concert halls	• Ancient monuments and	• Markets
• Cinemas	statues	• Shopping facilities
• Exhibitions	• Ecclesiastical buildings	
• Museums and art galleries	• Harbours	
• Theatres	• Historical street pattern	
	• Interesting buildings	
Sports facilities	• Parks and green areas	
• Indoor and outdoor	• Water, canals and river fronts	
Amusement facilities	**Socio-cultural features**	**ADDITIONAL ELEMENTS**
• Bingo halls	• Folklore	
• Casinos	• Friendliness	• Accessibility and parking
• Festivities	• Language	facilities
• Night clubs	• Liveliness and ambience of the	• Tourist facilities:
• Organised events	place	information offices,
	• Local customs and costumes	signposts, guides, maps and
	• Security	leaflets

Figure 3.5: The elements of tourism
Source: Modified from Jansen-Verbeke (1986)

it is not without its difficulties. For example, in many cities, the so-called secondary elements of shops and restaurants may well be the main attractions for certain groups of visitors'. Nevertheless, the supply-side variables within the context of the urban tourism system help in understanding the interrelationships between supply and demand and the interaction between the consumers and the products. In this respect, it is also useful to identify what aspect of the 'leisure product' tourists consume; some may consume only one product (e.g. a visit to an art gallery) while others may consume what Jansen-Verbeke (1988) terms a 'bundle of products' (i.e. several products during their stay such as a visit to a theatre, museum and a meal in a restaurant).

Jansen-Verbeke (1986) examined this concept within the inner-city tourism system to identify the nature of tourists visiting the inner city and the organisations responsible for the promotion of the inner city as an area for tourists to visit. The role of organisations promoting urban areas for tourism is discussed in more detail in Chapter 6, but to explain Jansen-Verbeke's (1986) analysis it is useful to consider the relationship which she believes exists between the product, the tourist and the promoter. Promoters affect the relationship in two ways:

1 they build an image of the inner city and its tourists' resources to attract potential tourists, investors and employers;
2 the promotion of the inner city may also lead to direct product improvement.

Consequently, the model Jansen-Verbeke (1986) constructs (Figure 3.5) illustrates how different elements of the inner-city tourism system are interrelated and the significance of the inner city as a leisure product. However, the public and private sector have distinct roles to play in this context.

Table 3.6: Some reasons for government involvement in tourism

Economic reasons
- to improve the balance of payments in a country;
- to attract foreign exchange;
- to aid regional (or local) economic development;
- to diversify the economy;
- to increase income levels;
- to increase state revenue from taxes;
- to generate new employment opportunities.

Social and cultural reasons
- to achieve social objectives related to 'social tourism' to ensure the well-being and health of families and individuals;
- to protect cultural mores, traditions, resources and heritage;
- to promote a greater cultural awareness of an area and its people;
- to promote international understanding.

Environmental reasons
- to undertake the stewardship of the environment and tourism resources to ensure that the agents of development do not destroy the future basis for sustainable tourism development;
- to create a natural resource which will serve to attract tourists.

Political reasons
- to further political objectives by promoting the development of tourism in order to broaden the political acceptance of a government among visitors;
- to control the development process associated with tourism;
- to protect the public interest and the interests of minorities;
- to further political ideology.

Sources: Jenkins and Henry (1982); D.G. Pearce (1989); Hall (1994); Hall and Jenkins (1995)

by measures that work within the price system. Across the globe almost every industry has been supported at various times by subsidies, the imposition of tariff regulations, taxation concessions, direct grants and other forms of government intervention, all of which serve to affect the price of goods and services and therefore influence the distribution of income, production and wealth. The size or economic importance of the tourism industry, so commonly emphasised by the public and private sectors, is no justification in itself for government intervention; within market-driven economies justification must lie in some aspect of: (1) market failure; (2) market imperfection; or (3) public/social concerns about market outcomes. Therefore, implicit in each justification for intervention is the view that government offers a corrective alternative to the market (Hall and Jenkins 1998).

The role of the state as entrepreneur in tourist development is closely related to the concept of the 'devalorisation of capital' (Damette 1980). The 'devalorisation of capital' is the process by which the state subsidises part of the cost of production, for instance, by assisting in the provision of infrastructure or by investing in a tourism project where private venture capital is otherwise unavailable. In this process what would have been private costs are transformed into public or social costs. The provision of infrastructure, particularly transport networks, is regarded as crucial to the development of tourist destinations (Page 1999). There are numerous formal and informal means for government at all levels to assist in minimising the costs of production for tourism developers. Indeed, the offer of government assistance for development is often used to encourage private investment in a particular region or tourist project; for instance, through the provision of cheap land or government-backed low-interest loans.

As well as acting as entrepreneurs, governments can also stimulate tourism in several ways: first, financial incentives such as low-interest loans or a depreciation allowance on tourist accommodation or infrastructure, although 'their introduction often reflected both the scarcity of domestic investment funds and widespread ambition to undertake economic development programmes' (Bodlender and Davies 1985, quoted in D.G. Pearce 1992b: 11); second, sponsoring research for the benefit of the tourism industry rather than for specific individual organisations and associations; third, marketing and promotion generally aimed at generating tourism demand, although it may also take the form of investment promotion aimed at encouraging capital investment for tourism attractions and facilities (Hall 1995).

One of the more unusual features of tourism promotion by government tourism organisations is that they have only limited control over the product they are marketing, with very few actually owning the goods, facilities and services that make up the tourism product (D.G. Pearce 1992b). This lack of control is perhaps testimony to the power of the public good argument used by industry to justify continued maintenance of government funding for destination promotion. However, it may also indicate the political power of the tourism lobby, such as industry organisations, to influence government tourism policies (Hall and Jenkins 1995).

Throughout most of the 1980s and the early 1990s, 'Thatcherism' (named after Conservative Prime Minister Margaret Thatcher) in the United Kingdom and 'Reaganism' (named after Republican President Ronald Reagan) in the United States, saw a period of retreat by central government from active intervention. At the national level, policies of deregulation, privatisation, free trade, the elimination of tax incentives and a move away from discretionary forms of macro-economic intervention, were and have been the hallmarks of a push towards 'smaller' government and lower levels of government intervention. Given such demand for smaller government in western society in recent years, there have been increasing demands from government and economic rationalists for greater industry self-sufficiency in tourism marketing and promotion. The political implications of such an approach for the tourism industry are substantial. As Hughes (1984: 14) noted, 'The advocates of a free enterprise economy would look to consumer freedom of choice and not to governments to promote firms; the consumer ought to be sovereign in decisions relating to the allocation of the nation's resources.' Such an approach means that lobbyists in the tourism industry may do better by shifting their focus on the necessity of government intervention to issues of externalities, public goods and merit wants rather than employment and the balance of payments (Hall 1994). 'Such criteria for government intervention have a sounder economic

base and are more consistent with a free-enterprise philosophy than employment and balance of payments effects' (Hughes 1984: 18). Nevertheless, as D.G. Pearce (1992b: 8) recognised, 'general destination promotion tends to benefit all sectors of the tourist industry in the place concerned; it becomes a "public good". . . . The question of "freeloaders" thus arises, for they too will benefit along with those who may have contributed directly to the promotional campaign.'

In many cases, the state's involvement is to ensure a policy of intervention so that political objectives associated with employment generation and planning are achieved, although this varies from one country to another and from city to city according to the political persuasion of the organisation involved. D.G. Pearce (1989: 44) rightly acknowledges, however, that

> the public sector then is by no means a single entity with clear cut responsibilities and well-defined policies for tourist development. Rather, the public sector becomes involved in tourism for a wide range of reasons in a variety of ways at different levels and through many agencies and institutions . . . [and] there is often a lack of coordination, unnecessary competition, duplication of effort in some areas and neglect in others.

SPATIAL ANALYTICAL APPROACHES TO THE SUPPLY OF TOURISM FACILITIES

Much of the research on tourism supply in relation to facilities and services is descriptive in content, based on inventories and lists of the facilities and where they are located. In view of the wide range of literature that discusses the distribution of specific facilities or services, it is more useful to consider only two specific examples of how such approaches and concepts may be used to derive generalisations of patterns of tourism activity.

The Tourism Business District

Within the literature on the supply of urban tourism, Ashworth (1989) reviews the 'facility approach' which offers researchers the opportunity to map the location of specific facilities, undertaking inventories of facilities on a city-wide basis. The difficulty with such an approach is that the users of urban services and facilities are not just tourists, since workers and residents as well as recreationists may use the same facilities. Therefore, any inventory will be only a partial view of the full range of facilities and potential services tourists could use. One useful approach is to identify the areas in which the majority of tourist activities occur and to use it as the focus for the analysis of the supply of tourism services in such a multi-functional city which meets a wide range of uses for a wide range of users (see Chapter 5). This avoids the individual assessments of the location and use of specific aspects of tourism services such as accommodation (Page and Sinclair 1989), entertainment facilities such as restaurants (S.L.J. Smith 1983b, 1989) and night-life entertainment facilities (Ashworth *et al.* 1988) and other attractions. This approach embraces the ecological approaches developed in human geography to pinpoint regions within cities as a basis to identify the processes shaping the patterns.

The ecological approach towards the analysis of urban tourism dates back to Gilbert's (1949) assessment of the development of resorts, which was further refined by Barrett (1958). The outcome is a resort model where accommodation, entertainment and commercial zones exist and the central location of tourism facilities were dominant elements. The significance of such research is that it identifies some of the features and relationships which were subsequently developed in urban geography and applied to tourism and recreation. The most notable study is Stansfield and Rickert's (1970) development of the Recreational Business District (RBD). This study rightly identifies the multifunctional land use of the central areas of cities, including tourism and recreational activities, in relation to the central area for business (Central Business District (CBD)). Meyer-Arendt (1990) also expands this notion in the context of the Gulf of Mexico coastal resorts, while D.G. Pearce (1989) offers a useful critique of these studies. The essential

ideas in the RBD have subsequently been extended to urban and resort tourism to try to explain where the location and distribution of the range of visitor-oriented functions occur in space.

Burtenshaw *et al.*'s (1991) seminal study of tourism and recreation in European cities deals with the concept of the Central Tourist District (CTD) where tourism activities in cities are concentrated in certain areas. This has been termed the TBD by Getz (1993a: 583–4), who argues that it is

> The concentration of visitor-oriented attractions and services located in conjunction with urban central businesses (CBD) functions. In older cities, especially in Europe, the TBD and CBD often coincide with heritage areas. Owing to their high visibility and economic importance, TBDs can be subjected to intense planning by municipal authorities. . . . The form and evolution of TBDs reveals much about the nature of urban tourism and its impacts, while the analysis of the planning systems influencing TBDs can contribute to concepts and methods for better planning of tourism in urban areas.

Therefore, TBDs are a useful framework in which to understand the supply components of urban tourism and how they fit together. Figure 3.6, based on Getz's (1993a) analysis of the TBD, is a schematic model in which the functions rather than geographical patterns of activities are considered. This model illustrates the difficulty of separating visitor-oriented services from the CBD and use of services and facilities by residents and workers. Yet as Jansen-Verbeke and Ashworth (1990) argue, while tourism and recreational activities are integrated within the physical, social and economic context of the city, no analytical framework exists to determine the functional or behavioural interactions in these activities. They argue that more research is needed to assess the extent to which the clustering of tourism and recreational activities can occur in cities without leading to incompatible and conflicting uses from such facilities. While the TBD may offer a distinctive blend of activities and attractions for tourist and non-tourist alike, it is important to recognise these issues where tourism clusters in areas such as the TBD. Even so, the use of street entertainment and special events and festivals (Getz 1997) may also add to the ambience

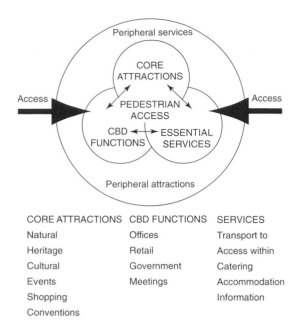

CORE ATTRACTIONS
Natural
Heritage
Cultural
Events
Shopping
Conventions

CBD FUNCTIONS
Offices
Retail
Government
Meetings

SERVICES
Transport to
Access within
Catering
Accommodation
Information

Figure 3.6: The tourism business district
Source: Based on Getz (1993a)

and sense of place for both the city worker and visitor. By having a concentration of tourism and non-tourism resources and services in one accessible area within a city, it is possible to encourage visitors to stay there, making it a place tourists will want to visit, as is the case in the West End of London (Page and Sinclair 1989). However, the attractions in urban areas are an important component in the appeal to potential visitors.

Tourism attractions

Attractions are an integral feature of urban tourism, which offer visitors passive and more active occupations on which to spend their time during a visit. They also comprise a key component of Jansen-Verbeke's (1986) 'primary element' (Figure 3.5). Recent studies have adapted descriptive analyses of specific types of attraction (e.g. Law 1993) rather than exploring their relationship with urban tourists. Lew (1987: 54) acknowledges that 'although the importance of tourist attractions is readily recognised, tourism researchers and

theorists have yet to fully come to terms with the nature of attractions as phenomena both in the environment and the mind'. As a result, Lew's (1987) study and Leiper's (1990) synthesis and conceptual framework of 'Tourist Attraction Systems' remain among the most theoretically informed literature published to date. Lew (1987) identifies three perspectives used to understand the nature of tourist attractions. These are:

1 *The ideographic perspective*, where the general characteristics of a place, site, climate, culture and customs are used to develop typologies of tourism attractions, involving inventories or general descriptions. For example, Standard Industrial Classification codes (SICs) are one approach used to group attractions (see S.L.J. Smith 1989). These approaches are the ones most commonly used to examine tourist attractions in the general tourism literature.

2 *The organisational perspective*, in contrast, tends to emphasise the geographical, capacity and temporal aspects (the time dimension) of attractions rather than the 'managerial notions of organisation' (Leiper 1990: 175). This approach examines scales ranging from the individual attraction to larger areas and their attractions.

3 *The cognitive perspective* is based on 'studies of tourist perceptions and experiences of attractions' (Lew 1987: 560). P.L. Pearce (1982: 98) recognises that any tourist place (or attraction) is one capable of fostering the feeling of being a tourist. Therefore, the cognitive perspective is interested in understanding the tourists' feelings and views of the place or attraction.

The significance of Lew's (1987) framework is that it acknowledges the importance of attractions as a research focus, although Leiper (1990) questions the definition of attractions used by many researchers. He pursues the ideas developed by MacCannell (1976: 41), that an attraction incorporates 'an empirical relationship between a tourist, a sight and a marker, a piece of information about a sight'. A 'marker' is an item of information about any phenomenon which could be used to highlight the tourist's awareness of the potential existence of a tourist attraction.

This implies that an attraction has a number of components, while conventional definitions consider only the sight (Leiper 1990: 177). In this respect, 'the tourist attraction is a system comprising three elements: a tourist, a sight and a marker' (Leiper 1990: 178). Although sightseeing is a common tourist activity, the idea of a sight really refers to the nucleus or central component of the attraction (Gunn 1972). In this context a situation could include a sight where sightseeing occurs, but it may also be an object, person or event. Based on this argument, Leiper (1990: 178) introduces the following definition of a tourist attraction as 'a system comprising three elements: a tourist or human element, a nucleus or central element, and a marker or informative element. A tourist attraction comes into existence when the three elements are interconnected.' On the basis of this alternative approach to attractions, Leiper (1990) identifies the type of information which is likely to give meaning to the tourist experience of urban destinations in relation to their attractions.

These ideas were developed further in Leiper's model of a tourist attraction system (Figure 3.7), breaking the established view that tourists are not simply 'attracted' or 'pulled' to areas on the basis of their attractions. Instead, visitors are motivated to experience a nucleus and its markers in a situation where the marker reacts positively with their needs and wants. Figure 3.7 identifies the linkages within the model and how tourist motivation is influenced by the information available and the individual's perception of their needs. Thus, an attraction system may develop only when the following have become connected:

- a person with tourist needs;
- a nucleus (a feature or attribute of a place that tourists seek to visit);
- a marker (information about the nucleus).

This theoretical framework has a great deal of value in relation to understanding the supply of urban tourism resources for visitors. First, it views an attraction system as a subsystem of the larger tourism system in an urban area. Second, it acknowledges the integral role for the tourist as consumer – without the tourist (or day tripper) the system would not exist. Third, the systems approach offers a convenient social science framework in which to understand how urban destinations attract visitors, with different markers and nuclei to attract specific groups of visitors. Having examined the significance of different approaches towards the analysis of tourism supply in urban areas, attention turns to the significance of different components of Jansen-Verbeke's leisure product and tourism destinations.

TOURIST FACILITIES

Among the 'secondary elements' of the leisure product in urban areas, four components emerge as central to servicing tourist needs. These are:

1 accommodation;
2 catering;
3 shopping;
4 conditional elements.

Accommodation

Tourist accommodation performs an important function in cities: it provides the opportunity for visitors to stay for a length of time to enjoy the locality and its attractions, while their spending contributes to the local economy. Accommodation forms a base for the tourists' exploration of the urban (and non-urban) environment. The tendency for establishments to locate in urban areas is illustrated in Figure 3.8, which is based on the typical patterns of urban hotel location in West European cities (Ashworth 1989; see also the seminal paper by Arbel and Pizam (1977) on urban hotel location). Figure 3.8 highlights the importance of infrastructure and accessibility when hotels are built to serve specific markets, i.e. the exhibition and conference market will need hotels adjacent

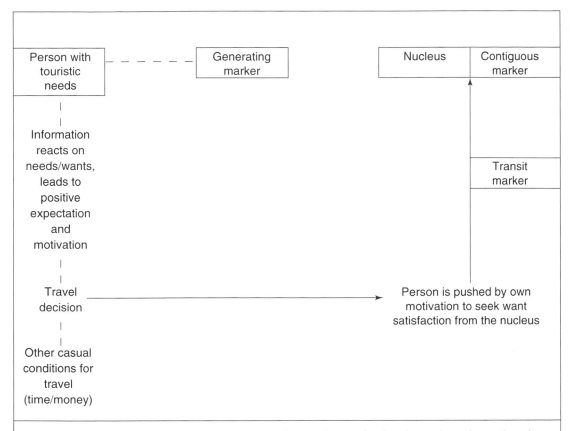

Figure 3.7: A model of a tourism attraction system
Source: Based on Leiper (1990)

to a major conference and exhibition centre, as Law (1996) emphasised.

The accommodation sector within cities can be divided into serviced and non-serviced sectors (Figure 3.9). Each sector has developed in response to the needs of different markets, and a wide variety of organisational structures have emerged among private sector operators to develop this area of economic activity. As D.G. Pearce (1989) notes, many large chains and corporations now dominate the accommodation sector, using vertical and hori-zontal forms of integration to develop a greater degree of control over their business activities (see McVey (1986) for a more detailed discussion). (A useful set of studies which focus on the issue of tourist accommodation may be found in Goodall 1989.)

Catering facilities

Ashworth and Tunbridge (1990) note that catering facilities are among the most frequently used

INSIGHT: Towards geographical analyses of hospitality: research agendas

While the geographer has predominately focused on the spatial and cultural implications of catering, there is a well-developed hospitality literature which has examined the historical evolution of the hospitality trades (Walton 2000). Critical debates associated with the 'McDonald-isation' of society (Ritzer 1993) and linked to globalisation, where the principles of fast food restaurants are dominating society, especially hospitality (e.g. the use of technology in place of people, service standardisation, set rules and procedures and clear division of labour) have introduced predictability into hospitality services globally. For the tourist experience, a global and spatial homogeneity associated with the McDonaldisation concept raises important cultural questions related to the type of experience being produced and consumed by tourists. In new conceptualisations of hospitality, Lashley challenges existing concerns with hospitality as a narrowly defined commercial activity, namely 'the

provision of food and/or drink and/or accommo-dation away from home' (Lashley 2000: 3). Preferring new approaches, Lashley (2000: 4) introduces a new breadth of definition with the use of the social, private and commercial domains of hospitality (Figure 3.10). Each domain represents one aspect of hospitality which is both independent and overlapping. From the social domain, the social setting of hospitality shapes the production and consumption of food/drink/ accommodation. In the private domain, the issues of hospitality and the host–guest encounter and cultural context of these relationships become important. In the commercial domain, the focus is on the production of hospitality services and their consumption as an economic activity.

For the geographer, much of the research has been conceived in the empiricist tradition and primarily concerned with employment in hos-pitality, its spatial form and processes shaping the supply of hospitality businesses. Again, this area

Figure 3.10: The domains of hospitality activities
Source: Modified from Lashley (2000: 4)

of research is particularly underdeveloped and is certainly well situated to utilise a wide range of research approaches (Walle 1997) and agendas ranging from an empiricist mode to new cultural geographies. Indeed, the growing interest in the relationships between tourist, food production, regionalisation and wine is certainly opening new domains for the spatially inclined (Hall *et al.* 2000; Hall and Mitchell 2002). Therefore, with a range of processes operating (e.g. globalisation and McDonaldisation) and concerns for the meaning of hospitality in a postmodern society (Williams 2000), it is clear that the geographers have been ominous by their absence from debates in this area.

Tourist shopping

The English Historic Town Forum's (1992) study on retailing and tourism highlights many of the relationships between 'tourism and retail activity [which] are inextricably linked to historic towns with three-quarters of tourists combining shopping with visiting attractions. . . . The expenditure is not only on refreshments and souvenirs, as might be expected, but also on clothing and footwear, stationery and books' (English Towns Forum 1992: 3). The study also emphasises the overall significance of the environmental quality in towns which is vital to the success of urban tourism and retailing. In fact the report argues that, 'for towns wishing to maintain or increase leisure visitor levels, the study reveals a number of guide-lines. For example, cleanliness, attractive shop fronts and provision of street entertainment are all important to tourists' (English Historic Towns Forum 1992: 3).

Unfortunately, identifying tourist shopping as a concept in the context of urban tourism is difficult, since it is also an activity undertaken by other users such as residents. Jansen-Verbeke (1990, 1991) considers the motives of tourists and their activities in a range of Dutch towns. She makes a number of interesting observations on this concept. However, the range of motives associated with tourism and leisure shopping are complex: people visit areas due to their appeal, and shopping may be a spontaneous as well as a planned activity. Even so, the quality and range of retail facilities may be a useful determinant of the likely demand for tourism and leisure shopping: the longer the visitor is enticed to stay in a destination, the greater the likely spending in retail outlets.

One important factor which affects the ability of cities to attract tourism and leisure shoppers is the retail mix – namely the variety of goods, shops and presence of specific retailers. For example, the English Historic Towns Forum (1992) notes that over 80 per cent of visitors consider the retailing mix and general environment of the town to be the most important attraction of the destination. Although the priorities of different tourist market segments vary slightly, catering, accessibility (e.g. availability of car-parking, location of car-parks and public transport), tourist attractions and the availability of visitor information shape the decision to engage in tourism and leisure shopping. The constant search for the unique shopping experience, especially in conjunction with day trips in border areas and neighbouring countries (e.g. the UK cross-channel tax-free shopping trips from Dover to Calais) are well-established forms of tourism and leisure shopping.

The global standardisation of consumer products has meant that the search for the unique shopping experience continues to remain important. The growth of the North American shopping malls and tourist specific projects (Lew 1985, 1989; Getz 1993b) and the development in the UK of out-of-town complexes (e.g. the Metro Centre in Gateshead and Lakeside at Thurrock, adjacent to the M25) have extended this trend. For example, in the case of Edmonton Mall (Canada), Jansen-Verbeke (1991) estimates that 10 per cent of the total floor space is used for leisure facilities with its 800 shops and parking for 27,000 cars. Such developments have been of great concern for many cities as out-of-town shopping has reduced the potential in-town urban tourism in view of the competition they pose for established destinations. The difficulty with most existing studies of leisure shopping is that they fail to disentangle the relationships between the actual activity tourists undertake and their perception of the environment. For this reason, Jansen-Verbeke (1991) distinguishes between intentional shopping and intentional leisure shopping in a preliminary attempt to explain how and why tourists engage in this activity; she also suggests that several criteria need to be considered to distinguish between intentional shopping and intentional leisure and tourism (Table 3.7).

For many destinations, finding the right mix between shops, leisure facilities and tourist attractions to appeal to a wide range of visitors and residents involves a process of development and promotion to attract investment in town centres. This also recognises the potential for using shopping as a marketing tool by the tourism industry in towns and cities. The English Historic Towns Forum (1992) emphasised this relationship, as 75 per cent of visitors to the cities surveyed combined tourism and shopping.

Only certain shopping centres have the essential ingredients to be promoted as tourism and day trip destinations. The image and manner in which these places are promoted is assuming growing significance. Historic cities in Europe have many of the key ingredients in terms of the environment, facilities, tourism attractions and the ability to appeal to distinct visitor audiences. Many successful cities in Western Europe have used tourism and leisure shopping to establish their popularity as destinations as a gradual process of evolution. For example, research by Page and Hardyman (1996) examines the concept of town centre management as one attempt to address the impact of out-of-town shopping malls and complexes as a threat to tourism and leisure spending in town centres. Their research found that based on concepts developed in North America, town centres can identify their users more closely and undertake in-town improvements to attract the user as a means of developing leisure shopping. In particular, improvements to town centres by

Table 3.7: Criteria to be considered in distinguishing between intentional shopping and intentional leisure and tourism

Behaviour pattern of visitors
- trip length – short, possibly longer;
- length of stay – limited or rather unplanned;
- time of stay – a few hours during the day, an evening, a full day;
- kinds of activity – window shopping, intentional buying, drinking, eating, various leisure activities, cultural activities, sightseeing;
- expenditure – goods, possibly some souvenirs, drinks, meals, entrance fees to leisure facilities.

Functional characteristics of the environment
- wide range of retail shops, department stores, catering, leisure and other facilities, tourist attractions, spatial clustering of facilities;
- parking space and easy access;
- street retailing, pedestrian priority in open spaces.

Quality of the environment
- image of the place, leisure setting, display of goods on the street, street musicians and artists;
- accessibility during leisure time, including weekends and evenings;
- aesthetic value, image of maintenance and safety;
- architectural design of buildings, streets, shops, windows, sign boards, lighting;
- social effective value, liveliness of the open space;
- animation, entertainment, amusement and surprise.

Hospitableness of the environment
- social, visual, physical;
- orientation, information, symbolism, identification.

Source: Jansen-Verbeke (1991: 9–10)

city authorities have acted as catalysts to this process by:

- establishing pedestrian precincts;
- managing parking problems and implementing park-and-ride schemes to improve access and convenience;
- marketing the destination based around an identifiable theme, often using the historical and cultural attractions of a city;
- investing in new and attractive indoor shopping galleries, improving facades, the layout and design of the built environment and making the environment more attractive.

The English Historic Towns Forum (1992: 12) identify the following factors which tourism and leisure shoppers deemed important:

- the cleanliness of the town;
- pedestrian areas/pavements which are well maintained;
- natural features such as rivers and parks;
- the architecture and facades/shop fronts;
- street furniture (seating and floral displays);
- town centre activities (e.g. outdoor markets and live entertainment).

One illustration of the effect of specific factors which tourists may view as important is evident from the Tidy Britain Group's qualitative study of the cleanliness of capital cities in Europe and the conditions at major tourist sites. The survey examined litter levels and environmental problems, awarding points for cleanliness. While the results of such surveys may be highly variable due to the sampling methodology, London featured as the overall winner in relation to the criteria used. Although Berne's 'The Bear Pit' emerges as the most clean tourist site among those locations surveyed (while Athens' Syntagma Square came bottom of the league), the environment around other facilities visited and used by tourists (e.g. shopping streets, railway stations and parliament buildings) provide additional insights into the environmental quality of those areas which tourists also visit. Although it is difficult to place a great deal of store by *ad-hoc* and random surveys such as the Tidy Britain Group, it does illustrate the point that cleanliness, litter and the perceived quality of the local environment may influence tourist views, particularly those seeking to visit shopping streets in major cities such as Oxford Street (London), Puerto del Sol (Madrid), Rue de Neuve (Brussels), Kalverstraat (Amsterdam), Bahnhof Platz (Berne), George Street (Dunedin), Ermou (Athens), Boulevard Haussman (Paris), Kurfustendamm (Berlin) and Via del Corso (Rome). The impressions which shoppers form of the environmental quality of urban areas may also influence other potential visitors, since word-of-mouth communication is a powerful force in personal recommendation of shopping areas.

Changes that alter the character of the town, where it becomes more tourist oriented, are sometimes characterised by the development of speciality and gift/souvenir shops and catering facilities in certain areas. However, as Owen (1990) argues, many traditional urban shopping areas are in need of major refurbishment, and tourism may provide the necessary stimulus for regeneration. Recent developments such as theme shopping (Jones Lang Wooten 1989) and festival market places (Sawicki 1989) are specialised examples of how this regeneration has proceeded in the UK and North America.

The next decade, therefore, would seem to be set for tourism and leisure shopping development to further segment markets by seeking new niches and products. Jansen-Verbeke (1991) describes the 'total experience' as the future way forward for this activity – retailers will need to attract tourism and leisure spending using newly built, simulated or refurbished retailing environments with a variety of shopping experiences. Keown's (1989) experience is that the opportunity to undertake a diverse range of retail activities in a locality increases the tourist's propensity to spend. However, the growing saturation of retailing provision in many industrialised countries may pose problems for further growth in tourism and leisure shopping due to the intense competition for such spending. Urban tourism destinations are likely to have to compete more aggressively for such spending in the new millennium.

The conditional elements

The last feature which Jansen-Verbeke (1986) views as central to the city's 'leisure product' is the conditional elements, such as transport, physical infrastructure and the provision of signposting. Unless adequate infrastructure is provided, tourists will be reluctant to divert from established patterns of visitor activity and tourism and leisure shopping will fail to materialise.

CONCLUSION

This chapter has examined a range of issues and concepts associated with the analysis of recreation and tourism supply issues. One interesting comparison which appears to hold true is Smith's (1983a) criticisms of recreational research being applicable to tourism due to the simplistic conceptualisation of the subject matter. In fact, Britton's (1980a, 1991) innovative and theoretically derived analyses offer a fresh and welcome attempt to rethink the geography of tourism, particularly the production side which has been notoriously descriptive and somewhat naive in its borrowing of geographical concepts while making no contribution to theory. This chapter has achieved two purposes: the first is to show how the geographer approaches the spatial complexity of supply issues in both recreation and tourism, while introducing some of the concepts, methods and ways of thinking about supply. Second, it has detailed the importance of developing a more meaningful assessment of tourism and the production system by situating the supply of tourism and recreation within the contexts of concepts of core and periphery, consumption and production, and tourism as a capitalist activity.

QUESTIONS

- How have geographers conceptualised recreational supply?
- What techniques and tools have geographers used to examine the supply of recreational facilities?
- What is the role of Britton's (1991) geography of production and consumption in the analysis of tourism?
- Are the majority of studies of tourism supply descriptive and based on empirical data rather than theoretical models?

READING

In terms of recreational supply, the following are useful introductions to the subject:

Countryside Agency (1999) *The State of the Countryside 1999*, Cheltenham: The Countryside Agency.
Evans, G. (1998) 'Urban leisure: Edge city and the new leisure periphery', in M. Collins and I. Cooper (eds) *Leisure Management: Issues and Applications*, Wallingford: CAB International, pp. 113–38.
Morgan, R., Jones, T. and Williams, A. (1993) 'Opinions and perceptions of England and Wales Heritage coast beach users: Some management implications from the Glamorgan Heritage Coast, Wales', *Journal of Coastal Research*, 9(4): 1083–93.

For a good review of conceptual issues on the supply of tourism services and facilities see:

Agarwal, S., Ball, R., Shaw, G. and Williams, A. (2000) 'The geography of tourism production: Uneven disciplinary development', *Tourism Geographies*, 2 (3): 241–63.

For studies of specific supply issues in different environments see:

Carter, R. (1982) 'Coastal caravan sites in Northern Ireland 1960–1980', *Irish Geography*, 15: 123–6.
Ilbery, B., Bowler, I., Clark, G., Crockett, A. and Shaw, A. (1998) 'Farm-based tourism as an alternative farm enterprise. A case study from the Northern Pennines, England', *Regional Studies*, 32 (4): 355–64.
Smith, R.A. (1992) 'Review of integrated beach resort development in South East Asia', *Land Use Policy*, 211–17.

For two useful historical reviews of recreational and tourism/hospitality service provision see:

Maver, I. (1998) 'Glasgow's public parks and the community 1850–1914', *Urban History*, 25(3): 323–47.
Walton, J. (2000) 'The hospitality trades: A social history', in C. Lashley and A. Morrison (eds) *In Search of Hospitality: Theoretical Perspectives and Debates*, Oxford: Butterworth-Heinemann, pp. 56–76.

4

THE IMPACTS OF TOURISM
AND RECREATION

The growth of international and domestic tourism has been matched by a corresponding increase in the numbers of those who study tourism and its impacts. Indeed, it may even be said that tourism research is one of the academic growth industries of the late twentieth century (Hall 1995). The literature on tourism has expanded enormously with the result that research has become 'highly fragmented, with researchers following separate and often divergent paths' (Mathieson and Wall 1982: 2). Nevertheless, one of the major areas of interest for geographers, as well as other tourism researchers, is the impacts of tourism and recreation.

Tourism and recreation cannot be studied in isolation from the complex economic, environmental, political and social milieux in which they occur (Runyan and Wu 1979). If geographers are to make a valid contribution to the study of tourism and recreation and their impacts it is vital that they are aware of the widest possible implications of such events for host communities, particularly as concerns over the sustainability of tourism and recreation grow (Butler 1990, 1991; Hall and Lew 1998). This has therefore meant that there has been substantial interchange of ideas, frameworks and methodologies between geographers and non-geographers in analysing the impacts of tourism and recreation.

There are a number of ways of categorising the impacts of tourism. One of the most common is that used by Mathieson and Wall (1982), which divided impacts into economic, social and physical (environmental categories). A more detailed break-down of the impacts of tourism has been used by Getz (1977), Ritchie (1984) and Hall (1992b). An overview of these categories is provided in Table 4.1 where they are categorised in terms of their positive or negative nature for a destination community. However, it should be noted that such a division is not absolute, as whether something is seen as positive or negative will depend on the goals and value position of an individual with respect to different types of tourism development. This chapter will provide a broad overview of the development of frameworks to manage recreation and tourism impacts, the impacts of tourism and recreation, and some of the main issues which arise out of the analysis and management of impacts.

IMPACTS – RECREATION RESOURCE MANAGEMENT

Resource management for recreational purposes is a useful tool with which to begin understanding the relationships between recreational and tourist impacts, sites and the action needed to address conflicts, namely planning (Seeley 1973), a theme explored in Chapter 9. In this context, resource management is concerned with the way the geographical approach meshes with the multidisciplinary contributions to understanding how resources need to be managed. Glyptis (1989a) made a fundamental assumption which many recreational texts overlook: that few recreational activities make use of resources that are solely recreational. Indeed, recreation is often juxtaposed

Table 4.1: Positive and negative dimensions of the impacts of tourism on host communities

Type of impact	Positive	Negative
Economic dimensions Economic	• Increased expenditures • Creation of employment • Increase in labour supply • Increase in standard of living • Increase in investment	• Localised inflation • Real estate speculation • Failure to attract tourists • Better alternative investments • Capital outflows • Inadequate estimation of costs of tourism development • Undesirable opportunity costs including transfer of funds from health and education
Tourism/commercial	• Increased awareness of the region as a travel/tourism destination • Increased knowledge concerning the potential for investment and commercial activity in the region • Creation of new facilities, attractions and infrastructure • Increase in accessibility	• Acquisition of a poor reputation as a result of inadequate facilities, improper practices or inflated prices • Negative reactions from existing enterprises due to the possibility of new competition for local manpower and government assistance
Socio-cultural impacts Social/cultural	• Increase in permanent level of local interest and participation in types of activity associated with event • Strengthening of regional values and traditions	• Commercialisation of activities which may be of a personal or private nature • Modification of nature of event or activity to accommodate tourism • Potential increase in crime • Changes in community structure • Social dislocation
Psychological	• Increased local pride and community spirit • Increased awareness of non-local perceptions	• Tendency toward defensive attitudes concerning host regions • High possibility of misunderstandings leading to varying degrees of host/visitor hostility
Political/administrative	• Enhanced international recognition of region and values • Development of skills among planners	• Economic exploitation of local population to satisfy ambitions of political elite • Distortion of true nature of event to reflect values of political system • Failure to cope • Inability to achieve aims • Increase in administrative costs • Use of tourism to legitimatise unpopular decisions • Legitimation of ideology of local elite
Environmental impacts Physical/environmental	• Development of new facilities • Improvement of local infrastructure • Conservation of heritage • Visitor management strategies	• Environmental damage • Changes in natural processes • Architectural pollution • Destruction of heritage • Overcrowding • Changed feeding and breeding habits of wildlife

Source: After Getz (1977); Mathieson and Wall (1982); Ritchie (1984); Hall (1992b)

in relation to forestry, agriculture, water supply, conservation and a host of competing activities that each make use of socially constructed leisure spaces. Consequently, the issue of multiple use of resources, as discussed in Chapter 3, is an underlying principle which recreation resource management seeks to accommodate.

Glyptis (1989) examined the contemporary context of recreation resource management, observing that four major influences could be discerned:

1 The belief that recreation is the right of every citizen.
2 Social change, particularly an ageing population and the changing demand for specific forms of recreation.
3 Changing economic and political doctrines which have seen debates associated with the demise of post-war notions of full employment and leisure as non-work or of less significance than work.
4 Strategic planning by public sector recreation agencies in relation to the previous three influences.

Within a UK context, the added changes in the 1980s under the Thatcher government saw the privatisation of many forms of recreation and leisure provision, a theme discussed later in Chapter 5 in terms of urban parks. What was critical here was the changing public policy framework within public service provision in leisure in the UK and other countries. Aitchison (1997) reviewed the impact of such changes, acknowledging the effect on access for women and other target groups.

Research has examined the introduction of Compulsory Competitive Tendering (CCT) which has been seen as naive and ill-thought out. Coalter (1998) pointed to the emphasis on economy and financial efficiency while neglecting non-financial performance measures such as the contribution of recreational outputs to a community's quality of life. Even simple notions of recreational supply, reviewed in Chapter 3, related to equity of access, and community needs do not appear to be met in many cases of CCT contracts. Simplistic measures of expressed demand have also not been evaluated systematically. Thus political and ideological changes in government can have a major bearing on the nature and approach to recreation resource management.

Both Chubb and Chubb (1981) and Patmore (1983) provided excellent appraisals of recreational behaviour, the resource requirements and the complex interplay of forces shaping recreational resource management from a geographical stand-point (Masser 1966–67). What emerged from the wide range of geographical contributions to recreational resource analysis during the 1960s, 1970s and 1980s was that the fundamental starting point for any discussion is demand. Reiterating the discussion in Chapter 2, data from site surveys and overall levels of participation in time and space as a dynamic process provide the baseline information for resource management. It is then a question of establishing the impact of specific activities.

Understanding the extent of impacts such as the effect on natural resources, social and psychological impacts arising from overcrowding, traffic congestion, aesthetic intrusions and conflict between recreational activities illustrate how the resource is being impacted upon. Even today, some 27 years since Burton's (1974) innovative study of carrying capacity of Cannock Chase, Staffordshire, UK, its methodological and conceptual value remains high despite innovations in mapping and analysis with GIS. Indeed, the interest in pursuing critical spatial concepts such as overcrowding and tolerance to visitor numbers has seen only a growing interest by geographers since the 1970s, especially in the context of rural recreation. In fact Robinson (1999: 270) argued that 'During the last three decades, work by geographers on the management of rural recreation and tourism have grown from a trickle to form a highly varied and substantial literature'. One notable example is O'Riordan and Paget's (1978) analysis of anglers and boaters where spatial tools were devised to achieve multiple use of the resource.

Probably one of the greatest challenges facing recreational resource planners in a non-urban context is the impact of the motor car in the post-war period. Many novel studies in the 1960s and 1970s (e.g. Hall 1972; Wall 1971, 1972) highlighted both the greater spatial reach and flexibility of access to recreational sites afforded by the car. Even so, the car is not a surrogate for individual mobility and recreational resource use, although as Page (1998, 1999) highlighted, the car is one of the major issues facing the recreational planner, especially in national parks (Eaton and Holding 1996). Within an urban context, Glyptis (1989a) also observed that the car was highly correlated with the use of sports facilities in the 1970s by middle-class males contributing to inequalities in access. Mobility and access to transport does limit certain social groups from enjoying the wider continuum of outdoor recreation opportunities, particularly those living in deprived inner-city environments, a feature constantly reiterated in urban recreation and summarised by Williams (1995: 35) thus: 'The net effect of car ownership is that participation rates in sports and outdoor recreations are significantly higher in households with access to a car.'

In the case of Loch Lomond, the pressure has come from another form of transport: recreational boating (see Bisset *et al.* 2000; Dickinson 2000). Recreational boat pressure, as in the case of The Broads in East Anglia (see Page 1999), has also posed concerns in terms of environmental pollution (Bannan *et al.* 2000). This concern has been heightened by the recent designation of the area as part of Scotland's first national park – the Loch Lomond and Trossachs National Park (see Page and Dowling 2001). For resource managers, much of the concern is with the use and management of individual sites, where specific tools such as site closure, rejuvenation, reconfiguring visitor flows on sites and discriminatory measures such as placing obstacles are used. In this respect, vehicles such as the private car have been prohibited or closely controlled to minimise impacts. At a practical level, recreation resource management involves maintaining and enhancing sites and the geographer has a valid role to play in understanding visitor behaviour, usage patterns, potential conflicts and spatial measures which can harmonise multiple use. This provides fundamental information to feed into the management and planning process.

CARRYING CAPACITY

Carrying capacity is one of the most complex and confusing concepts which faces the geographer in seeking to understand recreation sites and their ability to support a certain level of usage. In many early applications of the concept, it was viewed as

Plate 4.1: Footpath erosion, White Cliffs of Dover, Kent. How much of this erosion is due to recreational versus tourist use?

Plate 4.2: Historic sites such as the Acropolis in Greece also suffer visitor pressure and erosion of the built fabric.

a management tool to protect sites and resources from excessive use, while also seeking to balance usage with recreational enjoyment for participants. In many respects, it is a precursor of the much wider concept of 'sustainability' which has now embraced both recreation and tourism (see Hall and Lew 1998; Page *et al.* 2001). One early definition of carrying capacity by the Countryside Commission (1970: 2), with its central precept of the long-term capacity of resources and human activity, embodied the dual characteristics of protection and use: the level of recreation use an area can sustain without an unacceptable degree of deterioration of the character and quality of the resource or recreation experience. This was followed by an identification of four types of recreational carrying capacity: physical, economic, ecological and social carrying capacity.

The notion of physical carrying is primarily concerned with quantitative measures of the number of people or usage a site can support, primarily being a design concept. This may also act as a constraint on visitor use by deliberately limiting access to sites. The notion of economic carrying capacity is primarily concerned with multiple use of resources (Pigram and Jenkins 1999), particularly its compatibility with the site and wider management objectives for the site. The notion of ecological (or what Lavery (1971a) terms 'environmental capacity') is primarily 'concerned with the maximum level of recreational use, in terms of numbers and activities, that can be accommodated by an area or ecosystem before an unacceptable or irreversible decline in ecological values occur' (Pigram and Jenkins 1999: 91). The chief problem here lies in what individuals and groups construe as acceptable change. In an early study by Dower and McCarthy (1967) of Donegal, Eire, they estimated the environmental capacity which recreational and tourism resources could support at any point in time. Lavery (1971a) developed these ideas, based on subsequent work by Furmidge (1969) and Houghton Evans and Miles (1970) to produce a series of suggested space standards for environmental capacity (Table 4.2). Although this table may be criticised for using such absolute

values of capacity, it is notable that it provides a starting point for discussing how many visitors can support a site and how many might be too many. While critics have questioned the notion of fixed capacity for individual sites, it should be stressed that carrying capacity will only ever be one element of a management strategy for outdoor recreation. What Table 4.2 shows is the need to move beyond environmental capacity to recognise the significance of users, visitor satisfaction and the role of perception – embodied in the last notion – of social carrying capacity.

Social carrying capacity, often referred to as perceptual, psychological or behavioural carrying capacity, was defined by Pigram and Jenkins (1999: 93) as 'the maximum level of recreational use, in terms of numbers and activities, above which there is a decline in the quality of the recreation experience, from the point of view of the recreation participant'. The basic principles inherent in this approach relate to the ability of individuals and groups to tolerate others, their activities and the level of acceptability. Patmore (1973: 241) summed this up as 'the number of people (a site) can absorb before the latest arrivals perceive the area to be full and seek satisfaction elsewhere'. This has both a spatial and temporal dimension, embodied in the

Table 4.2: Suggested space standards for environmental capacity

Type of recreation area	Notional environmental capacity
Major scenic route	20 persons per mile
Minor scenic route	4 persons per mile
Major scenic feature	20 persons per square mile
Major historic site	30 persons per square mile
Woodland area	100 persons per square mile
Picnic area	60 persons per square mile
Enclosed land	50 persons per square mile
Rough or hill land	5 persons per square mile
Coast or lake shore (basic level)	50 persons per square mile
Attractive and accessible coast/beach	400 persons per mile

Source: Lavery (1971a: 46)

study by Glyptis (1981). One of the fundamental concepts here is the extent to which crowding impacts upon visitor satisfaction.

Developing a carrying capacity for a site involves at least eight steps (Hall and McArthur 1998):

1 Specify management objectives or standards for the state of the heritage resource to be maintained or attained and the type of experience to be provided.
2 Identify current levels of use for a defined period (e.g. hour, day, week, month, year).
3 Identify indicators for the biophysical, socio-cultural, psychological and managerial components.
4 Measure the current state of each indicator.
5 Identify apparent relationships between the state of the indicator and the level of use.
6 Make value judgements about the acceptability of the various impacts.
7 Determine a carrying capacity that is more, the same or less than current visitation.
8 Implement management strategies to ensure carrying capacity is not breached.

An example of the establishment of a carrying capacity is the Angkor World Heritage Site in Cambodia. A capacity of 300 to 500 visitors at any one time has been established, with an annual capacity set at 500,000; which assumes visitors will make two visits to the site during their stay (Wager 1995).

The most defendable carrying capacity is an estimate representing a compromise between individual capacities for each component. For example, suppose there was a biophysical carrying capacity set at 50 visits per day, a socio-cultural capacity set at 100 visits per day, a psychological capacity set at 80 visits a day and a managerial capacity set at 90 visits a day. If each component was valued equally, then an overall carrying capacity may be set at 80 visits per day. However, the typical scenario is one where the overall figure is influenced by the most sensitive or threatened factor, so in this example the capacity may be set at 50 visits per day (Hall and McArthur 1998).

Despite the concept of carrying capacity being over 30 years old, it remains in practice, although highly elusive to successfully implement.

> It is commonly recognised that there are no fixed or standard tourism carrying capacity values. Rather, carrying capacity varies, depending upon place, season and time, user behaviour, facility design, patterns and levels of management, and the dynamic character of the environments themselves. Moreover, it is not always possible to practice to separate tourism activity from other human activities.
>
> (Ceballos-Lacuarain 1996: 131)

Indeed, it is relatively easy to argue that there is no such thing as a single carrying capacity for any given site and that any capacity put forward is highly subjective and thus difficult to defend. A good example of the judgemental limitation is

Plate 4.3: Visitor management tools have been introduced to the Waitakere Ranges, Auckland to control erosion.

Green Island in far North Queensland. Concern over current crowding resulted in a carrying capacity being set at 1,900 visitors per day or no more than 800 at any one time (Queensland Department of Environment and Heritage 1993). Green Island currently receives some 300,000 visits per year. If the maximum daily level was reached every day, Green Island would receive 693,500 visitors in a year, over twice the current level (Hall and McArthur 1998). Nevertheless, the notion of carrying capacity has made a methodological and practical contribution to recreational and tourism resource management and has been at the heart of a number of visitor management tools in natural areas. Yet management ideas are changing as new debates within the recreational literature emerge, particularly regarding the limits of acceptable change framework (Newsome *et al.* 2002).

INSIGHT: The Recreation Opportunity Spectrum

The Recreation Opportunity Spectrum (ROS) is a conceptual framework to clarify the relationship between recreational settings, activities and experiences (Clark and Stankey 1979). It is premised on the assumption that quality is best assured through the provision of a diverse array of opportunities. The ROS provided a conceptual framework for thinking about how to create a diversity of recreation experiences, rather than just provide standard recreational facilities (Driver 1989).

A ROS is developed by identifying a spectrum of settings, activities and opportunities that a given region may contain. For example, a national park may contain a spectrum of settings that range from easily accessible, highly developed areas and facilities, to remote, undeveloped areas with no facilities. A museum might have a spectrum ranging from a complex set of transcripts in a quiet corner with detailed supporting information, to a crowded gift shop selling rubber frogs and filled with the sound of new age music. The information relating to each setting is entered into a tabular format to present the characteristics of the site, the type of activities undertaken and the opportunities available alongside each other. Comparisons can then be made across sites to determine what sort of core opportunities appear to be provided and the under- or over-supply to specific activities and opportunities. The ROS can therefore be very useful at reviewing then repositioning the type of visitor experiences most appropriate to a recreation or natural heritage site (Hall and McArthur 1998).

Management factors considered when determining which recreational class a setting should be categorised to include:

- access (e.g. difficulty, access system (roads and trails) and means of conveyance);
- the non-recreational resource;
- on-site management (e.g. extent, complexity and facilities);
- social interaction;
- acceptability of visitor impact (e.g. magnitude and prevalence);
- regimentation.

The standard range of recreational classes established by ROS are: developed; semi-developed; semi-natural; and natural.

Perhaps the key limitation to the use of the ROS is its emphasis on the setting at the expense of the type of visitor. Part of the reason for this is the influence of earlier cultures from the landscape planning and architecture professions that suggested visitor management could be largely addressed through site and facility design. Lipscombe (1993) suggests that while the ROS was extensively marketed in the early 1980s it has not been widely adopted by heritage managers in the late 1980s and early 1990s (Hall and McArthur 1998).

THE LIMITS OF ACCEPTABLE CHANGE

The Limits of Acceptable Change (LAC) system began with the fundamentals of the Recreation Opportunity Spectrum and initial principles of carrying capacity. Its designers then shifted the focus from a relationship between levels of use and impact to identifying desirable conditions for visitor activity to occur in the first place, as well as management actions required to protect or achieve the conditions (Clarke and Stankey 1979; Stankey and McCool 1984). The LAC implies an emphasis on establishing how much change is acceptable, then actively managing accordingly. The LAC model avoids the use/impact conundrum by focusing on the management of the impacts of use (Stankey *et al.* 1985). The model informs management whether the conditions are within acceptable standards; that is, that current levels and patterns of use are within the capacity of the host environment. When conditions reach the limits of acceptable change they have also reached the area's capacity under current management practices. Management is then equipped with a logical and defensible case to implement strategic actions before any more use can be accommodated. One action may be to limit use.

The LAC system is based on a nine-stage process:

1 Identification of area concerns and issues.
2 Definition and description of opportunity classes.
3 Selection of indicators for conditions.
4 Inventory of resource and social conditions.
5 Specification of standards for indicators.
6 Identification of alternative opportunity class allocations.
7 Identification of management actions for each alternative.
8 Evaluation and selection of the preferred option.
9 Implementation of actions and monitoring of conditions.

Prosser (1986a) identified a number of key strengths of the LAC system as being:

- emphasis on explicit, measurable objectives;
- promotion of a diversity of visitor experiences;
- reliance on quantitative field-based standards;
- flexibility and responsiveness to local situations;
- opportunity for public involvement;
- minimisation of regulatory approaches;
- a framework for managing conditions.

Unfortunately, only a few LAC systems have been generated and successfully implemented, mostly in wilderness areas of North America and, to a small extent, in one or two natural areas in Australia (Hall and McArthur 1998). The most critical aspect of the development of the LAC system has been establishing stakeholder endorsement and support (Prosser 1986b). Stakeholders from the local tourism sector and community can provide valuable input into desired conditions and acceptable standards, and are usually essential in providing the economic and political support necessary to maintain monitoring programmes and implement management decisions. The failure to establish sufficient stakeholder support has largely occurred because the LAC was created by natural area managers, for natural area managers (Stankey *et al.* 1985). According to Hall and McArthur (1998), the culture of the LAC is not attuned to attracting wider stakeholder involvement, and provides three examples of problems in its implementation. First, the use of the term 'limits' within the title, which the tourism industry has interpreted as being discouraging to growth and thus business. Second, the conventional narrow focus on the condition of the physical environment and, to some extent, the nature of the visitor experience. Other critical dimensions such as characteristics of the visitor market, socio-cultural aspects of the local community and economic activity associated with the tourism industry are not included. Third, the lack of co-operative involvement of the tourism sector in identifying indicators and standards that are acceptable to the industry. Without this involvement the monitoring results become prone to conjecture, particularly if they reveal surprising or controversial implications. However, if the culture of the LAC system was diversified and its

INSIGHT: The Tourism Optimisation Management Model (TOMM)

The Tourism Optimisation Management Model (TOMM) is one of the most recent and relatively untried models to monitor and manage visitors (McArthur 1996, 2000b; Hall and McArthur 1998). The conceptual emphasis of the TOMM is on achieving optimum performance rather than limiting activity. The TOMM positions a range of influences in the heritage–visitor relationship to focus on sustainability of the heritage, viability of the tourism industry and empowerment of stakeholders. The TOMM has borrowed the key strengths of the Visitor Impact Management Model (VIMM) developed by the United States National Parks and Conservation Association (Graefe 1989, 1991) and LAC, then broadened their focus into fields linked with the tourism industry and local community. Besides environmental and experiential elements, the TOMM addresses characteristics of the tourist market, economic conditions of the tourism industry and socio-cultural conditions of the local community. The expansion recognises the complex inter-relationships between heritage management, the tourism industry and supporting local populations. In this respect the TOMM is more politically sensitive to the forces which shape visitation and subsequent impacts (McArthur 2000a, 2000b).

The TOMM contains three main components: context analysis, a monitoring programme and a management response system (Manidis Roberts Consultants 1996; McArthur 2000b). The context analysis identifies the current nature of community values, tourism product, tourism growth, market trends and opportunities, positioning and branding. This information is collected through literature reviews, face-to-face interviews with relevant expertise, and a community workshop. The context analysis also identifies alternative scenarios for the future of tourism, used later to test the validity of the model.

The second stage of the development of a monitoring programme is the development of a monitoring programme. The basis for monitoring is a set of optimal conditions which tourism and visitor activity should create (rather than impacts they should avoid). In this way the model avoids setting limits, maximum levels or carrying capacities, and can offer the tourism industry opportunities to develop optimal sustainable performance. The monitoring programme is essentially designed to measure how close the current situation is to the optimal conditions. The measurement yardstick is a set of indicators (one for each optimal condition). Table 4.3 provides a list of assessment criteria for selecting the most appropriate indicators for a TOMM. Each indicator has a benchmark and an acceptable range for it to be expected to operate within. Table 4.4 provides an example of the desired outcomes and their supporting indicators and acceptable ranges; in this instance they are environmentally orientated. The data generated from the monitoring programme are then plotted to determine whether or not the status is within the acceptable range. Annual performance is presented via report charts already displaying benchmarks, and a relatively simple table that is principally designed to quickly reflect whether or not each indicator is within its acceptable range. The presentation of data is therefore designed to provide a 'quick and dirty look' that all stakeholders can utilise (Hall and McArthur 1998).

The third stage of development is a management response system. This system involves the identification of poor performing indicators, the exploration of cause and effect relationships, the identification of results requiring a response and the development of management response options. The first part of the response system is to annually identify which indicators are not performing within their acceptable range. This involves reviewing the report charts to identify and list each indicator whose annual performance

Table 4.3: Assessment criteria for selecting indicators for Tourism Optimisation Management Model on Kangaroo Island (KI)

Criteria	Explanation	Example
Degree of relationship with actual tourism activity	The indicator needs to have a clear relationship with tourism activity to be relevant to the model	The number of fur seals at Seal Bay is more relevant than the number of possums at Stokes Bay
Accuracy	The indicator needs to represent the desired condition accurately	The number of traffic accidents is more accurate than the perception of parking difficulties
Utility	The indicator is more worthwhile if it generates additional insights	Visitation (number of visitors) has greater utility than perception of crowding
Availability of data	The indicator is more worthwhile if data already exist and are accessible, rather than needing to be collected from scratch	Data on the level of expenditure are more available than operator profit
Cost to collect and analyse	The indicator is more worthwhile if it requires minimal additional human resources to collect and analyse	The level of direct tourism employment is cheaper to monitor than the number of tourism products developed by local suppliers in response to tourist demand

Source: McArthur (2000a)

Table 4.4: Management objectives and potential indicators for assessing the quality of the environment on Kangaroo Island

Optimal conditions	Indicators	Acceptable range
The majority of the number of visits to the island's natural areas occur in visitor service zones.	• The proportion of KI visitors to the island's natural areas who visit areas zoned specially for managing visitors	65 to 100% of visitors
Ecological processes are maintained or enhanced in areas where tourism activity occurs.	• Net overall cover of native vegetation at specific sites	0 to 5% increase in native vegetation from base case
Major wildlife populations attracting visitors are maintained and/or enhanced in areas where tourism activity occurs.	• Number of seals at designated tourist site • Number of hooded plover at designated tourist site • Number of osprey at designated tourist site	0 to 5% annual increase in number sighted
The majority of tourism accommodation operations have implemented some form of energy and water conservation practice.	• Energy consumption/visitor night/visitor • Water consumption/visitor night/visitor	3 to 7 kilowatts 20 to 40 litres of water

Source: McArthur (2000a)

data are outside its acceptable range. It also involves identifying the degree of the discrepancy and whether the discrepancy is part of a longer term trend. The trend is determined by reviewing previous annual data that have been entered on to the report charts. A qualitative statement is then entered under the degree of discrepancy. The second part in the response mechanism is to explore cause and effect relationships. The essential question relating to cause and effect is whether the discrepancy was principally induced by tourism activity or other effects such as the actions of local residents, initiatives by other industries, and regional, national or even global influences. The third part in the system simply involves nominating whether a response is required. Specific choices for the response might include a tourism-oriented response, a response from another sector, or identification that the situation is beyond anyone's control.

The fourth and final part involves developing response options, dependent upon whether they:

- require a response from a non-tourism sector (this involves identifying the appropriate body responsible, providing them with the results and suggesting a response on the matter);
- were out of anyone's control (in this instance no response is required);
- require a response from the tourism sector (this involves generating a series of management options for consideration, such as additional research to understand the issue, modification to existing practices, site-based development, marketing and lobbying.

After the tourism-related options are developed the preferred option is tested by brainstorming how the option might influence the various indicators. This requires the reuse of the predicted performance and management response sections of the model. Once several years of data are collected the model can be transferred to a simple computer program to streamline the reporting, predicting and testing of options.

The final application of the model is to test potential options or management responses to a range of alternative scenarios. The first form of testing for application is the performance of a sample of individual indicators. The second form of testing the model's performance is against several potential future scenarios that have already been developed and presented in the contextual analysis. The testing helps ensure that the model has some degree of predictive capability.

The first TOMM was produced in late 1996 and implemented during 1997 (Hall and McArthur 1998; McArthur 2000a). It spanned public and private land in South Australia's Kangaroo Island, and was co-funded by the Federal and South Australian Tourism Departments, and the South Australian Department of Environment and Natural Resources. The TOMM has attracted support not only from its three public sector funders, but from local government, the local tourism association, the tourism industry, conservation groups and members of the local community (Hall and McArthur 1998; McArthur 2000a). This has been achieved because of several key characteristics, including:

- the TOMM covers a range of dimensions to the heritage–visitor relationship;
- a wide range of stakeholders collect data and therefore 'own' part of the intellectual property;
- the results of the monitoring are produced in easy-to-follow formats so that any untrained eye can pass over them and broadly deduce the health of the heritage–visitor relationship;
- management strategies can be jointly determined through shared understandings of the current situation and emerging trends.

ened it may be better able to
t opportunities it was originally
(McCool and Cole 1997).

ECONOMIC ANALYSIS

Within tourism and recreation research, 'until recently, attention has concentrated on the more obvious economic impacts with comparatively little consideration being given to the environmental and social consequences of tourism' (Mathieson and Wall 1982: 3–4). However, considerable debate has arisen over methodological problems in the economic analysis of such events, particularly in the use of economic multipliers and cost–benefit analysis (Archer 1976, 1977a, b, 1984; Murphy 1985; D.G. Pearce 1989), the evaluation of opportunity cost (Vaughan 1977), and the relationship of tourism and recreation to regional development and employment (Royer *et al*. 1974; Doering 1976; Frechtling 1977; Hudman 1978; Ellerbrook and Hite 1980; Williams and Shaw 1988).

Many economic impact studies focus on what is known as the 'multiplier effect'. This effect is concerned with 'the way in which expenditure on tourism filters throughout the economy, stimulating other sectors as it does so' (D.G. Pearce 1989: 205). Several different types of multiplier are in use, each with their own emphasis (Archer 1977a, b, 1982). However, the multiplier may best be regarded as 'a coefficient which expresses the amount of income generated in an area by an additional unit of tourist spending' (Archer 1982: 236). It is the ratio of direct and secondary changes within an economic region to the direct initial change itself. In this context geographers have not played a major role, although multiplier analysis is not devoid of a spatial component with its linkage to regional science and its spatial concerns for quantitative analysis of areas and locations. In some cases, geographers have not pursued the regional analytical approaches of the economists in measuring and analysing tourist activity in a spatial context due to the prevailing geographic paradigms in human geography in the 1960s and 1970s. Although economic geography

has overlapped with economics in some cases, tourism and recreation is not an area where this occurred on a wide scale. Likewise, collaborative research between geographers and economists has not emerged as a theme in research until comparatively recently. This is often because each subject area has its own concepts, language, approach and few obvious intersections in the research field because tourism and recreation remained a fringe area for research in the 1960s and 1970s for both geographers and economists.

The economic impacts of tourism and recreation are usually classified as being either primary or secondary in nature (Archer 1982). Primary or direct impacts are those economic impacts which are a direct consequence of visitor spending (e.g. the purchase of food and beverages by a tourist in a hotel). Secondary impacts may be described as being either indirect or induced. Indirect impacts are those arising from the response of money in the form of local business transactions (e.g. the new investment of hotel owners in equipment and supplies). Induced impacts are those arising from the additional income generated by further consumer spending (e.g. the purchase of goods and services by hotel employees). For each round of spending per unit of initial visitor expenditure leakage will occur from the regional economy until little or no further re-spending is possible. Therefore, the recreation or tourism multiplier is a measure of the total effects (direct plus secondary effects) which result from the additional tourist or recreational expenditure. However, despite their extensive use, it should be noted that 'multipliers are difficult to calculate precisely under the best circumstances. They require substantial amounts of very detailed data. The methods used are also difficult and require a high degree level of statistical and/or macro-economic expertise' (Smith 1995: 16; see also Saeter 1998).

The size of the visitor multiplier will vary from region to region and will depend on a number of factors, including:

- the size of area of analysis;
- the proportion of goods and services imported into the region for consumption by visitors;

- the rate of circulation;
- the nature of visitor spending;
- the availability of suitable local products and services;
- the patterns of economic behaviour for visitor and local alike.

As a measure of economic benefit from recreation and tourism, the multiplier technique has been increasingly subject to question, particularly as its use has often produced exaggerated results (Archer 1977a, 1982; Cooper and Pigram 1984; Frechtling 1987; D.G. Pearce 1989). Nevertheless, despite doubts about the accuracy of the multiplier technique, substantial attention is still paid to the results of economic impact studies by government and the private sector as a measure of the success of tourism development or as a way of estimating the potential contribution of a proposed development in order to justify policy or planning decisions. As Smith (1995: 16) noted: 'Regrettably, the abuses of multipliers often seem to be as frequent as legitimate uses – thus contributing further to the industry's lack of credibility.'

The size of the tourist multiplier is regarded as a significant measure of the economic benefit of visitor expenditure because it will be a reflection of the circulation of the visitor dollar through an economic system. In general, the larger the size of the tourist multiplier the greater the self-sufficiency of that economy in the provision of tourist facilities and services. Therefore, a tourist multiplier will generally be larger at a national level than at a regional level, because at a regional level leakage will occur in the form of taxes to the national government and importation of goods and services from regions. Similarly, at the local level, multipliers will reflect the high importation level of small communities and tax payments to regional and national governments (Hall 1995).

According to Murphy (1985: 95), 'for practical purposes it is crucial to appreciate that local multiplier studies are just case studies of local gains and no more' and several questions remain unanswered about the real costs and benefits of tourism on local and regional development. Indeed, a major question should be: Who are the winners and losers in tourism development? As Coppock (1977b: 1.1) argued in relation to the use of tourism as a tool for economic development:

> Not only is it inevitable that the residents of an area will gain unequally from tourism (if indeed they gain at all) and probable that the interests of some will actually be harmed, but it may well be that a substantial proportion does not wish to see any development of tourism.

INSIGHT: The economic impact of events

An area which has seen considerable attention by geographers (e.g. Shaw 1985; Getz 1991a, b; Hall 1992b; Hall and Hodges 1996) is the impact of hosting staged, short-term attractions, usually referred to as hallmark, special or mega events (Ritchie 1984; Ritchie and Yangzhou 1987; Hall 1989). The hallmark event is different in its appeal from the attractions normally promoted by the tourist industry as it is not a continuous or seasonal phenomenon. Indeed, in many cases the hallmark event is a strategic response to the problems that seasonal variations in demand pose for the tourist industry (Ritchie and Beliveau 1974). Although the ability of an event 'to achieve this objective depends on the uniqueness of the event, the status of the event, and the extent to which it is successfully marketed within tourism generated regions' (Ritchie 1984: 2). As with other areas of research on the economic impacts of tourism, the analysis of hallmark events has been characterised by overstated large benefit–cost ratios (Hall 1989, 1992b; Getz 1991b). Several reasons may be cited for this:

- there has been a failure to account for the economic impact that would have occurred anyway but has switched from one industry to another;
- there has been an 'unfortunately common mistake of attributing all the benefits received from the event to government expenditure, instead of establishing the marginal impact of that contribution' (Burns and Mules 1986: 8, 10);
- the taxation benefits of expenditure generation have been counted as additional to the multiplier 'flow-ons' when they have already been included;
- 'output' rather than 'value-added' multipliers, which can result in major overestimates of the economic impact of events, are frequently uncritically used;
- there has been a general failure to delimit the size of the regional economy that is to be studied. The smaller the area to be analysed, the greater will be the number of 'visitors' and hence the greater would be the estimate of economic impact.

One of the primary justifications used by government in the encouragement of tourism development is that of tourism's potential employment benefits (D.G. Pearce 1992a; Hall 1994; Jenkins *et al.* 1998). However, as Hudson and Townsend (1992: 64) observed, there is

> a growing involvement of local authorities in policies to sustain existing tourist developments and encourage new ones, although often the actual impacts of tourism on local employment and the economy are imperfectly understood. The direction of causality between growing employment and increasing policy involvement is often obscure and in any case variable.

One of the ironies of the perceived employment benefits of tourism and recreation is that areas which have tourism as a mainstay of the local economy tend to have high levels of unemployment. For example, two of Australia's major destination areas, the Gold Coast and the Sunshine Coast in Queensland, have had unemployment rates significantly above the national average (Mullins 1984, 1990). Such a situation is often regarded by local politicians as an 'imported problem', by which 'the unemployed flock into these cities for the "good life". Yet data . . . on interstate transferees on unemployment benefits shows that the net number remaining in the Gold Coast and Sunshine Coast over any 12 month period barely makes 1 per cent of these cities unemployed' (Mullins 1990: 39). Instead of 'dole-bludger' (an Australian term which refers to people who deliberately seek unemploy-ment benefits rather than paid employment) and surfer migration, the answer to the unemployment situation rests on the nature of the two regions' economies. The economies of both areas are founded on two unstable industries: tourism, which is seasonal, and construction, which is cyclical and is itself related to actual or predicted tourist flows. Therefore, as Mullins (1990: 39) reported, 'high rates of unemployment seem inevitable', although as the economic base of the regions diversifies, unemployment levels should fall.

Another major consideration in the potential contribution of tourism to the national economy is the organisation and spatial allocation of capital and, in particular, the penetration of foreign or international capital. The distribution and organisation of capital and tourists is also spread unevenly between and within regions; indeed, tourism is often seen as a mechanism for redistributing wealth between regions (D.G. Pearce 1990a, 1992a). Geographers have long noted the manner in which tourism tends to distribute development away from urban areas towards those regions in a country which have not been developed (e.g. Christaller 1963), with the core–periphery nature of tourism being an important component of political-economy approaches towards tourism (Britton 1980a, 1980b, 1982), particularly with respect to tourism in the island microstates of the Pacific (Connell 1988; Lea 1988) and the Caribbean (Weaver 1998).

More recently, geographers have begun to critically analyse tourism with reference to issues of economic restructuring, processes of globalisation and the development of post-Fordist modes of production (e.g. Britton 1991; Hall 1994; Debbage and Ioannides 1998; Milne 1998; Williams and Shaw 1998). Tourism is a significant component of these shifts which may be described as 'post-industrial' or 'post-Fordist', which refers to the shift from an industrial to an information technology/service base. In addition, tourism is part of the globalisation of the international economy, in which economic production is transnational, interdependent and multipolar, with less and less dependence on the nation state as the primary unit of international economic organisation. As Williams and Shaw (1998: 59) recognise:

> The essence of tourism is the way in which the global interacts with the local. For example, mass tourism emphasises a global scan for destinations for global (or at least macro-regional) markets, while some forms of new tourism seek to exploit the individuality of places. These global–local relationships are not static but are subject to a variety of restructuring processes.

The notion of the 'globalisation' of tourism implies its increasing commodification. The tourist production system simultaneously 'sells' places in order to attract tourists, the means to the end (travel and accommodation) and the end itself (the tourist experience). Therefore, tourism finds itself at the forefront of an important recent dynamic within capitalist accumulation in terms of the creation and marketing of experiences. Tourists 'are purchasing the intangible qualities of restoration, status, lifestyle signifier, release from the constraints of everyday life, or conveniently packaged novelty' (Britton 1991: 465). Within this setting, place is therefore commodified and reduced to an experience and images for consumption. However, while place promotion is recognised as increasingly important for tourism and recreation (see Chapter 5), there have been insufficient attempts, with the exception of some of the authors noted above, to locate such issues within the context of mainstream tourism studies or tourism geography.

Related to the economic analysis of tourism has been the study of the forecasting of visitor demand and the marketing of the tourist product. Several studies of hallmark events, for example, have attempted to deal with the problem of forecasting visitor demand (see Ritchie and Aitken 1984; Hall 1992b). Nevertheless, substantial methodological problems still remain; and 'although relatively sophisticated statistical measures have been used, forecasts of tourism demand can produce only approximations' (Uysal and Crompton 1985: 13). Many of the early studies of the effects of tourism were restricted to economic analyses and enumerated the financial and employment benefits which accrued to destination areas as a result of tourism development. However, since the late 1970s a number of studies have emerged that examine the socio-cultural impacts of tourism which cast a more negative light on tourism's development capacities (Mathieson and Wall 1982).

THE ANALYSIS OF TOURISM'S SOCIAL IMPACTS

The social impact of tourism refers to the manner in which tourism and travel effects changes in collective and individual value systems, behaviour patterns, community structures, lifestyle and the quality of life (Hall 1995). The major focus of research on the social impacts of tourism is on the population of the tourist destination rather than on the tourist generating area and the tourists themselves, although significant work is also done in this area particularly with respect to outdoor recreationists. The variables which contribute to resident perceptions of tourism may be categorised as either extrinsic or intrinsic (Faulkner and Tideswell 1996). Extrinsic variables refer to factors which affect a community at a macro level (e.g. stage of tourism development, the ratio between tourists and residents, cultural differences between tourists and residents, and seasonality). Intrinsic variables are those factors which may vary in association with variations in the characteristics of individuals in a given population (e.g. demographic characteristics, involvement in tourism and proximity to tourist activity) (Hall 1998).

Researchers from a number of disciplinary backgrounds have conducted work on the social impacts of tourism. For example, interest in tourism marketing strategies and increased concern for the social consequences of tourism led to the social psychology of tourism becoming a major area of research (e.g. P. Pearce 1982; Stringer 1984; Stringer and Pearce 1984). Research has focused on aspects of the tourist experience as diverse as tourism and culture shock (Furnham 1984), and tourist–guide interaction (P. Pearce 1984). Research in the marketing of the tourist product sees attention being paid to the demand, motivations and preferences of the potential tourist (e.g. Jenkins 1978; Van Raaij and Francken 1984; Kent *et al.* 1987; D.G. Pearce 1989; Smith 1995), the evaluation of the tourist product and potential tourist resources (e.g. Ferrario 1979a, b; Gartner 1986; Smith 1995), the intended and unintended use of tourist brochures (e.g. Dilley 1986), the utility of market segmentation for specific targeting of potential consumers (e.g. Murphy and Staples 1979; Smith 1995), and tourist and recreationist satisfaction. In the latter area, geographers have done a substantial amount of work in the outdoor recreation and back-country use field, particularly with respect to the effects of crowding on visitor satisfaction (e.g. Shelby *et al.* 1989; see also Chapter 7).

Marketing research acts as a link between economic and psychological analysis of tourism (Van Raaij 1986) and gives notice of the need for a wider understanding of the social impact of tourism on visitor and host populations. Research on the social psychology of tourism has run parallel with the research of behavioural geographers in the area, with there being increased interchange between the two fields in recent years (e.g. Jenkins and Walmesley 1993; see also Walmesley and Lewis 1993).

Interestingly, the development of a more radical critique of behaviour in geography also has parallels in the social psychology of tourism as well. For example, the research of Uzzell (1984) on the psychology of tourism marketing from a structural-

Plate 4.4: Taman Min theme park, Jakarta. Does this represent local culture or a manufactured culture?

ist perspective offered a major departure from traditional social psychology. Uzzell's (1984) alternative formulation of the role of social psychology in the study of tourism has been reflected in much of the research conducted in anthropological, geographical (e.g. Britton 1991) and sociological approaches to the social impacts of tourism (e.g. Urry 1990, 1991).

The early work of Forster (1964), Cohen (1972, 1974, 1979a, b), Smith and Turner (1973) and MacCannell (1973, 1976), along with the more recent contribution by Urry (1990) has provided the basis for formulating a sociology of tourism, while Smith (1977) and Graburn (1983) have provided a useful overview of anthropology's contributions to the study of tourism. The research of geographers such as Young (1973), Butler (1974,

1975, 1980), D.G. Pearce (1979, 1981), Mathieson and Wall (1982) and Murphy (1985) has also yielded significant early insights into tourism's social impacts.

Many studies of the social impacts of tourism have focused on the impact of tourism on the Third World (UNESCO 1976). This research is no doubt necessary, yet caution must be used in applying research findings from one culture to another. Nevertheless, problems of cultural change and anxiety, social stress in the host community, and social dislocation resulting from changes to the pattern of economic production, may be identified in a wide number of studies undertaken in a variety of cultures and social settings (e.g. Farrell 1978; Mathieson and Wall 1982; Clary 1984; Oglethorpe 1984; Meleghy *et al.* 1985; Lea 1988; Getz 1993c; Shaw and Williams 1994; Hall and Page 1996; Weaver 1998).

The social costs of tourism to the host community will vary according to the characteristics of both visitor and host (Pizam 1978). However, tourism does undoubtedly cause changes in the social character of the destination (Long 1984). These changes may be related to the seasonality of tourism (Hartmann 1984), the nature of the tourist (Harmston 1980), the influence of a foreign culture (Mathieson and Wall 1982), and/or to the disruption of community leisure space (O'Leary 1976). An appreciation by planners of the social costs of tourism is essential for both financial and social reasons. Rejection of visitors by segments of the host community may well result in a decline in the attractiveness of the tourist destination, in addition to the creation of disharmony within the host community (Murphy 1985; Getz 1994b; Page and Lawton 1997).

Tourism development may initiate changes in government and private organisations (Baldridge and Burnham 1975) in order to cater for the impact of tourism. For instance, additional law enforcement officers may be required (Rothman *et al.* 1979), while special measures may be needed to restrict dislocation created by increased rents and land values (Cowie 1985). Geographers have long emphasised the importance of meaningful community participation in the decision-making process that surrounds the formulation of tourism policy and development (e.g. Butler 1974, 1975; Brougham and Butler 1981; Pearce 1981; Getz 1984; Murphy 1985). Furthermore, studies, such as those of Keller (1984) and Shaw (1985, 1986), indicate that the social impacts of tourism are complex and need to be examined within the context of the various economic, environmental, political and social factors that contribute to tourism development in a destination (Mings 1978; Runyan and Wu 1979; Wu 1982; D.G. Pearce 1989).

Community attitudes towards tourism invariably simultaneously reveal both positive and negative attitudes towards tourism (Butler 1975). For example, various positive and negative attitudes towards tourism were indicated in several studies of resident attitudes towards tourism in northern New South Wales, Australia, in the 1980s (Hall 1990). Pigram (1987) utilised Doxey's (1975) irridex scale of euphoria, apathy, annoyance and antagonism to investigate resident attitudes in the resort town of Coffs Harbour (Table 4.5). According to Pigram, 'the overwhelming majority felt that the economic and otherwise benefits of tourism outweighed the disadvantages' (1987: 67). Despite the overall favourable or apathetic response of residents, several negative reactions towards

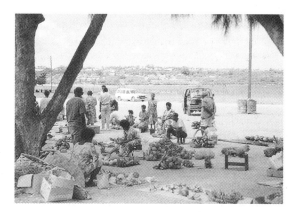

Plate 4.5: Market scene, Vanuatu. Local communities can benefit from visitors if they are encouraged to patronise local facilities rather than being cocooned in the environmental bubble of resort hotels.

Plate 4.6: Denarau Island, Fiji. A resort hotel where all the services are self-contained and interaction with the local population is minimised.

Table 4.5: Resident reaction to tourists in Coffs Harbour

Irridex scale	Survey scale	(% response)
Euphoria	Friendly	29
Apathy	No worry	58
Annoyance	Nuisance	10
Antagonism	Rude/unbearable	3

Source: After Pigram (1987: 68)

tourism did emerge from the study. According to Pigram (1987), the greatest impact of tourism on the local community was the perceived increase in the cost of goods and services because of the presence of tourists. The respondents also indicated that they believed that petty crime was also worse during the tourist season, an observation supported by Walmesley *et al.*'s (1981, 1983) study of crime in the region during the late 1970s. Furthermore, the natural environment of the Coffs Harbour area was perceived as slightly worse as a result of tourism with the greatest impact being on the beaches. However, opportunities for public recreation were perceived as the attribute of community life registering the most significant improvement as a result of tourism (Pigram 1987).

Resident attitudes are undoubtedly a key component in the identification, measurement and analysis of tourism impacts. However, investigation of community attitudes towards tourism is not just an academic exercise. Such attitudes are also important in terms of the determination of local policy, planning and management responses to tourism development and in establishing the extent to which public support exists for tourism (D.G. Pearce 1980; Page and Lawton 1997). For example, Getz (1994b) argued that resident perceptions of tourism may be one factor in shaping the attractiveness of a destination, where negative attitudes may be an indicator of an area's ability to absorb tourism. Although Getz suggests that 'identification of causal mechanisms is a major theoretical challenge, and residents can provide the local knowledge necessary to link developments with their consequences' (1994b: 247), it assumes that residents are sufficiently aware, perceptive and able to articulate such views to decision-makers and planners. Nevertheless, negative resident perceptions may lead to adverse reactions towards tourism and create substantial difficulties for the development of further facilities and infrastructure (Page and Lawton 1997). For example, although communities with a history of exposure to tourism may adapt and change to accommodate its effects (Rothman 1978), active or passive support or opposition may exist at any given time, as interest groups take political action to achieve specific objectives in relation to tourism (Murphy 1985; Hall and Jenkins 1995).

In locations where the original community is 'swamped' by large-scale tourism development in a relatively short space of time, disruption to the community values of the original inhabitants is more likely to occur (Hudson 1990a, 1990b). Table 4.6 details the costs and benefits of such tourism development in Broome, Western Australia. However, it must be emphasised that resident attitudes to tourism development will be influenced by where they fit into the existing social and economic order, their personal gains from the development process, and/or their response to the changing environment in light of their pre-existing values and attitudes (Hudson 1990b). In addition, it should be noted that while individuals may perceive there to

Table 4.6: Costs and benefits of tourism development in Broome, Australia

Costs	Benefits
• Marginalisation of the Aboriginal and coloured people • Too much power in vested interests • Destruction of multicultural flavour of the town and the original form of Shinju Matsuri • Increased racism • High accommodation costs/shortage • High local prices • Less friendly/more local conflicts • Environmental impacts (e.g. dune destruction) • Loss of historical character of town and imposition of artificially created atmosphere • More crime/domestic violence	• Expansion of new services and businesses • More infrastructure and community facilities • More sealed roads and kerbing and guttering • Increased variety of restaurants/entertainment • Restoration of Broome architecture • Better health system • Tidier town

Source: Hudson (1990b: 10)

be negative tourism impacts, they may still be favourable towards tourism's overall benefits to the community. Faulkner and Tideswell (1996) referred to this phenomenon as the 'altruistic surplus' and suggested that this could be the result of a mature stage of tourism development in a destination region whereby residents have adapted to tourism through experience and migration.

In addition to attitudinal studies, a number of other approaches and issues are of interest to the geographer. For example, historical studies of tourism may indicate the role tourism has in affecting attitudes and values with a destination community (e.g. Wall 1983a; Butler and Wall 1985). Studies of tourism policy may assist in an understanding of the way governments develop strategies to manage the negative impacts of tourism and in the overall manner that tourism is used in regional development (e.g. Papson 1981; Kosters 1984; Oglethorpe 1984; Hall and Jenkins 1995). Another area of tourism's social impact which has received more attention in recent years is that of health (Clift and Page 1996). Researchers have examined the spatial misinformation provided by travel agents when advising clients of the potential health risks they may face when travelling to Pacific Island destinations (Lawton *et al.* 1996; Lawton and Page 1997). What such research shows is the vital role of understanding place, space and the geography of risk in relation to the epidemi-

ology of disease. While geographers have studied disease for many years, making the link between travel and disease is a comparatively new development (Clift and Page 1996). For example, tourism may assist in the spread of disease, while tourists themselves are vulnerable to illness while travelling. Indeed, one of the major focal points for geographers' research on tourist health in recent years has been the spread of AIDS and its association with sex tourism. In fact there is growing evidence that the geographer will continue to develop expertise in this area and a major contribution could be made at a public policy level in the rapid dissemination of disease alerts to GPs and health professionals through the use of GIS technology. Important collaborations have been forged between geographers, tourism and health researchers to ensure this area expands the frontiers of knowledge (Clift and Page 1996).

Prostitution has also been related to tourism in both historical and contemporary settings, with research being focused on tourism in the less developed countries (Jones 1986), issues of gender (Kinnaird and Hall 1994), and sex tourism in particular (Ryan and Hall 2001). Yet prostitution and sex tourism's significant connection to western tourism should also be noted. For example, tourist promotion may highlight the more licentious attributes of a tourist destination. As Bailie (1980: 19–20) commented:

INSIGHT: Trafficking, sex tourism and slavery

Mobility is an integral part of the process of globalisation. However, one of the more unsavoury aspects of mobility is the extent to which there has been an increase in the extent of trafficking in women and children, often as sex workers. According to Human Rights Watch (1999), a United States-based non-government organisation, 'Trafficking, the illegal and highly profitable transport and sale of human beings across or within international borders for the purpose of exploiting their labor, is a human rights abuse with global dimensions' with many thousands of women and girls around the world being lured, abducted or sold into forced prostitution, forced labour, domestic service, or involuntary marriage. Trafficking is therefore closely related to the wider issue of sexual slavery (Matsui 1999). Indeed, Barry (1984: 40) argues that 'female sexual slavery is present in ALL situations where women or girls cannot change the immediate conditions of their existence; where regardless of how they got into those conditions they cannot get out; and where they are subject to sexual violence and exploitation'. Nevertheless, Barry does point to the significance of the exploitation that the loss of individual control brings in many situations where prostitution exists.

Many well-publicised media accounts of sex tourism in Thailand in particular have noted the extent to which women and girls have been bonded into prostitution often through agents and brothel owners making loans or payments to relatives (see e.g. Bishop and Robinson 1998; Matsui 1999). However, the selling of women into prostitution is not isolated to Thailand – it is a global phenomena in which the female body is objectified into a commodity to be bought and sold – it is the (il)logical extent of the objectification of labour in which not only are humans seen purely as a unit of sexual labour which is under the control of their 'owner', but it also represents the denial of self of one human by another (Ryan and Hall 2001). Indeed, in South-East Asia much of the demand for sex tourism is through intra-regional travel or from domestic travellers, with many of the border regions being areas in which brothels and other illegal activities are concentrated.

The Executive Director, Women's Rights Division of Human Rights Watch argues that the number of persons trafficked each year is impossible to determine, but it is clearly a large-scale problem, with estimates ranging from hundreds of thousands to millions of victims worldwide (Ralph 2000). The International Organization for Migration has reported on cases of trafficking in South-East Asia, East Asia, South Asia, the Middle East, Western Europe, Eastern Europe, South America, Central America and North America. For example, the United States State Department estimates that each year between 50,000 and 100,000 women and children are trafficked into the United States. Many women are trafficked to work in brothels, about half are trafficked into bonded sweatshop labour or domestic servitude. Once in the United States, the women who work in brothels typically are rotated from city to city to evade law enforcement, keep the women disoriented and give clients fresh faces (Rosenfried 1997). In her testimony before the Senate Committee on Foreign Relations, Ralph (2000) reported that 'in August 1999, a trafficking ring was broken up in Atlanta, Georgia that authorities believe was responsible for transporting up to 1000 women from several Asian countries into the United States and forcing them to work in brothels across the country'.

Tourism promotion in magazines and newspapers promises would-be vacationers more than sun, sea, and sand; they are also offered the fourth 's' – sex. Resorts are advertized under the labels of 'hedonism', 'ecstacism', and 'edenism'. . . . One of the most successful advertizing campaigns actually failed to mention the location of the resort: the selling of the holiday experience itself and not the destination was the important factor.

The extent of the relationship between crime and tourism has also been examined by several geographers (e.g. Nichols 1976; Walmesley *et al.* 1981, 1983), with research on Australian hallmark events also examining the relationship between increased visitor numbers and crime rates (Hall *et al.* 1995).

Another area to which geographers have been paying increasing attention is the relationship between tourism and indigenous peoples in both developed and less developed nations. While anthropology has focused considerable attention on the impacts and effects of tourism on indigenous peoples (e.g. V.L. Smith, 1977, 1992), geographers have assisted greatly in broadening the research agenda to include greater consideration of the way in which indigenous peoples interact with wildlife, the relationship between indigenous peoples and ecotourism and national parks, tourism and land rights, and indigenous business development (e.g. Nelson 1986; Nickels *et al.* 1991; Mercer 1994; Butler and Hinch 1996; Lew and van Otten 1997).

One of the most important concepts in humanistic geography is that of a 'sense of place'. A sense of place arises where people feel a particular attachment or personal relationship to an area in which local knowledge and human contacts are meaningfully maintained. 'People demonstrate their sense of place when they apply their moral or aesthetic discernment to sites and locations' (Tuan 1974: 235). However, people may only consciously notice the unique qualities of their place when they are away from it or when it is being rapidly altered.

The sense of place concept is of significance to tourism development for a number of reasons. The redevelopment and re-imaging of communities for tourism purposes (see Chapter 5) may force long-term residents to leave and may change the character of the community (Ley and Olds 1988).

In these instances, the identification of residents with the physical and social structure of the neighbourhood may be deeply disturbed, leading to a condition of 'placelessness' (Relph 1976). Residents of destinations which find themselves faced with rapid tourism development may therefore attempt to preserve components of the townscape including buildings and parks in order to retain elements of their identity.

The conservation of heritage is often a reaction to the rate of physical and social change within a community. Generally, when people feel they are in control of their own destiny they have little call for nostalgia. However, the strength of environment and heritage conservation organisations in developed nations is perhaps a reflection of the desire to retain a sense of continuity with the past (Lowenthal 1975, 1985). In addition, the protection of historic buildings and the establishment of heritage precincts can also effect a significant economic return to destinations because of the desire of many visitors to experience what they perceive as authentic forms of tourism (Konrad 1982; Hall and McArthur 1996).

PHYSICAL ENVIRONMENTAL IMPACTS

One of the areas of major interest for geographers is the impacts of tourists and recreationists on the physical environment. The reason for this lies in part in the nature of geography, which has a strong tradition of study of the interactions of humans with their environment (Mitchell and Murphy 1991). Indeed, the impacts of tourism and recreation on the physical environment and the subsequent resource analysis is one area where human and physical geographers find common ground in studying visitor issues (Johnston 1983b). However, another reason is the sheer significance of the physical environment for the recreation and tourism industry. As Mathieson and Wall (1982: 97) commented: 'In the absence of an attractive environment, there would be little tourism. Ranging from the basic attractions of sun, sea and sand to the undoubted appeal of historic sites and structures, the environment is the foundation of the tourist industry.'

The relationship between tourism and the environment is site and culture dependent and will likely change through time and in relation to broader economic, environmental and social concerns. As noted in the previous chapter, the recognition of something as a resource is the result of human perception, so it is also with the recognition that there are undesirable impacts on a environmental resource.

Increasing attention has been given to the impacts that tourism and recreation may have on the environmental and physical characteristics of a host community since the early 1970s (Walter 1975; Organisation for Economic Co-operation and Development 1980; Murphy 1985; Smith 1995). Interest in this area of applied geography is partly a response to the growth of tourism and the sheer impact that increased numbers of visitors will have on specific sites. However, concern has also developed because of the activities of environmental interest groups which have often provided an advocacy role for geographers in terms of arguing the results of the research and scholarship in direct involvement in the planning and policy process. The rise of the environmental movement has not only led to improvements in conservation practices but has also encouraged public interest in natural areas. However, 'environmentalism' and 'environmentalist' are oft-used terms that are frustratingly vague. According to O'Riordan and Turner (1984: 1):

> Although environmentalists are not the only people who object to much of what they interpret as modern-day values, aspirations and ways of life, it is probably fair to say that one of the two things which unite their disparate perceptions is a wish to alter many of the unjust and foolhardy features they associate with modern capitalism of both a state and private variety. The other common interest is a commitment to cut waste and reduce profligacy by consuming resources more frugally. Environmentalists do not agree, however, about how the transition should be achieved.

Nevertheless, despite confusion about what is meant by an environmentally 'responsible' approach to tourism development, it is apparent that the protection of the natural and cultural resources upon which tourism is based is essential for the sustainable development of a location (Hall and Lew 1998).

There is no fundamental difference in conducting research on the effects of tourism on the natural environment and research on the environmental impacts of recreation. The footprints of a recreationalist are the same as that of the tourist. The majority of research has been undertaken on the effects of tourism and recreation on wildlife and the trampling of vegetation, with relatively little attention being given to impacts on soils and air and water quality (Wall and Wright 1977; Mathieson and Wall 1982; Edington and Edington 1986; Parliamentary Commissioner for the Environment 1997).

The majority of studies have examined the impacts of tourism and recreation on a particular environment or component of the environment rather than over a range of environments. According to Mathieson and Wall (1982: 94), 'there has been little attempt to present an integrated approach to the assessment of the impacts of tourism'. However, there is clearly a need to detect the effects of tourism on all aspects of an ecosystem. For example, the ecology of an area may be dramatically changed through the removal of a key species in the food chain or through the introduction of new species, such as trout, for enhanced benefits for recreational fishermen, or game for hunters (Hall 1995). In addition, it is important to distinguish between perceptions and actual impacts of tourism. For example, many visitors believe an environment is healthy as long as it looks 'clean and green'. The ecological reality may instead be vastly different; an environment may be full of invasive introduced species which, although contributing to a positive aesthetic perception, may have extremely negative ecological implications. For example, while New Zealand promotes its tourism very strongly on the basis of its 'clean, green' image, the reality is quite different with respect to many tourist locations which may have very few indigenous species present and may have very low biodiversity (Parliamentary Commissioner for the Environment 1997).

Research on impacts has focused on particular regions or environments which has limited the ability to generalise the findings from one area to another. In addition, research on visitor impacts is comparatively recent and is generally of a reactionary nature to site-specific problems. We therefore rarely know what conditions were like before tourists and recreationalists arrived. Few longitudinal studies exist by which the long-term impacts of visitation can be assessed. Therefore, there are a number of significant methodological problems which need to be addressed in undertaking research on the environmental affects of tourism (Mathieson and Wall 1982: 94):

- the difficulty of distinguishing between changes induced by tourism and those induced by other activities;
- the lack of information concerning conditions prior to the advent of tourism and, hence, the lack of a baseline against which change may be measured;
- the paucity of information on the numbers, types and tolerance levels of different species of flora and fauna;
- the concentration of researchers upon particular primary resources, such as beaches and mountains, which are ecologically sensitive.

Nevertheless, despite the difficulties that have emerged in studying the relationship between tourism and the natural environment, it is apparent that 'a proper understanding of biological, or more specifically, ecological factors can significantly reduce the scale of environmental damage associated with recreational and tourist development' (Edington and Edington 1986: 2).

Tourism and recreation can have an adverse impact on the physical environment in numerous ways; for example, the construction of facilities that are aesthetically unsympathetic to the landscape in which they are situated, what D.G. Pearce (1978: 152) has described as 'architectural pollution', and through the release of air- and water-borne pollutants. Tourist or special-event facilities may change the character of the urban setting. Indeed, the location of a facility or attraction may be deliberately exploited in an attempt to rejuvenate an urban area through the construction of new infrastructure, as with the 1986 Vancouver Expo and the 1987 America's Cup in Fremantle (Hall 1992b) (see Chapter 5). The promotion of tourism without the provision of an adequate infrastructure to cope with increased visitor numbers may well cause a decline in urban environmental quality, for instance, in the impacts of increased traffic flows (Schaer 1978). However, there are a wide range of tourism and recreation impacts on the urban physical environment (Table 4.7) that may have substantial implications for the longer term sustainability of a destination which are only now being addressed in the tourism literature (Page 1995a; Hinch 1996).

Many of the ecological effects of tourist facilities may well take a long time to become apparent because of the nature of the environment, as in the case of the siting of marinas or resorts (Hall and Selwood 1987). The impact of outdoor recreation on the environment has been well documented (Wall and Wright 1977; Mathieson and Wall 1982) and is discussed further in Chapter 7. However, research on the physical impacts of tourism on the environment is still at a relatively early stage of development and presents an important area of future research, particularly with respect to sustainable tourism development (Hall and Lew 1998). Where the geographer has employed techniques from environmental science such as Environmental Assessment (EA), the spatial consequences of tourism and recreation activity have not always been fully appreciated. For example, Page (1992) reviewed the impact of the Channel Tunnel project on the natural and built environment and yet the generative effects of new tourist trips had been weakly articulated in the mountains of documents describing the effects to be mitigated, failing to recognise how this might impact on destination areas. Again, planners and researchers had failed to recognise how recreational and tourist behaviour cannot easily be incorporated into spatially specific plans for individual infrastructure projects which will have knock-on effects for other parts of the

Table 4.7: The impact of tourism on the urban physical environment

1   *The urban physical environment*
   • land lost through tourism development which may have been used for other purposes
   • changes to urban hydrology

2   *Visual impact*
   • development of tourism/leisure districts
   • introduction of new architectural styles
   • potential reinforcement of vernacular architectural forms
   • potential contribution to population growth

3   *Infrastructure*
   • potential overloading of existing urban infrastructure with the following utilities and developments:
      – roads
      – railways
      – car-parking
      – electricity and gas
      – sewage and water supply
   • provision of new infrastructure
   • additional environmental management measures to accommodate tourists and adapt areas for tourist use

4   *Urban form*
   • changes to land use as residential areas are replaced by accommodation developments
   • alterations to the urban fabric from pedestrianisation and traffic management schemes which have been constructed to accommodate visitation

5   *Restoration*
   • the restoration and conservation of historic sites and buildings
   • reuse of the facades of heritage buildings

Source: After Page (1995a: 147)

tourism system. Page (1999) also reviews the role of geographers in developing more meaningful appraisals of environmental impacts resulting from tourist transport and the need to scrutinise private sector claims of minimising environmental impacts. Nevertheless, tourism's impacts on the natural environment have often been exaggerated. This is because the impacts of tourism have often failed to be distinguished from other forms of development impact or even such factors as overpopulation, poor agricultural practice or poor resource management. This is not to say that tourism has not affected the environment. Yet, what is often at issue are aesthetic or cumulative impacts rather than effects that can be related solely to tourism development. Indeed, to focus on tourism as a form of negative impact on the natural environment is to miss the far greater environmental problems which arise from other forms of economic development, such as depletion of fisheries and forest resources and the loss of biodiversity, and the overall lack of monitoring and management of many environments.

For example, in the South Pacific, a region threatened by major environmental problems (Hall and Page 1996), there has been no systematic study of the environmental impacts of tourism over the region as a whole. Data and information are highly fragmented (Milne 1990). Baseline data, i.e. information regarding the condition of the natural environment prior to tourism development, is invariably lacking. Even in Australia, one of the most economically developed nations in the region, information about the environmental impacts of tourism is relatively poor and, where it does exist, it tends to be available for areas, such as national parks or reserves, which are under government control, rather than for private lands (Hall 1995). In addition, development specific reports, such as

Plate 4.7: The America's Cup Village, Auckland. This development led to environmental improvements for the area.

environmental impact statements on resort or tourism developments, required by law in many western countries, are often not required in the countries of the South Pacific because environmental planning legislation is still being developed (Minerbi 1992; Hall and Page 1996).

Minerbi (1992) recorded a number of environmental and ecological impacts associated with tourism development on Pacific islands (Table 4.8). The range of tourism-related impacts is similar to that for many other environments (Mathieson and Wall 1992; Edington and Edington 1986). However, in the case of Pacific islands, tourism impacts may be more problematic because tourism is concentrated on or near the ecologically and geomorphologically dynamic coastal environment. Due to the highly dynamic nature of the coastal environment and the significance of mangroves and the limited coral sand supply for island beaches in particular, any development which interferes with the natural system may have severe consequences for the long-term stability of the environment. The impact of poorly developed tourism projects on the sand cays (coral sand islands) of the Pacific, for example, has been well documented:

- near-shore vegetation clearing exposes the island to sea storm erosion and decreases plant material decomposition on the beach, thereby reducing nutrient availability for flora and fauna;
- manoeuvring by bulldozer (instead of hand clearing) results in scarring and soil disturbance and makes sand deposits loose and vulnerable to erosion;
- excessive tapping of the fresh ground-water lens induces salt-water intrusion which then impairs vegetation growth and human water use and renders the cay susceptible to storm damage and further erosion;
- sewage outfall in shallow water and reef flats may lead to an excessive buildup of nutrients, thereby causing algal growth which may eventually kill coral;
- sea-walls built to trap sand in the short-term impair the natural seasonal distribution of sand

resulting, in the long run, in a net beach loss and a reduction of the island land mass;
- boat channels blasted in the reef act as a sand trap; in time they fill with sand which is no longer circulating around the island; in turn this sand is replaced by other sand eroded from the vegetated edges, changing the size and shape of the island and in time threatening the island's integrity (Baines 1987).

Another component of the coastal environment in the Pacific and in other tropical and subtropical areas which are substantially affected by tourism is the clearing and dredging of mangroves and estuaries for resorts. Mangroves and estuarine environments are extremely significant nursery areas for a variety of fish species. The loss of natural habitat due to dredging or infilling may therefore have a dramatic impact on fish catches. In addition, there may be substantial impacts on the whole of the estuarine food chain with a subsequent loss of ecological diversity. A further consequence of mangrove loss is reduced protection against erosion of the shoreline thereby increasing vulnerability to storm surge. Therefore, removal of mangroves will not only have an adverse impact on the immediate area of clearance, but will also affect other coastal areas through the transport of greater amounts of marine sediment (Clarke 1991).

In concluding his examination of the impacts of tourism development on Pacific islands, Minerbi (1992: 69) was scathing in his criticism of the environmental impacts of tourism:

Resorts and golf courses increase environmental degradation and pollution. Littering has taken place on beaches and scenic lookouts and parks. Marine sanctuaries have been overrun and exploited by too many tourists. Resorts have interfered with the hydrological cycle by changing groundwater patterns, altering stream life, and engaging in excessive groundwater extraction. Coastal reefs, lagoons, anchialine ponds, wastewater marshes, mangroves, have been destroyed by resort construction and by excessive visitations and activities with the consequent loss of marine life and destruction of ecosystems. Beach walking, snorkeling, recreational fishing, boat tours and anchoring have damaged coral reefs and grasses and have disturbed near shore aquatic life. . . . Tourism

Table 4.8: Environmental and ecological impacts of tourism on the Pacific islands

Environmental degradation and pollution
- Degradation and pollution of the environment due to golf courses
- Pollution by littering

Destruction of habitats and damage to ecosystems
- Poorly managed tourism may result in destruction of high-quality natural environments
- Unmanaged human interference of specific species of fauna and flora
- Dynamite blasting and overfishing

Loss of coastal and marine resources
- Interference with inland and coastal natural processes
  - excessive ground-water extraction by large resorts induces salt-water intrusion and deterioration of water quality and recharge of the aquifer
- Coastal ecosystem damage and destruction through tourism development
- Terrestrial runoff and dredging on coastal areas
  - damage to coral reef and marine resources caused by the construction of tourist infrastructure such as runways, marinas, harbours, parking areas and roads, and use of coral limestone in hotels and resort developments
- Destruction by tourist activities
  - destruction of coral reefs, lagoons, mangroves, salt-water marshes and wetlands due to excessive visitation and/or unmanaged exploitation of those resources
  - disturbance to near shore aquatic life due to thrill crafts and boat tours
- Introduced exotic species
  - increased sea and air inter-island traffic creates the danger of accidental importation of exotic species, which can be very destructive to indigenous flora and fauna
  - tourism enterprises alter the integrity of the environment and encroach on local lifestyles with imported exotic species for safari hunting
- Damage to sand cay ecosystems
- Damage to mangrove ecosystems
- Damage to coastal rainforest ecosystems
- Loss of sandy beaches and shoreline erosion
  - loss of sandy beaches due to onshore development and construction of seawalls

Coastal pollution
- Waste-water discharge and sewage pollution
- Coastal water pollution and siltation due to near shore resort construction and runoff from resort areas results in the destruction of natural habitat, coral and feeding grounds for fish
- Marine and harbour pollution
  - coastal oil pollution due to motorised vehicles and ships

Surface water and ground-water diversion
- Diversion of streams and water sources from local use to resort use, with resulting decline in water availability for domestic and other productive uses and farming, particularly taro cultivation

Source: After Minerbi (1992); see also Milne (1990) and Weiler and Hall (1992)

has presented itself as a clean and not polluting industry but its claims have not come true.

Such expressions of concern clearly give rise to questions regarding how sustainable tourism can really be and the need to provide limits on the expansion of tourism and corresponding human impact. Indeed, observation of the potential combined pressures of the social and environmental impacts of tourism has long led researchers to speculate as to whether there exists a carrying capacity for tourist destinations (e.g. Hall 1974; McCool 1978; Getz 1983) (see Chapters 7 and 8).

INSIGHT: Tourism and coral reefs

One of the most obvious ways in which tourism-related development has impacted on the coastal environment is the affect of tourism and tourist activities on coral reefs. 'Coral reefs are very vulnerable, and adverse human activities may result in a lower capacity to regenerate, or the death of entire coral colonies' (Tourism Council of the South Pacific 1988: 12). Tourists can directly impact on coral reefs in a number of ways. Skin divers and snorklers can damage coral by hitting it with their fins. In order to restrict such damage, Vanuatu has been actively educating divers on the importance of maintaining correct buoyancy. In other parts of the Pacific, such as Australia's Great Barrier Reef, reef walking by tourists at low tide has resulted in substantial damage to sections of the reef within easy shore access.

The growth of coastal tourism in the Red Sea has also had substantial impacts on coral reefs in terms of both the effects of construction and infrastructure development as well as the direct affects of snorkelling and diving. According to Hawkins and Roberts (1994), approximately 19 per cent of Egypt's reefs were substantially affected by tourism in the early 1990s, but this figure was expected to rise to over 30 per cent by the year 2000. Given the accessibility of the coastlines of Israel, Egypt and Jordan and the development plans of government, substantial increases in environmental impacts were reported. For example, Israel plans a further 43 per cent increase in coastal tourism, Jordan 100 per cent and Egypt a massive eleven-fold expansion. Of the planned expansion in Egypt, 55 per cent is designated around the established resorts of Hurgharda and Sharm-el-Sheikh. Hawkins and Roberts (1994) reported that tourist-related development had already caused substantial damage to inshore reefs near to Hurgharda from infilling, sedimentation and over-fishing for marine curios. Elsewhere in the region, construction of tourist facilities and infrastructure was also beginning to modify reef habitats which up until the early 1990s was generally restricted to the direct effects of diving and snorkelling. While the growth in the numbers of arrivals to the Red Sea area appeared to be sustainable for the planned developments, the authors concluded that the massive expansion planned throughout the northern Red Sea substantially threatened the reef ecosystem and warned that unless the pace of tourist development is reduced, the carrying capacity of coral reefs would be exceeded with widespread reef degradation the likely result (Hawkins and Roberts 1994).

The major indirect aspect of tourism's impacts on coral reefs is therefore the environmental effects of urban and resort development, land clearing and pollution. Pollutants may come from both land (e.g. resorts) and marine sources (e.g. tourist boats). Land-based pollution is often in the form of excessive nutrients from sewage and fertilisers. While both of these types of pollution may come from non-tourism sources, it should be noted that septic tanks or inadequate sewage systems at resorts, or fertiliser run-off from golf-courses may substantially impact on reef systems (Kuji 1991). Excessive nutrients promote algal growth at the expense of coral, leading to the smothering of coral and its eventual death. Similarly, sedimentation leads to silting and water cloudiness, which cuts off sunlight to the coral reef, also killing it. In the case of the Cape Tribulation Road constructed near Daintree in Northern Queensland by the state government in the mid-1980s in an effort to develop tourism, sedimentation on adjacent coral reefs increased more than six-fold in comparison with undisturbed catchments in the same area (Hopley *et al.* 1993).

Yet regardless of the empirical validity of the notion of carrying capacity (Wall 1983b), attention must clearly be paid by planners to the ability of an area to absorb tourism in relation to the possibilities of environmental and social degradation (see Chapter 9).

CONCLUSION

The purpose of this chapter has been to give a brief account of some of the potential economic, social and environmental impacts of tourism and recreation. This provides a framework for the discussion of specific forms of tourism and recreation in Chapters 5–8. Tourism and recreation needs to be well managed in order to reduce possible adverse impacts (Murphy 1982). In turn, good management is likely to be related to the level of understanding of tourism and recreation phenomena. There is clearly a need to go beyond the image of tourism and recreation, and develop rigorous integrated economic, environmental, social and political analyses.

Geographers have contributed much to the understanding of the impacts of tourism and recreation, particularly with respect to the impacts on the physical environment and the spatial fixity of such effects. What the geographer has contributed is a better understanding of the wider consequences of individual impacts and their cumulative effect on the natural environment. However, there has been considerable exchange of approaches and methodologies through the various social sciences, which means that the demarcation line between geographical and other approaches has become increasingly fuzzy. This is clearly the case when using multidisciplinary techniques such as EA which has been enhanced by the use of GIS to improve the precision and location of the spatial awareness of impacts. One notable example during the 1980s and 1990s was the planning for the UK's high-speed rail link between London and the Channel Tunnel where GIS was used to model the optimum route for a tourist-transport infrastructure project, and where political changes and lobbying directly altered the geographical routing and distribution of its impacts (Goodenough and Page 1994). Nevertheless, no one discipline will have all the answers. Given the complex nature of tourism phenomena, particularly with respect to 'solving' environmental problems, the development of multidisciplinary approaches towards recreation and tourism may provide an appropriate starting point for the development of more sustainable forms of tourism.

QUESTIONS

- What are the key factors in determining the accuracy of the assessment of the economic impacts of tourism?
- What may determine the acceptability of a recreation resource management model to stakeholders?
- Why are the impacts of tourism on the natural environment poorly assessed?
- Is tourism necessarily a negative impact on a destination?

READING

Although now somewhat dated, one of the most influential books on understanding the impacts of tourism is:

Mathesion, A. and Wall, G. (1982) *Tourism: Economic, Physical and Social Impacts*, London: Longman.

Most general textbooks and recreation on tourism will include overview chapters on the impacts of tourism (e.g. Davidson and Maitland 1997; Williams 1998). Interesting regional perspectives on the impacts of tourism are to be found in:

Hall, C.M. and Page, S.J. (eds) (1996) *Tourism in the Pacific: Cases and Issues*, London: International Thomson Business Press.

Hall, C.M. and Page, S.J. (eds) (2000) *Tourism in South and South-East Asia: Cases and Issues*, Oxford: Butterworth Heinemann.

Excellent recent books which deal with the environmental dimensions of tourism and recreation and their management include:

Fennell, D. (1999) *Ecotourism: An Introduction*, London: Routledge.

Holden, A. (2000) *Environment and Tourism*, London: Routledge.

Newsome, D., Moore, S. and Dowling, R. (2002) *Natural Area Tourism: Ecology, Impacts and Management*, Clevedon: Channel View Press.

5

URBAN RECREATION
AND TOURISM

Urbanisation is a major force contributing to the development of towns and cities, where people live, work and shop (see Johnston *et al.* (1994) for a definition of the term 'urbanisation'). Towns and cities function as places where the population is concentrated in a defined area, and economic activities locate in the same area or nearby, to provide the opportunity for the production and consumption of goods and services in capitalist societies. Consequently, towns and cities provide the context for a diverse range of social, cultural and economic activities which the population engage in, and where tourism, leisure and entertainment form major service activities. These environments also function as meeting places, major tourist gateways, accommodation and transportation hubs, and as central places to service the needs of visitors. Most tourist trips will contain some experience of an urban area; for example, when an urban dweller departs from a major gateway in a city, arrives at a gateway in another city-region and stays in accommodation in an urban area. Within cities, however, the line between tourism and recreation blurs to the extent that at times one is indistinguishable from the other, with tourists and recreationalists using the same facilities, resources and environments although some notable differences exist. Therefore, many tourists and recreationalists will intermingle in many urban contexts. While most tourists will experience urban tourism in some form during their holiday, visits to friends and relatives, business trips or visits for other reasons (e.g. a pilgrimage to a religious shrine such as Lourdes in an urban area), recreationalists

will not use the accommodation but frequent many similar places as tourists. This chapter seeks to examine some of the ways geographers conceptualise, analyse and research urban recreation and tourism, emphasising their contribution to understanding the wider context in which such activities take place. One key feature of the chapter is the emphasis on five specific aspects of geographical enquiry:

1 description;
2 classification;
3 analysis;
4 explanation;
5 application of theoretical and conceptual issues to practical problem-solving contexts.

According to Coppock (1982), the geographer's principal interest in the geographical analysis of leisure provides a useful starting point in understanding the areas of research which have also been developed in urban recreation and tourism research in that they examine

> the way in which . . . pursuits are linked to the whole complex of human activities and physical features that determine the distinctive characters of places and region, and the interactions between such pursuits and the natural and man-made environments in which they occur . . . [and] the study of the spatial interactions between participants and resources probably represents the most significant contribution the geographer can make.
>
> (Coppock 1982: 2–3)

The focus on the behavioural aspects of recreational and tourism behaviour together with the planning, and more recently, the management implications of such activities in the urban environment have become fruitful areas for geographical research.

GEOGRAPHICAL APPROACHES TO URBAN RECREATION

Despite the growth in geographical research on leisure and recreation (Coppock 1982), the focus on urban issues remained neglected, as Patmore (1983: 87) noted, in that 'in the past geographers, with their inherently spatial interest, have tended to concentrate on outdoor recreation in rural areas, where spatial demands, and spatial conflicts have been the greatest'. This is a strange paradox according to Patmore (1983: 87) since:

> the greatest changes in recreation habits in the last fifty years have taken place in two opposing directions. High personal mobility has extended opportunities away from the home and brought a growing complexity to the scale and direction of leisure patterns. Conversely, the home has come to provide for a greater range of leisure opportunities, and home-centred leisure has acquired a greater significance. The family has become socially more self-sufficient, its links with the immediate community and with its own extended kinship network weaker. Social independence has been underpinned by greater physical independence of homes in the expanding suburban communities, by the weakening need for communal space that comes with lower housing densities and the command of greater private space.

For the geographer, understanding the spatial implications of such processes and the geographical manifestation of the urban recreational demand for and the supply of resources requires the use of concepts and methodologies to understand the complexity and simplify the reality of recreational activities to a more meaningful series of concepts and constructs. However, one area that has been largely neglected in reviews of urban recreational activities is the historical dimension. Although Towner (1996) provides an all-embracing review of tourism and leisure in a historical context, it is important to acknowledge the significance of social, political, economic and geographical factors which shaped the evolution of modern-day urban recreation. For this reason, no analysis of urban recreation can commence without an understanding of the historical and geographical processes associated with its development (See Bailey (1989) for a review of the historical leisure research in the UK). By focusing on the development of modern-day recreation in cities since their rapid expansion in the early nineteenth century, it is possible to examine many changes to the form, function and format of urban recreation and its spatial occurrence in the nascent urban–industrial cities and conurbations in England and Wales.

THE EVOLUTION OF URBAN RECREATION IN BRITAIN

Within the context of towns and cities, Williams (1995: 8) argues that 'urban populations engage in most of their leisure activities within the same urban area in which they live. The geographical patterns of residence are translated very readily into a pattern of recreation that is focused upon the urban environment, purely by the fact that most people spend the majority of their leisure time in, or close to the home.' This indicates that the patterns of residence and recreation are closely related. The current-day patterns of recreation and the ways in which they developed in Britain are fundamental to any understanding of the development of recreational opportunities in urban areas. According to Williams (1995), these passed through three district phases: (1) Foundation; (2) Consolidation; and (3) Expansion.

Phase 1: foundation

During the nineteenth century, public provision for urban recreational activities emerged through legislative provision (e.g. the number of urban parks in Britain increased from 19 between 1820 and 1850, to 111 between 1850 and 1880 (Conway 1991)), while innovations in town planning and urban design led to improved quality of streets and housing areas, expanding the space for recreation.

In addition, the nineteenth century saw the social geography of towns and cities in England and Wales (Lawton 1978) develop with social patterns of segregation and suburbanisation fuelled by urban growth. This also affected the development of recreational opportunities as cities expanded during the late nineteenth and early twentieth centuries.

Phase 2: consolidation

The period 1918 to 1939 saw a growth in more specialised forms of urban recreational land uses stimulated by legislation such as the rise of the Small Holdings and Allotments Act (1908), which expanded the range and type of amenity space in towns and cities, while other gaps in provision (e.g. the National Playing Fields Association formed in 1925) recognised the need for space in urban areas to support the role of sport. Likewise, the 1937 Physical Training and Recreational Act effectively signalled the emergence of public sector aid from central government for local authority provision of playing fields, gymnasia and swimming baths.

Phase 3: expansion

During the post-war period several key trends emerged including 'greater levels and diversity of provision in which traditional resources established in earlier phases have been augmented by new forms of provision designed to reflect the diversity and flexibility of contemporary recreational tastes' (Williams 1995: 20). In fact, one common theme is the recognition of recreation as an element in statutory planning procedures as the range and consumption of land for recreational purposes increased. However, according to Williams (1995: 21), in the absence of theoretical approaches to describing and explaining the pattern of recreation resources in urban areas, the approach to the task must inevitably become empirical, outlining the typical patterns of provision where older parks and recreation grounds are concentrated towards the core of the settlement (see the case of Leicester, p. 167), while newer parks and grounds associated

with inter-war and post-1945 housing produce further significant zones of provision to the periphery of the city. The outer edges of the built area are important for provision of extensive facilities such as sports grounds and golf courses.

While these conclusions are typical of recreational land use patterns in many towns and cities in England and Wales, one must question the extent to which a purely empirical analysis truly explains the spatial development of recreational resources in Britain's urban areas. For this reason it is valuable to consider the social, economic and political processes which contributed to the spatial organisation and occurrence of urban recreation in such areas in the period after 1800, because traditional empirical analyses are devoid of the diversity of people and users of such resources. For this reason, a series of historical snapshots taken in 1800, the 1840s, 1880s, 1920s, 1960s and post-1960s help to explain how present-day patterns were shaped.

URBAN RECREATION: A SOCIO-GEOGRAPHIC PERSPECTIVE

According to Clark and Crichter (1985), during the evolution of a capitalist society such as Britain, the analysis of leisure and recreation has traditionally emphasised institutional forms of provision, while each social class has its own history of organised and informal leisure and recreation. The predominant urban histories are those of male leisure, with female leisure and recreation structured around the family with free-time activities associated with the family, the street and neighbourhood in working-class society. Within historical analyses of urban recreation during the evolution of mass urban society in Victorian and Edwardian Britain, the emergence of distinctive forms of urban recreation and leisure and their spatial occurrence within different social areas of cities has been associated with a number of concepts, the most notable being 'popular culture' (see Williams (1976) for a discussion of popular culture). As Clark and Crichter (1985: 55) argue, 'the early nineteenth century was to bring a dramatic transformation to the form . . .

and context of popular culture, imposing very different parameters of time and space, rhythms and routines, behaviour and attitude, control and commerce'. However, the resulting changes cannot simply be conceptualised as a straightforward linear progression since different influences and cross-currents meant that this transformation affected different people and areas at different rates and in varying degrees.

Clark and Crichter (1985) provide a useful historical analysis of leisure and recreational forms in Britain during the nineteenth and twentieth centuries, with the emphasis on the urban forms and political factors, forms of social control (Donajgrodski 1978) and the underlying development and functioning of an urban capitalist society; leisure and recreational forms emerged as a civilising and diversionary process to maintain the productive capacity of the working classes as central to the continued development of capitalism. Therefore, the geographical patterns and manifestation of urban recreation and leisure for all social classes in the British city in the nineteenth and twentieth centuries has to be viewed against the background of social, economic and political processes which conditioned the demand and supply of leisure and recreation for each social class.

According to Billinge (1996: 450), 'Perhaps the single newest element in the townscape after the general regulation of the street, was the park, and more specifically the recreation ground . . . [since] the urban park, as distinct from the garden square, was essentially a nineteenth century phenomenon' and a symbol of civic pride. As Maver (1998: 346) argued, 'the development of Glasgow's public parks . . . sparked municipal interest during the 1850s, given the recognised impact of parks in improving the amenity value of middle-class residential areas'. The acknowledged role of parks as the 'lungs of the city', as a haven from industrialisation, was an attempt to recreate notions of community well-being. In Young's (1996) analysis of the development of San Francisco's city parks between 1850 and 1920, the main proponents of park development were a middle- to upper-class elite who embodied notions of parks contributing to well-being, reflecting elements of nature which were balanced and inherently good.

Billinge (1996: 444) recognised the way in which the Victorians engineered the term 'recreation' 'to perfection, they gave it a role and a geography. Confined by time, defined by place and regulated by content, recreation and the time it occupied ceased to be possessions freely enjoyed and became instead, obligations dutifully discharged.' The Victorians established a system of approved urban leisure and recreation activities and, as Billinge (1996) recognised, these were allocated to appropriate times and places. In spatial terms, this led to a reconfiguration of the Victorian and Edwardian town and its hinterland to accommodate new, organised and, later, informal recreational and leisure pursuits in specific spaces and at nominated places. In fact, the natural corollary of this in the late nineteenth century was the rise of the English seaside resort (Gilbert 1939, 1949, 1954; Walton 1983; Towner 1996). As Billinge (1996: 447) argued, it was 'the provision of set aside resorts for the masses at the scale of the whole township: the seaside resort where behaviour inappropriate in any other occasion could be loosed to burn itself out'. This can be viewed as a further example of the way in which Victorian society sought to exercise both a degree of social and spatial control of recreational spaces and activities among its populace. This created a social necessity for recreation as freedom from work: a non-work activity to recreate body and soul, to be refreshed for the capitalist economic system, with its regulated time discipline of a place for everything, and everything in its place.

For this reason, it is pertinent to consider the key features of Clark and Crichter's (1985) historical synthesis of urban leisure and recreation in Britain, since it helps to explain how changes in society shaped the modern-day patterns of urban recreation. Clark and Crichter (1985) adopt a cross-section approach to analyse key periods in nineteenth- and twentieth-century British urban society to emphasise the nature of the changes and type of urban recreation and leisure pursuits. It also helps to explain how the evolution of urban places and recreational activities emerged.

THE 1800s

As emphasised earlier in this chapter, Britain was in the process of emerging from a pre-industrial state. While cities were not a new phenomenon (Clark 1981), the movement of the rural population to nascent cities meant that the traditional boundary between work and non-work among the labouring classes was increasingly dictated by the needs of factory or mechanised production. Therefore, pre-industrial flexibility in the work–non-work relationship associated with cottage industries and labouring on the land changed. This led to a clearer distinction between work and non-work time, as time discipline emerged as a portent force during the industrial revolution (Pred 1981). In the pre-industrial, non-urbanised society, leisure and recreational forms were associated with market days, fairs, wakes, holidays, religious and pagan festivals which provided opportunities for sport. While the 1800s are often characterised by brutish behaviour and ribaldry, civilising influences emerged in the form of Puritanism to engender moral sobriety and spatial changes associated with the enclosure movement, which removed many strategic sites of customary activity.

In contrast, the geographical patterns of recreation of the ruling classes:

> eschewed contact with lower orders. Its forms were as yet disparate. Shooting, hunting and horse racing . . . the major flat race classics date from the 1770s onwards. . . . For the increasingly influential urban bourgeoisie, the theatre, literature, seaside holidays and music hall denoted more rational forms of leisure which depended for their decorum on the exclusion of the mass of the population.
>
> (Clark and Crichter 1985: 55)

THE 1840s

In historical analysis, this period is often characterised as a period of deprivation for the urban working classes. Endemic poverty, associated with rapid urbanisation and inadequate housing, poor living standards and limited infrastructure culminated in high rates of mortality, disease and exploitation of the labouring classes through long hours of work (twelve-hour, six-day weeks) (Page 1988). In terms of urban leisure and recreation, the pre-industrial opportunities for pursuits decreased as did the legal outlets, with many customary pastimes suppressed so that popular culture was conditioned through legislative changes. For example, the 1834 New Poor Law Act (Rose 1985) aimed to control the movement of 'travelling balladeers', 'entertainers' and 'itinerant salesmen' all of whom were deemed as vagabonds and returned to their parish of origin. Similarly, the 1835 Highways Act was intended to remove street nuisances such as street entertainers and traders while the 1835 Cruelty to Animals Act sought to suppress working-class pastimes involving animals, thereby driving many activities underground and leading to the emergence of a hybrid range of recreational activities including popular theatre, pantomime and circuses. In the late 1840s, railway excursions pioneered by Thomas Cook also developed. In addition, a range of rational recreation pursuits emerged in purpose-built facilities made possible by Parliamentary Acts including the Museums Act (1845), the Baths and Wash Houses Act (1846) and the Libraries Act (1850). Social theorists argue that such legislation may have acted as a form of social control (Donajgrodski 1978), to tame a new industrial workforce while demarcating recreation and work. Furthermore, the 1840s saw the emergence of the Victorian concept of domesticity and a bourgeois culture, with the use of a gender separation of male and female work.

THE 1880s

While the early Victorian period saw the establishment of urban recreational facilities, improved working conditions and living standards in the mid- to late Victorian period were accompanied by greater municipal provision (Briggs 1969). Yet as Clark and Crichter (1985) argue, four processes were at work in the 1850s and 1860s which led to significant changes in the 1880s:

1 a rise of middle-class urban recreation which excluded the working classes;
2 the expansion of local government's role in leisure and recreational provision;
3 an increasing commercialisation and greater capitalisation of urban recreation, relying upon mass audiences and licensing (e.g. the rise of football), which also required large areas of land;
4 attempts by the working classes to organise urban recreation according to their own aspirations.

By the 1880s, the pattern of urban conurbations had emerged in England which focused on London, the West Midlands, West Yorkshire, Merseyside and Tyneside (Lawton 1978). In addition to these trends in urban recreation, the rise of urban middle-class recreational pursuits centred on religion, reading, music and annual holidays reflected a more rational form of recreational activity. Nevertheless, the 1870s saw the growth in public parks and by 1885, nearly 25 per cent of the urban population had access to public libraries. At the same time, informal urban recreation based on the street- and neighbourhood-based activities largely remains invisible in documentary sources and official records, although limited evidence exists in the form of autobiographies and oral history. For example, Roberts' (1971, 1976) *The Classic Slum* observed that the pub played a major role in informal recreation in Victorian and Edwardian Salford where a community of 3,000 people had 15 beer houses. Through sexual segregation it was possible to observe the rise of male-only urban recreational pursuits in the 1880s. Yet the street life and neighbourhood forms of recreation remained unorganised and informal despite the institutionalisation, segmentation and emergence of a customer–provider relationship in Victorian urban recreational pursuits.

THE 1920s

In Britain, the 1920s are frequently viewed as the era of mass unemployment with social class more spatially defined in the urban environment. While the 1900s saw the rising patronage of the cinema, with 3,000 cinemas operating in Britain by 1926 and audiences of 20 million, with many people visiting the cinemas up to twice a week, this pursuit increasingly met the recreational needs of women as it displaced the Victorian music-hall, being more heavily capitalised and more accessible in terms of price and social acceptability. The ideological separation of work and home was firmly enshrined in the 1920s, with a greater physical separation and the rise of annual holidays and day trips using charabancs and the car. Spectator sports also retained large audiences although the social segregation of urban recreation based on social class, mass markets and institutional provision characterised this era.

THE 1960s AND BEYOND

Clark and Crichter (1985) identified six distinct trends occurring from the 1960s on:

1 rising standards of domestic consumption;
2 family-centred leisure;
3 the decline of public forms of urban leisure and recreation;
4 emergence of a youth culture;
5 the establishment of ethnic leisure and recreation culture;
6 increased state activity in prescribed spheres of urban recreation and a growing commercial domination of leisure institutions and services.

This has been well reviewed in the sociological literature (see Pahl 1975).

In terms of urban recreation, various debates exist in relation to the changes induced by a post-industrial society and the implications for urban recreation. Social theorists point to the concomitant changes induced by economic, occupational and technological change, associated with the demise of manufacturing and the rise of the service sector in towns and cities, affecting the pattern of life and recreational activities of urban populations associated with a growing polarisation of wealth and opportunity. Williams (1995: 213) outlines the impact of such changes for post-industrial towns and cities, as older central areas of towns decayed as they lost their economic rationale. In some cases this has led to the creation of space for recreation, as high-density housing and industry has been removed and urban regeneration results.

Williams (1995) also points to the effect of the rise of environmentalism since the 1960s, reflected in the concept of the 'green city' where redundant space is 'greened' to enhance the quality of the city environment while adding recreational opportunities (e.g. greenways, linear parks, green wedges and natural corridors). The greening of cities also has a wider concern with the sustainability of urban life. Williams (1995) also argues that a range of factors militate against the continued well-being of urban recreation provision, many of which are associated with political change outlined in detail by Page *et al*. (1994). A greater concern with financial costs of publicly provided services and more efficient service delivery and the introduction of Compulsory Competitive Tendering (CCT) (Benington and White 1988; Page *et al*. 1994) has characterised public and private sector recreational provision in urban areas in the 1980s and 1990s. Henry (1988) argued that the outcome will be determined by the political climate and philosophy prevailing in public sector environments, fluctuating between a limited role for the state characterised by right-wing ideology, to one based on principles of social equity and significant levels of public intervention influenced by principles of equality.

Indeed, Curry (2000) noted that the growth of community participation in outdoor recreation opportunities in urban areas resulted from threats posed by the freeing up of the planning system in the 1980s and 1990s, with the progressive loss of less formal open space. One of the main pressures on local authorities to sell vacant land for development saw a similar neglect of existing open spaces (Open Space Society 1992). The rise of partnerships with community groups in an era of declining municipal provision was reflected in the former Countryside Commission (now the Countryside Agency) initiative in 1996 to create 1,000 millennium greens by the year 2000. Although this ambitious target was subsequently modified to 250 greens, a stimulus was the competitively funded 50 per cent grant towards site acquisition and creation works (with 50 per cent to be generated from the local community). A Millennium Green (MG) could be located in or on the edge of a city, town, suburb, village or hamlet, and be up to 30 acres in size. The Countryside Agency received £10 million of Lottery Funding from the Millennium Commission and each green had to meet the following basic criteria:

- The site is to be held on trust as a permanent resource for the local community, normally through purchase or donation of the freehold.
- There is public support for the proposal, which also demonstrates that the Millennium Green is needed and that it will make a substantial contribution to the life of the community.
- Anyone may use any part of the land on foot, for informal enjoyment and play.
- Local people will be able to reach the Millennium Green safely and conveniently from their home.
- The community has viable and convincing proposals for the long-term management of the site.
- The Millennium Green could not happen without Millennium Commission funding and convincing proposals from the community (Countryside Agency 2000).

Priority was granted to proposals creating new areas of green space, and by late 1998 252 Site Preparation Grants had been awarded, of which 120 received full funding from partnerships. By 1999, 843 groups had made an initial application (Curry 2000). A comparison of the spatial distribution of Country Parks and MGs, both of which are the main post-war state initiatives to create national recreation sites, revealed an interesting pattern. The Country Parks were haphazard and sporadic in their distribution and the pattern of MGs is not dissimilar.

Many of the initiators of MGs were from the more affluent sections of society, and beneficiaries may be returning to politics of Victorian park founding observed by Maver (1998) in Glasgow. Here the politics of voluntary involvement and activity may simply reinforce patterns of inequality in recreational provision, reflecting political processes and other factors (e.g. human agency) shaping the landscape and pattern of leisure spaces.

Having briefly examined the evolution of urban recreational opportunities in Britain since the 1880s, it is pertinent to focus on one example which typifies the development processes in time and space, notably the evolution of parks and open space. This is considered in relation to one particular city in Britain: Leicester.

CASE STUDY: The evolution of parks and open space in Victorian Leicester

The development of open space in towns and cities in Britain traditionally evolved through the emergence of commons and walks prior to the nineteenth century, followed by private squares and greens for the wealthy classes. While towns and cities remained small in scale, the populations were able to enjoy recreation in the surrounding rural areas (Clark 1981). Urban industrial growth in the industrial revolution transformed the spatial form of towns and cities, as open land was consumed for economic and residential development. Two specific legislative changes during Victorian Britain contributed to the development of large parks, namely the Select Committee on Public Walks (1833) and the Health of Towns (1840), in a period of concern for the health and social well-being of the labouring classes. As Strachan and Bowler (1976) acknowledged, early park development was prompted by donations from industrialists and landowners, and four pieces of legislation enabled local authorities to purchase land for park development, notably:

1 the Towns Improvement Act (1847);
2 the Public Health Act (1848);
3 the Public Parks, Schools and Museums Act (1871);
4 the Public Improvements Act (1860).

While Edwardian and subsequent legislation enhanced park development, including the 1909 Housing and Town Planning Act and Town and Country Planning Acts of 1932 and 1947, the Victorian era was important in terms of the development of large-scale parks and open space.

PARK DEVELOPMENT IN VICTORIAN LEICESTER

Leicester expanded as a Victorian city where its population grew from 18,445 in 1801 to 64,829 in 1851 and 174,624 in 1891 and 211,579 in 1901. While Pritchard (1976) and Page (1988) examine the spatial development of the city (Figure 5.1), and constraints and opportunities for urban development, the city retained a medieval pattern of land development up until the 1800s. The poorly drained River Soar constrained development to the west of the river and also by owners of estates who refused to sell land for development. Most early urban growth in the 1800s occurred to the east and north-east. Prior to 1850, two open spaces existed: St Margaret's Pasture, a 13-acre (5.2 ha) meadow to the north of the urban area and at South Fields racecourse established in 1806 (Figure 5.2). In 1838, the city council provided 40 acres (16 ha) of land at South Fields at Welford to form the first public recreation ground, although only eight acres (3.2 ha) remains today. This was complemented by a series of private gardens and squares laid out from 1785 at the town council's request along New Walk, which today forms the sole surviving urban

Figure 5.1: The expansion of Leicester in the nineteenth century

pedestrian way in England (Strachan and Bowler 1976: 279).

With the growth in population by 1851, urban development occurred to the west of the Soar and the city council developed four parks and recreation grounds (Figure 5.2) between 1880 and 1900. Victoria Park (27.6 ha), established in 1882 on city-owned land, was made possible by the relocation of the city's racecourse from South Fields to Oadby. Abbey Meadows (22.8 ha) purchased in 1877, which fulfilled the purpose of draining a marsh area unsuitable for building, resulted in an ornamental park. The third park, aimed at providing open space access for the fast-growing suburb of Highfields, led to the development of 13.6 ha at Spinney Hill with a formal park in 1885. The fourth major park, established in the western suburbs, saw the development of the new parks estate (71.2 ha) in 1899. Each park was developed in the tradition of Victorian formal use with fountains, bandstands, gardens and open stretches of grass. In the case of Abbey Park, boating, river views, greenhouses and formal flower beds attracted users from across the city. To complement formal park provision, recreation grounds were also established in 1892, at Belgrave (4.8 ha) and Fosse Road (4.4 ha) in 1897.

POST-VICTORIA PARK DEVELOPMENT

In 1902, the Aylestone site (8 ha) was purchased as a recreation ground which was followed by a lull until the 1920s. During the period 1900 to 1920, small open spaces in the town centre led to the establishment of three ornamental gardens (Castle, Westcotes and St George's Church), two playgrounds and a small park at Westcotes. After 1920, further urban expansion led to the establishment of six multi-purpose parks with sports facilities, the largest at Braunstone (66.8 ha) in 1925 on the periphery of the city as a focal point of a large inter-war council estate. In contrast, other parks developed in the inter-war period were located in private housing areas such as Humberstone (8 ha) in 1928, Knighton (32.9 ha) in 1937 and Evington (17.6 ha) in 1949 in eastern and south suburbs. To balance the geographical distribution of provision, two large recreation grounds were opened at Rushey Fields (11.4 ha) in 1921 and Aylestone Playing Fields (33.2 ha) in 1946; a number of smaller open spaces were also developed on new council estates at Braunstone Park and Humberstone and a number of amenity open spaces amounting to 40.8 ha. In the post-war period, attention in

Leicester City Council shifted towards provision of small neighbourhood and local facilities as key features of new council estates. Only a limited number of larger open spaces were created on land unsuitable for residential development (e.g. Netherhall's 12.8 ha site in 1958 and Ingold's 5.6 ha site in 1970). Amenity open space was also incorporated into 13 council estates providing 105.6 ha of open space. A number of small village parks and playgrounds in old villages (e.g. Old Humberstone) contributed to the 27 parks and recreation grounds opened between 1950 and 1975. Since 1975, Leicester City Council has maintained an active role in enhancing open space and park provision to the point where in 1994, it maintained 1,200 ha of parkland and open space. This represented one-fifth of the total area of the city, an extremely high level of provision by European and North American standards.

Figure 5.3 shows the current distribution of urban parks in Leicester. By 2000, this had risen to 3000 ha of public open space, comprising country parks, formal parks, gardens, wetlands, allotments (see Thorpe (1970) and Crouch (1989a, b), for a discussion of allotments as a form of recreation) and woodlands. This is complemented by the provision of gardens with houses which perform an important recreational function (Halkett 1978) in the wider leisure context of the home (Glyptis and Chambers 1982). However, the dominant element is parkland. The City of Leicester Local Plan aim is to have public open space within 500 m of every home. Within new residential developments, the City Council require developers to provide 1.6 ha of open space per 1,000 people housed. As a result Leicester recreation space is an average of only 2.9 km from the city centre for parks/gardens, 3.6 km for recreation grounds, 3.5 km for playing fields, 3.7 km for sports grounds and 4.6 km for golf-courses, illustrating the role of low cost land for such facilities. Thus, as Williams (1995) argues, the level of recreational opportunity in modern-day Leicester increases with distance

METHODS OF ANALYSING URBAN RECREATION

Within the limited literature on urban recreation, the geographer has developed a number of concepts used within human geography and applied them in a recreational context to understand how the supply of recreational resources fits within the broader recreational context. For example, the use of the concept of a 'hierarchy of facilities' (Patmore 1983) highlights the catchment relating to the users' willingness, ability and knowledge of the facility or resource (Smith 1983a). What the hierarchy concept does is allow one to ascertain what type of catchment a recreational resource has at different spatial scales, taking into account users' willingness to travel to use them. Constraints of time and distance act as a friction on the potential use of resources. The outcome is an ordered pattern of resources which serve specific catchments depending on their characteristics, whereby the typical levels of provision may include:

- the neighbourhood level (a community centre);
- local areas (e.g. a recreation ground);
- regions within cities;
- a city-wide level (e.g. an art gallery).

An illustration of such a hierarchy for urban open space is illustrated in Table 5.1. The result is an ordered provision, each with its own set of users meeting the needs and aspirations of users which will vary in time and space. Within any urban context the challenge for recreational planning is to match the supply and demand for such resources.

Table 5.1: Hierarchical pattern of public open space

Type and main function	Approximate size and distance from home	Characteristics
Regional park Weekend and occasional visits by car or public transport	400 hectares 3.2–8 km	Large areas of natural heathland, common woodland and parkland. Primarily providing for informal recreation with some non-intensive active recreations. Car-parking at strategic locations.
Metropolitan park Weekend and occasional visits by car or public transport	60 hectares 3.2 km but more when park is larger than 60 hectares	Either natural heath, common, woods or formal parks providing for active and passive recreation. May contain playing fields, provided at least 40 hectares remain for other pursuits. Adequate car-parking.
District parks Weekend and occasional visits on foot, by cycle, car or short bus trip	20 hectares 1.2 km	Landscaped settings with a variety of natural features providing for a range of activities, including outdoor sports, children's play and informal pursuits. Some car-parking.
Local parks For pedestrian visitors	2 hectares 0.4 km	Providing for court games, children's play, sitting out, etc. in a landscaped environment. Playing fields if the park is large enough.
Small local parks Pedestrian visits especially by old people and children, particularly valuable in high-density areas	2 hectares 0.4 km	Gardens, sitting-out areas and children's playgrounds.
Linear open space Pedestrian visits	Variable Where feasible	Canal towpaths, footpaths, disused rail lines, etc., providing opportunities for informal recreation.

Source: Williams (1995)

One further technique which Patmore (1983) advocated for urban recreation is the resource inventory, whereby the range of existing resources is surveyed and mapped in relation to the catchment population. This population may then be compared to existing recommended levels of provision set by organisations for recreational provision. For example, the National Playing Fields Association in the UK recommended 2.4 ha of space per 1,000 population, 'excluding school playing fields except where available for general use, woodlands and commons, ornamental gardens, full-length golf courses and open spaces where the playing of games by the general public is either discouraged or not permitted' (Patmore 1983: 118).

Patmore (1983) outlined the range of urban recreational resources and facilities and provides a detailed spatial analysis of their occurrence and level of provision within the UK in terms of:

- capital intensive facilities (those with modest land requirements but a high capital cost – and those with a high capital cost where the land requirement is extensive);
- parks and open spaces;
- golf courses.

Williams (1995) adds an interesting array of other contexts including:

- the home;
- the street;
- gardens and allotments;
- playgrounds;
- other sporting contexts.

Table 5.2: Summary and explanation of key variables deployed within the recreation resource typology

Variable	Sub-categories	Explanation
Design	Purpose-built	Resource is designed for specific recreational uses
	Adapted	Resource has been converted to a recreational use from a previous function
	Annexed	Resource is not designed nor intended for recreational use, but will be used as such by some groups
Organisational	Formal	Resource has a structured design/layout and/or management
	Informal	Resource has no such structure
Function	Single	Resource has one intended recreational function
	Multi	Resource has a diversity of intended recreational functions
	Shared	Resource has a variety of functions of which recreation is one
Space/use characteristics	Extensive	Individual recreational functions range over large areas with generous use of space
	Intensive	Functions are concentrated with little or no unused/wasted space
Scale	Large	Over 10 acres in extent
	Medium	Between 2 and 10 acres in extent
	Small	Below 2 acres in extent
Catchment	City-wide	Resource draws use from across the urban area
	District	Resource draws use primarily from its district
	Local	Resource draws use primarily from its neighbourhood
Source of provision	Public	Funded/managed by government at either local or national level
	Private	Funded/managed by private individuals/groups for their own use
	Voluntary	Funded/managed by groups acting as co-operatives, clubs or societies, for the use of members

Source: Williams (1995)

To assist in understanding the spatial analysis of these resources and their interrelationship in an urban context, Williams (1995) developed a typology of urban recreational resources. To achieve this, and to incorporate the perception and use of the resource by urban users, he uses seven variables to construct a simple typology (Table 5.2). However, as Patmore (1983: 98) rightly argues, patterns of facility use are not related to location alone: effective access is not synonymous with convenience of location. As a result, barriers to urban recreational use include:

- *physical barriers* based on factors such as age, stage in the family life cycle (e.g. dependent children) and physical access;
- *financial barriers* include direct economic constraints due to costs of participation such as admission or membership costs (e.g. golf club fees) which may raise issues related to the public sector's role in provision;
- *social barriers* often reinforce the financial barriers whereby lower socio-economic groups do not participate due to financial barriers. Even when such barriers are removed, the image of participation still has cultural and social barriers (e.g. opera-going);
- *transport* can be a deterrent to urban recreational participation where access is limited by car ownership or where a short journey by bus may be difficult and costly in time for public transport users.

Using the key variables, which reflect basic resource attributes, Williams (1995) devised a practical typology of urban recreational resources as illustrated in Table 5.3. The challenge for recreational provision in any urban context is the planning and management undertaken to ensure that principles of equity and equal access are permitted where possible.

URBAN RECREATIONAL PLANNING

According to Patmore (1983: 117–18):

It may be possible to view [urban recreation] provision in a rational, hierarchical frame, to develop models for that precision that equate access and opportunity in a spatial pattern with mathematical precision, but reality

Table 5.3:   Basic typology of outdoor recreation facilities in urban areas

	Public facilities Formal	Informal	Private/voluntary facilities Formal	Informal	By particular groups
Large scale City-wide catchment	Major parks Major sports fields/stadia Municipal golf courses	Major commons Major urban woodland Major water space Urban country parks	Private golf courses		Major shopping centres Major transport centres, e.g. airports, stations
Medium scale District catchment	Recreation grounds Small parks	Urban greenways Minor urban woodland Minor water space Cycleways	Sports clubs, e.g. bowls or cricket		
Small scale local catchment	Children's play areas			Domestic gardens	Local streets/ pavements Waste ground Grass verges

Source: Williams (1995)

rarely gives an empty canvas where such a model can be developed in an unfettered form. Rather, reality is conditioned by the accident of historic legacy, by the fashions of spending from the public purse and by the commercial dictates of the public sector.

In geographical terms, urban recreational provision in town and cities grew in an *ad-hoc* fashion, and in many Western European contexts the task of city planners in the 1960s and 1970s was to tidy up the decades of incremental growth. In the UK, one solution used was to create 'leisure directorates' in city councils to amalgamate public recreation interests into one consolidated department. As Burtenshaw *et al.* (1991) argued, the consolidation of recreation activities in the public sector led to debates on the extent to which such activities should be a commercial or municipal enterprise. In fact, no one coherent philosophy has been developed, with individual cities deciding the precise range of activities which should be publicly funded.

Yet the 1980s and 1990s have seen the main changes in urban recreational provision and planning, as the following case study shows.

CASE STUDY: The management, planning and provision of urban parks in the 1990s. The example of Newham, East London

There has been a comparative neglect of urban parks by leisure and recreation researchers. Much of the research undertaken in the UK pre-dates the legislation and changes introduced in the late 1980s. Previous research has not examined the realities facing public sector leisure provision in the late 1980s and early 1990s although previous studies of urban parks have established their significance in metropolitan areas. Duffield and Walker (1983) produced a detailed review of research on urban parks which included a number of notable studies (e.g. Greater London Council 1968; Balmer 1973; Bowler and Strachan 1976). Previous studies of urban park use indicated that their catchments were localised and informal, fulfilling short-distance and short-stay recreational needs (Patmore 1983). Since the early 1980s, research on urban parks has focused on historical reconstructions of urban park development, user-based research (including behavioural and perception-type studies), research on park planning, access-related studies, and a growing interest in the application of management principles to parks.

The largest single area of research on urban parks has focused on the accessibility (Harrison 1983) and behavioural-type studies, exemplified by Burgess *et al.* (1988a, 1988b, 1988c) and those undertaken by Milton Keynes Development Corporation (1988, 1989). In addition, Gregory (1988) and Grahn (1991) examined the attitudes and psychological constructs of different socio-economic groups using parks and open spaces, while Grocott (1990) considered the role of public participation in the design and creation of community parks. There has also been a growing interest in the management issues associated with urban parks. One major development which has altered the philosophy and delivery of leisure services in local authorities concerns the management of services through a unified Leisure Services Department. These departments have created a new organisational structure for leisure service provision to accommodate the additional administrative functions created by the Local Government Act (1988). However, critics have argued that this new organisational structure may actually lead to fragmentation and poor integration in service provision, owing to the increased bureaucracy and centralised management of service provision by administrators rather than practitioners, who had daily contact with clients.

Accompanying organisational changes in leisure service provision since 1988 is a new ethos of service quality and quality assurance. This has permeated the delivery of public services. Barber (1991) examined the significance of management plans of parks and the role of local accountability, identifying individual park managers as the most effective personnel to ensure that the delivery of park-based services contributed to the quality of life in the local area. However, being responsive to the local needs has an economic cost and this may not always be compatible with the pursuit of efficiency in service provision. Morgan (1991) acknowledged the growing importance of consumer orientation in the planning and management process for parks and open spaces, to ensure community needs and desires were adequately considered. The increased use of attitude surveys and monitoring of urban park planning and management by local authorities is a direct response to the new ethos pervading public service provision. Yet research monitoring has a significant resource implication at a time of public sector restrictions on local government expenditure. The growing interest in urban park management is reflected in Welch's (1991) survey which documents many of the issues facing local authorities in the 1990s including park safety, CCT, park-related legislation, recreation management and risk management. Against this background, attention now turns to London in terms of open space provision and the London Borough of Newham as a context in which to understand the role of spatial analysis.

URBAN PARK PROVISION IN LONDON

Research on recreation and leisure in London has hitherto attracted little interest at a city-wide level following the abolition of the Greater London Council (GLC) in 1986, which had included leisure and recreation in its strategic planning function. Since 1986 each London borough's Unitary Development Plan is the framework for the formulation of policies to guide the provision of parks and open spaces. Leisure and recreation still remain a neglected aspect of London's diverse economic, social and cultural activities. Major studies of London's urban geography and expanding service sector (e.g. Hoggart and Green 1991) fail to acknowledge the significance of leisure service provision, although Bennett (1991: 212–13) did examine the London boroughs' statutory responsibility for leisure and recreation provision. The scale and nature of open space provision in London was set out in the Greater London Development Plan (Greater London Council 1968). Table 5.1 outlines the type of hierarchy of parks and open space provision envisaged in the late 1980s within the revised Greater London Development Plan.

Provision was based on a hierarchical principle, with different parks fulfilling various functions according to their size and distance from the users' homes. The concept of variety in park supply was to be achieved by the diversity of functions offered by parks in the capital, emphasising the social principle that parks of equal status were to be accessible to all sections of London's population. According to Burgess et al. (1988a), research in Greenwich questioned the suitability of a hierarchical system of park provision at the local area level, arguing that local communities did not recognise parks in terms of the differing functions that the GLC park hierarchy assigned to them. They claimed that most people in their survey felt that open spaces closest to their home failed to meet their leisure needs. This is a considerable problem for local authority leisure service departments, when the scale of public expenditure on open space and parks provision is examined on a London-wide scale. The extent to which financial resources are meeting local recreational needs is an important issue in view of the prioritisation of open space and park budgets of different local authorities across the capital.

According to the Chartered Institute of Public Finance and Accountancy (1990) in 1990 to

1991, local authority leisure expenditure in London amounted to almost £66 million gross on open space and park provision from a total leisure budget of £106 million. The scale and distribution of expenditure highlights the overriding importance and priority attached by local authorities to open spaces and park provision. Furthermore, in 1990 to 1991, £48 million of the total £66 million expenditure by London's local authorities on open space and park provision was spent on hired or contracted-out services administered through CCT procedures (Audit Commission 1993). Clearly urban parks form a publicly funded service, since only £6.5 million of the total expenditure on open space and park provision in London was generated as income. In view of the scale of public expenditure on open spaces and parks, it is appropriate to consider the extent to which the leisure needs of London's population are fulfilled beyond the amenity value of such resources. There is increasing concern by quangos, such as the Audit Commission, on cost-effective ways of delivering public services, and local authority leisure service departments are no exception to this. Within this context, it is pertinent to consider the extent to which the delivery of park-based services is responsive to local needs in one area of London: the London Borough of Newham.

THE LONDON BOROUGH OF NEWHAM

Leisure provision and urban parks

Newham is an east London borough with a population of 212,170 (1991). As one of the larger London boroughs, covering 3,637 ha, it comprises a number of distinct communities. The borough is a diverse multiracial area (Table 5.4) with a variety of economic and social contrasts, including part of London Docklands in the south, and pockets of deprivation and unemployment

elsewhere (Hoggart and Green 1991). In many respects, Newham has a range of inner-city characteristics with an outer London location.

A large number of the borough's main open spaces and parks were established in the Victorian and Edwardian period, with subsequent additions in the inter-war and post-war periods. The existing provision of open space and parks comprises 180 ha of parks and open space, some 4.9 per cent of the total area of the borough.

Newham Council performs a number of roles in terms of leisure provision, with responsibility based in the Leisure Services Department established in 1984. Newham's Leisure Development Strategy (1990–94) sets out the Council's objectives for leisure in the 1990s, which are focused on partnership schemes to enhance leisure opportunities for both residents and visitors to Newham. To guide the development and implementation of the Leisure Development Strategy, a Leisure Services Development Plan (1990–94) has also been produced. This is to ensure that the main objectives and tasks associated with the delivery of leisure services by different units within the Leisure Services Department can be provided according to the following principles: equal opportunity, service quality, customer choice and value for money.

Table 5.4: Ethnic origins of Newham's population

	%
UK White	57.7
Black Caribbean	7.2
Black African	5.6
Black Other	1.6
Indian	13.0
Pakistani	5.9
Bangladeshi	3.7
Chinese	0.8
Other groups	4.4
Total population in 1991	212,170

Source: OPCS (1992)

identified in the Leisure Services Development Plan. The financial resource implications of the Park Client Unit's progress towards key objectives are identified in the Leisure Services Development Plan. The Unit also has to recognise the implications of other council policies and initiatives such as *Newham's Policy for the Environment: A Consultation Document* (Newham Borough Council 1991a) which affects open space and park provision, since it aims to:

> preserve, develop and maintain a greener environment for Newham making it a more attractive, safer and cleaner place to live and work in. Parks, open spaces and play areas improve the local environment and provide people with opportunities for exercise, community and cultural activities, sport, quiet relaxation in natural surroundings. The protection of trees and other vegetation contributes to (*sic*) quality of the local environment and is an essential contribution to the reduction of global warming.
> (London Borough of Newham 1991a: 41)

In addition, the Park Client Unit must be aware of other Leisure Service Department policies such as the new ethos of customer care and satisfaction to ensure that 'everyone in Newham wants to be a customer of Leisure Services, and that every customer is a satisfied customer' (Newham Borough Council 1991b: 9). However, for the Park Client Unit to translate such an objective into reality for leisure provision at the local area level required a fundamental reassessment of the most appropriate organisational structure to deliver leisure services to local communities. One of the key functions for the Park Client Unit is to undertake research to identify areas for service development and to ensure quality service provision is delivered in practice at the local level, as opposed to remaining an element of a broad leisure strategy. For this reason, the Park Client Unit explored their information needs prior to assessing and monitoring consumer satisfaction in the delivery of park services. It is within this context that a research project was undertaken to establish a source of systematically derived data on park use and satisfaction in the borough.

The absence of existing information of park use in the borough reflects the current pressures facing local authorities who often lack adequate resources to deal with the expanding functions of local government. Therefore, the research reported here identifies areas of user concern and satisfaction within a number of park environments, to establish a baseline for further monitoring and research on parks and user groups.

NEWHAM URBAN PARK USER SURVEY

Methodology

The primary objective of the research for Newham's Park Client Unit was to examine a range of themes related to park use including client type, patterns of weekly, seasonal and annual use, attitudes towards amenity value, and management issues relating to the maintenance and development of the parks. One key task was to compile a questionnaire survey which was suitably sensitive to incorporate the beliefs and attitudes of park users across the borough. To achieve this objective, six parks were selected (Figure 5.4a) so that a number of larger urban parks and smaller parks and recreation grounds were included in the review.

The survey method, based on a detailed questionnaire, was designed to interview users within the recreational environment in which they felt at ease, by conducting a random sample of users within the park rather than to deter users with a closely monitored entry/exit survey.

A total of 463 interviews were conducted within the parks on a Saturday and Tuesday in late March 1992. The majority of interviews lasted between 15 and 40 minutes and were undertaken between 09.00 and 17.00 hours, achieving a reasonable distribution of responses despite the variable weather conditions.

Results: key findings and discussion

Of the 463 people interviewed, the sample was drawn from Central Park (29.7 per cent), Plashet Park (27 per cent), New Beckton Park (2.3 per cent), Little Ilford Park (11.8 per cent), West Ham Lane Recreation Ground (11.8 per cent) and West Ham Memorial Ground (13 per cent). The parks selected yielded a useful cross-section of opinions on a weekday and at a weekend, with equal numbers of male and female respondents drawn from a variety of age groups (Table 5.6). The largest single group of users (23.5 per cent) were aged 26 to 35 years, following by the 17 to 25 age group (18 per cent) and over 65 years (16 per cent) with approximately 36 per cent aged 36 to 65 years.

The ethnic origins of the respondents revealed a particular bias towards people of UK origin (71 per cent) followed by those of Afro-Caribbean origin (11 per cent) and people of Asian origin (8.5 per cent). A small number of respondents were of Irish descent (2.5 per cent). Only 1.5 per cent of respondents were from other ethnic groups while a small number of people did not respond to this question (5.5 per cent). The sample was reasonably representative of the UK-born and Afro-Caribbean population. It was the Asian population who were under-represented. One possible explanation for the low number of Asian users in the sample was the underlying racial tension within the borough in the weeks preceding the survey, a feature noted by Burgess *et al.* (1988a) in another London borough, where racial harassment constrained park use among users of Asian descent.

The main user groups were young mothers with children playing in a park, older age groups and young people aged 16 to 21 years. A significant number of users visited a park on a daily basis in the spring (56 per cent) and during the summer (50 per cent). This indicates that there were a regular group of users who made extensive use of the parks. The length of time spent in a park each day by 54 per cent of users was between 15 minutes and one hour. Most users visited the park alone (66 per cent), often meeting other people within the park. The majority of users also visited urban parks within the borough on a regular basis, and a minority (7 per cent) also made extensive use of local recreation grounds. The reasons mentioned for visiting the parks among 35 per cent of users were: to go for a walk; to enjoy the flowers and scenery; to walk the dog; and to play with their children. A significant number of respondents chose to visit a park because of its facilities and location. The parks sampled surveyed a distinct range of communities across the borough. For example, 91 per cent of users walked to the park, being located within five to ten minutes from their home. This is a feature noted in other urban park surveys (Patmore 1983). The majority of parks were located within easy access of the main centres of population in the borough. The postcode of the respondent indicated that their home address displayed a clear geographical bias towards the two largest parks within East Ham (Plashet and Central Park), which serve the major centres of population within the borough. This confirmed that the overwhelming pattern of use was local in relation to that catchment area.

Table 5.7 indicates that the recreational activities undertaken by the users reveal a bias towards passive leisure pursuits (walking the

Table 5.6: Age group of respondents

	Male	Female
16 years old	1	0
17–25	45	37
26–35	48	61
36–45	33	34
46–55	23	30
56–65	27	28
Over 65	43	30
Total	220	220

No response = 23

Table 5.7: Recreational activities of park users

	Number	Per cent
Walking the dog	131	29.0
Taking a short cut	119	26.0
Walking through	118	25.5
Playing with children	29	6.3
Playing sport/jogging	26	5.7
Sitting down	11	2.4
Meeting people	11	2.4
Other reasons	8	1.8
No response	10	2.2
Total	463	*

Note
* Total does not equal 100 owing to rounding error

dog, going for a walk and taking a short cut), compared to only 5.7 per cent of users who visited the park for active pursuits (sport or jogging). This illustrates one of the real functions of the parks: passive recreation, particularly in the older parks established in the late Victorian and Edwardian period. The establishment of Central and Plashet Park was primarily for walking and relaxation, as the design principles embodied in their layout reinforce this type of use. Therefore, other active recreational pursuits, such as sports, cannot easily be integrated within the existing layout.

Those parks developed in Newham after 1945 (for example, New Beckton Park) overcome some of these potential constraints by developing innovative layouts to provide a clear zoning of uses. Path layouts do not constrain the integration of passive and active pursuits which sometimes cause conflict in the older parks. Therefore, the parks surveyed contained a variety of layouts, resources and facilities for both passive and, to a lesser degree, active recreation. Recreation grounds tended to provide more opportunities for sport and games.

Most users did not explicitly recognise the problems associated with the layout of specific parks, tending to emphasise other factors such

as personal constraints. The most frequently mentioned reason (36 per cent) was the limited amount of time available to visit the park, indicating the extent to which leisure activities were accommodated within respondents' daily activities. Personal and child safety were also identified as potential constraints by only 8 per cent of users, although this may conceal the incidence of low usage rates by Asian groups due to the problem of perceived racial threats and harassment. Interestingly, 29 per cent of users claimed that there were no factors constraining their use.

IMPLICATIONS FOR MANAGING URBAN PARKS AND LOCAL LEISURE PROVISION

Urban parks perform an important social role, with the potential to provide an accessible leisure resource for metropolitan populations regardless of gender, race, age and disability. As a non-profit-making leisure resource, parks provide opportunities for planned and spontaneous leisure pursuits, being largely oriented towards passive rather than active forms of recreation. The results from the questionnaire survey have important implications for the management, development, planning and promotion of urban parks in Newham in terms of their ability to meet local leisure needs. The survey highlighted a number of potential problems related to the internal management process within Newham Council's Leisure Services Department and the external delivery of park services. The internal management of park services by the Park Client Unit would appear to be isolated from the central decision-making process within the Leisure Services Department, which in turn is also distant from the actual delivery of services. While the Park Client Unit is responsible for the day-to-day management of the parks and open spaces in Newham, there is little interaction between the users and providers of park services. To a certain extent this is a function of new management practices such as CCT, which devolve maintenance to contractors and remove opportunities for staff–user interaction and local park-based management. By reducing the Direct Service Organisation (DSO) input to park maintenance and management (see Welch 1991), Newham's urban parks are centrally planned and unable easily to incorporate the views and feelings of the users through a local park plan. This was one criticism which appeared in the questionnaire survey since different park users emphasised the importance of making improvements to parks in their locality. Within Newham there is no coherent and leisure-specific approach to park provision, with the Park Client Unit pulled in different directions by council policies embodied in the Leisure Development Strategy (1990–94), the borough's Unitary Development Plan and the Newham Policy for the Environment. Thus the Park Client Unit is responsible for the immediate management issues, although strategic planning and development functions are undertaken centrally. In practice there is no appropriate framework for local leisure planning since no specific management plans exist for individual parks. Therefore, park provision and management tends to accord with general principles of provision rather than innovative, locally determined plans (see Grocott 1990).

In terms of maintenance, the survey intimated that CCT procedures had reduced the quality and knowledge of staff employed on maintenance contracts resulting in a de-skilling process to achieve cost savings. Many respondents also felt that staffing levels were now at a critical level and this may actually inhibit their use of parks. If the experience in Newham is typical of other London boroughs, maintenance consumes a large proportion of the budget with capital expenditure on facility development dealt with through the borough's leisure development plan. Therefore, alterations to the park environment (for instance, safe play surfaces for children) have to be dealt with from central budgets rather then devolved budgets for local park managers to deploy in whatever way they feel necessary to meet local leisure needs. Although Newham Council is aware of these issues through different policies (see Table 5.5), progress is piecemeal and not determined according to expressed demand in local parks, owing to the existing lack of research of park use and user satisfaction.

Significant progress towards improving the park environment and diversity of leisure uses could be achieved by enhancing the interpretation of wildlife, horticulture, educational uses and the development of organised children's events. Users do not perceive parks as a static recreational resource only for passive use: they recognised multiple use and some of the conflicts which arise from a lack of activity-based zoning within specific parks. In many cases, users requested additional leisure facilities within local parks to facilitate active leisure pursuits. The most contentious issue within the survey was the 'dog-management problem'. It is evident that park use by dog owners should be identified as a discrete activity although it cannot easily be integrated within the existing layout of parks. Therefore, there need to be designated areas for dog walking which do not conflict with other uses. This will inevitably require a great deal of education of park users and changes in layout. The existing lack of dog-management measures appears to erode the amenity value of many parks and actually deters some parents from taking children to open spaces.

A greater variety of park events also need to be introduced to enhance the level of use and overcome inertia among non-park users. Promotion of the parks to provide leisure opportunities amongst non-users (for instance, ethnic minorities) is one area where action needs to be taken in view of the limited awareness of the council's *Parks for People* leaflet. Yet the extent to which these improvements may be implemented on a park-by-park basis ultimately depends on the

Leisure Service Department's prioritisation of capital spending on this leisure resource. The existing plans by the Park Client Unit are for piecemeal changes to the structure and layout of individual parks as funds become available. Yet given the significance of urban parks in the leisure lifestyles of urban populations, there seems to be some evidence to support a strategy of capital investment in existing parks to implement some of these changes, rather than the acquisition of additional open spaces which will inevitably place pressure on the distribution of maintenance budgets.

Urban parks are clearly an important and accessible local resource, which need to be planned and managed at the local level in relation to the individual park catchments and their users. This has major resource implications, since it requires a revaluation of how park-based leisure services are planned and delivered, as well as the most appropriate organisational structure to manage these public resources. Although parks are a non-commercial leisure resource, their development and management consume a significant proportion of the total leisure budget of local authorities. In the existing climate of financial restrictions on local authority spending, one has to consider whether the administration, organisation and management should be devolved to individual park managers. The management structure and organisation of Newham's Leisure Services Department has meant that service provision is somewhat distant from the local needs of different client groups. Even though individual units (for example, the Park Client Unit) fulfil the role of an intermediary in the provision, delivery and management of park-based services, the power base and allocation of resources remain under central control. Therefore, expenditure on urban parks is carefully monitored through a central financial accounting system to ensure maintenance is carried out within strict financial guidelines.

The situation in Newham appears to follow the organisation and management structure developed for leisure service provision in other metropolitan local authorities with large areas of open space and urban parks. Urban park provision by these public sector organisations is still based on traditional service delivery practices, being supply led rather than demand led. The impact of CCT has created a culture of financial management in the maintenance and management of these resources as political ideology has altered the framework for local leisure policy (Bramham and Henry 1985).

In a demand-led environment, the emphasis is on the efficient allocation and prioritisation of scarce public resources to meet a limited range of leisure needs, with user-pay philosophy affecting the provision of public services not deemed to be essential. These changes may be seen in Newham's Leisure Services Department and the Park Client Unit's approach to leisure provision, where it now has procedures in place for CCT and day-to-day management issues, and attention is now focusing on assessing user perceptions. Yet the full potential of urban parks is not being realised within the context of the rapid expansion of local authority leisure service departments (Veal and Travis 1979), if Newham's experience is representative of other localities. The major challenge facing local authority providers is to achieve financial savings in maintenance contracts for parks while devolving the management, planning and future development of the park infrastructure to a community-based form of planning which is adequately resourced and responsive to local needs.

Although parks are not as fashionable as capital-intensive leisure facilities, they are operated on a non-commercial basis and offer access to the entire population. Therefore, their value within the urban environment should be given greater recognition as they contribute to the wider public good of metropolitan populations compared with more specialised and targeted sport and leisure facilities. It is clear that further research is needed to establish how local leisure needs may be met in terms of park provision, so that park management plans focus attention on local areas and communities. Urban parks and open spaces are an important sustainable leisure resource which can accommodate multiple uses, being accessible to local communities which may not have access to countryside areas. They are an integral feature of the urban landscape and assume an important part of the daily lives of local communities.

SUMMARY POINTS

• The provision of open space and recreational opportunities in Newham is severely con-

strained by the availability of open space.
• The London Borough of Newham has practised open space provision as a priority in areas that are under-supplied.
• Political changes in the philosophy of urban space management have led to new ideologies in the planning, evaluation and development of parks for local people.
• Surveys of user needs provide invaluable data for planners to match park and open space provision to local needs.
• Similar issues of safety, usage by specific groups and the reasons for visiting parks emerge that compare with other national and international studies of urban parks.

This case study of urban parks integrates many of the concepts and ideas already developed in this chapter, concluding with a discussion on management and planning philosophy and the implementation of geographical principles.

URBAN TOURISM

The second part of this chapter examines the concept of urban tourism, reviewing the principal

Plate 5.1: Margate, Kent, *c.* 2000. A Victorian seaside resort which has passed through a series of stages of development and is now mainly a day-trip destination.

contributions towards its recognition as a tourism phenomenon worthy of study, and it also emphasises the scope and range of environments classified as urban destinations together with some of the approaches towards its analysis. It then considers a framework for the analysis of the tourist's experience of urban tourism which is followed by a discussion of key aspects of urban tourist behaviour: where do urban tourists go in urban areas, what activities do they undertake, how do they perceive these places and learn about the spatial attributes of the locality, and how is this reflected in their patterns of behaviour? Having reviewed these features, the chapter concludes with a discussion of service quality issues for urban tourism.

UNDERSTANDING THE NEGLECT OF URBAN TOURISM BY RESEARCHERS

Ashworth's (1989) seminal study of urban tourism acknowledges that a double neglect has occurred. Those interested in the study of tourism 'have tended to neglect the urban context in which much of it is set, while those interested in urban studies . . . have been equally neglectful of the importance of the tourist function of cities' (Ashworth 1989:

33). While more recent tourism textbooks (e.g. Shaw and Williams 1994) have expanded upon earlier syntheses of urban tourism research in a spatial context (e.g. D.G. Pearce 1987a), it still remains a comparatively unresearched area despite the growing interest in the relationship between urban regeneration and tourism (see Page (2000) and Page and Hall (2002) for a detailed review of the relationship of tourism and urban regeneration). The problem is also reiterated in a number of studies as one explanation of the neglect of urban tourism (see Vetter 1985; Page and Sinclair 1989). Despite this problem, which is more a function of perceived rather than real difficulties in understanding urban tourism phenomena, a range of studies now provide evidence of a growing body of literature on the topic (see Vetter 1985; Ashworth 1989, 1992a,b; Ashworth and Tunbridge 1990; Page 1995a, b, 2000; Law 1996; Murphy 1997; D.G. Pearce 1998, 1999). However, even though more publications are now appearing in the academic literature, it does not imply that urban tourism is recognised as a distinct and notable area of research in tourism studies. This is due to the tendency for urban tourism research to be based on descriptive and empirical case studies which do not contribute to a greater theoretical or methodological understanding of urban tourism. In fact, such an approach is perpetuated by certain disciplines which contribute to the study of tourism, where the case study method of approach does little more than describe the situation in each instance and fails to relate the case to wider issues to derive generalisations and to test hypotheses and assumptions within the academic literature. In this respect, the limited understanding is a function of the lack of methodological sophistication in tourism research noted in recent critiques of the subject (e.g. Pearce and Butler 1993).

According to Ashworth (1992a), urban tourism has not emerged as a distinct research focus: research is focused on tourism in cities and embodies Law's (1996) argument that urban tourism only exists in a recognisable form in large cities. This strange paradox may be explained by the failure by planners, commercial interest and residents to recognise tourism as one of the main economic rationales for cities. Tourism is often seen as an adjunct or necessary evil to generate additional revenue, while the main economic activities of the locality are not perceived as tourism related. Such negative views of urban tourism have meant that the public and private sectors have used the temporary, seasonal and ephemeral nature of tourism to neglect serious research on this theme. Consequently, a vicious circle exists: the absence of public and private sector research makes access to research data difficult, and the large-scale funding for primary data collection using social survey techniques, necessary to break the vicious circle, is rarely available. The absence of large-scale funding for urban tourism research reflects the prevailing consensus in the 1980s that such studies were unnecessary. However, with the pressure posed by tourists in many European tourist cities in the 1990s (e.g. Canterbury, London, York, Venice and Florence), this perception is changing now that the public and private sectors are belatedly acknowledging the necessity of visitor management (see English Tourist Board/Employment Department (1991), Gilbert and Clark (1997), Meethan (1997), and Snaith and Haley (1999) for a discussion of this issue) as a mechanism to enhance, manage and improve the tourist's experience of towns and places to visit. Nevertheless, as Ashworth (1992a: 5) argues: 'Urban tourism requires the development of a coherent body of theories, concepts, techniques and methods of analysis which allow comparable studies to contribute towards some common goal of understanding of either the particular role of cities within tourism or the place of tourism within the form and function of cities'. One way of assessing progress towards these objectives is to review the main approaches developed within the tourism literature.

APPROACHES TO URBAN TOURISM: GEOGRAPHICAL ANALYSIS

To understand how research on urban tourism has developed distinctive approaches and methodologies, one needs to recognise why tourists seek urban tourism experiences. Shaw and Williams (1994) argue that urban areas offer geographical concentration of facilities and attractions that are conveniently located to meet both visitor and resident needs alike. But the diversity and variety among urban tourist destinations has led researchers to examine the extent to which they display unique and similar features. Shaw and Williams (1994) identify three approaches:

1 the diversity of urban areas means that their size, function, location and history contribute to their uniqueness;
2 towns and cities are multi-functional areas, meaning that they simultaneously provide various functions for different groups of users;
3 the tourist functions of towns and cities are rarely produced or consumed solely by tourists, given the variety of user groups in urban areas.

Ashworth (1992a) conceptualises urban tourism by identifying three approaches towards its analysis, where researchers have focused on:

1 the supply of tourism facilities in urban areas, involving inventories (e.g. the spatial distribution of accommodation, entertainment complexes and tourist-related services), where urban ecological models have been used. In addition, the facility approach has been used to identify the tourism product offered by destinations;
2 the demand generated by urban tourists, to examine how many people visit urban areas, why they choose to visit and their patterns of behaviour, perception and expectations in relation to their visit;
3 perspectives of urban tourism policy, where the public sector (e.g. planners) and private sector agencies have undertaken or commissioned research to investigate specific issues related to their own interests in urban tourism.

More recently, attempts to interpret urban tourism theoretically have been developed by Mullins (1991) and Roche (1992). While these

Plate 5.2: A Cambridge college which is a major draw for tourist viewing.

studies do not have a direct bearing on attempts to influence or affect the tourist experience of towns and cities, their importance should not be neglected in wider reviews of urban tourism: they offer explanations of the sudden desire of many towns and cities with a declining industrial base to look towards service sector activities such as tourism. Both studies examine urban tourism in the context of changes in post-industrial society and the relationship with structural changes in the mode of capitalist production. In other words, both studies question the types of process now shaping the operation and development of tourism in post-industrial cities, and the implications for public sector tourism and leisure policy. One outcome of such research is that it highlights the role of the state, especially local government, in seeking to develop service industries based on tourism and leisure production and consumption in urban areas, as a response to the restructuring of capitalism which has often led to employment loss in the locality. It also illustrates the significance of place-marketing in urban tourism promotion (Ashworth and Voogd 1990a, b; Gold and Ward 1994; Gold and Gold 1995; Hall 1997b) as destinations seek to reinvent and redefine themselves in the market for cultural and heritage tourism (Houinen 1995; Judd 1995; Bramwell and Rawding 1996; Chang et al. 1996; Schofield 1996; Dahles 1998; Hall and McArthur 1998).

Mullins' (1991) concept of tourism urbanisation is also useful as it assists in developing the following typology of urban tourist destinations:

- capital cities;
- metropolitan centres, walled historic cities and small fortress cities;
- large historic cities;
- inner-city areas;
- revitalised waterfront areas;
- industrial cities;
- seaside resorts and winter sport resorts;
- purpose-built integrated tourist resorts;
- tourist-entertainment complexes;
- specialised tourist service centres;
- cultural/art cities.

(After Page 1995b: 17)

This typology illustrates the diversity of destinations which provide an urban context for tourist visits, and highlights the problem of deriving generalisations from individual case studies without a suitable conceptual framework. For this reason, it is pertinent to focus on the concept of the 'tourist experience of urban tourism' as a framework to assess some as the experiential aspects of this phenomenon.

THE TOURIST EXPERIENCE OF URBAN TOURISM

There is a growing literature on tourist satisfaction (e.g. Ryan 1995), and what constitutes the experiential aspects of a tourist visit to a locality. In the context of urban tourism, the innovative research by Graefe and Vaske (1987) offers a number of important insights as well as a useful framework. Graefe and Vaske (1987) acknowledge that the 'tourist experience' is a useful term to identify the experience of an individual which may

be affected 'by individual, environmental, situational and personality-related factors as well as the degree of communication with other people. It is the outcome which researchers and the tourism industry constantly evaluate to establish if the actual experience met the tourist's expectations' (Page 1995a: 24). Operationalising such a concept may prove difficult in view of the complex array of factors which may affect the visitor experience (Figure 5.5). For example, where levels of overcrowding occur at major tourist sites (e.g. Canterbury, Venice, St Paul's Cathedral, London and the Tower of London), this can have a negative effect on visitors who have a low tolerance threshold for overcrowding at major tourist sites. Yet conversely, other visitors may be less affected by use levels thereby illustrating the problem within tourism motivation research – predicting tourists' behaviour and their responses to particular situations. In fact Graefe and Vaske (1987: 394) argue that 'the effects of increasing use levels on the recreation/tourist experience can be explained only partially . . . as a function of use level'. Therefore, the individual tourist's ability to tolerate the behaviour of other people, level of use, the social situation and the context of the activity are all important determinants of the actual outcome. Thus, evaluating the quality of the tourist experience is a complex process which may require careful consideration of the factors motivating a visit (i.e. how tourists' perception of urban areas makes them predisposed to visit particular places), their actual patterns of activity and the extent to which their expectations associated with their perceptions are matched in reality (Page 1995a: 25). For this reason, attention now turns to some of the experiential aspects of urban tourists' visits and the significance of behavioural issues influencing visitor satisfaction. In view of the diversity of tourists visiting urban areas, it is useful to define the market for urban tourism.

- the weather conditions at the time of visit
- the standard and quality of accommodation available
- the cleanliness and upkeep of the city
- the city's aesthetic value (i.e. its setting and beauty)
- the tourists' personal safety from crime
- accessibility of attractions and points of interest in the city
- the extent to which local people welcome visitors in a warm manner
- the ability of tourism employees to speak foreign languages
- the range of cultural and artistic amenities
- the ambience of the city environment as a place to walk around
- the level of crowding and congestion
- the range of nightlife and entertainment available
- the range of restaurants and eating establishments in the city
- the pleasurability of leisure shopping
- the price levels of goods and services in the city
- the level of helpfulness among local people
- the adequacy of emergency medical care

Figure 5.5: Factors to consider in evaluating the urban tourism experience
Source: Modified from Haywood and Muller (1988)

INSIGHT: Tourism in capital cities

Capital cities represent a special case of urban tourism. As Canada's National Capital Commission (NCC) observed, 'The combination of political, cultural, symbolic and administrative functions is unique to national capitals' (NCC 2000b: 9). The capital functions as 'the political centre and symbolic heart of the country. It is the site of crucial political decision-making, yet it is also a setting for the nation's culture and history, where the past is highlighted, the present displayed and the future imagined.' Although such statements are obviously significant in political and cultural terms the wider significance of capital city status for tourism has been grossly under-researched and, perhaps, under-appreciated (Taylor *et al.* 1993; Hall 2000). Nevertheless, capital status is important. As capitals provide an administrative and political base of government

operations there will therefore be spin-off effects for business travel in terms of both those who work in the capital and those who are seeking to lobby government or influence decisions. In addition to business-related travel, capital cities are also significant for tourism because of their cultural, heritage and symbolic roles. They are frequently home to some of the major national cultural institutions while also tending to have a significant wider role in the portrayal, preservation and promotion of national heritage and which showcase national culture (Therborn 1996). Such a concentration of arts and cultural institutions will therefore have implications for the travel and activity behaviour of culturally interested tourists as well as contributing to the image of a city as a whole. If capital status is lost it can have a significant affect on visitor numbers, as in the case of the transfer of the German national capital from Bonn to Berlin after the reunification of Germany where Berlin has witnessed a dramatic increase in overnight stays and Bonn a decline.

The use of the notion of a capital in terms of branding and culture is significant for tourism both in terms of place promotion and attracting high-yielding cultural tourists. Indeed, given the growth of place marketing in an increasingly competitive global economic environment such a development is logical in terms of branding places and place competition. However, for the purpose of this discussion the notion of a capital is related primarily to political, administrative and symbolic functions which operate at a national or provincial level. Indeed, as Dubé and Gordon (2000: 6) observed, 'Planning for cities that include a seat of government often involves political and symbolic concerns that are different from those of other urban areas'. The historical development of capital cities may also provide them with a significant transport gateway or hub function (e.g. London and Paris).

A good example of the relationship between capital city status and tourism is Ottawa in Canada, declared capital of the new Canadian Confederation in 1867. Tourism now contributes well over a billion Canadian dollars to the Ottawa region economy and makes a substantial contribution to employment as well as government taxes. Ottawa is an excellent example of Gottmann's (1983) observation that 'capital cities often act as hinges between different regions of a country'. Ottawa lies at the border between French- and English-speaking Canada, a history of interaction between labour and capital, as well as being at a location where different ecological regions also coincide (NCC 1999). There are a number of primary benefits of visiting Ottawa that are unique to a capital city. In a survey conducted in 1991 85 per cent of respondents agreed that it was a good way for young people to learn about their country, while the oppor-

tunity to learn about Canada was cited as important by 57 per cent of respondents (NCC 1991). Indeed, a unique characteristic that is shared among all visitors to Ottawa-Hull is 'the desire to visit national cultural institutions and physical landmarks that symbolize and reflect all of Canada' (NCC 1991: v). According to the NCC (1999: 63): 'The function of a national cultural institution (e.g., museum) is to display, protect and explain past, present and future national phenomena and human achievements. National cultural institutions are also used to communicate social, cultural, political, scientific, technical, or other knowledge through various media.'

The main avenue for Canadian government actions to reinforce the role of Ottawa's capital city status is the National Capital Commission (NCC), which has the mission 'To create pride and unity through Canada's Capital Region' (NCC 2000a: 5). Established in 1959, the NCC is a Crown corporation governed by a national board of directors (the Commission) and reports to the Canadian Parliament through the Minister of Canadian Heritage.

Although the NCC is clearly not primarily a tourist organisation its actions and policies over the years have created both substantial tourism resources for the region in the form of attractions as well as imaging the city through its promotional and marketing campaigns. The significance of the NCC for tourism cannot be overstated. As Tunbridge (1998: 95) observed,

> In an unmanaged state Ottawa's tourism resource would be modest: a physical environment recreationally attractive, but unexceptional in Canada; a historic ambience with distinctive elements, but weak by international standards; and an overall cultural environment which was in the 1960s the butt of jests . . . and a non-place to most further afield.

According to the NCC it 'exists to promote national pride through the creation of a great capital for an increasingly diverse body of Canadians' (2000a: 8). A key focus of achieving its strategic goals since the early 1990s has been the theme of renewal and the development of core area vision for the National Capital Region (NCR). In order to achieve its goals it has 'fostered the re-development of the By Ward Market, where a mix of commercial and residential uses has restored life and preserved the character of a unique heritage neighbourhood' and is looking to regenerate the Sparks Street mall area 'only a block from Parliament Hill. . . . It forms the interface of the "civic" and "capital" realms. It is an expression of Ottawa and, as such, of Canada. The revitalization of Sparks Street is therefore an important symbol of Canada's commitment to a vibrant future that is solidly rooted in the past' (NCC 2000a: 3) (see also Tunbridge (2000) for an excellent discussion of the redevelopment of the market area). Significantly, a future tourism focus is the development of the NCR 'as an ecodestination. . . . However, to respond successfully to the needs of future travellers – not just eco-tourists, but also increasing numbers of business people, convention-goers and seniors – the NCC must support the development of new Capital services and infrastructure' (NCC 2000a: 9). In addition, the NCC has developed a series of parkways in the Ottawa region that have a historic role as recreational and leisure corridors for motorists and cyclists. The parkways also link into the transitway system and act as 'gateways' to the NCR which remain, 'influencing the perception of visitors and to communicating the image and landscape of the Capital' (NCC 1998: 52).

THE URBAN TOURISM MARKET: DATA SOURCES

Identifying the scale, volume and different markets for urban tourism remains a perennial problem for researchers. Urban tourism is a major economic activity in many of Europe's capital cities but identifying the tourism markets in each area is problematic. Page (1995a) provides a detailed assessment of the principal international data sources on urban tourism, reviewing published statistics by the World Tourism Organisation and the Organisation for Economic Co-operation and Development. Such data sources commonly employ the domestic and international tourist use of accommodation as one measure of the scale of tourism activity. In the context of urban tourism, it requires researchers to have an understanding of spatial distribution of tourist accommodation in each country to identify the scale and distribution of tourist visits. In countries where the majority of accommodation is urban-based, such statistics may provide preliminary sources of data for research. While this may be relevant for certain categories of tourist (e.g. business travellers and holiday-makers), those visitors staying with friends and relatives within an urban environment would not be included in the statistics. Even where statistics can be used, they only provide a preliminary assessment of scale and volume and more detailed sources are needed to assess specific markets for urban tourism. For example, Page (1995a) reviews the different market segmentation techniques used by marketing researchers to analyse the tourism market for urban areas, which helps one to understand the types of visitors and motives for visiting urban destinations. Table 5.8 highlights two typologies developed within the tourism literature to acknowledge the significance of individual motives for visiting urban destinations. However, Jansen-Verbeke (1986) does point to the methodological problem of distinguishing between the different users of the tourist city. For example, Burtenshaw et al. (1991) discuss the concept of functional areas (Figure 5.6) within the city, where different visitors seek certain attributes for their city visit (e.g. the historic city, the culture city, the nightlife city, the shopping city and the tourist city) where no one group has a monopoly over its use. In other words, residents of the city and its hinterland, visitors and workers all use the resources within the tourist city, but some user groups

Table 5.8: Typologies of urban tourists

According to Blank and Petkovitch (1980) the motives for visiting urban areas can be classified thus:

- visiting friends and relatives
- business/convention visitation
- outdoor recreation activities
- entertainment and sightseeing activities
- personal reasons
- shopping
- other factors

while more recently Page (1995: 48) identified a broader range of motivations for visiting urban areas which includes:

- visiting friends and relatives
- for business travel
- conference and exhibition attendance
- educational reasons
- cultural and heritage tourism
- religious travel (e.g. pilgrimages)
- hallmark events attendance
- leisure shopping
- day trips

identify with certain areas more than others. Thus, the tourist city is a multi-functional area which complicates attempts to identify a definitive classification of users and the areas/facilities they visit.

Ashworth and Tunbridge (1990) prefer to approach the market for urban tourism from the perspective of the consumers' motives, focusing on the purchasing intent of users, their attitudes, opinions and interests for specific urban tourism products. The most important distinction they make is between use/non-use of tourism resources, leading them to identify international users (who are motivated by the character of the city) and incidental users (who view the character of the city as irrelevant to their use). This two-fold typology is used by Ashworth and Tunbridge (1990) to identify four specific types of users:

1 intentional users from outside the city-region (e.g. holiday-makers and heritage tourists);
2 intentional users from inside the city-region (e.g. those using recreational and entertainment facilities – recreating residents);
3 incidental users from outside the city-region (e.g. business and conference/exhibition tourists and those on family visits – non-recreating visitors);

Figure 5.6: Functional areas in the tourist city
Source: After Burtenshaw *et al.* (1991)

4   incidental users from inside the city-region (e.g. residents going about their daily activities – non-recreating residents).

Such an approach recognises the significance of attitudes and the use made of the city and services rather than the geographical origin of the visitor as the starting point for analysis. Although the practical problem with such an approach is that tourists tend to cite one main motive for visiting a city, any destination is likely to have a variety of user groups in line with Ashworth and de Haan's (1986) examination of users of the tourist-historic city of Norwich. Their methodology involved tourists self-allocating the most important motives for visiting Norwich. While 50 per cent of holiday-makers were intentional users of the historic city, significant variations occurred in the remaining markets using the historic city. But this does confirm the multi-use hypothesis advanced by Ashworth and Tunbridge (1990) which was subsequently developed in a geographical context by Getz (1993a). Having outlined some of the methodological issues associated with assessing the market for urban tourism, attention now turns to the behavioural issues associated with the analysis of tourist visits to urban areas.

URBAN TOURISM: BEHAVIOURAL ISSUES

Any assessment of urban tourist activities, patterns and perceptions of urban locations will be influenced by the supply of services, attractions and facilities in each location. Recent research has argued that one needs to understand the operation and organisation of tourism in terms of the production of tourism services and the ways in which tourists consume the products in relation to the locality, their reasons for consumption, what they consume and possible explanations for the consumption outcome as visitor behaviour. As Law (1993: 14) argues:

> tourism is the geography of consumption outside the home area; it is about how and why people travel to

consume . . . on the production side it is concerned to understand where tourism activities develop and on what scale. It is concerned with the process or processes whereby some cities are able to create tourism resources and a tourism industry.

One framework developed in the Netherlands by Jansen-Verbeke (1986) to accommodate the analysis of tourism consumption and production in urban areas is that of the 'leisure product'. The facilities in an urban environment may be divided into the 'primary elements', 'secondary elements' and 'additional elements' (see Jansen-Verbeke (1986) for a more detailed discussion of this approach). To distinguish between user groups, Jansen-Verbeke (1986) identified tourists' and recreationalists' first and second reasons for visiting three Dutch towns (Deneter, Kampen and Zwolle). The inner-city environment provides a leisure function for various visitors regardless of the prime motivation for visiting. As Jansen-Verbeke (1986: 88–9) suggests:

> On an average day, the proportion of visitors coming from beyond the city-region (tourists) is about one-third of all visitors. A distinction that needs to be made is between week days, market days and Sundays. Weather conditions proved to be important . . . the hypothesis that inner cities have a role to play as a leisure substitute on a rainy day could not be supported.

Among the different user groups, tourists tend to stay longer, with a strong correlation between 'taking a day out', sightseeing and 'visiting a museum' as the main motivations to visit. Nevertheless, leisure shopping was also a major 'pull factor' for recreationalists and tourists, though it is of greater significance for the recreationalists. Using a scaling technique, Jansen-Verbeke (1986) asked visitors to evaluate how important different elements of the leisure product were to their visit. The results indicate that there is not a great degree of difference between tourists' and recreationalists' rating of elements and characteristics of the city's leisure product. While recreationalists attach more importance to shopping facilities than to events and museums, the historical characteristics of the environment and decorative elements combined with other elements, such as markets, restaurants and the compact nature of the inner city, to attract visitors. Thus 'the conceptual approach to the system of inner-city tourism is inspired by common features of the inner-city environment, tourists' behaviour and appreciation and promotion activities' (Jansen-Verbeke 1986: 97). Such findings illustrate the value of relating empirical results to a conceptual framework for the analysis of urban tourism and the necessity of replicating similar studies in other urban environments to test the validity of the hypothesis, framework and interpretation of urban tourists' visitor behaviour. But how do tourists and other visitors to urban areas learn about, find their way around and perceive the tourism environment?

TOURIST PERCEPTION AND COGNITION OF THE URBAN ENVIRONMENT

How individual tourists interact and acquire information about the urban environment remains a relatively poorly researched area in tourism studies, particularly in relation to towns and cities. This area of research is traditionally seen as the forte of social psychologists with an interest in tourism, though much of the research by social psychologists has focused on motivation (e.g. Guy and Curtis (1986) on the development of perceptual maps). Reviews of the social psychology of tourism indicate that there has been a paucity of studies of tourist behaviour and adaptation to new environments they visit. This is somewhat surprising since 'tourists are people who temporarily visit areas less familiar to them than their home area' (Walmesley and Jenkins 1992: 269). Therefore, one needs to consider a number of fundamental questions related to:

- How will the tourists get to know the areas they visit?
- How do they find their way around unfamiliar environments?
- What features in the urban environment are used to structure their learning experience in unfamiliar environments?

- What type of mental maps and images do they develop?

These issues are important in a tourism planning context since the facilities which tourists use and the opportunities they seek will be conditioned by their environmental awareness. This may also affect the commercial operation of attractions and facilities, since a lack of awareness of the urban environment and the attractions within it may mean tourists fail to visit them. Understanding how tourists interact with the environment to create an image of the real world has been the focus of research into social psychology and behavioural geography (see Walmesley and Lewis 1993: 95–126). Geographers have developed a growing interest in the geographic space perception of all types of individuals (Downs 1970), without explicitly considering tourists in most instances. Behavioural geographers emphasise the need to examine how people store spatial information and 'their choice of different activities and locations within the environment' (Walmesley and Lewis 1993: 95). The process through which individuals perceive the urban environment is shown in Figure 5.7. While this is a simplification, Haynes (1980) notes that no two individuals will have an identical image of the urban environment because the information they receive is subject to mental processing. This is conditioned by the information signals they receive through their senses (e.g. sight, hearing, smell, taste and touch) and this part of the process is known as *perception*. As our senses may only comprehend a small proportion of the total information received, the human brain sorts the information and relates it to the knowledge, values and attitudes of the individual through the process of *cognition* (Page 1995a: 222). The final outcome of the perception and cognition process is the formation of a mental image of a place. These images are an individual's own view of reality, but they are important to the individual and group when making decisions about their experience of a destination, whether to visit again, and their feelings in relation to the tourist experience of place.

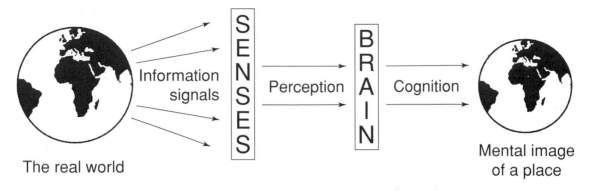

Figure 5.7: Perceptions of place

As Walmesley and Lewis (1993: 96) suggest, 'the distinction between perception and cognition is, however, a heuristic device rather than a fundamental dichotomy because in many senses, the latter subsumes the former and both are mediated by experience, beliefs, values, attitudes, and personality such that, in interacting with their environment, humans only see what they want to see'. Consequently, an individual tourist's knowledge of the environment is created in their mind as they interact with the unfamiliar environment they are visiting (or a familiar environment on a return visit).

According to Powell (1978: 17–18) an image of the environment comprises ten key features which include:

1 a spatial component accounting for an individual's location in the world;
2 a personal component relating the individual to other people and organisations;
3 a temporal component concerned with the flow of time;
4 a relational component concerned with the individual's picture of the universe as a system of regularities;
5 conscious, subconscious and unconscious elements;
6 a blend of certainty and uncertainty;
7 a mixture of reality and unreality;
8 a public and private component expressing the degree to which an image is shared;
9 a value component that orders parts of the image according to whether they are good or bad;
10 an affectional component whereby the image is imbued with feeling.

Among geographers, the spatial component to behavioural research has attracted most interest, and they derive much of their inspiration from the pioneering research by Lynch (1960). Lynch's research asked respondents in North American cities to sketch maps of their individual cities, and by simplifying the sketches, derived images of the city. Lynch developed a specific technique to measure people's urban images in which respondents drew a map of the centre of the city from memory, marking on it the streets, parks, buildings, districts and features they considered important. 'Lynch found many common elements in these mental maps that appeared to be of fundamental importance to the way people collect information about the city' (Hollis and Burgess 1977: 155). Lynch (1960) found five elements in the resulting maps after simplifying them. These were:

1 *Paths* which are the channels along which individuals move.
2 *Edges* which are barriers (e.g. rivers) or lines separating one region from another.
3 *Districts* which are medium to large sections of the city with an identifiable character.

4 *Nodes* which are the strategic points in a city which the individual can enter and which serve as foci for travel.
5 *Landmarks* which are points of reference used in navigation and way finding, into which an individual cannot enter.

(See Figure 5.8 for a schematic diagram of Lynchean landscape elements.)

The significance of such research for the tourist and visitor to the urban environment is that the information they collect during a visit will shape their image of the place, influencing their feelings and impressions of that place. Furthermore, this imageability of a place is closely related to the legibility, by which is meant the extent to which parts of the city may be recognised and interpreted by an individual as belonging to a coherent pattern. Thus a legible city would be one where the paths, edges, districts, nodes and landmarks are both clearly identifiable and clearly positioned relative to each other (Walmesley and Lewis 1993: 98).

Although there may sometimes be confusion among individuals regarding recognition of Lynchean urban landscape elements, it does help researchers to understand how individuals perceive

Figure 5.8: The Lynchean landscape of Armidale, New South Wales
Source: After Walmesley and Lewis (1993: 127)

the environment. Even so, Walmesley and Lewis (1993) review many of the issues associated with the methodology of imagery research and raise a range of concerns about deriving generalisations from such results. Such studies do have a role to play in understanding how people view, understand and synthesise the complexity of urban landscapes into images of the environment. Nevertheless, criticisms of spatial research of individual imagery of the environment are that it uses a 'borrowed methodology, a potpourri of concepts, and liberal doses of borrowed theory' (Stea and Downs (1979: 3), cited in Walmesley and Lewis 1993). In a tourism context, Walmesley and Jenkins (1992) observed that tourism cognitive mapping may offer a number of useful insights into how tourists learn about new environments and, for this reason, it is pertinent to consider how visitor behaviour may be influenced by the ability to acquire spatial knowledge and synthesise it into meaningful images of the destination to assist them in finding their way around the area or region.

TOURISM COGNITIVE MAPPING

Walmesley and Lewis (1993: 214) review the factors that affect visitor behaviour in terms of five interrelated factors which may initially shape the decision to visit an urban environment. These are:

1 antecedent conditions;
2 user aspirations;
3 intervening variables;
4 user satisfaction;
5 real benefits.

These factors will, with experience, raise or reduce the individual's desire for recreational (and tourism) activity. The opportunities and constraints on visitors' behaviour are affected by income, disposable time available and a host of other socio-economic factors. Research by Stabler (1990) introduces the concept of 'opportunity sets' where

the individual or family's knowledge of tourism opportunities is conditioned by their experience and the constraints on available time to partake in leisure and tourism activities.

Thus, once the decision is taken to visit an urban environment, the tourist faces the problem of familiarity/unfamiliarity of the location. It is the latter which tends to characterise most urban tourist trips, though visitors are often less hesitant about visiting urban destinations if they live in a town or city environment.

P.L. Pearce (1977) produced one of the pioneering studies of cognitive maps of tourists. Using data from sketch maps from first-time visitors to Oxford, England, the role of landmarks, paths and districts was examined. The conclusion drawn indicated that visitors were quick to develop cognitive maps, often by the second day of their visit. The interesting feature of the study is that there is evidence of an environmental learning process at work. Walmesley and Jenkins' (1992: 272) critique of P.L. Pearce's (1977) findings note that:

• the number of landmarks, paths and districts increased over time;
• the number of landmarks identified increased over a period of two to six days, while recognition of the number of districts increased from two to three days;
• the resulting sketch maps were complex with no one element dominating them.

A further study by P.L. Pearce (1981), examined how tourists came to know a route in Northern Queensland (a 340 km strip from Townsville to Cairns). The study indicated that experiential variables are a major influence upon cognitive maps. For example, drivers had a better knowledge than passengers, while age and prior use of the route were important conditioning factors. But as Walmesley and Jenkins (1992: 273) argue, 'very little concern has been shown for the cognitive maps of tourists' except for the work by Aldskogius (1977) in Sweden and Mercer (1971a) in Australia.

historical society, but all those ordinary people who appreciate these reminders of the past as they go about their daily business.' Indeed, Strong went on to note that 'Heritage identification and assessment is too important to be given to a group of experts. It should involve the whole community' (1997: 4).

- *Reducing uncertainty reduces time and costs and increases viability.*

  This fourth principle is extremely important for heritage conservation, particularly where the private sector is involved. Unfortunately, many heritage management agencies do not have a clear understanding of the economics of conservation, they do not have well-structured strategic plans which are open for evaluation, neither do they have an appreciation of the effectiveness of their expenditure in relation to their conservation objectives, if they have such objectives at all. Moreover, public heritage organisations typically do not have good estimates of forecasting expenditures and costs to meet objectives for given timelines. Indeed, their timeline often appears to be 'infinite'. They do not have good visitor records or details of expenditure patterns. They also fail to factor in costs of annual upkeep and maintenance. If they were operating on a commercial basis many of them would go bankrupt. From the private sector's perspective time is money, and even a casual observer of the economic behaviour of investors and commercial operators will realise that certainty is vital. However, heritage agencies trying to develop partnerships often seem to have no understanding of the needs of business.

SERVICE QUALITY ISSUES IN URBAN TOURISM

The competitive nature of urban tourism is increasingly being reflected in the growth in marketing and promotion efforts by towns and cities as they compete for a share of international and domestic tourism markets. Such competition has led to tourists' demands for higher standards of service provision and improved quality in the tourist experience. As Clewer *et al.* (1992) note, certain urban tourists (e.g. the German market) have higher expectations of service quality than do others. But developing an appropriate definition or concept of urban tourism quality is difficult due to the intangible nature of services as products which are purchased and consumed.

In the context of urban tourism, three key issues need to be addressed. First, place-marketing generates an image of a destination that may not be met in reality due to the problems of promoting places as tourist products. The image promoted through place-marketing may not necessarily be matched in reality through the services and goods which the tourism industry delivers. As a result, the gap between customers' perception of a destination and the bundle of products they consume is reflected in their actual tourist experience, which has important implications for their assessment of quality in their experience. Second, the urban tourism product is largely produced by the private sector either as a package or as a series of elements which are not easily controlled or influenced by the place-marketer. Third, there is a wide range of associated factors which affect a tourist's image of a destination, including less tangible elements like the environment and the ambience of the city which may shape the outcome of a tourist's experience. As a result, the customer's evaluation of the quality of the services and products provided is a function of the difference (gap) between expected and perceived service. It is in this context that the concept of service quality is important for urban tourism. Gilbert and Joshi (1992) present an excellent review of the literature, including many of the concepts associated with service quality. In the case of urban tourism, it is the practical management of the 'gap' between the expected and the perceived service that

Plate 5.3: The Dockland Light Railway is a major attraction for visitors.
Source: LDDC

requires attention by urban managers and the tourism industry. In reviewing Parasuraman *et al.*'s (1985) service quality model, Gilbert and Joshi (1992: 155) identify five gaps which exist between:

1   the expected service and the management's perceptions of the consumer experience (i.e. what they think the tourist wants) (Gap 1);
2   the management's perception of the tourist needs and the translation of those needs into service quality specifications (Gap 2);
3   the quality specifications and the actual delivery of the service (Gap 3);

4   the service delivery stage and the organisation/ provider's communication with the consumer (Gap 4);
5   the consumers' perception of the service they received and experienced, and their initial expectations of the service (Gap 5).

Gilbert and Joshi (1992) argue that the effective utilisation of market research techniques could help to bridge some of the gaps. For:

*   Gap 1 by encouraging providers to elicit detailed information from consumers on what they require;
*   Gap 2 by the management providing realistic specifications for the services to be provided which are guided by clear quality standards;
*   Gap 3 by the employees being able to deliver the service according to the specifications; these need to be closely monitored, and staff training and development is essential: a service is only as good as the staff it employs;
*   Gap 4 by the promises made by service providers in their marketing and promotional messages being reflected in the actual quality offered. Therefore, if a city's promotional literature promises a warm welcome, human resource managers responsible for employees in front-line establishments need to ensure that this message is conveyed to its customers;

Plates 5.4 and 5.5: Marketing images of London Docklands.
Source: LDDC

- Gap 5 by the major gap between the perceived service and delivered service being reduced through progressive improvements in the appropriate image which is marketed to visitors, and the private sector's ability to deliver the expected service in an efficient and professional manner.

Such an approach to service quality can be applied to urban tourism, as it emphasises the importance of the marketing process in communicating and dealing with tourists. To obtain a better understanding of the service quality issues associated with the urban tourist's experience of urban tourism, Haywood and Muller (1988) identify a methodology for evaluating the quality of the urban tourism experience. This involves collecting data on visitors' expectations prior to and after their city-visit by examining a range of variables (see Page (1995a) for a fuller discussion). Such an approach may be costly to operate, but it does provide a better appreciation of the visiting process, and they argue that cameras may also provide the day-to-day monitoring of city experiences. At a city-wide level, North American and European cities have responded to the problem of large visitor numbers and the consequences of mass tourism for the tourist experience by introducing Town Centre Management Schemes (see Page (1994a) for further details of this issue) and Visitor Management Schemes (see Page and Hardyman (1996) for more detail on the developments and application of such schemes).

While there is insufficient space here to review these new management tools to combat the unwieldy and damaging effect of mass tourism on key tourist centres in developed and developing countries, it is notable that many small historic cities in Europe are taking steps to manage, modify and in some cases deter tourist activities. A range of potential visitor management strategies utilised in urban destinations is outlined in Table 5.9. Yet before such measures can be taken to improve the tourist experience of urban tourism in different localities, Graefe and Vaske (1987) argue that the development of a management strategy is necessary to:

Plate 5.6: Crowding may have substantial impacts not only on the quality of the visitor experience but also on the attraction itself. Entrance to the cathedral precinct, Canterbury, Kent.

- deal with problem conditions which may impact on the tourist experience;
- identify the causes of such problems;
- select appropriate management strategies to deal with these problems.

(See Graefe and Vaske (1987) for more detail on the use of this approach to improve the tourist experience.)

THE SIGNIFICANCE OF URBAN TOURISM

Tourism's development in urban areas is not a new phenomenon. But its recognition as a significant activity to study in its own right is only belatedly gaining the recognition it deserves within tourism

Table 5.9: Applications of visitor management techniques

Visitor management technique	Application
Regulating access – by area	• All visitors are prohibited from visiting highly sensitive sites. • Different types and levels of use are regulated through zoning.
Regulating access – by transport	• Access is regulated to pedestrians only. • Access is regulated to pedestrians or by bicycle. • Public transport is the only allowable form of transport. • Centennial Park, Sydney, Australia has several 'car-free days' each year in which alternative ways to enter and move about the park must be found.
Regulating visitation – numbers and group size	• Regulations on total visitation per year, day or at any moment may be generated for a specific site. • Group size restrictions have been implemented in some European cathedrals.
Regulating visitation – type of visitor	• Some sites and attractions have a limit on visitation and the type of visitor. • Some urban attractions target older high and middle income groups and actively discourage other segments using strict controls on all accommodation and services, keeping prices high and scrutinising all marketing to maintain consistency.
Regulating behaviour	• Zoning in some cities and towns allocates different types of use to specified areas. • Restrictions on length of stay may be imposed. • Tour operators may be required to operate under a detailed set of guidelines of conduct for visitors. • Visitors must visit with a guide.
Regulating equipment	• Vehicular access may be restricted. • Loudspeakers may be restricted because of noise disturbance
Implementing entry or user fees	• Most heritage managers responsible for highly visited heritage sites now charge fees to access the site or use facilities at the site; influencing some visitors to choose whether to visit or find an alternative destination. • Some heritage sites offer days during low season when residents are offered free entry. • Cities may require tourism operators to pay for a permit or licence to access the heritage site, and operators must also collect entrance fees from each of their clients. • A portion of user fees collected is returned to local stakeholders as a means of demonstrating the value of tourism.
Modifying the site	• Some urban heritage sites may have specially designed walkways so as to reduce visitor impact. • The Castlemaine Jail, Victoria, Australia is privately run as a heritage tourism venture, with the prison workshops providing a conference venue, the dungeon kitchen providing a wine bar, the mess hall providing an à la carte restaurant, refurbished cells providing accommodation, and remaining cells being presented as they were originally used for guided tours to access.
Undertaking market research	• A study of the domestic and international visitor market may be conducted in order to identify the market segments most likely to visit urban tourism attractions.
Undertaking visitor monitoring and research	• Visitors may be asked to complete special 'day diary' forms to identify their motivations for visiting and the activities they undertook. • Visitors may be asked for their attitudes towards their experience and the performance of the respective heritage manager as a means of improving visitor management strategies. • Visitor impact monitoring and research is widely undertaken in sensitive urban heritage attractions.

Table 5.9: (*continued*)

Visitor management technique	Application
Undertaking marketing – promotional	• Visitation pressure may be relieved through the development, marketing and promotion of value-added alternative attractions. • Different urban tourism organisations may undertake common promotional activities in order to reinforce the profile of the destination.
Undertaking marketing – strategic information	• Tour guides can avoid sensitive areas by using a map and pictorial guide that identifies the best vantage points for attractions. • A walking 'trail selector' (brochure and map) may be developed to provide information on lightly used walking trails in order to redistribute use away from heavily used areas.
Implementing interpretation programmes and facilities	• Some urban tourism destinations may generate greater levels of visitor respect for the local culture through the provision of opportunities such as learning to cook with a local family or spending a night with a local family in a homestay. • Visitors may be taken on guided tours by local people who then convey their personal experiences and knowledge of the area to the visitor. This level of authenticity can greatly enhance the quality of the visitor experience.
Implementing education programmes and facilities	• Theme trails may be created to educate visitors about specific aspects of local history and culture. • Many urban heritage attractions have interpretation and signage encouraging appropriate behaviour.
Modifying the presence of heritage management	• Most museums strategically position security staff in corners and corridors to create a high profile when visitors are moving between exhibits and a low profile when they are studying an individual exhibit.
Encouraging and assisting alternative providers – tourism industry	• Some urban destination management organisations encourage the development of small-scale homestay accommodation and tours by local guides who are highly trained in heritage and interpretation, with profits therefore being reinvested in the local community.
Encouraging and assisting alternative providers – volunteers	• Many urban heritage attractions, such as museums and historic sites, have volunteer and friends' associations which assist in various aspects of management as well as providing a source of financial support. For example, the Karori Wildlife Sanctuary in Wellington, New Zealand is a private trust with a membership of several thousand people. A sizeable proportion of members volunteer to help build trails and act as guides, allowing the trust to reinvest funds into activities such as pest control and building a strong community base.
Concentrating on accredited organisations bringing visitors to a site	• National and regional accreditation programmes may be used to check on the appropriateness of tourism operator practices and the quality of facilities. For example, the Austrian Association of Green Villages requires accommodation providers to meet criteria and market co-operatively with others.

Source: After Hall and McArthur (1998)

studies. The reasons why tourists visit urban environments, to consume a bundle of tourism products, continues to be overlooked by the private sector, which often neglects the fundamental issue – cities are multi-functional places. Despite the growing interest in urban tourism research, the failure of many large and small cities which promote tourism to understand the reasons why people visit, the links between the various motivations, and the deeper reasons why people are attracted to cities, remains a fertile area for theoretically informed and methodologically sound research. Many cities are beginning to recognise the importance of monitoring visitor perceptions and satisfaction (e.g. Brocx 1994) and the activity patterns and behaviour of tourists (Survey Research Associates 1991). While such studies may have provided rich pickings for market research companies, all too often the surveys have been superficial, naive and devoid of any real understanding of urban tourism. For the public and private sector planners and managers with an interest, involvement or stake in urban tourism, the main concern continues to be the potential for harnessing the all-year-round appeal of urban tourism activity, despite the often short-stay nature of such visitors. Ensuring that such stays are part of a high-quality experience, where visitor expectations are realistically met through well-researched, targeted and innovative products continues to stimulate interest among tour operators and other stakeholders in urban tourism provision. Yet the urban tourism industry, which is so often fragmented and poorly co-ordinated, rarely understands many of the complex issues of visitor behaviour, the spatial learning process which tourists experience and the implications for making their visit as stress free as possible.

These concerns should force cities seeking to develop an urban tourism economy to reconsider the feasibility of pursuing a strategy to revitalise the city-region through tourism-led regeneration. All too often both the private and public sectors have moved headlong into economic regeneration strategies for urban areas, seeking a tourism component as a likely back-up for property and commercial redevelopment (see e.g. Lutz and Ryan 1996). The implications here are that tourism issues are not given the serious treatment they deserve. Where the visitors' needs and spatial behaviour are poorly understood and neglected in the decision-making process, it affects the planning, development and eventual outcome of the urban tourism environ-ment. The experience of waterfront areas in large cities is such that recent research which reviews the ambitious schemes to market tourism in London Docklands, to pull the centre of gravity and development in London to the east from the central tourism district in the west, resulted in developers underestimating the role of tourist behaviour (e.g. the inertia of tourists who would not travel east from St Katherine's Dock to areas en route to Greenwich). The result was a series of missed business opportunities and a range of business failures. Therefore, tourist behaviour, the tourism system and its constituent components need to be evaluated in the context of future growth in urban tourism to understand the visitor as a central component in the visitor experience. Managing the different elements of this experience in a realistic manner requires more attention among those towns and cities competing aggressively for visitors, using the quality experience approach as a new-found marketing tool. Future research needs to focus on the behaviour, attitudes and needs of existing and prospective urban tourists to reduce the gap between their expectations and the service delivered. But ensuring that the tourism system within cities can deliver the service and experience marketed through promotional literature in a sensitive and meaningful way is now one of the major challenges for urban tourism managers. The approach adopted by the tourism industry needs to be more proactive in its pursuit of high-quality visitor experiences rather than reactive towards individual problems that arise as a result of tourist dissatisfaction after a visit. Research has a vital role to play in understanding the increasingly complex reasons why tourists continue to visit urban environments and the factors which influence their behaviour and spatial activity patterns. While urban tourism continues to be a recognised and established form of tourism activity, research by the academic community and private sector has really paid only lip-service to what is a central feature of the tourism system in most developed and developing countries.

CONCLUSION

This chapter has reviewed the role of recreation and tourism within the context of an urban environment, where recreationalists and tourists inevitably use some of the same resources. This is best summarised by Burtenshaw *et al.*'s (1991) conceptualisation of different users and functional areas of the city, where no one group has a monopoly over its use. The urban environment is still a neglected field of research in relation to the geographer's analysis of tourism and recreation, and yet the methodologies, techniques and skills they possess can help both the public and private sector to understand how a range of research issues affect the functioning of the recreational and tourism system. For example, in recreational planning, issues of access, equality, need and social justice can easily be integrated into spatial analysis using secondary data. Where data do not exist, spatially orientated social surveys have proved to be extremely valuable in understanding the processes shaping and underpinning existing patterns of use and activity, provision and future development. However, this chapter has also demonstrated that applied geographical research (Sant 1982), for example, as illustrated by the case study of urban recreational provision in the London Borough of Newham, can be used to pose questions and address problem-solving tasks for managerial solutions as well as providing a basis for raising more fundamental questions about the nature of tourism and recreation in contemporary capitalist society.

QUESTIONS

- What are the key geographical approaches to the geography of urban recreation?
- What difficulties might exist in measuring the significance of urban tourism?
- Is it possible to reconcile social and economic values in conserving urban heritage?
- To what extent might urban recreation resources also act as resources for tourism?

READING

Useful recent texts on urban tourism include:

Law, C.M. (1993) *Urban Tourism: Attracting Visitors to Large Cities*, London: Mansell.
Page, S.J. (1995a) *Urban Tourism*, London: Routledge.
Page, S.J. and Hall, C.M. (2002) *Managing Urban Tourism*, Harlow: Pearson Education.

A profile of tourism in a number of cities can be found in:

Law, C.M. (ed.) (1996) *Tourism in Major Cities*, London: International Thomson Business Publishing.

Two recent papers by Pearce provide a useful overview of tourism in Paris:

Pearce, D.G. (1998) 'Tourism development in Paris: Public intervention', *Annals of Tourism Research*, 25(2): 457–76.
Pearce, D.G. (1999) 'Tourism districts in Paris: Structure and functions', *Tourism Management*, 19(1): 49–65.

A useful case study to complement the London Borough of Newham example on equality of access is:

Nicholls, S. (2001) 'Measuring accessibility and equity of public parks: A case study using GIS', *Managing Leisure*, 6(4): 201–19.

6

RURAL RECREATION AND TOURISM

As a focal point for geographical research, the recreational and tourism potential of rural areas is not a new theme for geographers to consider. The interest in rural areas has a long tradition (Owens 1984) but the problem remains that much of the research conducted, with a few exceptions (Page and Getz 1997; Sharpley and Sharpley 1997; Butler *et al.* 1998; Hall and O'Hanlon 1998), is now dated, fragmented and continues to view rural areas as either a recreational or a tourism resource. It fails to adopt a holistic view of the rural resource base as a multi-faceted environment capable of accommodating a wide range of uses (e.g. agriculture, industrialisation, recreation and tourism) and values. As Patmore (1983: 124) recognised, 'recreation use must compete with agriculture, forestry, water abstraction, mineral extraction and military training' within the rural environment which has both spatial implications for competing and complementary land uses as well as for the identification of the ways in which recreation and tourism may be accommodated in an ever-changing rural environment.

According to Coppock (1982: 8):

> the contribution to research that geographers have made has been focused primarily on outdoor recreation in the countryside. No clear distinction has been made between tourism and recreation which is not surprising in a small, densely settled country [Britain] where there is considerable overlap between the two; in any case, geographical studies in tourism have been much less numerous than those in outdoor recreation.

This is an assertion that, to a certain extent, still holds true for rural areas today. Butler *et al.* (1998: 2) argued that:

In many cases, however, the specific activities which are engaged in during leisure, recreation and tourism are identical, the key differences being the setting or location of the activities, the duration of time involved, and, in some cases, the attitudes, motivations and perceptions of the participants. In recent years the differences between recreation and tourism in particular, except at a philosophical level, have become of decreasing significance and distinctions increasingly blurred.

In fact, Pigram (1983) observed that it is 'where [such] space consumption and spatial competition and conflict are most likely to occur . . . that spatial organisation and spatial concerns become paramount, and so the geographer has a valuable role to play in considering rural recreation and tourism as a process and phenomenon which has spatial implications'. Pigram (1983: 15) further argued that the geographer cannot focus only on the spatial organisation and interaction which occurs, but also the 'imbalance or discordance between population related demand and environmentally related supply of recreation [and tourism] opportunities and facilities'. This point is reiterated by Hall (1995) who felt that the rural areas now host a wide range of activities undertaken in people's leisure time and to determine whether the activity is tourism or recreation may seem irrelevant. In contrast, Patmore (1983: 123) argued that 'outdoor recreation in rural areas rapidly achieves a distinctive character of its own and needs separate consideration for more than convention'. Either way, recreation and tourism are increasingly important activities in rural areas throughout the western world.

This chapter examines the growing interest from geographers in the way in which the rural environment is examined as a recreational and tourism resource together with some of the ways in which it has been conceptualised and researched. The chapter commences with a review of the concept of 'rural' and the ways in which geographers have debated its meaning and definition. This is followed by a discussion of the geographer's contribution to theoretical debate in relation to rural recreation and tourism. The contribution made by historical geography to the analysis of continuity and change in the rural environment and its consumption for leisure and tourism is briefly examined. The other contributions made by geographers to the analysis of recreation and tourism in rural environments is examined and a case study of tourism in Ireland is developed as a way of synthesising the geographer's interest in rural tourism.

IN PURSUIT OF THE CONCEPT OF 'RURAL'

Robinson's (1990) invaluable synthesis of rural change illustrates that the term 'rural' has remained an elusive one to define in academic research, even though popular conceptions of rural areas are based on images of rusticity and the idyllic village life. However, Robinson (1990: xxi–xxii) argued that:

> defining rural . . . in the past has tended to ignore common economic, social and political structures in both urban and rural areas. . . . In simple terms . . . 'rural' areas define themselves with respect to the presence of particular types of problems. A selective list of examples could include depopulation and deprivation in areas remote from major metropolitan centres; a reliance upon primary activity; conflicts between presentation of certain landscapes and development of a variety of economic activities; and conflicts between local needs and legislation emanating from urban-based legislators. Key characteristics of 'rural' are taken to be extensive land uses, including large open spaces of underdeveloped land, and small settlements at the base of the settlement hierarchy, but including settlements thought of as rural.

Therefore, research on rural recreation and tourism needs to recognise the essential qualities of what is 'rural'. While national governments use specific criteria to define 'rural', often based on the population density of settlements, there is no universal agreement on the critical population threshold which distinguishes between urban and rural populations. For the developed world, Robinson (1990) summarises the principal approaches used by sociologists, economists and other groups in establishing the basis of what is rural and this need not be reiterated here. What is important is the diversity of approaches used by many researchers who emphasise the concept of an urban–rural continuum as a means of establishing differing degrees of rurality and the essential characteristics of ruralness. Shaw and Williams (1994: 224) advocate the use of the concept of a rural opportunity spectrum, where the countryside is viewed as the location of a 'wide range of outdoor leisure and tourist activities, although over time the composition of these has changed'. Harrison (1991) highlighted the speed of change in rural areas, with the settings and activities undertaken in such areas changing rapidly in the 1970s and 1980s. Even so, such studies do little to establish a meaningful concept of what is meant by a rural setting.

In contrast, Hoggart's (1990) provocative article 'Let's do away with rural' argues that 'there is too much laxity in the treatment of areas in empirical analysis . . . [and] that the undifferentiated use of "rural" in a research context is detrimental to the advancement of social theory' (Hoggart 1990: 245), since the term 'rural' is unsatisfactory due to inter-rural differences and urban–rural similarities. Hoggart (1990) argued that general classifications of urban and rural areas are of limited value. For this reason, recent advances in social theory may offer a number of important insights into conceptualising the rural environment and tourism-related activities.

According to Cloke (1992), rural places have been traditionally associated with specific rural functions: agriculture, sparsely populated areas, geographically dispersed settlement patterns; and rurality has been conceptualised in terms of peripherality (see Page (1994c) for a discussion of tourism and peripherality), remoteness and dependence on rural economic activity. However, new approaches in social theory have argued that rural areas are inextricably linked to the national and international political economy. As Cloke (1992) rightly argues, changes in the way society and non-urban places are organised and function have rendered traditional definitions of rurality less meaningful due to the following changes:

- increased mobility of people, goods and messages have eroded the autonomy of local communities;
- delocalisation of economic activity makes it impossible to define homogeneous economic regions;
- new specialised uses of rural spaces (as tourist sites, parks and development zones) have created new specialised networks of relationships in the areas concerned, many of which are no longer localised;
- people who 'inhabit' a given rural area include a diversity of temporary visitors as well as residents;
- rural spaces increasingly perform functions for non-rural users and in these cases may be characterised by the fact that they exist independently of the action of rural populations (Mormont 1990: 31, cited in Cloke 1992).

Consequently, Mormont (1987) conceptualises rural areas as a set of overlapping social spaces, each with their own logic, institutions and network of actors (e.g. users and administrators). This reiterates many of the early ideas from behavioural scientists – that a rural space needs to be defined in terms of how the occupants perceive it, as a social construct where the occupiers of rural spaces interact and participate in activities such as recreation and tourism. In this context, recent developments in social theory imply that the nature and use of rural areas for activities such as recreation and tourism is best explained by examining the processes by which their meaning of 'rural' is 'constructed, negotiated and experienced' (Cloke 1992: 55). One approach favoured by Cloke (1992: 55) is the analysis of the way in which the

commodification of the countryside has occurred, leading to the rise of markets for rural products where:

> the countryside . . . [is] an exclusive place to be lived in; rural communities [are considered] as a context to be bought and sold; rural lifestyle [is something] which can be colonized; icons of rural culture [are commodities] can be crafted, packed and marketed; rural landscapes [are imbued] with a new range of potential from 'pay-as-you-enter' national parks, to sites for the theme park explosion; rural production [ranges] from newly commodified food to the output of industrial plants whose potential or actual pollutive externalities have driven them from more urban localities.

In this respect, rural areas are places to be consumed and where production is based on establishing new commodities or in reimaging and rediscovering places for recreation and tourism. Cloke (1992) cites privatisation in the UK as a major process stimulating this form of rural production focused on rural recreation and tourism. The new political economy influencing agriculture in the EC has also facilitated farm diversification into new forms of tourism accommodation (e.g. farmstays) and attractions. Yet the critical processes stimulating the demand for the mass consumption of rural products have been essential in effecting such changes. Urry (1988) points to changes in taste following the emergence of a new service class which have led to greater emphasis on consumption in rural environments. These tastes have also influenced other social groups who have adopted similar values in the consumption of rural areas including:

- the pursuit of a pastoral idyll;
- acceptance of cultural symbols related to the rural idyll;
- a greater emphasis on outdoor pursuits in such environments.

While the detailed social and cultural interpretations of such trends are dealt with in detail by Urry (1988), Poon (1989) illustrates the practical implications of such changes for the tourism industry. Poon (1989) interprets these changes in terms of a 'shift from an "old tourism" (e.g. the regimented and standardized holiday package) to a "new tourism" which is segmented, customized and flexible in both time and space'. In fact recent research on services has analysed the change in society from a 'Fordist' to 'Post-Fordist' stage which has involved a shift in the form of demand for tourist services from a former pattern of mass consumption 'to more individual patterns, with greater differentiation and volatility of consumer preferences and a heightened need for producers to be consumer-driven and to segment markets more systematically' (Urry 1991: 52). While recreational use of the countryside may not exhibit such a high degree of marketing and reinterpretation to develop novel and profitable experiences, Butler *et al.* (1998) do point to the increasing use of rural areas for such purposes which are juxtaposed with more traditional recreational and tourist uses. Nevertheless, Hummelbrunner and Miglbauer (1994) support both Poon's (1989) and Urry's (1991) assessments, arguing that these changes to the demand and supply of tourism services have contributed to the emergence of a 'new rural tourism'. From a supply perspective, this has manifested itself in terms of 'an increasing interest in rural tourism among a better-off clientele, and also among some holidaymakers as a growing environmental awareness and a desire to be integrated with the residents in the areas they visit' (Bramwell 1994: 3). This not only questions the need to move beyond existing concepts such as core and periphery with rural tourism as a simplistic consumption of the countryside, but also raises the question of how rural areas are being used to provide tourism and recreational experiences and how businesses are pursuing market-oriented approaches to the new era of commodification in rural environments. If the 1990s was a 'new era of commodifying rural space, characterised by a speed and scale of development which far outstrip farm-based tourism and recreation of previous eras' (Cloke 1992: 59), then a critical review of this process at an international and national scale is timely, to assess the extent and significance of rural tourism and recreation in the 1990s and into the new millennium.

CONCEPTUALISING THE RURAL RECREATION–TOURISM DICHOTOMY

One of the problems within the literature in recreation and tourism is that the absence of a holistic and integrated view of each area has continued to encourage researchers to draw a distinction between recreation and tourism as complementary and yet semantically different activities, without providing a conceptual framework within which to view such issues. Cloke (1992) overcomes this difficulty by observing that the relationship between rural areas and tourism and leisure activities has changed, with the activities being the dominant elements in many rural landscapes which control and affect local communities to a much greater degree than in the past. Therefore, while a critical debate has occurred in the tourism and recreational literature in terms of the similarity and differences between tourists and recreationists, it is the social, economic and spatial outcomes that are probably the most significant feature to focus on in the rural environment. However, there is still a need to recognise the magnitude and effect of recreational and tourist use because of the timing, scale, resource impact and implication of each use. But ultimately each use is a consumption of resources and space in relation to the user's discretionary leisure time and income. According to Shaw and Williams (1984), there are a range of issues to consider in relation to this debate. For example, in many countries, use of the countryside is a popular pastime (e.g. in 1990 the Countryside Commission found that 75 per cent of the population of England visited the countryside) and in such studies there is a clear attempt to avoid simplistic classifications of what constitutes tourist and recreationalist use. In fact Shaw and Williams (1994) prefer to use a more culturally determined definition to show that the use of rural landscapes for tourist and recreational purposes is conditioned by a wide range of social, economic and cultural meanings which affect the host area. Cultural definitions of urban and rural areas highlight not only the intrinsic qualities of the countryside which is significantly different from urban areas, but also the interpretation that 'there is nothing that is inherent in any part of the countryside that makes it a recreational resource' (Shaw and Williams 1994: 223). This recognises that there is a search for new meaning in a research context. In fact Butler *et al.* (1998: 8) would concur with this since:

> One of the major elements of change in rural areas has been the changes within recreation and tourism. Until the last two decades or so, recreational and tourist activities in rural areas were mostly related closely to the rural character of the setting.
>
> They were primarily activities which were different to those engaged in urban centers. . . . They could be characterised, at the risk of generalisation, by the following terms: relaxing, passive, nostalgic, traditional, low technological, and mostly non-competitive.

But in recent years this has been affected by changes to the meaning and use of rural environments, where the setting is no longer a passive component. Yet there is some support for not focusing on the rural setting; as Patmore (1983: 122) argued, 'there is no sharp discontinuity between urban and rural resources for recreation but rather a complete continuum from local park to remote mountain park'. If one maintains such an argument, it, to a certain extent, makes the geographer's role in classifying tourism and recreational environments and their uses for specific reasons and purposes rather meaningless if they are part of no more than a simple continuum of recreational and tourism resources, thereby denying new attempts to understand what motivates users to seek and consume such resources in a cultural context. To overcome this difficulty, Shaw and Williams (1994: 224) prefer to view 'rural areas as highly esteemed as locales for leisure and tourism' and their use is heavily contingent upon particular factors, especially social access, and the politics of countryside ownership. Yet these contingencies may only really be fully understood in the context of the developed world, according to Shaw and Williams (1994), by considering three critical concepts used by geographers: the rural opportunity spectrum, accessibility and time space budgets. However, prior to any discussion of such key concepts, it is pertinent to consider the historical dimension to

tourism and recreational pursuits in rural environments, since historical geographers emphasise continuity, change and the role of spatial separation of social classes in past periods as factors which affected the past use of rural locales.

THE GEOGRAPHER'S CONTRIBUTION TO THEORETICAL DEBATE IN RURAL CONTEXTS

Within any research area, progress is often gauged in terms of the extent to which the subject contributes to the development of theory. As Perkins (1993: 116) argued, a

> social scientist's primary role is to develop theories about society. Theories are sets of logically inter-related statements about phenomena, such as recreation and leisure. The reason for developing such theories is to help us understand the world humans make for themselves. It is on the basis of the understanding reached in the development of these theories that we plan and manage particular social phenomena.

As Owens (1984: 174) argued, 'during the mid-1970s there was a hiatus in leisure and recreation research which marked a profound change from the enthusiastic promotion of agency dependent ad hoc applied research to an evaluative phase characterised by introspection and self-criticism' since, prior to 1975, the generation of empirical case studies dominated the literature. After 1975 calls from North American researchers for a greater consideration of leisure behaviour and its contribution to theory was advocated. For example, critical reviews by researchers (e.g. Patmore 1977, 1978, 1979; Coppock 1980; Mercer 1979a; Patmore and Collins 1980, 1981), to name but a few, reiterated these criticisms, and Patmore (1977: 115) poignantly summarised the position where 'this review reveals continuing and glaring gaps in British research, not least in a better understanding of the nature and motivation of recreation demand and in the development of an effective body of integrative theory'.

A series of new texts in the 1980s (e.g. Kelly 1982; Smith 1983a; Torkildsen 1983) and the appearance of two major journals, *Leisure Studies* and *Leisure Sciences*, raised the need for more theoretically determined research, but only a limited range of studies by geographers focused on theoretical and conceptual issues (e.g. Owens 1984) while other disciplines contributed to the debate in a more vigorous and central manner (e.g. Graefe *et al.* 1984a). Despite large-scale research funding by government research agencies (e.g. the Social Science Research Council in the UK) in the 1970s and 1980s, a lack of concern for theory has meant that geographers have made little impact on the problem that

> the large body of rural outdoor recreation research has not been consolidated in more theoretical work but one wonders whether researchers have set themselves an intellectual challenge which they are unable to meet. Certainly, there is now a steady flow of publication, albeit mainly directed to traditional ends, and because of this the argument that lack of progress towards a theory of leisure and recreation simply reflects poor funding is now much less plausible.
>
> (Owens 1984: 176)

As a consequence, Perkins (1993: 116–17) suggests that 'there are four reasons for this neglect of theoretical geographical leisure research. The first is that within the discipline, leisure research is considered' to be unimportant when compared to the central concerns of economic, social and urban geography. The second reason is that very little research funding has been made available to geographers to pursue theoretical leisure research (see Perkins and Gidlow 1991). Third, much research has been British or North American in origin, 'where pressures between recreational uses of particular sites are very great . . . geographers have worked closely with recreational site managers to develop short to medium term management strategies for these areas'. Finally, recreation geographers 'have hardly participated in the theoretical debates which have thrived in their discipline since the 1970s' (Perkins 1993: 117).

In fact, Perkins (1993) offers one of the few attempts by geographers to rise to this challenge, using social theory, particularly structuration theory, and his research is valuable in relation to the understanding of locales for the analysis of human and spatial interaction. Locales comprise a range of settings which are different and yet connected through interactions. The interactions result from

> the life path of individuals . . . in ways that reflect patterns of production and consumption. These interactions result in a particular pattern of locales which have social and physical forms. Each life path is essentially an allocation of time between these different locales. A particular mode of production will emphasise dominant locales to which time must be allocated.
>
> (Perkins 1993: 126)

Within the theoretical literature on structuration, in a capitalist society, structure and human interaction are brought together through the concept of the locale. The dominant locales are:

- the home;
- work;
- school;

and they are settings in which consumption occur. Thus a leisure locale is a setting for interaction whereby 'people pursue leisure within the context of their life commitments and access to resources. Leisure interactions, of course, occur in and are influenced by places, and to this extent the leisure locale includes a spatial component' (Perkins 1993: 126). In such theoretically determined analyses, Perkins (1993) calls for the geographers of recreation to consider the position and internal organisation of the leisure locale in a rural setting, in relation to the dominant locales (i.e. the home, work and school) and other institutional locales such as religion and the arts. One possible mechanism for pursuing such theoretically determined research may be to employ new conceptualisations of geography using the new regional geography informed by structuration theory. Structuration theory and the new regional geography have emerged, emphasising producers of the interpenetration of structure and agency. Structure 'both constrains and enables people to take particular life paths, the collective effect of which is to produce and enable new members of society in their life paths . . . [where] geographical behaviour' (Perkins 1993: 117) affects people's specific situations. Therefore, the geographer in a rural setting would need to consider both structure and human interaction and how it is all brought together in the context of the locale (see Thrift (1977), Giddens (1984) and Perkins (1993) for more detail).

In the context of rural tourism, the theoretical analysis advocated by Perkins (1993) for rural recreation also has a relevance, particularly when one considers the debate engendered by Bramwell (1994: 2):

> does the physical existence of tourism in rural areas create a rural tourism that has a significance beyond the self-evident combination of particular activities in a specific place? In other words, do the special characteristics of rural areas help shape the pattern of tourism so that there is a particular rural tourism?

While the comments by Bramwell (1994) certainly highlight the need for more attention to the concept of the locale, Cloke (1992) indicates that structuration theory does have a role to play, although, as Perkins (1993) indicates, geographers may need to consider the value of humanistic research to ask questions that can address the issues raised by Bramwell (1994): How do people value rural areas and the relationships between locales? Unfortunately, much of the research published to date remains theoretically uninformed and empirically driven. As a result, much of the research on rural tourism by geographers has, with a number of exceptions, failed to contribute to a growing awareness of its role, value and significance in the wider development of tourism studies and its importance as a mainstay of many rural economies. In this context, Butler and Clark's (1992: 167) comments are relevant in that:

> The literature on rural tourism is sparse and . . . conceptual models and theories are lacking. . . . Many of the references in tourism are case studies with little theoretical foundation . . . or they focus on specific problems. . . . Some take a broader perspective focusing on issues and process. . . . There is, therefore a lack of theory and models placing rural tourism in a conceptual framework'.

Much of the research on rural tourism has been published in a diverse range of social science journals (e.g. *Sociologia Ruralis*, *Tourism Recreation Research*), reports and edited collections of essays which have been poorly disseminated as well as one or two specific texts (e.g. Sharpley 1993). Consequently, rural tourism has continued to be peripheral to the focus of tourism research while remaining poorly defined. It continues to be a general term which encapsulates a wide range of interest groups not only from tourism studies, but also from economics, planning, anthropology, geography, sociology and business studies. There has also been a lack of integration between these interest groups, each cultivating its own view and approach to rural tourism. As a result few researchers have attempted to define the concept of rural tourism.

TOWARDS A CONCEPT OF RURAL TOURISM

Keane *et al.*'s (1992) innovative, but little known study on rural tourism offers a number of insights into the definition of rural tourism acknowledging that there are a variety of terms used to describe tourism activity in rural areas: agritourism, farm tourism, rural tourism, soft tourism, alternative tourism and many others which have different meanings from one country to another. Keane also points out that it is difficult to avoid some of this confusion in relation to labels and definitions because the term 'rural tourism' has been adopted by the European Community to refer to the entire tourism activity in a rural area (Keane *et al.* 1992). One way of addressing this seemingly tautological proposition, that tourism in rural areas is not necessarily rural tourism when so many typologies exist for types of tourism that may or may not be deemed rural tourism, is to examine what makes rural tourism distinctive.

WHAT MAKES RURAL TOURISM DISTINCTIVE?

Lane (1994) discusses the historical continuity in the development of rural tourism and examines some of the key issues which combine to make rural tourism distinctive. Bramwell (1994: 3) suggests that despite the problems of defining the concept of 'rural', 'it may be a mistake to deny our common-sense thoughts that rural areas can have distinctive characteristics or that these can have consequences for social and economic interactions in the countryside'.

The views and perceptions people hold of the countryside are different from those of urban areas which is an important starting point for establishing the distinctiveness of rural tourism. Lane (1994) actually lists the subtle differences between urban and rural tourism, in which individual social representations of the countryside are a critical component of how people interact with rural areas. In fact, Squire (1994) acknowledges that both the social representations and personal images of the countryside condition whether people wish to visit rural areas for tourism, and what they see and do during their visit.

Lane (1994) also highlights the impact of changes in rural tourism since the 1970s, with far greater numbers of recreationalists and tourists now visiting rural areas. As Patmore's (1983) seminal study on recreation and leisure acknowledges, the impact of car ownership has led to a geographical dispersion of recreationalists and tourists beyond existing fixed modes of transport (e.g. railways). Consequently, tourism has moved away from a traditional emphasis on resorts, small towns and villages to become truly rural, with all but the most inaccessible wilderness areas awaiting the impact of the more mobile tourist. Despite this strong growth in the demand for rural tourism, Lane (1994) acknowledges the absence of any systematic sources of data on rural tourism, since neither the World Tourism Organisation nor OECD have appropriate measures. In addition, there is no agreement among member countries on how to measure this phenomenon. One way of establishing

the distinctive characteristics of rural tourism is to derive a working definition of rural tourism. Here the work by Lane (1994) is invaluable since it dismisses simplistic notions of rural tourism as tourism which occurs in the countryside. Lane (1994: 9) cites the following seven reasons why it is difficult to produce a complex definition of rural tourism to apply in all contexts:

1   Urban or resort-based tourism is not confined to urban areas, but spills out into rural areas.
2   Rural areas themselves are difficult to define, and the criteria used by different nations vary considerably.
3   Not all tourism which takes place in rural areas is strictly 'rural' – it can be 'urban' in form, and merely be located in a rural area. Many so-called holiday villages are of this type; in recent years, numerous large holiday complexes have been completed in the countryside. They may be 'theme parks', time shares or leisure hotel developments. Their degree of rurality can be both an emotive and a technical question.
4   Historically, tourism has been an urban concept; the great majority of tourists live in urban areas. Tourism can be an urbanising influence on rural areas, encouraging cultural and economic change, and new construction.
5   Different forms of rural tourism have developed in different regions. Farm-based holidays are important in many parts of rural Germany and Austria. Farm-based holidays are much rarer in rural USA and Canada. In France, the self-catering cottage, or gîte, is an important component of the rural tourism product.
6   Rural areas themselves are in a complex process of change. The impact of global markets, communications and telecommunication has changed market conditions and orientations for traditional products. The rise of environmentalism has led to increasing control by 'outsiders' over land use and resource development. Although some rural areas still experience depopulation, others are experiencing an inflow of people to retire or to develop new 'non-

traditional' businesses. The once clear distinction between urban and rural is now blurred by suburbanisation, long-distance commuting and second home development.

7 Rural tourism is a complex multi-faceted activity: it is not just farm-based tourism. It includes farm-based holidays but also comprises special-interest nature holidays and ecotourism, walking, climbing and riding holidays, adventure, sport and health tourism, hunting and angling, educational travel, arts and heritage tourism, and, in some areas, ethnic tourism. There is also a large general-interest market for less specialised forms of rural tourism. This area is highlighted by studies of the German tourism market, where a major requirement of the main holiday is the ability to provide peace, quiet and relaxation in rural surroundings.

Consequently, rural tourism in its purest form should be:

1 Located in rural areas.
2 Functionally rural – built upon the rural world's special features of small-scale enterprise, open space, contact with nature and the natural world, heritage, 'traditional' societies and 'traditional' practices.
3 Rural in scale – both in terms of buildings and settlements – and, therefore, usually small-scale.
4 Traditional in character, growing slowly and organically, and connected with local families. It will often be very largely controlled locally and developed for the long-term good of the area; and of many different kinds, representing the complex pattern of rural environment, economy, history and location (after Lane 1994).

Lane (1994: 16) argues that the following factors also have to be considered in defining rural tourism:

- holiday type;
- intensity of use;
- location;
- style of management;
- degree of integration with the community.

Using the continuum concept allows for the distinction to be made between those tourist visits which are specifically rural, and those which are urban, and those which fall in an intermediate category. Thus, any workable definition of rural tourism needs to establish the parameters of the demand for, and supply of, the tourism experience and the extent to which it is undertaken in the continuum of rural to urban environments. With these issues in mind, it is pertinent to examine the most influential studies published to date by historical geographers to illustrate how continuity and change in spatial patterns and processes of tourism and recreation activity contribute to the landscapes of rural leisure use in the present day.

RURAL RECREATION AND TOURISM IN HISTORICAL PERSPECTIVE

Rural environments, often referred to as the countryside or non-urban areas, have a long history of being used for tourism and recreational activities in both the developed and developing world, a feature frequently neglected in many reviews of rural areas. Towner (1996) documents many of the historical changes and factors which shaped tourism and leisure in the rural environment in Europe since 1540, observing how the rural landscape has been fashionable and developed for the use of social elites at certain times in history (e.g. the landed estates of the seventeenth and eighteenth centuries). Such a review provides an invaluable synthesis and point of reference on the history of tourism and recreation. For example, Towner (1996) reconstructs past geographies to show how the growth of towns and cities during the industrialisation of Europe led to an urbanised countryside around those nascent industrial centres (i.e. the construction of an urban fringe). Such patterns of recreational and tourism activity all combine to produce a wide variety of leisure and, more belatedly, tourism environments which exhibit elements of continuity in use, but also have been in a constant state of change. For example, Towner (1996: 45–6) characterises the pre-industrial period:

behaviour [saw] . . . a need to emphasise social science perspectives as a means to providing a more explicit task of managing use with supply'. The development of participation studies (e.g. The Outdoor Recreation Resources Review Commission in the USA and the General Household Survey in Britain) provided a new direction. Here the argument developed was that specific factors such as socio-demographic variables like age, sex, income and education shaped the spatial patterns of participation. Yet many early surveys proved to be only snapshots of recreational use and were not replicated on a regular basis, making comparisons difficult, while demand changed at such a rapid rate that forecasting exercises from such results was difficult to sustain. Such studies also failed to acknowledge the role of latent demand where such opportunities do not currently exist.

Site studies

In terms of studies of demand for rural recreation, these appear to have been the most numerous among geographers, with the site a spatial entity and the source of supply and ultimate object of demand. Such microscale studies of demand and supply proliferated due to the tendency for research agencies to fund individual site studies, and the publication of results in research articles offered researchers convenient research programmes. Such studies may be classified in terms of studies of demand, in relation to economic evaluation, carrying capacity and user perception. In terms of demand such studies used a range of innovative techniques, including participant observation (e.g. Glyptis 1979), while the geographer's preoccupation with patterns of usage together with a concern for methodological issues such as sampling and respondent bias (e.g. Mercer 1979a) also dominated the literature. The studies of economic evaluation have seen some geographers move into the realms of economics, with cost–benefit models developed and reviewed (e.g. Mansfield 1969), where demand is often conceptualised in terms of sensitivity to distance travelled, cost of travel and entrance fees to derive a simulated demand curve.

Yet research has questioned the rationality of recreational users in spatial patterns of behaviour and activity in models which assume distance minimisation is the sole pursuit for satisfaction (see S.L.J. Smith (1983a, 1995) for more detail).

Carrying capacity

According to Owens (1984: 166)

> the picture to emerge in the wake of the catalytic effect of demand-orientated site surveys is of a range of related but ill-coordinated empirical case studies. It is none the less possible to pick out several broad and important themes in the accumulated body of research. Two of the most important are seen in the burgeoning literature on carrying capacity and user perception studies.

Carrying capacity studies developed from the geographer's interest in the recreationist's impact on resources, as increased participation and the need among managers for greater resource protection provided a ready-made focus for applied geographical research. Yet carrying capacity is among one of the most difficult concepts to put into practice (Patmore 1983; Graefe et al. 1984a). Often one rarely knows what the true carrying capacity is until it has been exceeded. Mercer (1979a) acknowledges that any search for the concept of carrying capacity is futile, implying that a simple concept of carrying capacity may be developed which might be defined thus: 'recreation resources/ facilities will only be suitable for use by a certain number of people beyond which figure carrying capacity will be exceeded to the detriment of the resources and/or the users' experience' (Owens 1984: 167). In trying to put the concept into practice, a range of studies were developed to measure capacity (e.g. Dower and McCarthy 1967; Stankey 1973), with the attempt to differentiate between ecological, physical, social and psychological (or perceptual) capacity (see Chapter 4).

The other area of study noted by Owens (1984) was user perception studies. The greatest impetus for such studies emerged in the USA, particularly in relation to perception of wilderness areas (Stone and Taves 1957) with a specific management objective – the extent to which policies could be developed which would not adversely affect users' perceptions. Lucas' (1964) landmark study of Boundary Waters Canoe area saw users' opinions being canvassed which showed that some respondents had a more restricted view of wilderness than others and this assisted managers in developing land use zoning measures.

The key perception studies undertaken have focused on the following range of themes, although in practice a number of the studies have often been dealt with under more than one theme:

- perception of scenery and evaluation of landscape quality;
- perception of wilderness, wilderness management, and the psychology of wilderness experience;
- social and psychological carrying capacity;
- comparison of managers' and users' perceptions;
- social benefits of recreation, socialisation into leisure, quality of life elements in leisure experience;
- behaviour at sites and social meaning of recreation in relation to particular activities;
- perceived similarities between recreation activities and substitutability;
- psychological structure of leisure, leisure activity types, typology of recreation activity preferences.

(See Owen 1984 for more detail of these studies.)

Robinson (1990) also documented the behavioural differences between recreationalists in different countries, where there are cultural differences in the perception of rural aesthetics.

THE SUPPLY OF RURAL RECREATION

The types of studies developed and published reflect the geographer's interest in rural land use and the geographer's concern with the spatial distribution of resources which led to a range of studies of resource inventories and rural recreation.

According to Pigram (1983), for many people, the concept of resources is commonly taken to refer only to tangible objects in nature. An alternative way is to see resources not so much as material substances but as functions. In this sense resource functions are created by man through the selection and manipulation of certain attributes of the environment.

Resources are therefore constituted by society's subjective evaluation of their value and potential so that they satisfy recreational needs and wants. Earlier research by O'Riordan (1971: 4) still remains the most quoted definition of a resource: 'an attribute of the environment appraised by man to be of value over time within constraints imposed by his social, political, economic and institutional framework'. The recreational research by Clawson et al. (1960) still remains the popular conceptualisation of recreational resources, particularly in a rural context. Clawson et al. (1960) identified one of the standard approaches to recreational resources which has been developed and modified by geographers over the past 40 years: what constitutes a recreational resource, and how can you classify them so that effective planning and management can be developed? Clawson et al. (1960) distinguished between recreation areas and opportunity using a range of factors: location, size, characteristics, degree of use and extent of artificial development of the recreation resource. The result was the development of a continuum of recreational opportunities from user-orientated to resource-based with rural areas falling into resource-based and intermediate areas (i.e. the urban fringe). While geographers have reworked and refined such ideas the resource use remains one of the underlying tenets of the analysis of recreational resources (Simmons 1975). For example, Hockin et al. (1978) classified land-based recreational activities into:

- overnight activities (e.g. camping and caravanning);
- activities involving shooting;
- activities involving a significant element of organised competition (e.g. golf);

- activities involving little or no organised competition (e.g. angling, cycling, rambling, picnicking and wildlife observation).

This has moved on a stage from the continuum zoning concept of Clawson *et al.* (1960) to recognise the diversity of demand and how it did not necessarily fit into any one particular zone.

Coppock and Duffield (1975) outlined their principal contribution in terms of understanding what resources were used and consumed by recreationalists, the levels and volume of use, the capacity of resources to absorb recreationalists, the range of potential resources available, the role of resource evaluation and the techniques of resource evaluation developed by geographers, though their own experience was largely confined to major studies undertaken in Lanarkshire and Greater Edinburgh. By comparing Coppock and Duffield's (1975) synthesis with Patmore (1983), assessment of the geographer's principal concern with recreational resources may be seen to concentrate around three themes.

First there is the visual character of the resource itself, the very quality that gives stimulus and satisfaction. So much of the quality is intertwined with the theme of conservation and the composition of the rural landscape as a whole: for all its importance, however, that aspect is marginal to our purpose and will receive comparatively scant attention. The second theme is recreational opportunity, the direct use of the rural environment for recreational pursuits, both on sites with a uniquely recreational purpose and on those pursuits which recreation must compete directly and indirectly with other uses. The third theme is recreational variety, the variety of rural landscapes and the variety of recreational opportunity that each affords. It is this variety that is the geographer's concern; the frequent imbalance of recreational demand with resource supply, and the consequent compromises and patterns that such imbalance engenders (Patmore 1983: 164).

It is evident that the range of issues which have guided research exhibit a large degree of commonality. Patmore (1983) outlined the main themes

associated with the spatial analysis of rural recreational resources in terms of lost resources (to development and progress), preservation of resources, the active use and enjoyment of resources, the role of balancing conservation and use, and preservation and profit-recreation attractions. In addition, Patmore (1983) outlined the range of resources designed for rural recreation (e.g. forests, parks and the urban fringe), the use of linear resources (e.g. roads and footpaths), water resources and the coastal fringe each of which have a significant rural dimension. Among the early research on some of these themes was Coppock's (1966) landmark study which sought to summarise information on recreational land and water in Britain, while Duffield and Owen (1970) and Goodall and Whittow (1975) examined forest resources, and Tanner (1973, 1977) researched water resources.

A debate on the perception of scenery and its recreational value also emerged in the controversy over landscape evaluation (Penning-Rowsell 1973; Appleton 1974) which has an explicit recreational dimension and focused on the way people value the aesthetics of the landscape and different methodologies to understand the value and meaning of landscapes. The compilation of resource inventories by geographers focused on the supply of rural recreation resources, though there was little continuity in such research in the 1980s, with Pigram (1983) being critical of such studies where they had only a limited practical application.

THE IMPACT OF RURAL RECREATION

Robinson (1990: 270) observed that 'awareness and concern has grown over the environmental impact of recreational activity. In fact the growing severity of this impact reflects the concentrated form of rural recreation with distinctive foci upon a few "honey-pot" sites' where concentrated use may lead to adverse environmental impacts. In addition to direct impacts, the issue of conflict remains a consistent problem associated with recreational resources in the countryside. Many conflicts occur between recreation and agriculture

INSIGHT: Second homes

The utilisation of second homes represents a significant portion of the leisure activities of many tourists and day trippers in a number of countries around the world, and as such they are an integral, though often ignored component of both domestic and international tourism (Jaakson 1986). Second homes are defined by Shucksmith (1983: 174) as 'a permanent building which is the occasional residence of a household that usually lives elsewhere and which is primarily used for recreation purposes. This definition excludes caravans, boats, holiday cottages (rented for a holiday) and properties in major cities and industrial towns.'

Historically, the research into second homes has focused on motivational, planning, regional development and impact-related issues. Second homes development has emerged as a major issue in a number of countries, including Denmark, Sweden and Wales, where local communities have perceived second home purchase by 'outsiders' as being socially and economically invasive. However, despite their economic, social and cultural significance, geographical research on second homes has been highly variable in terms of regional studies and the maintenance of continued interest in second homes as a research issue. Two reasons may be put forward for this. First, the degree of research interest they generate may vary in relation to their value or impact, whether it be economic, social or environmental. Second, second home research may well have fallen out of fashion due to the development of other research interests, for example, the rise of interest in ecotourism. Regardless of these points there exists a large body of international research focusing specifically on, or around, second homes.

The boom period for research on second homes was the 1970s. Prior to this time research was undertaken primarily in North America (especially Canada), and Scandinavia where there is a strong tradition of second home ownership (Coppock

1977a) (see also the discussion of French geography in Chapter 1). During the 1970s an increase in the research undertaken from the United Kingdom culminated in Coppock's (1977a) benchmark publication *Second Homes: Curse or Blessing?* Even though a number of studies have been published since then, this text still remains the most comprehensive international overview of second homes.

Regional development is often advocated by local governments as one of the benefits of second homes development. Second homes provide a means for regional development through

- increasing direct visitor expenditure to the region (Tombaugh 1970; Ragatz 1977);
- the provision of infrastructure used for both home owners and other tourists (Jaakson 1986);
- the support of service and construction industries (Ragatz 1977; Shucksmith 1983);
- the opportunity for further regional development through owners retiring to their second home (Deller *et al.* 1997).

However, despite the opportunities second homes may provide for regional development, the actual contribution varies from location to location, with no consistent benchmark available from which to judge the effect that they will have, particularly in the long term (Fritz 1982). Though the benefits to a region of second home development are potentially high they may not always exceed the costs created for government in relation to increases in waste, health care and other services (Teisl and Reiling 1992), as well as the social and environmental impacts that may also occur.

As with all tourism development, second homes invariably bring a range of impacts to an area. Undesirable physical impacts may occur due to a lack of adequate infrastructure and planning; this includes lack of sewage systems, inappropriate site choice, excessive development and a failure to consider the excessive burden upon areas at peak holiday times (Mathieson and Wall 1982; Gartner 1987). The responsibility for these impacts usually lies with regional and local government which must put effective regulatory controls into place (Dower 1977; Shucksmith 1983). Local government may also have a significant role in relation to social impacts, as they can regulate development so as not to incur conflict between second homeowners and various groups. Examples of social conflict have included disagreement between locals and second home residents regarding levels of development (Jordan 1980; Gartner 1986; Green *et al.* 1996; D.G. Pearce 1998), conflict due to perceived social inequality (Gallent 1997), and competition for the use of land (Gallent 1997). Second homes, and the related issues of 'homes for locals', and the maintenance of services, are probably, more than most forms of tourism migration/settlement, the focus of contested space issues (Jordan 1980; Girard and Gartner 1993).

To understand the impacts of second homes, one must discover the motivations behind the decisions to have a second home. Second homeowners are motivated by a number of reasons,

many of which have to do with the specific amenity characteristics of a location including distance from primary residence, physical and social characteristics of the area and availability of recreational opportunities (Tombaugh 1970; Boschken 1975; Coppock 1977a; Ragatz 1977; D.G. Pearce 1998). However, one of the most significant aspects of second homeownership is the extent to which it is related to broader travel and lifestyle behaviour and the overall personal, spatial and temporal mobilities on individuals and families. The identification of a desirable second home environment tends to be related to an environmental search process of which travel is a key component. Holiday-making provides the opportunities to identify potential second home locations, while second homes may also be part of a wider lifestyle strategy that utilises second home purchase as a precursor to more permanent retirement or lifestyle migration. Indeed, recent renewed interest by geographers in second homes and their relationship to domestic and international migration suggests that second home tourism needs to be increasingly seen within the broader framework of mobility (Williams and Hall 2000; Hall and Williams 2001).

(Robinson 1999) which Shoard (1976) attributed to the *ad-hoc* manner in which recreational use of agricultural land has developed. For example, farmers are frequently dissatisfied with recreationalists' use of rights of way across their land due to the damage and problems caused by a minority of recreationalists (e.g. litter, harassment of stock and pollution). One problem which has emerged in New Zealand is the rise in the prevalence of giardia, a water-borne disease spread by recreationalists and tourists defecating and urinating in streams and water sources. By contrast, in Wales the Countryside Commission estimate that 16 million people use paths covering a wide scale and there is great potential for adverse environmental impacts and

conflict, aside from physical erosion and the subsequent need for ongoing protection from this erosion and, in some cases, the use of non-natural products (e.g. tarmac) to control it. However, as Owens (1984: 173) summarised:

In general, research has been problem-orientated to meet specific managerial requirements, with the consequence that ad hoc site studies proliferated without there being any particular intention of making a contribution to the development of testable theory. Interest has tended to focus on concepts (e.g. social carrying capacity) and the intricacies of methodology (e.g. attitude scales and factor analysis). Of course conceptual and methodological development is a vital part of research, but the main criticism here relates to the degree to which there has been introspection.

In view of these comments, attention is now turned to the geographer's contribution to the analysis of rural tourism.

RURAL TOURISM: SPATIAL ANALYTICAL APPROACHES

In the literature on rural tourism (e.g. Sharpley 1993; Page and Getz 1997; Sharpley and Sharpley 1997; Butler *et al.* 1998), there are few comparatively explicit spatial analytical approaches which make the geographer's perspective stand out above other social science contributions. While it is evident that research on demand, supply, impacts and management are evident, no well-developed literature exists. Probably the nearest synthesis one finds is the occasional section on tourism in rural geography texts (e.g. Robinson 1990) and a limited number of geography of tourism texts (e.g. Shaw and Williams 1994). For this reason, this section examines some of the more prominent contributions of geographers and is followed by a case study of tourism in Ireland.

THE IMPACT OF RURAL TOURISM

The literature on tourism impacts has long since assumed a central position within the emergence of tourism research, as early reviews by geographers confirm (e.g. Mathieson and Wall 1982). However, in a rural context, impact research has not been at the forefront of methodological and theoretical developments. One particular problem, as already noted, is the tendency for researchers to adopt well-established theoretical constructs and concepts from their own disciplinary perspective and apply them to the analysis of rural tourism issues. Within the social and cultural dimensions of rural tourism, the influence of rural sociology in the 1960s and 1970s (e.g. Bracey 1970) dominated sociological research while V.L. Smith's (1977) influential collection of anthropological studies of tourism highlighted the approaches adopted by anthropologists. Probably the most influential statement on the social and cultural impacts is Bouquet and Winter's (1987a) diverse anthology of studies of the conflict and political debates associated with rural tourism. For example, Bouquet and Winter (1987b) consider the relationship between tourism, politics and the issue of policies to control and direct tourism (and recreation) in the countryside in the post-war period. Geographers have largely remained absent from this area of study as Hall and Jenkins (1998) and Jenkins *et al.* (1998) indicate. Even so, non-spatial studies, such as Winter's (1987) study of farming and tourism in the English and Welsh uplands, argue for circumspection in advocating farm tourism as a solution to the socio-

Plates 6.1 and 6.2: In recent years, literary images such as James Herriot's Yorkshire have been used to market rural tourism as in the example of the fictitious Darrowby (Thirsk, North Yorkshire).

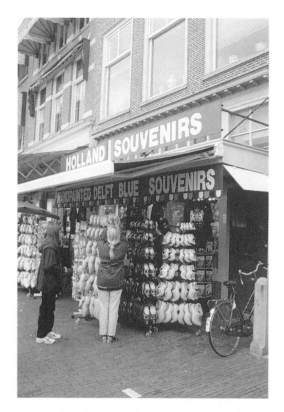

Plate 6.3: To what extent does tourism lead to cultural stereotyping and changed perceptions of cultural identity by both locals and tourists? Souvenir shop, Leyden, Holland.

economic development problems of 'less favoured areas', a conclusion which is widely endorsed by subsequent studies (e.g. Jenkins *et al.* 1998). Sociological studies offer an insight into the social implications of the spatially determined activities of tourists and recreationalists in remote areas, where they may contribute to farm incomes.

More recently, a number of researchers have sought to diversify the focus of social and cultural impact research to include concerns about the way in which tourism development may change rural cultures (e.g. Byrne *et al.* 1993) and the consumption of rural environments and cultures in relation to late modernity or the postmodern society which has a specific relevance for studies in geography. The role of women in rural tourism has also belatedly attracted interest as a highly seasonal and

unstable economic activity, since tourism offers one of the few employment opportunities to be taken up by women, which further contributes to the marginal status of women in the rural workforce. Similar arguments are also advanced by gender studies with a tourism component such as Redclift and Sinclair (1991), though few geographers have examined these issues. More recent studies by Edwards (1991) and Keane *et al.* (1992) also indicate the importance of community participation in tourism planning so that the local population, and women in particular, are not excluded from the benefits of rural tourism development. A particularly sensitive issue is that of indigenous people and traditional cultures, including land/resource rights and their roles as performers and entrepreneurs (Butler and Hinch 1996). Increasingly native people are becoming involved in tourism to help meet their own goals of independence and cultural survival, yet tourism development carries special risks for them (Hall 1996).

Considerable attention has been paid in the literature to residents' perceptions and attitudes towards tourism (in common with recreation research), including studies of small towns and rural areas (e.g. Allen *et al.* 1988; Long *et al.* 1990; Getz 1994a; Johnson *et al.* 1994) but few geographers have undertaken longitudinal studies of rural tourism's impact on the way communities view, interact, accept or deny tourism, though examples in urban areas are also limited (see Page 1997a). However, as Butler and Clark (1992: 180) conclude, an

> area where some research is needed is in the changing relationship between tourism and its host community. Rarely is tourism the sole rural economic activity. Over the last few decades the countryside has witnessed major changes in its social composition, the main symptoms being gentrification, new forms of social polarisation, and a domination by the service class. More research is needed on the relationship between the uneven social composition of the countryside, the spatially variable development of tourism, and the problematic relationship between the two.

It is somewhat ironic that with rural geographers making such a major contribution to rural studies, only a limited number have examined the implications in terms of social theory as well as the empirical dimensions of tourism development.

THE ECONOMIC IMPACT

The economic impact of rural tourism has been a fruitful area for research among a range of social scientists, often emphasising or challenging the role of tourism as a panacea for solving all the economic and social ills of the countryside although the major contribution of geographers has largely been in relation to the study of farm tourism. But as Butler and Clark (1992: 175) rightly acknowledge, tourism in rural areas is not necessarily the magical solution to rural development, given its

> income leakages, volatility, declining multipliers, low pay, imported labour and the conservatism of investors. The least favoured circumstance in which to promote tourism is when the rural economy is already weak, since tourism will create highly unbalanced income and employment distributions. It is a better supplement for a thriving and diverse economy than as a mainstay of rural development.

In a longitudinal study of the Spey Valley, Scotland, Getz (1981, 1986b, 1993c, 1994a, b) documents a rural area in which tourism has remained the economic mainstay. In this respect, Butler and Clark's (1992) research is useful in that it identifies the principal concerns in rural economic research and the role of tourism in development in relation to:

- income leakage;
- multipliers;
- labour issues (local versus imported and low pay);
- the limited number of entrepreneurs in rural areas;
- the proposition that tourism should be a supplement rather than the mainstay of rural economies.

The principal research in this area has been undertaken by economists such as Archer (1973, 1982) whose pioneering studies of multipliers have been used to establish the economic benefits of tourist expenditure in rural areas. While these studies have remained the baseline for subsequent research on rural tourism, few studies embrace a broad economic analysis to encompass the wide range of issues raised by Butler and Clark (1992). One possible explanation for this paucity of detailed economic studies of rural tourism may be related to the persistence of a 'farm tourism' focus.

Farm tourism

Farm tourism may offer one way of facilitating agricultural diversification. According to Evans (1992a), research on farm tourism can be divided into two categories. The first is an expanding literature concerned with 'differing types of farm diversification as a major option adapted by farm families to aid business restructuring, necessitated by falling farm incomes' (Evans 1992a: 140). The second is 'one devoted specifically to farm tourism and though these studies remain the most detailed, they are becoming increasingly dated' (Evans 1992a: 140). Evans (1992a) cited those by Davies (1971), Jacobs (1973), DART (1974), Bull and Wibberley (1976), Denman (1978) and Frater (1982) which all use 1970s data.

Evans (1992a) is critical of the second group of studies for their lack of definitional clarity, since they fail to distinguish between the accommodation and recreational components of farm tourism (Evans and Ilbery 1989). Evans (1992a: 140) rightly considers the analytical components of the studies to be too simplistic, focusing on expected economic costs and benefits of these enterprises, and the characteristics and attitudes of farm families to such development. Despite these problems with the farm tourism literature and concerns with its marketing, a major impediment to developing a more sophisticated understanding of farm tourism remains the absence of accurate national studies of the growth and development of farm tourism. However, Dernoi (1983) and Frater (1983) review the situation in Europe, Wrathall (1980) examines the development of France's *gîtes ruraux*, while Oppermann (1995) considers farm tourism in southern Germany, mapping and analysing the spatial distribution of the accommodation base. Vogeler (1977) discussed the situation in the United States, while Oppermann (1998) provided a valuable baseline survey of the New Zealand scene (see also Hall and Kearsley 2002).

A survey of England and Wales identified almost 6,000 farm businesses with accommodation. It also undertook a geographical analysis of the distribution of such accommodation, with South-West England, Cumbria, the Welsh border counties, North Yorkshire and the South-East coast of England popular locations for this activity. The upland areas and South-West England were the dominant locations, with a diversity of modes of operation (bed and breakfast, self-catering, camping and caravanning) and niche marketing used to satisfy particular forms of tourism demand (e.g. weekend breaks, week-long breaks and traditional two-week holidays). Evans (1992b) acknowledged the absence of national studies of why farm businesses have pursued this activity and the range of factors influencing their decision to undertake it. The survey also points to inherent contradictions in the existing literature, since its findings illustrate that larger farm businesses have also diversified into farm tourism (Ilbery 1991). While this is at odds with Frater's (1982) research it illustrates that family labour is widely used to service farm-based accommodation. Such research also highlights the capital requirements of farm tourism ventures and the role of marketing, financial advice and the need for external agents in establishing networks to develop their business. Even so, Maude and van Rest (1985) argue that due to the limited returns for small farmers and the constraints of existing planning legislation it is not a significant means of tackling the serious problem of low farm incomes in upland areas (see also Jenkins *et al.* 1998). Thus it is unlikely to improve the low-income problem of upland farmers in their Cumbria case study since they argue that farm tourism has been wrongly regarded as the main pillar in a diversified agricultural policy (Maude and van Rest 1985). Consequently, the continued debate and focus on farm tourism has detracted from a more critical debate on the wider signifi-cance of rural tourism within an economic context and the way it may be integrated into structuration theory and other contemporary theoretically informed analyses.

THE ENVIRONMENTAL EFFECTS OF RURAL TOURISM

The environmental impact of tourism has been extensively reviewed in the tourism literature and rural tourism has emerged as a prominent element, with the usual caveat that tourism is destructive in different degrees of the actual qualities which attract tourists. In a rural context, the growing pressure emerging from the development-intensive nature of tourism, and the expansion of mass tourism, has introduced many new pressures as 'new tourism' discovers the qualities of rural environments. In fact, the construction of theme parks in rural environments, second homes (Gartner 1987), timeshares, conference centres, holiday villages and designation of environments as special places to visit (e.g. national parks) have all contributed to the insatiable tourism appetite for rural environments. Bramwell (1991) highlights the concern for more responsible and environmental forms of rural tourism in the 1990s with the sustainability debate firmly focused on the rural environment. Bramwell (1991) examines the extent to which rural tourism policy in Britain has been integrated with concepts of sustainability, outlining the role of the English Tourist Board and Countryside Commission policy formulation process. The Countryside Commission points to the need for improving the public's understanding and care of the rural environment as outlined in their consultation paper 'Visitors to the Countryside'. A number of recent special issues of journals have also focused on sustainability and rural tourism (e.g. *Trends* 1994; *Tourism Recreation Research* 1991; *Journal of Sustainable Tourism* 1994) with geographers contributing to the debate (e.g. Butler and Hall 1998; Hall and Lew 1998). However, it is apparent that tourism in a rural context displays many of the features of the symbiotic relationship that exist between tourism

INSIGHT: Wine, food and tourism

Wine, food and tourism are all products which are differentiated on the basis of regional identity. Wine is often identified by its geographical origin (e.g. Burgundy, Champagne, Rioja) which, in many cases, has been formalised through a series of appellation controls in turn founded on certain geographical characteristics of a place (Moran 1993, 2000, 2001). Foods (e.g. cheese) are also identified by their place of origin. Similarly, tourism is also promoted by the attraction of regional or local destinations. It should therefore be of little surprise that the relationship between wine, food and tourism is extremely significant at a regional level through the contribution that regionality provides for product branding, place promotion and, through these mechanisms, economic development (Ilbery and Kneafsey 2000a, 2000b). As Moran (1993: 266) observed:

> Burgundy gives its name to one of the best known wines in the world but at the same time the region of Burgundy becomes known because of its wine. Moreover, the little bits of it, often only a few hectares, also derive their prestige from the wines that are produced there. In Burgundy, the process has developed to the extent that in order to capitalize on the reputation of their most famous wines many of the communes . . . have taken the name of their

most famous vineyard. Corton was added to make Aloxe-Corton, Montrachet to make both Puligny-Montrachet and Chassagne-Montrachet, Romanee to make Vosne-Romanee, St Georges to make Nuits-St Georges and so on.

The wine, food and tourism industries all rely on regional branding for market leverage and promotion (Hall *et al.* 1997/1998; Hall and Macionis 1998). Hall (1996b: 114) describes the importance of tourism place and wine appellation or region thus: 'there is a direct impact on tourism in the identification of wine regions because of the inter-relationships that may exist in the overlap of wine and destination region promotion and the accompanying set of economic and social linkages.' In addition, relationships between food and tourism are also created through the purchasing patterns of tourists which may have a significant impact on local production and the maintenance or expansion of the local farming economy (Reynolds 1993; Telfer and Wall 1996; Bell and Valentine 1997; Van Westering 1999).

Tourism has long been regarded as having the potential to contribute to regional development. However, ongoing economic restructuring and

Plate 6.4: Rural heritage is a significant attraction base for rural tourism. Sissinghurst, Kent.

Plate 6.5: Tourism may assist in the development of new rural industries through the creation of new markets. Vineyard development in Central Otago, New Zealand.

change in rural areas has increased the focus on tourism and how agricultural production may be enhanced through tourism demand. Moreover, these changes have been accompanied by the perceived need to retain or attract people in rural areas, maintain aspects of 'traditional' rural lifestyles and agricultural production, and conserve aspects of the rural landscape (Van Westering 1999). Many wine regions around the world have been affected by changed patterns of demand for wine and levels of tariff protection that has led to the planting of new grape varieties or, in some cases, loss of vineyards to other forms of production. Yet demand has also meant that some areas, particularly in New World wine regions such as Australia, Canada, New Zealand and the United States, have now been planted which had previously not been seriously considered for commercial wine production (Telfer 2000; Moran 2001). Within this context wine tourism is therefore emerging as an increasingly important component of rural diversification and development (Hall et al. 2000).

Strategies to integrate tourism and cuisine in order to promote economic development and the creation of sustainable food systems occur at national, regional and local levels (Hall and Mitchell 2002). Ideally, these levels should be integrated in order to maximise the likelihood of policy success. However, often the reality is that different levels of government and industry will undertake their own initiatives without consulting or co-operating with other levels. As Figure 6.1 indicates there are a number of mechanisms for promoting sustainable food systems utilising the relationship between wine and food, each of which operates most effectively at particular levels. Although intervention by the national and local state will occur at all levels it is very common for the policy activities at the higher level to be implemented at the lower level in order to achieve targeted regional and local development goals. This approach has been particularly common within the European Union and in federal states,

such as Australia, Canada and the United States (Hall et al. 2000; Telfer 2000).

At the national and regional level promotion and branding are extremely common strategies to link food with tourism. For example, in an effort to capitalise on and maximise the tourism potential of the wine industry, several Australian states have instituted specific wine and food tourism bodies to facilitate and co-ordinate the development of wine tourism (Hall and Macionis 1998). However, despite the ability of regions to brand themselves in terms of wine and food tourism the establishment of other forms of network relationships between food and wine producers and the tourism industry may be more problematic. Hall et al. (1997/1998) noted several barriers to creating effective links between wine producers and the tourism industry which can be extended to the majority of primary producers in Australia and New Zealand, including:

• the often secondary or tertiary nature of tourism as an activity in the wine industry;
• a dominant product focus of wine makers and wine marketers;
• a general lack of experience and understanding within the wine industry of tourism, and a subsequent lack of entrepreneurial skills and abilities with respect to marketing and product development;
• the absence of effective intersectoral linkages, which leads to a lack of inter- and intra-organisational cohesion within the wine industry, and between the wine industry and the tourism industry.

The Australian Bureau of Industry Economics (BIE) (1991a, b) identified four potential roles for government in the development of networks:

1 disseminating information on the opportunities created by networks;
2 encouraging co-operation within industries through industry associations;

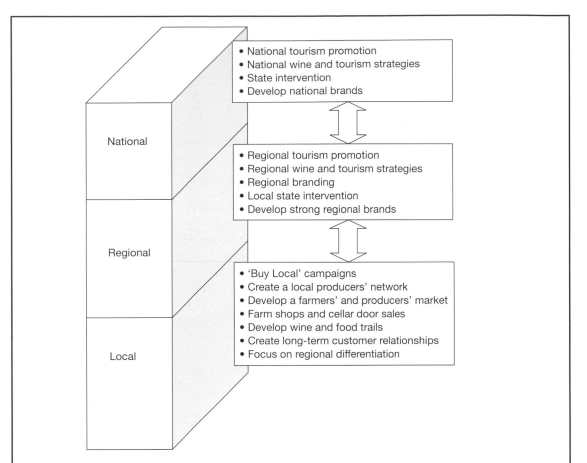

National
- National tourism promotion
- National wine and tourism strategies
- State intervention
- Develop national brands

Regional
- Regional tourism promotion
- Regional wine and tourism strategies
- Regional branding
- Local state intervention
- Develop strong regional brands

Local
- 'Buy Local' campaigns
- Create a local producers' network
- Develop a farmers' and producers' market
- Farm shops and cellar door sales
- Develop wine and food trails
- Create long-term customer relationships
- Focus on regional differentiation

Figure 6.1: Relationship between national, regional and local strategies

3 improving existing networks between the private sector and public sector agencies involved in research and development, education and training;

4 examining the effects of the existing legislative and regulatory framework on the formation, maintenance and breakup of networks relative to other forms of organisation, such as markets and firms.

In the case of wine and food tourism in Australia, the federal government directly utilised the first three roles in the creation of specific organisations and/or the provision of funding for research, education, co-operative strategies and mechanisms, and information provision. The BIE (1991a, b) considered information gaps to be a major factor in the impairment of network formation. Indeed, there are substantial negative attitudes towards tourism by wineries and some food producers, whereas tourism organisations tend to be far more positive towards the wine and food industry. This situation is reflective of Leiper's (1989, 1990) concept of tourism's partial industrialisation which suggests that businesses need to perceive they are part of the tourism industry before they will formally interact with tourism suppliers.

Several models of local network development are utilised in food systems (Figure 6.2). The

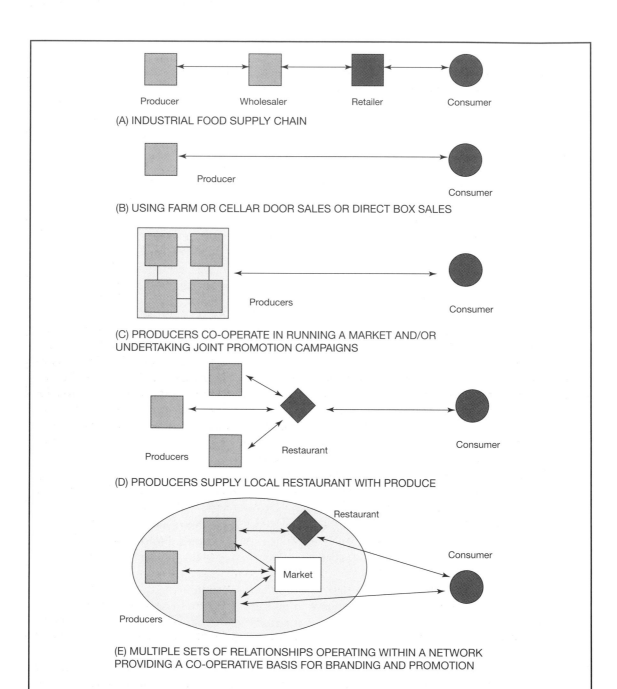

Figure 6.2: Creating different supply chains and local food systems

classic industrial model of the food supply chain of producer–wholesaler–retailer–consumer all linked through transport networks has provided for a relativly efficient means of distributing food but it has substantially affected the returns producers get as well as placing numerous intermediaries between consumers and producers. The industrial model has allowed for the development of larger farm properties, reduced labour costs and supported export industry but it has done little to promote sustainable economic development and food systems. In tourism terms this relationship has been utilised in national branding and promotion when multiple supply chains are bundled together to attract the foreign customer. One alternative is to create a direct relationship between producers and consumers. This may be done by direct marketing and 'box deliveries' (e.g. the delivery of a box of seasonal produce direct to the consumer). In relation to tourism an important direct relationship is the opportunity for the consumer to purchase at the farm or cellar door, allowing the consumer to experience where the produce is from and the people who grow or make it, thereby creating the potential for the development of long-term relationship marketing. Such direct sales are extremely popular with small wineries and horticultural producers and are often utilised by peri-urban and rural producers who are located close to urban centres where they can take advantage of the day-trip market. Nevertheless, such individual developments while useful at the business level and adding to the overall attractiveness and diversity of a location do not constitute a network relationship that can promote a region more effectively.

Co-operative relationships between producers provide the basis for the creation of producer networks that can pool resources to engage in local promotion and branding and undertaking research (Hall *et al.* 1997/1998). In addition, the pooling of resources can also lead to the development of new products such as produce markets. The impacts of farmers' markets on the regional economy and in generating employment may be substantial. For example, Farmers Markets Ontario (2001) estimate that in 1999 farmers' markets in the province attracted about a million shoppers a year, 90 per cent of whom came for the fresh produce. Over 25,000 people work in the markets sector with annual sales at all farmers' markets across Ontario exceeding Can$500 million and with an overall impact on the province's economy of over Can$1.5 billion. Another model of generating local food production is the use of a restaurant to act as the conduit by which local produce is presented to tourists. The development of local purchasing relationships by restaurants can have a substantial impact on local produce as it can assist in developing quality produce, allow producers to gain a clearer understanding of how their produce is being used, as well as providing a guaranteed sales outlet for their produce. In the case of the latter the knowledge of a guaranteed minimum income may allow producers the opportunity to expand production and find other markets for their produce. Finally, we arrive at the ideal model of multiple sets of producer and consumer relationships operating within a formal network structure which provides for branding and promotion as well as economic networking and resource sharing. A good example of this type of development is Tastes of Niagara in Ontario which is a Quality Food Alliance of Niagara food producers, wine makers, chefs, restaurateurs and retailers (http://www.tourismniagara.com/tastesofniagara/index.html). Established in 1993, members have joined together to promote the uniqueness of the region's agricultural products to consumers through the development and maintenance of high-quality regional produce, cuisine, events and service (see Telfer forthcoming).

Plate 6.6: Hunters, fisherpersons and walkers serve as an important source of income for many small villages in Scandinavia. Elga, Norway.

and the environment and is a key component of its very attraction to tourists. In order to illustrate some of the major issues raised in the above discussion, attention now turns to a case study of rural tourism in Ireland.

RECREATION, TOURISM AND SUSTAINABILITY

Ideas of sustainable development have been as influential in the area of rural policy as they have elsewhere (Murdoch 1993; Whatmore 1993). However, much of the discussion on applications of sustainability has been about individual components of rurality (e.g. attempts at developing sustainable agriculture), rather than a comprehensive approach to integrate the socio-cultural, economic and environmental components of both sustainability and rurality. For example, the Rural

---

CASE STUDY: Tourism in Ireland: peripherality and the rural environment

This case study seeks to illustrate the concepts and approaches which geographers have used to examine rural tourism in Ireland (e.g. supply, demand and spatial patterns) emphasising how it may assist in understanding the organisation of tourism and its development. The literature on tourism in Ireland has expanded in recent years, following the growing recognition of the country's potential as a tourist destination (Page 1994c; O'Connor and Cronin 1993; Deegan and Dineen 1996). As a tourist destination, Ireland (which in this case study is confined to Eire, the Republic of Ireland – see Figure 6.3) is a largely rural environment at a national level and serves as a major example of tourism development in a mainly rural environment, despite the expan-sion of urban and heritage tourism in small towns and cities (Page 1994d). In fact, Deegan and Dineen (1996: 111) aptly summarise the essential rural

qualities of Ireland thus: 'to some international tourists it [Ireland] represents the essence of Irish tourism – the beautiful countryside, the clean air, the friendly people, the relative solitude. It can be effective also in serenading a greater geographical spread of tourists.'

Within the context of the European Union, Ireland is an interesting example of a country which is peripheral to the traditional spatial concentrations of tourism-related activities. Existing studies of tourism in these areas have emphasised the concept of peripherality in relation to economic disadvantage and the emergence of 'problem regions' within the EU. Explanations of 'problem regions' have been based on how regions develop within a capitalist society and the way in which inequalities occur between 'core' (urban) areas and their 'periphery'. Although research on the political economy of

Figure 6.3: Ireland – location map
Source: McEniff (1996), reproduced courtesy of Travel and Tourism Intelligence

peripheral areas (e.g. Cooke 1986, 1989) has highlighted dependency relationships between core areas and their periphery, there has been an absence of theoretical research on how tourism functions in peripheral areas of the EU.

Consequently, a strange paradox exists: previous research on economic potential and peripherality in the EU (e.g. Keeble *et al.* 1982) has implied that geographical isolation is an obstacle to economic development, although such research did not acknowledge the complexity of service industries and their varied location requirements. Yet tourism plays 'an important role in the economy of remote rural areas because of the dispersed nature of tourism expenditure' (Grimes 1992: 28), and its potential to assist in regional development is widely acknowledged (D.G. Pearce 1988c, 1989, 1992a). The relative geographical isolation of an area in the context of the European space economy does not necessarily imply that successful tourism development is precluded: the tourism potential of an area, region or country is not necessarily conditioned by peripherality even though research on economic potential has inferred that geographical isolation is a constraint on economic development. Understanding the concept of peripherality is dependent upon the scale at which it is considered, and this can range from the international level (e.g. within the EU), to the national level (e.g. a country such as Ireland), down to the regional level (i.e. regions within one country) and local scale (i.e. within different parts of a region). Various countries perceived as peripheral within the EU have benefited from a growing internationalisation of tourism and the search for new tourist destinations in areas characterised as rural. Even so, this has to be set against the potential social and cultural impacts which tourism may generate in more rural areas and against the economic dependence of an industry which is notoriously fickle and subject to seasonal fluctuations (Brunt 1988).

THE GEOGRAPHER'S ANALYSIS OF PERIPHERALITY

The concept of peripherality is a useful starting point for the analysis of tourist destinations such as Ireland, although more detailed analysis of the context in which the tourism industry operates, recent trends and developments associated with tourism in the region, is equally important. Peripherality as a concept is not sufficiently developed within the existing literature on tourism in rural and marginal areas of the EU (see Seers *et al.* 1979), since much of the research has focused on the significance of agricultural and manufacturing activities in terms of the dependency relationship between peripheral areas and core regions (Crotty 1979; Seers and Ostrom 1982; Barry 1991). According to Clout (1987: 12), within the EU, core areas are characterised by a 'high density of population, good reservoirs of expertise, efficient means of access to communication systems allowing contact with the wider world' while peripheral areas are 'fragmented in spatial, economic and organisational terms and tend to be more susceptible than core zones to economic dependence' (Clout 1987: 13). Shaw and Williams (1990) review the literature on tourism, economic development and dependence, which emphasised the role of the entrepreneur and transnational corporations in influencing the nature of dependency relationships between core and peripheral areas (de Kadt 1979; O'Hearn 1989). Shaw and Williams (1990) also discuss geographical models of tourism and the dependency relationship (see also Britton 1980a, b; D.G. Pearce 1989), and for this reason it is pertinent to highlight a number of key concepts which have dominated the analysis of tourism and economic development.

The concepts of core and periphery are used in tourism research on economic development to show how different areas expand and develop within a capitalist system. The origin and application of such concepts may be attributed to the work of Friedmann (1966) which considered economic development and the emergence of a polarised pattern of growth as core areas expanded and developed at the expense of peripheral areas. The theoretical basis of such research has been extensively reviewed, particularly the dynamics of economic change and development (e.g. Lloyd and Dicken 1987; Phelps 1992). Townsend (1991: 315), however, has argued that due to the lack of research on services and economic development, there is a 'need and scope for the refinement of economic base theory' in view of its inability to accommodate the role of services. Since the initial work by Friedmann (1966), Seers *et al.* (1979) have examined peripheral areas and economic development further in terms of countries in the European periphery, such as the Irish Republic, and emphasised their geographical characteristics, and the extent to which economic and social problems resulted from peripherality. However, the 'core–periphery' concepts remain permanent in relation to research on economic development, since they form the basis for regional policy in the EU, which has aimed to reduce regional imbalances and economic disparities resulting from the historical pattern of economic development in the EU (Clout 1987). For example, the Commission of the European Community Fourth Periodic Report (1991) differentiated between regions in the EU according to the nature of their 'regional problem', with the Irish Republic forming a 'lagging region'. However, even when the concepts of core and periphery are developed in a more pluralistic framework (Clout 1987), they still constitute an oversimplification of a highly complex situation.

One particular problem with the application of core–periphery concepts to tourism and service industries is related to the question of the scale at which you analyse the geographical patterns of economic development in terms of the advanced stages of capitalism in the EU, since in 'many service industries . . . there is a major problem of specifying the boundary and content of many services' (Urry 1991: 2). Tourism services are primarily concerned with the provision of an intangible product or experience to meet the perceived needs of tourists compared to the more tangible products supplied by the primary and secondary sectors of the economy. Thus any attempt to theorise about the role of tourism, economic development and peripheral areas is notoriously difficult since core–periphery concepts cannot easily accommodate the complex role of tourism services in relation to changes in the organisation of contemporary society and the geographical preferences for different and varied tourist experiences. Recent research on services has analysed the change in society from a 'Fordist' to 'Post-Fordist' stage or organisation (Esser and Hirsch 1989) which has involved a shift in the form of demand for tourist services from a former pattern of mass consumption 'to more individual patterns, with greater differentiation and volatility of consumer preferences and a heightened need for producers to be consumer-driven and to segment markets more systematically' (Urry 1991: 52). These changes had led to a shift from an 'old tourism' (e.g. the regimented and standardised holiday package) to a 'new tourism' (Poon 1989) which is segmented, customised and flexible. Therefore, any explanation of tourism services and their role in peripheral areas needs to take account of new theoretical approaches to the production, consumption and delivery of tourist services, the interrelationships between these components and their impact on various localities. Consequently, while research on tourism urbanisation (Mullins 1991) has examined the consequences of concentrated tourist activity in urban areas, little theoretical work has been undertaken to examine the dispersed nature of tourist activity in relation to the growth of a new tourism, its development in peripheral areas and the implications for economic dependency. Therefore, the development of new theoretical explanations will also need to move beyond the geographical concepts of core and periphery in understanding the process of tourism development in areas perceived as peripheral.

THE DIMENSIONS OF PERIPHERALITY IN THE REPUBLIC OF IRELAND

Despite a number of notable international research publications (e.g. Anon. 1983; McEniff 1987, 1991, 1996; Baum 1989a, b; Euromonitor 1992; D.G. Pearce 1990, 1992b; Deegan and Dineen 1996), Ireland has been relatively neglected in the tourism literature. While the problem of peripherality has led certain researchers to observe that 'tourism . . . in Ireland would appear to be at an immediate and considerable disadvantage' (Pollard 1989: 301), significant progress has been made in overcoming this obstacle by expanding its international tourist arrivals in the late 1980s and early 1990s. By developing an expansionist policy towards inbound tourism and measures to redress the perceived 'peripherality' of Ireland's location in the EU, tourism has made a significant contribution to the national economy through tourist spending by building on the strengths and advantages of Ireland's geographical location and its distinctive tourism product (Bord Fáilte 1991a). Ireland's geographical position on the western margins of the EU is often viewed as peripheral (Mitchell 1970; Johnson 1987; Brunt 1988; Gillmore 1985; Carter and Parker 1989; Robinson 1991) and has been a powerful factor in shaping the economic fortunes of the Irish economy according to the national Development Plan 1989–1993. Grimes (1992), however, has argued that peripherality has been used as a mechanism to increase EU structural funds to address the perceived obstacles posed by relative geographical isolation and peripherality to economic development (Commission of the European Community 1991).

Ireland's role as a 'lagging region' in the EU is reflected in terms of its small population, estimated to be 3.6 million in 1996, equivalent to a population density of 50 per km which is the lowest in the EU. However, 'between 1979 and 1986 Ireland had the biggest population growth rate' (Grimes 1992: 23) in the EU or 5.1 per cent, fuelled by a high birth rate of 1.7 per cent per annum, the second highest in the EU. Ireland was also characterised by high rates of net internal migration, with an annual average loss of population of 3.4 per 1,000 induced in part by a high rate of unemployment of 14 per cent in 1990 (Economist Intelligence Unit 1991), which contributed to a continued outflow of skilled labour. Of the 1,120,000 people employed in Ireland in 1990, 15.4 per cent worked in agricultural-related activities, 26.9 per cent in manufacturing and 57.7 per cent in services, the latter having experienced a continued growth in the 1980s. As Grimes (1992: 25) acknowledged, 'economic performance in the Community has not been strong relative to that of other member countries' with GDP per head at 62.4 per cent of the EC average in 1989, which combined with a large public debt in an economy characterised by a high degree of openness (O'Hagan and Mooney 1983). Employment in the service sector expanded at a rate of 2.3 per cent per annum between 1971 and 1981, generating some 129,000 jobs, which was significant as services 'use relatively few imports and most of their demand remains in the economy' (Grimes 1992: 28) which was beneficial for the Irish economy where substantial leakages occur due to imports and profit repatriation by foreign companies. Furthermore, O'Riordan (1986) also noted that within the context of Ireland, services create more income and employment than other sectors of the economy, and therefore tourism has assumed an important role as a service industry (Bord Fáilte 1985).

TOURISM DEMAND AND IRELAND'S ECONOMY

In 1994, the Irish tourism industry earned I£2.18 bln from domestic and international tourist spending accounting for 6.8 per cent of GNP, with approximately 75 per cent of expenditure generated by overseas tourists. This made an important, though variable, contribution to the Irish economy within the context of the balance of payments (Gillmore 1985; Economist Intelligence Unit 1991) and employment generation (Deane 1987), where the number of full-time job equivalents in tourism rose from 69,000 in 1988 (Bord Fáilte 1989; Baum 1989b), to 82,000 in 1990 (McEniff 1991) and 94,000 in 1994 (McEniff 1996). The economic impact increased through a tourism multiplier effect of 1.72 (Fletcher and Snee 1989; Bord Fáilte 1990a). Baum (1989a: 141–2) examined the economic benefits of the tourism industry in the early 1980s.

The recent and sustained increase in tourist revenue is indicative of the Irish tourism industry's increased competitiveness, a higher quality of tourism product, the role of overseas marketing and promotion (Kassem 1987), and the development of Ireland's tourism infrastructure by Bord Fáilte and the private sector in the late 1980s, compared to a period of relative stagnation in the early 1980s (Gillmore 1985; Grimes 1992). A range of studies have described the historical development of tourism arrivals (e.g. Gillmore 1985; Brunt 1988; Pollard 1989), particularly in relation to improved accessibility (Brookfield 1955). According to McEniff (1996), in 1994, 68 per cent of Ireland's overseas visitors arrived by air, through the major gateways of Dublin, Shannon and Cork (see Figure 6.4). This tourist traffic comprised 1,488,000 visitors who travelled by cross-channel air services (between the UK and Ireland), 726,000 visitors using continental European air services and 242,000 visitors on transatlantic flights through Shannon. In contrast, 1,225,000 visitors used sea crossings from the UK and continental Europe to travel to Ireland. The emphasis on air travel is indicative of the recent deregulation of air routes and competitively priced air fares, especially between the UK and Ireland. The state airline Aer Lingus is an important agent in the development of tourism (Aer Lingus 1991) as 'its role in the direct and indirect promotion of the tourist industry is . . . of great significance' (Brunt 1988: 33–4). Improvements in transport infrastructure are also evident with the investment of I£73.3 million between 1989 and 1993 from the EU-funded Operational Programme on Peripherality to upgrade Irish imports. In fact between 1994 and 1999, the EU-funded Operational Programme on Peripherality planned to spend I£370 million on upgrading tourism infrastructure, which will increase to I£652 million if other public and private sector contributions occur.

In 1989, Ireland received 1.3 per cent of the EC's total international arrivals, and research on the origin of visitors has underlined the country's dependence on two major source areas – Great Britain (including Northern Ireland; see Barry and O'Hagan 1972) and continental Europe (Gillmore 1985) which accounted for 85 per cent of arrivals in 1994 and 75 per cent of revenue (McEniff 1996). The number of arrivals from continental Europe has more than doubled since 1985 (see Table 6.1) while the North American market has decreased in volume up to 1993 and then increased in 1994 (Grimes 1992; McEniff 1996), although it still forms an important source of revenue (O'Hagan and Harrison 1984a, b). The importance of different motives for international tourists visiting Ireland has been discussed in detail by Gillmore (1985), Brunt (1988), Pollard (1989) and McEniff (1991) and need not be reiterated here. More detailed studies have examined how special-interest tourism (Weiler and Hall 1992) has been developed in Ireland to diversify its tourism product and broaden the country's tourism appeal among niche markets such as social tourism (Champeaux 1987; McGrath 1989; Wilhelm 1990). Other forms of tourism, such as farm tourism (Fowler 1991), have been nurtured to develop alternative land uses, thereby diversifying the economic base in rural areas from agriculture to tourism despite the problems of seasonality and dependence (Ball 1989; McEniff 1991).

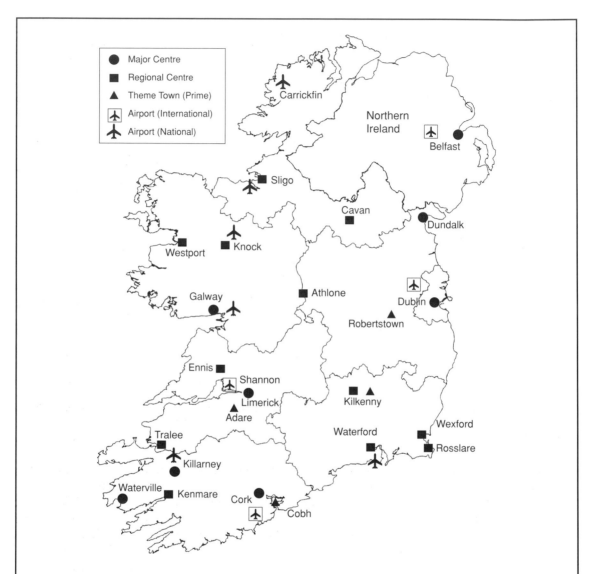

Figure 6.4: Major and regional tourism centres, theme towns and airports in the Republic of Ireland
Source: Redrawn from Department of Tourism and Transport (1989) and Deegan and Dineen (1996)

In contrast, domestic tourism (Gillmore 1985; Brunt 1988; Pollard 1989) and the role of out-bound Irish tourism (Brunt 1988; Fitzpatrick and Montague 1989) has received comparatively little attention despite the economic contribution of the 5.1 million domestic trips made in 1990 which generated I£342 million for the Irish economy. Although the number of domestic trips doubled between 1985 and 1990, due in part to the growth in short breaks, 'revenue receipts from domestic holidays in 1990 were estimated to be worth I£342 million, an increase of 86% in nominal terms since 1985 . . . average expenditure per holidaymaker has decreased in nominal and real

Table 6.1: Visitor arrivals in the Republic of Ireland by country of residence, 1985–94 (000s)

Country	1985	1986	1987	1988	1989	1990	1991	1992	1993	1994
UK:	1,704	1,716	1,802	2,090	2,396	2,355	2,266	2,315	2,397	2,668
Great Britain	1,119	1,130	1,236	1,508	1,716	1,785	1,746	1,765	1,857	2,038
Northern Ireland	585	586	566	582	680	570	520	550	540	630
Continental Europe:	334	337	390	408	547	744	841	874	945	988
France	95	89	113	111	138	198	220	220	242	231
West Germany	98	100	103	113	154	178	203	230	265	269
Italy	16	17	22	21	37	73	96	101	116	121
Netherlands	33	33	40	38	46	72	83	73	69	80
Spain	15	23	34	34	38	54	62	56	57	59
Switzerland	17	17	17	24	31	41	46	52	40	62
Belgium/Luxembourg	22	21	20	20	28	37	33	40	41	41
Norway/Sweden	10	11	11	12	18	26	27	26	32	33
Denmark	17	14	13	14	22	16	19	18	17	19
Other European	11	12	17	21	35	49	–	–	–	–
North America:	422	343	398	419	427	443	356	417	422	494
USA	392	309	367	385	385	402	321	374	376	449
Canada	30	34	31	34	42	41	35	43	46	45
Australia/New Zealand	37	36	37	46	62	69	–	–	–	–
Others	32	35	37	44	52	54	–	–	–	–
Total tourist numbers	2,529	2,467	2,664	3,007	3,484	3,665	3,571	3,724	3,888	4,309

Source: Page (1994c); McEniff (1996)

terms, falling in constant prices from I£99 per person in 1985 to I£81 in 1990' (McEniff 1991: 35). Brunt (1988: 86–7) examines the regional pattern of expenditure among the Irish population while Go (1991) emphasises the factors influencing outbound travel (e.g. social and work patterns, consumer tastes, leave entitlements and disposable income) and their sensitivity to fluctuations in the economic cycles, particularly in major urban areas (e.g. Dublin).

THE SUPPLY OF TOURISM RESOURCES IN IRELAND

Ireland's tourist product is based upon natural and man-made resources and an experience which is conditioned by the social and cultural environment (i.e. the people, their history, heritage, landscape and culture – see Keane 1972). The country's natural and man-made environment (Pollard 1989) reflects the aesthetic qualities of the Irish landscape (Foras Forbatha 1977), where 1.2 million ha of the landscape is classified as being of 'outstanding quality' (Mawhinney 1979), particularly in the more peripheral areas of the west of Ireland (Brunt 1988: 116) with its unpolluted, uncommercialised and scenic coastline, especially in the counties of Donegal, Clare and Kerry (Brady *et al.* 1972–73). Although urban tourism offers a contrast with the rural qualities of Ireland, Gillmore (1985: 312) identifies the principal preoccupations of visitors from a 1982 Bord Fáilte survey. The survey emphasised sightseeing, exploring the countryside and touring natural and cultural attractions as the main activities, highlighting the need to provide appropriate infrastructure and facilities to accommodate the rural and dispersed nature of many tourist activities (Plettner 1979). Mountain-based activities (Pollard 1989) and coastal-based activities also assumed an important role in tourists' use of rural environments. For example, Foras Forbatha's (1973) study of Brittas Bay highlighted the significance of coastal planning and the significance of 'carrying capacity' in these sensitive recreational and tourism environments, and Carter (1988) examines some of the pressures posed by tourism in the coastal environment. Stevens (1987) also provided an interesting insight in the context of coastal environments, in terms of the tourist potential of subterranean caverns. Gillmore (1985) also identifies other natural resource-based forms of tourism such as parks and forests, as do Bagnall et al. (1978) and Murphy and Gardiner (1983), while rivers and water-based resources are highlighted by Deblock (1986) and the expansion of activity holidays is examined by Lucas (1986). Cultural and historical attractions also form an important component of Ireland's tourist product (Roche and Murray 1978; Brennan 1990) with the potential to form an integrated heritage zone at conservation sites (Tubridy 1987). Gillmore (1985) provides a detailed discussion of these heritage resources in terms of archaeological remains, religious sites, historic properties, museums and their geographical distribution throughout Ireland, although there is a marked absence of research on tourist transportation, tourist activity patterns and the spatial distribution of tourist travel in Ireland in relation to 'circuit tourism' (see Forer and Pearce 1984; D.G. Pearce 1987a). Nevertheless, there has been a renewed interest in 'heritage tourism' with the recent Visitor Attraction Survey in Ireland in 1991 (Tourism Development International 1992) which discusses trends and the profile of visitors

and the proportion of heritage attractions among the stock of over 150 fee-paying attractions which received 4.5 million overseas and domestic visitors in 1991. Bord Fáilte (1990b) produced a strategy and action plan for heritage attractions and the analysis of their future development, marketing and management (Bord Fáilte 1992a, b). These studies also highlighted potential gaps in the range of heritage themes presented to visitors, the need for greater quality assurance and the integration of this form of tourism more fully into existing dispersed patterns of rural tourism, often based in remote, relatively inaccessible and peripheral locations outside of the main towns and cities where a network of 25 'heritage towns' were designated in 1991.

Accommodation also forms a critical component of tourism infrastructure in Ireland, and according to Gillmore (1985: 323), it is 'a prerequisite for tourism development . . . [but] in the late 1950s its amount and quality . . . [in Ireland] were major restrictions on the expansion of the industry'. The public and private sector has, to a certain extent, addressed these weaknesses, as recent studies of Ireland's accommodation and lodging industry have shown (Blackwell 1970; Baum 1989a; Pollard 1989). For example, Baum (1989a) identifies 4,383 lodging establishments in Ireland which employed 34,750 full- and part-time people in the serviced accommodation sector. In addition, Baum (1989b) discusses the diversity and significance of small, family-run establishments in the serviced accommodation sector and the key issues facing this sector of the tourism industry as they were poised for growth in the 1980s. CERT, the State Training Industry for Tourism, also examined management training initiatives for the hotel industry based on research it had undertaken on the accommodation sector (CERT 1987a, b, 1991), while it is also interesting to note that I£20 million from the EU European Social Fund between 1989 and 1993 was spent on tourism training.

Bord Fáilte also undertake such studies (e.g.

its analysis of interhotel trends; Bord Fáilte 1986), and Simpson Xavier Horwath (1990) have undertaken a more detailed review of recent trends in Ireland's hotel sector. In the non-serviced accommodation sector (Plettner 1979), research identified the type of facilities sought by tourists and the opportunities for architects in building forest cabins, farm building conversion and the potential of caravans and camp sites in Ireland and Northern Ireland. More recently, Fowler (1991) examined developments in farm tourism while Gillmore (1985) and Brunt (1988) focus on the largely unresearched issue of the impact of second homes in rural areas (see Coppock 1977a), particularly the ownership patterns, with the highest densities recorded in Wicklow-Wesford, Donegal, West Galway and South-West Ireland. Gillmore (1985) also examines the demand for second homes and the ownership patterns which were dominated by Dublin residents. In the case of second homeownership among Northern Ireland residents, there was a trend towards a significant concentration in the Donegal region while among continental European second home-owners, their properties were mainly located in South-West Ireland. Glebe (1978), for example, observes the tendency in West Cork and South Kerry for abandoned farms in coastal areas to be converted to second homes or retirement cottages. Brunt (1988: 116) acknowledges that 'although tourism contributes positively to the development of rural areas, there are problems which have to be recognised . . . (including) the problems of seasonality, the potential and actual conflict between tourism and competing land uses' induced through second home development. Therefore, with these potential problems in mind, it is pertinent to consider how the tourism industry is organised and managed in Ireland in order to address potential conflicts generated by tourism.

POLICY ISSUES IN IRISH TOURISM: THE CASE OF RURAL TOURISM

According to McEniff (1991: 37), 'the stance of the Irish government in relation to tourism is relatively interventionist', with the Department of Tourism and Transport responsible for policy formulation and funding the national tourism organisation, Bord Fáilte (Heneghan 1976). D.G. Pearce's (1990b) review identifies the organisational framework developed to manage, market, promote, plan, develop, research and regulate tourism in Ireland. As D.G. Pearce (1990b, 1992b) shows, Bord Fáilte's main expenditure is devoted to marketing and promotion, and McEniff (1991: 38) provides a useful analysis of state expenditure on tourism in the period 1987 to 1990 which emphasises the drop in the real value of the government allocation and the privatisation of former state interests in tourism (e.g. the B & I Ferry line in 1991).

In terms of the politics of tourism (Fianna Fail 1987), various state and semi-state agencies have performed important roles both directly and indirectly in relation to tourism (for example, the Office of Public Works is responsible for national parks and monuments). The government's National Development Plan 1989–1993 (Anon. 1989) highlighted the underlying rationale for state involvement in tourism:

- to double the number of international tourist arrivals;
- to increase revenue from tourism by I£500 mln between 1989 and 1993;
- to create an additional 25,000 jobs by 1993.

In order to achieve these objectives, the Irish government introduced an Operational Programme for Tourism 1989–1993 (Bord Fáilte 1991b) One of the main outcomes was the receipt of I£147 mln of EU aid from the 'European Regional Development Fund and the European Social Fund for investment in infrastructure, marketing and training to help meet these objectives' (McEniff 1991: 37) which continued with the 1994–1999 Programme. D.G. Pearce (1992b) provides a useful analysis of the ERDF assistance made available to Ireland's tourism industry and the dramatic change in fortunes from the situation in 1984, where no assistance had been granted, to the one in 1988, where 80 per cent of the total appropriations received by Ireland's tourism industry through the ERDF were made in that year alone. In fact, D.G. Pearce (1992b: 48) argued that this 'substantial increase in tourism projects in Ireland in 1988 reflects a broader change in official policy to tourism which saw a more positive stance being taken with regard to its role in the Irish economy', with the state putting forward tourism projects to the EU for ERDF funding, which had not been the case prior to 1988. Ireland's 'lagging region' status greatly assisted its ability to attract ERDF funds for tourism which were directed towards a range of infrastructure and attraction-related developments, especially in relation to the nation's heritage. For example, Bord Fáilte, which administered ERDF funds for tourism projects in Ireland between 1989 and 1993 (Bord Fáilte 1991b) and Stevens (1991) noted that over 33 per cent of this revenue was allocated to the development of Ireland's heritage resources although Bord Fáilte suggests that 'over 40% of the ERDF funds for tourism development are earmarked for the history and culture product and over 100 significant projects have been proposed' (Bord Fáilte 1992a: 1).

Gillmore (1985: 306) argued that 'one of the most important developments in tourism administration was the measure of decentralisation adopted in 1964 when Bord Fáilte established eight Regional Tourism Organisations (RTO)' and Mowat (1984) has examined the role of tourism administration in the development of tourist resources in North-West Ireland. While the eight RTOs were reduced to seven in 1984 to achieve economies in expenditure on tourism, this does reflect a regionalisation of tourism administration to address the 'growth in tourist traffic in the 1960s and the advent of the more mobile motoring holidaymaker following the widening of car ownership and the introduction of the first car ferries to the public in 1965' (D.G. Pearce 1990b: 138). In fact, the relationship between Bord Fáilte and the RTOs is indicative of a core–periphery relationship in terms of the management and power base for tourism marketing, development and promotion, especially since the ERDF funds are an additional source of funding to allocate to appropriate projects. D.G. Pearce (1990b) discusses the rationale, organisation and activities of the RTOs and their relationship with Bord Fáilte, particularly with regard to funding, visitor servicing, planning, development, marketing and promotion, and therefore these issues need not be reiterated here.

In terms of planning (Mawhinney and Bagnall 1976), D.G. Pearce (1990b) highlights the spatial component in relation to the designation of areas for conservation, developing some 81 tourism planning zones. The role of tourism development in expanding, improving and diversifying Ireland's tourism plant in terms of accommodation, attractions and infrastructure is apparent from the incentive grants and funding available from Bord Fáilte and government schemes (Bord Fáilte 1991a; McEniff 1991). For example, Bord Fáilte approved 275 projects with a total capital cost of I£529 million between 1987 and June 1991 under the Business Expansion Scheme, which provided tax relief for investment in tourism. Bord Fáilte also promoted agri-tourism to 'provide incentives to farmers and other rural dwellers towards the cost of providing facilities which will enhance the attractiveness of an area for tourists and meet clearly identified tourist demand' (Bord Fáilte 1991b), a scheme administered by the RTOs and Bord Fáilte to encourage rural economic development based on tourism. In addition, McEniff (1991) outlined the increased investment by licensed banks to the hospitality industry and the improvements made to accommodation facilities up to 1990. Pearce (1990b) also documents the marketing and promotional roles of Bord Fáilte and the RTOs and emphasises the significance of promoting the 'image of Ireland as a whole abroad . . . it is a national image, sometimes directed at specific interest groups, which has been promoted, presumably because this is seen as the most effective method of marketing a small country in large and competitive markets such as the UK, the USA and West Germany with a comparatively modest total budget' (D.G. Pearce 1990b: 42), reflecting some of the budgetary constraints faced by public sector tourism organisations at a time of expansion in the tourism industry.

Although public and private sector organisations are involved in the management of tourism in Ireland, various social, cultural and environmental impacts have arisen from tourist development. For example, Williams (1985) has examined the significance of native language speaking in the Gaeltacht areas of Ireland, and Gillmore (1985: 329) pointed to the positive benefits of tourism in such areas, despite the 'social disruption and diminution of cultural identity'. In contrast, O'Cinneide and Keane (1990) cite the example of the Inishowen peninsula and the initial reluctance of local entrepreneurs and tourist businesses to plan strategically and to promote tourism on a local area basis. However, McDermott and Horner (1978) examined second home conversion and development, which were used for tourist and recreational purposes, and they noted its positive contribution to rural renewal in Western Connemara, although there is a little agreement on the extent to which the advantages of second homeownership outweigh the disadvantages (Robinson 1990). Within the context of Ireland's Gaeltacht areas, it is interesting to note Whyte's (1978) observation that in a similar remote context – the Isle of Skye – local residents perceived the influx of English-speaking second homeowners as a threat to the Gaelic-speaking tradition. In an urban context the social impact of tourism has been observed where 'tourists visiting Dublin are at risk of victimisation in the capital in relation to crime' (Rottman 1989: 97).

In terms of environmental impacts, Gillmore (1985: 329) suggested that 'concern for tourism has been a vital force in promoting interest in environmental conservation in general and the protection of the landscape in particular'. Carter (1988), however, placed more emphasis on the environmental costs of tourism and argued that the 'value of Irish beaches and dunes to the economy makes it paradoxically [sic] that very little is done to manage the cost. In some places, management plans have been implemented, for example by the National Trust at Murlough, County Down but in far too many places, the beach environment has simply been allowed to deteriorate' (Carter 1989: 408). The recent designation of the Wicklow National Park has also seen a greater concern for the impact of tourism on the environment as the environmental impact statements for visitor centres in both Wicklow National Park (Brady et al. 1991) and Dun Chaoin, County Kerry (Environmental Impact Services Limited 1991) indicated. However, with the planned expansion of the volume of international tourism in Ireland, it is inevitable that the impacts generated by tourism will need further detailed research if the complexities of tourist–host interaction are to be more fully understood, especially regarding the extent to which Ireland's high-quality environmental attributes can be maintained through a careful policy of sustainable development in keeping with the character of the landscape and its acceptability to the local population.

Deegan and Dineen's (1996) recent synthesis of Irish tourism policy observes that there are examples of successful rural tourism initiatives in Ireland (Keane and Quinn 1990; Feeham 1992) particularly in relation to community development. Like the literature on rural tourism in general, Ireland exhibits many examples of a focus on farm tourism (O'Connor 1995, 1996) and accommodation initiatives such as 'Rent-an-Irish Cottage' (Share 1992). However, the LEADER programme in Ireland is one example of a policy initiative intended to assist with the development of rural tourism.

LEADER 1 PROGRAMME

LEADER is an EU programme intended to assist with alternative forms of development to replace declining agriculture incomes (Kearney *et al*. 1994; Jenkins *et al*. 1998). As Figure 6.5 shows, some 17 LEADER 1 areas were designated covering 61 per cent of Ireland and 44 per cent of funded projects were associated with rural tourism. Some 50 per cent of the I£70 million funds for LEADER 1 were devoted to these tourism projects, and 35 per cent of the projects were associated with accommodation. The evaluation of the LEADER 1 Programme observed that while net employment gains were targeted, major benefits were associated with qualitative improvements (e.g. capacity building in rural communities) since rural tourism

Figure 6.5: Distribution of LEADER 1 areas in the Republic of Ireland
Source: Deegan and Dineen (1996: 110)

development was identified by Deegan and Dineen (1996: 109) as a 'potent vehicle for local development, economic recovery, social progress and conservation of the rural heritage' although they note that the difference between LEADER 1 and other programmes which emphasised farm tourism were that they focused more on the process and confidence-building process in rural communities prior to launching rural tourism programmes.

However, Keane and Quinn (1990) observe that rural tourism in Ireland remains a fragmented topic with the state tourism organisation (Bord Fáilte) only belatedly supporting what has been viewed as a marginal activity. Yet it is far from a niche market, since one of the very attractions of the Irish tourism product is its rural idyll, despite its recognition that 'it has a marginal though important contribution to make to regional income distribution in areas of the country which have undeveloped tourism resources and are not on recognised tourist routes' (Deegan and Dineen 1996: 111), though LEADER 1 is probably best noted for the qualitative rather than quantitative contribution it made to improving rural tourism in Ireland. McEniff (1996: 61) also noted that 'because of the popularity of LEADER 1, aims to limit the proportion of funding allocated to tourism projects' is now enshrined in LEADER 2, while a number of other government schemes now aim to assist rural tourism development (e.g. The Operational Programme for Agriculture, Rural Development and Forestry).

SUMMARY POINTS

It is apparent from the review that the economic impact of tourism appears to have dominated the research agenda in Ireland, despite the growing interest in rural tourism, especially among geographers. Ireland is an interesting example of the way in which perceived inaccessibility, combined with the positive features of its remoteness and landscapes, has been harnessed through creative and innovative marketing to boost tourist arrivals. Air travel and increased sea routes from the UK and mainland Europe, together with more competitively priced air fares, have assisted in overcoming the geographical effects of peripherality while the country has benefited from EU funds to develop its tourism industry. The application of 'core–periphery' concepts to explain tourism development and activities in a country such as Ireland highlight a major weakness in the simple delimitation of urban and rural areas which research has criticised for failing to take account of the socio-economic conditions and processes at work (Hoggart 1988).

Both the public and private sector have emphasised the positive effects of tourism in terms of the increased volume of international arrivals and, to lesser degree, the benefits of domestic tourism. This imbalance in attention implies that other disciplines have either not publicised the results of their research to the same effect as those concerned with the economic impact or that there has been relatively little interest in the broader aspects of tourism. There is also a noticeable absence of research on the sustainability of tourism and its environmental effects to indicate the State's concern for this controversial issue. Although there have been some influential studies undertaken on tourism in Ireland, a greater emphasis is needed on rural tourism in order to understand the long-term effects of basing a significant element of the country's economy on tourism.

Managing tourism in a period of expansion during the 1990s required greater co-operation between the public and private sector tourism interests to ensure that critical components of the nation's heritage were not irrecoverably damaged. For example, the impact of tourism on Ireland's regional culture and the Gaelic language is a case in point. This is one of the distinctive characteristics of the Irish tourist product which needs to be protected and enhanced rather than eroded through the internationalisation of tourism. If 'Ireland is a tourist destination with a future . . . [with] its unspoilt environment . . . rich in the tourism resource of tomorrow . . . which the sophisticated tourist increasingly seeks . . . [and its] scenery, people and culture make for a unique holiday destination' (Bord Fáilte 1991b), it will need to sensitively manage the impact of the tourist and tourism at the start of the twenty-first century to maintain a delicate balance between attaining economic benefits from tourism and minimising the potentially detrimental impact on the Irish population, its distinctive Gaelic culture and its largely unspoilt natural environment.

White Paper entitled *Rural England: A Nation Committed to a Living Countryside* (Department of the Environment and Ministry of Agriculture, Fisheries and Food (DoE/MAFF) 1995), was the first specifically rural policy from a British government for 50 years (Blake 1996).

According to Butler and Hall (1998), in many western regions and countries the structure of the relative homogeneous and distinct rural systems of the post-Second World War period has been either destroyed or weakened. They argue that such weakness is a result of at least three types of restructuring, namely, the collapse of peripheral areas unable to shift to a more capital-intensive economy; the selective and reductionist process of industrialisation of the remaining agricultural sector; and the pressures of urban and ex-urban development. Butler and Hall (1998: 252) concluded that the result is a rural system suffering absolute decline along its extensive margins and the rural–urban interface, with the intervening core area weakened by decoupling of farm and non-farm sectors and the shift of decision making to urban based corporations and governments. Restructuring has created a fragmented and reduced rural system which seems to lack most of the criteria for sustainability in either economic or community terms.

Despite images to the contrary, rurality is no longer dominated by concepts of food production, and new uses of the countryside, particularly related to recreational and tourism activities, are redefining the idea of what constitutes the rural landscape. In Britain, as in many other industrialised countries, these uses are placing extreme pressures and creating new conflicts not only in terms of rural policy-making and their relationship to agriculture but also between themselves (Curry 1992). For example, Blake (1996) reports that, according to a Countryside Commission survey, 76 per cent of the English population visited the countryside in 1990. Such a high level of visitation inevitably leads to the transformation of villages, and the creation of tourist facilities and infrastructure. However, at the same time, 89 per cent of people now believe that the English countryside should be protected at all costs (presumably as long as this cost would not result in the exclusion of those who wanted it saved). In the case of the United Kingdom the outbreak of 'foot and mouth' disease in February 2001 has probably focused more attention on what is really happening in the countryside than ever before. As the story unfolded in the media it quickly became apparent that tourism was a far greater economic contributor to rural areas than was farming. Nevertheless, policy measures were still

Plate 6.7: Tourism has revitalised many former mining towns in the western United States through the development of resort and accommodation facilities. Telluride, Colorado.

being primarily developed in relation to the agricultural sector rather than the needs of the tourism sector to recover from the impacts of the measures to control the disease on tourist and recreational mobility and access to the countryside. In terms of issues of sustainability it will be extremely interesting what new management, policy and planning structures are put in place by the central and local governments in Britain in response to the economic and social crisis in the countryside that the disease has revealed to the wider public. According to Hall and Butler (1998), one of the major errors which policy-makers and academics have made with respect to tourism and recreation in rural areas is to treat them in isolation from the other factors which constitute the social, environmental and economic fabric of rural regions. Tourism needs to be appropriately embedded within the particular set of linkages and relationships which comprise the essence of rurality with tourism being recognised as but one component of the policy mix which government and the private sector formulate with respect to rural development. Hall and Butler (1998) argue that many regional authorities fail to recognise that it is the visual complexity of the rural landscape which generates amenity values for locals and visitors alike. In the attempt to generate economic development, a wider tax base and employment, inappropriate policies and strategies may be followed. Furthermore, 'Policy measures in one sector, such as the attraction of agribusinesses or large foreign investments to a region, may lead to a decline of the industrial value of the region to other industries, such as tourism and businesses which are based on adding-value to local primary production' (Hall and Butler 1998: 255). An integrated approach to rural resource development is therefore essential for sustainable rural development. As Jenkins (1997) observed with respect to rural Australia, government can best assist rural areas to meet the challenges of economic restructuring and change by supporting the development of 'soft infrastructure', such as education and entrepreneurial skills, and by attaching greater importance to the provision of relevant research to improve

decision-making, rather than specifically supporting programmes which encourage the production of brochures, walking trails and other small-scale local tourism initiatives, such as visitor centres.

CONCLUSION

This chapter has emphasised the development of geographical research in rural recreation and tourism and the major philosophical changes in emphasis from empirically derived analyses through to more socially derived analyses. The geographer has sometimes found it hard to distinguish between the context of recreation and tourism, as users consume the same resources in the rural environment (Jenkins and Pigram 1994). The 1960s and 1970s saw the development of a strong recreational geography of the rural environment emerge from the leading research of noteworthy authors such as Coppock, Duffield, Lavery and Glyptis within the UK and in North America, followed by the influential work of Smith (1983a). The disappointing feature is the lack of continuity and theoretical development after the 1970s to follow up and build upon the groundwork established in the 1960s and 1970s. One possible explanation may be derived from Chapter 1 with the denial of mainstream geography and its reluctance to embrace such research as critical to the conceptual and theoretical development of the discipline. This is certainly true in tourism up until the 1990s when research by mainstream human geographers such as Cloke began to cultivate critical social geographies of recreation and tourism in the countryside. Even so, one would expect that geographical research assessment exercises in countries such as the UK would do little to foster a spirit of mainstream incorporation of tourism and recreation into the discipline as it may be assessed under business and management rather than as a subgroup of geography. The nearest inroad is through the study groups of professional bodies such as the IBG and AAG where these developments have not been discouraged. Human geography in particular has been less accepting of such fringe subject areas and a consequence is that even when notable researchers have emerged in these areas they have not fostered the same stature or influence of the human geographers of the 1960s and 1970s who cultivated and really established rural recreation and tourism as a rich area of spatially contingent research. The scope of the studies reviewed and discussed in this chapter have a common theme associated with some of the problems associated with rural areas in general, namely peripherality. Yet, ironically, this can also be a major feature associated with place marketing of rural areas where the peaceful rural idyll is marketed and commodified around the concept of space and peripherality. The rural geographer has made some forays into this area of research but, more often than not, many of the texts on rural geography pay only limited attention to tourism and recreation despite its growing significance in economic, social and political terms. Indeed, the outbreak of foot and mouth disease in the United Kingdom in February 2001 has only served to highlight the critical importance of tourism for the countryside.

QUESTIONS

- How has the recent outbreak of foot and mouth disease in the United Kingdom affected tourism?

- Is rural tourism distinctive?
- To what extent should second homes be regarded as part of the geography of tourism and recreation in rural areas?
- To what extent is rural recreation and tourism dependent on amenity values?

READING

A useful recent collection of readings is:

Butler, R.W., Hall, C.M. and Jenkins, J. (eds) (1998) *Tourism and Recreation in Rural Areas*, Chichester: Wiley.

The chapter by Jenkins *et al.* provides a valuable overview of rural restructuring issues:

Jenkins, J., Hall, C.M. and Troughton, M. (1998) 'The restructuring of rural economies: rural tourism and recreation as a government response', in R. Butler, C.M. Hall and J. Jenkins (eds) *Tourism and Recreation in Rural Areas*, Chichester: Wiley, pp. 43–68.

For an overview of rural recreation issues see:

Pigram, J.J. and Jenkins, J. (1999) *Outdoor Recreation Management*, London: Routledge.

7

TOURISM AND RECREATION IN THE PLEASURE PERIPHERY
Wilderness and National Parks

Historically, wilderness has been one of the main sources of 'the other' in western society. Wilderness was what lay beyond the boundaries of a 'civilised', ordered landscape. Since the beginning of the nineteenth century however, wilderness and wild areas began to assume a more favourable impression under the influence of the romantic and transcendentalist movements which favoured wild nature as an antidote to an increasingly industrialised and technocratic society. More recently, the conservation and commodification of wilderness has become entwined with the growth of recreation and tourism which has seen national parks established not only for outdoor and adventure recreation enthusiasts but also as one of the main sites in which eco-tourism occurs.

Geographers have long played a significant role in understanding and contributing to the conservation of natural resources and natural areas and their relationship with recreation and tourist activities (e.g. Graves 1920; Marsh and Wall 1982; Sewell and Dearden 1989). Indeed, recreation and tourism has long been used as an economic justification for the conservation and legal protection of such areas. Geographers have contributed to an understanding of a number of different dimensions of the relationship between wilderness and national park concepts and recreation and tourism:

- the changing meaning of wilderness in western society;
- the environmental history of national parks and wilderness areas;
- the value of wilderness;

- the identification and inventory of wilderness;
- the demand for wilderness and natural areas, including visitor profiles, activities and behaviours;
- the development of wilderness and national park policy and the supply of wilderness and natural areas for recreation and tourist activities.

THE CHANGING MEANING OF WILDERNESS IN WESTERN SOCIETY

Definition presents a major problem in the identification of wilderness areas. Definition is important 'because it is the basis for common understanding and communication' and it 'provides a basis for putting a concept into action through creating and preserving a referent' (Gardner 1978: 7). However, wilderness is an elusive concept with many layers of meaning (Gardner 1978; Graber 1978). Tuan (1974: 112) has gone so far as to claim that 'wilderness cannot be defined objectively: it is as much a state of mind as a description of nature'. Wilderness has now become 'a symbol of the orderly progress of nature. As a state of mind, true wilderness exists only in the great sprawling cities'.

The problem of defining wilderness was summarised by Nash (1967: 1):

'Wilderness' has a deceptive concreteness at first glance. The difficulty is that while the word is a noun it acts like an adjective. There is no specific material object that is wilderness. The term designates a quality (as the '-ness' suggests) that produces a certain mood or feeling in a given individual and, as a consequence, may be assigned by that person to a specific place. Because of this subjectivity a universally acceptable definition of wilderness is elusive. . . . Wilderness, in short, is so heavily freighted with meaning of a personal, symbolic, and changing kind as to resist easy definition.

The meaning of wilderness has changed over time but several themes may be distinguished. The word 'wilderness' is derived from the old English word *wilddeoren* meaning 'of wild beasts', which in turn is derived from the Teutonic languages of Northern Europe. In German, for example, *Wildnis* is a cognate verb, and *Wildor* signifies wild game (Nash 1967: 2).

The Romance languages have no single word which expresses the idea of wilderness but rely instead on its attributes. In French the equivalent terms are *lieu desert* (deserted place) and *solitude inculte*, while in Spanish wilderness is *la naturaleza, immensidad* or *falts da cultura* (lack of cultivation). 'Italian uses the vivid *scene di disordine o confusione*' (Nash 1967: 2). The Latin root of desert, *de* and *serere* (to break apart, becoming solitary) connotes not only the loneliness and fear associated with separation but also an arid, barren tract lacking cultivation (Mark 1984: 3). Both the Northern European and the Mediterranean traditions define and portray wilderness as a landscape of fear, which is outside the safer bounds of human settlement (Tuan 1971, 1979). This image was taken up by Nash (1967: 2) who noted that the image of wilderness 'is that of a man [*sic*] in an alien environment where the civilization that normally orders and controls life is absent'.

The landscape of fear that dominated early attitudes towards wilderness was noted in the eighth-century classic *Beowulf* (Wright 1957), 'where *wildeor* appeared in reference to savage and fantastic beasts inhabiting a dismal region of forests, crags, and cliffs' (Nash 1967: 1). The translation of the Scriptures into English from Greek and Hebrew led to the use of wilderness as a description of 'the uninhabited, arid land of the Near East' (Nash 1967: 2–3). It was at this point that wilderness came to be associated with spiritual

values. Wilderness was seen as both a testing ground for man and an area in which man could draw closer to God.

The biblical attitude towards nature was an essential ingredient of the Judaeo-Christian or western attitude towards wilderness (Glacken 1967; Passmore 1974; Graber 1978; Attfield 1983; Pepper 1984; Short 1991). According to the dominant tradition within Judaeo-Christianity concerning humankind's relationship with nature, it was 'God's intention that mankind multiply itself, spread out over the earth, make its domain over the creation secure' (Glacken 1967: 151). This relationship is best indicated in Genesis 1:28 where God said to man, 'Be fruitful and multiply, and fill the earth and subdue it; and have dominion over the fish of the sea and over the birds of the air and over every living thing that moves upon the earth.'

To the authors of the Bible, wilderness had a central position in their accounts as both a descriptive and as a symbolic concept. To the ancient Hebrews, wilderness was 'the environment of evil, a kind of hell' in which the wasteland was identified with God's curse (Nash 1967: 14–15). Paradise, or Eden, was the antithesis of wilderness. The story of Adam and Eve's dismissal from the Garden of Eden, from a watered, lush paradise to a 'cursed' land of 'thorns and thistles' (Genesis 2:4), reinforced in western thought the notion that wilderness and paradise were both physical and spiritual opposites (Williams 1962). Isaiah (51:3), for instance, contains the promise that God will comfort Zion and 'make her wilderness like Eden, her desert like the garden of the Lord', while Joel (2:3) stated that 'the land is like the garden of Eden before them, but after them a desolate wilderness'.

The experience of the Israelites during the Exodus added another dimension to the Judaeo-Christian attitude towards wilderness. For 40 years the Jews, led by Moses, wandered in the 'howling waste of the wilderness' (Deuteronomy 32:10) that was the Sinai peninsula (Funk 1959). The wilderness, in this instance, was not only a place where they were punished by God for their sins but also a place where they could prove themselves worthy of the Lord and make ready for the promised land.

Indeed, it was precisely because it was unoccupied that it 'could be a refuge as well as a disciplinary force' (Nash 1967: 16).

The experience of the Exodus helped to establish a tradition of going to the wilderness 'for freedom and purification of faith' (Nash 1967: 16). Elijah spent 40 days in the wilderness in order to draw guidance and inspiration from God (1 Kings 19: 4–18). John the Baptist was the voice crying in the wilderness to prepare for the coming of the Messiah (Matthew 4:1), while Christ himself 'was led by the spirit into the wilderness to be tempted by the devil' (Matthew 4:1; Mark 1:12ff.). It was through the environment of evil and hardship, characteristic of the dominant Judaeo-Christian perception of the wilderness, that spiritual catharsis could occur, a sentiment that exists through to this day (Graber 1978). (See Chapter 6 on the role of wilderness areas in rural tourism.)

The example of the prophets venturing into the wilderness was followed by early Christian ascetics (Williams 1962). Hermits and monks established themselves in wilderness surroundings in order to avoid the temptations of earthly wealth and pleasure and to find a solitude conducive to spiritual ideals. As Tuan (1974: 148) recorded:

> The monastic community in the wilderness was a model of paradise set in an unredeemed world. Wilderness was often perceived as the haunt of demons but in the neighbourhood of the monastery it could acquire some of the harmony of redeemed nature and the animals in it, like their human suzerains in the monastery, lived in peace.

The desert ascetics drew on an appreciation of nature that sprang from the Bible itself. As Glacken (1967: 151) observed, 'The intense otherworldliness and rejection of the beauties of nature because they turn men away from the contemplation of God are elaborated upon far more in theological writings than in the Bible itself'. The desert monks lived in the solitude of the wilderness to remove themselves from man, not from nature. Psalm 104 provides one of the clearest statements of the existence of a sympathetic attitude in Christianity towards nature, noting that everything in nature has its place in a divine order: 'the high mountains are for the wild goats; the rocks are a refuge for the badgers' (Psalm 104:18). 'O Lord, how manifold are thy works! In wisdom hast thou made them all' (Psalm 104: 24). As Glacken (1967: 157) noted:

> It is not to be wondered at that Psalm 104 has been quoted so often by thinkers sympathetic to the design argument and the physico-theological proof for the existence of God. The life, beauty, activity, order, and reasonableness in nature are described without mysteries, joyously – even triumphantly. God is separate from nature but he may be understood in part from it.

The theme of the wisdom of the Lord being shown in the order of nature was similarly indicated elsewhere in the Bible. The psalmist in Psalm 8:1 exclaimed: 'O Lord, our Lord, how majestic is thy name in all the earth!' The notion that 'The heavens are telling the glory of God; and the firmament proclaims his handiwork' (Psalm 19:1) proved to be influential throughout Christendom in the Dark and Middle Ages, although by no means enabling a universally sympathetic attitude towards nature. Nature came to be regarded as a book which could reveal the works of the Lord in a manner similar to the Scriptures. In the early exegetical writings God was regarded as being made manifest in his works. 'There is a book of nature which when read along with the book of God, allows men to know and understand Him and his creation; not only man but nature suffered from the curse after the Fall; one may admire and love the beauty of the earth if this love and admiration is associated with the love of God' (Glacken 1967: 203).

This view of nature played an important role in establishing a favourable attitude towards wild country. St Augustine (in Glacken 1967: 204) wrote, 'Some people in order to discover God, read books. But there is a great book: the very appearance of created things.' Pulpit eloquence was 'adopted by medieval mystico-philosophical speculation, and finally passed into common usage' (Curtius 1953: 321, in Glacken 1967: 104).

Reading the book of nature for the word of God was eventually to lead to the reading of nature itself, but the notion of nature as a book was also to prepare the way for the development of a natural theology in the writings of St Francis of Assisi, St Bonaventura and Ramon Sibiude. To St Francis, living creatures were not only symbols, but were also 'placed on earth for God's own purposes (not for man's), and they, like man, praise God' (Glacken 1967: 216). St Francis' theology represented a revolutionary change in Christian attitudes towards nature because of the distinct break they make from the anthropocentric nature of earlier theology (White 1967). Upon the foundation built by the natural theologians and their intellectual heirs, such as John Ray and Gilbert White, came to be built the framework for the discovery of nature by the Romantic movement. Nevertheless, despite a continuing appreciation of nature as part of God's divine presence by some theologians, the dominant attitude in the Judaeo-Christian tradition until the seventeenth century was that true appreciation of God could only be gained by looking inwards, not out at nature. Nature was provided for man to utilise. Wilderness and wild lands were to be tamed and cultivated to display the divine order as interpreted by man.

The dominant Judaeo-Christian view of wilderness may be contrasted with that of eastern religions. In eastern thought, wilderness 'did not have an unholy or evil connotation but was venerated as the symbol and even the very essence of the deity' (Nash 1967: 20). The aesthetic appreciation of wild land began to change far earlier in the Orient than in the West. By the fourth century AD, for instance, large numbers of people in China had begun to find an aesthetic appeal in mountains, whereas they were still seen as objects of fear in Europe (Nicholson 1962; Tuan 1974).

Eastern faiths such as Shinto and Taoism 'fostered love of wilderness rather than hatred' (Nash 1982: 21). Shinto deified nature in favour of pastoral scenes. The polarity that existed between city and wilderness in the Judaeo-Christian experience did not exist outside European cultural tradition (Callicott 1982). Western civilisation has tended to dominate, rather than adapt, to its surrounding landscape whereas traditional eastern and non-European cultures have tended to attempt to blend into their surroundings. As Tuan (1974:

148) noted, 'In the traditions of Taoist China and pre-Dorian Greece, nature imparted virtue or power. In the Christian tradition sanctifying power is invested in man, God's vice regent, rather than nature.' However, it should be emphasised that Oriental civilisations, such as those of China, India and Japan, have had highly destructive impacts on the environment and will continue to do so.

The attitude of different cultures to nature and, hence, wilderness is important (Tuan 1971, 1979). As Eidsvik (1980, 1985) has recognised, wilderness has only recently taken on global meaning with the increasing dominance of western culture throughout the world. The perception of wilderness as an alien landscape of fear is derived from the Northern European set of attitudes towards nature, where the Judaeo-Christian perception of nature became combined with the Teutonic fear of the vast northern forests. It is perhaps of no coincidence therefore that the creation of designated wilderness areas began in lands occupied by peoples who have inherited European cultural attitudes. However, despite retaining something of its original attributes the meaning of wilderness has changed substantially over time and now incorporates wider scientific and conservation values. Table 7.1 portrays the development of the wilderness concept in the United States, Canada, New Zealand and Australia: those countries within which the idea of wilderness has been most influential in outdoor recreation and tourism policy and in the production and consumption of tourism experiences.

The classic example of changing popular attitudes towards wilderness is witnessed in the history of the evolution of the wilderness concept in the United States (Table 7.1). The founding fathers of the American colonies saw the wild lands before them in classical biblical terms, and although attitudes towards wilderness did change gradually through the seventeenth and eighteenth centuries it was not until the late eighteenth century that positive appreciation of American nature began to emerge. The political independence of the American nation found cultural expression in the extolment of the virtues of American natural scenery. However, a similar cultural expression was not to be found in colonial Canada where untamed nature still assumed the guise of a landscape of fear (Kline 1970). Nevertheless, America's cultural independence from the Old World produced a desire to laud the moral purity of the wild forests and mountains of the New World, untainted as they were by the domination of things European, a cultural movement which, perhaps somewhat ironically, sprang from the Romantic movement then sweeping Europe.

The American Romantic movement laid the groundwork upon which a popular appreciation of the value of wild land would come to be based. Artistic, literary and political perceptions of the importance of contact with wild nature provided the stimulus for the creation of positive cultural attitudes towards the American wilderness. Once positive attitudes towards primitive, unordered nature had developed then the emergence of individuals and societies dedicated to the preservation of wilderness values was only a short step away. However, an appreciation of the aesthetic values of wild land was countered by the utilitarian ethic that dominated American society.

The majority of Americans saw the land as an object to be conquered and made productive. The first reservations for the preservation of scenery therefore tended to be established in areas that were judged to be wastelands that had no economic value in terms of agriculture, grazing, lumbering or mining. The aesthetic value of wilderness was upheld by national parks and reserves which were intended to protect national scenic monuments that expressed the cultural independence of America in addition to providing for the development of the area through the tourist dollar. Monumentalism was characterised by the belief that natural sites, such as Niagara Falls or the Rockies, were grand, noble and elevated in idea and had something of the enduring, stable and timeless nature of the great architecture of Europe, and proved a significant theme in the establishment of American parks (Runte 1979).

Although the national parks in Australia, Canada and New Zealand did not assume the same importance as national monuments, their development nevertheless parallels that of the American park system. The themes of aesthetic romanticism, recreation and the development of 'worthless' or 'waste' lands through tourism characterised the creation of the first national parks in Australia, Canada and New Zealand. Banff National Park in Canada was developed by the Canadian Pacific Railroad as a tourist spa (Marsh 1985). New Zealand's first parks had lodges and hostels established within them that matched the tourist developments in the North American parks. Australia's first parks, particularly those of Queensland and Tasmania, were also marked by the influence of the desire of government to boost tourism. However, the Australian parks were also noted for their establishment, in unison with railway development, as areas where city-dwellers could find mental restoration in recreation and communion with nature (Hall 1985, 1992a).

With the closing of the American frontier at the end of the nineteenth century the preservation of America's remaining wilderness received new impetus. A massive but unsuccessful public campaign by wilderness preservationists led by John Muir to protect Hetch Hetchy Valley in Yosemite National Park from a dam scheme, a conservation-minded President (Theodore Roosevelt) in the White House, and the emergence of economically oriented 'progressive conservation' under the leadership of Gifford Pinchot all led to wilderness preservation becoming a matter of public importance in the United States.

The United States Forest Service and National Park Service responded to pressures from recreationalists for the creation of designated wilderness areas. Contemporaneously, the development of the science of ecology led to a recognition of the scientific importance of preserving wilderness. The various elements of wilderness preservation blended together in the inter-war years to lay a framework for the establishment of legally protected wilderness areas.

Economic conservation and the development of a scientific perception of wilderness was also influential in Australia, Canada and New Zealand. In Australia, the publication of George Perkins

Table 7.1: The development of the wilderness concept in the United States, Canada, New Zealand and Australia

Date	United States	Canada	New Zealand	Australia
Pre-1860	Major romantic influence on American art and literature			A 'New Britannia'
1832	Joseph Catlin calls for the creation of a 'nation's Park'			Aesthetic and utilitarian visions of the Australian landscape
1832	Arkansas Hot Springs reserved			Rapid clearfelling of land for agriculture and mining
1851	Transcendentalism – Thoreau's *Walking* proclaims that 'in Wildness is the preservation of the World'	Development of a romantic perception of the Canadian landscape		
1860	Romantic Monumentalism			
1864	George Perkins Marsh's *Man and Nature* is published, heralds the start of 'economic conservation'; Yosemite State Park established			Marsh's book well received in Australia; 1866 Jenolan Caves reserved
1870	Wilderness perceived as 'worthless land'			The need to conserve forests argued by Clarke, Goyder and von Mueller 'Scientific Vision'
1872	Yellowstone National Park established; John Muir begins writing and campaigning for wilderness preservation		1878 T. Potts publishes *National Domains*; 1881 *Thermal Springs Districts Act*	1879 Royal National Park established in New South Wales
1880	Rise of 'Progressive Conservation' led by Gifford Pinchot	1885 Banff Hot Springs Reserve declared	1887 Tongariro deeded to the New Zealand Government	Rise of the 'Bush Idyll' National Parks associated recreation and tourism 'Sydney or the Bush'
1890	F.J. Turner declares the end of the American frontier; Yosemite National Park created with help of railroads; *Forests Reserves Act 1891*	Strengthening of a romantic vision of nature in Canada and rise of progressive conservation; 1894 Algonquin Park established	1892 J. Matson calls for Australasian Indigenous Parks	1891 *National Park Act* (S.A.); 1892 *Tower Hill National Park Act* (Vic.)
1900	Cult of the Wilderness; Tourism a major motive for the establishment of parks in all four countries			
1905	U.S. Forest Service created			1905 *State Forests and National Parks Act* (Queensland)
1910		1911 *Dominion Forest Reserves and Parks Act*		
1913	Preservationists lose battle to prevent Hetch Hetchy being dammed			
1916	U.S. National Park Service created; Rise of Ecological Perspectives			1915 *Scenery Preservation Act* (Tas.); Growth of the 'Bushwalking Movement' under Myles Dunphy in NSW
1920	Forest Service areas retained as 'primitive lands'		Negative reaction to introduced animals in National Parks begins	
1926	Forest Service Wilderness Inventory			

Year			
			1927 Formation of the National Parks and Primitive Areas Council
1928	Forest Service Regulation L-20		
1930		1930 *National Parks Act*	
1934	Everglades National Park established		1934 Greater Blue Mountains National Park Scheme; Development of Snowy-Indi Proposal (NSW)
1937	Formation of the Wilderness Society		
1939	Forest Service 'U' Regulations		
1940			1944 *Kosciusko State Park Act*
1949	Keyser Report		
1950	Dinosaur National Monument Campaign	1952 *National Parks Act*	
1956	First Wilderness Bill	1955 *Wilderness Areas Act* (Ontario) 1955 *Reserves and Domains Act*	1957 Victorian National Park Authority created
1960	ORCC Report		
1962	*Wilderness Act* becomes law; Agencies begin implementation		1963 Kosciusko Primitive Area established (NSW); 1967 NSW National Parks and Wildlife Service created; Wilderness becomes a major policy issue: Little Desert, Great Barrier Reef, Fraser Island and Lake Pedder
1964	RARE I commences	1969 Study tour of National Parks Director to North America	
1970	Mounting pressure from tourists and commercial interests in national parks in all countries		1975 National Parks and Wildlife Service (Commonwealth) created
1974	*Eastern Wilderness Act*; RARE II commences; Bureau of Land Management commences inventory; 'Sagebrush Rebellion'; Provision for wilderness in Alaska	1977 *Reserves Act*	
1980	Major conflicts over wilderness preservation; 1984 South Moresby Island campaign	1980 *National Parks Act*; 1981 Wilderness Advisory Group established; 1984 new wilderness areas established; 1986 World Heritage listing for South Westland Park; 1987 Creation of Department of Conservation	1982 National Conservation Strategy; 1983 Franklin Dam Case; 1984 Calls for establishment of National Wilderness System; 1985 CONCOM discussion paper; 1987 Federal government acts to preserve the Wet Tropics, Kakadu, and the Lemonthyme and Southern Forests; 1987 NSW *Wilderness Act* passed
1990	Increased attention given to concept of ecotourism and sustainable tourism by governments and industry bodies		

Plate 7.1: Mount Cook National Park, New Zealand. Is it still within the perceived threshold of a wilderness experience given the large amount of people who visit it?

Marsh's (1864 (1965)) book *Man and Nature* stimulated the colonial governments into establishing forest reserves. In addition, significant scientists such as Baron von Mueller, and bodies such as the Australasian Association for the Advancement of Science argued for the preservation of native flora and fauna in both Australia and New Zealand. However, the first national parks in Australia were created for reasons of aesthetics, tourism and recreation with science gaining little recognition (Hall 1992a).

In Canada, progressive conservation proved influential in the creation of forest reserves, and it is significant to note that many of the early Canadian parks were established under forestry legislation. However, the preservation of wilderness lagged behind the efforts of the United States (Nicol 1969).

The declaration of the Wilderness Act in 1964 marked the beginning of the current legislative era of wilderness preservation in the United States. Under the Wilderness Act wilderness is defined as 'an area where the earth and its community of life are untrammelled by man, where man himself is the visitor that does not remain'. The four defining qualities of wilderness areas protected under the Act are that such areas:

1   generally appear to be affected by the forces of nature, with the imprint of man substantially unnoticeable;

2   have outstanding opportunities for solitude or a primitive and unconfined type of recreation;

3   have at least 5,000 acres or be of sufficient size as to make practical its preservation and use in an unimpaired condition;

4   may also contain ecological, geological or features of scientific, educational, scenic or historical value.

The protection of wilderness through legal means gave new impetus to the task of improving the process of defining and compiling a wilderness inventory as well as providing for its management, a process that is still continuing today in America as well as in countries such as Australia, which have tended to follow the American model for wilderness and national park protection. Although wilderness in New Zealand is given administrative protection under a variety of acts, there is no specific legislation for the preservation of wilderness. Similarly, until late 1987 with the passing of the New South Wales Wilderness Act, no wilderness legislation had been enacted in Australia (Hall 1992a). In Canada, wilderness areas have received a degree of protection under provincial legislation. However, as in Australia and New Zealand, there is no national wilderness act. Yet, in recent years increasing attention has been given to the implications of international heritage agreements, such as the World Heritage Convention, as a mechanism for the preservation of wilderness and other natural areas of international significance (Hall 1992a).

THE ENVIRONMENTAL HISTORY OF NATIONAL PARKS AND WILDERNESS AREAS

Environmental history is a field concerned with the role and place of nature in human life (Worster 1977). Research and scholarship on the environmental history of national parks and wilderness lies at the intersection of a number of fields of geographic and academic endeavour. Within geography, as with history, the increased awareness of the environment as a social, economic and political issue has led to geographers and historians attempting to chart the history of land use of a given region or site in order to increase understanding of its significance, values and present-day use. Such research is not just an academic exercise. As well as assisting in understanding how current natural resource management problems or user conflicts have developed, such research can also be used to develop interpretive material for visitors as part of a programme of heritage management, an area in which geographers are becoming increasingly involved (e.g. Ashworth and Tunbridge 1990; Tunbridge and Ashworth 1996; Hall and McArthur 1996, 1998). Cronan (1990) asserts that good work in environmental history incorporates three levels of analysis. These are the dynamics of natural ecosystems in time (ecology), the political economies that people erect within these systems (economy), and the cognitive lenses through which people perceive those systems (the history of ideas). Geographers, with their integrative approach to environment, cultural landscapes and land use, would therefore seem to be ideally poised to work in this area. As Mark (1996: 153) observed, 'Widening the scope of historical narrative has frequently resulted in more complex interpretation of the past and should point the way toward greater understanding of the past in heritage management.'

National parks are a major focus of heritage management but have been a relatively quiet backwater in traditional historical narrative. Environ-

mental history, however, can place them within the larger context of interaction between nature and culture (Griffiths 1991; Mark 1996). For example, a number of extremely valuable park histories which highlight the role of tourism and outdoor recreation in park development have been written on the Yellowstone (Haines 1977), Grand Canyon (Hughes 1978), Rocky Mountain (Buchholtz 1983), Olympic (Twight 1983), Sequoia and Kings Canyon (Dilsaver and Tweed 1990) and Yosemite (Runte 1990) national parks in the United States; the Albertan (Bella 1987) and the Ontario (Killan 1993) national park systems in Canada, and with useful national overviews being provided by Nelson (1970), Hall (1992a) and Dearden and Rollins (1993).

Substantial methodological research is called for when undertaking research on environmental and park histories. In the New Worlds of North America and the Antipodes, travel accounts written during the period of initial European settlement have been utilised by scholars interested in historic environments (Powell 1978). They often hope to establish a pre-European settlement landscape as a baseline from which to assess subsequent environmental change. One difficulty with using travel accounts, however, is that they are often written in places where the journalist is not actually travelling; instead the diarist is summarising past events at a convenient place (Mark 1996). Another problem is how to tie the usually limited detail (little of which could be utilised quantitatively) to specific localities. The paucity of locality information is often present in even the best accounts, such as those left by collectors of natural history specimens.

The only site-specific records available in many areas about presettlement landscapes are land survey notes. These have been helpful in establishing a historic condition of some forests, riparian habitats and grasslands. Their reliability varies, however, because there can be limitations associated with insufficient description, bias in recording data, contract fraud and land use prior to survey (Galatowitsch 1990). Another technique which is useful for developing a historical record of land use change or for reconstructing past environments or

Plate 7.2: Erosion on a walking trail in Noosa Heads, National Park, Queensland, Australia.

heritage sites is repeat photography (Rogers *et al.* 1984). However, while such techniques may be useful for specific sites or attractions the photographic record of 'ordinary' landscapes, i.e. those which were not subject to the interest of visitors as a view or panorama, is more difficult to construct because of incomplete records.

Cultural landscape documentation is somewhat narrower in scope than environmental history because the question of nature's character is not so central (Mark 1996). Nevertheless, it emphasises change over time and represents a way of integrating nature with culture. In a park setting, its emphasis becomes one of design, material, change, function and use, with one of its main effects on heritage management being the broadening of the focus of historic preservation beyond buildings to the associated landscape and environmental context (Mark 1991).

THE VALUES OF WILDERNESS

Decisions affecting environmental policies grow out of a political process (Henning 1971, 1974), in which 'value choice, implicit and explicit . . . orders the priorities of government and determines the commitment of resources within the public jurisdiction' (Simmons *et al.* 1974: 457). Therefore, in order to consider the means by which wilderness is utilised, it is essential to understand what the values of wilderness are. As Henning (1987: 293) observed: 'In the end, the survival of the wilderness will depend upon values being a respected factor in the political and governmental process.'

The value of wilderness is not static. The value of a resource alters over time in accordance with changes in the needs and attitudes of society. As noted above, ideas of the values of primitive and wild land have shifted in relation to the changing perceptions of western culture. Nevertheless, the dynamic nature of the wilderness resource does not prevent an assessment of its values as they are seen in present-day society. Indeed, such an evaluation is essential to arguments as to why wilderness should be conserved.

Broadly defined, the values of wilderness may be classified as being either anthropocentric or biocentric in nature. The principal emphasis of the anthropocentric approach is that the value of wilderness emerges in its potential for direct human use. In contrast, 'the biocentric perspective places primary emphasis on the preservation of the natural order'. The former approach places societal above ecological values and emphasises recreational and aesthetic rather than environmental qualities. Both perspectives focus on human benefits. However, 'the important distinction between them is the extent to which these benefits are viewed as being independent of the naturalness of wilderness ecosystems' (Hendee *et al.* 1978: 18).

A more radical, and increasingly popular, interpretation of the notion of the value of wilderness has been provided by what is often termed a deep ecology perspective (Godfrey-Smith 1979, 1980; Nash 1990; Oelschlaeger 1991). Deep ecologists argue that wilderness should be held as valuable not just because it satisfies a human need (instrumental value) but as an end in itself (intrinsically valuable). Instrumental anthropocentric values, derived from a Cartesian conception of nature, are regarded as being opposed to a holistic or systematic view 'in which we come to appreciate the symbiotic interdependencies of the natural world' (Godfrey-Smith 1979: 316). The holistic view broadly corresponds with the ecological conception of wilderness (Worster 1977; Nash 1990; Oelschlaeger 1991). However, it goes further by arguing that 'the philosophical task is to try and provide adequate justification . . . for a scheme of values according to which concern and sympathy for our environment is immediate and natural, and the desirability of protecting and preserving wilderness self-evident' (Godfrey-Smith 1979: 316), rather than justified purely according to human needs.

We can, however, provide – and it is important that we do so – an answer to the question: 'What is the use of wilderness?' We certainly ought to preserve and protect wilderness areas as gymnasiums, as laboratories, as stockpiles of genetic diversity and as cathedrals. Each of these reasons provides a powerful and sufficient instrumental justification for their preservation. But note how the very posing of this question about the utility of wilderness reflects an anthropocentric system of values. From a genuinely ecocentric point of view the question, 'What is the use of wilderness?' would be as absurd as the question, 'What is the use of happiness?' (Godfrey-Smith 1979: 319).

Hendee *et al.* (1978) identified three consistent themes in the values associated with wilderness: experiential, mental and moral restorational, and scientific. Experiential values highlight the importance of the 'wilderness experience' for recreationists and tourists (Scott 1974; Hamilton-Smith 1980; McKenry 1980). Several themes emerge in an examination of the wilderness experience including the aesthetic, the spiritual and the escapist (Table 7.2). Given its essentially personal nature, the wilderness experience is extremely difficult to define (Scott 1974). Nevertheless, the values recorded from writings on wilderness listed in Table 7.2 do point to the various aspects of the wilderness experience that are realised in human contact with wild and primitive lands.

Associated with the values of the wilderness experience is the idea that wilderness can provide mental and moral restoration for the individual in the face of modern civilisation (Carhart 1920; Boyden and Harris 1978). This values wilderness as a 'reservoir for renewal of mind and spirit' and

Table 7.2: Components of the wilderness experience

Component	Nature of experience	Examples
Aesthetic appreciation	Appreciation of wild nature	Leopold 1921, 1925; Marshall 1930; McKenry 1972a; Smith 1977; Hamilton-Smith 1980; Alexander 1984; Nash 1990.
Religious	The experience of God in the wilderness	McKenry 1972a; Hendee *et al.* 1978; Wright 1980; Hamilton-Smith 1980; Nash 1990.
Escapist	Finding freedom away from the constraints of city living	McKenry 1972a; Smith 1977; Hendee *et al.* 1978; Hamilton-Smith 1980; Hawes 1981.
Challenge	The satisfaction that occurs in overcoming dangerous situations and fully utilising physical skills	McKenry 1972a; Smith 1977; Gardner 1978; Hamilton-Smith 1980; Warboys 1980.
Historic/Romantic	The opportunity to re-live or imagine the experiences of pioneers of the 'frontier' that formed national culture	Leopold 1925; Smith 1977; Hamilton-Smith 1980; Ride 1980; Alexander 1984; Johnston 1985
Solitude	The pleasure of being alone in a wild setting	Lee 1977; Smith 1977; Hamilton-Smith 1980; Hawes 1981; Sinclair 1986.
Companionship	Paradoxically, in relation to the previous category, the desire to share the setting with companions	Lee 1977; Smith 1977; Hamilton-Smith 1980.
Discovery/Learning	The thrill of discovering or learning about nature in a natural setting	Smith 1977; Gardner 1978; Hamilton-Smith 1980.
Vicarious appreciation	The pleasure of knowing that wilderness exists without actually ever having seen it	McKenry 1977; Smith 1977; Hawes 1981; Johnston 1985.
Technology	Influence of technological change on outdoor activities	Marsh and Wall 1982.

INSIGHT: National parks and indigenous peoples

National parks are a western concept (Nash 1967, 1982). National parks have their origins in the New World desire to conserve nature and appropriately aesthetic landscapes for economic development through tourism (Hall 1992a; 2000b). Until recently, the creation of national parks was marked by the exclusion of aboriginal populations as undesirable elements in the 'natural' landscape. The drawing of boundaries between the natural parks and the rural human landscape available for agriculture, forestry, mining and/or grazing reflecting the Cartesian divide of western society has long sought to separate civilisation and wilderness. However, over the past three decades the separation between natural and cultural heritage has come to be seen as increasingly artificial. In part, this has been due to the renaissance of aboriginal and indigenous cultures in the New Worlds of North America and Australasia as well as greater assertion of native cultural values in post-colonial societies in Africa. Such developments have had enormous influence not only on the ways in which parks are managed but also on how they are established and recreated for tourist consumption.

The influence of the Romantic movement on the establishment of national parks was extremely significant (Hall 1992a). For example, the first call for the establishment of national parks in the US came in 1832 from an artist, George Catlin, who on seeing the slaughter of buffalo on the Great Plains described the waste of animals and humankind to be a 'melancholy contemplation', but he found it 'splendid' when he imagined that there might be in the future '(by some great protecting policy of government) . . . a magnificent park', which preserved the Animal and the North American Indian 'in their pristine beauty and wildness'. 'What a beautiful and thrilling specimen for America to preserve and hold up to the view of her refined citizens and the world, in future ages! A nation's Park, containing man and

beast, in all the wild and freshness of their nature's beauty!' Catlin's seminal call for 'a nation's park' highlighted the new mood in America towards wilderness. Almost exactly 40 years after Catlin's journal entry, President Ulysses S. Grant signed an Act establishing Yellowstone Park, creating the institution of which Catlin desired 'the reputation of having been the founder' (Catlin 1968: 8, 9).

Similarly, John Matson (1892) compared the efforts made in New Zealand to protect wildlife with the absence of such attempts in the Australian colonies and appealed for the creation of 'indigenous parks' in order to preserve the animal and bird life of Australasia. Significantly, Matson quoted a New Zealand 'poet', George Phipps Williams, to conclude his case for the preservation of wildlife and their habitat, in a manner which is reminiscent of Catlin:

Out in the wilderness is there no desolate space,
Which you may spare to the brutes of indigenous race?
Grant us the shelter we need from the pitiless chase.
Gone are the stateliest forms of the apteryx kind,
Short is the space that the kiwi is lagging behind;
Soon you shall painfully seek what you never shall find.
(George Phipps Williams, *A Plea of Despair*, in Matson 1892: 359)

Williams' comments, along with those of Catlin, may seem ill at ease with political and cultural sensibilities at the beginning of the twenty-first century. However, in the late nineteenth century such sentiments were commonplace. Maori, along with other aboriginal peoples, were seen as the remnant of a dying race and placing them in parks and reserves, so long as the land was not required for other economic purposes, was often seen as the most appropriate course of action. Despite the initial Romantic sentiments which helped create the momentum for the establishment of parks, humans, including the aboriginal peoples who had often created the park landscapes through their hunting and food-gathering practices, were excluded from the parks through loss of ownership and access rights, management and regulatory actions and policing strategies. Such measures were the result of ecological and cultural blindness at best, and outright racism and cultural imperialism at worst, with park boundaries serving as the demarcation between the natural and the cultural in European eyes.

Although the political status of aboriginal peoples is still a highly contested issue in many societies, substantial shifts have occurred in management practices with respect to aboriginal peoples and their role in national parks over the past 100 years. A number of broad social and political factors in relation to the overall rights of aboriginal peoples have contributed to these changes, including:

- a renaissance of aboriginal culture in a number of western countries which has led to renewed pride in traditional cultural practices;
- the withdrawal of colonial powers in African and Asian states and the development of new modes of administration and management;
- the assertion of ownership of and/or access to natural resources through treaty settlements and other legal channels;
- changed government policies with respect to native peoples which has led to greater economic and political self-determination;

- greater political influence of aboriginal peoples.

The management of national parks has been substantially affected and a number of changes have occurred at the micro-level in parallel to the shifts which have occurred at the macro-political level. Hall (2000c) identified several factors:

- a recognition that many supposedly 'natural' landscapes are the product of a long period of aboriginal occupancy which has created a series of ecological conditions and relationships which are dependent on certain types of human behaviour. This means that the traditional knowledge of native peoples becomes a vital ingredient in effective ecosystem management;
- growth of the tourist appeal of some indigenous cultural attractions.
- greater emphasis by park management authorities on the role of various stakeholder groups, including native peoples, in park management and the development of appropriate co-operative management strategies;
- changed park management practices and strategies which are aimed at specifically satisfying the concerns and needs of native peoples including, in some cases, the management of national park lands owned by native peoples which are then leased to park management agencies.

Dasmann's recognition of wilderness as a discrete land-use category did not appear in the IUCN's (1978) eventual categorisation of conservation areas. However, this does not imply that wilderness has only minimal value as a form of conservation land use. Rather it is a recognition of the difficulties in transferring the notion of wilderness from a North American to a more universal setting (Eidsvik 1985). Nevertheless, increased public awareness of the environment, sustainable develop-

ment, World Heritage areas, Biosphere Reserves and other sites of international conservation significance highlight the worldwide attention given to the preservation of the earth's remaining wilderness areas. Indeed, the IUCN General Assembly in 1984 recommended 'that all nations identify, designate and protect their wilderness areas on both public and private lands' (Resolution 16/34 in Eidsvik 1987: 19). Yet such measures need to have a basis by which wilderness may be identified if it is to succeed. Although a wilderness inventory has been undertaken in the United States, probably the most sustained research programme on wilderness identification occurred in Australia, and it is to this case study that we now turn.

Plate 7.3: National parks are often under enormous pressure in terms of visitor numbers. The Grand Canyon National Park, USA receives over five million visitors a year.

CASE STUDY: Wilderness inventory in Australia

One of the key elements in preserving wilderness is the identification of areas of high-quality wilderness that can be incorporated into a national wilderness system. In 1985 the Australian Conservation Foundation and other conservation groups, particularly the Wilderness Society, led the Working Group on Management of National Parks of the Australian Council of Nature and Conservation Ministers (CONCOM) to examine the establishment of a nationwide system of wilderness areas. CONCOM (1985: 7) recommended that 'an inventory of potential wilderness areas should be compiled by all states and Territories, where possible in consultation with user groups. The inventory would assess areas within existing parks and extend to other land if appropriate. It would be desirable for a consistent approach to be adopted for the surveys.' However, the hopes of CONCOM were not met. Despite both the quality and quantity of research, no consistent approach to evaluating wilderness in Australia has been accepted by all participants in the process of wilderness identification and management, although the Australian Heritage Commission's National Wilderness Inventory Program came closest. This situation may be due to the academic nature of most wilderness research, the geographic differences between

regions, the politics of wilderness preservation, or it may well derive from the intrinsic intangibility of wilderness (Hall 1987, 1992a). Nevertheless, the identification of primitive and remote areas will obviously be critical to the protection and management of wilderness.

WILDERNESS INVENTORIES

Planners and managers now require detailed information to assist in the identification of areas suitable for designation and protection as wilderness, to monitor the status of the resource, and to develop appropriate and effective management prescriptions. There is also a need for the capacity to assess the impact on wilderness of various development proposals so that alternatives may be examined and a suitable response determined.
(Lesslie *et al.* 1988a: iv)

Definition is the major problem in the inventory of wilderness. The definition, and its accompanying criteria, provide the source from which all else flows. Two different conceptions of wilderness are generally recognised, one anthropocentric, the other biocentric or ecocentric (see p. 258). From the anthropocentric view, wilderness is seen from a perspective in which human needs are considered paramount. Adherents of this approach tend to ascribe a recreational role to wilderness. In contrast, the biocentric approach defines 'wilderness in ecological terms and [equates] wilderness quality with a relative lack of human disturbance' (Lesslie and Taylor 1983: 10).

The recreational values of wilderness have tended to be dominant in wilderness literature (Hendee *et al.* 1978). This is partly the result of the 'Americanisation' of the wilderness concept, where the predominantly recreational perspective of American research has coloured most other studies, but it is also probably related to the way in which the wilderness concept has developed (Nash 1963; Smith 1977; Stankey 1989; Oelschlaeger 1991). Nevertheless, over recent years the biocentric concept of wilderness has become increasingly important in research. This increased priority is most likely related to the growth of importance of ecological research relative to recreational research in national park and reserve management and to a recognition that fauna and flora have an intrinsic right to exist (Nash 1990).

Table 7.5 demonstrates the major features of the wilderness inventories that had been carried out in Australia up until the early 1990s, by which time the methodology for the National Wilderness Inventory supported by the Australian Heritage Commission had become well developed. For each inventory the study area, wilderness definition, dimensional criteria, status of coastal areas, database and status of roadworks is recorded. The status of roadworks criterion is included because it provides a basis of comparison with the 'roadless area' concept which permeates American notions of wilderness and also illustrates one of the major problems in standardising wilderness criteria (Bureau of Land Management 1978). As Lesslie and Taylor (1983: 23) observed, 'road definition is a major point of contention in the general wilderness literature. Controversy centres on the qualities which make a high grade road an unacceptable intrusion into wilderness and a low

grade road a detrimental but nevertheless acceptable intrusion.'

The first Australian study of wilderness of any consequence, the wilderness study of eastern New South Wales and south-east Queensland by Helman *et al.* (1976; Jones 1978) was designed as a model for future Australian wilderness inventories and it was applied in Victoria (Feller *et al.* 1979) and Tasmania (Russell *et al.* 1979). However, the inventory procedures may not be valid for arid and semi-arid environments because they were undertaken in relatively humid, forested and mountainous environments (Lesslie and Taylor 1983); also, they failed to recognise the remoteness and primitiveness which constitute the key qualities of wilderness (Mark 1985). Stanton and Morgan's (1977) study of Queensland identified four key areas as fitting rigid conservation-based criteria. Twenty-four other areas were identified as being 'equivalent to the wilderness areas delineated by Helman *et al.* (1976) in their study of eastern Australia' (Morgan 1980).

Kirkpatrick's (1980) study of south-west Tasmania identified wilderness as a recreational resource, 'as land remote from access by mechanised vehicles, and from within which there is little or no consciousness of the environmental disturbance of western man' (Kirkpatrick and Haney 1980: 331). Kirkpatrick assigned absolute wilderness quality scores, which had not been attempted in Australian wilderness inventories, although it was characteristic of American ones. However, unlike the United States inventories, Kirkpatrick focused on the more readily quantifiable characteristics of wilderness: remoteness and primitiveness.

Remoteness and primitiveness are the two essential attributes of wilderness (Helburn 1977). Remoteness is measured 'as the walking time from the nearest access point for mechanised vehicles' while primitiveness, which 'has visual, aural and mental components', is 'determined from measures of the arc of visibility of any

Table 7.5: Australian wilderness inventories

Study and area	Definitions of wilderness	Dimensional criteria	Status of coastal areas	Status of roadworks	Database
Helman et al. 1976: Eastern New South Wales and south-east Queensland	Large area of land perceived to be natural, where genetic diversity and natural cycles remain essentially unaltered.	• A minimum core area of 25,000 ha; • a core area free of major indentations; • a core area of at least 10 km in width; and • a management (buffer) zone surrounding the core of about 25,000 ha or more.	Coastal areas were not required to meet the dimensional criteria as rigidly as inland areas, due to their linear characteristics and the type of ecosystems and recreation they support.	If roads do not seriously impair the user's perception of the wilderness or the natural functioning of the ecosystem and use can be controlled by management, their presence to a limited degree should not preclude wilderness status.	Landsat images in conjunction with DNM 1:250,000 maps. Aerial reconnaissance to check results.
Stanton and Morgan 1977: Queensland	An extensive pristine area with extremely limited access.	Size based on a core area defined as a day's walk from any access point. A minimum wilderness area (with no core) of about 40,000 ha.	No specific criteria.	Roadworks are incompatible with the strict definition of wilderness.	Aerial photographs at approximately 1:84,000, 1:1,000,000 maps.
Feller et al. 1979: Victoria	As for Helman et al.	As for Helman et al., with special criteria for semi-arid and mountain wilderness, a minimum area of about 150,000 ha for semi-arid wilderness and 50,000 ha for mountain wilderness.	Minimum area as close as possible to 50,000 ha; it may be smaller if • the core area is free of major indentations; • there is a buffer on the landward side of the core; • there is a reasonable length of coast included in the core.	• All two-wheel drive roads and substantial four-wheel drive tracks were excluded from the core. Substantial tracks were included only if they were dead-end and not often used; • sealed and gravel roads were excluded from the core and buffer; and • an acceptable density of tracks was determined for each wilderness.	DNM 1:100,000 maps, aerial photographs at 1:20,000 to 1:50,000. Additional information from Forests Commission, National Parks Service and Land Conservation Council maps. Some field checking was carried out.

Study	Definition	Coastal consideration	Roadworks	Data sources
Russell *et al.* 1979: Tasmania	As for Helman *et al.*	As for Helman *et al.* with special attention to exclusion of intrusions and the use of natural topographic boundaries to determine core area boundaries. Minimum areas of approximately 10,000 ha were also identified and delineated.	The core of a wilderness area with a coastal boundary may extend to the coastline with an as yet undefined buffer zone extending into the surrounding coastal waters.	The buffer zone boundary excluded all formed access roads and high-density or high-impact vehicular tracks. Vehicular roads and tracks were excluded from the inner core wilderness areas.	Lands Department 1:500,000, 1:250,000 geographic and 1:100,000 topographic maps. Land tenure maps at 1:100,000 and 1:250,000. Aerial photographs at 1:50,000. Some field checking.
Kirkpatrick 1980: south-west Tasmania	An area of land remote from access by mechanised vehicles and within which there is little or no consciousness of the environmental disturbances of western man.	Wilderness was assumed to exist in relatively undisturbed environments at places greater than 5 km or more from access point or human disturbance. Wilderness quality scores were derived from mathematical functions which represent the relationship between the intensity of the wilderness experience, the time/distance from the access point or nearest sign of human disturbance, and the proportion of the area of visibility occupied by signs of human disturbance.	No special consideration.	No roadworks are included in wilderness areas.	Lands Department 1:100,000 and 1:250,000 map series. Additional information from the National Parks and Wildlife Service and the South West Tasmanian Resource Survey.
Lesslie and Taylor 1983: South Australia	Land which is remote from and undisturbed by the presence and influences of settled people.	Wilderness quality was scaled according to four indicators: remoteness from settlement, remoteness from access, aesthetic primitiveness and bio-physical primitiveness. Wilderness quality was then expressed as classes: very high, high or moderately high. Additative and weighted additative procedures ranked sites according to their wilderness value. High-quality wilderness could then be distinguished.	No special consideration.	High-grade roads were regarded as access points while low-grade roads were treated as aesthetic disturbances. Wilderness quality relates to the density of linear structures (such as roadworks) per unit area. Four-wheel drive transport was seen as an appropriate wilderness travel mode in arid and semi-arid areas.	DNM 1:250,000 and 1:100,000 topographic series, Department of Lands 1:50,000 topographic series and South Australian Royal Automobile Association Touring maps.

continued

Table 7.5: (continued)

Study and area	Definitions of wilderness	Dimensional criteria	Status of coastal areas	Status of roadworks	Database
Hawes and Heatley 1985: Tasmania	• largely free of evidence of human artifacts, activity and disturbance; • remote from substantial human artifacts and areas where there is substantial human activity or disturbance; and • remote of access.	Land whose direct remoteness (the map distance between that point and the nearest intrusion) and access remoteness (the minimum time separation between that point and any access point) are d and t respectively, for a suitable choice of values d (km) and t (hours and days).	• Regular use of mechanised vehicles is regarded as a major intrusion; and • no special provision was made for the use of coastal areas by mechanised vehicles as it was assumed that use was still low due to the relative inaccessibility.	The following were regarded as major intrusions: • all roads, and all vehicular tracks accessible to and frequently used by off-road vehicles; • all areas where mechanised transport is intensively used or where the use of such transport has led or is likely to lead to the formation of permanent tracks or cause long-term environmental disturbance.	1:100,000 maps of Tasmania and 1:500,000 vegetation map of Tasmania; primitive country and wilderness were identified manually on 1:500,000 maps.
Lesslie et al. 1987; Preece and Lesslie 1987: Victoria	As for Lesslie and Taylor 1983.	Modification of Lesslie and Taylor methodology for ease of digitising, storing and spatially organising wilderness quality indicators through a grid cell framework. (National Wilderness Inventory State I).	No special consideration.	Three grades of road and track access were distinguished according to the level of access and the degree of use: major two-wheel-drive roads; minor two-wheel-drive roads; and four-wheel-drive tracks.	DNM 1:100,000 topographic maps, Department of Conservation Forests and Lands regional maps, RAC Victoria Guide maps, governmental reports, land tenure information and personal knowledge.
Lesslie et al. 1988: Tasmania	As for Lesslie et al. 1987.	National Wilderness Inventory Stage II, as for Lesslie et al. 1987.	No special consideration.	As for Lesslie et al. 1987.	National 1:250,000 topographic mapping grid of Tasmania, 1:100,000 topographic maps, 1:25,000 1:500,000 vegetation map topographic series, RAC Tasmania touring information, Forestry Commission 1:100,000 maps, large-scale aerial photography, Forestry Commission Tasmania GIS Forest type database.

Lesslie, Abrahams and Maslen 1991: Cape York Peninsula, Queensland	As for Lesslie et al. 1987.	National Wilderness Inventory Stage III.	No special consideration.	As for Lesslie et al. 1987	National 1:250,000 topographical mapping grid.
Lesslie, Maslen, Canty, Goodwins and Shields 1991: Kangaroo Island, South Australia	As for Lesslie et al. 1987.	National Wilderness Inventory: South Australia.	Lakes, rivers and oceans included as natural bodies.	In addition to the three grades utilised in previous National Wilderness Inventory stages a fourth grade of access was distinguished: very low – 'established but unconstructed vehicle access routes (e.g. beach access) and cleared lines; established walking tracks; cleared land' (p.10)	National 1:250,000 topographical mapping grid, 1:100,000 map series, Department of Lands 1:50,000 map series.
Manidis Roberts Consultants 1991: Western New South Wales	A wilderness area is a large tract of land remote at its core from access and settlement, substantially unmodified by modern technological society or capable of being restored to that state, and of sufficient size to make practical the long term protection of its natural system.	Combination of Helman et al. and National Wilderness Inventory methodology in order to indicate prospective wilderness areas.	Not applicable.	A paved road excludes the surrounding land from a wilderness classification. Tracks and loose surface roads are acceptable in small quantities, because it is possible to reduce the impact and restore the wilderness value. Walking tracks and maintenance tracks impacts are not considered to reduce wilderness value substantially.	Literature review, contacts within the network of conservation groups, 1:100,000 scale maps, by NATMAP and the Central Mapping Authority.

DNM: Division of National Mapping
RAC: Royal Automobile Club
Source: Hall (1992a: 12–17)

disturbance . . . and the distance to the nearest disturbance' (Kirkpatrick and Haney 1980: 331). The identification of remoteness and primitiveness as the essential attributes of a wilderness area helped create the methodological basis for the wilderness inventory of South Australia by Lesslie and Taylor (1983, 1985) and provides the basis for a national survey of wilderness.

Lesslie and Taylor (1983) saw previous wilderness inventory procedures as unsatisfactory because they sought to express a relative concept in absolute terms. They identified four indicators of wilderness quality: remoteness from settlement, remoteness from access, aesthetic primitiveness (or naturalness) and biophysical primitiveness (or naturalness). These indicators were used to provide an inventory of relatively high-quality wilderness areas in South Australia. The attributes of remoteness and primitiveness may be expressed as part of a continuum which indicates the relative wilderness quality of a region (Figure 7.1). A continuum approach can accommodate the ecological and recreational characteristics of a far wider range of environments than can the inventories formulated for the higher rainfall areas of Australia (Lesslie and Taylor 1983; Hall and Mark 1985; Hall 1987; Lesslie *et al.* 1987; Lesslie 1991; Manidis Roberts Consultants 1991).

The variation in approaches to wilderness inventory in Australia is 'systematic of confusion concerning the definition of wilderness, since areas which satisfy biocentric considerations need not be consistent with areas which satisfy anthropocentric considerations' (Lesslie and Taylor 1983: 11). The area required to satisfy recreational criteria for wilderness may be much smaller than the area required for maintaining the ecological balance of a region (Valentine 1980). Therefore, the experiental criterion for wilderness remains substantially different to ecological criterion and the concept of 'wilderness experience' must be separated from that of 'wilderness area'. As Lesslie and Taylor (1983: 14) observed, there has been an 'almost universal tendency to confuse the *benefits derived from wilderness* with the *nature of wilderness itself*', a point of crucial importance in the delineation, inventory and management of wilderness. Hence, the two attributes which are definitive of wilderness, *remoteness* from the presence and influences of settled people, and *primitiveness*, the absence of environmental disturbance by settled people, need to be based at the high-quality end of the wilderness continuum in order to accommodate the anthropocentric and biocentric dimensions of wilderness (Taylor 1990; Lesslie 1991). In Australia, the methodology of Lesslie and Taylor (1983), and modified in the

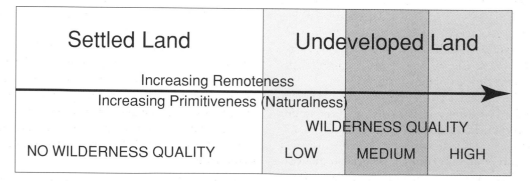

Figure 7.1: The wilderness continuum
Source: Hall (1992a)

1987 Victorian inventory (Lesslie *et al.* 1987; Preece and Lesslie 1987), comes closest to achieving this goal and has served as the model for other studies within the Australian Heritage Commission's National Wilderness Inventory (see below). Furthermore, Lesslie *et al.*'s (1987) methodology is able to indicate low-quality wilderness areas which are not indicated in an inventory along the lines of Helman *et al.* (1976), but which may nevertheless be of significant conservation and recreation value (Hall 1987).

In 1987 the Australian government, through the Australian Heritage Commission, initiated a National Wilderness Inventory (NWI) to provide information in order to improve decisions about wilderness conservation (Lesslie *et al.* 1991b). This action was 'a result of its concern over the rapid decline in area and quality of relatively remote and natural lands in Australia and in recognition that an inventory of the remaining resource was the necessary first step in formulating appropriate measures for conservation and management' (Lesslie *et al.* 1991a: 1). The NWI had three main emphases (Lesslie *et al.* 1988a): to compile a national wilderness database; to refine database maintenance procedures and analytical techniques; and to produce information relevant to policy and management issues. Several inventories were conducted under the auspices of the National Wilderness Inventory, including surveys of Victoria (Lesslie *et al.* 1987; Preece and Lesslie 1987); Tasmania (Lesslie *et al.* 1988a); South Australia (Lesslie *et al.* 1991b); and Queensland (Lesslie *et al.* 1991a). In 1990 the NWI was accelerated to provide a comprehensive coverage for the whole of Australia.

'The evaluation of wilderness in the National Wilderness Inventory is based upon the notion of wilderness quality as a continuum of remote and natural conditions from pristine to urban' (Lesslie *et al.* 1991b: 6). A spatial framework utilising the techniques of Geographic Information Systems (GIS) is used to sample variation in values of the four wilderness quality indicators.

There are two major advantages in using a GIS to formulate wilderness evaluation databases. First, the approach is open-ended: new data may be added and current data modified. Indeed, in Australia, 'information about access and landuse is often poorly recorded and lacking in currency. Even the most recently available information may be inaccurate and out of date. This makes the compilation of a reliable database difficult, particularly because of the necessary dependence on published sources for much of the required information' (Lesslie *et al.* 1991b: 13). Second, the process is spatially flexible, enabling scale to be matched to purpose. Furthermore, maps showing the distribution of wilderness identified in the inventory can be generated rapidly and efficiently in order to assist decision-making.

FROM IDENTIFICATION TO PRESERVATION

The purpose of wilderness inventory in Australia has, on the whole, been to identify areas of wilderness quality for the possible enactment of conservation measures by government. Inventories provide a systematic means of ensuring the designation areas of high environmental quality. 'Recognition of wilderness is the necessary first step towards protecting, appreciating and managing wilderness areas' (Manidis Roberts Consultants 1991: 2). However, identifying an area as wilderness does not, by itself, ensure that its wilderness qualities can be maintained; this may only be done through the appropriate legislation and management. 'Decisions of this kind are inevitably judgemental, requiring comparative assessments of the social worth of alternative and often conflicting landuse opportunities' (Lesslie *et al.* 1988a: v). Nevertheless, from a management perspective:

> The delimitation of wilderness management boundaries for any particular location is a separate question. The major point to be made here is that

via a list of variables that may be considered appropriate or inappropriate to wilderness recreation and tourism. A five-point Likert scale allowed respondents to express the extent to which each variable was considered acceptable or unacceptable. Higham noted that in 'classic' (i.e. high quality in terms of absence of human impact) wilderness terms it should be expected that these variables would be considered to violate or compromise qualities of wilderness recreation. However, only seven of the 21 variables listed received a generally negative response (a mean value less than 3.0). Thirteen variables returned mean values exceeding 3.0 indicating a generally favourable disposition within the sample frame (Table 7.6).

In Higham's (1997) study, 'Distance from civilisation' (mean = 4.0) is clearly an important aspect of wilderness recreation to most inbound tourists. The desire for remoteness is reinforced in the similar high regard for the scale of the location ('big

enough to take at least two days to walk across' mean = 3.8). However, there is also a desire for the provision of safeguard mechanisms to reduce risk, with the provision of search and rescue operations receiving the highest mean score (4.3) of all listed variables. The desire for swing bridges and walkwires over watercourses, signposting and well-marked and maintained tracks confirm the widely held desire for wilderness recreation in a natural but relatively safe and humanised environment.

Furthermore, the placement of restrictions upon access and group size, again inconsistent with the notion of wilderness as free from human influences, was widely considered acceptable by inbound visitors. The variables 'restricted access' and 'restricted group size' share a mean of 3.8, placing them favourably on Table 7.6. As Higham (1997: 83) observed, 'It is quite possible that positive disposition toward these variables derives from trampers visiting high profile tracks on which social

Table 7.6: Responses to variables listed in question 'Indicate whether you feel that the following activities/facilities are acceptable based on your perception of wilderness' (%)

Variable list	1	2	3	4	5	Mean
Search and rescue operations	4.0	3.1	16.6	21.2	49.1	4.3
Distant from towns and cities	4.0	6.7	19.8	22.6	45.1	4.0
Swing bridges/walkwires over rivers or streams	5.2	6.8	21.8	28.3	36.9	3.9
Restricted group size	10.5	9.5	16.6	24.9	33.5	3.8
Restricted access to prevent crowding	10.5	8.0	17.5	25.2	34.2	3.8
Big enough to take at least two days to walk across	8.9	6.8	18.8	24.3	39.4	3.8
Water provided in huts	14.3	7.9	17.7	22.3	36.9	3.6
Maintained huts and shelters	9.5	11.0	22.7	27.9	26.4	3.6
Toilet facilities	14.0	8.5	18.6	22.9	34.5	3.6
Exotic plants/trees (pines, thistles and foxgloves)	11.2	11.6	20.4	20.7	33.4	3.6
Signposts/information	7.0	12.8	24.8	24.5	29.4	3.6
Road access to the start of track	12.5	11.6	27.1	22.0	25.0	3.4
Maintained tracks (e.g. tracks cleared of fallen trees)	13.1	18.3	21.7	27.2	18.0	3.2
Developed camping sites	20.2	14.4	25.2	24.2	14.1	3.0
Grazing of stock (cattle, sheep)	31.2	15.9	25.7	11.9	11.3	2.7
Gas provided in huts for cooking	33.7	16.7	21.3	10.3	16.7	2.6
Stocking of animals and fish not native to NZ	40.1	20.7	21.0	4.6	7.7	2.4
Hunting/trapping	38.6	18.8	21.9	9.3	8.0	2.4
Motorised transport (powered vehicles, boats)	44.9	22.5	15.7	6.2	8.3	2.2
Plantation logging/mining/hydro development	52.8	18.1	16.6	4.3	4.0	2.0
Commercial recreation (e.g. guided tours)	52.7	20.1	13.1	5.5	6.4	2.0

Non-essential/unacceptable 1–2–3–4–5 Essential/acceptable
Where percentage figures do not total 100, the difference is explained by non-response to variables.

Source: Higham (1997: 82)

carrying capacities are being approached and, at times, exceeded.'

Only seven listed variables returned a mean response which indicated a generally negative disposition (Table 7.6). Six of these seven variables described activities that were likely to present associated social or physical impacts. These included commercial recreation and motorised transport, and grazing of stock and hunting/trapping and plantation logging, respectively. The seventh such variable, 'gas provided in huts for cooking', is exceptional in that it described the provision of a facility that may ease the passage of visitors in back-country locations. This was the only such variable that was generally rejected by inbound tourists, all other visitor provisions and facilities (huts, shelters, the provision of water and toilet facilities) being considered generally acceptable or compatible with wilderness recreation and tourism.

Higham's (1997) research raises important questions about the role of accessibility to wilderness areas. Indeed, issues of access are now presenting major management problems in wilderness and national parks. For many years access to wilderness was restricted by both the nature of the terrain and the capacity of individuals to travel there. Up until the Second World War the main means of access to most national parks was by train, with many of the national parks in the New World actually being developed in association with the railroads (Runte 1974a, 1974b, 1979; Hall 1992a). However, in the post-war period there was a substantial increase in the proportion of personal car ownership, thereby increasing accessibility to parks. National park management agencies also promoted themselves to the public through 'parks for the people campaigns'. Herein though lies the critical situation in which many parks and wilderness managers now find themselves. National parks were originally established to provide both recreational enjoyment and conservation (Hall 1992a). The founders of the park movement, though, such as John Muir, could never have imagined the almost continuous growth in demand for park access from tourists and recreationists seeking to escape the urban environment. The situation now sees traffic jams occurring in some parks, congestion on walking tracks, displacement of local users by tourists, increased pollution and other adverse environmental impacts, and reduced visitor satisfaction (e.g. Hall and McArthur 1996, 1998; Higham 1997; Kearsley 1997). Within this context, therefore, park and wilderness managers are now seeking both a better understanding of their visitors and how they may be satisfied, and strategies to find a better match between visitor needs and the capacities of the resource to be used, yet to retain the values that attract people in the first place (Hall and McArthur 1998).

Historically, tourist profiles have been generated to assist in the planning and management of visitor demand at a particular destination, attraction or site. Analysing tourist demand has traditionally been based on one of two main approaches: a socio-economic approach and a psychological or psychographic approach (see Chapter 2). The socio-economic approach attempts to establish a correlation between a visitor's actions at a particular destination and their social position (Lowyck et al. 1992). Mathieson and Wall (1982) argue that visitor attitudes, perceptions and motivations at a destination are influenced by socio-economic characteristics such as age, education, income, residence and family situation. Representative of this form of research is Blamey's (1995) study of international ecotourists to Australia, a country which has paid particular attention to promoting its natural features to tourists in recent years (Hall 1995).

According to Blamey (1995), Japanese and other Asian tourists are the most common inbound visitors to national parks on an absolute basis (21 and 19 per cent respectively of all such visitors), although they have the lowest propensities to do so on a per visit basis. Visitors from Switzerland have the highest propensity to visit natural areas (74 per cent) followed by Germany, Canada, Scandinavia and other European countries (all above 65 per cent). In addition, the economic expenditure of nature-based tourists may be substantial. Blamey (1995) reported that in 1993 the average expenditure per trip for international visitors undertaking bushwalks during their stay was Aus.$2,824 in amount of the economic multipliers generated by tourism. Successful reduction of multiplier leakage requires local participation in development planning and outside assistance with the provision of necessary infrastructure, training and credit.

Ecotourism, tourism and recreation in natural environments can undoubtedly bring economic benefits to both communities on the periphery and to the wholesalers and suppliers of such experiences, and it is for this reason that increasing attention is being given to the supply of the experience of wild nature (Fennell 1999).

SUPPLYING THE WILDERNESS AND OUTDOOR RECREATION EXPERIENCE

In many ways the idea that one can 'supply' a wilderness or outdoor recreation experience seems at odds with the implied freedom of wilderness. However, the tourism industry is in the business of producing such experiences, while national parks and wilderness areas, by virtue of their formal designation, are places which have been defined as places where such experiences may be found. One of the most important transformations in the production of leisure on the periphery has been the way in which the initial construction of national parks as places of spectacular scenery and national monuments for the few were transformed into places of mass recreation in the 1950s and 1960s and to places of tourist commodification in the 1980s and 1990s, particularly through the notion of ecotourism.

A number of different meanings applied to the concept of 'ecotourism' (Valentine 1992; Hall 1995; Weaver 1998) which range from 'shallow' to 'deeper' statements of the tourism environment relationship:

- ecotourism as any form of tourism development which is regarded as environmentally friendly and has the capacity to act as a branding mechanism for some forms of tourist products;
- ecotourism as 'green' or 'nature-based' tourism which is essentially a form of special interest

tourism and refers to a specific market segment and the products generated for that segment;
- ecotourism as a form of nature-based tourism that involves education and interpretation of the natural environment and is managed to be ecologically and culturally sustainable.

The Australian Office of National Tourism (1997), for example, defined ecotourism as 'nature-based tourism that involves interpretation of the natural and cultural environment and ecologically sustainable management of natural areas'.

> Ecotourism is seen as ecologically and socially responsible, and as fostering environmental appreciation and awareness. It is based on the enjoyment of nature with minimal environmental impact. The educational element of ecotourism, which enhances understanding of natural environments and ecological processes, distinguishes it from adventure travel and sightseeing.
> (Office of National Tourism 1997)

Many countries around the world are now focusing on the supply of an ecotourism product (Fennell 2000). Unfortunately, much of the ecotourism promotion best fits into the shallow end of the ecotourism spectrum, in that much of it revolves around the branding of a product or destination rather than seeking to ensure sustainability. Indeed, one of the greatest problems of ecotourism is the extent to which such experiences can be supplied without a limit on the number of people who visit natural areas, as visitation may lead not only to environmental damage, but also to perceptions of crowding thereby reducing the quality of the experience. As Kearsley *et al.* (1997: 71) noted, 'From the viewpoint of tourism . . . it is the impact of tourists upon tourists that has increasingly led to concern. Issues of crowding, displacement and host community dissatisfaction have risen to prominence.'

Crowding is a logical consequence of rising participation in outdoor recreation and nature-based tourism activities (Gramann 1982). It should therefore be of no great surprise that crowding is the most frequently studied aspect of wilderness recreation (Shelby *et al.* 1989). Indeed, many issues in wilderness management and outdoor recreation,

Plate 7.4: Access to national parks and other places of scenic beauty is a problem. Should cars be allowed within national parks or should they be kept outside? Many national parks now suffer problems of traffic congestion more typically associated with urban centres.

such as satisfaction, desired experiences, carrying capacity and displacement are all related to the primary issue of crowding. Furthermore, social carrying capacity is increasingly being recognised as the most critical of all types of carrying capacity, since ecological impacts can often be controlled by management actions other than limiting use levels; for example, facilities may be extended and made more effective, and physical capacities are usually high (Shelby and Heberlein 1984).

Importantly, crowding should not be confused with density. Density refers to the number of individuals in a given area while crowding refers to the evaluation of a certain density (Graefe *et al.* 1984a, b). In a review of 35 studies of crowding, Shelby *et al.* (1989) identified four sources of variation in perceptions of crowding:

1 *Temporal variation* – either in terms of time or season within which outdoor recreation activities are taking place. For example, weekends and public holidays are likely to experience higher than average use densities thereby resulting in inflated perceptions of crowding.
2 *Resource availability* – variation of resource availability (e.g. the opening and closing of tracks in alpine areas) may act to alter the presence of people at recreational sites.

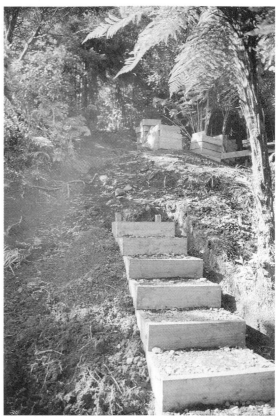

Plate 7.5: In order to minimise erosion caused by large visitor numbers in natural areas, substantial site and trail hardening may have to be undertaken as here in the Waitakere Regional Park, Auckland, New Zealand. However, what effects does such work have on the visitor experience and does the increased ease of access actually encourage yet more visitation?

3 *Accessibility* – distance (expressed in terms of time, cost, spatial or perceived distance) will affect crowding and densities, particularly if there is little or no recreation resource substitution.
4 *Management strategies* – management can intervene directly (e.g. use restrictions), or indirectly (e.g. de-marketing) to reduce visitor numbers at recreation sites.

Shelby *et al.* (1989) also investigated the hypothesis that crowding perceptions would vary according to the type of recreational use, although they were not able to resolve this hypothesis. However, recent research by Higham (1996) indicates that recreational use history is a substantial factor in influencing perceptions of crowding.

Concerns over crowding are closely related to issues of social carrying capacity in wilderness and outdoor recreation areas. Social carrying capacity in recreation areas 'has typically been defined as a use level beyond which some measure of experiential quality becomes impaired' (Graefe *et al.* 1984b: 500). However, as Chapter 6 noted, there is no 'absolute value' of social carrying capacity, there is no single response to specific levels of use in a particular area. Instead, indicators of social or behavioural capacity will be dependent on the management objectives for a given recreation site (Greafe *et al.* 1984a). Shelby and Heberlein (1986: 21) therefore refined this definition to read: 'Social carrying capacity is the level of use beyond which social impacts exceed acceptable levels specified by evaluative standards.'

Several factors have been identified as influencing crowding norms, with a number of variables contributing to the interpretation of increasing recreational use density as perceived crowding (Manning 1985):

- visitor characteristics: motivations, preferences and expectations, previous use experiences, visitors' attitudes towards wilderness;
- characteristics of those encountered: type and size of groups encountered, behaviour of those encountered, perceptions of alikeness;
- situational variables: type of area and location within an area.

Manning (1985) concluded that crowding norms are extremely diverse, yet the significance of visitor characteristics as a factor and the psychographic variables which comprise this factor indicate the possibility of a high degree of agreement being reached on crowding norms within particular subsets of the recreational population. This latter possibility highlights the importance of managers having a good understanding of the psychographic and demographic profiles of their visitor base in order to optimise levels of visitor satisfaction and attainment of management objectives (Hall and McArthur 1998).

Density alone provides no measure of visitor satisfaction. Satisfaction will be determined by expectations, prior experiences and commitment to the recreational activity. Perceptions of crowding are therefore influenced by use densities, but this relationship is mediated by a range of other factors and variables (Graefe *et al.* 1984a). Indeed, a range of reactions or coping strategies are possible in recreationalist response to decreased recreational satisfaction, which may result not only from crowding, but also from such factors as littering, noise and worn out camp sites (e.g. Anderson and Brown 1984). Such reactions include:

- modifying behavioural patterns (e.g. by camping rather than using developed facilities);
- changing time of visit or use (e.g. visiting in shoulder or off-peak periods in order to avoid conflicts with other users);
- changing perceptions, expectations and recreation priorities (also referred to as product shift (Shelby *et al.* 1988), e.g. developing a new set of expectations about a recreational setting in order to maintain satisfaction);
- recreational displacement, where those who are most sensitive to recreational conflicts seek alternative sites to achieve desired outcomes.

Of the above strategies, recreational displacement is probably the most serious from the manager's perspective as displacement appears to be a reality of wilderness use regardless of the level of recreational experience (Becker 1981; Anderson and Brown 1984). Therefore, increases in numbers of visitors to wilderness and other natural areas, particularly at a time when such areas have to cope with their promotion as places for ecotourism experiences as well as the pressures of traditional recreation users, may lead to a decline in wilderness qualities as users are displaced from site to site. For example, in the case of major walking tracks in the South Island of New Zealand, Kearsley (1997: 95) observes:

National parks and scenic areas

A   Coramandel Range
B   Raukumara Range
C   Egmont National Park
D   Whanganui National Park
E   Tongariro National Park
F   Pirongia Forest Park
G   Northland Forest Park
H   Tairarua Ranges
I   Ruahine Range
J   Kaimangua Forest Park
K   Kaweka Forest Park
L   Urewera National Park
M   North-West Nelson Forest Park
N   Mount Richmond Forest Park
O   Nelson Lakes National Park
P   Victoria Forest Park
Q   Hamner Forest Park
R   Lake Sumner Forest Park
S   Arthur's Pass National Park
T   Mount Cook National Park
U   Mount Aspiring National Park
V   Fiordland National Park
W   Catlins Forest Park
X   Westland National Park

Figure 7.2: National parks and scenic areas in New Zealand frequented by international tourists

In a context where there is a clear hierarchy of sites, as in Southern New Zealand, displacement down the hierarchy is an all-too-likely possibility . . . the very large increase in overseas users of the Routeburn has displaced some domestic recreationists (and perhaps some tourists) to second tier tracks such as the Hollyford or Dart-Rees, or, indeed, out of tramping altogether. Similarly, their arrival might displace others yet further down the hierarchy to even less well known places, and there is a danger that trampers might be forced into wild and remote environments that are beyond their safe capacity.

One consequence of this, if it is happening, is increased visitor pressure on more remote locations and displacement of moderate wilderness purists to a limited reservoir of pristine sites . . . with obvious physical impacts. A second consequence is the effect upon host community satisfaction, as domestic recreationists are displaced by overseas visitors [Figure 7.2]. Both of these consequences have serious implications for the sustainability of tourism.

The case of crowding and other variables which influence visitor satisfaction and behaviour, including displacement, highlights the significance of understanding the factors of supply and demand of the recreation and tourist experience (see Chapters 2 and 3). Just as importantly they indicate the need for sound planning and management practice in trying to achieve a balance between the production and consumption of tourism and recreation, particularly in environmentally sensitive areas.

CONCLUSION

This chapter has highlighted a number of areas in which geographers have contributed to research and scholarship in the tourism and recreation periphery. From the Topophilia of Tuan (1974), the sacred space of Graber (1978) and the breathtaking historical analysis of Glacken (1967), geographers have been at the forefront not only of understanding the human relationship to the natural environment and wild lands in particular, but also to the behaviours of tourists and recreationists in the wilderness. In addition, geographers have assisted in developing techniques to identify wilderness areas, undertake environmental histories and to cast light on their values.

As a resource analyst, the geographer therefore 'seeks to understand the fundamental characteristics of natural resources and the processes through which they are allocated and utilised' (Mitchell 1979: 3). The geographer's task is also relayed by Coppock (1970: 25), who has made remarks of direct relevance to a better understanding of the relationship between tourism, recreation and wilderness conservation: 'A concern with problem solving and with the processes of human interaction with resources, particularly in respect of decision making, will powerfully assist a more effective geographical contribution to conservation.'

QUESTIONS

- Is wilderness only a concept of the New World or does the concept also have relevance to western Europe?
- Is the methodology of Australia's national wilderness inventory easily transferable to other countries?
- What are the main factors which influence crowding norms?

READING

On wilderness see:

Nash, R. (1982) *Wilderness and the American Mind*, 3rd edn, New Haven, CT: Yale University Press.
Oelschlaeger, M. (1991) *The Idea of Wilderness: From Prehistory to the Age of Ecology*, New Haven, CT: Yale University Press.
Hall, C.M. (1992a) *Wasteland to World Heritage: Preserving Australia's Wilderness*, Carlton: Melbourne University Press.

For a recent excellent overview on national parks and tourism around the world see:

Butler, R. and Boyd, S. (eds) (2000) *Tourism and National Parks*, Chichester: John Wiley.

8

COASTAL AND MARINE
RECREATION AND TOURISM

The coastal environment is a magnet for tourists and recreationists although its role in leisure activities has changed in time and space, as coastal destinations have developed, waned, been reimaged and redeveloped in the twentieth century. The coastal environment is a complex system which is utilised by the recreationist for day trips, while juxtaposed to these visits are those made by the domestic and international tourist. In an early attempt to identify the complexity of the coastline for tourism, Pearce and Kirk (1986) identified three elements to the coastal environment: the *hinterland* (where accommodation and services are provided); the *transit* zone (i.e. dunes) and the *recreational activity* zone (beach and sea). This model typifies much of the research by geographers prior to the 1990s: to observe, record, synthesise and model recreational and tourism phenomena in pursuit of an explanation of the spatial relationships and nature of the coast. In Lavery's (1971b) analysis of resorts, the distinction between recreation and tourism blurred but the coastal resort was a dominant element of the observed patterns and models of tourism activity. The pursuit of explanations of the spatial structure of coastal tourism and preoccupation with the resort morphology has led to the replication of a multiplicity of studies that look at the similarities and differences between resorts in different parts of the world. As D.G. Pearce (1988: 11) rightly concluded: 'In stressing the physical form tourism takes along the coast, geographers have largely neglected the way tourists actually use this space. The questions of where and how coastal tourists spend their time appear to

have been taken for granted for they have rarely been addressed explicitly nor examined in any detail.' This assessment may equally be applied to the recreational activities of visitors to the coastal environment since this neglect is not germane to tourism alone. This was confirmed by Patmore (1983: 209) since 'For such extensive resource, it has been little studied in any comprehensive fashion'.

Ocean and coastal tourism is widely regarded as one of the fastest growing areas of contemporary tourism (Pollard 1995; Kim and Kim 1996; Orams 1999). While tourism development has been spatially focused on the beach for much of the past 50 years, as witnessed, for example, in the slogan of the four 'S's of tourism – sun, sand, surf and sex – the coastal and the marine environment as a whole has become one of the new frontiers and fastest growing areas of the world's tourism industry (Miller and Auyong 1991). The exact numbers of marine tourists remain unknown. Nevertheless, the selling of 'sun, sand and surf experiences', the development of beach resorts and the increasing popularity of marine tourism (e.g. fishing, scuba diving, windsurfing and yachting) has all placed increased pressure on the coast, an area for which use may already be highly concentrated in terms of agriculture, human settlements, fishing and industrial location (Miller 1993; ESCAP 1995a, 1995b). However, because of the highly dynamic nature of the coastal environment any development which interferes with the natural coastal system may have severe consequences for the long-term stability of the environment (Cicin-Sain and Knecht 1998).

Indeed, the United States National Oceanic and Atmospheric Administration (1997) recognised that:

> Of all the activities that take place in coastal zones and the near-shore coastal ocean, none is increasing in both volume and diversity more than coastal tourism and recreation. Both the dynamic nature of this sector and its magnitude demand that it be actively taken into account in government plans, policies, and programs related to the coasts and ocean. Indeed, virtually all coastal and ocean issue areas affect coastal tourism and recreation either directly or indirectly. Clean water, healthy coastal habitats, and a safe, secure, and enjoyable environment are clearly fundamental to successful coastal tourism. Similarly, bountiful living marine resources (fish, shellfish, wetlands, coral reefs, etc.) are of critical importance to most recreational experiences. Security from risks associated with natural coastal hazards such as storms, hurricanes, tsunamis, and the like is a requisite for coastal tourism to be sustainable over the long term.

The concept of coastal tourism embraces the full range of tourism, leisure and recreationally oriented activities that take place in the coastal zone and the offshore coastal waters. These include coastal tourism development (accommodation, restaurants, food industry and second homes), and the infra-structure supporting coastal development (e.g. retail businesses, marinas and activity suppliers). Also included are tourism activities such as recreational boating, coast- and marine-based ecotourism, cruises, swimming, recreational fishing, snorkelling and diving (Miller and Auyong 1991; Miller 1993). Marine tourism is closely related to the concept of coastal tourism but also includes ocean-based tourism such as deep-sea fishing and yacht cruising. Orams (1999: 9) defines marine tourism as including 'those recreational activities that involve travel away from one's place of residence and which have as their host or focus the marine environment (where the marine environment is defined as those waters which are saline and tide-affected)'. Such a definition is significant, for as well as having a biological and recreational base it also emphasises that consider-ation of the elements of marine and coastal tourism must include shore-based activities, such as land-based whale watching, reef walking, cruise ship supply and yachting events, within the overall ambit of marine tourism.

This chapter seeks to review the principal ways in which the geographer has approached the coastal and marine environment. In particular, it highlights the reluctance of geographers to adopt a holistic understanding, whereby recreation and tourism are analysed as competing and yet complementary activities using the same resource base. The chapter commences with a discussion of the way in which the coast, and the beach in particular, was created by recreationalists and tourists. Like wilderness areas, the comparatively recent discovery of the coast as a potential resource for leisure use illustrates that leisure resources are – *created*: they exist in a latent form until their discovery, recognition and their development leads to their use. In most geographical analyses of the coastline as such a resource, the value of a historical approach is acknowledged in virtually every textbook on resorts. And yet the geographer has been largely remiss in addressing this vital theme – how the resource was discovered and developed. It developed in the human consciousness, supplanting perceptions of the coastal zone as a repulsive environment once the lure of the seaside marked a changing sensibility in society. For this reason, historical reconstructions of coastal environment need to recognise the way in which the resource was discovered, popularised and developed, and assumed a cultural significance in society.

THE COASTLINE AS A RECREATION AND TOURIST RESOURCE: ITS DISCOVERY AND RECOGNITION AS A LEISURE RESOURCE

According to Lenĉlek and Bosker (1999: xx):

> The beach as we know it is, historically speaking, a recent phenomenon. In fact, it took hundreds of years for the seashore to be colonised as the pre-eminent site for human recreation. . . . A proscenium for history, the beach has become a conspicuous signpost against which Western culture has registered its economic, aesthetic, sexual, religious, and even technological milestones.

This illustrates the changing perception of a natural resource for leisure through history: the

European acceptance of the beach embodied notions of utility which replaced a reverence for the sea and images of nature dominating human existence in the littoral zone. In the Romantic period the beach represented a site for pleasure, spiritual exercise and a positive experience. The symbolic value of the beach was also incorporated in poetry, landscape painting and created a new sensibility and practices. This brought new social, psychological, economic and spatial prestige to a landscape as a place of leisure and pleasure (see Lenĉlek and Bosker's (1999) stimulating cultural history of the beach for more detail). In Corbin's (1995) *The Lure of the Sea: The Discovery of the Seaside 1750–1840*, the dramatic changes in western attitudes towards the sea, the seaside and the landscape are reviewed in a European context. As a French translation of the European literature, it provides a fascinating reconstruction of those elements in western society which contributed to the discovery of the coast as a leisure resource (i.e. Romanticism) and the impact on perceptions of the seaside. The publication of Jane Austen's *Sanditon* in 1817, heralded as the first 'seaside' novel, was a parody of coastal tourism as a fashion-driven experience with health and recuperative benefits. What is significant in Corbin's (1995) thesis is the discovery of the pleasure qualities of the coast and the transformation from 'the classical period [which] knew nothing of the attraction of seaside beaches, the emotion of a bather plunging into the waves, or the pleasures of a stay at the seaside. A veil of repulsive images prevented the seaside from exercising its appeal' (Corbin 1995: 1). What the period 1750 to 1840 witnessed was a fundamental reassessment of the ways in which leisure time and places were used with the evolution of the seaside holiday. Within that evolutionary process the beach was invented as part of a resort complex. The beach developed as the activity space for recreation and tourism, with distinct cultural and social forms emerging in relation to fashions, tastes and innovations in resort form. The development of piers, jetties and promenades as formal spaces for organised recreational and tourism activities led to new ways of experiencing the sea. The coastal environment, resort and the beach have been an enduring resource for tourism and recreation since the 1750s in western consciousness, with its meaning, value to society and role in leisure time remaining a significant activity space.

Indeed, the beach 'invites watchers to unearth not only the dominant, culturally elite themes of a period, but its popular sensibilities: a blank piece of real estate on which each wave of colonizers puts up its own idea of paradise' (Lenĉlek and Bosker 1999: xx): in short the coast represents a liminal landscape in which the juncture of pleasure, recreation and tourism are epitomised in the postmodern consumption of leisure places. The beach is an environment where hordes are prepared to tolerate overcrowding to experience the man–nature environmental landscape – being at one with nature so that the three 'S's' (sun, sea and sand) can be experienced in the tourist and recreationalist consciousness and pursuit of the liminal existence.

THE GEOGRAPHER'S CONTRIBUTION TO THE ANALYSIS OF COASTAL RECREATION AND TOURISM

The coast has emerged as one of the popular, yet hidden and underplayed elements in the geographer's application of the hallmark traits of spatial analysis, observation and explanation. From the early context for economic geography, such as Hötelling's (1929) model of ice-cream sellers on the beach to Weaver's (2000) model of resort scenarios, the coast has assumed a significance as a context for research, but not as a veritable resource for the legitimate analysis of tourism and recreation. This dependence on the coast as a laboratory for the analysis of spatial concepts, interdependencies and the application of geographical methodologies does not adequately reflect the cultural and leisure significance of the beach and coastline in recreational and tourism activity in time and space. To the contrary, locating a landmark study which embodies the coastline as one of the most significant resources for recreation and tourism is notoriously difficult. The literature is fragmented, with tourism and recreational geographers seemingly obdurate given their reluctance to move this theme higher up the research agenda to fully appreciate its wider significance in modern-day patterns and consumption of day trips and holiday-making. Despite the fact that the coast remains one of the most obvious contexts for tourism and recreation, it is poorly understood. Research is reliant on a host of very dated and highly disjointed studies of the coastal environment. Despite the publication of two important studies in the 1990s (Fabbri 1990; Wong 1993b), the area has barely moved forward in the mainstream tourism literature, with *ad-hoc* studies published in non-tourism sources. Even in D.G. Pearce's (1995) review of coastal tourism, much of the emphasis was on spatial patterns, resort morphology, the significance of the seafront and planning issues.

This is extremely problematic for both tourism and recreation studies and geographers. The early interest in coastal tourism and recreation (e.g. Gilbert 1939; Patmore 1968; Lavery 1971b; Pearce and Kirk 1986) has not been accompanied by a sustained interest and, as a result, the research published has been highly specialised (see Table 8.1) and not been situated in a wider ecosystem/environmental context where the interconnections and sustainability of coastal environments can be understood in a holistic context.

Where research has been published, it has made significant contributions to advancing knowledge on the coastal-leisure interface, where physical processes are entwined with human action on a dynamic and volatile resource base. What Table 8.1 shows in this context is that the geographer has contributed to the historical analysis of resorts (in conjunction with seminal studies by social historians such as Walton (1983), and have formulated models to describe the process of development and change. The main dynamics of change, combined with temporal and spatial seasonality embodied in tourist and recreational travel to the coast, have remained an enduring theme in the geographer's analysis of this resource for leisure. The recreational and tourist behaviour which occurs in the coastal

environment has also generated a number of seminal studies (i.e. Mercer 1972; Cooper 1981), while the physical geographers have made valid studies of the processes affecting vulnerable coastal environments. This has been complemented by studies of the pattern and impact of resort development which raises important conservation issues associated with the human–environment interactions in these environments. Finally, geographers have also made useful contributions to the policy, planning and management of coastal environments. But what marks this area out in the geography of recreation and tourism is the sparse nature of these studies within the mainstream literature, with the entire theme seeming almost unfashionable and knowledge often being based on findings from studies published in the 1960s, 1970s and 1980s, despite the significance of Fabbri's (1990) and Wong's (1993b) collection of papers on the topic by geographers and non-geographers. As a result, the following section examines the different contributions geographers have made and the significance to increasing our knowledge of the coast in the formation of distinct leisure and tourism geographies.

THE HISTORICAL ANALYSIS OF RECREATION AND TOURISM IN THE COASTAL ZONE

In many geographical analyses of recreation (e.g. Lavery 1971c; Patmore 1973, 1983) and tourism (e.g. Towner 1996; Williams 1998), the English seaside resort is a popular topic for discussion. Indeed, Williams and Shaw's (1998) interesting analysis of the rise and fall of the English seaside or coastal resort examined two principal concerns of the historical geographer and contemporary tourism geographer: continuity and change in the development, organisation and prospects for the resort. Most analyses of the English seaside resort by geographers (e.g. Patmore 1968) refer to the seminal studies by Gilbert (1939, 1949) and the doctoral thesis by Barrett (1958). Despite these influential studies, the most notable contributions

Table 8.1: Illustrations of the geographer's contribution to the analysis of coastal recreation and tourism

Theme	Example(s)
The historical analysis of recreation and tourism in the coastal zone	Gilbert (1939), The development of coastal resorts Patmore (1968), Spa resorts in Britain Naylon (1967), The development of tourism in Spain Robinson (1976), Geography of tourism and resort development Barke and Towner (1996), The evolution of tourism in Spanish resorts Towner (1996), Synthesis of the process of development of resorts and patterns of tourism
Models of recreation and tourism	Hötelling (1929), Locational geography and the beach Stansfield and Rickert (1970), The recreational business district Miossec (1972), The process of resort development Britton (1982), Model of post-colonialist development of resort development Weaver (2000), Destination development scenarios Jeans (1990), Analysis of beach resort morphology in England and Australia Pigram (1977), Analysis of beach resort morphology
Tourist and recreationalist travel to the coast	Wall (1971, 1972), Patterns of travel by Hull car owners Patmore (1971), Routeways and tourist/recreational travel Mercer (1972), Recreational use of Melbourne beaches
Tourist and recreationalist behaviour	Cooper (1981), The behaviour and activities of tourists in Jersey Coppock (1977a), Second homeownership Pearce (1998), Tourist time budget study in Vanuatu Walmesley and Jenkins (1994), Perception of coastal areas Wong (1990), Recreational activities in coastal areas of Singapore Tunstall and Penning-Rowsell (1998), Beach user perceptions in England
Geomorphology of coasts and inter-relationship with tourism/recreation	May (1993), Survey of South England Morris (1996), Environmental management in coastal Spain
Coastal processes and the relationship and impact on tourism/recreation activity	Burns *et al.* (1990), Analysis of coastal processes affecting the SW Cape coastline in South Africa Kirkby (1996), Recreation and the quality of coastal water in Spain
Resort development	Carter (1982), Caravan site development in Ireland Pearce (1978), The form and function of French resorts Wong (1986, 1993a), The development of island tourism in Peninsula Malaysia Morrison and Dickinson (1987), The Costa Brava in Spain
Conservation of coastal environment	Miossec (1993), The coastal conservation measures developed in France White *et al.* (1997), Special Area Management and coastal tourism resources in Sri Lanka
Human/Environment interactions within coastal environments	Carter *et al.* (1990), Man's impact on the Irish coastline McDowell *et al.* (1990), Man's impact on the Costa del Sol Edwards (1987), Ecological impacts of tourism on heritage coasts in the UK
The management and planning of coastal areas for recreation and tourism	Nielsen (1990), Constructing a recreational beach in Denmark Ghelardoni (1990), Planning the Aquitane coastline in France for tourism Pearce and Kirk (1986), Carrying capacity for coastal tourism Carter (1988), The coastline as an area to manage for recreation and tourism
Other contributions	Dumas (1982), The commercial structure of Benidorm Kim and Kim (1996), Overview of coastal and marine tourism in Korea Penning-Rowsell *et al.* (1992), Economics of coastal management

to the analysis of English resorts came from the social and economic historians, such as Walton (1983) and the geographical analysis by Towner (1996). What these studies emphasise are the role of historical sources, such as the census, development plans, advertising, photographic archives and other documentary sources in reconstructing the recreational and tourism environments in coastal areas in the Victorian, Edwardian and subsequent periods. Specific phenomena, such as the English holiday camp, examined by Ward and Hardy (1986), are also charted using similar sources.

In each of the studies of the English seaside resort, geographers have sought to map and analyse the changing dynamics of resort development. In these analyses, the preconditions for resort development (see Bescancenot *et al.* 1978), the role of stakeholders, developers and planners have been examined, and D.G. Pearce (1995a) reviews many of the French geographers' contributions to coastal tourism research. In the analysis of Spanish tourism by Barke *et al.* (1996), a number of useful historical reconstructions of coastal tourism exist (e.g. Barke and Towner 1996; Walton and Smith 1996), which review the emergence of coastal areas in the era during and after the Grand Tour. The late nineteenth- and early twentieth-century patterns of coastal tourism in Spain, and the dynamics of tourist circuits, were reconstructed from historical guidebooks. The relationship of tourist circuits, the evolution of the Spanish railway system and the development of tourist accommodation highlighted the consumption of leisure resources, particularly the evolution of seaside resorts. Walton and Smith (1996: 57) concluded that 'The importance of the quality of local government to resort success has been strongly apparent in studies of English resorts, but its role in San Sebastian was even more impressive'. More recent evaluations of coastal resources, such as the development of England and Wales Heritage Coastline (Romeril 1984, 1988), has also emerged as a resource with a historical connotation. In other countries (e.g. the USA and Australia), historical studies of coastal tourism and recreation (see Pigram 1977; Miller 1987; Pigram and Jenkins 1999) have considered resorts, their life

cycles and development in a longitudinal context. The historical geography of specific resorts has provided a focal point for research, where a range of factors explain why resorts developed where they developed, why they develop and the pace and scale of change.

MODELS OF COASTAL RECREATION AND TOURISM

As already mentioned, model building is one of the hallmarks of the logical positivist traditions in human geography (see Johnston 1991). In the early studies of coastal recreation and tourism (e.g. Gilbert 1939), the major contribution to spatial knowledge was predicated on developing models which had a universal or more general application. By far the most extensive review of models of coastal recreation and tourism is D.G. Pearce (1995a).

D.G. Pearce (1995a) reviewed models of resort development, acknowledging the role of historical antecedents (e.g. the role of developers in developing resorts for different social classes). Using the resort life cycle developed by Butler (1980), various factors were used to explain similarities and differences in development paths and the resulting morphological structure of the resort. D.G. Pearce (1995a) identified the problem of tourism functions being added to existing urban centres in coastal locations where a day trip market may also exist. What Pearce concluded was that 'a spectrum of coastal resorts exists, ranging from those with a wholly tourist function, notably the new planned resorts, to those where a significant amount of tourist activity occurs alongside a variety of other functions' (D.G. Pearce 1995a : 137). Interestingly, this reiterates the earlier typology developed by Lavery (1971c) in a recreational context, where a similar notion of a continuum was implicit but not explicitly developed. What D.G. Pearce (1995a) could also have added is that the recreational market in many resorts will numerically outnumber the tourist market, though the behaviour of the former is very much climatically conditioned and opportunistic.

Among the most widely cited models of the resort is Stansfield and Rickert's (1970) discussion of the impact of consumption on resort morphology. Their resulting model, identified as the Recreational Business District (RBD), utilised earlier concepts from urban morphology models where central place functions of urban centres exist. The RBD, as distinct from the CBD, was viewed as the locale for recreational services and activities. Stansfield and Rickert (1970: 215) defined the RBD as 'the seasonally oriented linear aggregation of restaurants, various specialty food stands, candy stores and a varied array of novelty and souvenir shops which cater to visitors' leisurely shopping needs'. Although the model was based only on two New Jersey seaside resorts, the important distinction for current cultural interest in coastal recreation and tourism was that the RBD was not only an economic manifestation but a social phenomenon. Similar relationships between the CBD, which is spatially detached from the RBD in resorts, was an important focus for research in the 1970s and 1980s. Had such models been developed in the 1990s, the research agenda and formulation of the model framework would have been very different. A greater emphasis would be placed upon the supply dynamics which created the RBD (i.e. the role of capital), the cultural and social meaning attached to the tourist, and recreationalists' experience of the RBD as a place in time and space (see Britton (1991) for a fuller discussion of these ideas). It would not be viewed in a static context, since the processes of change and evolution of the RBD to accommodate consumer tastes would also be emphasised.

In the emerging tourist destinations in South-East Asia (see Hall and Page 2000), the RBD is a more complex phenomenon where the addition of hawker stalls, souvenir sellers and the informal economy combine to create a distinct entertainment district. D.G. Pearce (1995a) identified the addition of a night-life function in Patong, Phuket (Thailand) where the commodification of sex tourism is an additional function evident in the RBD (see Ryan and Hall (2001) for further discussion). Research by planners, most notably R.A. Smith (1991, 1992b), observed that in integrated resort development in South-East Asia, the RBD function is incorporated as a key function. Land-use zoning and the spatial separation of accommodation from the RBD to increase resort carrying capacity in locations such as Cancun (Gormsen 1982) highlighted the use of spatial concepts to manage tourist development. Pigram's (1977) influential study of morphological changes in Surfers Paradise (Queensland, Australia) between 1958 and 1975 recognised the spatial separation of the RBD and CBD. Yet relatively little interest has been shown in models of beach use, with a notable exception (Jeans 1990) where a semiotic model was developed. This model distinguished between the resort which represented culture and the sea which represented nature. What emerged was a transitional zone between culture and nature, a zone of 'ambiguity' – the beach. A second axis of meaning was also recognised, where the beach zone had a social periphery, where nonconformists (i.e. semi-nude and nude bathers and surfers) inhabited the area. This further refines Pearce and Kirk's (1986) model, though it was valuable in identifying the complexities of understanding the different types of carrying capacity of the resort and wider coastal zone.

TOURIST AND RECREATIONAL TRAVEL TO THE COAST

Within the tourism literature, the role of transport as a facilitating mechanism to explain tourist travel, patterns of tourism and development have only belatedly been acknowledged (Page 1994b, 1998, 1999). There are a number of seminal studies (e.g. Patmore 1968) in explaining the development of spas. Similarly, Pearson's (1968) study of the evolution of coastal resorts in East Lincolnshire illustrated the geographers' interest in the transport dimension. Patmore's (1971: 70) recognition that 'Deep-rooted in the very concept of outdoor recreation is the "journey to play", the fundamental movement linking residence or workplace to recreation resource. Such movement varies in scale, in duration and frequency'. A similar analogy may also be applied to tourism, and the geographer has utilised a wide range of concepts from transport geography to analyse the patterns of travel for coastal activity by recreationalists and tourists. As Patmore (1971) recognised, it is the identification of the routeways (the lines of movement) and the link to nodes of intensive leisure activity which have preoccupied the geographers' analysis of tourism and recreational travel, seeking to model and understand this phenomenon (Mansfield 1969; Colenutt 1970). As Patmore (1971: 72) argued, 'The crux of recreational planning is therefore the location, design and management of a relatively limited number of sites devoted wholly or partially to recreation, together with a concern for the routes which link them both to each other and to the residences of the users'.

For the coastal environment, it has been the mobility afforded by the car (Wall 1971, 1972) which has posed many of the resulting pressures, planning problems and conflicts in environments that are constrained in the number of visitors they can absorb. Wall (1971) recognised that holiday-makers generate a considerable proportion of the road traffic in resorts. As Wall (1971) poignantly and ironically commented: 'One of the major advantages of automobile travel is that it appears to be quite cheap. The capital expenditure involved in the purchase of an automobile is likely to be large, but having incurred this outlay, the cost of additional increments of travel is comparatively small' (Wall 1971: 101). The irony in 2001 is the £3 gallon of petrol in the UK, but this has not constrained the recreational or tourist use of the car for pleasure travel. The car remains convenient and flexible, and adds a degree of readily available mobility which is not constrained by public transport timetables. Probably the greatest constraint for the car is in accommodating the space demand in relation to recreational and tourist routeways in coastal environments (i.e. parking space). There is also growing evidence from the public sector of pressure in some coastal environments to exclude the car from certain areas. The car may reduce what the geographer terms 'the friction of distance', making coastal environments attractive and accessible to urban-dwellers. However, one has to place the coastal environment in the wider recreational and tourist context of participation levels. Patmore (1971: 76–7) aptly summarised this issue where 'The nearest seaside or open moorland may lure people from conurbations six times a year, while the local park is used every day to exercise the dog'. This hierarchy of tourism and leisure resources can often be overlooked.

Access to the coastal environment is a key term, though as Patmore (1971) argued it was a relative term, since improvements in transport routes and technology may directly change the nature of the access. The historical geographer's emphasis on the role of railway companies in Victorian Britain has identified their function in developing major visitor hinterlands for specific coastal resorts. Even some 150 years later, coastal resorts still have a limited reliance upon the rail network as a source of visitors, although the car is by far the most important mode of travel for recreational trips. The coastal environment and the routeways developed along coastlines, with viewing areas and a network of attractions, may also be a major recreational resource. For example, on the upper North Island of New Zealand, the collaboration between regional tourism organisations (see Page *et al.* 1999) created the Pacific Coastal Highway scenic drive. Not only did this utilise coastal routeways that receive comparatively limited traffic outside of the main summer season, but it also reduced congestion on other routeways between Auckland and the Bay of Islands.

Geographers have also examined one other contentious element of movement in coastal environments: the use of recreational footpaths (Huxley 1970). These are a major routeway resource, a linear recreational resource that often transects a variety of other leisure resources, from the coastline to the built environment through to the countryside. Many countries contain dense networks of footpaths, with Patmore (1971) referring to an estimated 120,000 miles in England and Wales. The issue is contentious, especially in coastal environments where the coastline is adjacent to privately owned land, and access is carefully guarded. In England and Wales, the designation of Heritage Coasts (Romeril 1988) has improved access issues and provided an opportunity for management agreements to be developed between private land-owners and planners.

TOURIST AND RECREATIONAL BEHAVIOUR: USE AND ACTIVITY PATTERNS IN COASTAL ENVIRONMENTS

Among the influential studies by geographers from the 1970s were the development of a behavioural geography and its application to recreation and tourism, especially in relation to coastal environments. Mercer (1971a: 51) summarised the significance of the behavioural perspective where 'The values and attributes of any outdoor recreation site, whether a local neighbourhood park or major wilderness area are perceived somewhat differently by numerous sub-groups within society'. Mercer (1971a) outlined the recreationalists' decision-making process (subsequently modified by Pigram 1983), and the meaning attached to tourism and recreational experiences. Mercer's (1970) analysis of recreational trips to beaches in Melbourne highlighted the urban resident's vague notion of the outdoor recreational opportunities open to them. The role of image in choosing beach environments is an important factor, and may override concerns of overcrowding and even pollution. Perceived distance and accessibility are also important factors affecting recreational search behaviour, and may account for why certain coastal environments attract large crowds and others do not. In England and Wales, the coast is no more than 120 km away for the most inland population, and, building on the model by Pearce and Kirk (1986), it is evident that the coast contains a variety of recreational environments: the shore, beach and the marine environment (Orams 1999). Each resource is perceived in a variety of ways by different individuals and groups, and the potential for resource conflict is high unless research can harmonise the needs and wishes of multiple resource users.

There is also a need to understand fundamental differences in the user's perception of the developed coastal resort and the nature of the natural environment, such as the beach, sea and coastline, because as Patmore (1983: 209) remarked, 'the coast is the epitome of the wider problems of recreational use' of resources. The behaviour and activities of coastal tourists and recreationalists are therefore vital to understanding the nature of the problems and impacts which occur. The use of coastal environments is very much temporarily contingent on the availability of leisure time as holidays and free time at weekends. This led Patmore (1983: 158) to argue that 'on a day-to-day basis, holidaymakers' patterns of activities within the holiday area differ, but little from the use of day visitors. . . . Little attention, however, has been given to the sequence of those activities as the holiday progresses.' One of the seminal studies which addressed this topic was Cooper's (1981) analysis of holiday-maker patterns of behaviour in Jersey. As a laboratory for tourism research, Jersey offers many attractions, for it is almost a closed system with a limited number of resorts, attractions and defined tourist itineraries.

What Cooper (1981) observed was a spatial and temporal pattern of tourist use of the coastal environment and non-coastal resources. For example, the holiday begins at the tourist's accommodation to maximise uncertainty in visiting unknown places. As a result, at St Heliers (the location of two-thirds of the island's accommodation stock), 75 per cent of tourists surveyed spent their first day in the town. After that point, a growing spatial awareness of coastal resources develops, and the two most popular beaches (St Brelade's Bay and Gorey) are visited on days two and three. The touring of the island to derive spatial familiarity with the tourist resources also occurred on days two and three. As spatial knowledge of the island develops, smaller and lesser known recreational sites were visited. What Cooper's (1981) research highlighted was a wave pattern in visitation, as visitors' use of resources (especially the use of the coastal environment) moves down the hierarchy, spreading to a wider distribution of sites. This reveals a classic geographical diffusion process and offers a great deal of advice for planners and coastal management.

Plate 8.1: Dover's Marine Parade. Accommodation developed in the Victorian period for coastal and cross-channel travel.

Plate 8.2: Blackpool Pier. The Victorians built piers to enable promenading as well as to represent man dominating and taming nature (i.e. the coast and sea).

D.G. Pearce (1988a) continued the interest in tourist behaviour using a time budget methodology in 1985 in Vanuatu (South Pacific) to extend Cooper's (1981) research on the tourists filtering down the hierarchy of sites. This behavioural research had an explicit spatial focus – patterns of tourist circulation. The problem with Pearce's (1988a) island-based study was the geographically constrained activity patterns of visitors, with resort hotels at Vila dominating the activities.

Probably one of the most interesting studies published by geographers in recent years was Tunstall and Penning-Rowsell's (1998) review of the English beach. As they observed

> England's beaches and coasts have a special place in the nation's consciousness. A day at the English beach is a particularly notable experience, full of rituals, symbolism, nostalgia and myths. The holiday at the coast, or the day visit, brings special activities, enjoyment and memories that virtually no other recreational experience provides. The English beach, with its particular characteristics and contexts, holds special meanings for those it attracts, and creates experiences which have life-long echoes.
>
> (Tunstall and Penning-Rowsell 1998 : 319)

In their analysis of the beach, they precisely identify it as the inter-tidal zone, the area which occurs above the high-watermark where beach material exists (i.e. sand, shingle and mud). The significance of the coast is epitomised in the UK Day Visits Survey, with over 137 million visits a year in England to rural areas, seaside resorts and the coastline. Cultural geographies of the beach and coastal environment (i.e. Shields 1991) mark the change, continuity and endurance of the beach as a social construction. In the post-war period, the English coastline has also attracted a growing retirement migration (see Cosgrove and Jackson (1972) for an early analysis of this trend in the UK), increasing the recreational appeal of these environments. This is complemented by the rise of second homeownership in coastal locations (Coppock 1977a). Some coastal resorts have also sought to diversify their appeal, with the development of conference and convention business (Shaw and Williams 1997). What Tunstall and Penning-Rowsell (1998) recognised was that the coastal resort, and particularly the beach/seawall/promenade which protects the RBD from nature, is a costly infrastructure that needs ongoing investment.

Using a longitudinal research technique which focused on 15 beaches in England over a decade, preferences towards beaches and protection methods to consider the values attached to beaches were examined. A model of beach users' attitudes and values was developed to explain the factors which contribute to the values attached to beaches. The role of recreational constraints (i.e. time and income), frequency of visitation, cost of visit, tastes and values (i.e. subjective enjoyment value) and the values assigned to specific resorts and beaches were incorporated into the model. A range of popular and less popular beaches were examined with some commercial resort towns and smaller towns included. Each location had the potential to experience beach erosion problems. Among the main factors motivating beach visits to popular recreational sites were the cleanliness of the site, type of beach material available, the natural setting and familiarity with the site. In the case of undeveloped coasts such as Spurn Head (Humberside), the quietness and natural setting were important attractions. The convenience of access and a number of other factors were important (albeit in varying degrees according to the place visited) as pull factors, including:

- the town and its facilities;
- quality of the sea front promenade;
- characteristics of the beach;
- the coastal scenery;
- scenery and places to visit in the hinterland;
- suitability of the sea for swimming and paddling;
- convenience of the journey;
- cost of the trip.

(Modified from Tunstall and
Penning-Rowsell 1998)

What Tunstall and Penning-Rowsell's (1998) study confirm is Patmore's (1983) earlier assertion on the diversity of coastal resources and reasons for visiting them. The coast, the sea, the seashore and landscape are all integral elements associated with the social, aesthetic and cultural meaning attached to the coast. However, 'There is considerable diversity in what attracted visitors to particular places but it is clear that seafront elements were more important at almost all locations than other aspects of the resort' (Tunstall and Penning-Rowsell 1998: 323). What detracted from visitation at specific sites were sewage, cleanliness, litter and the water-bathing quality, though as Morgan (1999) found, even the visitors' perception of these issues

was complex to deconstruct and explain, since perception and behaviour were not necessarily rational and predictable.

In temporal and spatial terms, Tunstall and Penning-Rowsell (1998) found that beach visits are not only experienced differently but have different meanings. This varied according to residents, day visitors and tourists. For residents, the beach was a local leisure resource, a regular and routine element of their everyday lives (similar to parks for urban-dwellers). For the day visitor, the beach was construed as a special event, an occurrence perhaps experienced only a couple of times a year. For holiday-makers, it is a special experience, but one often repeated with tourists who return to the same location year on year. What is culturally significant with a beach visit is the way in which it can enable the visitor to recollect childhood memories and a process repeated through time by families. It also marks a social occasion, with large proportions arriving by car as groups of two to four. In the summer season, beach visits are interconnected with families and young children. Even so, the beach readily accommodates solitary visitors, and in some locations up to one-third of users were unaccompanied. In this respect, the beach can function like a park with its ability to accommodate a multitude of users.

The amount of time spent at the beach varied by resort, with the majority of people spending less

Plate 8.3: Tourist beach in Tahiti, illustrating the diversity of tourist activities.

than four hours on the beach. It was typically between two and four hours in duration. Beach activities included a diversity of marine activities (sailboarding, jetskiing for a minority) through to a common range of activities including:

- sitting/sunbathing/picnicking on the beach;
- sitting/sunbathing/picnicking on the promenade;
- swimming/paddling;
- walking/strolling on the promenade/cliffs;
- long walks of 3 km or more;
- informal games or sports;
- walking the dog;
- playing with sand, stones and shells.

(Modified from Tunstall and Penning-Rowsell 1998)

This shows that while activities are important, so is relaxing and passive pastimes. This seminal study by Tunstall and Penning-Rowsell (1998: 330) not only recognised that 'English beaches are important to the English' but that environmental concerns for pollution and the quality of the resource are important to recreationalists, tourists and residents alike. The following assessment by Tunstall and Penning-Rowsell (1998: 331) really encapsulates the wider meaning, significance and value of the beach.

> The English seaside and its beaches are special because they are special places to play, to relax, to exercise or to enjoy. They bring back memories – mainly of families and childhood. They are places of discovery and adventure, and contact with nature. Their meanings come from these imaginings and these activities, and from the repeated visits to the same familiar and reassuring locales. Their beaches have a coherence that derives from their enduring physical character – waves, tides sand and noise and from the assemblage of features that keeps them there: the sea-wall, the promenade and the groynes. Each is understood and valued, for their timelessness and familiarity.

A number of novel studies of beach behaviour by non-geographers have also been undertaken (Carr 1999) which explore the youth market and their behaviour within resorts (e.g. Ford and Eiser 1996), particularly the meaning and significance of the beach and liminality. What Carr (1999) emphasised

was that there were comparatively few gendered differences in leisure and tourism activities among visitors aged 18 to 24 years of age. In fact, these results appear to confirm the findings of Tunstall and Penning-Rowsell (1998), in that the resort and beach are major attractions for coastal tourism. Other studies published in non-geographical journals (e.g. Morgan *et al.* 1993) have also examined issues of perception among beach users, but the literature is increasingly scattered across a wide range of coastal-related journals which are not necessarily tourism- or recreation-related. However, Morgan's (1999) examination of beach rating systems for tourist beaches highlighted the contribution which coastal researchers can make to understanding the perception of beach users.

By using beach awards, such as the European Blue Flag, the Seaside Award and Good Beach Guide (Marine Conservation Society 1998), there are indications of a growing interest in the promotion of beach tourism in relation to quality measures (Williams and Morgan 1995). Even so, poor public knowledge of these rating schemes and their significance, even though in the EU the number of Blue Flag beaches increased from 1,454 in 1994 to 1,927 in 19 countries in 1998. Morgan (1999) assessed 70 beaches in Wales and concluded that beaches are different, with users having different

Plate 8.4: Modifying a mangrove swamp at Denarau Island, Fiji to build a resort complex has meant erosion measures are necessary now the ecosystem has been changed.

preferences in line with Tunstall and Penning-Rowsell's (1998) study.

ENVIRONMENTAL PERSPECTIVES ON COASTAL RECREATION AND TOURISM

The environment for coastal leisure pursuits has seen the geographer make a number of influential contributions from a range of perspectives. In the early analysis of the coastline for tourism and recreation, Cosgrove and Jackson (1972) identified the vital characteristic which makes the coast a major focal point for geographical analysis: it is a zonal resource, with activities concentrated at specific places, making management a key issue in time and space. Although the coast may have a number of different resource designations (e.g. Heritage Coastline and Area of Outstanding Natural Beauty in England and Wales), the impacts of tourism and recreation are multi-faceted. In the wide-ranging study by the German Federal Agency for Nature Conservation (1997), the dominant coastline regions globally were the Mediterranean, the Caribbean, the Gulf of Mexico, the Indian Ocean islands, Australasia and the Pacific Islands. In this context, the coastal resource is a global environmental issue which is complex, diverse and not simply reduced to beach resorts, as the discussion has alluded so far. (See Visser and Njunga's (1992) examination of the Kenyan coastline where the ecological diversity in the coastal environment comprises coral reefs, sea grass and seaweed beds, mangrove forests, sand-dunes and inland tropical forests.)

According to the German Federal Agency for Nature Conservation (1997), coastal tourism environments may be categorised as follows:

- oceanic islands;
- coral reefs;
- offshore waters;
- mangroves;
- near-coastal wetlands;
- sandy beaches;
- coastal dunes.

In terms of the environments under the greatest recreational and tourism pressure are sandy beaches followed by coastal dunes (see Nordstom *et al.* (2000) for a review of management practices to restore dunes). Within a European context, the principal erosion and sedimentation processes affecting coastal environments are related to natural processes including:

- wave and tidal action;
- geomorphological factors (e.g. rivers which impact upon the river mouth and deltas);
- meteorological factors (e.g. wind and storms);
- changes in sea-level;
- geological processes (e.g. seismic and volcanic activity).

In addition, the European coastline is also subjected to a great number of environmental stresses, to the point where some researchers consider it to be under the greatest pressure of any coastal environment globally (German Federal Agency for Nature Conservation 1997). As a consequence, the pressures from the natural environment are being compounded by:

- large-scale pollution by oil spills;
- the development of harbours;
- increasing shore erosion caused by sediment processes are interrupted by building on the coastline;
- high levels of freshwater removal which is causing salt-water to encroach upon the water-table;
- increasing impacts from tourism and recreational activities. Approximately 100 million tourists visit the European coastline annually, a figure which could rise to 230 million by 2030.

Some of the visible signs of environmental deterioration include water pollution, and the rise of algal blooms. This problem is exacerbated by sewage pollutants where nutrient enrichment leads to algal blooms. In the Mediterranean between 1900 and 1990 there was a 75 per cent loss of sand dunes in France and Spain due to sand loss. This is a clear indication of the scale of the problem in relation to tourism which is sand- and beach-dependent. How has the geographer contributed to the wider under-standing, analysis and debates associated with coastal environments for recreation and tourism?

The physical geographer (e.g. May 1993) has examined the geomorphological characteristics which underlie the creation of existing coastal environments. In the case of the Cape coastline in South Africa, Burns *et al.* (1990) indicated the need to develop tourism according to sound environ-mental principles. They argued that the physical characteristics of soft shorelines need to be recog-nised, and near-shore and aeolian sediment trans-port regimes must be understood and quantified. This highlighted the active nature of the littoral zone of coastlines, so that long-term shore erosion can be reduced to create recreational environments. What emerges from much of the literature on beach erosion, particularly dune erosion, is that inter-vention is a costly strategy. In the case of Florida 'there has been a tendency to build so close to the shoreline as possible: Florida is no exception. Such actions have destroyed dunes, wetlands and beaches which formed protective barriers against storms and floods' (Carter 1990: 8). In the historical analysis of coastline destruction in Florida, Carter (1990: 8–9) examined the speed of environmental degradation where

> The first shoreline buildings were beach houses in the dunes. Very often the seawardmost dunes were lowered or removed altogether to give a view of the sea. Very soon, house owners became aware of shoreline changes, especially natural erosion, and began to protect against it. Much of this protection was unapproved, unsightly and ineffective. Along the east coast, bulkheads and groynes were common after 1925, yet by the mid 1930s, much of the duneline was destroyed. . . . It quickly became clear that such an approach was exacerbating erosion, and there was mounting pressure for official assistance . . . Florida became a natural laboratory for shore protection devices, including inlet bypassing and back-passing, beach nourishment and diverse species of revetments, breakwaters and groynes . . . Not all were successful.

What emerged from Carter's (1990) study was that by the 1980s, of the 870 km of Florida's coastline, 40 per cent of the coastline with sand dunes was under threat which also affected roads, houses and other development. Much of the impact is recreation and tourism-related, since in areas where no recreation occurs, no erosion exists. In the case of Denmark, Nielsen (1990) examined the positive enhancement of the environment with the creation of Koege Bay Beach Park in 1980 to meet the recreational needs of the Greater Copenhagen area. Using land reclamation methods, including extensive beach nourishment, a new beach environment was created. Some 5 million cubic metres of sand were used, dredged from lagoon areas and a 20 m wide dyke was built of sand to a height of 3 m above sea-level. Various environmental management measures were needed, including sluices for the lagoon environment to prevent stagnant water. A programme of planting on the dunes was also implemented to stabilise the resource. By developing the beach park to fit the underlying geomorphology, it represents a good example of an attempt to develop a sustainable leisure resource although it is not without environ-mental effects. However, the time frame is too short at this stage to observe long-term consequences and impacts or to assess the extent to which it is a truly sustainable resource. What is clear is that where significant demand exists in close proximity to an urban population, the creation of a local resource may act as a honey-pot and attract a significant number of visitors, taking pressure off other sites.

What Nielsen (1990) identified was the close involvement in physical geographers' monitoring and evaluation of coastal processes to understand how the coastal geomorphology will respond to such a radical change – the creation of a new recreational environment. In a detailed coastal geomorphological study of the German coastline, Kelletat (1993) documented the major beach nourishment needed for islands along the German North Sea coast. This was due to tourism, recre-ation and storms. However, in a study of Sylt Island, the growth of tourism has also provided the impetus and funding for coastal tourism on islands of the German North Sea coast (Kelletat 1993).

A range of other studies (e.g. D.G. Pearce 1988a; Carter *et al.* 1990; McDowell *et al.* 1990) have also documented the recreation, the production of coastal recreation strategies and coastal management plans to co-ordinate decision-making in the coastal zone. The diverse range of interest groups associated with coastal environments highlights the complexity of developing management plans where collaboration, communication and management solutions are introduced to control tourist and recreational use.

One related aspect of the geographers' interest in the coastal environment has been the development of resorts and planning measures to manage these physical impacts. In a conceptual context, the dynamics of resort development and change have hinged on the Butler (1980) model, and subsequent criticisms (e.g. Cooper and Jackson 1989; Cooper 1990) and concerns with the post-stagnation phase (Agarwal 1994; Priestley and Mundet 1998). This distinguishes between the land use and physical planning and management measures needed for the coastal environment and strategic planning measures needed to ensure the long-term prosperity, viability and development of the resort. The concern with land use and planning measures has been well documented in Inskeep (1994), D.G. Pearce (1989, 1995b) with specific examples of planning measures implemented in resort development documented by Meyer-Arendt (1990) and Wong (1986, 1990). In a detailed study by Penning-Rowsell et al. (1992), the economic cost of coastal protection schemes for recreation and other purposes and various valuation techniques were reviewed.

One of the most recent syntheses of coastal recreation management was produced by Goodhead and Johnson (1996) where the planning issues affecting recreation and tourism activity in the marine environment were reviewed in a UK context. Although not developed by geographers, the text offers a useful range of perspectives on the planning process for marine and coastal documenting land use change but really neglects the key point: the coast, the beach and the resort are major cultural icons in a postmodern society, retaining much of their value, meaning and significance from previous eras. In this context, the experience of the coast, the beach, the resort and of the place are socially and culturally conditioned. There is a continuity in the transmission and formation of values of the beach and coast which may help to explain the ongoing love affair the recreationalist and tourist has with such special 'places'. In historical terms, the resort morphology, rules, meanings and behaviour embodied in the coastal environment have changed in line with what society will tolerate, condone and legitimate. But these special, highly valued, natural and man-made environments remain central to the recreational and tourist experience of leisure places and space. For most social groups, the coastline is a social leveller, a free resource to be enjoyed and consumed according to the vagaries of the season and weather.

INSIGHT: Cruise tourism

Cruise tourism has become significant for a number of ports because cruise tourists are higher yield tourists, spending, on average, much higher amounts per day than other categories of international tourists (Dwyer and Forsyth 1996, 1998; Ritter and Schafer 1999). In a study of cruise tourism in Australia Dwyer and Forsyth (1996) reported that home-porting cruise ships in Australia, with a marketing emphasis on flycruise packages for inbound tourists, had the greatest potential for generating large expenditure inflows to Australia. In addition, they reported that because of leakages due to foreign ownership and foreign sourcing of inputs, the average expenditure per passenger per cruise injected into the Australian economy is twice as great for the coastal as opposed to the international cruise. Nevertheless, there is significant debate over the impacts of cruise ships. Ritter and Schafer (1999), for example, argue that the ecological impact of cruises is low; spending by individual tourists high, and accultural processes minimal, and claim that although the number of jobs directly created as a result of cruises is low, it compares very favourably against most other forms of travel as a sustainable development option. In contrast, Marsh and Staple (1995) in a study of cruise tourism in the Canadian Arctic concluded that given the environmental fragility of much of the region and the vulnerability of small, remote, largely aboriginal communities to impact, great care should be exercised in using the area for cruise tourism. Similarly, in examining some of the cultural dimensions of the cruise ship experience, Wood (2000) argued that the global nature of the cruise market has meant that cruise ships have become examples of 'globalisation at sea' with corresponding deterritorialisation, cultural theming and simulation. In addition, concern over the environmental impacts of cruise ships led the United States Environmental Protection Agency (EPA) to host a series of meetings in 2000 to solicit input from the public, the cruise ship industry and other stakeholders on the issue of discharges from cruise ships. These meetings were part of an information-gathering effort on the part of the agency to prepare an in-depth assessment of environmental impacts and existing and potential measures to abate impacts from these discharges. Cruise discharges are currently regulated through a combination of domestic and international pollution prevention laws and the EPA was assessing whether these laws adequately protect the environment and whether there are gaps in coverage or in application of these laws which may pose a risk to the environment (Rethinking Tourism Project 2000).

CONCLUSION

The coastal environment has been neglected in one sense by the geographer, where recreational and tourism activity have not been understood in the wide context of the resource, its use, impacts and planning needs. The recent development of studies by Tunstall and Penning-Rowsell (1998) has re-established the geographers' major contribution to the analysis of coastal recreation and tourism, building on seminal studies by Fabbri (1990) and Wong (1993b). Yet even these are not cited as mainstream studies or recognised for their synthesising role in bringing together different disciplines to disseminate a diverse and rich range of experience and knowledge of coastal processes, impacts, applied research and concerns about the leisure use of fragile coastal environments. The coastline needs to be moved higher up the geographers' research agenda in tourism and recreation, reiterating Patmore's (1983) criticism of the comparative neglect of this issue. Given the value and significance attached to the beach and coast observed by Tunstall and Penning-Rowsell (1998), it is evident that the coast is a major recreational environment. The association with resorts and the geographers' preoccupation with resort models and development should arguably be directed to a fuller understanding of the impact of man on the coastal environment, particularly the interference with coastal processes and the resulting measures needed to redress the consequences for the coastal environment.

There is no doubt that the coastal environment is facing a wide range of environmental pressures not least of which is the intensity of use. This, combined with environmental impacts from human activity, poses many severe planning problems for one simple reason: the scale and rate of change associated with coastal processes (e.g. erosion) are rapid, as the examples provided by Carter (1990) and Kelletat (1993) have shown. This requires costly remedial action, particularly in the case of beach nourishment and in coastal protection schemes where the natural environment is directly altered by tourist and recreational development.

Given the potential impacts of tourism on the coastal environment it is therefore not surprising that organisations such as ESCAP (1995a, 1995b) have been trying to encourage sustainable forms of coastal development in Asia and the Pacific. Sustainable development of coastal tourism is recognised as being dependent on:

1 good coastal management practices (particularly regarding proper siting of tourism infrastructure and the provision of public access);
2 clean water and air, and healthy coastal eco-systems;
3 maintaining a safe and secure recreational environment through the management of coastal hazards (such as erosion, storms, floods), and the provision of adequate levels of safety for boaters, swimmers and other water users;
4 beach restoration efforts that maintain the recreational and amenity values of beaches;
5 sound policies for wildlife and habitat protection.

(NCAA 1997)

However, such a statement, while laudable, fails to reflect the complexities and difficulties of the management and regulation of tourism with respect to the physical environment. Unfortunately, there is usually little or no co-ordination between programmes that promote and market tourism and those that aim to manage coastal and marine areas (Smith 1994; Hudson 1996). Environmental or planning agencies often fail to understand tourism, while tourism promotion authorities tend not to be involved with the evaluation of its effects or its planning and management. Implementation strategies often fail to recognise the interconnections that exist between agencies in trying to manage environmental issues, particularly when, as in the case of the relationship between tourism and the environment, responsibilities may cut across more traditional lines of authority. Therefore, one of the greatest challenges facing coastal managers is how to integrate tourism development within the ambit of coastal management, and thus increase the likelihood of long-term sustainability of the coast as a whole (White *et al.* 1997; Cicin-Sain and Knecht 1998). Nevertheless, solving such dilemmas will clearly be of importance to many countries in the region which has substantial emphasis on marine and coastal tourism, particularly when environmental quality becomes another means to achieve a competitive edge in the tourism market place.

The coastal environment has a great deal of potential for the cultural and social geographer to explore the value and role of tourism and recreation in these leisure places. There is also a role for applied geographers to combine their skills with planners, to understand, explain and develop planning measures to safeguard these threatened environments. The coastal environment is one of the best examples where geographers can harness their ability to construct a holistic understanding of the human and physical environment in a coastal context, where the interactions, impacts and measures needed to ameliorate negative effects can be addressed. The past 30 years have, with a few notable exceptions, not seen the geographical fraternity rise to this challenge and lead the coastal research agenda in a tourism and recreational context. One would hope, indeed expect, geographers to engage their skills, building on a long tradition of the geographers' involvement with the recreational and tourism use of the coast.

QUESTIONS

- Why is the coastline such a popular area for recreationalists and tourists globally?
- What techniques have geographers used to examine tourist use of the coastline, and how effective are they in explaining the motivation for such activities?
- What are the environmental problems associated with the coastal environment as a recreational and tourist resource?
- What are the planning and management measures which have been successful in reconciling the use of coastal environments with the need for preservation and recuperation of the resource base?

READING

In terms of the environmental impact of tourism and recreational activities in coastal environments, see:

Baldwin, J. (2000) 'Tourism development, wetland degradation and beach erosion in Antigua, West Indies', *Tourism Geographies*, 2(2): 193–218.

Fabbri, P. (ed.) (1990) *Recreational Uses of Coastal Areas: A Research Project of the Commission on the Coastal Environment*, Dordrecht: Kluwer.

German Federal Agency for Nature Conservation (ed.) (1997) *Biodiversity and Tourism: Conflicts on the World's Seacoasts and Strategies for Their Solution*, Berlin: Springer.

Wong, P. (1999) 'Adaptive use of a rock coast for tourism – Mactan Island, Philippines', *Tourism Geographies*, 1(2): 226–43.

9

TOURISM AND RECREATION PLANNING AND POLICY

Geographers have long been interested in planning. Indeed, a number of academic departments combine geography and planning, while many geography students have gone on to specialise in planning as a professional career. Planning and the associated area of policy analysis are therefore substantive areas of applied geographical research, particularly as geographers have sought to make their work more relevant to the society in which they work (Johnston 1991).

It should therefore come as no surprise that tourism and recreation planning and policy have long been major areas of interest for geographers. This chapter examines the nature of recreation and tourism planning and policy and then goes on to discuss the contributions that geographers have made in these fields, particularly with respect to the role of planning and policy at a regional or destination level. More specific applications in recreational and tourism planning have been introduced in earlier chapters and so this chapter discusses many of the principles, concepts and geographical contributions to the field as a whole.

RECREATION PLANNING POLICY

According to Henry and Spink (1990: 33), the 'treatment of leisure planning in the literature can be described as unsystematic and fragmented. At the outset it is important to make the distinction between the organisational planning which commercial bodies in leisure and recreation conduct, and statutory planning which the public sector

undertake, where the public good is normally the underlying rationale. The public sector is often charged with the management and maintenance of facilities, locational issues and wider strategic goals for the population'. To understand the evolution of recreation planning and the role of public sector agencies, it is useful to briefly examine the historical context.

THE EVOLUTION OF LEISURE AND RECREATION PLANNING

In many industrialising nations, the nineteenth century saw the intervention by philanthropists and reformers to address the squalor and living conditions of the working population, embodied in government legislation. Environmental improvement was predicated on the notion that it had a positive effect on the human condition. This shaped government legislation where a wide range of utopian, humanitarian and determinist attitudes (see Taylor 1999) were reflected in the debates on improvement. In the UK, the 1909 Housing and Town Planning Bill highlighted the need for government intervention to generate more socially appropriate forms of land use which market forces would not address (i.e. public open space). Table 9.1 summarises the subsequent role of the state in town and planning in relation to leisure, where political ideology shaped the nature of state intervention in the UK. In a rural context, the 1968 Countryside Act established a network of country parks, picnic sites, nature trails and bird sanctuaries.

Table 9.1: State intervention: town and country planning and leisure

	1800–1900	1918–19	1919–39	1939–45	1960s	1980s
Chronology state	*Laissez-faire* 'property'	Minimal intervention 'conservative' depression reconstruction		Welfare state reformism austerity consensus	Corporate state	'Enterprise' small state Crisis | Modernisation Monetarism
Planning acts	1909	1919	1932	1947	1968	1980 1986
Objectives	Improve health and housing	Reconstruct Stop sprawl Protect 'Country'		Reform Socialise Control	Organise Develop Integrate growth	Minimal state Reduce public sector Encourage private development
Forms	Possible schemes for new building	Schemes for 20,000+ population		Physical plans (6 in. to mile) Development controlled	Socio-economic Diagrammatic plans	Enterprise Zones Simplified Planning Zones
Aims	Improve	Restrict		Construct	Reorganise	Facilitate
Leisure	Private provision	Protection of some green spaces		Detailed planning of amenity provision	Broad outline of amenity provision	Market supported Decentralised provision
Implications	Commercially profitable facilities Public and private benefaction of leisure spaces	Largely ineffective attempts to check urban sprawl and preserve rural areas		Reconstruction of town centres Land use structured Specific allocation of leisure spaces	Liveable cities aim General land use implications	Pressures on central spaces Job creation supported in tourism and leisure

Source: Henry and Spink (1990: 56)

This was accompanied by the state's division of planning powers into two levels of local government: structure plans came under county and regional authorities, with a view to a 10- to 20-year timeframe and framework for local plans which were the responsibility of district authorities. Despite subsequent modifications in the 1980s and 1990s in the 'retreat from state planning', these two levels of planning remain. They can also be discerned in many other countries. Much of their concern has been with land use planning and site-specific planning for recreation, since this has been the public sector concern: the ordering of leisure space and provision through time.

RECREATION PLANNING: THE CONCERN WITH SPACE AND PLACE

According to Pigram and Jenkins (1999: 270), 'In the planning of recreation space, the aim should be to provide a range of functional and aesthetically pleasing environments for outdoor recreation, which avoid the friction of unplanned development, without lapsing into uniformity and predictability'. Since people decide on recreation participation as a discretionary use of time and on a voluntary basis, planning is beset by a wide range of factors that need to be considered. One of the most persuasive issues is the trends and tastes in leisure and outdoor recreation. Here the problem is in matching potential demand to the supply of recreation space, while a growing sophistication among recreation users means issues such as quality and satisfaction are also important in public sector provision.

There is also a temporal and cyclical factor which is often overlooked, namely that in times of economic downturn, recreation assumes a new dimension in the amelioration of hardship (Glyptis 1989b). At the same time, such economic stringencies may also put the public sector under increased pressure in terms of its priorities for resource allocation (i.e. what is the opportunity cost of additional expenditure on leisure provision). At the local planning level, different local authorities will have varying levels of commitment to recreation provision, which will also vary according to the political persuasion of the elected politicians that varies in time and space.

Against this background, planners need to understand societal changes, namely demographic trends, lifestyle changes (see the early study by Havighurst and Feigenbaum 1959), social attitudes to recreation and the increasing demands of ethnic groups (Floyd 1998; Johnson *et al.* 1998) and the disabled and other minority groups to achieve equity goals in local planning for leisure (Shinew and Arnold 1998). In many countries, notably the USA, Canada, New Zealand, Britain and Australia, issues of cultural pluralism and a multicultural population pose new challenges to conventional notions of recreation planning. Probably one of the greatest technological innovations that now exist to assist planners in integrating these new perspectives into social and land use planning is GIS. It enables planners to spatially integrate the demand and supply of recreation and to evaluate possible locational issues and outcomes. This is also invaluable in modelling resource degradation (see Bahaire and Elliott-White (1999) for more detail). In essence, GIS operates on spatial data which have a standard geographical frame of reference. It also utilises attribute data, which are statistical and non-locational. GIS allows planners to link planning goals to basic geographical issues such as location, trends through time, patterns at specific points in time and an ability to model issues such as recreational impacts (see Briggs and Tantrum (1997) for specific recreational applications and Kliskey and Kearsley (1993) for an application to wilderness perception mapping in New Zealand).

Pigram and Jenkins (1999) argued that a more strategic approach to recreation planning is needed but much of the existing practise of planning is concerned with geographical issues of the availability of recreational opportunities, the location of services and facilities. Although recreation planning should be a complex process, its application in the public sector often remains a simplistic activity, focused on the provision of specific facilities rather than the wider context of recreation opportunity, desire and provision. According to Robinson (1999), eight approaches to planning for leisure may be discerned and a number of them utilise spatial principles (see Table 9.2). Even in seemingly advanced recreational contexts such as the Netherlands with an enviable reputation for recreation planning, Dietvorst (1993: 84) argued that 'During the 1980s it was realised that public tastes had changed and that the amenities for outdoor recreation in many ways no longer satisfied demand'. This reflected the changing policy framework which

Table 9.2: Approaches to planning for leisure

Approach	Content
1 Standards	Planning based on per capita specifications of levels of provision laid down by some authoritative body. Usually based on demand estimates.
2 Gross demand	Estimation of broad demand levels based on existing national or regional participation surveys. This is the most basic of demand estimation approaches but can be varied to consider local socio-demographic conditions.
3 Spatial approaches	Localised demand estimation incorporating consideration of facility catchment areas. This extends the gross demand approach when considering the question of facility location.
4 Hierarchies of facilities	Recognises that different types and scales of facility have different catchment areas. Especially relevant for planning new communities and for facilities involving spectator audiences.
5 Grid or matrix approach	Examines impacts of all of an authority's leisure services on all social groups via impact evaluation.
6 Organic approach	Strategy development based on assessment of existing service provision and spatial gaps in demand. It is incremental rather than comprehensive and is common within the private sector.
7 Community development approach	Planning and policy development based on community consultation
8 Issues approach	Plans based on initial identification of 'key issues' rather than comprehensive needs/demand assessment. Corresponds to SWOT (strengths, weaknesses, opportunities, threats) analysis. Most common for *ad-hoc*, one-off projects.

Source: Based on Veal (1993: 92–3 in Robinson (1999: 260))

saw a convergence of interest towards recreation and tourism with common goals in terms of provision (Jansen-Verbeke and Dietvorst 1987). Indeed, Dietvorst (1993) criticised the strong normative planning framework prevailing in the Netherlands as not offering flexible and market-oriented forms of outdoor recreation. What is clear is that the state, its agencies (e.g. the newly amalgamated Countryside Agency in the UK) (see Coalter (1990) for more detail on agencies) have a wide remit for the management and planning of outdoor recreation resources given the diversity and extent of recreational environments (Figure 9.1), while the statutory planning framework is based on the twin goals of development plans and development control (Ravenscroft 1992). Even so, Ravenscroft (1992: 135) concluded that

the whole framework upon which planning has been predicated has, for the most part, tended to neglect recreation. By largely basing development plans on

land use zoning, it has tended to subjugate multiple uses in favour of primary ones. . . . This means that in areas where provision for recreation is seen as important, such as National Parks, primary uses such as agriculture and forestry still dominate . . . [and] the reactive nature of the planning process means that opportunities to secure recreation provision are not taken up.

In fact, the political processes associated with local authority recreation planning and issues such as planning gain are increasingly being used by developers as betterment payments for the right to develop, making recreation and community benefit a tool to exercise leverage on planning applications.

TOURISM PLANNING AND POLICY

The partially industrialised nature of tourism means that tourism, like the environment, should be regarded as a meta-problem which represents highly

Figure 9.1: The Countryside Agency's designated and defined interests

interconnected planning and policy 'messes' (Ackoff 1974) which cut across fields of expertise and administrative boundaries and, seemingly, become connected with almost everything else. Tourism, therefore, 'is merely an acute instance of the central problem of society' (P. Hall 1992: 249) of creating a sense of the whole which can then be effectively planned and managed. Nevertheless, planning for tourism is still regarded as important because its effects are so substantial and potentially long-standing. Indeed, concern with making tourism, along with all development, sustainable has provided an even greater imperative for developing relevant tourism planning frameworks (Hall 2000a). Yet despite use by tourism researchers of the evolving network paradigm in management literature (e.g. Selin 1993, 1998; Selin and Chavez 1994; Jamal and Getz 1995; Buhalis and Cooper 1998) there has been, given the central role of government in tourism promotion and development, surprisingly little reference to the wider planning public policy literature which analyses what has been, until recently, a 'neglected' aspect of contemporary administration and policy-making (O'Toole 1997).

Planning for tourism has traditionally focused on land use zoning, site development, accommodation and building regulations, the density of tourist development, the presentation of cultural, historical and natural tourist features, and the provision of infrastructure including roads and sewage (Getz 1987). However, in recent years, tourism planning has adapted and expanded to include broader environmental and socio-cultural concerns, and the need to develop and promote economic development strategies at local, regional and national scales, particularly within an increasingly globalised tourism environment (Hall 2000a).

The diverse nature of recreation and tourism has meant that the industry is difficult for policy-makers and planners to define and grasp conceptually. This has meant that there have been substantial difficulties for policy-makers to develop appropriate policies, while the co-ordination of the various elements of the recreation and tourism product has been extremely difficult (Hall 1994; Hall and Jenkins 1995). Yet, somewhat paradoxically, it is the very nature of the industry, particularly the way in which local communities, their culture and lifestyles, and the environment are part of the broad leisure product which makes planning so important (Murphy 1985) and, perhaps, academically appealing (Hall et al. 1997).

Planning and policy-making are 'filtered through a complex institutional framework' (Brooks 1993: 79). However, the institutional arrangements for tourism have received little attention in the tourism literature (Pearce 1992b; Hall and Jenkins 1995; Hall 2000a). Institutions may be thought of as a set of rules which may be explicit and formalised (e.g. constitutions, statutes and regulations) or implicit and informal (e.g. organisational culture, rules governing personal networks and family relationships). Thus institutions are an entity devised to order interrelationships between individuals or groups of individuals by influencing their behaviour. As a concept and as an aspect of tourism policy-making, institutions cast a wide net; they are extensive and pervasive forces in the tourism policy system. In a broad context, O'Riordan (1971: 135) observed that:

> One of the least touched upon, but possibly one of the most fundamental, research needs in resource management [and indeed, tourism management] is the analysis of how institutional arrangements are formed, and how they evolve in response to changing needs and the existence of internal and external stress. There is growing evidence to suggest that the form, structure and operational guidelines by which resource management institutions are formed and evolve clearly affect the implementation of resource policy, both as to the range of choice adopted and the decision attitudes of the personnel involved.

Institutions therefore 'place constraints on decision-makers and help shape outcomes ... by making some solutions harder, rather than by suggesting positive alternatives' (Simeon 1976: 574). As the number of check-points for policy increase, so too does the potential for bargaining and negotiation. In the longer term, 'institutional arrangements may themselves be seen as policies, which, by building in to the decision process the need to consult particular groups and follow particular procedures, increase the likelihood of some kinds of decisions and reduces that of others' (Simeon 1976: 575). For example, new government departments may be established as part of the growth in the activity and influence of government, particularly as new demands, such as environmental concerns, reach a high priority on the political agenda.

> The setting up of entirely new government departments, advisory bodies or sections within the existing administration is a well established strategy on the part of governments for demonstrating loudly and clearly that 'something positive is being done' with respect to a given problem. Moreover, because public service bureaucracies are inherently conservative in terms of their approach to problem delineation and favoured mode of functioning . . . administrative restructuring, together with the associated legislation, is almost always a significant indicator of public pressure for action and change.
>
> (Mercer 1979b: 107)

The implications of the structure and nature of the tourist industry are not merely academic as it is difficult for government to develop policies and design institutions for a policy area that is hard to determine (Jenkins 1994). Indeed, quality information concerning the tourist industry is relatively limited when compared to the collection of information on other industries and sectors of the economy. Hall and Jenkins (1995) even hypothesise that there is an element of inexperience in tourism policy formulation and implementation, as much government activity in the tourist industry is relatively recent when compared with other traditional concerns of government, such as economics, manufacturing and social welfare, and suggests that tourism public policies are therefore likely to be *ad hoc* and incremental. Indeed, Hall (2000a) in a review of the role of government in New Zealand tourism identified three government agencies with primary responsibilities with respect to tourism policy and over 30 agencies with secondary responsibilities, with there typically being very little formal tourism policy co-ordination between the various agencies. Such a situation though should not be surprising, since the nature of tourism means that it cuts across a range of government responsibilities which make policy and planning co-ordination inherently difficult unless a lead agency is clearly identified.

WHAT IS TOURISM PLANNING?

What is planning? 'Planning is a process, a process of human thought and action based upon that thought – in point of fact, forethought, thought for the future – nothing more or less than this is planning, which is a very general human activity' (Chadwick 1971: 24). Similarly, according to Hall (1982a: 303), planning 'should aim to provide a resource for democratic and informed decision-making. This is all planning can legitimately do, and all it can pretend to do. Properly understood, this is the real message of the systems revolution in planning and its aftermath.' Hall's (1982a) observation reflects Johnston's (1991: 209) comment that underlying the geographer's involvement in planning and policy is 'the basic thesis that geographers should be much more involved in the creation and monitoring and policies', yet, as he went on to note, 'what sort of involvement?', a point discussed in Chapter 1.

As a general field of research, tourism planning has mirrored broader trends within the urban and regional planning traditions (e.g. Getz 1986a, 1987; Hall 2000a) primarily because it has been focused on destination planning rather than individual tourism business planning. Moreover, planning for tourism tends to reflect the economic, environmental and social goals of government and, increasingly, industry interests, at which ever level the planning process is being carried out (Hall *et al.* 1997).

Planning for tourism occurs in a number of forms (development, infrastructure, promotion and marketing); structures (different government and non-government organisations); scales (international, national, regional, local and sectoral) and times (different time scales for development, implementation and evaluation). However, planning is rarely exclusively devoted to tourism *per se*. Instead, planning for tourism tends to be 'an amalgam of

Table 9.4: Tourism planning approaches: assumptions, problem definition, methods and models

Planning tradition	Underlying assumptions and related attitudes	Definition of the tourism planning problem	Some examples of related methods	Some examples of related models
Boosterism	• tourism is inherently good • tourism should be developed • cultural and natural resources should be exploited • industry as expert • development defined in business/corporate terms	• how many tourists can be attracted and accommodated? • how can obstacles be overcome? • convincing hosts to be good to tourists	• promotion • public relations • advertising • growth targets	• demand forecasting models
Economic	• tourism equal to other industries • use tourism to: create employment, earn foreign revenue and improve terms of trade, encourage regional development, overcome regional economic disparities • planner as expert • development defined in economic terms	• can tourism be used as a growth pole? • maximisation of income and employment multipliers • influencing consumer choice • providing economic values for externalities • providing economic values for conservation purposes	• supply–demand analysis • benefit–cost analysis • product–market matching • development incentives • market segmentation	• management processes • tourism master plans • motivation • economic impact • economic multipliers • hedonistic pricing
Physical/spatial	• tourism as a resource user • ecological basis to development • tourism as a spatial and regional phenomenon • environmental conservation • development defined in environmental terms • preservation of genetic diversity	• physical carrying capacity • manipulating travel patterns and visitor flows • visitor management • concentration or dispersal of visitors • perceptions of natural environment • wilderness and national park management • designation of environmentally sensitive areas	• ecological studies • environmental impact assessment • regional planning • perceptual studies	• spatial patterns and processes • physical impacts • resort morphology • LAC (limits of acceptable change) • ROS (recreational opportunity spectrum) • TOS (tourism opportunity spectrum) • destination life cycles

Community	• need for local control • search for balanced development • search for alternatives to 'mass' tourism development • planner as facilitator rather than expert • development defined in socio-cultural terms	• how to foster community control? • understanding community attitudes towards tourism • understanding the impacts of tourism on a community • social impact	• community development • awareness and education • attitudinal surveys • social impact assessment	• ecological view of community • social/perceptual carrying capacity • attitudinal change • social multiplier
Sustainable	• integration of economic, environmental and socio-cultural values • tourism planning integrated with other planning processes • holistic planning • preservation of essential ecological processes • protection of human heritage and biodiversity • inter and intra-generational equity • achievement of a better balance of fairness and opportunity between nations • planning and policy as argument • planning as process • planning and implementation as two sides of the same coin • recognition of political dimension of tourism	• understanding the tourism system • setting goals, objectives and priorities • achieving policy and administrative co-ordination in and between the public and private sectors • co-operative and integrated control systems • understanding the political dimensions of tourism • planning for tourism that meets local needs and trades successfully in a competitive marketplace	• strategic planning to supersede conventional approaches • raising producer awareness • raising consumer awareness • raising community awareness • stakeholder input • policy analysis • evaluative research • political economy • aspirations analysis • stakeholder audit • environmental analysis and audit • interpretation	• systems models • integrated models focused on places and links and relationships between such places • resources as culturally constituted • environmental perception • business ecology • learning organisations

Sources: After Getz (1987); Hall *et al.* (1997); Hall (1999) with being relevant to community needs. The most well-known exemplar of this approach is the work of Murphy (1985).

A community approach to tourism planning is an attempt to formulate a 'bottom-up' form of planning, which emphasises development *in* the community rather than development *of* the community. Under this approach, residents are regarded as the focal point of the tourism planning exercise not the tourists, and the community, which is often equated with a region of local government, is usually used as the basic planning unit. Nevertheless, substantial difficulties will arise in attempting to implement the concept of community planning in tourist destinations. As Dowling (1993: 53) noted, 'research into community attitudes towards tourism is reasonably well developed, although incorporation of such views into the planning process is far less common'. For example, Jenkins (1993) identified seven impediments to incorporating public participation in tourism planning:

1 the public generally has difficulty in comprehending complex and technical planning issues;
2 the public is not always aware of or understands the decision-making process;
3 the difficulty in attaining and maintaining representativeness in the decision-making process;
4 the apathy of citizens;
5 the increased costs in terms of staff and money;
6 the prolonging of the decision-making process;
7 adverse effects on the efficiency of decision-making.

One notable exception here is the research reported by Page and Lawton (1997) which sought to incorporate residents' views as part of the planning process for tourism in a local area.

As the above discussion indicates, one of the major difficulties in implementing a community approach to tourism planning is the political nature of the planning process. Community planning implies a high degree of public participation in the planning process. However, public participation implies that the local community will have a degree of control over the planning and decision-making process. Therefore, a community approach to tourism planning implies that there will be a need for partnership in, or community control of, the tourism development process.

Yet power is not evenly distributed within a community, and some groups and individuals will therefore have the ability to exert greater influence over the planning process than others (Hall and Jenkins 1995). Therefore, in some circumstances, the level of public involvement in tourism planning may be more accurately described as a form of tokenism in which decisions or the direction of decisions have already been prescribed by government. Communities rarely have the opportunity to say 'no' (Hall 1995). Nevertheless, as Murphy (1985: 153) argued: 'If tourism is to become the successful and self-perpetuating industry many have advocated, it needs to be planned and managed as a renewable resource industry, based on local capacities and community decision making', with an increased emphasis being given to the interrelated and evolutionary nature of tourist development.

More recently, geographers have become concerned with the development of sustainable approaches towards tourism (Hall and Lew 1998). Sustainable tourism planning is therefore an integrative form of tourism planning, which bears much similarity to the many traditionally applied concerns of the geographer as resource manager (Mitchell 1979). Sustainable tourism planning seeks to provide lasting and secure livelihoods with minimal resource depletion, environmental degradation, cultural disruption and social instability. The approach therefore tends to integrate features of the economic, physical/spatial and community traditions.

The concern for equity, in terms of both intra- and intergenerational equity, in sustainable development means that not only should we be concerned with the maintainance of 'environmental capital' (Jacobs 1991) but also the maintenance and enhancement of social capital (Healey 1997), in terms of the rich set of social networks and relationships that exist in places, through appropriate policies and programmes of social equality and political participation (Blowers 1997). Such an approach has considerable implications for the structure of tourism planning and policy-making. To fulfil the sustainable goal of equity, decision-making processes will need to be more inclusive of the full range of values, opinions and interests that surround tourism developments and tourism's overall contribution to development, and provide a clearer space for public argument and debate (Smyth 1994). As Evans (1997: 8) argued, 'if environmental planning for sustainability . . . is to be anywhere near effective, the political processes of public debate and controversy, both formal and informal, will need to play a much more significant role than has hitherto been the case'.

Dutton and Hall (1989) identified five key elements of sustainable tourism planning: co-operative and integrated control systems, development of industry co-ordination mechanisms, raising consumer awareness, raising producer awareness, and strategic planning to supersede conventional approaches.

CO-OPERATIVE AND INTEGRATED CONTROL SYSTEMS

In a typical planning process, stakeholders are consulted minimally, near the end of the process, and often via formal public meetings. 'The plan that results under these conditions tends to be a prescriptive statement by the professionals rather than an agreement among the various parties'; by contrast, an interactive style 'assumes that better decisions result from open, participative processes' (Lang (1988) in Wight 1998: 87). An integrative planning approach to tourism planning and management at all levels (from the regional plan to individual resort projects) would assist in the distribution of the benefits and costs of tourism development more equitably, while focusing on improved relationships and understanding between stakeholders may also assist in agreement on planning directions and goals. However, co-operation alone will not foster commitment to sustainable development without the incentive of increased mutual benefits.

One of the most important aspects of co-operative and integrated control systems is the selection of indicators of sustainability. The role of an indicator is to make complex systems understandable. An effective indicator or set of indicators helps a destination, community or organisation determine where it is, where it is going and how far it is from chosen goals. Sustainability indicators provide a measure of the long-term viability of a destination or community based on the degree to which its economic, environmental and social systems are efficient and integrated (Gill and Williams 1994; Hall 1999). However, indicators are useful only in the context of appropriately framed questions (Hall and McArthur 1998). In choosing indicators, one must have a clear understanding of planning goals and objectives. For example, a typology of indicators might include:

- economic, environmental and social indicators (measuring changes in the state of the economy, environment and society);
- sustainability indicators (measuring distance between that change and a sustainable state of the environment);
- sustainable development indicators (measuring progress to the broader goal of sustainable development in a national context).

There has been a tendency to pick indicators that are easiest to measure and reflect most visible change; therefore important concerns from a holistic perspective of tourism development, such as the social and cultural impacts of tourism, may be dropped. In addition, appropriate indicators may not be selected because organisations might not want to be held accountable for the results of evaluations (Hall and McArthur 1998). According to Wight (1998), indicators to reflect desired conditions and use should ideally:

- be directly observable;
- be relatively easy to measure;
- reflect understanding that some change is normal, particularly in ecological systems, and be sensitive to changing use conditions;

- reflect appropriate scales (spatial and temporal);
- have ecological, not just institutional or administrative boundaries;
- encompass relevant structural, functional and compositional attributes of the ecosystem;
- include social, cultural, economic and ecological components;

- reflect understanding of indicator function/type (e.g. baseline/reference, stress, impact, management, system diagnostic);
- relate to the vision, goals and objectives for the destination region;
- be amenable to management.

INSIGHT: The changing role of government and sustainability

Changes in government's role as interest protector has major implications for tourism and sustainability. As Blowers (1997: 36) noted in the case of the United Kingdom, 'the long period of privatisation, deregulation, cuts in public expenditure and attacks on local government have resulted in a "democratic deficit" – a dispersal of power to unelected quangos and business interests – and have led to unsustainable developments', a critique also reflected in the comments of Haughton and Hunter (1994: 272):

> The unregulated market approach, being relatively amoral, can allow individuals to be immoral. The ethical dimension is important since the market does not provide a sufficient basis for the resolution of the profound moral issues which face us every day; it can play a part in avoiding distorted decision making by individuals and organizations, but alone it cannot reconcile all of the environmental problems facing society.

The above comments highlight the need to see partnership and collaboration between government and the private sector within the context of the public interest as opposed to the market interest. Incorporation of a wider range of inputs into the policy process would lead to the formation of issue networks as opposed to sub-governments. Issue networks are structures of interaction among participants in a policy area that are marked by their transience and the absence of established centres of control (Heclo 1978). According to Heclo (1978: 102), the term 'issue network' describes

a configuration of individuals concerned about a particular aspect of an issue and the term policy community is used more broadly to encompass the collection of issue networks within a jurisdiction. Both describe the voluntary and fluid configuration of people with varying degrees of commitment to a particular cause.

One of the great problems in examining the role of interest groups in the tourism policy-making process is deciding what the appropriate relationship between an interest group and government should be (Hall and Jenkins 1995). At what point does tourism industry membership of government advisory committees or of a national, regional or local tourism agency represent a 'closing up' of the policy process to other interest groups rather than an exercise in consultation, co-ordination, partnership or collaboration? As Deutsch (1970: 56) recognised,

> this co-operation between groups and bureaucrats can sometimes be a good thing. But it may sometimes be a very bad thing. These groups, used to each other's needs, may become increasingly preoccupied with each other, insensitive to the needs of outsiders, and impervious to new recruitment and to new ideas. Or the members of the various interest group elites may identify more and more with each other and less and less with the interests of the groups they represent.

The relationship between the tourism industry and government tourism agencies clearly raises questions about the extent to which established policy processes lead to outcomes which are in the 'public interest' and which contribute to sustainability rather than meeting just narrow sectoral interests. Mucciaroni (1991: 474) noted that 'client politics is typical of policies with diffuse costs and concentrated benefits. An identifiable group benefits from a policy, but the costs are paid by everybody or at least a large part of society'. As Hall and Jenkins (1995) argued, tourism policy is one such area, particularly in terms of the costs of tourism promotion and marketing. However, the implications of this situation also affect the overall sustainability of tourism and of communities. In reviewing the tourism and collaboration literature, Hall (1999) concluded that the present focus by government tourism agencies on partnership and collaboration is laudable. 'But the linguistic niceties of partnership and collaboration need to be challenged by focusing on who is involved in tourism planning and policy processes and who is left out. . . . Unless there are attempts to provide equity of access to all stakeholders then collaboration will be one more approach consigned to the lexicon of tourism planning clichés.' Therefore, the policy arguments surrounding networks and collaboration need to be examined within broader ideas of the appropriate role of government and changing relationships and expectations between government and communities.

DEVELOPMENT OF INDUSTRY CO-ORDINATION MECHANISMS

While a range of formal and informal tourism industry bodies exist in almost every country in the world, few of these address such complex issues as sustainable development. The support by industry groups of environmental codes is perhaps indicative of possible directions if common needs can be agreed upon. However, for such guidelines to be effective, it must be ensured that they do not constitute a 'lowest common denominator' approach to development and implementation (Hall 1995). Therefore, government and public interest groups tend to use their influence to encourage greater industry co-ordination on planning issues by creating structures and processes which enable stakeholders to talk to each other and create effective relationships and partnerships. In many ways such measures are easier to achieve at a local level because the range of stakeholders which need to be incorporated into co-ordinating bodies will be narrower. In addition, contact at the local level provides a greater capacity for face-to-face contact to occur and therefore trust-building to develop (Hall 2000a).

Co-ordination refers to formal institutionalised relationships among existing networks of organisations, interests and/or individuals, while co-operation is 'characterized by informal trade-offs and by attempts to establish reciprocity in the absence of rules' (Mulford and Rogers 1982: 13). Often, the problem of developing co-ordinated approaches towards tourism planning and policy problems, such as the meta-problem of sustainability, is identified in organisational terms (e.g. the creation of new organisations or the allocation of new responsibilities to existing ones). However, such a response does not by itself solve the problem of bringing various stakeholders and interests together which is an issue of establishing collaborative processes. Instead, by recognising the level of interdependence that exists within the tourism system (Hall 2000a), it may be possible for 'separate, partisan interests to discover a common or public interest' (Friedmann 1973: 350). For example, moves towards the implementation of an 'ecosystem management' approach among United States government natural resource management agencies has opened up new ways of thinking about heritage and natural area management (Hall and McArthur 1998). Notions of collaboration, co-ordination and partnership are separate, though closely related, ideas within the emerging network paradigm. Networks refer to the development of linkages between actors (organisations and individuals) where linkages become more formal-ised towards maintaining mutual interests. The nature of such linkages exists on a continuum ranging from 'loose' linkages to coalitions and more lasting structural arrangements and relationships. Mandell (1999) identifies a continuum of such collaborative efforts as follows:

- linkages or interactive contacts between two or more actors;
- intermittent co-ordination or mutual adjust-ment of the policies and procedures of two or more actors to accomplish some objective;
- *ad hoc* or temporary task force activity among actors to accomplish a purpose or purposes;
- permanent and/or regular co-ordination between two or more actors through a formal arrangement (e.g. a council or partnership) to engage in limited activity to achieve a purpose or purposes;
- a coalition where interdependent and strategic actions are taken, but where purposes are narrow in scope and all actions occur within the participant actors themselves or involve the mutually sequential or simultaneous activity of the participant actors;
- a collective or network structure where there is a broad mission and joint and strategically interdependent action. Such structural arrange-ments take on broad tasks that reach beyond the simultaneous actions of independently operating actors.

However, as Mandell (1999: 8) cautions:

> because we as professionals are eager to achieve results, we often look for prescriptions or answers as to how to solve ongoing dilemmas . . . it is tempting for both academics and practitioners to try to develop a model of success that will fit this complex world. In this regard, the concepts of networks and network structures can easily become the next in line for those in the field to 'latch onto' and use wholesale. Although it may be tempting to do so, this 'one size fits all' type of modelling does not take into consideration the myriad of factors and events that must be understood before these concepts can be of much use in the 'real world'.

RAISING CONSUMER AWARENESS

One of the hallmarks of tourism, and other industries, in recent years has been the increased consumer demand for 'green' or 'environmentally friendly' products; such demand is often related to increased consumer awareness of environmental and social issues associated with trade and tourism. However, in many cases, the difference between a sustainable and non-sustainable tourism operation may be difficult for consumers to detect, partic-ularly if the greening of tourism is regarded more as a branding device than a fundamental change in product development.

One development which is usually regarded as an indicator of increased consumer awareness is the development of tourist codes of behaviour in order to minimise the negative impacts of tourists on the social and physical environment (Hall and Lew 1998). For example, Valentine (1992) cites the example of the Audubon Society, one of the largest conservation groups in the United States, which has developed the Audubon Travel Ethic in order to draw attention to the appropriate behaviours and ethics to which individuals travelling with the Society should follow:

1 The biota shall not be disturbed.
2 Audubon tours to natural areas will be sus-tainable.
3 The sensibilities of other cultures will be respected.
4 Waste disposal shall have neither environmental nor aesthetic impacts.
5 The experience a tourist gains in travelling with Audubon will enrich his or her appreciation of nature, conservation and the environment.
6 The effect of an Audubon tour will be to strengthen the conservation effort and enhance the natural integrity of places visited.
7 Traffic in products that threaten wildlife and plant populations shall not occur.

However, while consumer awareness is impor-tant and may result in shifts in tourism product, particularly if one believes the old adage that the consumer is king, fundamental changes are also required on the supply side of the tourism equation.

RAISING PRODUCER AWARENESS

According to Hall (1995), greater attention has been given to meeting the demands of different consumer segments than the needs of the supplier of the tourist product. As with the raising of consumer awareness, much attention has been given to the production of environmental codes of conduct or practice for tourism associations (Hall and McArthur 1998). For example, extensive guidelines have been developed for tourism operators in the Antarctic (Hall and Johnston 1995). However, such guidelines, while undoubtedly influencing the actions of some tourism operators, may need to be backed up by government regulation and environmental planning legislation if they are to have any overall effect on development practices. For example, where such codes of conduct are voluntary, what practical measures exist to punish operators who do not subscribe to them?

INSIGHT: The International Association of Antarctica Tour Operators (IAATO)

IAATO (www.iaato.org) was founded in August 1991 by seven charter members (Enzenbacher 1992) and now includes most of the main cruise lines which operate in the Antarctic. In 2001 IAATO had 14 full members, six provisional members, one probational member, and 14 associate members. IAATO members meet annually in conjunction with the National Science Foundation/Antarctic Tour Operators Meeting; attendance is compulsory as memberships, by-laws and other important issues are discussed. It is estimated that IAATO members carry approximately 70 per cent of all Antarctic tourists (Enzenbacher 1995). As Claus (1990, in Enzenbacher 1995: 188) noted, 'Over the past few years we have been involved in Antarctic policy meetings, US Congressional hearings and scientific conferences, not only in the US but in Australia and New Zealand as well, where we have taken a leading role in the environmental protection of Antarctica'. IAATO has two sets of guidelines: the first is addressed to Antarctica tour operators (1993a), the second is directed at Antarctica visitors (1993b). IAATO tour operator guidelines are intended for crew and staff members of Antarctic tour companies. The agreed principles contained within aim at increasing awareness and establishing a code of behaviour that minimises tourism impacts on the environment. The willingness of industry members to co-operate with Antarctic Treaty Parties in regulating tourism is crucial to the protection of the Antarctic environment given that the Antarctic is transnational space within which domestic laws are complicated in their application (Keage and Dingwall 1993; Hall and Johnson 1995). Tour operators maintain that current IAATO guidelines are adequate, noting that tourists often serve as effective guardians of the wildlife and environment. Yet, as Enzenbacher (1995: 188) noted, 'it is not clear that self-regulation sufficiently addresses all issues arising from tourist activity as no neutral regulatory authority currently exists to oversee all Antarctic operators'. Infractions of IAATO guidelines by members have been documented, but it is not known to what extent the environment was seriously affected by them (Enzenbacher 1992).

STRATEGIC PLANNING TO SUPERSEDE CONVENTIONAL APPROACHES

Strategic planning is becoming increasingly important in tourism (e.g. Dowling 1993). Strategic planning aims to be proactive, responsive to community needs, to incorporate implementation within a single planning process, and to be ongoing. A 'strategy' is a means to achieve a desired end. Strategic planning is the process by which an organisation effectively adapts to its management environment over time by integrating planning and management in a single process. The strategic plan is the document which is the output of a strategic planning process, it is the template by which progress is measured and which serves to guide future directions, activities, programmes and actions. The outcome of the strategic planning process is the impact the process has on the organisation and its activities. Such impacts are then monitored and evaluated through the selection of appropriate indicators as part of the ongoing revision and readjustment of the organisation to its environment. Strategic planning therefore emphasises the process of continuous improvement as a cornerstone of organisational activity in which strategic planning is linked to management and operational decision-making. According to Hall and McArthur (1998) there are three key mechanisms to achieving strategic planning which differentiate it from conventional planning approaches:

- a planning framework which extends beyond organisational boundaries and focuses on strategic decisions concerning stakeholders and resources;
- a planning process that stimulates entrepreneurial and innovative thinking;
- an organisational values system that reinforces managers and staff commitment to the organisational strategy.

Effective strategic planning for sustainable tourism recognises the importance of factors that affect the broad framework within which strategies are generated, such as institutional arrangements, institutional culture and stakeholder values and attitudes. These factors are significant because it is important to recognise that strategic plans will be in line with the legislative powers and organisational structures of the implementing organisation(s) and the political goals of government. However, it may also be the case that once the strategic planning process is underway, goals and objectives formulated and the process evaluated, the institutional arrangements may be recognised as being inadequate for the successful achievement of sustainable goals and objectives. In addition, it must be recognised that in order to be effective, the strategic planning process needs to be integrated with the development of appropriate organisational values (see Hall and Jenkins (1995) on the role of values in planning and policy). Indeed, with respect to the significance of values it may be noted that the strategic planning process is as important as its output, i.e. a plan. By having an inclusive planning process by which those responsible for implementing the plan are also those who helped formulate it, the likelihood of 'ownership' of the plan and, hence, effective implementation will be dramatically increased (Heath and Wall 1992; Hall and McArthur 1996).

A strategic planning process may be initiated for a number of reasons (Hall and McArthur 1998), including:

- *Stakeholder demands* – Demand for the undertaking of a strategic plan may come from the pressure of stakeholders (e.g. environmental conservation groups or government).
- *Perceived need* – The lack of appropriate information by which to make decisions or an appropriate framework with which to implement legislative requirements may give rise to a perception that new management and planning approaches are required.
- *Response to crisis* – The undertaking of strategic planning exercises is often the result of a crisis in the sense that the management and planning system has failed to adapt to aspects of the

management environment (e.g. failure to conserve the values of an environmentally significant site from visitor pressures).

- *Best practice* – Visitor managers can be proactive with respect to the adoption of new ideas and techniques. Therefore, a strategic planning process can become a way of doing things better.
- *Adaptation, innovation and the diffusion of ideas* – Individuals within an organisation can encourage strategic planning processes as part of the diffusion of ideas within and between responsible management agencies.

Strategic planning is rarely initiated for a single reason. However, it is important to understand as much as possible why a particular planning process is being initiated, as this helps the participants understand the expectations which have been created. Once underway, strategic planning is designed to be iterative. In other words, planning systems are meant to be able to adapt and change; they learn how to be effective in terms of the most appropriate set of goals, objectives, actions, indicators, institutional arrangements and practices. In this sense, strategic planning from the perspective of sustainable tourism seeks to reflect in an organisational context the principles of appropriate adaptation and change which exist in the ecological relationships they are so often attempting to maintain. In addition, strategic approaches place great store on understanding the policy environment within which tourism planning operates, and it is to this that we will now briefly turn.

INSIGHT: Singapore: *Tourism 21*

Why should anybody come to Singapore to begin with? What did we have? . . . We only had a name, then Raffles Hotel, and what? A few quaint habits and customs and the mediums and the temples, and the Indian with his *kavadi* walking over heated charcoal . . . that is not going to bring in six million [tourists]. [Instead], we *created the attraction*. We created the interest that brought the six million tourists. We developed a marketing strategy . . . [a]nd made ourselves useful to the world.

(Senior Minister Lee Kuan Yew, cited in *The Straits Times Weekly Edition*, 16 June 1993, in Teo and Chang 1999: 117)

As tourist taste and markets have changed over time, 'Singapore has constantly strove to recreate its resources in order to remain competitive' (Teo and Chang 1999: 117). The government's changing focus over time has been reflected in shifts in tourism policy; from the development of local resources in the 1986 plan to the creation of a 'regional tourism economy' in 1996 (Chang 1998). However, regardless of changes in marketing strategies, the government has consistently sought to emphasise and reinforce Singapore's location as a gateway to South-East Asia and as a transport hub. As Teo and Chang (1999) observed, as an air travel hub, a business centre and a node for tourism/lifestyle companies, the foundation of Singapore's ability to survive in the tourism business is to take advantage of its sophisticated infrastructure to position itself as a gateway.

In 1996 Singapore set itself a target of 10 million arrivals and S\$16 billion in tourism receipts at the end of the year 2000 (Hall 1997). In order to achieve these goals Singapore launched a new tourism plan *Tourism 21: Vision of a Tourism Capital* in July 1996 (Singapore Tourism Board 1996). The goal of the plan is to make Singapore the tourism hub of South-East Asia. In order to achieve this, six strategic thrusts were identified:

1 *Redefining tourism*: widening the focus of tourism from destination marketing to developing Singapore as a tourism business centre and a tourism hub.
2 *Reformulating the product*: developing new themes, events and infrastructure, and linking Singapore products with those of the region.

3   *Developing tourism as an industry*: adopting a cluster development approach, creating investment incentives, and developing a competent tourism workforce, information networks and branding strategies.

4   *Configuring new tourism space*: encourage tourism-related investment overseas by Singaporean companies and develop partnerships with neighbouring countries in product development.

5   *Partnering for success*: encourage tourism development partnerships at all levels.

6   *Championing tourism*: the STPB will take on an enlarged role as a one-stop tourism agency with activities in tourism business development as well as its traditional promotional function.

The Singapore Tourism Promotion Board's name will eventually change to the Singapore Tourism Board to reflect its new role.

Singapore received a total of 7,691,090 visitors in 2000, the highest number of visitors ever recorded. Visitor arrivals from most of the regions, namely Asia, Europe, Oceania and the Americas, also reached historical highs. Given the impact of the Asian economic crisis on tourism in the region this figure was a substantial achievement and testimony to Singapore's tourism planning strategy. Details of the plan are available from the Singapore Tourism Board's website (http://www.stb.com.sg).

TOURISM POLICY

As with planning, geographers have long held a substantial interest in policy-making, although such concerns have only recently found substantial expression in the tourism sphere (e.g. Fagence 1990, 1991; D.G. Pearce 1992a, 1992b; Hall and Jenkins 1995). Public policy is the focal point of government activity. Public policy 'is whatever governments choose to do or not to do' (Dye 1992: 2). This definition covers government action, inaction, decisions and non-decisions as it implies a deliberate choice between alternatives. For a policy to be regarded as public policy, at the very least it must have been processed, even if only authorised or ratified, by public agencies (Hall *et al.* 1997). Public policy-making, including tourism policy-making, is first and foremost a political activity. Public policy is influenced by the economic, social and cultural characteristics of society, as well as by the formal structures of government and other features of the political system. Policy is therefore a consequence of the political environment, values and ideologies, the distribution of power, institutional frameworks, and of decision-making processes (Hall and Jenkins 1995; Hall *et al.* 1997) (Figure 9.2).

Tourism public policy is whatever governments choose to do or not to do with respect to tourism (Hall and Jenkins 1995). However, as a number of studies by geographers have indicated (e.g. McKercher 1993c, 1997; Jenkins 1997), pressure groups (e.g. tourism industry associations, conservation groups, community groups), community leaders and significant individuals (e.g. local government councillors), members of the bureaucracy (e.g. employees within tourism commissions or regional development agencies) and others (e.g. academics and consultants) influence and perceive public policies in significant and often markedly different ways.

Research on tourism policy research may generally be divided into two main types of theory: that which adopts prescriptive models and that which adopts descriptive models (Mitchell 1989; Hall 1994; Hall and Jenkins 1995). 'Prescriptive or normative models seek to demonstrate how [planning and] policy making should occur relative to pre-established standards', whereas 'descriptive models document the way in which the policy process actually occurs' (Mitchell 1989: 264). Prescriptive (normative) models serve as a guide to an ideal situation. The majority of references to

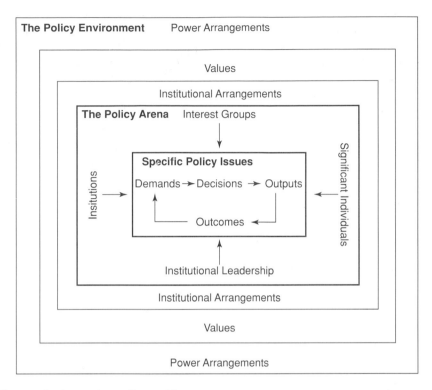

Figure 9.2: Elements in the tourism policy-making process

policy- and decision-making in the tourism literature have tended to utilise a prescriptive model of
policy-making which demonstrates how tourism
policy- and decision-making should occur relative
to pre-established standards (e.g. Murphy 1985).
The prescriptive–rational approach assumes that a
dichotomy exists between the policy-making
process and administration and the existence of
'Economic Man [*sic*]', whereby individuals can
'identify and rank goals, values and objectives', and
'can choose consistently among them after having
collected all the necessary data and systematically
evaluated them' (Mitchell 1979: 296). However,
while these may be useful rational models against
which to compare reality, they do not provide
detailed insights into the real world of planning and
its associated set of values, power and interests.
Instead, approaches, methods and techniques need
to be evaluated within the context of the goals,
objectives and outcomes of tourism planning and

development (Hall and Jenkins 1995; Hall *et al.*
1997).

Descriptive approaches give rise to explanations
about what happened during the decision-making,
planning and policy-making processes. Case studies
are an important component of descriptive tourism
research as they help analysts understand the effects
that such factors as choice, power, perception,
values and process have on tourism planning and
policy-making. As Mitchell (1979: 42) recorded,
'much research in resource analysis has been based
upon one-shot case studies'. The main criticism of
the case study method is 'claimed to be its reliance
upon historical–descriptive chronology and lack
of consistency in scope, context and conceptual
cohesiveness' (Davis 1981: 8). However, although
a single case study 'will rarely be sufficient for a full
inquiry', the duplication of studies may well suggest
fundamental relationships and generalisations
(Mitchell 1979: 43). Indeed, 'it cannot be claimed

that the case evidence is entirely definitive or utterly representative' (Davis 1981: 7), but case studies do present the researcher with the capacity to highlight certain problem areas within the scope of the objectives to be gained in this thesis. This attitude is reflected in the recreation research of La Page (cited in Mercer 1973: 42): 'For sound research planning, I would gladly swap all the "highly significant" correlation coefficients of the past 10 years for a couple of good case studies that yielded some solid conceptual insight to build on.'

Under a descriptive approach, emphasis is therefore placed on understanding the various elements of the policy process and how it arrives at certain outputs and outcomes. As W.I. Jenkins (1978: 16) argued, 'for many process is a central, if not the central, focus, to the extent that they argue that a conceptual understanding of the policy process is fundamental to an analysis of public policy'. Therefore, for the descriptive analysis of tourism policy

> to explain policy maintenance and policy change, one needs to explore the socio-political conditions in which the political system operates, examining in particular the extent to which outputs are conditioned by external influences. Thus . . . the vital task of the policy analyst is to explore the links between the environment, the political system and policy outputs and impacts.
>
> (W.I. Jenkins 1978: 26–7)

Unfortunately, the understanding of the tourism policy process is rather limited as the area has not received a great deal of emphasis until recently, although geographers have been making a substantial contribution to the field (e.g. Pearce 1992b; Hall and Jenkins 1995). Nevertheless, an understanding of the way in which government utilises tourism as a policy mechanism may be extremely valuable not only in terms of improving the policy-making and planning process, but also in terms of improving the conditions of the people who are affected by such policies.

For example, tourism as a policy response to the economic problems of rural areas in developed countries has gone through a number of phases in recent years (Jenkins *et al.* 1998). Until the mid-1980s rural tourism was primarily concerned with commercial opportunities, multiplier effects and

employment creation (e.g. Canadian Council on Rural Development 1975). In the late 1980s policy guidance shifted to the message that the environment is a key component of the tourism industry. Under this notion, 'tourism is an additive rather than extractive force for rural communities' (Curry 1994: 146). Tourism was regarded as 'sustainable', stressing the intrinsic value of the environment and, in some countries, the rural community as a tourist resource. (Although in Australia sustainability was defined primarily in ecological terms (Hall 1995).)

In the late 1980s and early 1990s an additional layer to the policy responses of government to tourism and regional development has been added which returns to the earlier economic concerns (e.g. D.G. Pearce 1992a). This is the perception of rural tourism as a major mechanism for arresting the decline of agricultural employment and therefore as a mechanism for agricultural diversification (Rural Development Commission 1991a, 1991b). In the case of Europe, for example, we see the identification of specific rural development areas (Pearce 1992a; Jenkins *et al.* 1998). Rural tourism has also been given substantial emphasis in Australia, New Zealand and North America because of its development potential (Butler *et al.* 1998). For example, as the Australian Commonwealth Department of Tourism (1993: 24) noted:

> Diversification of traditional rural enterprises into tourism would provide considerable benefits to local rural economies including:
>
> - wider employment opportunities;
> - diversifying the income base of farmers and rural towns;
> - additional justification for the development of infrastructure;
> - a broader base for the establishment, maintenance and/or expansion of local services;
> - scope for the integration of regional development strategies;
> - an enhanced quality of life through extended leisure and cultural opportunities.

Yet despite government enthusiasm for tourism as a mechanism to counter problems arising out of rural restructuring and depopulation, the success of these policies has been only marginally successful, with the greatest growth from tourism- and recreation-related industries occurring in the larger rural service centres and the rural–urban fringe, arguably those areas which least need the benefits that tourism can bring (Butler *et al.* 1998; Jenkins *et al.* 1998). Why has this occurred?

To a great extent it relates to a failure by government to understand the nature of tourism and its relationship with other sectors of the economy and the policy and planning process itself. First, all the dimensions of development need to be considered. Second, it implies the need for us to be aware of the various linkages that exist between the elements of development. Third, it also implies that 'successful' regional development will require co-ordination and, at times, intervention, in order to achieve desired outcomes. Fourth, it also means that tourism should not be seen as the be-all and end-all of regional development, but instead should be utilised as an appropriate response to the real needs of rural regions. As Getz (1987: 3–4) stated, tourism 'can be a tool in regional development or an agent of disruption or destruction'. Or, to put it another way, to quote an article from Canada: 'Those who think a bit of Victorian architecture and an overpriced cappuccino bar are going to turn their community into a gold mine are in for a disappointment' (Threndyle 1994). However, the problems of rural tourism and recreation development have long been recognised. For example, as Baum and More (1966: 5) stated with respect to the American experience in the early 1960s:

> there are and there will be increasing opportunities for [tourism] development, but this industry should not be considered to be a panacea for the longstanding problems of substantial and persistent unemployment and underemployment besetting low-income rural areas. . . . The successful development of a particular [tourism] enterprise or complex of enterprises requires the same economic considerations as the planning and development of economic activities in other sectors.

The starting point with respect to determining successful regional tourism development is deciding in the first place what the objectives should be and how a community is going to get there. Such a decision should not be made by the tourism industry alone. As Long and Nuckolls (1994: 19) noted:

Pro-active, community-driven planning, that goes beyond developing and promoting the static supply side of tourism, is essential for successful development of a sustainable tourism industry. Furthermore, tourism plans must be integrated into broader strategies for community, economic and regional development and management. Communities that fail to organise resources and strategically plan for tourism will likely be faced with short term, haphazard development, resulting in long term, negative economic, social and environmental impacts.

An understanding of tourism policy processes therefore lies at the heart of broader goals of rural and regional development. Yet, as Hall and Jenkins (1998) argued, the formulation and implementation of rural tourism and recreation public policies present several conundrums. Unrealistic expectations of tourism's potential are unfortunately combined with ignorance or wilful neglect by decision-makers of the potentially adverse economic, environmental and social consequences of tourist development that threaten to curtail its benefits. Yet, as Duffield and Long (1981: 409) observed, 'Ironically, the very consequences of lack of development, the unspoilt character of the landscape and distinctive local cultures, become positive resources as far as tourism is concerned.' Government involvement in rural tourism development is therefore quite unsuccessful:

> Management decisions for the allocation of related outdoor recreation resources are seldom guided by strategic policy frameworks. Decisions are typically made in a reactive manner in response to various pressures from groups competing for the same resource or lobbying for different management of a particular resource. . . . Even in Europe, where rural tourism has been increasingly promoted over the last decade as an important mechanism for regional economic development and European integration, substantial problems have emerged with respect to policy formulation and implementation.
>
> (Hall and Jenkins 1998: 28)

The reason for such failures lies in a lack of understanding of policy processes: 'while the goals of rural tourism development are fairly clear at the regional level, little research has been conducted on the most appropriate policy mix to achieve such objectives and there is often minimal monitoring and evaluation of policy measures' (Hall and Jenkins 1998). Therefore, for each location within which regional development objectives are being sought through the development of tourism, there are a range of policy measures available (Table 9.5). Five different measures were identified:

1 *regulatory instruments* – regulations, permits and licences that have a legal basis and which require monitoring and enforcement;
2 *voluntary instruments* – actions or mechanisms that do not require expenditure;
3 *expenditure* – direct government expenditure to achieve policy outcomes;
4 *financial incentives* – including taxes, subsidies, grants and loans, which are incentives to undertake certain activities or behaviours and which tend to require minimal enforcement;
5 *non-intervention* – where government deliberately avoids intervention in order to achieve its policy objectives.

The selection of the most appropriate measure or, more likely, a range of measures, is dependent on the particular circumstances of each region. There is no universal 'best way'; each region or locale needs to select the appropriate policy mix for its own development requirements. However, this does not mean that the policy and planning process occurs in a vacuum. Rather the attention to policy and planning processes has the intent of making such processes as overt as possible, so that the values, influence and interests of various stakeholders are relatively transparent. There is no perfect planning or policy process, yet we can, through the geographer's contribution, help make it more relevant to the people who are affected by tourism development and continually strive for improvement.

CONCLUSION

This chapter has provided a broad overview of the tourism and recreation planning and policy process. It has noted the various strands of tourism planning, and emphasised the particular contri-

bution of geographers to the physical/spatial, community and sustainable approaches to tourism planning.

The reasons for focusing on tourism which is not as well developed or articulated in local, regional and national development plans beyond statements and broad objectives contrasts with recreational planning which has a much longer history of development and application. In fact if the experience of urban areas is considered, one can see the emergence of recreational planning in the nineteenth century in the UK with the role of the public sector in park development, the provision of libraries and other items to meet the wider public good. What geographers have contributed to recreational planning is the synthesis and analysis of good practice, rather than being actively involved as academics, beyond a research role, to assist public and private sector bodies in locational analysis and land use planning. This chapter has therefore placed a great deal of emphasis on the importance of policy analysis, especially from a descriptive approach. This does not mean that prescription is without value, rather it argues that prescription must be seen in context, with particular reference to those who are in any way affected by policy statements.

In looking at the application of policy analysis to tourism issues we have therefore almost come full circle. The interests which have long concerned tourism and recreation geographers that are applied and relevant to the needs of the subjects of our research remain, and it is to these issues that we will return in the final chapter.

QUESTIONS

* Is there anything that makes planning for tourism distinct from other forms of planning?
* Why is recreation planning such an integral component of resource management?
* What are the institutional arrangements for tourism and recreation in your country? Describe them and their interrelationships between the national, regional and local level.

Table 9.5: Rural tourism development policy instruments

Categories	Instruments	Examples
Regulatory instruments	1 Laws	Planning laws can give considerable power to government to encourage particular types of rural tourism development through, for example, land use zoning
	2 Licences, permits and standards	Regulatory instruments can be used for a wide variety of purposes at local government level, e.g. they may set materials standards for tourism developments, or they can be used to set architectural standards for heritage streetscapes or properties
	3 Tradeable permits	Often used in the United States to limit resource use or pollution. However, the instrument requires effective monitoring for it to work
	4 Quid pro quos	Government may require businesses to do something in exchange for certain rights, e.g. land may be given to a developer below market rates, or a development is of a particular type or design
Voluntary instruments	1 Information	Expenditure on educating the local public, businesses or tourists to achieve specific goals, e.g. appropriate recreational behaviour
	2 Volunteer associations and non-governmental organisations	Government support of community tourism organisations is very common in tourism. Support may come from direct grants and/or by provision of office facilities. Examples of this type of development include local or regional tourist organisations, heritage conservation groups, mainstreet groups, tour guide programmes, or helping to establish a local farmstay or homestay association
	3 Technical assistance	Government can provide technical assistance and information to businesses with regard to planning and development requirements
Expenditure	1 Expenditure and contracting	This is a common method for government to achieve policy objectives as government can spend money directly on specific activities. This may include the development of infrastructure, such as roads, or it may include mainstreet beautification programs. Contracting can be used as a means of supporting existing local businesses or encouraging new ones
	2 Investment or procurement	Investment may be directed into specific businesses or projects, while procurement can be used to help provide businesses with a secure customer for their products
	3 Public enterprise	When the market fails to provide desired outcomes, governments may operate their own businesses, e.g. rural or regional development corporations or enterprise boards. If successful, such businesses may then be sold off to the private sector
	4 Public–private partnerships	Government may enter into partnership with the private sector in order to develop certain products or regions. These may take the form of a corporation which has a specific mandate to attract business to a certain region, for example
	5 Monitoring and evaluation	Government may allocate financial resources to monitor rural economic, environmental and socio-economic indicators. Such measures may not only be valuable to government to evaluate the effectiveness and efficiency of rural tourism development objectives but can also be a valuable source of information to the private sector as well
	6 Promotion	Government may spend money on promoting a region to visitors either with or without financial input from the private sector. Such promotional activities may allow individual businesses to reallocate their own budgets, reducing planned expenditure on promotion

Table 9.5: (continued)

Categories	Instruments	Examples
Financial incentives	1 Pricing	Pricing measures may be used to encourage appropriate behaviour or to stimulate demand, e.g. use of particular walking trails, lower camping or permit costs
	2 Taxes and charges	Governments may use these to encourage appropriate behaviours by both individuals and businesses, i.e. pollution charges. Taxes and charges may also be used to help fund infrastructure development, e.g. regional airports
	3 Grants and loans	Seeding money may be provided to businesses to encourage product development or to encourage the retention of heritage and landscape features
	4 Subsidies and tax incentives	Although subsidies are often regarded as creating inefficiencies in markets they may also be used to encourage certain types of behaviour with respect to social and environmental externalities, e.g. heritage and landscape conservation, that are not taken into account by conventional economics
	5 Rebates, rewards and surety bonds	Rebates and rewards are a form of financial incentive to encourage individuals and businesses to act in certain ways. Similarly, surety bonds can be used to ensure that businesses act in agreed ways, if they don't then the government will spend the money for the same purpose
	6 Vouchers	Vouchers are a mechanism to affect consumer behaviour by providing a discount on a specific product or activity, e.g. to shop in a rural centre
Non-intervention	1 Non-intervention (deliberate)	Government deciding not to directly intervene in sectoral or regional development is also a policy instrument, in that public policy is what government decides to do and not do. In some cases the situation may be such that government may decide that policy objectives are being met so that their intervention may not add any net value to the rural development process and that resources could be better spent elsewhere

Source: After Hall and Jenkins (1998: 29–32)

- What is the appropriate relationship between government and the tourism industry in the formulation of tourism policy?

READING

There are several classic works that relate to tourism planning. In particular see the work of Gunn (1972, 1988 and more recent editions) and the work of Murphy:

Murphy, P.E. (1985) *Tourism: A Community Approach*, New York: Methuen.
Murphy, P.E. (1988) 'Community driven tourism planning', *Tourism Management*, 9(2): 96–104.

For a traditional approach to resort and tourism planning see:

Inskeep, E. (1991) *Tourism Planning: An Integrated and Sustainable Development Approach*, New York: Van Nostrand Reinhold.

Hall (2000a) is a more theoretically informed work which attempts to integrate planning and policy concerns at different scales of analysis. A more practical guide to tourism planning and dealing with stakeholders is:

Hall, C.M. and McArthur, S. (1998) *Integrated Heritage Management*, London: The Stationery Office.

A recent useful work on British tourism policy is:

Church, A., Ball, R., Bull, C. and Tyler, D. (2000) 'Public policy engagement with British tourism: The national, local and the European Union', *Tourism Geographies*, 2 (3): 312–36.

Recent works with more of a recreational planning emphasis include:

Cope, A., Doxford, D. and Probert, C. (2000) 'Monitoring visitors to UK countryside resources: The approaches of land and recreation resource management organisations to visitor monitoring', *Land Use Policy*, 17: 59–66.

Ferreira, S. and Harmse, A. (1999) 'The social carrying capacity of Kruger National Park, South Africa: Policy and practice', *Tourism Geographies*, 1(3): 325–42.

Wezenaar, H. (1999) 'Leisure land-use planning and sustainability in the new town of Almere, The Netherlands', *Tourism Geographies*, 1(4): 460–76.

10

THE FUTURE

Speaking only as one individual, I feel strongly that I should not go into research unless it promises results that would advance the aims of the people affected and unless I am prepared to take all practicable steps to help translate the results into action.

(White 1972: 102)

As the various chapters in this book have indicated, geographers have made substantial contributions to the understanding of tourism and recreation. However, as noted in Chapter 1, the geographers who are working in the field are, increasingly, not based in geography departments but instead are located in departments of tourism and recreation or leisure, environmental studies or business. Indeed, the authors, while still regarding themselves as geographers, were working in faculties of business as this manuscript was being completed.

Such a situation is a reflection of several things: the growth of tourism and recreation as a separate, legitimate area of academic endeavour; the poor standing in which studies of tourism and recreation have generally been held within academic geography, and the applied nature of much work in tourism and recreation geography, which has meant a professional career in the public and private sectors for many geography graduates in the field. Such a situation clearly raises substantial questions about what the future of the subdiscipline will be. As Johnston (1991: 2) recognised: 'It is the advancement of knowledge – through the conduct of fundamental research and the publication of its original findings – which identifies an academic discipline; the nature of its teaching follows from the nature of its research.'

This final chapter will briefly revisit the place of tourism and recreation geography in the applied geography tradition. It will then discuss the contributions that geography can bring to the study of tourism and recreation and highlight a possible future for the field.

GEOGRAPHY – THE DISCIPLINE: DIRECTION AND PROGRESS

According to Johnston (1985b: 326), 'geographers, especially but not only human geographers, have become parochial and myopic in recent decades' and have been accompanied by a disengagement from close field contact and a global concern with human phenomena. The disengagement from the region has been seen as a mechanism to synthesise systematic investigations. In seeking to advance the discipline, Johnston (1985b) argued that geographers need both a theoretical appreciation of the general processes of the capitalist mode of production and an empirical appreciation of the social formations that result. The discipline versus detachment from the skills of fieldwork, observation and description continue to remain fundamental weaknesses, and in many respects the 'core' elements of a geographical education at university level now reflect the often fragmented specialisation that characterises many geography curricula. In fact, geography is a subject in retreat in many contexts, particularly in Australia where the specialisation function has now led to the dissipation of geography departments and the emergence of more multidisciplinary groupings focused on environmental science, for example. In the UK, the declining enrolments being experienced by many geography departments has been attributed to the rapid growth in tourism and recreation studies with the focus on business, management and vocationalism and a declining interest at the post-16 level in schools and colleges. Geography is perceived as having failed to move with the times to integrate a greater vocationalism and applied focus, and in many cases to offer students a practical, real-world engagement with society. Even though the rise of GIS and its application to planning and problem-solving has assisted in real-world problem-solving, the main body of the discipline has often not engaged students in fundamental elements of the real world through fieldwork and practical knowledge.

In the United States the position of geography may be slightly more positive thanks in great part to the growth of government and industry awareness of the value of GIS; nevertheless, as the President of the Association of American Geographers noted, there is only a very limited presence of geography in the elite universities and institutions (Cutter 2000). While the authors may agree with Cutter's remarks that 'The lack of formal geography (courses, an undergraduate minor, major, or graduate study) in many of the most prestigious universities in the nation is a missed opportunity for these elite institutions of higher education' (Cutter 2000: 3), such a comment also reflects the failings of geography and geographers to effectively communicate their interests and contributions in a wide range of contemporary issues and subjects, including tourism and recreation.

Although the new synthesis of applied geography (Pacione 1999b) outlines the way in which some geographers perceive themselves and their contribution to research, this is not being adequately communicated to students, particularly in the marginalisation of applied geography as a hybrid according to concerns purists and qualitative researchers have about social and cultural theory as their analytical framework. Nevertheless, it is important to revisit applied geography and to

provide some illustrations of how tourism and recreational geographers make contributions to 'problem-solving', 'policy-analysis' and the wider public good. Pacione (1999b) in his protocol for applied geographical analysis (Figure 10.1) outlines the DEEP process: Description, Explanation, Evaluation and Prescription, which may be followed by Implementation and Monitoring.

REVISITING APPLIED GEOGRAPHY

Within the literature on the geography of recreation and tourism there have been comparatively few studies which have emphasised how the tourism and recreation geographer has made a valuable contribution to the wider development of 'applied geography'. According to Sant (1982), the scope of applied geography comprises a concern with policy-making and the monitoring of problems. More specifically it focuses on 'the sense of the problem, the contribution to decision making and policy, the monitoring of actions and the evaluation of plans. But these are common to all applied social sciences' (Sant 1982: 3) and so the geographer must ensure that s/he can make a distinctive contribution through the use of approaches, tools, techniques or skills which other social scientists, consultants and policy-makers do not possess, if it is regarded as important that a geographical approach survives.

All too often the application of geographical skills in commercial and non-commercial contexts has been poorly developed. There are notable exceptions in the history of geographical thought where the skills of spatial analysis have been used for practical and commercial purposes, particularly in colonial times where the pursuit of resource inventories and mapping assisted in imperialist expansion in new territories (see Johnston 1991). In the post-war period some aspects of geography clearly dissipated to new disciplines such as town planning while the greater social science involvement and expansion of geographical subject matter saw geographers lose some of their competitive edge which had been gained in the pre- and inter-war

Figure 10.1: The DEEP process for applied geographical analysis
Source: Pacione (1999b)

years. In recent times, some geographers have made transitions into the public and private sector where their skills have been in high demand (e.g. GIS), and some have made major contributions to public policy formulation and analysis in recreation and tourism (e.g. Patmore 1983). There has been the development of new specialisms which have emerged from a geographical tradition with an explicit public and commercial dimension. Recre-ation and tourism are two examples which have furnished many opportunities for the geographer to apply their skills in a wider context than academia, although this has not always meant that they have been particularly successful in capitalising on such opportunities.

While geographers still make a substantial contri-bution to planning, this contribution is perhaps not widely acknowledged by society at large. Similarly,

GIS is increasingly being usurped by marketers, while the contribution of geographers to tourism and recreation is now adding far more of an academic base for the field of tourism and recreation studies than it is for geography. Should we care? The answer we believe is 'yes'. As the book stated at the outset by imitating the title of Massey and Allen's (1984) work: *Geography Matters!*, the geography of tourism and recreation also matters. One of the problems however is that we are often not very good at convincing other people that we do. In fact declining enrolments in geography at university level in the UK have been attributed to the growth of interest in cognate subjects like tourism and recreation, though this is part of a growing interest in vocational subjects such as business studies as previously mentioned. Given increasing demands for the development of sustainable forms of tourism on the one hand and a relevant academic geography on the other, geography and geographers have an important role to play. In some senses those geographers who have moved to business schools to pursue their interest in tourism and recreation have at least managed to retain a spatial component to such curricula.

CONTRIBUTIONS

According to Stamp (1960: 9), 'the unique contribution of the geographer is the holistic approach in which he sees the relationship between man and his [*sic*] environment'. This statement is just as relevant to the application of geography to problem-solving today as it was when originally written. Indeed, perhaps more so given the size of the environmental, social and economic problems we face. Doornkamp (1982) posed a range of questions related to the role of applied geography, and two of these are of significance to tourism and recreation:

- Is the geographical contribution sufficiently unique to make it worth pursuing?
- How, in the commercial world, can the work of the applied geographer be sold?

These two questions highlight the need for geographers to assess what inherent skills they have which may be of value in an applied context. While accepting that the nature of geographical training in the 1990s may be somewhat different from that in the 1970s and 1980s, Table 10.1 does still provide a useful assessment of how the geographer can contribute to problem-solving. While skills are important in addressing problems, Doornkamp (1982) and Dawson and Doornkamp's (1973) research in applied geography provides many key pointers to the value of a spatial approach. He highlights the need to separate knowledge from the ability to use skills. During a geographical education, exposure to the systematic elements of the discipline in human and physical geography combines with practical and fieldwork in spatial techniques, which, together with regional studies, is where many of the former elements can be synthesised. This continues to provide the core of knowledge for the geographer and more advanced training then focuses on a specialised study in a particular subdiscipline of geography. It is often at this point that the cross-over between geography and other social science disciplines occurs when the knowledge base becomes shared. The problem within business schools is that the spatial component is often extremely watered down to a basic conceptualisation of place, space and environment. At the same time, the inquisitive nature of geographical research, particularly the interest in human–environment relationships at a variety of spatial scales, often means that the geographer pursues a holistic perspective not often found in other disciplines. Yet conveying this to the new generation of students interested in the business applications of recreation and tourism requires the geographer to not only sell the value of a synthesising holistic approach, but to also move forward to meet the new challenge for applied geography in a new millennium. Equally, the geographer also has a formidable challenge in convincing colleagues and researchers in mainstream geography of the validity and intellectual rigour associated with research in recreation and tourism.

Table 10.1: The skills of a geographer

- To think in spatial terms.
- To be able to assess the implications of the distribution of any one 'landscape' characteristic.
- To be able to think about more than one distribution at a time – and to perceive from this any likely generic links between the items under study.
- To be able to change the scale of thinking according to the needs of the phenomena or problems being analysed.
- To be able to add the dimension of time as appropriate.
- To be able to place phenomena within a 'model' or 'systems' framework.
- To be able to comprehend and initiate thinking that links the human and physical systems operating in the landscape.
- To 'read' and 'understand' landscape.
- To be able to use certain techniques, for example:
  - To acquire information through fieldwork, map analysis or from remote sensing sources – with an emphasis on spatial distributions and relationships.
  - To be able to handle and analyse large data sets, incomplete data sets, spatial data or time-based data, through quantitative methods using computer technology.
  - To be equally at home in a literary search amongst archives and historical records.
  - To be able to monitor landscape components, and to be able to submit them to further analyses as appropriate.
  - To present information with clarity, and especially in map form.
  - To utilise technological developments such as GIS to assist in gaining a holistic view of the problem in hand.
- To be able to provide a statement of one's findings which integrates one's own knowledge with that of allied disciplines.

Source: After Doornkamp (1982: 7)

But harnessing this training and the range of skills acquired in order to apply them in a problem-solving context requires one important prerequisite. According to Doornkamp (1982: 9), this is an ability to see the problem from the point of view of the person who needs a solution. Having convinced this person of their ability to conceptualise the problem in their terms, in order to provide a solution three principal factors need to be considered:

1 The research must be framed and reported in a manner which the client requires: it needs to be as concise and as thorough as possible. It is not to be a thesis or academic research paper. Otherwise the client will simply not recommend or use the organisation again. This is a principal failing for many academics who are unable to bridge the industry–academic interface.

2 Personal relationships of trust and respect need to be built up in a commercial environment, often framed around numerous meetings and regular interfacing; and the work must be professionally presented, being easy to read, targeted at the audience intending to read it, and precise and unambiguous.

3 Even where the client is a non-paying customer (i.e. if the research is undertaken as a contribution to the local community), such criteria are equally important. Otherwise, the outside world's image of the geographer will remain one of the ivory tower academic perceived as being distant from the real world and problem-solving contributions they can make. Likewise, academics need to be willing to incorporate changes on drafts and to recognise that in this environment their view is not necessarily without reproach. This is nowhere more the case than in recreation and tourism where an explicit business dimension is incorporated into such research.

It is fair to agree with Doornkamp's (1982: 26) analogy that practising geographers left the discipline in the immediate post-war period and joined the commercial world, calling themselves planners. A similar move may be occurring in recreation and tourism, with the movement of staff to business schools and specialist tourism and/or recreation departments either from academic positions in departments of geography or after completion of their graduate studies. The 'professional practice' side of the discipline of geography has continued to lose out to other disciplines even when its skills are more relevant and analytical. Interfacing with the real world has meant that a small proportion of recreation and tourism geographers have made a steady transition to professional practice without compromising their academic integrity and reputation. While payment for their services may have filled some of their peers and contemporaries with horror, recreation and tourism are commercial activities. In some cases, not using the label 'geographer' can have a great deal of benefit when interfacing with recreation and tourism businesses, since the public perception of geographers is not of practitioners making commercial or social contributions to society. So in summary, it is clear that applied geography problem-solving in recreation and tourism contexts can enhance the geographer's skills and relationship with society. In the longer term, it may help address the public image of the discipline as one of major value to research in applied fields such as tourism.

But ultimately the main barrier to geographers using their skills for an applied purpose is their own willingness and ability to interface in commercial and public contexts where they can be heard, listened to, taken seriously and their skills harnessed. In many cases, there is often a belated recognition of the value of such skills when a client uses such a person. Therefore, the public face of geography can only be enhanced if it embraces recreation and tourism as legitimate subdisciplines of a post-industrial society/geography that can have a major contribution to make in various applied contexts.

THE ROLE OF GIS AND TOURISM: A TOOL FOR APPLIED GEOGRAPHIC RESEARCH

GIS, developed by advances in computer hardware and software (such as ArcInfo), incorporates more sophisticated systems to search, query, present and analyse data in a spatial context. Table 10.2 outlines the capabilities of a GIS and its role in enabling geographers to assist decision-makers in making planning decisions. In fact, Butler (1992) outlined some of the possible problem-solving roles of GIS in tourism as shown in Table 10.3. What is evident from Table 10.3 is the application of GIS to tourism planning, particularly in tourism and recreational resource management, as well as in tourism marketing (Elliott-White and Finn 1998). The ability

Table 10.2: Capabilities of a Geographical Information System

Examples of functional capabilities of a GIS	Examples of basic questions that can be investigated using a GIS (after Rhind 1990)		Examples of tourism applications
Data entry, storage and manipulation	Location	What is at?	Tourism resource inventories
Map production	Condition	Where is it?	Identifying most suitable locations for development
Database integration	Trend	What has changed?	Measuring tourism impacts
Data queries and searches	Routing	Which is the best route?	Visitor management/flows
Spatial analysis	Pattern	What is the pattern?	Analysing relationships associated with resource use
Spatial modelling	Modelling	What if . . .?	Assessing potential impacts of tourism development

Source: Bahaire and Elliott-White (1999: 161)

Table 10.3: Problems of tourism and the potential of Geographical Information Systems (based on Butler 1992: 33)

Problems of tourism	Nature of problem	GIS application
Ignorance	Of dimensions, nature, power of tourism, i.e. by key decision-makers and communities	A key point is that stakeholders do not have the types of information needed to assert their point of view. Using GIS for the *systematic inventory* of tourism resources and analysis of *trends* can help ameliorate this problem.
Lack of ability	To determine levels of sustainable tourism development given the fuzziness of the concept	GIS can be used to monitor and control tourism activities once levels of development deemed appropriate and acceptable by stakeholders have been determined. By integrating tourism, environmental, socio-cultural and economic data GIS facilitates the identification and monitoring of indicators of sustainable development.
Lack of ability	To manage and control development – associated with uses, capabilities, capacities	GIS can be used to identify suitable locations for tourism development, identify zones of conflict/complementarity.
Lack of appreciation	That tourism is an industry and causes impacts which cannot be easily reversed	GIS can be used to *stimulate* and *model* spatial outcomes of proposed developments. To sensitise stakeholders to externalities associated with their actions, e.g. visibility analysis, network analysis, gravity models.
Lack of appreciation	That tourism is dynamic and causes change as well as responding to change, i.e. tourism is just a part of a wider development process which can produce intra- and inter-industry conflict which may destroy the tourism resource	GIS enables the *integration* of datasets representing socio-economic development and environmental capital within a given spatial setting. GIS sits comfortably on top of integrated and strategic spatial planning.
Lack of agreement	Over levels of appropriate development, control and direction	GIS functions as a decision support system – to produce more informed arguments and (hopefully) facilitate compromise and resolution. However, this presupposes the existence of a coherent planning and development control framework.

Source: Bahaire and Elliott-White (1999: 162)

to incorporate the dynamics of tourism and recreational activity and its effect on tourism and recreational resources has a major role to play. As Boyd and Butler (1996) observed, GIS can be used to identify suitable areas for ecotourism in Northern Ontario. The process of employing a GIS involved the inventory mapping, buffering (which is the identification of areas of human intrusion) with overlaps to map the appropriate areas for ecotourism. A very early application of GIS in the

UK by Duffield and Coppock (1975) was associated with the development of the Tourism and Recreation Information Package (TRIP) to assist with tourism planning in Scotland. What the use of GIS highlights is which agency is the most appropriate framework for tourism and recreation planning, as outlined in Chapter 9, given the decline in strategic planning in the 1980s and 1990s. What Bahaire and Elliot-White's (1999) review of GIS and its use in tourism reveals is a passivity in the geographers' impact and influence. The problem is that the technique is valuable, but few geographers are making the fundamental linkage with public sector planning agencies, political decision-makers and policy-makers (see Page *et al.* (1999) for a discussion of this issue in relation to Maori tourism in New Zealand). The 1970s and early 1980s saw recreational and tourism geographers (e.g. Coppock, Patmore and Glyptis in the UK) play a vital role in advancing the geographer's role in policy-making and planning at all levels in the public sector. Yet in the 1990s and the new millennium, this lead has not been carried on by the new generation of geographers. While there are exceptions to the rule, the discipline and sub-discipline of tourism and recreation has not made a major impact with political decision-makers. To illustrate how geographers can engage with decision-makers, policy analysts and influence planning, the following insight examines both the process and application of geographical research to a problem-solving context.

INSIGHT: Analysing the scale, extent and impact of tourist safety issues in New Zealand's adventure tourism industry (Tim Bentley and Stephen J. Page)

During the 1990s, New Zealand's adventure tourism industry expanded which comprises a range of activities outlined in Tables 10.4 and 10.5. As a result of the growth of this sector of the tourism industry, the nature of the risks and problems inherent in adventure activities increased and a series of highly publicised fatalities occurred. Despite the existence of a no-fault accident compensation scheme (ACC) within New Zealand (see Page and Meyer 1996), policy-makers engaged a tourism consultant to evaluate the scale, extent and nature of adventure tourism accidents (Page 1997b). This followed a policy document which examined the extent to which government intervention in the form of legislation or self-regulation by the industry should be pursued.

The consultancy report (Page 1997b) examined the range of available data sources which existed to review the extent of accidents (see Bentley and Page (2001) for more detail), particularly deficiencies in data sources, to assess issues of accident causation and diagnosis. The main findings of the report confirmed the earlier research by Page and Meyer (1996) that adventure tourism accidents were predominantly located in a number of locations in the North and South Islands of New Zealand. Yet the imprecise nature of the records which existed did not permit a detailed spatial and temporal analysis. The existing records also indicated that knowledge of adventure tourism accidents was both deficient and incomplete. At the same time, policy-making decisions under a government which favoured minimal state intervention, promoted self-regulation and industry codes of conduct.

As a consequence of the incomplete state of knowledge on this issue and continued support and involvement of policy-makers in this area, a concerted programme of research was undertaken. To examine the multidisciplinary nature of this research problem, a multidisciplinary research team comprising a geographer, a statistician, an ergonomist and safety management researcher was assembled to understand the wider dimensions of the adventure tourism accident problem so that the policy advice proffered was based on a holistic analysis.

The first stage of the research programme involved the identification of the factors associated with tourist accidents and highlighted the deficiencies in knowledge from the tourist operator and tourist perspective. The spatial distribution of operators to the survey (see Bentley *et al.* (2000) for more detail) confirmed the geographical pattern evident from Page and Meyer's

Table 10.6: Injuries per million participation hours groups and mean client injury-incidence rates by activity sector

Activity	Zero injuries (%)	'Low' injury group <100 IMPH [1] (%)	'Moderate' injury group 100–499 IMPH (%)	'High' injury group 500+ IMPH (%)	IMPH mean
All terrain vehicles	40	20	20	0	25
Adventure education	25	75	0	0	33
Ballooning	100	0	0	0	0
Black-water rafting	33	0	0	67	483
Bungy-jumping	20	40	40	0	117
Caving	0	0	0	100	6,636
Cycle touring	0	0	40	60	7,401
Diving	25	50	25	0	125
Eco tour	89	11	0	0	5
Fishing	0	0	50	50	3,164
Guided walking	80	13	7	0	20
Horse riding	30	30	20	20	718
Jet boating	60	20	20	0	33
Kayaking	83	13	4	0	14
Marine encounter	43	43	14	0	48
Mountain recreation	36	27	18	18	216
Quad biking	0	0	0	100	3,096
Scenic flight	89	11	0	0	7
Skydiving/parasailing	100	0	0	0	0
Wind-surfing	80	0	20	0	50
White-water rafting	30	0	40	30	537
Total % for accident groups	55	18	14	13	

Note
[1] Injuries per million participation hours.

Source: Bentley *et al.* (2000)

THE ROLE OF THE GEOGRAPHER IN THE NEW MILLENNIUM: WHITHER TOURISM AND RECREATION?

The previous Insight illustrated how tourism and recreation issues are viewed, taught and researched within and outside the discipline (see Pacione's (1999b) excellent review of applied geography for a critique of the scope and extent of the geographer's engagement with real-world issues). Yet often the perceived domain of the geographer – the quest for investigations associated with environment, man, place and space – is not necessarily viewed by other social scientists and non-academics in the same way. Indeed, a multidisciplinary approach to problems such as those in the previous Insight underpinned and informed by a spatial analytical approach often provides an understanding beyond that achieved by the geographer working in isolation. One consequence of building multidisciplinary research teams peopled by non-geographers is a growing disciplinary marginalisation by other geographers and the stated 'gatekeepers' within the subdiscipline. This can impair the wider assimilation of the research area within the subdiscipline and within the wider context of geography as a discipline. This is somewhat ironic at a time when tourism and recreation have experienced rapid growth as activities within global, national and local space economies. Further, with tourism and recreation comprising major components of the service economies of many countries, it is somewhat surprising that the contribution of geographers to understanding this phenomenon is still constrained by perceptions within the discipline of what is appropriate to study and research as serious topics of geographical investigation.

Both authors of this book are probably viewed as 'outsiders' in the wider geographical domain of consciousness that now besets the discipline, even though there is a growing strength of interest in tourism and recreation. The major 'internal' problem facing the discipline is related to the tension between positivism and humanism/the new cultural geography and army of geographers turned social theorists. This fragmentation, or internal realignment to develop careers related to the latest bandwagon (a theme the authors were frequently confronted with in the 1980s and early 1990s in relation to tourism and recreation) has certainly made a geographical education a less unified and structured process. Disciplinary fragmentation and communication within the wider domain of geography creates barriers and constraints to the wider integration of this exciting, dynamic and fast-changing area of research. The fundamental difference between the authors as 'outsiders' and the new social theorists is that the authors utilise applied geographical concepts and analysis to study tourism and recreation. One of the central messages implicit in this book is that it is inappropriate to simply decry previous paradigms as redundant and analytically bankrupt: within tourism and recreation geography, the early studies established many of the central tenets and building blocks of the subdiscipline. This is reflected in the richness of the literature reviewed throughout the book, and the value it has added to spatial analysis of tourism. The discontinuities between positivism, humanism, critical social theory and Marxism may enrich a geographical awareness of how to interpret the real world, but it does not produce a skill set among graduates which can broadly be termed spatial analysis. Indeed the emergence of GIS as the new 'saviour' of the discipline, in terms of relevance, practical application and as a recruiter of students in the information age (see Forer 1999) certainly gave the discipline a new lease of life at the end of the twentieth century. The effect has also been to create a new specialisation that is not a core element of the discipline, since it is the 'applied' domain and not the theoretically derived core of the purists.

These constant revolutions in geographical knowledge and thinking pose a central question for the student of tourism and recreation: What is the role of the geographer? Is there a role? How is that role mediated, nurtured and negotiated within the discipline, outside the discipline and how does the geographer engage political influence to ensure the profile, relevance and continued survival of the subject?

One way of engaging in this debate is through introspection – or through a refocusing of attention on the possible contribution which specific approaches to geography may make to problem-solving (i.e. the applied perspective). For example, if one returns to the previous case study of adventure tourism accidents, much of the data were derived from a positivist perspective. So what were the key findings? What patterns of accident causation occurred? What issues do the data not show? Would a series of maps have aided the analysis and interpretation of the data? What other elements of research would you have addressed? Does the absence of a theoretical framework invalidate the work since the research developed a conceptual framework to only understand the immediate problems? Or, should we be concerned at all with applied problem-solving?

These questions are a useful starting point, to assess the role of the geographer beyond the synthesising role and integrating ability to harmonise a wide range of social science perspectives. Bennett (1985) warned of the dangers of such an approach since it may contribute to a loss of identity among geographical contributions, as other disciplines and their methodologies overtake the spatial focus.

What is clear from the case study example is that the quest for relevance, understanding and explanation cannot solely be achieved from the logical positivist approach to research. It can be as blind as it is revealing: it can obscure understanding and explanation – it is only a partial focus on a problem and its solution. Thus, the non-positivist or humanist perspective needs to be used as a counterweight to expand, develop, question and reinterpret the positivist paradigm. In this context, Powell (1985) re-examines the four main concerns of the geographer which remain as relevant 16 years on. These are:

1 *Space* – what is the human meaning and experience of space?
2 *Place* – as a centre of action and intention in relation to human activity, where perception, human activity and changes in the life course of individuals and groups occur.
3 *Time* – how it is fundamental to human activity, action and the interaction with humans and their environment, in terms of resource conflict in outdoor recreation and their use of leisure time.
4 *People* – as the fundamental focus in a relevant 'human geography'.

These four central themes characterise the geographer's focus and, even though it is specific to the way the humanist views the world, place, space and time which is different to the positivist, they are key elements in establishing research questions and a particular view of the world. Therefore, in the new millennium, tourism and recreational geographers are increasingly being divided into the positivist–humanistic camps, with the ongoing quest for relevance, explanation and recognition of their respective contributions to a spatially relevant subject. At a personal level, the authors recognise the criticisms of applied geography as critiqued and debated by Pacione (1999a, b) and would proffer the following role for the geographer in a wider leisure context: to utilise an applied analytical science with its focus on space, place, time and people with a view to problem-solving, understanding and explanation. One important qualification needs to be added, however: to adopt a radical critique, such as Peet (1977a, b), will likely not contribute to a wider public-policy debate for geographers and an ability to improve the human condition, albeit from within the capitalist system. This is not to say that the authors are not empathetic with such a perspective – far from it. However, we would argue that to actually improve the human condition (and we remain such unreconstructed children of the Enlightenment that we still see this as a goal of geography and ourselves as academics), one needs to engage and communicate with stakeholders, most especially the wider public and those who are affected by our work, in a language which is broadly understandable and not the domain of arcane, inward-looking academic sub-communities.

This does not mean we seek the corporatisation of the university nor that we wish just to talk the language of industry – it means we need to argue and communicate in a manner which can be understood in the public sphere. As a consequence, geography can be relevant to society, to the needs of policy-makers, planners, communities, individuals and to the future of the planet. In the tourism–recreation context, the skills of the geographers are increasingly being harnessed, recognised and utilised within academia. Ironically, it is often when geographers drop the label of 'geography' and move to an applied academic environment such as a business school or planning department, that their skills gain a greater acceptance, legitimacy and validity with political decision-makers. Introspection, the pursuit of navel gazing and much of the discipline's detachment from the real world of politics, decision-making and problem-solving to improve the human condition has not gained the subject widespread societal support.

To the discipline's ideologues, the gatekeepers of knowledge, its leaders and scholars, tourism and recreation will continue to remain a fringe activity – amorphous and seemingly didactic in its conception of space, place and environment. Yet in a changing postmodern society where consumption is a basic element associated with the growth of tourism, leisure and recreation, a discipline which does not embrace this new domain of study is regulating itself to a 'non-relevant', esoteric and increasingly distant position. Recreational activity and tourism per se are now culturally embedded in the lifestyles of much of the world's population. This may be a function of globalisation, westernisation or other socially contingent processes; if they wish to pursue them it is a reality: it exists – and poses new research agendas and opportunities for a generation of geographers. The area is exciting, ever-changing, socially, economically, politically and environmentally challenging. Understanding the dynamics, processes, elements of change and wider meaning and value of recreation and tourism in society has opened so many avenues for spatial and multidisciplinary research. For the main discipline, these opportunities should be fostered, nurtured and encouraged since the area has the potential to engage not only students, but the wider public decision-makers and politicians. Geographers can make a difference, even if it is in a liberal market-driven economy, making gradual changes to the status quo. Geography is relevant, intellectually challenging and capable of developing the wider context of leisure studies, so that recreation and tourism are respectable areas of study within the discipline, and increasingly outside of the discipline, with geographers working in business schools, public and private sector contexts in the development of this area of study.

INSIGHT: The future – the ageing population

Currently, 11 per cent of the world's population is aged 60 and above. By 2050, one in five will be 60 years or older; and by 2150, one in three will be 60 years or older. However, the older population itself is ageing. The health revolution, which has given millions of elderly persons relatively good health well into their eighties, has also helped drive tourism's growth in general and health-related travel in particular. The population of 45- to 64-year-olds will grow nearly five times faster than the total population between 2000 and 2010; between 2010 and 2030, the population over 65 will grow eight times faster than the total population (Tarlow and Muehsam 1992). The increase in the number of very old people (aged 80+ years) between 1950 and 2050 is projected to grow by a factor of from eight to ten times on the global scale. On current trends, by 2150, about one-third of the older population will be 80 years or older. As well as a general ageing of the world's population there are also substantial regional differences in the aged population. For example, currently one in five Europeans is 60 years or older, but one in twenty Africans is 60 years or older. In some developed countries today, the proportion of older persons is close to one in five. According to the United Nations, during the first half of the next century that proportion will reach one in four and, in some countries, one in two (United Nations, Division for Social Policy and Development 1998). Given that the vast majority of the world's tourists come from the developed countries, such a demographic shift will clearly have substantial implications for the international health tourism industry. Not only may particular types of tourism continue to grow in popularity, such as cruising, but second homes and retirement homes and the provision of health facilities for retirees may become increasingly important in destination development strategies. For example, areas of the European Mediterranean and the Iberian Peninsula and the south-west United States and Florida are already subject to substantial seasonal and permanent retirement migration (e.g. Williams et al. 1997) that is designed to further healthy retirement lifestyles.

In the United States the number of persons aged 65 and above has grown faster than the general population. The Travel Industry Association of America estimated that by the year 2000 the elderly will comprise approximately a quarter of the nation's population (Tarlow and Muehsam 1992). With people living longer following retirement, the lifestyles of the mature traveller will have a substantial influence on the development and supply of tourism infrastructure. For example, *Modern Maturity*, a North American lifestyles journal for the over-fifties, surveyed its subscribers about their travel habits and preferences. Over 37 per cent travelled three to five times a year, 46 per cent preferred car travel over any other type of transportation, 42 per cent indicated that the purpose of their trip was to relax, 39 per cent preferred just their partner as a travelling companion, 46 per cent preferred to go to museums over any other tourist attraction, and 67 per cent stayed in hotels (Modern Maturity 1999: 12). This group will not only have the most available free time of any segment of the population, but it will also have the greatest amount of disposable income. Already, travellers over age 60 make up well over 30 per cent of all room nights sold within the American lodging industry. Older travellers spend more nights away from home (8.2) than do travellers under age 50 (4.8), according to the American Association of Retired Persons (AARP). The financially and physically able elderly will significantly increase the demand for leisure travel with health-related tourism being a significant component of growth in the retired travel market (Tarlow and Muehsam 1992).

TRANSFORMATIONS?

As this book has indicated, the geography of tourism and recreation, as with the discipline as a whole, has undergone considerable change since it began in the 1930s. This is to be expected, since geography, as with any discipline, adapts and reacts in relation to the society and culture within which it operates (see Chapter 1). The case for understanding the changing nature of tourism and recreation 'contextually closely parallels the case made by realists for appreciating all human activity; the operation of human agency must be analysed within the constraining and enabling conditions provided by its environment' (Johnston 1991: 280). In this sense the environment for the study of tourism and recreation must be positive given the growth of international tourism and the role it now plays within government policy-making. Given the significance of globalisation, mobility, postmodernism, post-Fordism and localisation to contemporary social theory it should also be no surprise that many human geographers and other social scientists are now discovering tourism and recreation as having some significance for social change. Indeed, the emerging paradigm of mobility which is acting to link research in tourism geography with that of migration, and is also connecting geographers, sociologists and demographers, appears to be a research direction potentially rich in possibiliities (see e.g. Urry 2000; Williams and Hall 2000; Hall and Williams 2001). However, previous work in the area is often ignored while many authors discussing contemporary tourism phenomena, particularly in an urban or rural setting, seem to think that all tourists and tourism are the same and fail to perceive the complexity of the phenomena they are investigating.

It would also be true to note that many tourism and recreation geographers find the discovery of 'their' field by social theory and cultural studies somewhat amusing given that they have been ignored for so long. Others will also find it threatening given that their own work bears all the hallmarks of traditional spatial science, excellent maps, flows and patterns but little role for more critical examination of tourism phenomena.

The geography of tourism and recreation therefore bears the hallmarks of much Anglo-North American geography in terms of the tensions that exist between the different approaches within the discipline. Such tensions, if well managed, can be extremely healthy in terms of the debate they generate and the 'freshness' of the subject matter. However, if not well managed and if external influences become too attractive, splits will occur.

Research and scholarship in the geography of tourism and recreation are now at this stage. Unless greater links are built between the subdiscipline and the discipline as a whole then, potentially, much of the field will be swallowed up by the rapidly expanding field of tourism studies which bears many of the hallmarks of being a discipline in its own right. Even if only in terms of student numbers, such a shift would have substantial implications for geography as already mentioned above.

The geography of tourism and recreation is at a crossroads. It is to be hoped that a situation will not develop where those concerned with social theory will stay in geography and those who do not will go to the business and tourism schools. An understanding of social theory by itself will not provide geography graduates with jobs. However, the integration of some of the central concerns of social theory, and the central concerns of the geographer – sites, places, landscapes, regions and national configurations, and the spatial arrangements and relationships that interconnect them – with the subject of tourism and recreation will lead to the development of a more relevant applied area of geography that can better contribute to all its stakeholders. To this end we can only reiterate the words of Gilbert White (and break the rule we tell our students of not finishing in your own words!) as a guiding light for a relevant tourism and recreation geography:

> Speaking only as one individual, I feel strongly that I should not go into research unless it promises results that would advance the aims of the people affected and unless I am prepared to take all practicable steps to help translate the results into action.
>
> (White 1972: 102)

QUESTIONS

- Is geography a relevant subject to study in the twenty-first century as a basis for understanding tourism and recreational phenomena?
- What is applied geography and how does it relate to tourism and recreation?
- How has the geographer contributed to the wider public-policy and problem-solving approach to tourism and recreation research? Has this been at the expense of academic credibility within the discipline?
- What is the role of GIS in tourism and recreational research?

READING

For a critical review of the role of geography as a discipline see:

Johnston, R.J. (1985) 'Introduction: Exploring the future of geography', in R.J. Johnston (ed.) *The Future of Geography*, London: Methuen, pp. 3–26.

Meyer-Arendt, K. (2000) 'Commentary: Tourism geography as the subject of North American Doctoral dissertations and Masters theses, 1951–98', *Tourism Geographies*, 2(2): 140–57.

On the role of applied geography and the scope/extent of the geographer's engagement with 'real-world problems' and the wider public policy arena see:

M. Pacione (ed.) (1999) *Applied Geography: Principles and Practice*, London: Routledge.
This is a very good comprehensive overview of the geographers' attempts to engage with research issues outside of academia. For more applied examples, see journals such as *Tourism Geographies, Tourism Management, Journal of Sustainable Tourism* and *Current Issues in Tourism* which contain articles where similar applied research has been conducted within a spatially analytical framework.

On the use of GIS in tourism and recreational research see:

Tarrant, M. and Cordell, H. (1999) 'Environmental justice and the spatial distribution of outdoor recreation sites: An application of geographic information systems', *Journal of Leisure Research*, 31(1): 18–34.

Taylor, P.J. (1985) 'The value of a geographical perspective', in R.J. Johnston (ed.) *The Future of Geography*, London: Methuen, pp. 92–110.

Van der Knaap, W. (1999) 'Research report: GIS-oriented analysis of tourist time–space patterns to support sustainable tourism development', *Tourism Geographies*, 1(1): 56–69.

REFERENCES

Aaker, D. and Day, G. (1986) *Marketing Research*, New York: Wiley.

Abercrombie, P. (1938) 'Geography, the basis of planning', *Geography*, 20(3): 196–200.

Ackerman, E.A. (1963) 'Where is a research frontier?', *Annals of the Association of American Geographers*, 53: 429–40.

Ackoff, R.L. (1974) *Redesigning the Future*, New York: Wiley.

Adler, S. and Brenner, J. (1992) 'Gender and space: Lesbians and gay men in the city', *International Journal of Urban and Regional Research*, l6: 24–34.

Aer Lingus (1991) *Report and Accounts for the Year Ended March 1991*, Dublin: Aer Lingus Group.

Agarwal, S. (1994) 'The resort cycle revisited: Implications for resorts', in C. Cooper and A. Lockwood (eds) *Progress in Tourism, Recreation and Hospitality Management Volume 5*, London: Belhaven Press, pp. 194–208.

Aitchison, C. (1997) 'A decade of compulsory competitive tendering in the UK sport and leisure services: Some feminist perspectives', *Leisure Studies*, 16: 85–105.

Aitchison, C. (1999) 'New cultural geographies: The spatiality of leisure, gender and sexuality', *Leisure Studies*, 18: 19–39.

Aitchison, C., Macleod, N. and Shaw, S. (2000) *Leisure and Tourism Landscapes: Social and Cultural Geographies*, London: Routledge.

Aldskogius, H. (1968) 'Modeling the evolution of settlement patterns: Two case studies of vacation house settlement', *Geografiska regionstudie*, 6, Uppsala: Geografiske institutionen.

Aldskogius, H. (1977) 'A conceptual framework and a Swedish case study of recreational behaviour and environmental cognition', *Economic Geography*, 53: 163–83.

Alexander, K. (1984) 'In search of the spirit of wilderness', *Habitat*, 12(5): 3–5.

Allen, L.R., Long, P.T., Perdue, R.R. and Kieselbach, S. (1988) 'The impact of tourism development on residents' perceptions of community life', *Journal of Travel Research*, 27(1): 16–21.

Anderson, D.H. and Brown, P.J. (1984) 'The displacement process in recreation', *Journal of Leisure Research*, 16(1): 61–73.

Anderson, J. (1971) 'Space-time budgets and activity studies in urban geography and planning', *Environment and Planning*, 3(4): 353–68.

Anderson, S., Smith, C., Kinsey, R. and Wood, J. (1990) *The Edinburgh Crime Survey: First Report*, Edinburgh: Scottish Office.

Anon. (1983) 'National Report No. 86, Ireland', *International Tourism Quarterly*, 3: 27–36.

Anon. (1989) *National Development Plan 1989–1992*, Dublin: Stationery Office.

Anon. (1994) 'Special issue on sustainable rural tourism development', *Trends*, 31(1).

Appleton, I. (1974) *Leisure Research and Policy*, Edinburgh: Scottish Academic Press.

Arbel, A. and Pizam, A. (1977) 'Some determinants of hotel location: The tourists' inclination', *Journal of Travel Research*, 15 (winter): 18–22.

Archer, B. (1973) *The Impact of Domestic Tourism*, Cardiff: University of Wales Press.

Archer, B.H. (1976) 'Uses and abuses of multipliers', in W.W. Swart and T. Var (eds) *Planning For Tourism Development: Quantitative Approaches*, New York: Praeger, pp. 115–32.

Archer, B.H. (1977a) 'The economic costs and benefits of tourism', in B.S. Duffield (ed.) *Tourism a Tool for Regional Development*, Leisure Studies Association Conference, Edinburgh, 1977, Edinburgh: Tourism and Recreation Research Unit, University of Edinburgh, pp. 5.1–5.11.

Archer, B.H. (1977b) *Tourism Multipliers: The State of the Art*, Occasional Papers in Economics, No. 11, Bangor: University of Wales Press.

Archer, B.H. (1978) 'Tourism as a development factor', *Annals of Tourism Research*, 5: 126–41.

Archer, B.H. (1982) 'The value of multipliers and their policy implications', *Tourism Management*, 3: 236–41.

Archer, B.H. (1984) 'Economic impact: Misleading multiplier', *Annals of Tourism Research*, 11: 517–18.

Archer, J. and Yarman, I. (1991) *Nature Conservation in Newham*, London Ecology Unit: Ecology Handbook 17.

Argawal, S., Ball, R., Shaw, G. and Williams, A. (2000) 'The geography of tourism production: Uneven disciplinary development', *Tourism Geographies*, 2(3): 241–63.

Argyle, M. (1996) *The Social Psychology of Leisure*, London: Penguin.

Ashworth, G.J. (1989) 'Urban tourism: An imbalance in attention', in C.P. Cooper (ed.) *Progress in Tourism, Recreation and Hospitality Management*, Vol. 1, London: Belhaven Press, pp. 33–54.

Ashworth, G.J. (1992a) 'Is there an urban tourism?', *Tourism Recreation Research*, 17(2): 3–8.

Ashworth, G.J. (1992b) 'Planning for sustainable tourism: A review article', *Town and Planning Review*, 63(3): 325–29.

Ashworth, G.J. (1999) 'Heritage tourism: A review', *Tourism Recreation Research*, 25(1): 19–29.

Ashworth, G.J. and Dietvorst, A. (eds) (1995) *Tourism and Spatial Transformations*, Wallingford: CAB International.

Ashworth, G.J. and Ennen, E. (1998) 'City centre management: Dutch and British experiences', *European Spatial Research and Policy*, 5(1): 1–15.

Ashworth, G.J. and de Haan, T.Z. (1986) 'Uses and users of the tourist–historic city', *Field Studies*, 10, Groningen: Faculty of Spatial Sciences.

Ashworth, G.J. and Tunbridge, J.E. (1990) *The Tourist–Historic City*, London: Belhaven Press.

Ashworth, G.J. and Tunbridge, J.E. (1996) *Dissonant Heritage*, Chichester: Wiley.

Ashworth, G.J. and Voogd, H. (1988) 'Marketing the city: Concepts, processes and Dutch applications', *Town Planning Review*, 59(1): 65–80.

Ashworth, G.J. and Voogd, H. (1990a) *Selling the City*, London: Belhaven Press.

Ashworth, G.J. and Voogd, H. (1990b) 'Can places be sold for tourism?', in G.J. Ashworth and B. Goodall (eds) *Marketing Tourism Places*, London: Routledge, pp. 1–16.

Ashworth, G.J. and Voogd, H. (1994) 'Marketing of tourism places: What are we doing?', in M. Uysal (ed.) *Global Tourist Behaviour*, New York: International Press, pp. 5–20.

Ashworth, G.J., White, P.E. and Winchester, H.P. (1988) 'The red light district in the West-European City: A neglected aspect of the urban landscape', *Geoforum*, 19(2): 201–12.

Attfield, R. (1983) *The Ethics of Environmental Concern*, Oxford: Blackwell.

Audit Commission (1993) *Realising the Benefits of Competition: The Client for Contracted Services*, London: HMSO.

Austin, M. (1974) 'The evaluation of urban public facility location: An alternative to cost–benefit analysis', *Geographical Analysis*, 6: 135–46.

Bagnall, U., Gillmore, D. and Phipps, J. (1978) 'The recreational use of forest land', *Irish Forestry*, 35: 19–34.

Bahaire, T. and Elliott-White, M. (1999) 'The application of geographical information systems (GIS) in sustainable tourism planning', *Journal of Sustainable Tourism*, 7(2): 159–74.

Bailey, M. (1989) 'Leisure, culture and the historian: Reviewing the first generation of leisure historiography in Britain', *Leisure Studies*, 8: 107–27.

Bailie, J.G. (1980) 'Recent international travel trends in Canada', *Canadian Geographer*, 24(1): 13–21.

Baines, G.B.K. (1987) 'Manipulation of islands and men: Sand-cay tourism in the South Pacific', in S. Britton and W.C. Clarke (eds) *Ambiguous Alternative: Tourism in Small Developing Countries*, Suva: University of the South Pacific, pp. 16–24.

Baldridge, J.V. and Burnham, R.A. (1975) 'Organizational innovation: Individual, organizational, and environmental impacts', *Administrative Science Quarterly*, 20: 165–76.

Ball, R.M. (1989) 'Some aspects of tourism, seasonality and local labour markets', *Area*, 21: 35–45.

Balmer, K. (1971) 'Urban open space and outdoor recreation', in P. Lavery (ed.) *Recreation Geography*, Newton Abbot: David and Charles, pp. 112–26.

Balmer, K. (1973) *Open Space in Liverpool*, Liverpool: Liverpool Corporation.

Bandura, A. (1977) 'Self-efficacy: Toward a unifying theory of behavioural change', *Psychological Review*, 84: 191–215.

Bannan, M., Adams, C. and Pirie, D. (2000) 'Hydrocarbon emissions from boat engines: Evidence of recreational boating impact on Loch Lomond', *Scottish Geographical Journal*, 116(3): 245–56.

Barbaza, Y. (1966) *Le paysage humain de la Costa Brava*, Paris: A. Colin.

Barber, A. (1991) *Guide to Management Plans for Parks and Open Spaces*, Reading: Institute of Leisure and Amenity Management.

Barbier, B. and Pearce, D.G. (1984) 'The geography of tourism in France: Definition, scope and themes', *GeoJournal*, 9(1): 47–53.

Baretje, R. (1982) 'Tourism's external account and the balance of payments', *Annals of Tourism Research*, 9(1): 57–67.

Barke, M. and Towner, J. (1996) 'Exploring the history of leisure and tourism in Spain', in M. Barke, J. Towner and M. Newton (eds) *Tourism in Spain: Critical Issues*, Wallingford: CAB International, pp. 189–212.

Barke, M., Towner, J. and Newton, M. (eds) (1996) *Tourism in Spain: Critical Issues*, Wallingford: CAB International.

Barnes, B. (1982) *T.S. Kuhn and Social Science*, London: Macmillan.

BarOn, R. (1984) 'Tourism terminology and standard definitions', *Tourist Review*, 39(1): 2–4.

BarOn, R. (1989) *Travel and Tourism Data: A Comprehensive Research Handbook on the World Travel Industry*, London: Euromonitor.

Baron-Yellés, N. (1999) *Le tourisme en France: territoires et stratégies*, Paris: A. Colin.

Barrett, J. (1958) *The Seaside Resort Towns of England and Wales*, unpublished Ph.D. thesis, London: University of London.

Barry, F. (1991) 'Industrialisation strategies for developing countries: Lessons from the Irish experience', *Development Policy Review*, 9: 85–98.

Barry, K. (1984) *Female Sexual Slavery*, New York: New York University Press.

Barry, K. and O'Hagan, J. (1972) 'An econometric study of British expenditure in Ireland', *Economic and Social Review*, 3: 143–61.

Baum, E.L. and Moore, E.J. (1966) 'Some economic opportunities and limitations of outdoor recreation enterprises', in G.W. Cornwall and C.J. Holcomb (eds) *Guidelines to the Planning, Developing, and Managing of Rural Recreation Enterprises*, Bulletin 301, Blacksburg: Cooperative Extension Service, Virginia Polytechnic Institute, pp. 52–64.

Baum, T. (1989a) 'Managing hotels in Ireland: Research and development for change', *International Journal of Hospitality Management*, 8: 131–44.

Baum, T. (1989b) 'Scope for the tourism industry and its employment impact in Ireland', *Service Industries Journal*, 9: 140–51.

Baum, T. (ed.) (1993) *Human Resource Issues in International Tourism*, Oxford: Butterworth Heinemann.

Becker, R.H. (1981) 'Displacement of recreational users between the Lower St. Croix and Upper Mississippi Rivers', *Journal of Environmental Management*, 13(3): 259–67.

Belford, S. (1983) 'Rural tourism', *Architects Journal*, 178: 59–71.

Bell, D. and Valentine, G. (eds) (1997) *Consuming Geographies; We Are Where We Eat*, London: Routledge.

Bell, M. (1977) 'The spatial distribution of second homes: A modified gravity model', *Journal of Leisure Research*, 9(3): 225–32.

Bella, L. (1987) *Parks for Profit*, Montreal: Harvest House.

Benington, J. and White, J. (eds) (1988) *The Future of Leisure Services*, Harlow: Longman.

Benko, G. and Strohmmayer, U. (1997) *Space and Social Theory: Interpreting Modernity and Postmodernity*, Oxford: Blackwell.

Bennett, R. (1985) 'Quantification and relevance?', in R. Johnston (ed.) *The Future of Geography*, London: Methuen, pp. 211–24.

Bennett, R. (1991) 'Rethinking London government', in K. Hoggart and D. Green (eds) *London: A New Metropolitan Geography*, London: Edward Arnold.

Bentley, T. and Page, S.J. (2001) 'Scoping the extent of tourist accidents in New Zealand', *Annals of Tourism Research*, 28(3): 705–26.

Bentley, T., Page, S.J. and Laird, I. (2000) 'Safety in New Zealand's adventure tourism industry: The client accident experience of adventure tourism operators', *Journal of Travel Medicine*, 7(5): 239–45.

Bentley, T., Page, S.J., Meyer, D. and Chalmers, D. (2001) 'The role of adventure tourism recreation injuries among visitors to New Zealand: An exploratory analysis using hospital discharge data', *Tourism Management*, 22(4): 373–81.

Bescancenot, J., Mounier, J. and Laverne, F. (1978) 'Climatological conditions for coastal tourism: A comprehensive research method', *Morois*, 99: 357–82.

Bevins, M., Brown, T., Cole, G., Hock, K. and LaPage, W. (1974) *Analysis of the Campground Market in the Northeast*, USDA, Forest Service Bulletin 679, Burlington, VT: University of Vermont Agricultural Experimental Station.

Billinge, M. (1996) 'A time and place for everything: An essay on recreation, re-creation and the Victorians', *Journal of Historical Geography*, 22(4): 443–59.

Bishop, R. and Robinson, L.S. (1998) *Night Market: Sexual Cultures and the Thai Economic Miracle*, London and New York: Routledge.

Bisset, N., Grant, A. and Adams, C. (2000) 'Long term changes in recreational craft utilisation on Loch Lomond', *Scottish Geographical Journal*, 116(3): 257–66.

Bitner, M.J. (1992) 'Servicescapes: The impact of physical surroundings on customers and employees', *Journal of Marketing*, 56(2): 57–71.

Bitner, M.J., Booms, B.H. and Tetreault, M.S. (1990) 'The service encounter: Diagnosing favourable and unfavourable incidents', *Journal of Marketing*, 54(2): 71–84.

Blackwell, J. (1970) 'Tourist traffic and the demand for accommodation: Some projections', *Economic and Social Review*, 1: 323–43.

Blake, J. (1996) 'Resolving conflict? The rural white paper, sustainability and countryside policy', *Local Environment*, 1(2), 211–18.

Blamey, R.K. (1995) *The Nature of Ecotourism*, Occasional Paper No. 21, Canberra: Bureau of Tourism Research.

Blamey, R.K. and Braithwaite, V.A. (1997) 'A social values segmentation of the potential ecotourism market', *Journal of Sustainable Tourism*, 5(1): 29–45.

Blank, U. and Petkovich, M. (1980) 'The metropolitan area: A multifaceted travel destination complex', in D. Hawkins, E. Shafer and J. Ravelstad (eds) *Tourism Planning and Development*, Washington, DC: George Washington University Press, pp. 393–405.

Blom, T. (2000) 'Morbid tourism – a postmodern market niche with an example from Althrop', *Norsk Geografisk Tidsskrift*, 54(1): 29–36.

Blowers, A. (1997) 'Environmental planning for sustainable development: The international context', in A. Blowers and B. Evans (eds) *Town Planning Into the 21st Century*, London: Routledge, pp. 34–53.

Bodewes, T. (1981) 'Development of advanced tourism studies in Holland', *Annals of Tourism Research*, 8(1): 35–51.

Boo, E. (1990) *Ecotourism: The Potentials and Pitfalls*, 2 Vols, Washington, DC: World Wildlife Fund.

Bord Fáilte (1985) *Employment in Tourism*, Dublin: Bord Fáilte.

Bord Fáilte (1986) *The Irish Hotel Industry, 1985 Manual for Inter Hotel Comparison*, Dublin: Bord Fáilte.

Bord Fáilte (1988a) *Bord Fáilte's Strategy for Growth*, Dublin: Bord Fáilte.

Bord Fáilte (1988b) *The Regional Tourism Organisations*, Dublin: Bord Fáilte.

Bord Fáilte (1989) *Tourism and the Economy*, Dublin: Bord Fáilte.

Bord Fáilte (1990a) *Economic Benefits of Tourism*, Dublin: Bord Fáilte.

Bord Fáilte (1990b) *Developing Heritage Attractions*, Dun Laoghaire Conference, Dublin: Bord Fáilte.

Bord Fáilte (1991a) *Co-Operative Marketing Guide 1992: Targeting Irish Tourism Opportunities at Home and Overseas*, Dublin: Bord Fáilte.

Bord Fáilte (1991b) *Investment Opportunities in the Irish Tourism and Leisure Industry*, Dublin: Bord Fáilte.

Bord Fáilte (1992a) *Heritage Attraction Development: A Strategy to Interpret Ireland's History and Culture for Tourism*, Dublin: Bord Fáilte.

Bord Fáilte (1992b) *Heritage and Tourism: Second Conference on the Development of Heritage Attractions in Ireland*, Dublin: Bord Fáilte.

Boschken, H. (1975) 'Second home subdivision: Market suitability for recreational and pastoral use', *Journal of Leisure Research*, 7(1): 63–72.

Bote Gomez, V. (1996) 'La investigacion turistica espanola en economia y geografia', *Estudios Turisticos*, Special Issue.

Bouquet, M. (1987) 'Bed, breakfast and an evening meal: Commensality in the nineteenth and twentieth century farm household in Hartland', in M. Bouquet and M. Winter (eds) *Who From Their Labours Rests? Conflict and Practice in Rural Tourism*, Aldershot: Avebury.

Bouquet, M. and Winter, M. (eds) (1987a) *Who From Their Labours Rests? Conflict and Practice in Rural Tourism*, Aldershot: Avebury.

Bouquet, M. and Winter, M. (1987b) 'Introduction: Tourism, politics and practice', in M. Bouquet and M. Winter (eds) *Who From Their Labours Rests? Conflict and Practice in Rural Tourism*, Aldershot: Avebury, pp. 1–8.

Bowler, I. and Strachan, A. (1976) *Parks and Gardens in Leicester*, Leicester: Recreation and Cultural Services Department, Leicester City Council.

Boyd, S. and Butler, R. (1996) 'Seeing the forest through the trees: Using GIS to identify potential ecotourism sites in Northern Ontario', in L. Harrison and W. Husbands (eds) *Practising Responsible Tourism: International Case Studies in Tourism Planning, Policy and Development*. Chichester: Wiley, pp. 380–403.

Boyden, S.V. and Harris, J.A. (1978) 'Contribution of the wilderness to health and wellbeing', in G. Mosley (ed.) *Australia's Wilderness: Conservation Progress and Plans, Proceedings of the First National Wilderness Conference*, Australian Academy of Science, Canberra, 21–23 October 1977, Hawthorn: Australian Conservation Foundation, pp. 34–7.

Boyer, M. (1996) *L'invention du tourisme*, Paris: Le Seuil.

Bracey, H. (1970) *People and the Countryside*, London: Routledge & Kegan Paul.

Bradshaw, J. (1972) 'The concept of social need', *New Society*, 30(3): 640–3.

Brady, Shipman and Martin (1991) *Wicklow Mountain's National Park Visitor Centre Environmental Impact Statement*, Dublin: Brady, Shipman and Martin.

Brady, Shipman, Martin and Hyde, N. (1972–73) *National Coastline Study*, Dublin: Bord Fáilte and Foras Forbartha.

Bramham, P. and Henry, I. (1985) 'Political ideology and leisure policy in the United Kingdom', *Leisure Studies*, 4: 1–19.

Bramwell, B. (1991) 'Sustainability and rural tourism policy in Britain', *Tourism Recreation Research*, 16(2): 49–51.

Bramwell, B. (1993) *Tourism Strategies and Rural Development*, Paris: OECD.

Bramwell, B. (1994) 'Rural tourism and sustainable rural tourism', *Journal of Sustainable Tourism*, 2: 1–6.

Bramwell, B. and Rawding, L. (1996) 'Tourism marketing images of industrial cities', *Annals of Tourism Research*, 23(2): 201–21.

Brennan, E. (ed.) (1990) *Heritage: A Visitor's Guide*, Dublin: Stationery Office.

Briggs, A. (1969) *Victorian Cities*, Middlesex: Pelham.

Briggs, D. and Tantrum, D. (1997) *Using GIS for Countryside Management: The Experience of National Parks*, Cheltenham: Countryside Commission.

Bristow, R., Leiber, S. and Fesenmaier, D. (1995) 'The compatibility of recreation activities in Illinois', *Geografiska Annaler B*, 77(1): 3–15.

British Tourist Authority (1993) *Guidelines for Tourism to Britain 1993–97*, London: British Tourist Authority.

British Travel Association and University of Keele (1967 and 1969) *Pilot National Recreation Survey*, Keele: University of Keele.

Britton, S.G. (1980a) 'A conceptual model of tourism in a peripheral economy', in *South Pacific: The Contribution of Research to Development and Planning*, NZ MAB Report No. 6, Christchurch: NZ National Commission for UNESCO/Department of Geography, pp. 1–12.

Britton, S.G. (1980b) 'The spatial organisation of tourism in a neo-colonial economy: A Fiji case study', *Pacific Viewpoint*, 21: 144–65.

Britton, S.G. (1982) 'The political economy of tourism in the Third World', *Annals of Tourism Research*, 9(3): 331–58.

Britton, S.G. (1991) 'Tourism, capital and place: Towards a critical geography of tourism', *Environment and Planning D: Society and Space*, 9: 451–78.

Brocx, M. (1994) *Visitor Perceptions and Satisfaction Study Winter 1993*, Auckland: Tourism Auckland.

Brookfield, H. (1955) 'Ireland and the Atlantic ferry', *Irish Geography*, 3: 69–78.

Brooks, S. (1993) *Public Policy in Canada*, Toronto: McClelland and Stewart.

Brougham, J.E. and Butler, R.W. (1981) 'A segmentation analysis of resident attitudes to the social impacts of tourism', *Annals of Tourism Research*, 8: 569–90.

Brown, R.M. (1935) 'The business of recreation', *Geographical Review*, 25: 467–75.

Brunt, B. (1988) *The Republic of Ireland*, London: Paul Chapman.

Bryant, C. (1989) 'Entrepreneurs in the rural environment', *Journal of Rural Studies*, 5(4): 337–48.

Buchholtz, C.W. (1983) *Rocky Mountain National Park: A History*, Boulder, CO: Colorado Associated University Press.

Buhalis, D. and Cooper, C. (1998) 'Competition or co-operation? Small and medium sized tourism enterprises at the destination', in E. Laws, B. Faulkner and G. Moscardo (eds) *Embracing and Managing Change in Tourism: International Case Studies*, London: Routledge, pp.324–46.

Bull, A. (1991) *The Economics of Travel and Tourism*, London: Pitman.

Bull, C. and Wibberley, G. (1976) *Farm Based Recreation in South-East England: Studies in Rural Land Use Report 12*, London: Wye College, University of London.

Bull, P. and Church, A. (1994) 'The hotel and catering industry of Great Britain during the 1980s: Sub-regional employment change, specialisation and dominance', in C.P. Cooper and A. Lockwood (eds) *Progress in Tourism, Recreation and Hospitality Management*, Vol. 5, Chichester: Wiley, pp. 248–69.

Bureau of Industry Economics (1991a) *Networks: A Third Form of Organisation*, Discussion Paper 14, Canberra: Bureau of Industry Economics.

Bureau of Industry Economics (1991b) 'Networks: A third form of organisation', *Bulletin of Industry Economics*, 10: 5–9.

Bureau of Land Management (1978) *Wilderness Inventory Handbook: Policy, Direction, Procedures, and Evidence for Conducting Wilderness Inventory on the Public Lands*, Washington, DC: US Department of the Interior, Bureau of Land Management.

Burgess, J., Harrison, C. and Limb, M. (1988a) 'People, parks and the urban green: A study of popular meanings and values for open spaces in the city', *Urban Studies*, 26: 455–73.

Burgess, J., Harrison, C. and Limb, M. (1988b) 'Exploring environmental values through the medium of small groups. Part one: Theory and practice', *Environmental and Planning A*, 20: 309–26.

Burgess, J., Harrison, C. and Limb, M. (1988c) 'Exploring environmental values through the medium of small groups. Part two: Illustrations of a group at work', *Environment and Planning A*, 20: 457–76.

Burkart, A. and Medlik, S. (1974) *Tourism, Past, Present and Future*, Oxford: Heinemann.

Burkart, A. and Medlik, S. (1981) *Tourism, Past Present and Future*, 2nd edn, London: Heinemann.

Burnet, L. (1963) *Villégiature et tourisme sue les côtes de France*, Paris: Hachette.

Burns, J.P.A. and Mules, T.L. (1986) 'A framework for the analysis of major special events', in J.P.A. Burns, J.H. Hatch and T.L. Mules (eds) *The Adelaide Grand Prix: The Impact of a Special Event*, Adelaide: The Centre for South Australian Economic Studies, pp. 5–38.

Burns, M., Barwell, L. and Heinecken, T. (1990) 'Analysis of critical coastal processes affecting recreation and tourism development opportunities along South-Western Cape coastline', in P. Wong (ed.) *Tourism vs Environment: The Case for Coastal Areas*, Dordrecht: Kluwer, pp. 19–32.

Burtenshaw, D., Bateman, M. and Ashworth, G.J. (1991) *The City in West Europe*, 2nd edn, Chichester: Wiley.

Burton, R. (1974) *The Recreational Carrying Capacity of the Countryside*, Occasional Publication No. 11, Keele: Keele University Library.

Burton, T. (1966) 'A day in the country – a survey of leisure activity at Box Hill in Surrey', *Chartered Surveyor*, 98(7): 378–80.

Burton, T. (1971) *Experiments in Recreation Research*, London: Allen & Unwin.

Burton, T.L. (1982) 'A framework for leisure policy research', *Leisure Studies*, 1: 323–35.

Butler, R.W. (1974) 'The social implications of tourist developments', *Annals of Tourism Research*, 2: 100–11.

Butler, R.W. (1975) 'Tourism as an agent of social change', in F. Helleiner (ed.) *Tourism as a Factor in National and Regional Development*, Occasional Papers in Geography, No. 4, Peterborough: Trent University, pp. 89–50.

Butler, R.W. (1980) 'The concept of a tourist area cycle of evolution, implications for management of resources', *Canadian Geographer*, 24(1): 5–12.

Butler, R.W. (1990) 'Alternative tourism: Pious hope or Trojan horse', *Journal of Travel Research*, 28(3): 40–5.

Butler, R.W. (1991) 'Tourism, environment, and sustainable development', *Environmental Conservation*, 18(3): 201–9.

Butler, R.W. (1992) 'Alternative tourism: The thin edge of the wedge', in V.L. Smith and W.R. Eadington (eds) *Tourism Alternatives: Potentials and Problems in the Development of Tourism*, Philadelphia: University of Pennsylvania Press, pp. 31–46.

Butler, R.W. (1998) 'Sustainable tourism – looking backwards in order to progress?', in C.M. Hall and A. Lew (eds) *Sustainable Tourism Development: A Geographical Perspective*, London: Addison Wesley Longman, pp. 25–34.

Butler, R.W. and Clark, G. (1992) 'Tourism in rural areas: Canada and the UK', in I. Bowler, C. Bryant and M. Nellis (eds) *Contemporary Rural Systems in Transition*, Volume 2: *Economy and Society*, Wallingford: CAB International.

Butler, R.W. and Hall, C.M. (1998) 'Conclusion: The sustainability of tourism and recreation in rural areas', in R. Butler, C.M. Hall and J. Jenkins (eds) *Tourism and Recreation in Rural Areas*, Chichester: Wiley, pp. 249–58.

Butler, R.W. and Hinch, T. (eds) (1996) *Tourism and Indigenous Peoples*, London: International Thomson Publishing.

Butler, R.W. and Wall, G. (1985) 'Themes in research on the evolution of tourism', *Annals of Tourism Research*, 12: 287–96.

Butler, R.W., Hall, C.M. and Jenkins, J. (eds) (1998) *Tourism and Recreation in Rural Areas*, Chichester: Wiley.

Byrne, A., Edmondson, R. and Fahy, K. (1993) 'Rural tourism and cultural identity in the West of Ireland', in B. O'Connor and M. Cronin (eds) *Tourism in Ireland: A Critical Analysis*, Cork: Cork University Press, pp. 233–57.

Caffyn, A. and Lutz, J. (1999) 'Developing the heritage tourism product in multi-ethnic cities', *Tourism Management*, 20(2): 213–21.

Calais, S.S. and Kirkpatrick, J.B. (1986) 'The impact of trampling on the natural ecosystems of the Cradle Mt. Lake St. Claire National Park', *Australian Geographer*, 17: 6–15.

Callicott, J.B. (1982) 'Traditional American Indian and Western European attitudes toward nature: An overview', *Environmental Ethics*, 4: 293–318.

Campbell, C.K. (1966) *An Approach to Recreational Geography*, B.C. Occasional Papers No. 7.

Canadian Council on Rural Development (1975) *Economic Significance of Tourism and Outdoor Recreation for Rural Development*, Working Paper, Ottawa: Canadian Council on Rural Development.

Cannon, J. (1987) 'Issues in sampling and sample design – a managerial perspective', in J.B. Ritchie and C. Goeldner (eds) *Travel, Tourism and Hospitality Research: A Handbook for Managers and Researchers*, New York: Wiley, pp. 101–16.

Carhart, A.H. (1920) 'Recreation in the forests', *American Forests*, 26: 268–72.

Carlson, A.S. (1938) 'Recreation industry of New Hampshire', *Economic Geography*, 14: 255–70.

Carlson, A.W. (1978) 'The spatial behaviour involved in honeymoons: The case of two areas in Wisconsin and North Dakota', *Journal of Popular Culture*, 11: 977–88.

Carr, N. (1999) 'A study of gender differences: Young tourist behaviour in a UK coastal resort', *Tourism Management*, 20: 223–28.

Carter, R. (1982) 'Coastal caravan sites in Northern Ireland 1960–1980', *Irish Geography*, 15: 123–6.

Carter, R. (1988) *Coastal Environments*, London: Academic Press.

Carter, R. (1990) 'Recreational use and abuse of the coastline of Florida', in P. Fabbri (ed.) *Recreational Uses of Coastal Areas*, Dordrecht: Kluwer, pp. 3–18.

Carter, R. and Parker, A. (1989a) 'Resources and management of Irish coastal waters and adjacent coasts', in R. Carter and A. Parker (eds) *Ireland: Contemporary Perspectives on a Land and its People*, London: Routledge, pp. 393–420.

Carter, R. and Parker, A. (eds) (1989b) *Ireland: Contemporary Perspectives on a Land and its People*, London: Routledge.

Carter, R., Eastwood, D. and Pollard, J. (1990) 'Man's impact on the coast of Ireland', in P. Wong (ed.) *Tourism vs Environment: The Case for Coastal Areas*, Dordrecht: Kluwer, pp. 211–25.

Cater, E.A. (1993) 'Ecotourism in the third world: Problems for sustainable development', *Tourism Management*, 14(2): 85–90.

Cater, E.A. and Lowman, G. (eds) (1994) *Ecotourism: A Sustainable Option?*, Chichester: Wiley.

Catlin, G. (1968) 'An artist proposes a National Park', in R. Nash (ed.) *The American Environment: Readings in the History of Conservation*, Reading: Addison-Wesley, pp. 5–9.

Ceballos-Lascuarain, H. (1996) *Tourism, Ecotourism and Protected Areas: The State of Nature Based Tourism Around the World and Guidelines for its Development*, Gland: IUCN.

CERT (1987a) *Management in the Hotel Industry*, Dublin: Bord Fáilte.

CERT (1987b) *Scope of the Tourism Industry in Ireland*, Dublin: CERT.

CERT (1991) *A Profile of Employment in the Tourism Industry in Ireland: non food/accommodation sectors*, Dublin: CERT.

Chadwick, G. (1971) *A Systems View of Planning*, Oxford: Pergamon Press.

Chadwick, R. (1987) 'Concepts, definitions and measures used in travel and tourism research', in J.R. Brent Ritchie and C. Goeldner (eds) *Travel, Tourism and Hospitality Research: A Handbook for Managers and Researchers*, New York: Wiley, pp. 47–62.

Chadwick, R. (1994) 'Concepts, definitions and measures used in travel and tourism research', in J.R. Brent Ritchie and C. Goeldner (eds) *Travel, Tourism and Hospitality Research: A Handbook for Managers and Researchers*, 2nd edn, New York: Wiley, pp. 65–80.

Champeaux, J.P. (1987) 'Le marché du tourisme social en Europe', *Espaces*, 86: 17–20.

Chang, T. (1998) 'Regionalism and tourism: Exploring integral links in Singapore', *Asia Pacific Viewpoint*, 39(1): 73–94.

Chang, T. and Yeoh, B. (1999) 'New Asia-Singapore: Communicating local cultures through global tourism', *Geoforum*, 30(2): 101–15.

Chang, T. C. (2000) 'Singapore's Little India: A tourist attraction in a contested landscape', *Urban Studies*, 37(2): 343–66.

Chang, T.C., Milne, S., Fallon, D. and Pohlmann, C. (1996) 'Urban heritage tourism: The global–local nexus', *Annals of Tourism Research*, 23: 1–19.

Chapin, F. (1974) *Human Activity Patterns in the City*, New York: Wiley.

Charlton, C. and Essex, S. (1996) 'The involvement of District Councils in tourism in England and Wales', *Geoforum*, 27 (2): 175–92.

Chartered Institute of Public Finance and Accountancy (1990) *Leisure and Recreation Statistics 1990–91 Estimates*, London: Chartered Institute of Public Finance and Accountancy.

Christaller, W. (1933) *Die Zentralen Orte in Söddent-schland*, Jena.

Christaller, W. (1963) 'Some considerations of tourism location in Europe: The peripheral regions – under-developed countries – recreation areas', *Regional Science Association Papers*, 12: 95–105.

Chubb, M. and Chubb, H. (1981) *One Third of Our Time? An Introduction to Recreation Behaviour and Resources*, New York: Wiley.

Church, A. (1988) 'Urban regeneration in London's Docklands: A five year policy review', *Environment and Planning C: Government and Policy*, 6: 187–208.

Church, A. (1990) 'Transport and urban regeneration in London Docklands', *Cities: The International Journal of Urban Policy and Planning*, 7(4): 289–303.

Cichetti, C. (1971) 'Some economic issues in planning urban recreation facilities', *Land Economics*, 47: 14–23.

Cicin-Sain, B. and Knecht, R.W. (1998) *Integrated Coastal and Ocean Management: Concepts and Experiences*, Washington, DC: Island Press.

Clark, J. and Crichter, C. (1985) *The Devil Makes Work: Leisure in Capitalist Britain*, Basingstoke: Macmillan.

Clark, P. (ed.) (1981) *Country Towns in Pre-industrial England*, Leicester: Leicester University Press.

Clark, R.N. and Stankey, G.H. (1979) *The Recreation Opportunity Spectrum: A Framework for Planning, Management and Research*, USDA Forest Service, General Technical Report PNW-98.

Clarke, W.C. (1991) 'Time and tourism: An ecological perspective', in M.L. Miller and J. Auyong (eds) *Proceedings of the 1990 Congress on Coastal and Marine Tourism*, Honolulu: National Coastal Research and Development Institute, pp. 387–93.

Clary, D. (1984a) 'Coastal tourism: Research methods', *Revue de Geographie de Lyon*, 59(1/2): 63–72.

Clary, D. (1984b) 'The impact of social change on a leisure region, 1960–1982: A study of Nord Pays D'Auge', in J. Long and R. Hecock (eds) *Leisure, Tourism and Social Change*, Dunfermline: Centre for Leisure Research, Dunfermline College of Physical Education, pp. 51–6.

Clary, D. (1993) *Le tourisme dans l'espace français*, Paris: Editions du CRNS.

Clawson, M. (1958) *Statistics on Outdoor Recreation*, Washington, DC: Resources for the Future.

Clawson, M. and Knetsch, J. (1966) *The Economics of Outdoor Recreation*, Baltimore, MD: Johns Hopkins University Press.

Clawson, M. and Knetsch, J. (1968) *The Economics of Outdoor Recreation*, Baltimore, MD: Johns Hopkins University Press.

Clawson, M., Held, R. and Stoddart, C. (1960) *Land for the Future*, Baltimore, MD: Johns Hopkins University Press.

Clewer, A., Pack, A. and Sinclair, M.T. (1992) 'Price competitiveness and inclusive tour holidays', in P. Johnson and B. Thomas (eds) *Choice and Demand in Tourism*, London: Mansell, pp. 123–44.

Clift, S. and Page, S.J. (eds) (1996) *Health and the International Tourist*, London: Routledge.

Cloke, P. (1992) 'The countryside', in P. Cloke (ed.) *Policy and Change in Thatcher's Britain*, Oxford: Pergamon Press, pp. 269–96.

Cloke, P. and Perkins, H. (1999) 'Cracking the canyon with the awesome foursome: Representation of adventure tourism in New Zealand', *Environment and Planning D: Society and Space*, 16: 185–218.

Clout, H.D. (1987) 'Western Europe in context', in H.D. Clout (ed.) *Regional Development in Western Europe*, 3rd edn, London: David Fulton, pp. 3–18.

Coalter, F. (1990) 'The "mixed economy" of leisure: The historical background to the development of the commercial, voluntary and public sectors of the leisure industries', in I. Henry (ed.) *Management and Planning in the Leisure Industries*, Basingstoke: Macmillan, pp. 3–32.

Coalter, F. (1993) 'Sports participation: Price or priorities?', *Leisure Studies*, 12: 171–82.

Coalter, F. (1998) 'Leisure studies, leisure policy and social citizenship: The failure of welfare or the limits of welfare?', *Leisure Studies*, 17: 21–36.

Cohen, E. (1972) 'Towards a sociology of international tourism', *Social Research*, 39: 164–82.

Cohen, E. (1974) 'Who is a tourist? A conceptual clarification', *Sociological Review*, 22: 527–55.

Cohen, E. (1979a) 'Rethinking the sociology of tourism', *Annals of Tourism Research*, 6: 18–35.

Cohen, E. (1979b) 'A phenomenology of tourist experiences', *Sociology*, 13: 179–201.

Cohen, E. (1983) 'Thai girls and farang men', *Annals of Tourism Research*, 9: 403–8.

Cole, D.N., Petersen, M.E. and Lucas, R.C. (1987) *Managing Wilderness Recreation Use: Common*

Problems and Potential Solutions, USDA Forest Service General Technical Report INT–230, Utah: Intermountain Forest and Range Experiment Station.

Colenutt, R. (1970) *An Investigation into the Factors Affecting the Pattern of Trip Generation and Route of Choice of Day Visitors to the Countryside*, Ph.D. thesis (unpublished), Bristol, University of Bristol.

Commission of the European Community (1991) *Fourth Periodic Report on the Social and Economic Situation and Development of the Regions of the Community*, Luxemburg: Commission of the European Community.

Committee of the Federal Republic of Germany for the IGU (ed.) (2000) *German Geographical Research 1996–1999: Bibliography of Publications in Geographical Series*, Trier: Dokumentationszentrum für deutsche Landeskunde, Universität Trier.

Commonwealth Department of Tourism (1993) *Rural Tourism, Tourism Discussion*, Paper No. 1, Canberra: Commonwealth Department of Tourism.

Conforti, J. (1996) 'Ghettos as tourism attractions', *Annals of Tourism Research*, 23(4): 830–42.

Connell, J. (1988) *Sovereignty and Survival: Island Microstates in the Third World*, Research Monograph No.3, Sydney: Department of Geography, University of Sydney.

Conway, H. (1991) *People's Parks: The Design and Development of Victorian Parks in Britain*, Cambridge: Cambridge University Press.

Cooke, K. (1982) 'Guidelines for socially appropriate tourism development in British Columbia', *Journal of Travel Research*, 21(1): 22–8.

Cooke, P. (ed.) (1986) *Global Restructuring, Local Responses*, London: Economic and Social Research Council.

Cooke, P. (1989) *Localities: The Changing Face of Urban Britain*, London: Unwin Hyman.

Cooper, C.E. (1947) 'Tourism', *Journal of Geography*, 46: 115–20.

Cooper, C.P. (1981) 'Spatial and temporal patterns of tourist behaviour', *Regional Studies*, 15: 359–71.

Cooper, C.P. (1987) 'The changing administration of tourism in Britain', *Area*, 19(3): 249–53.

Cooper, C.P. (1990) 'Resorts in decline: The management response', *Tourism Management*, 11: 63–7.

Cooper, C.P. (1992) 'The life cycle concept and tourism', in P. Johnson and B. Thomas (eds) *Choice and Demand in Tourism*, London: Mansell, pp.145–160.

Cooper, C.P. (1994) 'Product lifecycle', in S.F. Witt and L. Moutinho (eds) *Tourism Marketing and Management Handbook*, Englewood Cliffs, NJ: Prentice Hall, pp.145–60.

Cooper, C.P. and Jackson, S. (1989) 'Destination life cycle: The Island of Man case study', *Annals of Tourism Research*, 16(3): 377–98.

Cooper, C.P., Fletcher, J., Gilbert, D.G. and Wanhill, S. (1993) *Tourism: Principles and Practice*, London: Pitman.

Cooper, M.J. and Pigram, J.J. (1984) 'Tourism and the Australian economy', *Tourism Management*, 5(1): 2–12.

Cope, A., Doxford, D. and Probert, C. (2000). 'Monitoring visitors to UK countryside resources: The approaches of land and recreation resource management organisations to visitor monitoring', *Land Use Policy*, 17: 59–66

Coppock, J.T. (1966) 'The recreational use of land and water in rural Britain', *Tidschrift voor Economische en Sociale Geografie*, 57: 81–96.

Coppock, J.T. (1970) 'Geographers and conservation', *Area*, 2, 24–26.

Coppock, J.T. (1974) 'Geography and public policy: Challenges, opportunities and implications', *Transactions of the Institute of British Geographers*, 63: 1–16.

Coppock, J.T. (1976) 'Geography and public policy: Challenge, opportunities and implications', in J.T. Coppock and W. Sewell (eds) *Spatial Dimensions of Public Policy*, Oxford: Pergamon.

Coppock, J.T. (ed.) (1977a) *Second Homes: Curse or Blessing?*, Oxford: Pergamon Press.

Coppock, J.T. (1977b) 'Tourism as a tool for regional development', in B.S. Duffield (ed.) *Tourism: A Tool for Regional Development*, Edinburgh: Tourism and Recreation Research Unit, University of Edinburgh, pp. 1.2–1.5.

Coppock, J.T. (1980) 'The geography of leisure and recreation', in E.H. Brown (ed.) *Geography Yesterday and Tomorrow*, London: Royal Geographical Society, pp. 243–79.

Coppock, J.T. (1982) 'Geographical contributions to the study of leisure', *Leisure Studies*, 1: 1–27.

Coppock, J.T. and Duffield, B. (1975) *Outdoor Recreation in the Countryside: A Spatial Analysis*, London: Macmillan.

Coppock, J.T. and Sewell, W. (1976) *Spatial Dimensions of Public Policy*, Oxford: Pergamon.

Corbin, A. (1995) *The Lure of the Sea: The Discovery of the Seaside 1750–1840*, London: Penguin.

Corner, J. and Harvey, S. (eds) (1991) *Enterprise and Heritage: Crosscurrents of National Culture*, London and New York: Routledge.

Cornish, V. (1930) 'The claim of the coast', *Geography*, 15(5): 384–7.

Cornish, V. (1934) 'A national park at the Lands End', *Geography*, 19(4): 288–91.

Cornwall, G.W. and Holcomb, C.J. (eds) (1966) *Guidelines to the Planning, Developing, and Managing of Rural Recreation Enterprises*, Bulletin 301, Blacksburg: Cooperative Extension Service, Virginia Polytechnic Institute.

Corsi, T.M. and Harvey, M.E. (1979) 'Changes in vacation travel in response to motor fuel shortages and higher prices', *Journal of Travel Research*, 17(4): 6–11.

Cosgrove, I. and Jackson, R. (1972) *The Geography of Recreation and Leisure*, London: Hutchinson.

Council of Nature Conservation Ministers (CONCOM) Working Group on Management of National Parks (1985) *Identification and Management of Wilderness Areas in Australia*, Discussion Paper, Canberra: CONCOM.

Council of Nature Conservation Ministers (CONCOM) Working Group on Management of National Parks (1986) *Guidelines for Reservation and Management of Wilderness Areas in Australia*, Canberra: CONCOM.

Countryside Agency (2000) *The State of the Countryside 1999*, Cheltenham: The Countryside Agency.

Countryside Commission (1970) *Countryside Recreation Glossary*, London: Countryside Commission.

Countryside Commission (1974) *Advice Note on Country Parks*, Cheltenham: Countryside Commission.

Countryside Commission (1983) *A Management Plan for the Green Belt Area in Barnet and South Havering*, CCP 147, Cheltenham: Countryside Commission.

Countryside Commission (1988) *Countryside Management in the Urban Fringe*, CCP 136, Cheltenham: Countryside Commission.

Countryside Commission (1992) *Enjoying the Countryside – Policies for People*, CCP 371, Cheltenham: Countryside Commission.

Coventry, N. (1998) 'December dive', *Inside Tourism*, March: 1.

Cowie, I. (1985) 'Housing policy options in relation to the America's Cup', *Urban Policy and Research*, 3: 40–1.

Crandall, R. (1980) 'Motivations for leisure', *Journal of Leisure Research*, 12: 45–54.

Crawford, D. and Godbey, G. (1987) 'Reconceptualising barriers to family leisure', *Leisure Sciences*, 9: 119–27.

Crawford, D., Jackson, E. and Godbey, G. (1991) 'A hierarchical model of leisure constraints', *Leisure Sciences*, 13: 309–20.

Crisler, R.M. and Hunt, M.S. (1952) 'Recreation regions in Missouri', *Journal of Geography*, 51(1): 30–9.

Crompton, J.L. (1979) 'An assessment of the image of Mexico as a vacation destination', *Journal of Travel Research*, 17(fall): 18–23.

Crompton, J.L. and Richardson, S.L. (1986) 'The tourism connection where public and private leisure services merge', *Parks and Recreation*, October: 38–44, 67.

Crompton, J.L. and Van Doren, C. (1976) 'Amusement parks, theme parks, and municipal leisure services: Contrasts in adaption to cultural change', *Journal of Physical Education and Recreation*, 47: 18–22.

Cronan, W. (1990) 'Modes of prophecy and production: Placing nature in history,' *Journal of American History*, 76(4): 1122–31.

Crotty, R. (1979) 'Capitalist colonialism and peripheralisation: The Irish case', in D. Seers, B. Schaffer and M.L. Kiljunen (eds) *Under-developed Europe: Studies in Core–Periphery Relations*, Totowa, NJ: Humanities Press, pp. 225–35.

Crouch, D. (1989a) 'Patterns of cooperation in the cultures of outdoor leisure – the case of allotments', *Leisure Studies*, 8(2): 189–99.

Crouch, D. (1989b) 'The allotment, landscape and locality', *Area*, 21(3): 261–7.

Crouch, D. (1999a) 'Introduction: Encounters in leisure/tourism', in D. Crouch (ed.) *Leisure/Tourism Geographies: Practices and Geographical Knowledge*, London: Routledge, pp. 1–16.

Crouch, D. (ed.) (1999b) *Leisure/Tourism Geographies: Practices and Geographical Knowledge*, London: Routledge.

Crouch, D. (2000) 'Places around us: Embodied lay geographies in leisure and tourism', *Leisure Studies*, 19(2): 63–76.

Crouch, G. (1994) 'The study of tourism demand: A review of findings', *Journal of Travel Research*, 33(1): 2–21.

Csikszentmihalyi, M. (1975) *Beyond Boredom and Anxiety*, San Francisco, CA: Jossey Bass.

Curry, N. (1992) 'Recreation, access, amenity and conservation in the United Kingdom: The failure of integration', in I.R. Bowler, C.R. Bryant and M.D. Nellis (eds) *Contemporary Rural Systems in Transition*, Vol. 2, Wallingford: CAB, pp.141–54.

Curry, N. (1994) *Countryside Recreation: Access and Land Use Planning*, London: E&FN Spon.

Curry, N. (2000) 'Community participation in outdoor recreation and the development of Millennium Greens in England', *Leisure Studies*, 19(1): 17–35.

Cushman, G., Veal, A. and Zuzanek, J. (eds) (1996a) *World Leisure Participation: Free Time in the Global Village*, Wallingford: CAB International.

Cushman, G., Veal, A. and Zuzanek, J. (eds) (1996b) 'National participation surveys: An overview', in G. Cushman, A. Veal and J. Zuzanek (eds.) *World Leisure Participation: Free Time in the Global Village*, Wallingford: CAB International, pp. 1–15.

Cutter, S. (2000) 'President's column: Bring geography back to Harvard and Yale and . . .', *AAG Newsletter*, 35(10): 2–3.

Cybriwsky, R. (1999) 'Changing patterns of urban public space: Observations and assessments from the Tokyo and New York metropolitan areas', *Cities: The International Journal of Urban Policy and Planning*, 4: 223–31.

d'Hauteserre, A. (1996) 'A response to Dimitri Ioannides, "Strengthening the ties between tourism and economic geography: a theoretical agenda"', *Professional Geographer*, 48(2): 218–19.

Dahles, H. (1998) 'Redefining Amsterdam as a tourism destination', *Annals of Tourism Research*, 25: 55–69.

Damette, F. (1980) 'The regional framework of monopoly exploitation: new problems and trends', in J. Carney, R. Hudson and J.R. Lewis (eds) *Regions in Crisis*, London: Croom Helm.

Dann, G. (1981) 'Tourist motivation: An appraisal', *Annals of Tourism Research*, 8 (2): 187–219.

Dann, G. (1993) 'Limitations in the use of nationality and country of residence variable', in D. Pearce and R. Butler (eds) *Tourism Research: Critique and Challenges*, London: Routledge, pp. 88–112.

DART (1974) *Farm Recreation and Tourism in England and Wales*, Report to the Countryside Commission, English Tourist Board and Wales Tourist Board, Publication No. 14, CCP 83, Cheltenham: Countryside Commission.

Dasmann, R.F. (1973) *Classification and Use of Protected Natural and Cultural Areas*, IUCN Occasional Paper No.4, Morges: International Union for Conservation of Nature and Natural Resources.

Davidson, R. and Maitland, R. (1997) *Tourism Destinations*, London: Hodder & Stoughton.

Davies, E. (1971) *Farm Tourism in Cornwall and Devon – Some Economic and Physical Considerations*, Report No. 184, Exeter: Agricultural Economics Unit, University of Exeter.

Davies, E. (1987) 'Planning in the New Zealand National Parks', *New Zealand Geographer*, 43(2): 73–8.

Davis, B. (1981) *Characteristics and Influence of the Australian Conservation Movement*, unpublished Ph.D. thesis, Hobart: University of Tasmania.

Dawson, J. and Doornkamp, J. (eds) (1973) *Evaluating the Human Environment: Essays in Applied Geography*, London: Edward Arnold.

De Kadt, E. (ed.) (1979) *Tourism – Passport to Development?*, Oxford: Oxford University Press.

Deane, B. (1987) 'Tourism in Ireland: An employment growth area', *Administration*, 35: 337–49.

Dearden, P. (1993) 'Cultural aspects of tourism and sustainable development: Tourism and the hilltribes of Northern Thailand', in J.G. Nelson, R. Butler and G. Wall (eds) *Tourism and Sustainable Development: Monitoring, Planning and Managing*, Waterloo: Department of Geography, University of Waterloo.

Dearden, P. and Rollins, R. (eds) (1993) *Parks and Protected Areas in Canada: Planning and Management*, Toronto: Oxford University Press.

Deasy, G.F. (1949) 'The tourist industry in a north woods county', *Economic Geography*, 25(2): 240–59.

Deasy, G.F. and Griess, P.R. (1966) 'Impact of a tourist facility on its hinterland', *Annals of the Association of American Geographers*, 56(2): 290–306.

Debarbieux, B. (1995) *Tourisme et montagne*, Paris: Economica.

Debbage, K.G. (1990) 'Oligopoly and the resort cycle in the Bahamas', *Annals of Tourism Research*, 18(2): 251–68.

Debbage, K.G. (1991) 'Spatial behaviour in a Bahamian resort', *Annals of Tourism Research*, 18(2): 251–68.

Debbage, K.G. and Ioannides, D. (eds) (1998) *The Economic Geography of the Tourism Industry*, London: Routledge.

Deblock, A. (1986) 'Tourisme et pàche', *Espaces*, 82: 22–5.

Deegan, J. and Dineen, D. (1996) *Tourism Policy and Performance*, London: International Thomson Publishing.

Deem, R. (1986) *All Work and No Play? The Sociology of Women and Leisure*, Milton Keynes: Open University Press.

Del Casino, V. and Hanna, S. (2000) 'Representations and identities in tourism map spaces', *Progress in Human Geography*, 24(1): 23–46.

Deller, S.C, Marcouiller, D.W and Green, G.P. (1997) 'Recreational housing and local government finance', *Annals of Tourism Research*, 24(3): 687–705.

Denman, R. (1978) *Recreation and Tourism in Farms, Crofts and Estates*, Report to the Highlands and Islands Development Board and the Scottish Tourist Board, Edinburgh.

Department of Regional Economic Expansion (1972) *The Canada Land Inventory: Land Capability Classification for Outdoor Recreation*, Report No. 6, Ottawa: Queens Printer for Canada.

Department of the Environment (1990) *Tourism and the Inner City*, London: HMSO.

Department of the Environment and Ministry of Agriculture, Fisheries and Food (DoE/MAFF) (1995) *Rural England: A Nation Committed to a Living Countryside*, London: HMSO.

Department of Tourism (1993) *Rural Tourism, Tourism Discussion Paper No.1*, Canberra: Department of Tourism.

Department of Tourism and Transport (1989) *Improving the Performance of Irish Tourism: A Summary Report*, Dublin: Stationery Office.

Deprest, F. (1997) *Enquê sur le tourisme de masse: l'écologie face au territoire*, Paris: Belin.

Dernoi, L.A. (1983) 'Farm tourism in Europe', *Tourism Management*, 4(3): 155–66.

Deutsch, K. (1970) *Politics and Government: How People Decide Their Fate*. Boston, MA: Houghton Mifflin.

Dewailly, J. and Flament, E. (eds) (1993) *Géographie du tourisme et des loisirs*, Paris: SEDES.

Dickinson, G. (2000) 'The use of Loch Lomond area for recreation', *Scottish Geographical Journal*, 116(3): 231–44.

Dietvorst, A. (1993) 'Planning for outdoor recreation and tourism in The Netherlands', in H. van Lier and P. Taylor (eds) *New Challenges in Recreation and Tourism Planning*, Amsterdam: Elsevier Science.

Dietz, T. and Kwaad, F. (2000) *Dutch Geography 1996–2000*, Utrecht, NL: International Geographical Union.

Dilley, R.S. (1986) 'Tourist brochures and tourist images', *The Canadian Geographer*, 30(1): 59–65.

Dilsaver, L.M. and Tweed, W.C. (1990) *Challenge of the Big Trees: A Resource History of Sequoia and Kings Canyon National Park*s, Three Rivers: Sequoia Natural History Association.

Ding, P. and Pigram, J. (1995) 'Environmental audits: An emerging concept for sustainable tourism development', *Journal of Tourism Studies*, 2: 2–10.

Dingsdale, A. (1986) 'Ideology and leisure under socialism: The geography of second homes in Hungary', *Leisure Studies*, 5: 35–55.

Doering, T.R. (1976) 'A reexamination of the relative importance of tourism to state economies', *Journal of Travel Research*, 15(1): 13–17.

Donajgrodski, A. (ed.) (1978) *Social Control in Nineteenth Century Britain*, London: Croom Helm.

Doorne, S. (1998) *The Last Resort: A Study of Power and Participation on the Wellington Waterfront*, unpublished Ph.D. thesis, Department of Tourism and Services Management, Victoria University of Wellington.

Doornkamp, J. (1982) *Applied Geography*, Nottingham Monographs in Applied Geography No. 1, Department of Geography, University of Nottingham.

Doren, C., Priddle, G. and Lewis, J. (1979) *Land and Leisure: Concepts and Methods in Outdoor Recreation*, London: Methuen.

Douglas, N. and Douglas, N. (1996) 'Tourism in the Pacific: Historical factors', in C.M. Hall and S.J. Page (eds) *Tourism in the Pacific: Issues and Cases*, London: International Thomson Business Press, pp. 19–35.

Dower, M. (1965) *The Challenge of Leisure*, London: Civic Trust.

Dower, M. (1977) 'Planning aspects of second homes', in Coppock, J.T. (ed.) *Second Homes: Curse or Blessing*, Oxford: Pergamon Press.

Dower, M. and McCarthy, P. (1967) 'Planning for conservation and development', *Journal of the Royal Town Planning Institute*, 53(1): 99–105.

Dowling, R.K. (1993) 'Tourism planning, people and the environment in Western Australia', *Journal of Travel Research*, 31(4): 52–8.

Dowling, R.K. (1997) 'Plans for the development of regional ecotourism: Theory and practice', in C.M. Hall, J. Jenkins and G. Kearsley (eds) *Tourism Planning and Policy in Australia and New Zealand: Cases, Issues and Practice*, Sydney: Irwin Publishers, pp. 110–26.

Downs, R.M. (1970) 'Geographic space perception: Past approaches and future prospects', *Progress in Geography*, 2: 65–108.

Downs, R.M. and Stea, D. (1973) *Image and Environment*, New York: Aldine.

Doxey, G.V. (1975) 'A causation theory of visitor–resident irritants: Methodology and research inferences', in *Proceedings of the Travel Research Association 6th Annual Conference*, San Diego: Travel Research Association, pp. 195–8.

Driver, B.L. (1989) 'Recreation Opportunity Spectrum: A framework for planning, management and research', in *Proceedings of a North American Workshop on*

Visitor Management in Parks and Protected Areas, Waterloo: Tourism Research and Education Centre, University of Waterloo and Environment, Canada Park Service, pp. 127–58.

Dubaniewicz, H. (1976) 'An appraisal of the natural environment of the Ködz Region for the needs of economic development and recreation', *Geographica Polonica*, 34: 265–71.

Dubé, P. and Gordon, G. (2000) 'Capital cities: Perspectives and convergence', *Plan Canada*, 40(3): 6–7.

Duffield, B. (1984) 'The study of tourism in Britain – a geographical perspective', *GeoJournal*, 9(1): 27–35.

Duffield, B. and Coppock, J. (1975) 'The delineation of recreational landscapes: The role of computer-based information systems', *Transactions of the Institute of British Geographers*, 66(2): 141–8.

Duffield, B. and Long, J. (1981) 'Tourism in the Highlands and Islands of Scotland: Rewards and conflicts', *Annals of Tourism Research*, 8(3): 403–31.

Duffield, B. and Owen, M. (1970) *Leisure + Countryside = : A Geographical Appraisal of Countryside Recreation in Lanarkshire*, Edinburgh: University of Edinburgh.

Duffield, B. and Walker, S. (1983) *Urban Parks and Open Spaces: A Review*, Edinburgh: Tourism and Recreation Research Unit.

Dumas, D. (1982) 'Le commerce de detail dans une grande station touristique balneaire espagnole: Benidorm', *Annales de Géographie*, 506: 486–9.

Dunning, J. and McQueen, M. (1982) *Transnational Corporations in International Tourism*, New York: United Nations.

Dutton, I. and Hall, C.M. (1989) 'Making tourism sustainable: The policy/practice conundrum', in *Proceedings of the Environment Institute of Australia Second National Conference*, Melbourne: Environment Institute of Australia, pp. 196–296.

Dwyer, L. and Forsyth, P. (1996) 'Economic impacts of cruise tourism in Australia', *Journal of Tourism Studies*, 7(2): 36–43.

Dwyer, L. and Forsyth, P. (1998) 'Economic significance of cruise tourism', *Annals of Tourism Research*, 25(2): 393–415.

Dye, T. (1992) *Understanding Public Policy*, 7th edn, Englewood Cliffs, NJ: Prentice Hall.

Eagles, P. (1992) 'The travel motivations of Canadian ecotourists', *Journal of Travel Research*, 31(2): 3–7.

Eaton, B. and Holding, D. (1996) 'The evaluation of public transport alternatives to the car in British National Parks', *Journal of Transport Geography*, 4(1): 55–65.

Economist Intelligence Unit (EIU) (1991) *Ireland Country Profile*, London: Economist Intelligence Unit.

Edington, J.M. and Edington, M.A. (1986) *Ecology, Recreation and Tourism*, Cambridge: Cambridge University Press.

Edwards, J. (1987) 'The UK heritage coasts: An assessment of the ecological impacts', *Annals of Tourism Research*, 14: 71–87.

Edwards J. (1991) 'Guest–host perceptions of rural tourism in England and Portugal', in M.T. Sinclair and M.J. Stabler (eds) *The Tourism Industry: An International Analysis*, Wallingford: CAB International, pp. 143–64.

Eidsvik, H.K. (1980) 'National parks and other protected areas: Some reflections on the past and prescriptions for the future', *Environmental Conservation*, 7(3): 185–90.

Eidsvik, H.K. (1985) 'Wilderness policy – an international perspective', paper presented at the *National Wilderness Resources Conference*, Fort Collins, Colorado, July.

Eidsvik, H.K. (1987) *Categories Revision – A Review and a Proposal, Commission on National Parks and Protected Areas*, Morges: International Union for the Conservation of Nature and Natural Resources.

Eiselen, E. (1945) 'The tourist industry of a modern highway, US16 in South Dakota', *Economic Geography*, 21: 221–30.

Ellerbrook, M.J. and Hite, J.C. (1980) 'Factors affecting regional employment in tourism in the United States', *Journal of Travel Research*, 18(3): 26–32.

Elliott-White, M. and Finn, M. (1998) 'Growing in sophistication: The application of GIS in post-modern marketing', *Journal of Travel and Tourism Marketing*, 7(1): 65–84.

Elson, M. (1977) *A Review and Evaluation of Countryside Recreation Site Surveys*, Cheltenham: Countryside Commission.

Elson, M. (1979) *The Leisure Use of Green Belts and Urban Fringes*, London: Sports Council and Social Science Research Council.

Elson, M. (1986) *Green Belts: Conflict Mediation in the Urban Fringe*, London: Heinemann.

Elson, M. (1993) 'Sport and recreation in the green belt countryside', in S. Glyptis (ed.) *Leisure and the Environment: Essays in Honour of Professor J.A. Patmore*, London: Belhaven Press, pp. 131–7.

English Historic Towns Forum (1992) *Retailing in Historic Towns: Research Study 1992*, London: Donaldsons.

English Tourist Board/Employment Department (1991)

Tourism and the Environment: Maintaining the Balance, London: English Tourist Board.

Environmental Impact Services Limited (1991) *Great Blasket Island National Park Visitor Centre*, Dun Chaoirsn, Co. Kerry, Dublin: Environmental Impact Services Limited.

Enzenbacher, D.J. (1992) 'Antarctic tourism and environmental concerns', *Marine Pollution Bulletin*, 25(9–12): 258–65.

Enzenbacher, D.J. (1995) 'The regulation of Antarctic tourism', in C.M. Hall and M. Johnston (eds) *Polar Tourism: Tourism in the Arctic and Antarctic Regions*. Chichester: John Wiley & Sons, pp. 179–216.

Erkip, F. (1997) 'The distribution of urban public services: The case of parks and recreational services in Ankara', *Cities: The International Journal of Urban Policy and Planning*, 14(6): 353–61.

ESCAP (1995a) *Guidelines on Environmentally Sound Development of Coastal Tourism*, ST/ESCAP/1371, Bangkok: ESCAP.

ESCAP (1995b) *Planning Guidelines on Coastal Environmental Management*, ST/ESCAP/1316, Bangkok: ESCAP.

Escourrou, P. (1993) *Tourisme et Environnement*, Paris: SEDES.

Esser, J. and Hirsch, J. (1989) 'The crisis of fordism and the dimensions of a "post-fordist" regional and urban structure', *International Journal of Urban and Regional Research*, 13: 417–37.

Ettema, D.F. and Timmermans, H.J.P. (1997) *Activity-based Approaches to Travel Analysis*, Oxford: Pergamon Press.

Euromonitor (1992) *European Tourism Report*, London: Euromonitor.

Evans, B. (1997) 'From town planning to environmental planning', in A. Blowers and B. Evans (eds) *Town Planning Into the 21st Century*, London and New York: Routledge, pp. 1–14.

Evans, G. (1998) 'Urban leisure: Edge city and the new leisure periphery', in M. Collins and I. Cooper (eds) *Leisure Management: Issues and Applications*, Wallingford: CAB International, pp. 113–38.

Evans, N.J. (1992a) 'Advertising and farm-based accommodation: A British case study', *Tourism Management*, 13(4): 415–22.

Evans, N.J. (1992b) 'The distribution of farm-based accommodation in England and Wales', *Journal of the Royal Agricultural Society of England*, 153: 67–80.

Evans, N.J. (1992c) 'Towards an understanding of farm-based tourism in Britain', in A.W. Gilg (ed.) *Progress in Rural Policy and Planning*, Vol. 2, London: Belhaven Press.

Evans, N.J. and Ilbery, B.W. (1989) 'A conceptual framework for investigating farm-based accommodation and tourism in Britain', *Journal of Rural Studies*, 5(3): 257–66.

Evernden, N. (1992) *The Social Creation of Nature*, Baltimore, MD: Johns Hopkins University Press.

Ewert, A. and Hollenhurst, S. (1989) 'Testing the adventure model: Empirical support for a model of risk recreational participation', *Journal of Leisure Research*, 21: 124–9.

Fabbri, P. (ed.) (1990) *Recreational Use of Coastal Areas: A Research Project of the Commission on the Coastal Environment*, International Geographical Union, Dordrecht: Kluwer.

Fagence, M. (1990) 'Geographically-referenced planning strategies', *Journal of Environmental Management*, 3(1): 1–18.

Fagence, M. (1991) 'Geographic referencing of public policies in tourism', *Revue de Tourisme*, 3(3): 8–19.

Farmers Markets Ontario (2001) history http://www. fmo.reach.net/history.html

Farrell, B.H. (ed.) (1978) *The Social and Economic Impact of Tourism on Pacific Communities*, Santa Cruz: Centre for South Pacific Studies, University of California.

Faulkner, B. and Tideswell, C. (1996) 'Gold Coast resident attitudes toward tourism: The influence of involvement in tourism, residential proximity, and period of residence', in G. Prosser (ed.) *Tourism and Hospitality Research: Australian and International Perspectives*, Canberra: Bureau of Tourism Research, pp. 19–36.

Featherstone, M. (1987) 'Leisure, symbolic power and the life course', in J. Horne, D. Jary and A. Tomlinson (eds) *Sport, Leisure and Social Relations*, London: Routledge & Kegan Paul, pp. 113–38.

Fedler, A. (1987) 'Introduction: Are leisure, recreation and tourism interrelated?', *Annals of Tourism Research*, 14(3): 311–13.

Feehan, J. (ed.) (1992) *Tourism on the Farm*, Dublin: Environmental Institute, University College.

Feller, M., Hooley, D., Dreher, T., East, I. and Jung, R. (1979) *Wilderness in Victoria: An Inventory*, Monash Publications in Geography No. 21, Clayton: Department of Geography, Monash University.

Fennell, D. (1999) *Ecotourism: An Introduction*, London: Routledge.

Ferguson, M. and Munton, R. (1978) *Informal Recreation in the Urban Fringe: Provision and Management of Sites in London's Green Belt*, Working Paper No.

2, Land for Informal Recreation, London: Department of Geography, University College.

Ferguson, M. and Munton, R. (1979) 'Informal recreation sites in London's green belt', *Area*, 11: 196–205.

Ferrario, F.F. (1979a) 'The evaluation of tourist resources: An applied methodology part I', *Journal of Travel Research*, 17(3): 18–22.

Ferrario, F.F. (1979b) 'The evaluation of tourist resources: An applied methodology part II', *Journal of Travel Research*, 17(4): 24–9.

Fesenmaier, D.R. and Lieber, S.R. (1987) 'Outdoor recreation expenditure and the effects of spatial structure', *Leisure Sciences*, 9(1): 27–40.

Fianna Fail (1987) *Putting Growth Back into Tourism*, Dublin: Fianna Fail.

Filoppovich, L. (1979) 'Mapping of recreational development around a large city', *Soviet Geography*, 20: 361–9.

Fines, K. (1968) 'Landscape evaluation: A research project in East Sussex', *Regional Studies*, 2(1): 41–5.

Finn, A. and Erden, T. (1995) 'The economic impact of a mega-multi mall: Estimation issues in the case of West Edmonton Mall', *Tourism Management*, 16(5): 367–73.

Finnveden, B. (1960) 'Den dubbla bosattingen och sommermigrationen: Exempel från Hallandskustens fritidsbebyggelse', *Svensk Geografisk årsbok*, 36: 58–84.

Fisher, D., Lewis, J. and Priddle, G. (eds) (1974) *Land and Leisure: Concepts and Methods in Outdoor Recreation*, Chicago, IL: Maaroufa Press.

Fitton, M. (1976) 'The urban fringe and the less privileged', *Countryside Recreation Review*, 1: 25–34.

Fitton, M. (1979) 'Countryside recreation – the problems of opportunity', *Local Government Studies*, 5: 57–90.

Fitzpatrick, J. and Montague, M. (1989) 'Irish Republic outbound', *Travel and Tourism Analyst*, 6: 40–55.

Fletcher, J. and Snee, H.R. (1989) 'Tourism multiplier efforts', in S.F. Witt and L. Moutinho (eds) *Tourism Marketing and Management Handbook*, Hemel Hempstead: Prentice Hall, pp. 529–31.

Flognfeldt, T. (1998) 'A spectator's view of the results of the development of an Olympic host town, before and after the games', *Festival Management & Event Tourism*, 5: 93–4.

Floor, H. (1990) *Aktiviteten Systemen en Bereikboaheid*, Amsterdam: Siswo.

Floyd, M. (1998) 'Getting beyond marginality and ethnicity: The challenge for race and ethnic studies in leisure research', *Journal of Leisure Research*, 30(1): 3–22.

Foras Forbartha (1973) *Brittas Bay: A Planning and Conservation Study*, Dublin: Foras Forbartha.

Foras Forbartha (1977) *Inventory of Outstanding Landscapes in Ireland*, Dublin: Foras Forbartha.

Ford, N. and Eiser, J. (1996) 'Risk and liminality: The HIV-related socio–sexual interaction of young tourists', in S. Clift and S.J. Page (eds) *Health and the International Tourist*, London: Routledge, pp. 152–78.

Forer, P. (1999) 'Fabricating space', in R. Le Heron, L. Murphy, P. Forer and M. Goldstone (eds) *Explorations in Human Geography: Encountering Place*, Auckland: Oxford University Press, pp. 85–117.

Forer, P. and Pearce, D.G. (1984) 'Spatial patterns of package tourism in New Zealand', *New Zealand Geographer*, 40: 34–42.

Forster, J. (1964) 'The sociological consequences of tourism', *International Journal of Comparative Sociology*, 5: 217–27.

Forsyte Research (2000) 'Topline results of the 1999 Domestic Travel Study', paper presented at the NZTIA Conference, 11 August, Wellington.

Fowler, J. (1991) 'Farm house holidays in Ireland', *Tourism Recreation Research*, 16: 72–5.

Frankel, O.H. (1978) 'The value of wilderness to science', in G. Mosley (ed.) *Australia's Wilderness: Conservation Progress and Plans, Proceedings of the First National Wilderness Conference, Australian Academy of Science, Canberra, 21–23 October, 1977*, Hawthorn: Australian Conservation Foundation, pp. 101–5.

Frater, J. (1982) *Farm Tourism in England and Overseas*, Research Memorandum 93, Birmingham: Centre for Urban and Regional Studies, University of Birmingham.

Frater, J. (1983) 'Farm tourism in England', *Tourism Management*, 4(3): 167–79.

Frechtling, D. (1976) 'Proposed standard definitions and classifications for travel research', *Marketing Travel and Tourism, Seventh Annual Conference Proceedings*, Boca Raton: Travel Research Association, pp. 59–74.

Frechtling, D.C. (1976) 'Travel as an employer in the state economy', *Journal of Travel Research*, 15(4): 8–12.

Frechtling, D.C. (1987) 'Assessing the impacts of travel and tourism – introduction to travel impact estimation', in J.R.B. Ritchie and C.R. Goeldner (eds) *Travel, Tourism and Hospitality Research: A Handbook for Managers and Researchers*, New York: Wiley, pp. 325–31.

Frechtling, D.C. (1996) *Practical Tourism Forecasting*, Oxford: Butterworth Heinemann.

Freeman, T.W. (1961) *A Hundred Years of Geography*, London: Gerald Duckworth.

Fretter, A.D. (1993) 'Place marketing: A local authority perspective', in G. Kearns and C. Philo (eds) *Selling Places: The City as Cultural Capital, Past and Present*, Oxford: Pergamon Press, pp. 163–74.

Friedmann, J. (1966) *Regional Development Policy: A case study of Venezuela*, Boston, MA: MIT Press.

Friedmann, J. (1973) 'A conceptual model for the analysis of planning behaviour', in A. Faludi (ed.) *A Reader in Planning Theory*, Oxford: Pergamon Press, pp. 344–70.

Fritz, R. (1982) 'Tourism, vacation home development and residential tax burden: A case of the local finances of 240 Vermont towns', *American Journal of Economics and Sociology*, 41(4): 375–85.

Fukaz, G. (1989) 'Hungary: More work, less leisure', in A. Olszewska and K. Roberts (eds) *Leisure and Lifestyle: A Comparative Analysis of Free Time*, London: Sage, pp. 39–46.

Funk, R.W. (1959) 'The wilderness', *Journal of Biblical Literature*, 78: 205–14.

Furmidge, J. (1969) 'Planning for recreation in the countryside', *Journal of the Royal Town Planning Institute*, 55 (2): 62–7.

Furnham, A. (1984) 'Tourism and culture shock', *Annals of Tourism Research*, 11: 41–58.

Fyfe, N. and Banister, J. (1996) 'City watching: Closed circuit television surveillance in public spaces', *Area*, 28(1): 37–46.

Galatowitsch, S.M. (1990) 'Using the original land survey notes to reconstruct presettlement landscapes of the American West', *Great Basin Naturalist*, 50(2): 181–91.

Gale, F. and Jacobs, J.M. (1987) *Tourists and the National Estate Procedures to Protect Australia's Heritage*, Australian Heritage Commission Special Australian Heritage Publication Series No.6, Canberra: Australian Government Publishing Service.

Gallent, N. (1997) 'Improvement grants, second homes and planning control in England and Wales: A policy review', *Planning Practice and Research*, 12(4): 401–10.

Gannon, J. and Johnston, K. (1995) 'The global hotel industry: The emergence of continental hotel companies', *Progress in Tourism and Hospitality Research*, 1: 31–42.

Gardner, J.S. (1978) 'The meaning of wilderness: A problem of definition', *Contact – Journal of Urban and Environmental Affairs*, 10(1): 7–33.

Garner, C. (1996) 'Park life is given £50 million injection', *Independent*, 29 January.

Gartner, W.C. (1986) 'Temporal influences on image change', *Annals of Tourism Research*, 13: 635–44.

Gartner, W.C. (1987) 'Environmental impacts of recreational home developments', *Annals of Tourism Research*, 14(1): 38–57.

Gaviria, M. (1975) *Turismo de Playa en Espana*, Madrid: Edicione S. Turner.

German Federal Agency for Nature Conservation (ed.) (1997) *Biodiversity and Tourism: Conflicts on the World's Seacoasts and Strategies for Their Solution*, Berlin: Springer.

Getz, D. (1977) 'The impact of tourism on host communities: A research approach', in B.S. Duffield (ed.) *Tourism: A Tool for Regional Development*, Edinburgh: Tourism and Recreation Research Unit, University of Edinburgh, pp. 9.1–9.13.

Getz, D. (1981) 'Tourism and rural settlement policy', *Scottish Geographical Magazine*, 97 (December): 158–68.

Getz, D. (1983) 'Capacity to absorb tourism: Concepts and implications for strategic planning', *Annals of Tourism Research*, 10: 239–63.

Getz, D. (1984) 'Tourism, community organisation and the social multiplier', in J. Long and R. Hecock (eds) *Leisure, Tourism and Social Change*, Dunfermline: Centre for Leisure Research, Dunfermline College of Physical Education, pp. 85–100.

Getz, D. (1986a) 'Models in tourism planning towards integration of theory and practice', *Tourism Management*, 7(1): 21–32.

Getz, D. (1986b) 'Tourism and population change: Long term impacts of tourism in the Badenoch–Strathspey District of the Scottish Highlands', *Scottish Geographical Magazine*, 102(2): 113–26.

Getz, D. (1987) 'Tourism planning and research: Traditions, models and futures', paper presented at the *Australian Travel Research Workshop*, Bunbury, Western Australia, 5–6 November.

Getz, D. (1991a) *Festivals, Special Events, and Tourism*, New York: Van Nostrand Reinhold.

Getz, D. (1991b) 'Assessing the economic impacts of festivals and events: Research issues', *Journal of Applied Recreation Research*, 16(1): 61–77.

Getz, D. (1992) 'Tourism planning and destination life cycle', *Annals of Tourism Research*, 19: 752–70.

Getz, D. (1993a) 'Planning for tourism business districts', *Annals of Tourism Research*, 20: 583–600.

Getz, D. (1993b) 'Tourist shopping villages: Development and planning strategies', *Tourism Management*, 14(1): 15–26.

Getz, D. (1993c) 'Impacts of tourism on residents' leisure: Concepts, and a longitudinal case study of Spey Valley, Scotland', *Journal of Tourism Studies*, 4(2): 33–44.

Getz, D. (1994a) 'Students' work experiences, perceptions and attitudes towards careers in hospitality and tourism: A longitudinal case study in Spey Valley, Scotland', *International Journal of Hospitality Management*, 13(1): 25–37.

Getz, D. (1994b) 'Residents' attitudes towards tourism: A longitudinal study in Spey Valley, Scotland', *Tourism Management*, 15(4): 247–58.

Getz, D. (1997) *Event Management and Tourism*, New York: Cognizant.

Ghelardoni, P. (1990) 'Tourist planning along the coast of Aquitane, France', in P. Fabbri (ed.) *Recreational Use of Coastal Areas*, Dordrecht: Kluwer, pp. 191–8.

Gibson-Graham, J.K. (1996) *The End of Capitalism (as we knew it): A Feminist Critique of Political Economy*, Oxford: Blackwell.

Giddens, A. (1984) *The Constitution of Society: Outline of the Theory of Structuration*, Cambridge: Polity Press.

Giddens, A. (1990). 'Modernity and utopia', *New Statesmen and Society*, 2 November, pp. 20–2.

Gilbert, D. and Clark, M. (1997) 'An exploratory examination of urban tourism impact with reference to residents' attitudes in the cities of Canterbury and Guildford', *Cities: The International Journal of Urban Policy and Planning*, 14(6): 343–52.

Gilbert, D. and Joshi, I. (1992) 'Quality management and the tourism and hospitality industry', in C. Cooper and A. Lockwood (eds) *Progress in Tourism, Recreation and Hospitality Management*, Vol. 4, London: Belhaven Press, pp. 149–68.

Gilbert, E.W. (1939) 'The growth of inland and seaside health resorts in England', *Scottish Geographical Magazine*, 55: 16–35.

Gilbert, E.W. (1949) 'The growth of Brighton', *Geographical Journal*, 114: 30–52.

Gilbert, E.W (1951) 'Geography and regionalism', in G. Taylor (ed.) *Geography in the Twentieth Century*, London: Methuen.

Gilbert, E.W. (1954) *Brighton: Old Ocean's Bauble*, London, Methuen.

Gilg, A. (1985) *An Introduction to Rural Geography*, London: Edward Arnold.

Gill, A. and Williams, P.W. (1994) 'Managing growth in mountain tourism communities', *Tourism Management*, 15(3): 212–20.

Gillmore, D.A. (1985) *Economic Activities in the Republic of Ireland: A Geographical Perspective*, Dublin: Gill & Macmillan.

Girard, T.C. and Gartner, W.C. (1993) 'Second home second view: Host community perceptions', *Annals of Tourism Research*, 20(4): 685–700.

Glacken, C. (1967) *Traces on the Rhodian Shore, Nature and Culture in Western Thought from Ancient Times to the End of the Eighteenth Century*, Berkeley: University of California Press.

Glansberg, A. (1991) 'Revitalizing tourism in Northern Ireland', *Cornell Hotel and Restaurant Administration Quarterly*, 31: 28–30.

Glasson, J., Godfrey, K. and Goodey, B. with Absalom, H. and Van Der Borg, J. (1995) *Towards Visitor Impact Management: Visitor Impacts, Carrying Capacity and Management Responses in Europe's Historic Towns and Cities*, Aldershot: Avebury.

Glebe, G. (1978) 'Recent settlement desertion on the Beara and Iveragh peninsulas: A methodological approach', *Irish Geography*, 11: 171–6.

Glyptis, S. (1979) *Countryside Visitors: Site Use and Leisure Lifestyles*, unpublished Ph.D. thesis, Hull: University of Hull.

Glyptis, S. (1981a) 'Leisure life-styles', *Regional Studies*, 15: 311–26.

Glyptis, S. (1981b) 'People at play in the countryside', *Geography*, 66(4): 277–85.

Glyptis, S. (1981c) Room to relax in the countryside', *The Planner*, 67(5): 120–2.

Glyptis, S. (1989a) 'Recreational resource management', in C. Cooper (ed.) *Progress in Tourism, Recreation and Hospitality Management*, Vol. 1, London: Belhaven Press, pp. 135–53.

Glyptis, S. (1989b) *Leisure and Unemployment*, Milton Keynes: Open University Press.

Glyptis, S. (1991) *Countryside Recreation*, Harlow: Longman.

Glyptis, S. (1993) 'Leisure and the environment', in S. Glyptis (ed.) *Essays in Honour of Professor J.A. Patmore*, London: Belhaven Press, pp. 3–12.

Glyptis, S. and Chambers, D. (1982) 'No place like home', *Leisure Studies*, 1(3): 247–62.

Go, F. (1991) *Competitive Strategies for the International Hotel Industry*, Economist Intelligence Unit Special Report, London.

Go, F. and Pine, R. (1995) *Globalization Strategy in the Hotel Industry*, London: Routledge.

Godbey, G. (1976) *Recreation and Park Planning: The Exercise of Values*, Ontario: University of Waterloo.

Godfrey-Smith, W. (1979) 'The value of wilderness', *Environmental Ethics*, 1: 309–19.

Godfrey-Smith, W. (1980) 'The value of wilderness: A philosophical approach', in R.W. Robertson, P. Helman and A. Davey (eds) *Wilderness Management in Australia, Proceedings of a Symposium Held at the Canberra College of Advanced Education 19–23 July 1978*, Canberra: School of Applied Science, Canberra College of Advanced Education, pp. 56–71.

Gold, J. (1980) *An Introduction to Behavioural Geography*, Oxford: Oxford University Press.

Gold, J. and Gold, M. (1995) *Imaging Scotland: Tradition, Representation and Promotion in Scottish Tourism since 1750*, Aldershot: Ashgate.

Gold, J. and Ward, S. (eds) (1994) *Place Promotion: The Use of Publicity and Public Relations to Sell Places*, London: Belhaven Press.

Gold, S. (1973) *Urban Recreation Planning*, Philadelphia, PA: Lea & Febiger.

Gold, S. (1980) *Recreation Planning and Design*, New York: McGraw Hill.

Goodall, B. (ed.) (1989) 'Tourism accommodation: Special issue', *Built Environment*, 15(2).

Goodall, B. (1990) 'The dynamics of tourism place marketing', in G.J. Ashworth and B. Goodall (eds) *Marketing Tourism Places*, London: Routledge, pp. 259–79.

Goodall, B. and Whittow, J. (1975) 'Recreation requirements and forest opportunities', *Geographical Paper No. 378*, Reading: Department of Geography, University of Reading.

Goodenough, R. and Page, S.J. (1994) 'Evaluating the environmental impact of a major transport infrastructure project: The Channel Tunnel high speed rail link', *Applied Geography*, 14(1): 26–50.

Goodhead, T. and Johnson, D. (eds) (1996) *Coastal Recreation Management: The Sustainable Development of Maritime Leisure*, London: E&FN Spon.

Goodwin, M. (1993) 'The city as commodity: The contested spaces of urban development', in G. Kearns and C. Philo (eds) *Selling Places: The City as Cultural Capital, Past and Present*, Oxford: Pergamon Press, pp. 145–62.

Gormsen, E. (1982) 'Tourism as a development factor in tropical countries – a case study of Cancun, Mexico', *Applied Geography and Development*, 19: 46–63.

Gottmann, J. (1983) 'Capital cities', *Ekistics*, 50: 88–93.

Graber, K. (1997) 'Cities and the destination life cycle', in J.A. Mazanec (ed.) *International City Tourism: Analysis and Strategy*, London: Pinter, pp. 39–53.

Graber, L.H. (1978) *Wilderness as Sacred Space*, Monograph No. 8, Washington, DC: The Association of American Geographers.

Graburn, N.H.H. (1983) 'The anthropology of tourism', *Annals of Tourism Research*, 10: 9–33.

Graefe, A.R. (1989) 'Visitor management in Canada's national parks', in *Towards Serving Visitors and Managing Our Resources, Proceedings of A North American Workshop on Visitor Management in Parks and Protected Areas*, Waterloo: Tourism Research and Education Centre, University of Waterloo and Canada Parks Service.

Graefe, A.R. (1991) 'Visitor impact management: An integrated approach to assessing the impacts of tourism in national parks and protected areas', in A.J. Veal, P. Jonson and G. Cushman (eds) *Leisure and Tourism: Social and Environmental Change, Papers from the World Leisure and Recreation Association Congress, Sydney*, Sydney: University of Technology, pp. 74–83.

Graefe, A.R. and Vaske, J.J. (1987) 'A framework for managing quality in the tourist experience', *Annals of Tourism Research*, 14: 389–404.

Graefe, A.R., Vaske, J.J. and Kuss, F.R. (1984a) 'Social carrying capacity: An integration and synthesis of twenty years of research', *Leisure Sciences*, 6(4): 395–431.

Graefe, A.R., Vaske, J.J. and Kuss, F.R. (1984b) 'Resolving issues and remaining questions about social carrying capacity', *Leisure Sciences*, 6(4): 497–507.

Grahn, P. (1991) 'Landscaped in our minds: People's choice of recreative places in towns', *Landscape Research*, 16: 11–19.

Gramann, J.H. (1982) 'Toward a behavioural theory of crowding in outdoor recreation: An evaluation and synthesis of research', *Leisure Sciences*, 5(2): 109–26.

Grano, O. (1981) 'External influence and internal change in the development of geography', in D.R. Stoddart (ed.) *Geography, Ideology and Social Concern*, Oxford: Blackwell, pp. 17–36.

Graves, H.S. (1920) 'A crisis in national recreation', *American Forestry*, 26(July): 391–400.

Greater London Council (1968) *Surveys of the Use of Open Space*, Vol. 1, Greater London Council Research Paper 3, London: Greater London Council.

Greater London Council (1975) *Greater London Recreation Study*, London: Greater London Council.

Greater London Council (1976) *Greater London Recreation Study: Part 1, Demand*, London: Greater London Council.

Green, B. (1990) *Countryside Conservation*, London: Unwin Hyman.

Green, E., Hebron, S. and Woodward, D. (1987) *Leisure and Gender: A Study of Sheffield Women's Leisure Experiences*, Sheffield: The Sports Council/Economic and Social Research Council.

Green, E., Hebron, S. and Woodward, D. (1990) *Women's Leisure, What Leisure?*, London: Macmillan.

Green, G., Marcouiller, D., Deller, S., Erkkil, D. and Sumathi, N. (1996) 'Local dependency, land use attitudes, and economic development: Comparisons between seasonal and permanent residents', *Rural Sociology*, 61(3): 427–45.

Greenhut, M. (1956) *Plant Location in Theory and Practice*, Chapel Hill: University of North Carolina Press.

Gregory, J. (1988) *Perceptions of Open Space: A Report on Research Undertaken by the Urban Wildlife Group*, Birmingham: Urban Wildlife Trust.

Grekin, J. and Milne, S. (1996) 'Toward sustainable tourism development: The case of Pond Inlet, NWT', in R.W. Butler and T. Hinch (eds) *Tourism and Indigenous Peoples*, London: International Thomson Business Publishing, pp. 76–106.

Griffin, K. (1999) 'The inter-organisational relationships in Irish tourism', *Irish Geography*, 32(1): 57–72.

Griffith, D. and Elliot, D. (1988) *Sampling Errors on the IPS*, London: OPCS New Methodology Series.

Griffiths, T. (1991) 'History and natural history: Conservation movements in conflict', in D.J. Mulvaney (ed.) *The Humanities and the Australian Environment*, Canberra: Australian Academy of the Humanities, pp. 87–109.

Grimes, S. (1992) 'Ireland: The challenge of development in the European periphery', *Geography*, 77: 22–32.

Grinstein, A. (1955) 'Vacations: A psycho-analytic study', *International Journal of Psycho-Analysis*, 36: 177–86.

Grocott, A. (1990) 'Parks for people', *Leisure Management*, 8: 31–2.

Groome, D. and Tarrant, C. (1984) 'Countryside recreation: Achieving access for all?', *Countryside Planning Yearbook 1984*: 77–98.

Groundwork Foundation (1986) *Putting Wasteland to Good Use*, Birmingham: Groundwork Foundation.

Gunn, C. (1972) *Vacationscape: Designing Tourist Regions*, Austin: University of Texas.

Gunn, C. (1988) *Tourism Planning*, 2nd edn, London: Taylor & Francis.

Guo, L., Wu, B., Liu, F. and Fau, Y. (2000) 'Study on the tourist resources classification system and types evaluation in China', *Acta Geographica Sinica*, 55(3): 294–301.

Guthrie, H.W. (1961) 'Demand for goods and services in a world market', *Regional Science Association Papers*, 7: 159–75.

Guy, B.S. and Curtis, W.W. (1986) 'Consumer learning or retail environment: A tourism and travel approach', Conference paper presented at the American Academy of Marketing Conference, Tourism Services Marketing: Advances in Theory and Practice, Cleveland: American Academy of Marketing Conference, Cleveland University.

Haggett, P. (1979) *Geography: A Modern Synthesis*, New York: Harper & Row.

Haggett, P. (1986) 'Geography', in R.J. Johnston, D. Gregory and D.M. Smith (eds) *The Dictionary of Human Geography*, Oxford: Blackwell, pp. 175–8.

Haines, A.L. (1977) *The Yellowstone Story*, 2 vols, Yellowstone National Park: Yellowstone Library and Museum Association/Colorado Associated University Press.

Haley, A. (1979) 'Municipal recreation and park standards in the United States: Central cities and suburbs', *Leisure Sciences*, 2: 277–91.

Halkett, I. (1978) 'The recreational use of private gardens', *Journal of Leisure Research*, 10(1): 13–20.

Hall, C.M. (1985) 'Outdoor recreation and national identity: A comparative study of Australia and Canada', *Journal of Canadian Culture*, 2(2): 25–39.

Hall, C.M. (1987) 'Wilderness inventories in Australia', in A. Conacher (ed.) *Readings in Australian Geography, Proceedings of the 21st Institute of Australian Geographers' Conference*, Perth, 10–18 May 1986, Nedlands: Department of Geography, University of Western Australia, pp. 466–76.

Hall, C.M. (1989) 'The definition and analysis of hallmark tourist events', *GeoJournal*, 19(3): 263–8.

Hall, C.M. (1990) 'From cottage to condominium: Recreation, tourism and regional development in northern New South Wales', in D.J. Walmesley (ed.) *Change and Adjustment in Northern New South Wales: Department of Geography and Planning*, Armidale University of New England, pp. 85–99.

Hall, C.M. (1992a) *Wasteland to World Heritage: Preserving Australia's Wilderness*, Carlton: Melbourne University Press.

Hall, C.M. (1992b) *Hallmark Events: Impacts, Management and Planning*, London: Belhaven Press.

Hall, C.M. (1994) *Tourism and Politics: Policy, Power and Place*, London: John Wiley.

Hall, C.M. (1995) *Introduction to Tourism in Australia*, 2nd edn, South Melbourne: Longman Australia.

Hall, C.M. (1996a) 'Tourism and the Maori of Aoteroa/New Zealand', in R.W. Butler and T. Hinch (eds) *Tourism and Indigenous Peoples*, London: International Thomson Business Publishing, pp. 155–70.

Hall, C.M. (1996b) 'Wine tourism in New Zealand', in *Proceedings of Tourism Down Under II: A Tourism Research Conference*, Dunedin: University of Otago, pp.109–19.

Hall, C.M. (1997a) *Tourism in the Pacific: Development, Impacts and Markets*, 2nd edn, South Melbourne: Addison Wesley Longman.

Hall, C.M. (1997b) 'Geography, marketing and the selling of places', *Journal of Travel and Tourism Marketing*, 6(3/4): 61–84.

Hall, C.M. (1998) *Introduction to Tourism: Development, Dimensions and Issues*, 3rd edn, South Melbourne: Addison Wesley Longman.

Hall, C.M. (1999) 'Rethinking collaboration and partnership: A public policy perspective', *Journal of Sustainable Tourism*, 7(3/4): 274–89.

Hall, C.M. (2000a) *Tourism Planning: Policies, Processes and Relationships*, Harlow: Prentice Hall.

Hall, C.M. (2000b) 'Tourism and the establishment of national parks in Australia', in R. Butler and S. Boyd (eds) *Tourism and National Parks*, Chichester: John Wiley, pp. 29–38.

Hall, C.M. (2000c) 'Tourism, national parks and aboriginal populations', in R. Butler and S. Boyd (eds) *Tourism and National Parks*, Chichester: John Wiley, pp. 57–71.

Hall, C.M. (2001) 'Territorial economic integration and globalisation', in C. Cooper and S. Wahab (eds) *Tourism in the Age of Globalisation*, London: Routledge, pp. 22–44.

Hall, C.M. and Hodges, J. (1996) 'The party's great, but what about the hangover?: The housing and social impacts of mega-events with special reference to the Sydney 2000 Olympics', *Festival Management and Event Tourism*, 4(1/2): 13–20.

Hall, C.M. and Jenkins, J. (1995) *Tourism and Public Policy*, London: Routledge.

Hall, C.M. and Jenkins, J. (1998) 'The policy dimensions of rural tourism and recreation', in R. Butler, C.M. Hall and J. Jenkins (eds) *Tourism and Recreation in Rural Areas*, Chichester: Wiley, pp. 19–42.

Hall, C.M. and Johnston, M. (eds) (1995) *Polar Tourism: Tourism in the Arctic and Antarctic Regions*, Chichester: Wiley.

Hall, C.M. and Kearsley, G.W. (2002) *Tourism in Transition: New Zealand's Changing Tourism Environments, Strucutres and Markets*, Melbourne: Oxford University Press.

Hall, C.M. and Lew, A.A. (eds) (1998) *Sustainable Tourism Development: Geographical Perspectives*, Harlow: Addison Wesley Longman.

Hall, C.M. and McArthur, S. (1994) 'Commercial whitewater rafting in Australia', in D. Mercer (ed.) *New Viewpoints in Australian Outdoor Recreation Research and Planning*, Williamstown: Hepper Marriot and Associates Publishers, pp. 109–18.

Hall, C.M. and McArthur, S. (eds) (1996) *Heritage Management in Australia and New Zealand: The Human Dimension*, Sydney: Oxford University Press.

Hall, C.M. and McArthur, S. (1998) *Integrated Heritage Management*, London: The Stationery Office.

Hall, C.M. and Macionis, N. (1998) Wine tourism in Australia and New Zealand', in R.W. Butler, C.M. Hall and J.M. Jenkins (eds) *Tourism and Recreation in Rural Areas*, Chichester: John Wiley & Sons, pp. 267–98.

Hall, C.M. and Mark, S.R. (1985) *Saving All the Pieces: Wilderness and Inventory and Prospect in Western Australia, A Working Paper*, Nedlands: Department of Geography, University of Western Australia.

Hall, C.M. and Mitchell, R. (2002) 'The changing nature of the relationship between cuisine and tourism in Australia and New Zealand: from fusion cuisine to food networks', in A-M. Hjalager and G. Richards (eds) *Tourism and Gastronomy*, London: Routledge.

Hall, C.M. and Page, S.J. (eds) (1996) *Tourism in the Pacific: Cases and Issues*, London: International Thomson Business Publishing.

Hall, C.M. and Page, S.J. (eds) (2000) *Tourism in South and South-East Asia: Cases and Issues*, Oxford: Butterworth Heinemann.

Hall, C.M. and Selwood, H.J. (1987) 'Cup gained, paradise lost? A case study of the 1987 America's Cup as a hallmark event', in *Proceedings of the New Zealand Geography Society Conference*, Palmerston North: Department of Geography, Massey University.

Hall, C.M. and Williams, A.M. (eds) (2001) *Tourism and Migration*, Dordrecht: Kluwer.

Hall, C.M., Jenkins, J.M. and Kearsley, G. (eds) (1997) *Tourism Planning and Policy in Australia and New Zealand: Cases and Issues*, Sydney: Irwin Publishers.

Hall, C.M., Johnson, G. and Mitchell, R. (2000) 'Wine tourism and regional development', in C.M. Hall, E. Sharples, B. Cambourne and N. Macionis (eds) *Wine Tourism Around the World: Development, Management and Markets*, Oxford: Butterworth Heinemann.

Hall, C.M., Selwood, H.J. and McKewon, E. (1995) 'Hedonists, ladies and larrikins: Crime, prostitution and the 1987 America's Cup', *Visions in Leisure and Business*, 14(3): 28–51.

Hall, C.M., Cambourne, B., Macionis, N. and Johnson, G. (1997/1998) 'Wine tourism and network development in Australia and New Zealand: Review, establishment and prospects', *International Journal of Wine Marketing*, 9(2/3): 5–31.

Hall, C.M., Sharples, E., Cambourne, C. and Macionis, N. (eds) (2000) *Wine Tourism Around the World: Development, Management and Markets*, Oxford: Butterworth Heinemann.

Hall, D.R. (ed.) (1991) *Tourism and Economic Development in Eastern Europe and the Soviet Union*, London: Belhaven Press.

Hall, D.R. and O'Hanlon, L. (eds) (1998) *Rural Tourism Management: Sustainable Options*, Proceedings of an International Conference, 9–12 September, Scottish Agricultural College Auchincruive, Ayr.

Hall, J.M. (1972) 'Leisure motoring in Great Britain: Patterns and policies', *Geographica Polonica*, 24: 211–25.

Hall, J.M. (1974) 'The capacity to absorb tourists', *Built Environment*, 3: 392–7.

Hall, P. (1982a) *Urban and Regional Planning*, 2nd edn, Harmondsworth: Penguin.

Hall, P. (1982b) *Great Planning Disasters*, Harmondsworth: Penguin.

Hall, P. (1992) *Urban and Regional Planning*, 3rd edn London: Routledge.

Hall, P. (2000) 'The changing role of capital cities', *Plan Canada*, 40(3): 8–12.

Halseth, G. and Rosenberg, M.W. (1995) 'Cottagers in the urban field', *Professional Geographer*, 47: 148–59.

Hamilton-Smith, E. (1980) 'Wilderness: Experience or land use', in R.W. Robertson, P. Helman and A. Davey (eds) *Wilderness Management in Australia, Proceedings of a Symposium Held at the Canberra College of Advanced Education 19–23 July 1978*, Canberra: School of Applied Science, Canberra College of Advanced Education, pp. 72–81.

Harmston, F.K. (1980) 'A case study of secondary impacts comparing through and vacationing travelers', *Journal of Travel Research*, 18(3): 33–6.

Harris, C.C., McLaughlin, W.J. and Ham, S.H. (1987) 'Integration of recreation and tourism in Idaho', *Annals of Tourism Research*, 14(3): 405–19.

Harrison, C. (1980–81) 'Recovery of lowland grassland and heathland in Southern England from disturbance by trampling', *Biological Conservation*, 19: 119–30.

Harrison, C. (1981) *Preliminary Results of a Survey of Site Use in the South London Green Belt*, Working Paper No. 9, Land for Informal Recreation, London: Department of Geography, University College.

Harrison, C. (1983) 'Countryside recreation and London's urban fringe', *Transactions of the Institute of British Geographers*, 8: 295–313.

Harrison, C. (1991) *Countryside Recreation in a Changing Society*, London: TML Partnership.

Hart, W. (1966) *A Systems Approach to Park Planning*, Morges: International Union for the Conservation of Nature.

Hartmann, R. (1984) 'Tourism, seasonality and social change', in J. Long and R. Hecock (eds) *Leisure, Tourism and Social Change*, Dunfermline: Centre for Leisure Research, Dunfermline College of Physical Education, pp. 101–12.

Harvey, D. (1974) 'What kind of geography, for what kind of public policy', *Transactions of the Institute of British Geographers*, 63: 18–24.

Harvey, D. (1987) 'Flexible accumulation through urbanisation', *Antipode*, 19: 260–86.

Harvey, D. (1988) 'Voodoo cities', *New Statesman and Society*, 30 September, pp. 33–5.

Harvey, D. (1989a) 'From managerialism to entrepreneurialism: The transformation in urban governance in late capitalism', *Geografiska Annaler*, 71B: 3–17.

Harvey, D. (1989b) *The Condition of Postmodernity: An Enquiry into the Origins of Cultural Change*, Oxford: Blackwell.

Harvey, D. (1990) 'Between space and time: Reflection on the geographic information', *Annals Association of American Geographers*, 80: 418–34.

Harvey, D. (1993) 'From space to place and back again: Reflections on the condition of postmodernity', in J. Bird, B. Curtis, T. Putnam, G. Robertson and L. Tickner (eds) *Mapping the Futures: Local Cultures, Global Change*, London: Routledge, pp. 3–29.

Harwood, C. and Kirkpatrick, J.B. (1980) *Forestry and Wilderness in the South West*, rev. edn, Hobart: Tasmanian Conservation Trust.

Haughton, G. and Hunter, C. (1994) *Sustainable Cities*, London: Jessica Kingsley.

Havighurst, R. and Feigenbaum, K. (1959) 'Leisure and lifestyle', *American Journal of Sociology*, 64: 396–405.

Hawes, M. (1981) 'In search of wilderness that speaks to the heart', *Habitat*, 9(6): 3.

Hawes, M. and Heatley, D. (1985) *Wilderness Assessment and Management, A Discussion Paper*, Hobart: The Wilderness Society.

Hawkins, J.P. and Roberts, C.M. (1994) 'The growth of coastal tourism in the Red Sea: Present and future effects on coral reefs', *Ambio*, 23(8): 503–8.

Haynes, R. (1980) *Geographical Images and Mental Maps*, London: Macmillan.

Haywood, K.M. (1986) 'Can the resort–area life cycle be made operational?', *Tourism Management*, 7: 154–67.

Haywood, K.M. and Muller, T.E. (1988) 'The urban tourist experience: Evaluating satisfaction', *Hospitality Education and Research Journal*: 453–9.

Healey, P. (1997) *Collaborative Planning: Shaping Places in Fragmented Societies*, Basingstoke: Macmillan Press.

Heath, E. and Wall, G. (1992) *Marketing Tourism Destinations: A Strategic Planning Approach*, Chichester: Wiley.

Heclo, H. (1978) 'Issue networks and the executive establishment', in A. King (ed.) *Annual Review of Energy*, Vol.4, Palo Alto: Annual Reviews Inc.

Heeley, J. (1981) 'Planning for tourism in Britain', *Town Planning Review*, 52: 61–79.

Helber, L.E. (1988) 'The roles of government in planning in tourism with special regard for the cultural and environmental impact of tourism', in D. McSwan (ed.) *The Roles of Government in the Development of Tourism as an Economic Resource*, Seminar Series No.1, Townsville: Centre for Studies in Travel and Tourism, James Cook University, pp. 17–23.

Helburn, N. (1977) 'The wilderness continuum', *Professional Geographer*, 29: 337–47.

Helman, P.H. (1979) *Wild and Scenic Rivers: A Preliminary Study of New South Wales*, Occasional Paper No. 2, Sydney: New South Wales National Parks and Wildlife Service.

Helman, P.H., Jones, A.D., Pigram, J.J.J. and Smith, J.M.B. (1976) *Wilderness in Australia: Eastern New South Wales and South-East Queensland*, Armidale: Department of Geography, University of New England.

Hendee, J.C., Stankey, G.H. and Lucas, R.C. (1978) *Wilderness Management*, Miscellaneous Publication No. 1365, Washington, DC: US Department of Agriculture, Forest Service.

Henderson, K. (1997) 'A critique of constraints theory: A response', *Journal of Leisure Research*, 29(4): 453–7.

Hendry, L., Shucksmith, J., Love, J. and Glendinning, A. (1993) *Young People's Leisure and Lifestyles*, London: Routledge.

Heneghan, P. (1976) 'The changing role of Bord Fáilte 1960–1975', *Administration*, 24: 394–406.

Henning, D.H. (1971) 'The ecology of the political/administrative process for wilderness classification', *Natural Resources Journal*, 11: 69–75.

Henning, D.H. (1974) *Environmental Policy and Administration*, New York: American Elsevier Publishing Company.

Henning, D.H. (1987) 'Wilderness politics: Public participation and values', *Environmental Management*, 11(3): 283–93.

Henry, I. (1988) 'Alternative futures for the public leisure service', in J. Benington and J. White (eds) *The Future of Leisure Services*, Harlow: Longman, pp. 207–44.

Henry, I. (ed.) (1990) *Management and Planning in the Leisure Industries*, Basingstoke: Macmillan.

Henry, I. and Spink, J. (1990) 'Planning for leisure: The commercial and public sectors', in I. Henry (ed.) *Management and Planning in the Leisure Industries*, Basingstoke: Macmillan, pp.33–69.

Herbert, D.T. (1987) 'Exploring the work–leisure relationship: an empirical study of south Wales', *Leisure Studies*, 6: 147–65.

Herbert, D.T. (1988) 'Work and leisure: exploring a relationship', *Area*, 20 (3): 241–52.

Herbertson, A.J. (1905) 'The major natural regions', *Geographical Journal*, 25: 300–10.

Higgott, R. (1999) 'The political economy of globalisation in East Asia: The salience of "region building"', in K. Olds, P. Dicken, P.F. Kelly, L. Kong and H.W. Yeung (eds) *Globalisation and the Asia-Pacific: Contested Territories*, Warwickshire Studies in Globalisation Series, London: Routledge, pp. 91–106.

Higham, J.E.S. (1996) *Wilderness Perceptions of International Visitors to New Zealand: The Perceptual Approach to the Management of International Tourists Visiting Wilderness Areas within New Zealand's Conservation Estate*, unpublished Ph.D. thesis, Dunedin: Centre for Tourism, University of Otago.

Higham, J.E.S. (1997) 'Visitors to New Zealand's back-country conservation estate', in C.M. Hall, J. Jenkins and G. Kearsley (eds) *Tourism Planning and Policy in Australia and New Zealand*, Sydney: Irwin Publishers, pp. 75–86.

Higham, J.E.S. and Kearsley, G.W. (1994) 'Wilderness perception and its implications for the management of the impacts of international tourism on natural areas in New Zealand', in C. Ryan (ed.) *Tourism Down-under: A Tourism Research Conference*, 6–9 December, Palmerston North: Department of Management Systems, Massey University, pp. 505–29.

Hillman, M. and Whalley, A. (1977) *Fair Play for All: A Study of Access to Sport and Informed Recreation*, London: Political and Economic Planning Broadsheet No. 571.

Hinch, T.D. (1990) 'A spatial analysis of tourist accommodation in Ontario: 1974–1988', *Journal of Applied Recreation Research*, 15(4): 239–64.

Hinch, T.D. (1996) 'Urban tourism: Perspectives on sustainability', *Journal of Sustainable Tourism*, 4(2): 95–110.

Hockin, R., Goodall, B. and Whitlow, J. (1978) 'The site requirements and planning of outdoor recreation activities', *Geographical Paper No. 54*, Reading: University of Reading.

Hoggart, K. (1988) 'Not a definition of rural', *Area*, 20: 35–40.

Hoggart, K. (1990) 'Let's do away with rural', *Journal of Rural Studies*, 6: 245–57.

Hoggart, K. and Green D. (eds) (1991) *London: A New Metropolitan Geography*, London: Edward Arnold.

Holden, A. (2000) *Environment and Tourism*, London: Routledge.

Hollis, G.E. and Burgess, J.A. (1977) 'Personal London: Students perceive the urban scene', *Geographical Magazine*, 50(3): 155–61.

Hooper-Greenhill, E. (1992) *Museums and the Shaping of Knowledge*, London: Routledge.

Hopley, D., van Woesik, R., Hoyal, D.C.J.D., Rasmussen, C.E. and Steven, A.D.L. (1993) *Sedimentation Resulting From Road Development, Cape Tribulation Area*, Great Barrier Reef Marine Park Authority Technical Memorandum 24, Townsville: Great Barrier Reef Marine Park Authority.

Horne, J. (1998) 'Understanding leisure time and leisure space in contemporary Japanese society', *Leisure Studies*, 17: 37–52.

Horwath and Horwath (1986) *London's Tourism Accommodation in the 1990s*, London: Horwath and Horwath.

Hötelling, H. (1929) 'Stability in competition', *Economic Journal*, 39: 41–57.

Houghton Evans, W. and Miles, J. (1970) 'Environmental capacity in rural recreation areas', *Journal of the Royal Town Planning Institute*, 56(10): 423–27.

Houinen, G.(1995) 'Heritage issues in urban tourism: An assessment of new trends in Lancaster County', *Tourism Management*, 16(5): 381–8.

Hoyle, B.S. and Pinder, D. (eds) (1992) *European Port Cities in Transition*, London: Belhaven Press.

Hoyles, M. (1994) *Lost Connections and New Directions*, Working Paper No. 6, London: Comedia & Demos.

Hudman, L. (1978) 'Tourist impacts: The need for regional planning', *Annals of Tourism Research*, 9: 563–83.

Hudson, B. (1996) 'Paradise lost: A planner's view of Jamaican tourist development', *Caribbean Quarterly*, 42(4): 22–31.

Hudson, K. (1987) *Museums of Influence*, Cambridge: Cambridge University Press.

Hudson, P. (1990a) 'Stresses in small towns in northwestern Australia: The impact of tourism and development', paper presented at the 24th Institute of Australian Geographers Conference, University of New England, Armidale, September.

Hudson, P. (1990b) 'Structural changes in three small north-western Australian communities: The relationship between development and local quality of life', Paper presented at the Annual Conference of Regional Science Association, Australian and New Zealand section, Perth, December.

Hudson, R. and Townsend, A. (1992) 'Tourism employment and policy choices for local government', in P. Johnson and B. Thomas (eds) *Perspectives on Tourism Policy*, London: Mansell, pp. 49–68.

Hughes, H.L. (1984) 'Government support for tourism in the UK: A different perspective', *Tourism Management*, 5(1): 13–19.

Hughes, J.D. (1978) *In the House of Stone and Light: A Human History of the Grand Canyon*, Grand Canyon: Grand Canyon Natural History Association.

Hull, J. (1998) 'How sustainable is ecotourism in Costa Rica?' in C.M. Hall and A.A. Lew (eds) *Sustainable Tourism Development: Geographical Perspectives*, Harlow: Addison Wesley Longman, pp. 107–18.

Human Rights Watch (1999) *Trafficking*, http://www.hrw.org/about/projects/traffcamp/intro.html

Hummelbrunner, R. and Miglbauer, E. (1994) 'Tourism promotion and potential in peripheral areas: The Austrian case', *Journal of Sustainable Tourism*, 2: 41–50.

Hurst, F. (1987) 'Enroute surveys', in J.B. Ritchie and C. Goeldner (eds) *Travel Tourism and Hospitality Research: A Handbook for Managers and Researchers*, 1st edn, New York: John Wiley & Sons, pp. 401–16.

Huxley, T. (1970) *Footpaths in the Countryside*, Edinburgh: Countryside Commission for Scotland.

Ilbery, B. (1991) 'Farm diversification as an adjustment strategy on the urban fringe of the West Midlands', *Journal of Rural Studies*, 7(3): 2–18.

Ilbery, B. and Kneafsey, M. (2000a) 'Registering regional specialty food and drink products in the United Kingdom: the case of PDOs and PGIs', *Area*, 32(3): 317–25.

Ilbery, B. and Kneafsey, M. (2000b) 'Producer constructions of quality in regional speciality food production: A case study from South West England', *Journal of Rural Studies*, 16: 217–30.

Ilbery, B., Bowler, I., Clark, G., Crockett, A. and Shaw, A. (1998) 'Farm-based tourism as an alternative farm enterprise. A case study from the Northern Pennines, England', *Regional Studies*, 32(4): 355–64.

Industry Commission (1995) *Tourism Accommodation and Training*, Melbourne; Industry Commission.

Inskeep, E. (1991) *Tourism Planning: An Integrated and Sustainable Development Approach*, New York: Van Nostrand Reinhold.

Inskeep, E. (1994) *National and Regional Tourism Planning*, London: Routledge.

International Association of Antarctica Tour Operators (IAATO) (1993a) *Guidelines of Conduct for Antarctica Tour Operators as of November 1993*, Kent: IAATO.

International Association of Antarctica Tour Operators (IAATO) (1993b) *Guidelines of Conduct for Antarctica Visitors as of November 1993*, Kent: IAATO.

International Union for the Conservation of Nature and Natural Resources (IUCN) (1978) *Categories, Objectives and Criteria for Protected Areas, A Final Report Prepared by Committee on Criteria and Nomenclature Commission on National Parks and Protected Areas (CNPPA)*, Morges: International Union for Conservation of Nature and Natural Resources.

International Union of Tourism Organisations (IUOTO) (1974) 'The role of the state in tourism', *Annals of Tourism Research*, 1(3): 66–72.

Ioannides, D. (1992) 'Tourism development agents: The Cypriot resort cycle', *Annals of Tourism Research*, 19: 711–31.

Ioannides, D. (1995) 'Strengthening the ties between tourism and economic geography: A theoretical agenda', *Professional Geographer*, 47(1): 49–60.

Ioannides, D. (1996) 'Tourism and economic geography nexus: A response to Anne-Marie d'Hauteserre', *Professional Geographer*, 48(2): 219–21.

Isard, W. (1956) *Location and Space Economy*, Massachusetts: Massachusetts Institute of Technology Press.

Iso-Ahola, S. (1980) *The Social Psychology of Leisure and Recreation*, Springfield, IL: C. Thomas.

Jaakson, R. (1986) 'Second-home domestic tourism', *Annals of Tourism Research*, 13: 367–91.

Jackson, E. (1988) 'Leisure constraints: A survey of past research', *Leisure Sciences*, 10: 203–15.

Jackson, E. (1990) 'Variations in the desire to begin a leisure activity: Evidence of antecedent constraints', *Journal of Leisure Research*, 22: 55–70.

Jackson, E. (1994) 'Geographical aspects of constraints on leisure', *The Canadian Geographer*, 38: 110–21.

Jackson, E., Crawford, D. and Godbey, G. (1993) 'Negotiation of leisure constraints', *Leisure Sciences*, 15(1): 1–11.

Jackson, P. and Smith, S.J. (1984) *Exploring Social Geography*, London: Allen & Unwin.

Jacob, G. and Schreyer, R. (1980) 'Conflict in outdoor recreation: A theoretical perspective', *Journal of Leisure Research*, 12(4): 368–80.

Jacobs, C. (1973) *Farms and Tourism in Upland Denbighshire*, Tourism and Recreation Report 4, Denbighshire County Council.

Jacobs, M. (1991) *The Green Economy*, London: Pluto Press.

Jafari, J. and Aaser, D. (1988) 'Tourism as the subject of doctoral dissertations', *Annals of Tourism Research*, 15: 407–29.

Jamal, T.B. and Getz, D. (1995) 'Collaboration theory and community tourism planning', *Annals of Tourism Reseach*, 22: 186–204.

James, P.E. (1972) *All Possible Worlds: A History Of Geographical Ideas*, 1st edn, Indianapolis: The Odyssey Press.

Janiskee, R. and Mitchell, L. (1989), 'Applied recreation geography', in M. Kenzer (ed.) *Applied Geography Issues, Questions and Concerns*, Dordrecht: Kluwer Academic Publishers, pp. 151–64.

Jansen-Verbeke, M. (1986) 'Inner-city tourism: Resources, tourists and promoters', *Annals of Tourism Research*, 13(1): 79–100.

Jansen-Verbeke, M. (1988) *Leisure, Recreation and Tourism in Inner Cities. Explorative Case Studies*, Amsterdam l Nijmegen: Netherlands Geographical Studies 58.

Jansen-Verbeke, M. (1989) 'Inner cities and urban tourism in the Netherlands: New challenges for local authorities', in P. Bramham, I. Henry, H. Mommass and H. van der Poel (eds) *Leisure and Urban Processes: Critical Studies of Leisure Policy in Western European Cities*, London: Routledge, pp. 233–53.

Jansen-Verbeke, M., (1990) 'Leisure and shopping – tourism product mix', in G.J. Ashworth and B. Goodall (eds) *Marketing Tourism Places*, London: Routledge, pp. 128–37.

Jansen-Verbeke, M. (1991) 'Leisure shopping: A magic concept for the tourism industry', *Tourism Management*, 12 (1): 9–14.

Jansen-Verbeke, M. (1992) 'Urban recreation and tourism: Physical planning issues', *Tourism Recreation Research*, 17(2): 33–45.

Jansen-Verbeke, M. (1995) 'Urban tourism and city trips', *Annals of Tourism Research*, 22(3): 699–700.

Jansen-Verbeke, M. and Ashworth G.J. (1990) 'Environmental integration of recreation and tourism', *Annals of Tourism Research*, 17(4): 618–22.

Jansen-Verbeke, M. and Dietvorst, A. (1987) 'Leisure, recreation and tourism: A geographic view on integration', *Annals of Tourism Research*, 14: 361–75.

Jansen-Verbeke, M. and Rekom, J. (1996) 'Scanning museum visitors: Urban tourism marketing', *Annals of Tourism Research*, 23(2): 364–75.

Jeans, D. (1990) 'Beach resort morphology in England and Australia: A review and extension', in P. Fabbri (ed.) *Recreational Use of Coastal Areas*, Dordrecht: Kluwer, pp. 277–85.

Jenkins, C. and Henry, B. (1982) 'Government involvement in tourism in developing countries', *Annals of Tourism Research*, 9(4): 499–521.

Jenkins, J. (1993) 'Tourism policy in rural New South Wales – policy and research priorities', *GeoJournal*, 29(3): 281–90.

Jenkins, J. (1997) 'The role of the Commonwealth Government in rural tourism and regional development in Australia', in C.M. Hall, J. Jenkins and G. Kearsley (eds) *Tourism Planning and Policy in Australia and New Zealand: Cases, Issues and Practice*, Sydney: Irwin Publishers, pp. 181–91.

Jenkins, J. and Pigram, J. (1994) 'Rural recreation and tourism: Policy and planning', in D. Mercer (ed.) *New Viewpoints in Australian Outdoor Recreation Research and Planning*, Williamstown: Hepper Marriott & Associates, pp. 119–28.

Jenkins, J. and Prin, E. (1998) 'Rural landholder attitudes: The case of public recreational access to 'private' lands', in R. Butler, C.M. Hall and J. Jenkins (eds) *Tourism and Recreation in Rural Areas*, Chichester: Wiley, pp. 179–96.

Jenkins, J. and Walmesley, D.J. (1993) 'Mental maps of tourists: A study of Coffs Harbour, New South Wales', *GeoJournal*, 29(3): 233–41.

Jenkins, J., Hall, C.M. and Troughton, M. (1998) 'The restructuring of rural economies: Rural tourism and recreation as a government response', in R. Butler, C.M. Hall and J. Jenkins (eds) *Tourism and Recreation in Rural Areas*, Chichester: Wiley, pp. 43–68.

Jenkins, R.L. (1978) 'Family vacation decision-making', *Journal of Travel Research*, 16(spring): 2–7.

Jenkins, W.I. (1978) *Policy Analysis: A Political and Organizational Perspective*, New York: St Martin's Press.

Jessop, B. (1999) 'Reflections on globalisation and its (il)logic(s)', in K. Olds, P. Dicken, P.F. Kelly, L. Kong and H.W. Yeung (eds) *Globalisation and the Asia-Pacific: Contested Territories*, Warwickshire Studies in Globalisation Series, London: Routledge, pp.19–38.

Johnson, C., Bowker, J., English, D. and Worthen, D. (1998) 'Wildland recreation in the rural South: An examination of marginality and ethnic theory', *Journal of Leisure Research*, 30(1): 101–20.

Johnson, D., Snepenger, J. and Akis, S. (1994) 'Residents' perceptions of tourism development', *Annals of Tourism Research*, 21(3): 629–42.

Johnson, J.W. (1987) 'Republic of Ireland', in H.D. Clout (ed.) *Regional Development in Western Europe*, 3rd edn, London: David Fulton, pp. 285–306.

Johnston, R.J. (1983a) 'On geography and the history of geography', *History of Geography Newsletter*, 3: 1–7.

Johnston, R.J. (1983b) 'Resource analysis, resource management and the integration of human and physical geography', *Progress in Physical Geography*, 7: 127–46.

Johnston, R.J. (1985a) 'Introduction: Exploring the future of geography', in R.J. Johnston (ed.) *The Future of Geography*, London: Methuen, pp. 3–26.

Johnston, R.J. (1985b) 'To the ends of the earth', in R. Johnston (ed.) *The Future of Geography*, London: Methuen, pp. 326–38.

Johnston, R.J. (1986) 'Applied geography', in R.J. Johnston, D. Gregory and D.M. Smith (eds) The Dictionary of Human Geography, Oxford: Blackwell, pp. 17–20.

Johnston, R.J. (1991) Geography and Geographers: Anglo-American Human Geography Since 1945, 4th edn, London: Edward Arnold.

Johnston, R.J., Gregory, D. and Smith, D.M. (eds) (1986) The Dictionary of Human Geography, 2nd edn, Oxford: Blackwell.

Johnston, R.J., Gregory, D. and Smith, D.M. (eds) (1994) The Dictionary of Human Geography, 4th edn, Oxford: Blackwell.

Johnston, S. (1985) 'The beauty and significance of wild places', Habitat, 13(1), February, 27–8.

Jones Lang Wooten (1989) Retail, Leisure and Tourism, London: English Tourist Board.

Jones, A.D. (1978) 'Measuring our wilderness', Habitat, 6(2): 16–19.

Jones, D.R.W. (1986) 'Prostitution and tourism', in J.S. Marsh (ed.) Canadian Studies of Parks, Recreation and Tourism in Foreign Lands, Occasional Paper 11, Peterborough: Department of Geography, Trent University, pp. 241–8.

Jones, S.B. (1933) 'Mining tourist towns in the Canadian Rockies', Economic Geography, 9: 368–78.

Jones, T. (1994) 'Theme park development in Japan', in C. Cooper and A. Lockwood (eds) Progress in Tourism, Recreation and Hospitality Management, Vol. 6, Chichester: Wiley, pp. 111–25.

Jordan, J.W. (1980) 'The summer people and the natives: Some effects of tourism in a Vermont vacation village', Annals of Tourism Research, 7(1): 34–55.

Judd, D. (1995) 'Promoting tourism in US cities', Tourism Management, 16(3): 175–87.

Jung, B. (1994) 'For what leisure? The role of culture and recreation in post-communist Poland', Leisure Studies, 13(4): 262–76.

Jung, B. (1996) 'Poland', in G. Cushman, A. Veal and J. Zuzanek (eds) World Leisure Participation Free Time in the Global Village, Wallingford: CAB International, pp. 183–99.

Kabanoff, B. (1982) 'Occupational and sex differences in leisure needs and leisure satisfaction', Journal of Occupational Behaviour, 3: 233–45.

Kaltenborn, B.P. (1997) 'Recreation homes in natural settings: Factors affecting place attachment', Norsk Geografisk Tidsskrift, 51: 187–98.

Kaltenborn, B.P. (1998) 'The alternate home: Models of recreation home use', Norsk Geografisk Tidsskrift, 52: 121–34.

Kassem, M. (1987) Marketing of Tourism: An Investigation of the Application of Marketing Concepts and Practices in Promoting Egypt as a Tourist Destination in Britain and Ireland, unpublished Ph.D. thesis, University of Strathclyde.

Kay, R. and Alder, J. (1999) Coastal Planning and Management, London: E&FN Spon.

Kay, T. and Jackson, G. (1991) 'Leisure despite constraint: The impact of leisure constraints on leisure participation', Journal of Leisure Research, 23: 301–13.

Keage, P.L. and Dingwall, P.R. (1993) 'A conservation strategy for the Australian Antarctic Territory', Polar Record, 29(170): 242–4.

Keane, E.F. (1972) Irish Tourism: Industry in Strategic Change, Dublin: Bord Fáilte.

Keane, M.J. and Quinn, J. (1990) Rural Development and Rural Tourism, Galway: SSRC, University College.

Keane, M.J., Briassoulis, H. and van der Stratten, J. (1992) 'Rural tourism and rural development', in H. Briassoulis and J. van der Stratten (eds) Tourism and the Environment: Regional, Economic and Policy Issues, Environment and Assessment, Vol. 2, Dordrecht: Kluwer Academic Publishers, pp. 43–56.

Kearney, B., Boyle, G. and Walsh, J. (1994) EU Leader and Initiative in Ireland: Evaluation and Recommendations, Department of Agriculture, Food and Forestry, Dublin: Commission of the European Communities.

Kearns, G. and Philo, C. (eds) (1993) Selling Places: The City as Cultural Capital, Past and Present, Oxford: Pergamon Press.

Kearsley, G.W. (1990) 'Tourism development and the user's perceptions of wilderness in Southern New Zealand', Australian Geographer, 21(2): 127–40.

Kearsley, G.W. (1997) 'Managing the consequences of over-use by tourists of New Zealand's conservation estate', in C.M. Hall, J. Jenkins and G. Kearsley (eds) Tourism Planning and Policy in Australia and New Zealand, Sydney: Irwin Publishers, pp. 87–98.

Kearsley, G.W., Hall, C.M. and Jenkins, J. (1997) 'Tourism planning and policy in natural areas: Introductory comments', in C.M. Hall, J. Jenkins and G. Kearsley (eds) Tourism Planning and Policy in Australia and New Zealand, Sydney: Irwin Publishers, pp. 66–86.

Keeble, D., Owens, P. and Thompson, C. (1982) 'Regional accessibility and economic potential in the European Community', Regional Studies, 16: 419–32.

Keller, C.P. (1984) 'Centre–periphery tourism development and control', in J. Long and R. Hecock (eds) *Leisure, Tourism and Social Change*, Dunfermline: Centre for Leisure Research, Dunfermline College of Physical Education, pp. 77–84.

Kelletat, D. (1993) 'Coastal geomorphology and tourism on the German North Sea coast', in P. Wong (ed.) *Tourism vs Environment: The Case for Coastal Areas*, Dordrecht: Kluwer Academic, pp. 139–66.

Kelly, J. (1982) *Leisure*, Englewood Cliffs, NJ: Prentice Hall.

Kelly, P.F. and Olds, K. (1999) 'Questions in a crisis: The contested meanings of globalisation in the Asia-Pacific', in K. Olds, P. Dicken, P.F. Kelly, L. Kong and H.W. Yeung (eds) *Globalisation and the Asia-Pacific: Contested Territories*, Warwickshire Studies in Globalisation Series, London: Routledge, pp. 1–15.

Ken, S. and Rapoport, R. (1975) *Beyond Palpable Mass Demand – Leisure Provision and Human Demands: The Life Cycle Approach*, paper presented to Planning and Transport Research and Computation (International) Company Ltd, Summer Annual Meeting.

Kent, W.E., Meyer, R.A. and Reddam, T.M. (1987) 'Reassessing wholesaler marketing strategies: The role of travel research', *Journal of Travel Research*, 25(3): 31–3.

Kenzer, M. (ed.) (1989) *Applied Geography Issues, Questions and Concerns*, Dordrecht: Kluwer Academic.

Keogh, B. (1984) 'The measurement of spatial variations in tourist activity', *Annals of Tourism Research*, 11: 267–82.

Keown, C. (1989) 'A model of tourists' propensity to buy: The case of Japanese visitors to Hawaii', *Journal of Travel Research*, winter: 31–4.

Khan, N. (1997) 'Leisure and recreation among women of selected hill-farming families in Bangladesh', *Journal of Leisure Research*, 29(1): 5–20.

Killan, G. (1993) *Protected Places: A History of Ontario's Provincial Parks System*, Toronto: Dundurn Press.

Kim, K. (2000) 'Topics of human geography', in W. Yu and I. Son (eds) *Korean Geography and Geographers*, Seoul: Hanul Publishing, pp.195–265.

Kim, S. and Kim, J. (1996) 'Overview of coastal and marine tourism in Korea', *Journal of Tourism Studies*, 7(2): 46–53.

King, R. (1995) 'Tourism, labour and international migration', in A. Montanari and A.M. Williams (eds) *European Tourism: Regions, Spaces and Restructuring*, Chichester: Wiley, pp.177–90.

King, R., Warnes, A.M. and Williams A.M. (1998) 'International retirement migration in Europe', *International Journal of Population Geography*, 4(2): 91–112.

Kinnaird, V. and Hall, D. (eds) (1994) *Tourism: A Gender Analysis*, Chichester: Wiley.

Kirkby, S. (1996) 'Recreation and the quality of Spanish coastal waters', in M. Barke, J. Towner and M. Newton (eds) *Tourism in Spain: Critical Issues*, Wallingford: CAB International, pp. 189–212.

Kirkpatrick, J.B. (1980) 'Hydro-Electric development and wilderness: Report to the Department of the Environment', attachment to *Department of the Environment (Tas.), Assessment of the HEC Report on the Lower Gordon River Development Stage Two*, Hobart: Department of the Environment.

Kirkpatrick, J.B. and Haney, R.A. (1980) 'The quantification of developmental wilderness loss: The case of forestry in Tasmania', *Search*, 11(10): 331–5.

Kissling, C. (1989) 'International tourism and civil aviation in the South Pacific: Issues and innovations', *GeoJournal*, 19(3): 309–16.

Kline, M.B. (1970) *Beyond the Land Itself: Views of Nature in Canada and the United States*, Cambridge, MA: Harvard University Press.

Kliskey, A.D. and Kearsley, G.W. (1993) 'Mapping multiple perceptions of wilderness in southern New Zealand', *Applied Geography*, 13: 203–23.

Knafou, R. (1978) *Les stations de sports d'hiver des Alpes françaises. L'améagement de la montagne à la françaises*, Paris: Masson.

Knafou, R. (2000) Tourismes en France: Vivre de la diversité, in Union Géographique Internationale Comité National Français de Géographie, *Historiens & Geographes: Vivre en France dans la diversité*, Paris: Union Géographique Internationale Comité National Français de Géographie, pp. 367–84.

Knafou, R., Bruston, M., Deprest, F., Duhamel, P., Gay, J. and Sacareau, I. (1997) 'Une approache géographique du tourisme', *L'Espace géographique*, 3: 193–204.

Kneafsey, M. (1998) 'Tourism and place identity: A case study in rural Ireland', *Irish Geography*, 31(2): 111–23.

Knetsch, J. (1969) 'Assessing the demand for outdoor recreation', *Journal of Leisure Research*, 1(2): 85.

Konrad, V.A. (1982) 'Historical artifacts as recreational resources', in G. Wall and J. Marsh (eds) *Recreational Land Use*, Ottawa: Carleton University Press, pp. 393–416.

Koskela, H. and Pain, R. (2000) 'Revisiting fear and place: Women's fear of attack and the built environment', *Geoforum*, 31: 269–80.

Kosters, M.J. (1984) 'The deficiencies of tourism social science without political science: Comment on Richter', *Annals of Tourism Research*, 11: 609–13.

Kraas, F. and Taubmann, W. (eds) (2000) *German Geographical Research on East and Southeast Asia*, Sankt Augustin: Asgard-Verlag.

Kretchmann, J. and Eagles, P. (1990) 'An analysis of the motives of ecotourists in comparison to the general Canadian population', *Society and Leisure*, 13(2): 499–507.

Kreutzwiser, R. (1989) 'Supply', in G. Wall (ed.) *Outdoor Recreation in Canada*, Toronto: Wiley, pp. 21–41.

Kuji, T. (1991) 'The political economy of golf', *AMPO, Japan-Asia Quarterly Review*, 22(4): 47–54.

Kwiatkowska, A. (1999) 'Nomadic-symbolic and settle-consumer leisure practices in Poland', in D. Crouch (ed.) *Leisure/Tourism Geographies: Practices and Geographical Knowledge*, London: Routledge, pp. 126–36.

Lane, B. (1994) 'What is rural tourism?', *Journal of Sustainable Tourism*, 2: 7–21.

Lang, R. (1988) 'Planning for integrated development', in F.W. Dykeman (ed.) *Integrated Rural Planning and Development*, Sackville: Mount Allison University, pp. 81–104.

Lashley, C. (2000) 'Towards theoretical understanding', in C. Lashley and A. Morrison (eds) *In Search of Hospitality: Theoretical Perspectives and Debates*, Oxford: Butterworth Heinemann, pp. 1–17.

Latham, J. (1989) 'The statistical measurement of tourism', in C.P. Cooper (ed.) *Progress in Tourism, Recreation and Hospitality Management*, Vol. 1, London: Belhaven Press, pp. 57–76.

Lavery, P. (1971a) 'The demand for recreation', in P. Lavery (ed.) *Recreational Geography*, Newton Abbot: David and Charles, pp. 21–50.

Lavery, P. (1971b) 'Resorts and recreation', in P. Lavery (ed.) *Recreational Geography*, Newton Abbot: David and Charles, pp. 167–98.

Lavery, P. (ed.) (1971c) *Recreational Geography*, Newton Abbott: David and Charles.

Lavery, P. (1975) 'The demand for leisure: a review of studies', *Town Planning Review*: 185–200.

Law, C.M. (1988) 'Conference and exhibition tourism', *Built Environment*, 13(2): 85–92.

Law, C.M. (1992) 'Urban tourism and its contribution to economic regeneration', *Urban Studies*, 29(3/4): 599–618.

Law, C.M. (1993) *Urban Tourism: Attracting Visitors to Large Cities*, London: Mansell.

Law, C.M. (ed.) (1996) *Tourism in Major Cities*, London: International Thomson Business Publishing.

Law, S. (1967) 'Planning for outdoor recreation', *Journal of the Town Planning Institute*, 53: 383–6.

Lawton, G. and Page, S.J. (1997a) 'Evaluating travel agents' provision of health advice to tourists', *Tourism Management*, 18(2): 89–104.

Lawton, G. and Page, S.J. (1997b) 'Health advice to the travellers to the Pacific Islands: Whose responsibility?', in M. Oppermann (ed.) *Pacific Rim Tourism*, Wallingford: CAB International, pp. 184–95.

Lawton, G., Page, S. and Hall, C.M. (1996) 'The provision of health advice to tourists', paper presented at the International Geographical Union Conference, The Hague, August.

Lawton, R. (1978), 'Population and society 1730–1900', in R. Dodgson and R. Butlin (eds) *An Historical Geography of England and Wales*, London: Academic Press, pp. 291–366.

Lazzarotti, O. (1995) *Les loisirs à la conquête des espaces périurbains*, Paris: L'Harmattan.

Lea, J. (1988) *Tourism and Development in the Third World*, London: Routledge.

Lee, H. (2000) 'Applied geography', in W. Yu and I. Son (eds) *Korean Geography and Geographers*, Seoul: Hanul Publishing, pp.340–82.

Lee, R.G. (1977) 'Alone with others: The paradox of privacy in the wilderness', *Leisure Services*, 1: 3–19.

Leiper, N. (1984) 'Tourism and leisure: The significance of tourism in the leisure spectrum', *Proceedings of the 12th New Zealand Geography Conference*, New Zealand Geographical Society, Christchurch, pp. 249–53.

Leiper, N. (1989) *Tourism and Tourism Systems*, Occasional Paper No.1, Palmerston North: Department of Management Systems, Massey University.

Leiper, N. (1990) *Tourism Systems: An Interdisciplinary Perspective*, Palmerston North, New Zealand: Department of Management Systems Occasional Paper 2, Massey University.

Lenĉlek, L. and Bosker, G. (1999) *The Beach: The History of Paradise on Earth*. London: Pimlico.

Leopold, A. (1921) 'The wilderness and its place in forest recreational policy', *Journal of Forestry*, 19(7): 718–21.

Leopold, A. (1925) 'Wilderness as a form of land use', *Journal of Land and Public Utility Economics*, 1(4): 398–404.

Lesslie, R.G. (1991) 'Wilderness survey and evaluation in Australia', *Australian Geographer*, 22: 35–43.

Lesslie, R.G. and Taylor, S.G. (1983) *Wilderness in South Australia*, Occasional Paper No. 1, Adelaide: Centre for Environmental Studies, University of Adelaide.

Lesslie, R.G. and Taylor, S.G. (1985) 'The wilderness continuum concept and its implications for Australian wilderness preservation policy', *Biological Conservation*, 32: 309–33.

Lesslie, R.G, Abrahams, H. and Maslen, M. (1991a) *Wilderness Quality on Cape York Peninsula, National Wilderness Inventory: Stage III*, Canberra: Australian Heritage Commission.

Lesslie, R.G., Mackey, B.G. and Preece, K.M. (1987) *National Wilderness Inventory: A Computer Based Methodology for the Survey of Wilderness in Australia*, prepared for the Australian Heritage Commission, Canberra: Australian Heritage Commission.

Lesslie, R.G., Mackey, B.G. and Preece, K.M. (1988b) 'A computer-based method for the evaluation of wilderness', *Environmental Conservation*, 15(3): 225–32.

Lesslie, R G., Mackey, B.G. and Shulmeister, J. (1988a) *Wilderness Quality in Tasmania*, National Wilderness Inventory: Stage II, A report to the Australian Heritage Commission, Canberra: Australian Heritage Commission.

Lesslie, R.G., Maslen, M., Canty, D., Goodwins, D. and Shields, R. (1991b) *Wilderness on Kangaroo Island, National Wilderness Inventory: South Australia*, Canberra: Australian Heritage Commission.

Lew, A.A. (1985) 'Bringing tourists to town', *Small Town*, 16: 4–10.

Lew, A.A. (1987) 'A framework for tourist attraction research', *Annals of Tourism Research*, 14(4): 553–75.

Lew, A.A. (1989) 'Authenticity and sense of place in the tourism development experience of older retail districts', *Journal of Travel Research*, 27(4): 15–22.

Lew, A.A. and van Otten, G.A. (eds) (1997) *Tourism on American Indian Lands*, New York: Cognizant Communications Corporation.

Lew, A.A. and Wu, L. (eds) (1995) *Tourism in China: Geographic, Political and Economic Perspectives*, Boulder, CO: Westview Press.

Ley, D. and Olds, K. (1988) 'Landscape as spectacle: World's Fairs and the culture of heroic consumption', *Environment and Planning D*, 6: 191–212.

Li, Y. (2000) 'Geographical consciousness and tourism experience', *Annals of Tourism Research*, 27 (4): 863–83.

Limb, M. (1986) *Community Involvement in the Management of Open Space for Recreation in the Urban Fringe*, unpublished Ph.D. thesis, University of London.

Lindberg, K. and McKercher, B. (1997) 'Ecotourism: A critical overview', *Pacific Tourism Review*, 1: 65–79.

Linton, D. (1968) 'The assessment of scenery as a recreation resource', *Scottish Geographical Magazine*, 84(3): 219–38.

Lipscombe, N. (1993) 'Recreation planning: Where have all the frameworks gone?', in *Track to the Future, Managing Change in Parks and Recreation*, Cairns: Royal Australian Institute of Parks and Recreation.

Llewelyn-Davis Planning/Leisureworks (1987) *Tourism Development in London Docklands: Themes and Facts*, London: London Docklands Development Corporation.

Lloyd, P. and Dicken, P. (1987) *Location in Space: A Theoretical Approach to Human Geography*, 2nd edn, London: Harper & Row.

Locke, S. (1985) *Country Park Visitor Surveys: Lessons from a Study at Sherwood Forest and Rufford Country Parks, Nottinghamshire*, Cheltenham: Countryside Commission, CCP 180.

London Borough of Newham (1993) *Newham's Unitary Development Plan: Written Statement Parts One and Two*, East Ham, London: London Borough of Newham.

London Tourist Board (1987) *The Tourism Strategy for London*, London: London Tourist Board.

London Tourist Board (1988) *London Tourism Statistics*, London: London Tourist Board.

Long, J.A. (1984) 'Introduction – tourism and social change', in J. Long and R. Hecock (eds) *Leisure, Tourism and Social Change*, Dunfermline: Centre for Leisure Research, Dunfermline College of Physical Education, pp. 69–76.

Long, J.A (1987) 'Continuity as a basis for change: Leisure and male retirement', *Leisure Studies*, 6: 55–70.

Long, P.T. and Nuckolls, J.S. (1994) 'Organising resources for rural tourism development: The importance of leadership, planning and technical assistance', *Tourism Recreation Research*, 19(2): 19–34.

Long, P., Perdue, R. and Allen, L. (1990) 'Rural residents' perception and attitudes by community level of tourism', *Journal of Travel Research*, 29: 3–9.

Lösch, A. (1944) *Die Raümliche Ordnung der Wirtschaft*, Jena: Gustar Fischer.

Lovingwood, P. and Mitchell, L. (1978) 'The structure of public and private recreational systems: Columbia, South Carolina', *Journal of Leisure Research*, 10: 21–36.

Lowenthal, D. (1975) 'Past time, present place: Landscape and memory', *The Geographical Review*, 65: 1–36.

Lowenthal, D. (1985) *The Past is a Foreign Country*, Cambridge: Cambridge University Press.

Lowyck, E., Van Langenhove, L. and Bollaert, L. (1992) 'Typologies of tourist roles', in P. Johnson and T. Barry (eds) *Tourism Policy*, London: Mansell, pp. 13–32.

Lozato. J. (1985) *Géographie du tourisme*, Paris: Masson.

Lucas, P. (1986) 'Fishy business', *Leisure Manager*, 4: 18–19.

Lucas, R. (1964) 'Wilderness perception and use: The example of the Boundary Waters Canoe Area', *Natural Resources Journal*, 3(1): 394–411.

Lutz, R.J. and Ryan, C. (1997) 'The impact inner city tourism projects: The case of the International Convention Centre, Birmingham, UK', in P. Murphy (ed.) *Quality Management in Urban Tourism*, London: John Wiley, pp. 41–53.

Lynch, K. (1960) *The Image of the City*, Cambridge, MA: MIT Press.

McAlvoy, L. (1977) 'Needs and the elderly: An overview', *Parks and Recreation*, 12(3): 31–5.

McArthur, S. (1996) 'Beyond the limits of acceptable change – developing a model to monitor and manage tourism in remote areas', in *Tourism Down Under: 1996 Tourism Conference Proceedings*, Dunedin: Centre for Tourism, University of Otago.

McArthur, S. (2000a) *Visitor Management in Action: An Analysis of the Development and Implementation of Visitor Management Models at Jenolan Caves and Kangaroo Island*, unpublished Ph.D. thesis, Belconnen: University of Canberra.

McArthur, S. (2000b) 'Beyond carrying capacity: Introducing a model to monitor and manage visitor activity in forests', in X. Font and J. Tribe (eds) *Forest Tourism and Recreation: Case Studies in Environmental Management*, Wallingford: CAB International, pp. 259–78.

MacCannell, D. (1973) 'Staged authenticity: Arrangements of social space in tourist settings', *American Journal of Sociology*, 69: 578–603.

MacCannell, D. (1976) *The Tourist: A New Theory of the Leisure Class*, London: Macmillan.

McCool, S. (1978) 'Recreation use limits: Issues for the tourism industry', *Journal of Travel Research*, 17(2): 2–7.

McCool, S. and Cole, D. (1997) *Proceedings – Limits of Acceptable Change and related Planning Processes: Progress and Future Directions*, INT-GTR-371, Missoula: USDA, Forest Service, Rocky Mountain Research Station.

McDermott, D. and Horner, A. (1978) 'Aspects of rural renewal in Western Connemara', *Irish Geography*, 11: 176–9.

McDowell, A., Carter, R. and Pollard, J. (1990) 'The impact of man on the shoreline environment of the Costa del Sol, Southern Spain', in P. Wong (ed.) *Tourism vs Environment: The Case for Coastal Areas*, Dordrecht: Kluwer Academic, pp. 189–210.

McEniff, J. (1987) 'Republic of Ireland', *International Tourism Reports*: 5–26.

McEniff, J. (1991) 'Republic of Ireland', *International Tourism Reports*: 25–45.

McEniff, J. (1996) 'Ireland', *International Tourism Reports*, 1: 45–66.

McGahey, S. (1996) 'South Korea outbound', *Travel and Tourism Analyst*, 1: 17–35.

McGrath, F. (1989) 'Characteristics of pilgrims to Lough Derg', *Irish Geography*, 22: 44–7.

McIntosh, R.W. and Goeldner, C. (1990) *Tourism: Principles, Practices and Philosophies*, New York: Wiley.

McKenry, K. (1972a) *Value Analysis of Wilderness Areas*, Combined Universities Recreation Research Group, Monograph 2, Clayton: Monash University.

McKenry, K. (1972b) 'A history and critical analysis of the controversy concerning the Gordon River Power Scheme', in Australian Conservation Foundation, *Pedder Papers Anatomy of a Decision*, Parkville: Australian Conservation Foundation, Parkville, pp. 9–30.

McKenry, K. (1977) 'Value analysis of wilderness areas', in D. Mercer (ed.) *Leisure and Recreation in Australia*, Malvern: Sorrett Publishing, pp. 209–21.

McKenry, K. (1980) 'The beneficiaries of wilderness', in R.W. Robertson, P. Helman and A. Davey (eds) *Wilderness Management in Australia, Proceedings of a Symposium Held at the Canberra College of Advanced Education 19–23 July 1978*, Canberra: School of Applied Science, Canberra College of Advanced Education, pp. 82–91.

McKercher, B. (1993a) 'Some fundamental truths about tourism: Understanding tourism's social and environmental impacts', *Journal of Sustainable Tourism*, 1(1): 6–16.

McKercher, B. (1993b) 'The unrecognized threat to tourism: Can tourism survive sustainability', *Tourism Management*, 14(2): 131–6.

McKercher, B. (1993c) 'Australian conservation organisations' perspectives on tourism in National Parks: A critique', *GeoJournal*, 29(3): 307–13.

McKercher, B. (1997) 'Benefits and costs of tourism in Victoria's Alpine National Park: Comparing attitudes of tour operators, management staff and public interest group leaders', in C.M. Hall, J. Jenkins and G. Kearsley (eds) *Tourism Planning and Policy in Australia and New Zealand: Cases, Issues and Practice*, Sydney: Irwin Publishers, pp. 99–109.

McMillan, S. (1997) 'Balancing the books: Economic returns and corporate citizenship', mimeo of a paper presented at Business With Style: Adapting Heritage Buildings for Commercial Use, New South Wales Government, Heritage Office, Sydney.

McMurray, K.C. (1930) 'The use of land for recreation', *Annals of the Association of American Geographers*, 20: 7–20.

McMurray, K.C. (1954) 'Recreational geography', in P.E. James and C.F. Jones (eds) *American Geography: Inventory and Prospect*, Syracruse: Syracruse University Press, pp. 251–7.

McVey, M. (1986) 'International hotel chains in Europe: Survey of expansion plans as Europe is rediscovered', *Travel and Tourism Analyst*, September: 3–23.

Madge, C. (1997) 'Public parks and the geography of fear', *Tijdschrift Voor Economische en Sociale Geografie*, 88, 237–50.

Madsen, H. (1992) 'Place-marketing in Liverpool: A review', *International Journal of Urban and Regional Research*, 16(4): 633–40.

Maitiand, D. (1992) 'Space, vulnerability and dangers', *The Operational Geographer*, 9: 28–9.

Malamud, B. (1973) 'Gravity model calibration of tourist travel to Las Vegas', *Journal of Leisure Research*, 5(1): 13–33.

Mandell, M.P. (1999) 'The impact of collaborative efforts: Changing the face of public policy through networks and network structures', *Policy Studies Review*, 16(1): 4–17.

Manidis Roberts Consultants (1991) *National Estate NSW Wilderness Review*, Sydney: National Estate Grants Program, Department of Planning.

Manidis Roberts Consultants (1996) *Tourism Optimisation Management Model for Kangaroo Island*, Adelaide: South Australian Tourism Commission.

Manning, R.E. (1985) 'Crowding norms in backcountry settings: A review and synthesis', *Journal of Leisure Research*, 17(2): 75–89.

Mansfeld, Y. (1992) 'Industrial landscapes as positive settings for tourism development in declining industrial cities – the case of Haifa, Israel', *GeoJournal*, 28(4): 457–63.

Mansfield, N. (1969) 'Recreational trip generation', *Journal of Transport Economics and Public Policy*, 3(2): 152–64.

Marine Conservation Society (1998) *Readers Digest Good Beach Guide*, Newton Abbot: David and Charles.

Mark, S. (1984) *Wilderness Review in the East Mojave National Scenic Area, California*, unpublished M.Sc. thesis, South Oregon State College.

Mark, S. (1985) 'Wilderness inventory of Western Australia', *Environment W.A.*, 7(3): 30–2.

Mark, S. (1991) 'Planning and development at Rim Village', *in Administrative History, Crater Lake National Park, Oregon*, Seattle: US Department of the Interior, National Park Service.

Mark, S. (1996) 'Writing environmental and park histories', in C.M. Hall and S. McArthur (eds) *Heritage Management in Australia and New Zealand: The Human Dimension*, Melbourne: Oxford University Press, pp. 153–9.

Marketpower (1991) *A Report on the Structure of the UK Catering Industry*, London: Market Power.

Marsh, G.P. (1864 (1965)) *Man and Nature; Or, Physical Geography as Modified by Human Action*, ed. D. Lowenthal, Cambridge, MA: Belknap Press of Harvard University Press.

Marsh, J.G. (1983) 'Canada's parks and tourism: A problematic relationship', in P.E. Murphy (ed.) *Tourism in Canada: Selected Issues and Options*, Western Geographical Series, Vol. 21, Victoria: Department of Geography, University of Victoria, pp. 271–307.

Marsh, J.G. (1985) 'The Rocky and Selkirk Mountains and the Swiss connection 1885–1914', *Annals of Tourism Research*, 12: 417–33.

Marsh, J.G. and Staple, S. (1995) 'Cruise tourism in the Canadian Arctic and its implications', in C.M.Hall and M.E. Johnston (eds) *Polar Tourism: Tourism in the Arctic and Antarctic Regions*, Chichester: John Wiley & Sons, pp. 63–72.

Marsh, J.G. and Wall, G. (1982) 'Themes in the investigation of the evolution of outdoor recreation', in G. Wall and J. Marsh (eds) *Recreational Land Use, Perspectives on its Evolution in Canada*, Ottawa: Carleton University Press, pp. 1–12.

Marshall, R. (1930) 'The problem of the wilderness', *Scientific Monthly*, 30: 141–8.

Martin, W. and Mason, S. (1979) *Broad Patterns of Leisure Expenditure*, London: Sports Council and Social Science Research Council.

Maslow, A. (1954) *Motivation and Personality*, New York: Harper & Row.

Masser, I. (1966–67) 'The use of outdoor recreational facilities', *Town Planning Review*, 37(1): 41–53.

Massey, D. and Allen, J. (eds) (1984) *Geography Matters! A Reader*, Cambridge: Cambridge University Press.

Mathieson, A. and Wall, G. (1982) *Tourism: Economic, Physical and Social Impacts*, London: Longmans.

Matley, I.M. (1976) *The Geography of International Tourism*, Resource Paper No.76–1, Washington, DC: Association of American Geographers.

Matson, J. (1892) 'The Australasian indigenous park', *New Zealand Country Journal*, 16(4): 356–60.

Matsui, Y. (1999) *Women in the New Asia*, London: Zed Books.

Matthews, H.G. (1983) 'Editor's page: On tourism and political science', *Annals of Tourism Research*, 10(4): 303–6.

Maude, A.J.S. and van Rest, D. J. (1985) 'The social and economic effects of farm tourism in the United Kingdom', *Agricultural Administration*, 20: 85–99.

Maver, I. (1998) 'Glasgow's public parks and the community 1850–1914', *Urban History*, 25(3): 323–47.

Mawhinney, K. A. (1979) 'Recreation', in D.A. Gilmore (ed.) *Irish Resources and Land Use*, Dublin: Institute of Public Administration.

Mawhinney, K. A. and Bagnall, G. (1976) 'The integrated social economic and environmental planning of tourism', *Administration*, 24: 383–93.

May, V. (1993) 'Coastal tourism, geomorphology and geological conservation: The example of South Central England', in P. Wong (ed.) *Tourism vs Environment: The Case for Coastal Areas*, Dordrecht: Kluwer Academic, pp. 3–10.

Medlik, S. (1993) *Dictionary of Travel, Tourism and Hospitality*, Oxford: Butterworth Heinemann.

Meethan, K. (1997) 'York: Managing the tourist city', *Cities: The International Journal of Urban Policy and Planning*, 14(6): 333–42.

Melbourne Parks (1983) *A Survey of the Use of Selected Sites*, Melbourne: Melbourne and Metropolitan Board.

Meleghy, T., Preglau, M. and Tafertsofer, A. (1985) 'Tourism development and value change', *Annals of Tourism Research*, 12: 201–19.

Mercer, D. (1970) 'The geography of leisure: A contemporary growth point', *Geography*, 55(3): 261–73.

Mercer, D. (1971a) 'Perception in outdoor recreation', in P. Lavery (ed.) *Recreational Geography*, Newton Abbot: David and Charles, pp. 51–69.

Mercer, D. (1971b) 'Discretionary travel behaviour and the urban mental map', *Australian Geographical Studies*, 9: 133–43.

Mercer, D. (1972) 'Beach usage in the Melbourne region', *Australian Geographer*, 12(2): 123–9.

Mercer, D. (1973) 'The concept of recreational need', *Journal of Leisure Research*, 5: 37–50.

Mercer, D. (1979a) 'Outdoor recreation: Contemporary research and policy issues', in T. O'Riordan and R.D. Arge (eds) *Progress in Resource Management and Environmental Planning*, Vol. 1, New York: Wiley, pp. 87–142.

Mercer, D. (1979b) 'Victoria's land conservation council and the alpine region', *Australian Geographical Studies*, 17(1): 107–30.

Mercer, D. (1994) 'Native peoples and tourism: conflict and compromise', in W.F. Theobald (ed.) *Global Tourism: The Next Decade*, Boston, MA: Butterworth Heinemann, pp. 124–45.

Meyer-Arendt, K. (1990) 'Recreational Business Districts in Gulf of Mexico seaside resorts', *Journal of Cultural Geography*, 11: 39–55.

Meyer-Arendt, K. (2000) 'Commentary: Tourism geography as the subject of North American Doctoral dissertations and Masters theses, 1951–98', *Tourism Geographies*, 2(2): 140–57.

Meyer-Arendt, K. and Lew, A. (1999) 'A decade of American RTS geography', *Tourism Geographies*, 1(4): 477–87.

Michaud, J. (1983) *Le tourisme face à l'environnement*, Paris: PUF.

Michaud, J. (ed.) (1992) *Tourismes: chance pour l'économie, risque pour les sociétes?*, Paris: PUF.

Middleton, V. (1988) *Marketing in Travel and Tourism*, Oxford: Butterworth Heinemann.

Miller, M. (1987) 'Tourism in Washington's coastal zone', *Annals of Tourism Research*, 14(1): 58–70.

Miller, M. (1993) 'The rise of coastal and marine tourism', *Ocean and Coastal Management*, 21(1–3): 183–99.

Miller, M.L. and Auyong, J. (1991) 'Coastal zone tourism: A potent force affecting environment and society', *Marine Policy*, 15(2): 75–99.

Milne, S. (1990) 'The impact of tourism development in small Pacific Island states', *New Zealand Journal of Geography*, 89: 16–21.

Milne, S. (1998) 'Tourism and sustainable development: The global–local nexus', in C.M. Hall and A.A. Lew (eds) *Sustainable Tourism Development: Geographical Perspectives*, Harlow: Addison Wesley Longman, pp. 35–48.

Milton Keynes Development Corporation (1988) *Study of the Use and Perception of Parks in Milton Keynes*, Milton Keynes: Milton Keynes Recreation Unit Study 18.

Milton Keynes Development Corporation (1989) *Parks Visitor Survey*, Milton Keynes: Milton Keynes Recreation Unit Study 18.

Milward, H.B. (1996) 'Symposium on the hollow state: Capacity, control and performance in inter-organizational settings', *Journal of Public Administration Research and Theory*, 6(2): 193–5.

Minerbi, L. (1992) *Impacts of Tourism Development in Pacific Islands*, San Francisco, CA: Greenpeace Pacific Campaign.

Mings, R.C. (1978) 'The importance of more research on the impacts of tourism', *Annals of Tourism Research*, July/September: 340–4.

Ministry of Housing and Local Government (1955) *Green Belts*, HMSO: Circular 42/55.

Mitchell, B. (1989) *Geography and Resource Analysis*, 2nd edn, Harlow: Longman.

Mitchell, L. (1969a) 'Recreational geography: Evolution and research needs', *Professional Geographer*, 21(2): 117–19.

Mitchell, L. (1969b) 'Towards a theory of public urban recreation', *Proceedings of the Association of American Geographers*, 1: 103–8.

Mitchell, L. and Lovingwood, P. (1976) 'Public urban recreation: An investigation of spatial relationships', *Journal of Leisure Research*, 8: 6–20.

Mitchell, L.S. (1979) 'The geography of tourism: An introduction', *Annals of Tourism Research*, 9 (3): 235–44.

Mitchell, L.S. (1984) 'Tourism research in the United States: A geographical perspective', *GeoJournal*, 9: 5–15.

Mitchell, L.S. (1991) *A Conceptual Matrix for the Study of Tourism*, Les Cahiers du Tourisme, Aix en Provence: Centre des Haute Études Touristiques.

Mitchell, L.S. (1997) 'Rediscovering geography (i.e. RTS)', personal communication to Michael Hall, Friday, 13 June.

Mitchell, L.S. and Lovingwood, P. (1976) 'Public urban recreation: An investigation of spatial relationships', *Journal of Leisure Research*, 8: 6–20.

Mitchell, L.S. and Murphy, P.E. (1991) 'Geography and tourism', *Annals of Tourism Research*, 18(1): 57–70.

Mitchell, N.C. (1970) 'Irish ports, recent developments', in N. Stephens and R. Glassock (eds) *Irish Geographical Studies in Honour of E. Estyn Evans*, Belfast: Queen's University of Belfast, pp. 325–41.

Modern Maturity (1999) 'Results of travel survey', *Modern Maturity*, January: 12.

Montanari, A. and Williams, A.M. (eds) (1995) *European Tourism: Regions, Spaces and Restructuring*, Chichester: Wiley.

Moore, K., Cushman, G. and Simmons, D. (1995) 'Behavioural conceptualisation of tourism and leisure', *Annals of Tourism Research*, 22(1): 67–85.

Moran, W. (1993) 'Rural space as intellectual property', *Political Geography*, 12(3): 263–77.

Moran, W. (2000) 'Culture et nature dans la géogrphiede l'industrie vinicole néo-zélandaise', *Annales de geographie*, 614–15: 525–51.

Moran, W. (2001) 'Terroir – the human factor', *Australian and New Zealand Wine Industry Journal of Oenology, Viticulture, Finance and Marketing*, 16(2): 32–51.

Morgan, C. and King, J. (1966) *Introduction to Psychology*, New York: McGraw Hill.

Morgan, G. (1980) 'Wilderness areas in Queensland: The rakes approach', in R.W. Robertson, P. Helman and A. Davey (eds) *Wilderness Management in Australia, Proceedings of a symposium held at the Canberra College of Advanced Education, 19–23 July 1978*, Natural Resources, School of Applied Science, Canberra College of Advanced Education, Canberra, pp. 103–7.

Morgan, G. (1991) *A Strategic Approach to the Planning and Management of Parks and Open Space*, Reading: Institute of Leisure and Amenity Management.

Morgan, R. (1999) 'A novel, user-based rating system for tourist beaches', *Tourism Management*, 20: 393–410.

Morgan, R., Jones, T. and Williams, A. (1993) 'Opinions and perceptions of England and Wales Heritage coast beach users: Some management implications from the Glamorgan Heritage Coast, Wales', *Journal of Coastal Research*, 9(4): 1083–93.

Mormont, M. (1987) 'Tourism and rural change', in M. Bouquet and M. Winter (eds) *Who From Their Labours Rest? Conflict and Practice in Rural Tourism*, Aldershot: Avebury, pp. 35–44.

Morris, A. (1996) 'Environmental management in coastal Spain', in M. Barke, J. Towner and M. Newton (eds) *Tourism in Spain: Critical Issues*, Wallingford: CAB International, pp. 213–28.

Morrison, A. and Dickinson, G. (1987) 'Tourist development in Spain: Growth versus conservation on the Costa Brava', *Geography*, 72: 16–25.

Mosley, J.G. (1983) 'Australia's World Heritage areas', *Habitat*, 11(1): 16–26.

Moutinho, L. (1987) 'Consumer behaviour in tourism', *European Journal of Marketing*, 21(10): 3–44.

Mowat, P. (1984) *The Administrative Factor in the Development of Tourist Resources and Markets in North-West Ireland*, unpublished D. Phil. thesis, New University of Ulster, Coleraine.

Mowforth, M. and Munt, I. (1997) *Tourism and Sustainability*, London: Routledge.

Mowl, G. and Turner, J. (1995) 'Women, gender leisure and place: Towards a more "humanistic" geography of women's leisure', *Leisure Studies*, 14: 102–16.

Mucciaroni, G. (1991) 'Unclogging the arteries: The defeat of client politics and the logic of collective action', *Policy Studies Journal*, 19(3–4): 474–94.

Mulford, C.L. and Rogers, D.L. (1982) 'Definitions and models', in D.L. Rogers and D.A. Whetten (eds) *Interorganizational Coordination: Theory, Research and Implementation*, Ames: Iowa State University Press.

Müller, D.K. (1999) *German Second Home Owners in the Swedish Countryside*, Umeå and Ostersund: Etour, Vetenskapliga bokserien.

Mullins, G. and Heywood, J. (1984) *Unobtrusive Observation: A Visitor Survey Technique*, Columbus, OH: Ohio Agricultural Research Development Circular, Ohio Agricultural Development Centre No 20.

Mullins, P. (1984) 'Hedonism and real estate: Resort tourism and Gold Coast development', in P. Williams (ed.) *Conflict and Development*, Sydney: Allen & Unwin.

Mullins, P. (1990) 'Tourist cities as new cities: Australia's Gold Coast and Sunshine Coast', *Australian Planner*, 28(3): 37–41.

Mullins, P. (1991) 'Tourism urbanization', *International Journal of Urban and Regional Research*, 15: 326–43.

Murdoch, J. (1993) 'Sustainable rural development: Towards a research agenda', *Geoforum*, 24 (3): 225–41.

Murphy, L. and Le Heron, R. (1999) 'Encountering places, peoples and environments: Introducing human geography', in R. Le Heron, L. Murphy, P. Forer and M. Goldstone (eds) *Explorations in Human Geography: Encountering Place*, Auckland: Oxford University Press, pp. 1–23.

Murphy, P.E. (1982) 'Tourism planning in London: An exercise in spatial and seasonal management', *Tourist Review*, 37: 19–23.

Murphy, P.E. (1985) *Tourism: A Community Approach*, New York: Methuen.

Murphy, P.E. (1988) 'Community driven tourism planning', *Tourism Management*, 9(2): 96–104.

Murphy, P.E. (1994) 'Tourism and sustainable development', in W. Theobold (ed.) *Global Tourism: The Next Decade*, Oxford: Butterworth Heinemann, pp. 274–90.

Murphy, P.E. (ed.) (1997) *Quality Management in Urban Tourism*, International Western Geographical Series, Chichester: Wiley.

Murphy, P.E. and Keller, C.P. (1990) 'Destination travel patterns: An examination and modelling of tourism patterns on Vancouver Island, British Columbia', *Leisure Sciences*, 12(1): 49–65.

Murphy, P.E. and Rosenblood, L. (1974) 'Tourism: An exercise in spatial search', *Canadian Geographer*, 18(3): 201–10.

Murphy, P.E. and Staples, W.A. (1979) 'Life cycle concept in marketing research', *Journal of Consumer Research*: 12–22.

Murphy, R.E. (1963) 'Geography and outdoor recreation: An opportunity and an obligation', *Professional Geographer*, 15(5): 33–4.

Murphy, W. and Gardiner, J.J. (1983) 'Forest recreating economics', *Irish Forestry*, 40: 12–19.

Nash, R. (1963) 'The American wilderness in historical perspective', *Journal of Forest History*, 6(4): 2–13.

Nash, R. (1967) *Wilderness and the American Mind*, New Haven, CT: Yale University Press.

Nash, R. (1982) *Wilderness and the American Mind*, 3rd edn, New Haven, CT: Yale University Press.

Nash, R. (1990) *The Rights of Nature: A History of Environmental Ethics*, Leichhardt: Primavera Press.

National Capital Commission (1991) *NCR Visitor Survey, Volume 1 – Analysis of Findings*, conducted for the National Capital Commission by Gallup Canada, National Capital Commission, Ottawa.

National Capital Commission (1998) *A Capital in the Making*, Ottawa: National Capital Commission.

National Capital Commission (1999) *Plan for Canada's Capital: A Second Century of Vision, Planning and Development*, Ottawa: National Capital Commission.

National Capital Commission (2000a) *Summary of the Corporate Plan 2000–2001 to 2004–2005*, Ottawa: National Capital Commission.

National Capital Commission (2000b) *Planning Canada's Capital Region*, Ottawa: National Capital Commission.

National Oceanic and Atmospheric Administration (NCAA) (1997) *1998 Year of the Ocean – Coastal Tourism and Recreation*, Discussion paper, (http://www.yoto98.noaa.gov/yoto/meeting/tour_rec_316.html)

Naylon, J. (1967) 'Tourism – Spain's most important industry', *Geography*, 52: 23–40.

Nelson, J.G. (1973) 'Canada's national parks – Past, present and future', *Canadian Geographical Journal*, 86(3): 68–89.

Nelson, J.G. (1982) 'Canada's national parks: past, present and future', in G. Wall and J.S. Marsh (eds) *Recreational Land Use Perspectives on its Evolution in Canada*, Carleton Library Series, Ottawa: Carleton University Press, pp. 41–61.

Nelson, J.G. (1986) *An External Perspective on Parks Canada Strategies*, Occasional Paper No.2, Waterloo: University of Waterloo Parks Canada Liaison Committee, University of Waterloo.

Nelson, J.G. (ed.) (1970) *Canadian Parks in Perspective*, Montreal: Harvest House.

Neulinger, J. (1981) *The Psychology of Leisure*, Springfield: C. Thomas.

New Zealand Tourism Board (1991a) *Tourism in the 90s*, Wellington: New Zealand Tourism Board.

New Zealand Tourism Board (1991b) *New Zealand Domestic Tourism Study*, Wellington: New Zealand Tourism Board.

New Zealand Tourism Board (1995) *New Zealand Tourism in the 90s*, Wellington: New Zealand Tourism Board.

New Zealand Travel and Publicity Department (1987) *The New Zealand Domestic Travel Study 1986–1987: General Report*, Wellington: New Zealand Travel and Publicity Department.

Newham Borough Council (1991a) *Newham's Policy for the Environment: A Consultation Document*, London: Borough of Newham.

Newham Borough Council (1991b) *Shaped for Success: Leisure Development Strategy 1990–94*, London: Borough of Newham.

Newsome, D., Moore, S. and Dowling, R. (2002) *Natural Area Tourism: Ecology, Impacts and Management*, Clevedon: Channel View Press.

Ngoh, T. (1985) 'Guidelines for the harmonisation of international tourism statistics among PATA member countries', in *The Battle for Market Share: Strategies in Research and Marketing*, 16th Annual Conference Tourism and Travel Research Association, Salt Lake City: Graduate School of Business, University of Utah, pp. 291–306.

Nichols, L.L. (1976) 'Tourism and crime', *Annals of Tourism Research*, 3: 176–81.

Nicholson, M.H. (1962) *Mountain Gloom and Mountain Glory*, New York: Norton.

Nicholson-Lord, D. (1994) 'Space for green reinvention', *The Independent*, 4 April.

Nickels, S., Milne, S. and Wenzel, G. (1991) 'Inuit perceptions of tourism development: The case of Clyde River, Baffin Island, NWT', *Etudes/Inuit/Studies*, 15(1): 157–69.

Nicol, J.I. (1969) 'The National Parks movement in Canada', in J.G. Nelson and R.C. Scace (eds) *The Canadian National Parks: Today and Tomorrow*, Vol. 1, Studies in Land Use History and Landscape Change National Park Series, Calgary: Department of Geography, University of Calgary, pp. 35–52.

Nielsen, N. (1990) ' Construction of a recreational beach using the original coastal morphology, Koege Bay, Denmark', in P. Fabbri (ed.) *Recreational Use of Coastal Areas*, Dordrecht: Kluwer, pp. 177–90.

Nordstrom, K., Lampe, R. and Vandemark, L. (2000) 'Reestablishing naturally functioning dunes on developed coasts', *Environmental Management*, 25(1): 37–51.

Norkunas, M.K. (1993) *The Politics of Memory: Tourism, History, and Ethnicity in Monterey, California*, Albany: State University of New York Press.

O'Cinneide, M. and Keane, M.J. (1990) 'Applying strategic planning to local economic development: The case of the Connemara Gaeltacht, Ireland', *Town Planning Review*, 61: 475–86.

O'Connor, B. and Cronin, M. (eds) (1993) *Tourism in Ireland: A Critical Analysis*, Cork: Cork University Press.

O'Connor, P. (1995) 'Tourism and development in Ballyhoura: women's business?', *Economic and Social Review*, 26(4): 369–401.

O'Connor, P. (1996) *Invisible Players? Women, Tourism and Development in Ballyhoura*, Limerick: Women's Studies, Department of Government and Society, University of Limerick.

O'Dell, A. (1935) 'European air services, June 1934', *Geography*, 19(4): 288–91.

O'Hagan, J. and Harrison, M. (1984a) 'UK and US visitor expenditure in Ireland: Some econometric findings', *Economic and Social Review*, 15: 195–207.

O'Hagan, J. and Harrison, M. (1984b) 'Market share of US tourist expenditure in Europe: An econometric analysis', *Applied Economics*, 16: 919–31.

O'Hagan, J. and Mooney, D. (1983) 'Input–output multipliers in a small open economy: An application to tourism', *Economic and Social Review*, 14: 273–9.

O'Hearn, D. (1989) 'The Irish case of dependency, an exception to exceptions?', *American Sociological Review*, 54: 578–96.

O'Leary, J.T. (1976) 'Land use definition and the rural community: Disruption of community leisure space', *Journal of Leisure Research*, 8: 263–74.

O'Riordan, T. (1971) *Perspectives on Resource Management*, London: Pion Press.

O'Riordan, T. and Paget, G. (1978) *Sharing Rivers and Canals*, Study 16, London: Sports Council.

O'Riordan, T. and Turner, R.K. (eds) (1984) *An Annotated Reader in Environmental Planning and Management*, Oxford: Pergamon Press.

O'Riordan, W.K. (1986) 'Service sector multipliers', *Irish Banking Review*: 30–40.

O'Toole, L. (1997) 'Treating networks seriously: Practical and research based agendas in public administration', *Public Administration Review*, 57(1): 45–52.

Oc, T. and Tiesdell, S. (eds) (1997) *Safer City Centres: Reviving the Public Realm*, London: Chapman and Hall.

Oelschlaeger, M. (1991) *The Idea of Wilderness: From Prehistory to the Age of Ecology*, New Haven, CT: Yale University Press.

Office for National Statistics (2000) *Social Trends 30*, London: The Stationery Office.

Office of National Tourism (1997) *Ecotourism*, Tourism Facts No. 16, May (http://www.tourism. gov.au/new/cfa/cfa_fs16.html (accessed 31 December)).

Office of Population Censuses and Surveys (OPCS) (1992) *1991 Census: Inner London*, London: OPCS.

Oglethorpe, M. (1984) 'Tourism and development in the Maltese Islands', in J. Long and R. Hecock (eds) *Leisure, Tourism and Social Change*, Dunfermline: Centre for Leisure Research, Dunfermline College of Physical Education, pp. 121–34.

Ohmae, K. (1995) *The End of the Nation State: The Rise of Regional Economies*, New York: HarperCollins and The Free Press.

Olszewska, A. (1989) 'Poland: The impact of the crisis on leisure patterns', in A. Olszewska and K. Roberts (eds) *Leisure and Lifestyle: A Comparative Analysis of Free Time*, London: Sage, pp. 17–38.

Olwig, K. and Olwig, K. (1979) 'Underdevelopment and the development of "natural" parks ideology', *Antipode*, 11(2): 16–25.

Open Space Society (1992) *Making Space: Protecting and Creating Open Space for Local Communities*, Oxfordshire: Open Space Society.

Oppermann, M. (1992) 'International tourist flows in Malaysia', *Annals of Tourism Research*, 19(3): 482–500.

Oppermann, M. (1993) 'German tourists in New Zealand', *The New Zealand Geographer*, 49(1): 31–4.

Oppermann, M. (1994) 'Regional aspects of tourism in New Zealand', *Regional Studies*, 28: 155–67.

Oppermann, M. (1995) 'Holidays on the farm: A case study of German hosts and guests', *Journal of Travel Research*, 33: 57–61.

Oppermann, M. (1998) 'Farm tourism in New Zealand', in R. Butler, C.M. Hall and J. Jenkins (eds) *Tourism and Recreation in Rural Areas*, Chichester: Wiley, pp. 225–35.

Oppermann, M. and Chon, K. (1997) *Tourism in Developing Countries*, London: International Thomson Business Publishing.

Orams, M. (1999) *Marine Tourism*, London: Routledge

Organisation for Economic Co-operation and Development (1980) *The Impact of Tourism on the Environment*, Paris: Organisation for Economic Co-operation and Development.

Outdoor Recreation Resources Review Commission (1962) *Outdoor Recreation for America*, Washington, DC: Government Printing Office.

Ovington, J.D. and Fox, A.M. (1980) 'Wilderness – a natural asset', *Parks*, 5(3): 1–4.

Owen, C. (1990) 'Tourism and urban regeneration', *Cities: The International Journal of Urban Policy and Planning*, August: 194–201.

Owens, P. (1984) 'Rural leisure and recreation research: A retrospective evaluation', *Progress in Human Geography*, 8: 157–85.

Pacione, M.(1999a) 'Applied geography: In pursuit of useful knowledge', *Applied Geography*, 19: 1–12.

Pacione, M. (1999b) 'In pursuit of knowledge: The principles and practice of applied geography', in M. Pacione (ed.) *Applied Geography: Principles and Practice*, London: Routledge, pp.3–18.

Pacione, M. (ed.) (1999c) *Applied Geography: Principles and Practice*, London: Routledge.

Page, S.J. (1988) *Poverty in Leicester 1881–1911: A Geographical Perspective*, unpublished Ph.D. thesis, Department of Geography, University of Leicester.

Page, S.J. (1989) 'Tourist development in London Docklands in the 1980s and 1990s', *GeoJournal*, 19(3): 291–5.

Page, S.J. (1992) 'Perspectives on the environmental impact of the Channel Tunnel on tourism', in C. Cooper and A. Lockwood (eds) *Progess in Tourism, Recreation and Hospitality Management*, Vol. 4, London: Belhaven Press, pp. 82–102.

Page, S.J. (1994a) 'European bus and coach travel', *Travel and Tourism Analyst*, 1: 19–39.

Page, S.J. (1994b) *Transport for Tourism*, London: Routledge.

Page, S.J. (1994c) 'Perspectives on tourism and peripherality: A review of tourism in the Republic of Ireland', in C. Cooper and A. Lockwood (eds) *Progress in Tourism, Recreation and Hospitality Management*, Vol. 5, Chichester: Wiley, pp. 26–53.

Page, S.J. (1994d) 'Developing heritage tourism in Ireland in the 1990s', *Tourism Recreation Research*, 19(2): 79–90.

Page, S.J. (1995a) *Urban Tourism*, London: Routledge.

Page, S.J. (1995b) 'Waterfront revitalisation in London: Market-led planning and tourism in London Docklands', in S. Craig-Smith and M. Fagence (eds) *Recreation and Tourism as a Catalyst for Urban Waterfront Development*, Westport, CT: Greenwood Publishing, pp. 53–70.

Page, S.J. (1997a) 'Urban tourism: Analysing and evaluating the tourist experience', in C. Ryan (ed.) *The Tourist Experience: A New Introduction*, London: Cassell, pp. 112–35.

Page, S.J. (1997b) *The Cost of Accidents in the Adventure Tourism Industry*, Consultant's Report for the Tourism Policy Group, Ministry of Commerce, Wellington.

Page, S.J. (1998) 'Transport for recreation and tourism', in B. Hoyle and R. Knowles (eds) *Modern Transport Geography*, 2nd edn, Chichester: Wiley, pp. 217–40.

Page, S.J. (1999) *Transport and Tourism*, London: Addison Wesley Longman.

Page, S.J. (2000) 'Urban tourism', in C. Ryan and S.J. Page (eds) *Tourism Management: Towards the New Millennium*, Oxford: Pergamon, pp. 197–202.

Page, S.J. and Dowling, R. (2001) *Ecotourism*, Harlow: Pearson Education.

Page, S.J. and Getz, D. (eds) (1997) *The Business of Rural Tourism: International Perspectives*, London: International Thomson Business Press.

Page, S.J. and Hall, C.M. (2002) *Managing Urban Tourism*, Harlow: Pearson Education.

Page, S.J. and Hardyman, R. (1996) 'Place marketing and town centre management: A new tool for urban revitalisation', *Cities: The International Journal of Urban Policy and Planning*, 13 (3): 153–64.

Page, S.J. and Lawton, G. (1997) 'The impact of urban tourism on destination communities: Implications for community tourism planning in Auckland', in C.M. Hall, J. Jenkins and G. Kearsley (eds) *Tourism Planning and Policy in Australia and New Zealand: Cases, Issues and Practice*, Sydney: Irwin Publishers, pp. 209–26.

Page, S.J. and Meyer, D. (1996) 'Tourist accidents: An exploratory analysis', *Annals of Tourism Research*, 23(3): 666–90.

Page, S.J. and Sinclair, M.T. (1989) 'Tourism accommodation in London: Alternative policies and the Docklands experience', *Built Environment*, 15(2): 125–37.

Page, S.J. and Thorn, K. (1997) 'Towards sustainable tourism planning in New Zealand: Public sector planning responses', *Journal of Sustainable Tourism*, 5(1): 59–78.

Page, S.J. and Thorn, K. (1998) 'Sustainable tourism development and local government in New Zealand', in C.M. Hall and A. Lew (eds) *The Geography of Sustainable Tourism: Approaches, Issues and Experiences*, Harlow: Addison Wesley Longman, pp. 173–84.

Page, S.J., Forer, P. and Lawton, G. (1999) 'Tourism and small business development: Terra incognita', *Tourism Management*, 20(3): 435–59.

Page, S.J., Nielsen, K. and Goodenough, R. (1994) 'Managing urban parks: User perspectives and local leisure needs in the 1990s', *Service Industries Journal*, 14(2): 216–37.

Page, S.J., Brunt, P., Busby, G. and Connell, J. (2001) *Tourism: A Modern Synthesis*, London: Thomson Learning.

Pahl, R.E. (1975) *Whose City? And Further Essays in Urban Society*, Harmondsworth: Penguin.

Pain, R. (1997). 'Social geographies of women's fear of crime', *Transactions of the Institute of British Geographers*, 22: 231–44.

Panchuk, S. and Yudina, Y. (1977) 'Cottage settlements and garden cooperatives in the Moscow area', *Soviet Geography*, 18: 329–38.

Papson, S. (1981) 'Spuriousness and tourism: Politics of two Canadian provincial governments', *Annals of Tourism Research*, 8: 220–35.

Parasuraman, A., Zeithmal, V. and Berry, L. (1985) 'A conceptual model of service quality and its implications for future research', *Journal of Marketing*, 49(4): 41–50.

Parker, S. (1999) *Leisure in Contemporary Society*, Wallingford: CAB International.

Parliamentary Commissioner for the Environment (1997) *Management of the Environmental Effects Associated With the Tourism Sector*, Wellington: Office of the Parliamentary Commissioner for the Environment.

Passmore, J. (1974) *Man's Responsibility for Nature*, London: Duckworth.

Patmore, J.A. (1968) 'The spa towns of Britain', in R. Beckinsale and J. Houston (eds) *Urbanization and its Problems*, Oxford: Blackwell, pp. 47–69.

Patmore, J.A. (1970) *Land and Leisure*, Newton Abbot: David and Charles.

Patmore, J.A. (1971) 'Routeways and recreation', in P. Lavery (ed.) *Recreational Geography*, Newton Abbot: David and Charles, pp. 70–96.

Patmore, J.A. (1973) 'Recreation', in J. Dawson and J. Doornkamp (eds) *Evaluating the Human Environment: Essays in Applied Geography*, London: Edward Arnold, pp. 224–48.

Patmore, J.A. (1977) 'Recreation and leisure', *Progress in Human Geography*, 1: 111–17.

Patmore, J.A. (1978) 'Recreation and leisure', *Progress in Human Geography*, 2: 142–7.

Patmore, J.A. (1979) 'Recreation and leisure', *Progress in Human Geography*, 3: 126–32.

Patmore, J.A. (1980) 'Recreation and leisure', *Progress in Human Geography*, 4: 91–8.

Patmore, J.A. (1983) *Recreation and Resources: Leisure Patterns and Leisure Places*, Oxford: Blackwell.

Patmore, J.A. and Collins, M. (1981) 'Recreation and leisure', *Progress in Human Geography*, 5(1): 87–92.

Patmore, J.A. and Rodgers, J. (eds) (1972) *Leisure in the North-West*, Salford: North-West Sports Council.

Pearce, D.G. (1978) 'Form and function in French resorts', *Annals of Tourism Research*, 6: 245–72.

Pearce, D.G. (1979) 'Towards a geography of tourism', *Annals of Tourism Research*, 6: 245–72.

Pearce, D.G. (1981) *Tourist Development*, Harlow: Longman.

Pearce, D.G. (1986) 'The spatial structure of coastal tourism: A behavioural approach', paper presented at the International Geographical Union Commission on the Geography of Tourism and Leisure, Palma de Mallorca.

Pearce, D.G. (1987a) *Tourism Today: A Geographical Analysis*, Harlow: Longman.

Pearce, D.G. (1987b) 'Motel location and choice in Christchurch', *New Zealand Geographer*, 43(1): 10–17.

Pearce, D.G. (1988a) 'The spatial structure of coastal tourism: A behavioural approach', *Tourism Recreation Research*, 13(2): 11–14.

Pearce, D.G. (1988b) 'Tourist time-budgets', *Annals of Tourism Research*, 15: 106–21.

Pearce, D.G. (1988c) 'Tourism and regional development in the European Community', *Tourism Management*, 9: 11–22.

Pearce, D.G. (1989) *Tourist Development*, 2nd edn, Harlow: Longman.

Pearce, D.G. (1990a) 'Tourism, the regions and restructuring in New Zealand', *Journal of Tourism Studies*, 1(2): 33–42.

Pearce, D.G. (1990b) 'Tourism in Ireland: Questions of scale and organisation', *Tourism Management*, 11: 133–51.

Pearce, D.G. (1992a) 'Tourism and the European regional development fund: The first fourteen years', *Journal of Travel Research*, 30: 44–51.

Pearce, D.G. (1992b) *Tourist Organisations*, Harlow: Longman.

Pearce, D.G. (1993a) 'Comparative studies in tourism research', in D. Pearce and R. Butler (eds) *Tourism Research: Critiques and Challenges*, London: Routledge, pp. 113–34.

Pearce, D.G. (1993b) 'Domestic tourist travel patterns in New Zealand', *GeoJournal*, 29(3): 225–32.

Pearce, D.G. (1995a) *Tourism Today: A Geographical Analysis*, 2nd edn, Harlow: Longman.

Pearce, D.G. (1995b) 'Planning for tourism in the 90s: An integrated, dynamic, multi-scale approach', in R.W. Butler and D.G. Pearce (eds) *Change in Tourism: People, Places, Processes*, London: Routledge, pp. 229–44.

Pearce, D.G. (1998) 'Tourism development in Paris: Public intervention', *Annals of Tourism Research*, 25(2): 457–76.

Pearce, D.G. (1999a) 'Towards a geography of the geography of tourism: Issues and examples from New Zealand', *Tourism Geographies*, 1(4): 406–24.

Pearce, D.G. (1999b) 'Tourism districts in Paris: Structure and functions', *Tourism Management*, 19(1): 49–65.

Pearce, D.G. and Butler, R.W. (eds) (1993) *Tourism Research: Critiques and Challenges*, London: Routledge.

Pearce, D.G. and Kirk, D. (1986) 'Carrying capacities for coastal tourism', *Industry and Environment*, 9(1): 3–6.

Pearce, D.G. and Mings, R. (1984) 'Geography, tourism and recreation in the Antipodes', *GeoJournal*, 9(1): 91–5.

Pearce, J.A. (1980) 'Host community acceptance of foreign tourists: strategic considerations', *Annals of Tourism Research*, 7: 224–33.

Pearce, P.L. (1977) 'Mental souvenirs: A study of tourists and their city maps', *Australian Journal of Psychology*, 29: 203–10.

Pearce, P.L. (1981) 'Route maps: A study of travellers' perceptions of a section of countryside', *Journal of Environmental Psychology*, 1: 141–55.

Pearce, P.L. (1982) *The Social Psychology of Tourist Behaviour*, Oxford: Pergamon.

Pearce, P.L. (1984) 'Tourist guide interaction', *Annals of Tourism Research*, 11: 129–46.

Pearce, P.L. (1993) 'The fundamentals of tourist motivation', in D. Pearce and R. Butler (eds) *Tourism Research: Critique and Challenges*, London: Routledge.

Pearson, R. (1968) 'Railways in relation to resort development in East Lincolnshire', *East Midland Geographer*, 4: 281–95.

Peet, R. (ed.) (1977a) *Radical Geography: Alternative Viewpoints on Contemporary Social Issues*, London: Methuen.

Peet, R. (1977b) 'The development of radical geography in the United States', *Progress in Human Geography*, 1: 240–63.

Penning-Rowsell, E. (1973) *Alternative Approaches to Landscape Appraisal and Evaluation*, Planning Research Group, Report No. 11, Enfield: Middlesex Polytechnic.

Penning-Rowsell, E. (1975) 'Constraints on the application of landscape evaluation', *Transactions of the Institute of British Geographers*, 66: 49–55.

Penning-Rowsell, E., Green, C., Thompson, P., Coker, A., Tunstall, S., Richards, C. and Parker, D. (1992) *The Economics of Coastal Management: A Manual of Benefit Assessment Techniques*, London: Belhaven Press.

Pepper, D. (1984) *The Roots of Modern Environmentalism*, London: Croom Helm.

Perdue, R. (1985) 'The 1983 Nebraska Visitor Survey: Achieving a high response rate', *Journal of Travel Research*, 24(2): 23–6.

Perkins, H. (1993) 'Human geography, recreation and leisure', in H. Perkins and G. Cushman (eds) *Leisure, Recreation and Tourism*, Auckland: Longman Paul, pp. 116–29.

Perkins, H. and Gidlow, B. (1991) 'Leisure research in New Zealand: Patterns, problems and prospects', *Leisure Studies*, 10: 93–104.

Phelps, N. (1992) 'External economies, agglomeration and flexible accumulation', *Transactions of the Institute of British Geographers*, 17: 35–46.

Pigram, J.J. (1977) 'Beach resort morphology', *Habitat International*, 2(5–6): 525–41.

Pigram, J.J. (1980) 'Environmental implications of tourism development', *Annals of Tourism Research*, 7: 554–83.

Pigram, J.J. (1983) *Outdoor Recreation and Resource Management*, Beckenham: Croom Helm.

Pigram, J.J. (1985) *Outdoor Recreation and Resource Management*, 2nd edn, London: Croom Helm.

Pigram, J.J. (1987) *Tourism in Coffs Harbour: Attitudes, Perceptions and Implications*, Coffs Harbour: North Coast Regional Office, Department of Continuing Education, University of New England.

Pigram, J.J. (1990) 'Sustainable tourism: Policy considerations', *Journal of Tourism Studies*, 1(2): 2–9.

Pigram, J.J. and Jenkins, J. (1999) *Outdoor Recreation Management*, London: Routledge.

Pimlico Li, Y. (2000) 'Geographical consciousness and tourism experience', *Annals of Tourism Research*, 27(4): 863–83.

Piperoglou, J. (1966) 'Identification and definition of regions in Greek tourist planning', *Regional Science Association Papers*, pp. 169–76.

Piven, F. (1995) 'Is it global economics or neo-laissez-faire?' *New Left Review*, 213: 107–14.

Pizam, A. (1978) 'Tourism's impacts: The social costs to the destination community as perceived by its residents', *Journal of Travel Research*, 16(4): 8–12.

Place, S.E. (1998) 'How sustainable is ecotourism in Costa Rica?', in C.M. Hall and A.A. Lew (eds) *Sustainable Tourism Development: Geographical Perspectives*, Harlow: Addison Wesley Longman, pp. 107–18.

Plettner, H.J. (1979) *Geographical Aspects of Tourism in the Republic of Ireland*, Research paper 9, Galway: Social Sciences Research Centre, University College.

Plog, S. (1974) 'Why destination areas rise and fall in popularity', *The Cornell Hotel and Restaurant Administration Quarterly*, 15(November): 13–16.

Plog, S. (1977) 'Why destination areas rise and fall in popularity', in E. Kelly (ed.) *Domestic and International Tourism*, Wellesey, MA: Institute of Certified Travel Agents.

Pollard, J. (1989) 'Patterns in Irish tourism', in R.W.G. Carter and A.J. Parker (eds) *Ireland: Contemporary Perspectives on a Land and its People*, London: Routledge, pp. 301–30.

Pollard, J. (1995) 'Tourism and the environment', in P. Breathnach (ed.) *Irish Tourism Development*, Maynooth: Geographical Society of Ireland, pp. 61–77.

Pompl, W. and Lavery, P. (eds) *Tourism in Europe: Structures and Development*, Wallingford: CAB International.

Poon, A. (1989) *Tourism, Technology and Competitive Strategies*, Wallingford: CAB International.

Porter, M. (1980) *Competition in Global Industries*, Boston, MA: Harvard Business School Press.

Potier, F. and Cazes, G. (1996) *Le tourisme urbain*, Paris: PUF.

Potier, F. and Cazes, G. (1998) *Le tourisme et la ville: expériences européennes*, Paris: L'Harmattan.

Powell, J.M. (1978) *Mirrors of the New World: Images and Image – Makers in the Settlement Process*, Canberra: Australian National University Press.

Powell, J. (1985) 'Geography, culture and liberal education', in R. Johnston (ed.) *The Future of Geography*, London: Methuen, pp. 307–25.

Pratt, A. (1998) 'The cultural industries production system: A case study of employment change in Britain, 1984–91', *Environment and Planning A*, 29: 1953–74.

Pred, A. (1981) 'Production, family and free-time projects: A time-geographic perspective on the individual and societal changes in nineteenth century US cities', *Journal of Historical Geography*, 7: 3–86.

Preece, K.M. and Lesslie, R.G. (1987) *A Survey of Wilderness Quality in Victoria*, Melbourne/ Canberra: Ministry for Planning and Environment (Vic) and Australian Heritage Commission.

Priestley, G. and Mundet, L. (1998) 'The post-stagnation phase of the resort cycle', *Annals of Tourism Research*, 25(1): 85–111.

Pritchard, A. and Morgan, N. (2000) 'Privileging the male gaze – gendered tourism landscapes', *Annals of Tourism Research*, 27(4): 884–905.

Pritchard, R. (1976) *Housing and the Spatial Structure of the City*, Cambridge: Cambridge University Press.

Prosser, G. (1986a) 'The limits of acceptable change: An introduction to a framework for natural area planning', *Australian Parks and Recreation*, Autumn: 5–10.

Prosser, G. (1986b) 'Beyond carrying capacity: Establishing limits of acceptable change for park planning', in *Developing Communities into the 21st Century: Proceedings from the 59th National Conference of the Royal Australian Institute of Parks and Recreation*, Melbourne: Royal Australian Institute of Parks and Recreation, pp. 223–33.

Queensland Department of Environment and Heritage (1993) *Green Island and Reef Management Plan*, Cairns: Department of Environment and Heritage.

Ragatz, R.L. (1977) 'Vacation homes in rural areas: Towards a model for predicting their distribution and occupancy patterns', in J.T. Coppock (ed.) *Second Homes: Curse or Blessing*, Oxford: Pergamon Press.

Ralph, E. (2000) *Oppose the Trafficking of Women and Children*, Testimony before the Senate Committee on Foreign Relations Subcommittee on Near Eastern and South Asian Affairs by Regan E. Ralph, Executive Director, Women's Rights Division, Human Rights Watch, International Trafficking of Women and Children, 22 February.

Rapoport, R.N. and Rapoport, R. (1975) *Leisure and the Family Life Cycle*, London: Routledge & Kegan Paul.

Ravenscroft, N. (1992) *Recreation Planning and Development*, Basingstoke: Macmillan.

Redclift, N. and Sinclair, M.T. (eds) (1991) *Working Women: International Perspectives on Labour and Gender Ideology*, London: Routledge.

Reilly, W. (1931) *The Law of Retail Gravitation*, New York: Putnam Press.

Relph, E. (1976) *Place and Placelessness*. London: Pion.

Relph, E. (1981) *Rational Landscapes and Humanistic Geography*, London: Croom Helm.

Restaurant Brands (1997) *Restaurant Brands New Zealand Ltd. Prospectus 1997*, Auckland: F R Partners Limited and Merrill Lynch and Company.

Rethinking Tourism Project (2000) 'EPA solicits public input on cruise ship discharges', *EPA Water News. Electronic Newsletter*, 29 August.

Reynolds, P.C. (1993) 'Food and tourism: Towards an understanding of sustainable culture', *Journal of Sustainable Tourism*, 1(1): 48–54.

Rhodes, R.A.W. (1997) 'From marketisation to diplomacy: It's the mix that matters', *Australian Journal of Public Administration*, 56(2): 40–53.

Richards, G. (1995) 'Politics of national tourism policy in Britain', *Leisure Studies*, 14(3): 153–73.

Ride, W.D.L. (1980) 'Wilderness: An Australian perspective', in R.W. Robertson, P. Helman and A. Davey (eds) *Wilderness Management in Australia, Proceedings of a Symposium Held at the Canberra College of Advanced Education 19–23 July 1978*, Occasional Papers in Recreational Planning, Natural Resources, School of Applied Science, Canberra: Canberra College of Advanced Education, pp. 35–45.

Rink, D.R. and Swan, J.E. (1979) 'Product life cycle research: Literature review', *Journal of Business Research*, 78: 219–42.

Riordan, J. (1982) 'Leisure: The state and the individual in the USSR', *Leisure Studies*, 1(l): 65–80.

Ritchie, J.R.B. (1975) 'Some critical aspects of measurement theory and practice in travel research', in R. McIntosh and C. Goeldner, *Tourism Principles, Practices and Philosophies*, New York: Wiley, pp. 437–51.

Ritchie, J.R.B. (1984) 'Assessing the impact of hallmark events: Conceptual and research issues', *Journal of Travel Research*, 23(1): 2–11.

Ritchie, J.R.B. and Aitken, C. (1984) 'Assessing the impacts of the 1988 Olympic Winter Games: The research program and initial results', *Journal of Travel Research*, 22(3): 17–25.

Ritchie, J.R.B. and Beliveau, D. (1974) 'Hallmark events: An evaluation of a strategic response to seasonality in the travel market', *Journal of Travel Research*, 14 (fall): 14–20.

Ritchie, J.R.B. and Yangzhou, H. (1987) 'The role and impact of mega-events and attractions on national and regional tourism: A conceptual and methodological overview', 37th Annual Congress of the International Association of Scientific Experts in Tourism, Calgary: AIEST.

Ritter, W. and Schafer, C. (1999) 'Cruise-tourism: A chance of sustainability', *Tourism Recreation Research*, 23(1) 65–71.

Ritzer, G. (1993) *The McDonaldization of Society*, Thousand Oaks, CA: Pine Forge.

Roberts, K. (1999) *Leisure in Contemporary Society*, Wallingford: CAB International.

Roberts, R. (1971) *The Classic Slum: Salford Life in the First Quarter of the Century*, Penguin: Harmondsworth.

Roberts, R. (1976) *A Ragged Schooling: Growing Up in the Classic Slum*, London: Fontana.

Robinson, D. (1991) 'Living with peripherality', *Transport*, November/December: 177–85.

Robinson, G.M. (1990) *Conflict and Change in the Countryside*, London: Belhaven Press.

Robinson, G.M. (1999) 'Countryside recreation management', in M. Pacione (ed.) *Applied Geography: Principles and Practice*, London: Routledge, pp. 257–73.

Robinson, G.W. (1972) 'The recreational geography of South Asia', *The Geographical Review*, 62(4): 561–73.

Robinson, H. (1976) *A Geography of Tourism*, Harlow: Longman.

Roche, F. W. and Murray, J. A. (1978) *Tourism and Archaeology: A Study of Wood Quay*, Dublin: McIver.

Roche, M. (1992) 'Mega-events and micro-modernisation: On the sociology of the new urban tourism', *British Journal of Sociology*, 43(4): 563–600.

Rodgers, H. (1973) 'The demand for recreation', *Geographical Journal*, 13(9): 467–73.

Rodgers, H. (1969) *British Pilot National Recreation Survey Report No 1*, London: British Travel Association/University of Keele.

Rodgers, H. (1977) 'The leisure future: Problems of prediction', in J. Settle (ed.) *Leisure in the North-West: A Tool for Forecasting*, Manchester: Sports Council Study No 11.

Rodgers, H. (1993) 'Estimating local leisure demand in the context of a regional planning strategy', in S. Glyptis (ed.) *Leisure and the Environment: Essays in Honour of Professor J. A. Patmore*, London: Belhaven Press, pp. 116–30.

Rodgers, H. and Patmore, J.A. (eds) (1972) *Leisure in the North-West*, Manchester: North-West Sports Council.

Rogers, G.F., Malde, H.E. and Turner, R.M. (1984) *Bibliography of Repeat Photography for Evaluating Landscape Change*, Salt Lake City: University of Utah Press.

Romeril, M. (1984) 'Coastal tourism – the experience of Great Britain', *Industry and Environment*, 7(1): 4–7.

Romeril, M. (1988) 'Coastal tourism and the Heritage Coast programme in England and Wales', *Tourism Recreation Research*, 13(2): 15–19.

Rose, M. (ed.) (1985) *The Poor and the City: The English Poor Law in its Urban Context 1834–1914*, Leicester: Leicester University Press.

Rosemary, J. (1987) *Indigenous Enterprises in Kenya's Tourism Industry*, Geneva: UNESCO.

Rosenfried, S. (1997) 'Global sex slavery', *San Francisco Examiner*, 6 April.

Rothman, R.A. (1978) 'Residents and transients: Community reaction to seasonal visitors', *Journal of Travel Research*, 16(3): 8–13.

Rothman, R.A., Donnelly, P.G. and Tower, J.K. (1979) 'Police departments in resort communities: Organizational adjustments to population undulation', *Leisure Sciences*, 2: 105–18.

Rottman, D. (1989) 'Crime in geographical perspective', in R.W.G. Carter and A.J. Parker (eds) *Ireland: Contemporary Perspectives on a Land and its People*, London: Routledge, pp. 87–111.

Rowntree, S. and Lavers, G. (1951) *English Life and Leisure: A Social Study*, London: Longmans, Green & Co.

Royer, L.E., McCool, S.F. and Hunt, J.D. (1974) 'The relative importance of tourism to state economies', *Journal of Travel Research*, 11(4): 13–16.

Rubio, (1998–99) 'La imagen geográphica del turismo en Espana (1962–1998): Creónica breve de una gran expansión', *Boletín de la Real Sociedad Geográfica*, 134–5: 67–103.

Rudkin, B. and Hall, C.M. (1996) 'Unable to see the forest for the trees: Ecotourism development in Solomon Islands', in R. Butler and T. Hinch (eds) *Tourism and Indigenous Peoples*, London: International Thomson Business Publishing, pp. 203–26.

Runte, A. (1972a) 'How Niagara Falls was saved: The beginning of aesthetic conservation in the United States', *The Conservationist*, 26(April–May): 32–5, 43.

Runte, A. (1972b) 'Yellowstone: It's useless, so why not a park', *National Parks and Conservation Magazine: The Environment Journal*, 46(March): 4–7.

Runte, A. (1973) '"Worthless" lands – our national parks: The enigmatic past and uncertain future of America's scenic wonderlands', *American West*, 10(May): 4–11.

Runte, A. (1974a) 'Pragmatic alliance: Western railroads and the national parks', *National Parks and Conservation Magazine: The Environmental Journal*, 48(April): 14–21.

Runte, A. (1974b) 'Yosemite Valley Railroad highway of history', *National Parks and Conservation Magazine: The Environmental Journal*, 48(December): 4–9.

Runte, A. (1977) 'The national park idea: Origins and paradox of the American experience', *Journal of Forest History*, 21(2): 64–75.

Runte, A. (1979) *National Parks The American Experience*, Lincoln: University of Nebraska Press.

Runte, A. (1990) *Yosemite: The Embattled Wilderness*, Lincoln: University of Nebraska Press.

Runyan, D. and Wu, C. (1979) 'Assessing tourism's more complex consequences', *Annals of Tourism Research*, 6: 448–63.

Rural Development Commission (1991a) *Tourism in the Countryside: A Strategy for Rural England*, London: Rural Development Commission.

Rural Development Commission (1991b) *Meeting the Challenge of Rural Adjustment: A New Rural Development Commission Initiative*, London: Rural Development Commission.

Russell, J.A., Matthews, J.H. and Jones, R. (1979) *Wilderness in Tasmania: A Report to the Australian Heritage Commission*, Occasional Paper 10, Hobart: Centre for Environmental Studies, University of Tasmania.

Ryan, C. (1991) *Recreational Tourism: A Social Science Perspective*, London: Routledge.

Ryan, C. (1995) *Researching Tourism Satisfaction: Issues, Concepts, Problems*, London: Routledge.

Ryan, C. (ed.) (1997) *The Tourist Experience: A New Introduction*, London: Cassell.

Ryan, C. and Hall, C.M. (2001) *Sex Tourism: Travels in Liminality*, London: Routledge.

Sadler, D. (1993) 'Place-marketing, competitive places and the construction of hegemony in Britain in the 1980s', in G. Kearns and C. Philo (eds) *Selling Places: The City as Cultural Capital, Past and Present*, Oxford: Pergamon Press, pp. 175–92.

Saeter, J.A. (1998) 'The significance of tourism and economic development in rural areas: A Norwegian case study', in R. Butler, C.M. Hall and J. Jenkins (eds) *Tourism and Recreation in Rural Areas*, Chichester: Wiley, pp. 237–47.

Samdahl, D. and Jekubovich, N. (1997) 'A critique of leisure constraints: Comparative analyses and understandings', *Journal of Leisure Research*, 29(4): 430–52.

Sant, M. (1982) *Applied Geography*, Harlow:Longman.

Sawicki, D. (1989) 'The festival marketplace as public policy', *Journal of the American Planning Association*, summer: 347–61.

Schaer, U. (1978) 'Traffic problems in holiday resorts', *Tourist Review*, 33: 9–15.

Schofield, P. (1996) 'Cinematographic images of a city: Alternative heritage tourism in Manchester', *Tourism Management*, 17(5): 333–40.

Schwarz, C.F., Thor, E.C. and Elsner, G.H. (1976) *Wildland Planning Glossary*, Washington, DC: US Department of Agriculture, Forest Service.

Scott, N.R. (1974) 'Towards a psychology of the wilderness experience', *Natural Resource Journal*, 14: 231–7.

Seaton, A. and Bennett, M. (eds) (1996) *Marketing Tourism Products*, London: International Thomson Business Publishing.

Seeley, I. (1983) *Outdoor Recreation and the Urban Environment*, Basingstoke: Macmillan.

Seers, D. and Ostrom, K. (eds) (1982) *The Crisis of the European Regions*, New York: St Martin's Press.

Seers, D., Schaffer, B. and Kiljunen, M. (eds) (1979) *Underdeveloped Europe: Studies in Core–Periphery Relations*, Sussex: Harvester Press.

Selin, S. (1993) 'Collaborative alliances: New interorganizational forms in tourism', *Journal of Travel and Tourism Marketing*, 2(2/3): 217–27.

Selin, S. (1998) 'The promise and pitfalls of collaborating', *Trends*, 35(1): 9–13.

Selin, S. and Chavez, D. (1994) 'Characteristics of successful tourism partnerships: A multiple case study design', *Journal of Park and Recreation Administration*, 12(2): 51–62.

Selke, A.C. (1936) 'Geographic aspects of the German tourist trade', *Economic Geography*, 12: 206–16.

Selwood, H.J. and Hall, C. (1986) 'The America's Cup: A hallmark tourist event', in J.S. Marsh (ed.) *Canadian Studies of Parks, Recreation and Tourism in Foreign Lands*, Occasional Paper 11, Peterborough: Department of Geography, Trent University.

Sessa, A. (1993) *Elements of Tourism*, Rome: Catal.

Sewell, W.R.D. and Dearden, P. (1989) *Wilderness: Past, Present and Future*, special issue of *Natural Resources Journal*, 29: 1–222.

Shackelford, P. (1980) 'Keeping tabs on tourism: A manager's guide to tourism statistics', *International Journal of Tourism Management*, 1(3): 148–57.

Share, B. (1992) *Shannon Departures: A Study in Regional Initiatives*, Dublin: Gill & Macmillan.

Sharpley, R. (1993) *Tourism and Leisure in the Countryside*, Managing Tourism Series, No. 5, Huntingdon: Elm Publications.

Sharpley, R. and Sharpley, J. (1997) *Rural Tourism*, London: International Thomson Business Publishing.

Shaw, B.J. (1985) 'Fremantle and the America's Cup . . . the spectre of development?', *Urban Policy and Research*, 3: 38–40.

Shaw, B.J. (1986) *Fremantle W.A. and the America's Cup: The Impact of a Hallmark Event*, Working Paper No. 11, London: University of London, Australian Studies Centre, Institute for Commonwealth Studies.

Shaw, D.J. (1979) 'Recreation and the socialist city', in R. French and F. Hamilton (eds) *The Socialist City: Spatial Structure and Urban Policy*, Chichester: Wiley, pp. 119–44.

Shaw, G. and Williams, A.M. (1990) 'Tourism, economic development and the role of entrepreneurial activity', in C. Cooper (ed.) *Progress in Tourism, Recreation and Hospitality Management*, Vol. 2, London: Belhaven Press, pp. 67–81.

Shaw, G. and Williams, A.M. (1994) *Critical Issues in Tourism: A Geographical Perspective*, Oxford: Blackwell.

Shaw, G. and Williams, A.M. (eds) (1997) *The Rise and Fall of British Coastal Resorts: Cultural and Economic Perspectives*, London: Mansell.

Shaw, G., Agarwal, S. and Bull, P. (2000) 'Tourism consumption and tourist behaviour: A British perspective', *Tourism Geographies*, 2(3): 264–89.

Shaw, S., Bonen, A. and McCabe, J. (1991) 'Do more constraints mean less leisure? Examining the relationship between constraints and participation', *Journal of Leisure Research*, 23: 286–300.

Shelby, B. and Heberlein, T.A. (1984) 'A conceptual framework for carrying capacity', *Leisure Sciences*, 6: 433–51.

Shelby, B. and Heberlein, T.A. (1986) *Carrying Capacity in Recreation Settings*, Corvallis: Oregon State University Press.

Shelby, B., Bregenzer, N.S. and Johnston, R. (1988) 'Displacement and product shift: Empirical evidence from Oregon Rivers', *Journal of Leisure Research*, 20(4): 274–88.

Shelby, B., Vaske, J.J. and Heberlein, T.A. (1989) 'Comparative analysis of crowding in multiple locations: Results from fifteen years of research', *Leisure Sciences*, 11(4): 269–91.

Shields, R. (1991) *Places on the Margin: Alternative Geographies of Modernity*. London: Routledge.

Shinew, K. and Arnold, M. (1998) 'Gender equity in the leisure services field', *Journal of Leisure, Research*, 30(2): 177–94.

Shoard, M. (1976) 'Fields which planners should conquer', *Forma*, 4: 128–35.

Short, J.R. (1991) *Imagined Country: Society, Culture and Environment*, London: Routledge.

Shucksmith, M. (1983) 'Second homes: A framework for policy', *Town Planning Review*, 54(2): 174–93.

Shurmer-Smith, P. and Hannam, K. (1994) *Worlds of Desire, Realms of Power: A Cultural Geography*, London: Arnold.

Sidaway, R. and Duffield, B. (1984) 'A new look at countryside recreation in the urban fringe', *Leisure Studies*, 3: 249–71.

Simeon, R. (1976) 'Studying public policy', *Canadian Journal of Political Science*, 9(4): 558–80.

Simmons, D.G. (1997) *National Profiles: Domestic Tourism Prototype Survey*, Lincoln: Lincoln University.

Simmons, I. (1974) *The Ecology of Natural Resources*, London: Edward Arnold.

Simmons, I. (1975) *Rural Recreation in the Industrial World*, London: Edward Arnold.

Simmons, R., Davis, B.W., Chapman, R.J. and Sager, D.D. (1974) 'Policy flow analysis: A conceptual model for comparative public policy research', *Western Political Quarterly*, 27(3): 457–68.

Simpson Xavier Horwath (1990) *Irish Hotel Industry Review*, Dublin: Simpson Xavier Horwath.

Sinclair, J. (1986) 'Counting the loss of wilderness', *Habitat*, 14(3): 14–15.

Sinclair, M.T. (1991) 'The economics of tourism', in C. Cooper (ed.) *Progress in Tourism, Recreation and*

Hospitality Management, Vol. 3, London: Belhaven Press, pp. 1–27.

Sinclair, M.T. and Stabler, M. (eds) (1992) *The Tourism Industry: An International Analysis*, Wallingford: CAB International.

Singapore Tourism Board (STB) (1996) *Tourism 21: Vision of a Tourism Capital*, Singapore: STB.

Slee, W. (1982) *An Evaluation of Country Park Policy*, Gloucestershire Papers in Local and Rural Planning No. 16, Cheltenham: GLOSCAT.

Smith, D.M. (1977) *Human Geography: A Welfare Approach*, London: Edward Arnold.

Smith, M. and Turner, L. (1973) 'Some aspects of the sociology of tourism', *Society and Leisure*, 3: 55–71.

Smith, P.E. (1977) 'A value analysis of wilderness', *Search*, 8(9): 311–17.

Smith, R.A. (1991) 'Beach resorts: A model of development evolution', *Landscape and Urban Planning*, 21: 189–210.

Smith, R.A. (1992a) 'Beach resort evolution: Implications for planning', *Annals of Tourism Research*, 19: 304–22.

Smith, R.A. (1992b) 'Review of integrated beach resort development in South East Asia', *Land Use Policy*, 211–17.

Smith, R.A. (1994) 'Planning and management for coastal eco-tourism in Indonesia: A regional perspective', *Indonesian Quarterly*, 22(2): 148–57.

Smith, R.V. and Mitchell, L.S. (1990) 'Geography and tourism: A review of selected literature', in C. Cooper (ed.) *Progress in Tourism, Recreation and Hospitality Management*, Vol. 2, London: Belhaven Press, pp. 50–66.

Smith, S.J. (1987) 'Fear of crime: Beyond a geography of deviance', *Progress in Human Geography*, 11: 1–23.

Smith, S.L.J. (1983a) *Recreational Geography*, Harlow: Longman.

Smith, S.L.J. (1983b) 'Restaurants and dining out: Geography of a tourism business', *Annals of Tourism Research*, 10(4): 515–49.

Smith, S.L.J. (1987) 'Regional analysis of tourism resources', *Annals of Tourism Research*, 14: 253–73.

Smith, S.L.J. (1989) *Tourism Analysis*, Harlow: Longman.

Smith, S.L.J. (1995) *Tourism Analysis*, 2nd edn, Harlow: Longman.

Smith, S.L.J. and Brown, B.A. (1981) 'Directional bias in vacation travel', *Annals of Tourism Research*, 8: 257–70.

Smith, V.L. (ed.) (1977) *Hosts and Guests: The Anthropology of Tourism*, Philadelphia: University of Pennsylvania Press.

Smith, V.L. (ed.) (1992) *Hosts and Guests: An Anthropology of Tourism*, 2nd edn, Philadelphia: University of Pennsylvannia Press.

Smyth, H. (1994) *Marketing the City: The Role of Flagship Developments in Urban Regeneration*, London: E&FN Spon.

Snaith, T. and Haley, A. (1999) 'Resident opinions of tourism development in the historic city of York, England', *Tourism Management*, 20(5): 595–603.

Soja, E.W. (1989) *Postmodern Geographies: The Reassertion of Space in Critical Social Theory*, London: Verso.

Solecki, W. and Welch, J. (1995) 'Urban parks: Green spaces or green walls?', *Landscape and Urban Planning*, 32: 93–106.

Sopher, D. (1968) 'Pilgrim circulation in Gujurat', *The Geographical Review*, 58: 392–45.

Spencer, J. and Thomas, W. (1948) 'The hill stations and summer resorts of the Orient', *The Geographical Review*, 38: 637–51.

Squire, S.J. (1993) 'Valuing countryside: Reflections on Beatrix Potter tourism', *Area*, 25(1): 5–10.

Squire, S.J. (1994) 'Accounting for cultural meanings: The interface between geography and tourism studies revisited', *Progress in Human Geography*, 18: 1–16.

Stabler, M. (1990) 'The concept of opportunity sets as a methodological framework for the analysis of selling tourism places: The industry view', in G.J. Ashworth and B. Goodall (eds) *Marketing Tourism Places*, London: Routledge, pp. 23–41.

Stamp, D. (1948) *The Land of Britain: Its Use and Misuse*, Harlow: Longman.

Stamp, D. (1960) *Applied Geography*, London: Penguin.

Stankey, G.H. (1973) *Visitor Perception of Wilderness Carrying Capacity*, USDA, Forest Service Research Paper, INT–42, Ogden, UT: Intermountain Forest and Range Experiment Station.

Stankey, G.H. (1989) 'Beyond the campfire's light: Historical roots of the wilderness concept', *Natural Resources Journal*, 29: 9–24.

Stankey, G.H. and McCool, S.F. (1984) 'Carrying capacity in recreational settings: Evolution, appraisal, and application', *Leisure Sciences*, 6(4): 453–73.

Stankey, G.H. and Schreyer, R. (1987) 'Attitudes toward wilderness and factors affecting visitor behaviour: A state of knowledge review', in *Proceedings – National Wilderness Research Conference: Issues, State of Knowledge and Future Directions*, General Technical Report INT–220, Ogden, UT: Intermountain Research Station, pp. 246–93.

Stankey, G.H., Cole, D.N., Lucas, R.C., Petersen, M.E. and Frissell, S. (1985) *The Limits of Acceptable Change System for Wilderness Planning*, USDA, Forest Service Research Paper, INT–176, Ogden, UT: Intermountain Forest and Range Experiment Station.

Stansfield, C. A. and Rickert, J.'E. (1970) 'The recreational business district', *Journal of Leisure Research*, 2(4): 213–25.

Stanton, J.P. and Morgan, M.G. (1977) *Project 'RAKES' – A Rapid Appraisal of Key and Endangered Sites, Report No. 1: The Queensland Case Study*, A Report to the Department of Environment, Housing and Community Development, Armidale: School of Natural Resources, University of New England.

Stationery Office (1999) *Regional Trends* 34, London: Stationery Office.

Stea, R. and Downs, R. (1970) 'From the outside looking in at the inside looking out', *Environment and Behaviour*, 2: 3–12.

Stebbins, R.A. (1979) *Amateurs: On the Margin Between Work and Leisure*, Beverly Hills, CA: Sage Publications.

Stebbins, R.A. (1982) 'Serious leisure: A conceptual statement', *Pacific Sociological Review*, 25: 251–72.

Stevens, T. (1987) 'Going underground', *Leisure Management*, 7: 48–50.

Stevens, T. (1991) 'Irish eyes are smiling', *Leisure Management*, 11: 46–8.

Stockdale, J.E. (1985) *What is Leisure? An Empirical Analysis of the Concept of Leisure and the Role of Leisure in People's Lives*, London: Sports Council.

Stoddart, D.R. (1981) 'Ideas and interpretation in the history of geography', in D.R. Stoddart (ed.) *Geography, Ideology and Social Concern*, Oxford: Blackwell, pp. 1–7.

Stoffle, R.W., Last, C. and Evans, M. (1979) 'Reservation-based tourism: Implications of tourist attitudes for Native American economic development', *Human Organization*, 38(3): 300–6.

Stone, G. and Taves, M. (1957) 'Research into the human element in wilderness use', *Proceedings of the 1956 Meeting of the Society of American Foresters*, pp. 26–32.

Strachan, A. and Bowler, I. (1976) 'The development of public parks in the City of Leicester', *East Midland Geographer*, 6: 275–83.

Stringer, P. (1984) 'Studies in the socio-environmental psychology of tourism', *Annals of Tourism Research*, 11: 147–66.

Stringer, P. and Pearce, P.L. (1984) 'Towards a symbiosis of social psychology and tourism studies', *Annals of Tourism Research*, 11: 5–18.

Strong, R. (1997) 'External factors: State and local government controls; community expectations', mimeo of paper presented at Business With Style: Adapting Heritage Buildings for Commercial Use, New South Wales Government, Heritage Office, Sydney.

Survey Research Associates (1991) *London Docklands Visitor Survey: Summary of Findings*, London: London Docklands Development Corporation.

Takeuchi, K. (1984) 'Some remarks on the geography of tourism in Japan', *GeoJournal*, 9(1): 85–90.

Talbot, M. (1979) *Women and Leisure*, London: Sports Council/Social Science Research Council Joint Panel on Leisure and Recreation Research.

Tanner, M. (1971) 'The planning and management of water recreation areas', in P. Lavery (ed.) *Recreational Geography*, Newton Abbot: David and Charles, pp. 197–214.

Tanner, M. (1973) 'The recreational use of inland waters', *Geographical Journal*, 139: 486–91.

Tanner, M. (1977) *Recreational Use of Water Supply Reservoirs in England and Wales*, Research Report No. 3, London: Waterspace Amenity Commission.

Tarlow, P.E. and Muehsam, M.J. (1992) 'Wide horizons: Travel and tourism in the coming decades', *The Futurist*, 26(5): 28–33.

Tarrant, M. and Cordell, H. (1999) 'Environmental justice and the spatial distribution of outdoor recreation sites: An application of geographic information systems', *Journal of Leisure Research*, 31(1): 18–34.

Taylor, D. (1999) 'Central Park as a model for social control: Urban parks, social class and leisure behaviour in nineteenth century America', *Journal of Leisure Research*, 31(4): 426–77.

Taylor, G. (ed.) (1951) *Geography in the Twentieth Century*, London: Methuen.

Taylor, J., Legellé, J.G., and Andrew, C. (eds) (1993) *Capital Cities: International Perspectives/Les capitales: Perspectives internationales*, Ottawa: Carleton University Press.

Taylor, P.J. (1985) 'The value of a geographical perspective', in R.J. Johnston (ed.) *The Future of Geography*, London: Methuen, pp. 92–110.

Taylor, R., Shumaker, S. and Gottfredson, S. (1985) 'Neighbourhood-level links between physical features and local sentiments. Deterioration, fear of crime and confidence', *Journal of Architectural and Planning Research*, 2: 261–75.

Taylor, S.G. (1990) 'Naturalness: The concept and its application to Australian ecosystems', *Proceedings of the Ecological Society of Australia*, 16: 411–18.

Teisl, M. and Reiling, S. (1992) 'Measuring tourism impacts at the community level. The impact of tourism on local government public service expenditures' (www.msue.edu/msue/imp/modtd/33519758.htr)

Telfer, D.J. (2000) 'The Northeast Wine Route: Wine tourism in Ontario, Canada and New York State', in C.M. Hall, E. Sharples, B. Cambourne and N. Macionis (eds) *Wine Tourism Around the World: Development, Management and Markets*, Oxford: Butterworth Heinemann, pp. 253–71.

Telfer, D.J. (forthcoming) 'Tastes of Niagara: Building strategic alliances between tourism and agriculture', *International Journal of Hospitality and Tourism Administration*.

Telfer, D.J. and Wall. G. (1996) 'Linkages between tourism and food production', *Annals of Tourism Research*, 23(3): 635–53.

Teo, P. and Chang, T.C. (2000) 'Singapore: Tourism development in a planned context', in C.M. Hall and S.J. Page (eds) *Tourism in South and South-East Asia: Cases and Issues*, Oxford: Butterworth Heinemann, pp.117–28.

The Countryside Agency (1999) *The State of the Countryside 1999*, Cheltenham: The Countryside Agency.

Therborn, G. (1996) *Monumental Europe: The National Years of the Iconography of European Capital Cities*, Gothenberg: University of Gothenberg.

Thoreau, H.D. (1854 (1968)) *Walden*, Everyman's Library, London: Dent.

Thorpe, H. (1970) 'A new deal for allotments: Solutions to a pressing land use problem', *Area*, 3: 1–8.

Threndyle, S. (1994) 'Towns in transition: Careful tourism-planning can soften the blows of changing times in resource-based economies, but there's no panacea', *Georgia Straight*, 22–29 July.

Thrift, N. (1977) *An Introduction to Time Geography*, Norwich: Catmog 13.

Thurot, J.M. and Thurot, G. (1983) 'The ideology of class and tourism confronting the discourse of advertising', *Annals of Tourism Research*, 10: 173–89.

Tillman, A. (1974) *The Program Book for Recreation Professionals*, Palo Alto: National Press Books.

Timmermans, H.J.P. and Morgansky, M. (eds) (1999) 'Direct marketing: Where the old meets the new', *Journal of Business Research* (special issue), 45: 247–304.

Tombaugh, L.W (1970) 'Factors influencing home location', *Journal of Leisure Research*, 2(1): 54–63.

Torkildsen, G. (1983) *Leisure and Recreation Management*, London: E & FN Spon.

Torkildsen, G. (1992) *Leisure and Recreation Management*, 3rd edn, London: E & FN Spon.

Tourism Council of the South Pacific (1988) *Nature Legislation and Nature Conservation as a Part of Tourism Development in the Island Pacific: A Report Covering Cook Islands, Fiji, Kiribati, Niue, Papua New Guinea, Solomon Islands, Tonga, Tuvulu, Vanuatu and Western Samoa*, Suva: Tourism Council of the South Pacific.

Tourism Development International (1992) *Visitors to Tourist Attractions in Ireland in 1992*, Dublin: Tourism Development International.

Towner, J. (1985) 'The Grand Tour: A key phase in the history of tourism', *Annals of Tourism Research*, 12(3): 297–333.

Towner, J. (1996) *An Historical Geography of Recreation and Tourism in the Western World 1540–1940*, Chichester: Wiley.

Townsend, A. (1991) 'Services and local economic development', *Area*, 23: 309–17.

Townsend, P. (1979) *Poverty in the UK: A Survey of Household Resources and Standards of Living*, Harmondsworth: Penguin.

Tuan, Yi-Fu (1971) *Man and Nature*, Washington, DC: Commission on College Geography, Association of American Geographers.

Tuan, Yi-Fu (1974) *Topophilia: A Study of Environmental Perception, Attitudes, and Values*, Englewood Cliffs, NJ: Prentice Hall.

Tuan, Yi-Fu (1979) *Landscapes of Fear*, New York: Pantheon.

Tubridy, M. (ed.) (1987) *Heritage Zones: The Co-existence of Agriculture, Nature Conservation and Tourism: The Clonmacnoise Example*, Environmental Science Unit, Occasional Publication, Dublin: Trinity College.

Tunbridge, J.E. (1998) 'Tourism management in Ottawa, Canada: Nurturing in a fragile environment', in D. Tyler, Y. Guerrier and M. Robertson (eds) *Managing Tourism in Cities: Policy, Process and Practice*, London: Wiley, pp. 91–108.

Tunbridge, J.E. (2000) 'Heritage momentum or maelstrom? The case of Ottawa's Byward Market', *International Journal of Heritage Studies*, 6(3): 269–91.

Tunbridge, J.E. and Ashworth, G.J. (1996) *Dissonant Heritage: The Management of the Past as a Resource in Conflict*, Chichester: Wiley.

Tunstall, S. and Penning-Rowsell, E. (1998) 'The English beach: Experience and values', *Geographical Journal*, 164(3): 319–32.

Twight, B. (1983) *Organizational Values and Political Power: The Forest Service Versus the Olympic National Park*, University Park: The Pennsylvania State University Press.

Tyler, D., Guerrier, Y. and Robertson, M. (eds) (1998) *Managing Tourism in Cities: Policy, Process and Practice*, Chichester: Wiley.

UNESCO (1976) 'The effects of tourism on socio-cultural values', *Annals of Tourism Research*, November/December: 74–105.

United Nations (UN) (1994) *Recommendations on Tourism Statistics*, New York: United Nations.

United Nations, Division for Social Policy and Development (1998) *The Ageing of the World's Population*, New York: United Nations (http://www.un.org/esa/socdev/agewpop.htm)

United States Department of the Interior (1978) *National Urban Recreation Study*, Washington, DC: United States Department of the Interior.

Unwin, K. (1976) 'The relationship of observer and landscape in landscape evaluation', *Transactions of the Institute of British Geographers*, 66: 130–4.

Urry, J. (1987) 'Some social and spatial aspects of services', *Society and Space*, 5: 5–26.

Urry, J. (1988) 'Cultural change and contemporary holidaymaking', *Theory, Culture and Society*, 5: 35–55.

Urry, J. (1990) *The Tourist Gaze: Leisure and Travel in Contemporary Societies*, London: Sage.

Urry, J. (1991) 'The sociology of tourism', in C.P. Cooper (ed.) *Progress in Tourism, Recreation and Hospitality Management*, Vol. 3, London: Belhaven Press, pp. 48–57.

Urry, J. (2000) *Sociology Beyond Societies: Mobilities for the Twenty-First Century*, London: Routledge.

Uysal, M. (1998) 'The determinants of tourism demand: A theoretical perspective', in D. Ioannides and K. Debbage (eds) *The Economic Geography of the Tourist Industry: A Supply-side Analysis*, London: Routledge, pp. 79–95.

Uysal, M. and Crompton, J.L. (1985) 'An overview of approaches to forecasting tourist demand', *Journal of Travel Research*, 23(4): 7–15.

Uzzell, D. (1984) 'An alternative structuralist approach to the psychology of tourism marketing', *Annals of Tourism Research*, 11: 79–100.

Valentine, G. (1989) 'The geography of woman's fear', *Area*, 21(4): 385–90.

Valentine, G. (1990) 'Women's fear and the design of public space', *Built Environment*, 16(4): 288–303.

Valentine, P. (1980) 'Tropical rainforest and the wilderness experience', in V. Martin (ed.) *Wilderness*, Findhorn: Findhorn Press, pp. 123–32.

Valentine, P. (1984) 'Wildlife and tourism: Some ideas on potential and conflict', in B. O'Rourke (ed.) *Contemporary Issues in Australian Tourism, 19th Institute of Australian Geographer's Conference and International Geographical Union Sub-Commission on Tourism in the South West Pacific*, Sydney: Department of Geography, University of Sydney, pp. 29–54.

Valentine, P. (1992) 'Review. Nature-based tourism', in B. Weiler and C.M. Hall (eds) *Special Interest Tourism*, London: Belhaven Press.

Van der Knaap, W. (1999) 'Research report: GIS-oriented analysis of tourist time–space patterns to support sustainable tourism development', *Tourism Geographies*, 1(1): 56–69.

Van Raaij, W.F. (1986) 'Consumer research on tourism: Mental and behavioural constructs', *Annals of Tourism Research*, 13: 1–10.

Van Raaij, W.F. and Francken, D.A. (1984) 'Vacation decisions, activities, and satisfactions', *Annals of Tourism Research*, 11: 101–13.

Van Westering, J. (1999) 'Heritage and gastronomy: The pursuits of the "new" tourist', *International Journal of Heritage Studies*, 5(2): 75–81.

Vaughan, D.R., Farr, H. and Slee, W. (2000) 'Estimating and interpreting the local economic benefits of visitor spending', *Leisure Studies*, 19(2): 95–118.

Vaughan, D.R. (1977) 'Opportunity cost and the assessment and development of regional tourism', in B.S. Duffield (ed.) *Tourism: A Tool for Regional Development*, Edinburgh: Tourism and Recreation Research Unit, University of Edinburgh, pp. 8.1–8.9.

Veal, A. (1987) *Leisure and the Future*, London: Unwin & Hyman.

Veal, A. and Travis, T. (1979) 'Local authority leisure services – the state of play', *Local Government Studies*, 5: 5–16.

Veal, A.J. (1992) *Research Methods for Leisure and Tourism: A Practical Guide*, Harlow: Longman.

Vendenin, Y. (1978) 'Evolution of the recreational functions of a territory', *Soviet Geography*, 19: 646–59.

Vetter, F. (ed.) (1985) *Big City Tourism*, Berlin: Dietrich Verlag.

Vickerman, R. (1975) *The Economics of Leisure and Recreation*, London: Macmillan.

Vidal, J. (1994). 'Parks: Who needs them?', *The Guardian*, 21 July.

Visser, N. and Njunga, S. (1992) 'Environmental impacts of tourism on the Kenya coast', *Industry and Environment*, 15(3/4): 42–52.

Vogeler, I. (1977) 'Farm and ranch vacationing', *Journal of Leisure Research*, 9: 291–300.

Wager, J. (1995) 'Developing a strategy for the Angkor World Heritage site', *Tourism Management*, 16 (7): 515–23.

Waitt, G. (1997) 'Selling paradise and adventure: Representations of landscape in the tourist advertising of Australia', *Australian Geographical Studies*, 35(1): 47–60.

Waitt, G. and McGuirk, P.M. (1997) 'Marking time: Tourism and heritage representation at Millers Point, Sydney', *Australian Geographer*, 27(1): 11–29.

Wall, G. (1971) 'Car-owners and holiday activities', in P. Lavery (ed.) *Recreational Geography*, Newton Abbot: David and Charles, pp. 97–111.

Wall, G. (1972) 'Socio-economic variations in pleasure trip patterns: The case of Hull car-owners', *Transactions of the Institute of British Geographers*, 57: 45–58.

Wall, G. (1983a) 'Atlantic City tourism and social change', *Annals of Tourism Research*, 10: 555–6.

Wall, G. (1983b) 'Cycles and capacity: A contradiction in terms?', *Annals of Tourism Research*, 10: 268–70.

Wall, G. (ed.) (1989) *Outdoor Recreation in Canada*, Toronto: Wiley.

Wall, G. and Marsh, J. (eds) (1982) *Recreational Land Use, Perspectives on its Evolution in Canada*, Ottawa: Carleton University Press.

Wall, G. and Wright, C. (1977) *The Environmental Impacts of Outdoor Recreation*, Publication Series No. 11, Waterloo: Department of Geography, University of Waterloo.

Wall, G., Dudycha, D. and Hutchinson, J. (1985) 'Point pattern analysis of accommodation in Toronto', *Annals of Tourism Research*, 12(4): 603–18.

Walle, A. (1997) 'Quantitative versus qualitative tourism research', *Annals of Tourism Research*, 24 (3): 524–36.

Walmesley, D.J. and Jenkins, J. (1992) 'Tourism cognitive mapping of unfamiliar environments', *Annals of Tourism Research*, 19(3): 268–86.

Walmesley, D.J. and Jenkins, J. (1994) 'Evaluations of recreation opportunities: Tourist impacts of the New South Wales North Coast', in D. Mercer (ed.) *New Viewpoints in Australian Outdoor Recreation Research and Planning*. Melbourne: Hepper Marriot and Associates, pp. 89–98.

Walmesley, D.J. and Lewis, G.J. (1993) *People and Environment: Behavioural Approaches in Human Geography*, 2nd edn, Harlow: Longman.

Walmesley, D.J., Boskovic, R.M. and Pigram, J.J. (1981) *Tourism and Crime*, Armidale: Department of Geography, University of New England.

Walmesley, D.J., Boskovic, R.M. and Pigram, J.J. (1983) 'Tourism and crime: An Australian perspective', *Journal of Leisure Research*, 15: 136–55.

Walsh, K. (1988) 'The consequences of competition', in J. Bennington and J. White (eds) *The Future of Leisure Services*, Harlow: Longman, pp. 37–56.

Walter, R.D. (1975) *The Impact of Tourism on the Environment*, ARRA Monograph 7, Melbourne: Australian Recreation Research Association.

Walton, J. (1983) *The English Seaside Resort: A Social History 1750–1914*, Leicester: Leicester University Press.

Walton, J. (2000) 'The hospitality trades: A social history', in C. Lashley and A. Morrison (eds) *In Search of Hospitality: Theoretical Perspectives and Debates*, Oxford: Butterworth Heinemann, pp. 56–76.

Walton, J. and Smith, J. (1996) 'The first century of beach tourism in Spain: San Sebastian and the Playas del Norte from the 1830s to the 1930s', in M. Barke, J. Towner and M. Newton (eds) *Tourism in Spain: Critical Issues*, Wallingford: CAB International, pp. 189–212.

Ward, C. and Hardy, D. (1986) *Goodnight Campers: The History of the British Holiday Camp*, London: Mansell.

Warr, M. (1985) 'Fear of rape among urban women', *Social Problems*, 32: 238–50.

Weaver, D. (1998) *Ecotourism in the Less Developed World*, Wallingford: CAB International.

Weaver, D. (2000) 'A broad context model of destination development scenarios', *Tourism Management*, 21: 217–34.

Weiler, B. (1991) *Ecotourism: Conference Proceedings*, Canberra: Bureau of Tourism Research.

Weiler, B. and Hall, C.M. (1991) 'Meeting the needs of the recreation and tourism partnership: A comparative study of tertiary education programmes in Australia and Canada', *Leisure Options: Australian Journal of Leisure and Recreation*, 1(2): 7–14.

Weiler, B. and Hall, C.M. (eds) (1992) *Special Interest Tourism*, London: Belhaven Press.

Welch, D. (1991) *The Management of Urban Parks*, Harlow: Longman.

Westover, T. (1985) 'Perceptions of crime and safety in three midwestern parks', *Professional Geographer*, 37: 410–20.

Whatmore, S. (1993) 'Sustainable rural geographies', *Progress in Human Geography*, 17(4): 538–47.

White, A., Barker, V. and Tantrigama, G. (1997) 'Using integrated coastal management and economics to conserve coastal tourism resources in Sri Lanka', *Ambio*, 26(6): 335–44.

White, G. (1972) 'Geography and public policy', *Professional Geographer*, 24: 101–4.

White, K. and Walker, M. (1982) 'Trouble in the travel account', *Annals of Tourism Research*, 9(1): 37–56.

White, L., Jr (1967) 'The historical roots of our ecological crisis', *Science*, 155(10 March): 1203–7.

Whitehead, J.W.R. (1993) *The Making of the Urban Landscape*, Oxford: Blackwell.

Whyte, D. (1978) 'Have second homes gone into hibernation?', *New Society*, 45: 286–8.

Wight, P.A. (1993) 'Sustainable ecotourism: Balancing economic, environmental and social goals within an ethical framework', *Journal of Tourism Studies*, 4(2): 54–66.

Wight, P.A. (1995) 'Sustainable ecotourism: Balancing economic, environmental and social goals within an ethical framework', *Tourism Recreation Research*, 20(1): 5–13.

Wight, P.A. (1998) 'Tools for sustainability analysis in planning and managing tourism and recreation in the destination', in C.M. Hall and A.A. Lew (eds) *Sustainable Tourism Development: A Geographical Perspective*, Harlow: Addison Wesley Longman, pp. 75–91.

Wilhelm, K. (1990) *Journeys: The Dynamics of Specialty Tourists to Ireland*, unpublished Ph.D. thesis, University of Maryland College Park.

Williams, A. (2000) 'Consuming hospitality: Learning from post-modernism?', in C. Lashley and A. Morrison (eds) *In Search of Hospitality: Theoretical Perspectives and Debates*, Oxford: Butterworth Heinemann, pp. 217–32.

Williams, A. and Zelinsky, W. (1970) 'On some patterns of international tourism flows', *Economic Geography*, 46(4): 549–67.

Williams, A.M. and Hall, C.M. (2000) 'Tourism and migration: New relationships between production and consumption', *Tourism Geographies*, 2(1): 5–27.

Williams, A.M. and Hall, C.M. (2001) 'Tourism, migration, circulation and mobility: The contingencies of tme and place', in C.M. Hall and A.M. Williams (eds) *Tourism and Migration*, Dordrecht: Kluwer.

Williams, A.M. and Morgan, R. (1995) 'Beach awards and rating systems', *Shore and Beach*, 63(4): 29–33.

Williams, A.M. and Shaw, G. (1998) 'Tourism and the environment: Sustainability and economic restructuring', in C.M. Hall and A.A. Lew (eds) *Sustainable Tourism Development: Geographical Perspectives*, Harlow: Addison Wesley Longman, pp. 49–59.

Williams, A.M. and Shaw, G. (eds) (1988) *Tourism and Economic Development: Western European Experiences*, London: Belhaven Press.

Williams, A.M. and Shaw, G. (eds) (1991) *Tourism and Economic Development: Western European Experiences*, 2nd edn, London: Belhaven.

Williams, A.M., King. R. and Warnes, A.M. (1997) 'A place in the sun: International retirement migration from Northern to Southern Europe', *European Urban and Regional Studies*, 4: 15–34.

Williams, C.H. (1985) *Language Planning, Marginality and Regional Development in the Irish Gaeltacht*, Discussion paper in Geolinguistics No. 10, Stoke-on-Trent: Department of Geography and Recreation Studies, North Staffordshire Polytechnic.

Williams, D. and Kaltenborn, B. (1999) 'Leisure places and modernity: The use and meaning of recreational cottages in Norway and the USA'. in D. Cronin (ed.) *Leisure/Tourism Geographies: Practices and Geographical Knowledge*, London: Routledge, pp. 214–31.

Williams, G.H. (1962) *Wilderness and Paradise in Christian Thought*, New York: Harper & Brothers.

Williams, R. (1976) *Keywords*, London: Fontana.

Williams, S. (1995) *Recreation in the Urban Environment*, London: Routledge.

Williams, S. (1998) *Tourism Geography*, London: Routledge.

Williams, W.M. (1979) 'Some applications in social geography', in P. Whiteley (ed.) *Geography*, London: Sussex Books, pp. 115–26.

Willis, A. (1992) *Women and Crime. Key Findings from the Report on Crime Prevention in the Leicester City Challenge Area*, Leicester: School of Social Work, Leicester University.

Winsberg, M.P. (1966) 'Overseas travel by American civilians since World War II', *Journal of Geography*, 65: 73–9.

Winter, M. (1987) 'Farm-based tourism and conservation in the uplands', *Ecos: A Review of Conservation*, 5(3): 10–15.

Winterbottom, D. (1967) 'How much urban space do we need', *Journal of the Royal Town Planning Institute*, 53: 144–7.

Withington, W. (1961) 'Upland resorts and tourism in Indonesia: Some recent trends', *The Geographical Review*, 51: 418–23.

Withyman, W. (1985) 'The ins and outs of international travel and tourism data', *International Tourism Quarterly*, Special Report No. 55.

Witt, S. and Martin, C. (1989) 'Demand forecasting in tourism and recreation', in C.P. Cooper (ed.) *Progress in Tourism, Recreation and Hospitality Management*, Vol. 1, London: Belhaven Press, pp. 4–32.

Witt, S. and Martin, C. (1992) *Modelling and Forecasting Demand in Tourism*, London: Academic Press.

Witt, S., Brooke, M. and Buckley, P. (1991) *The Management of International Tourism*, London: Routledge.

Wolfe, R.J. (1951) 'Summer cottages in Ontario', *Economic Geography*, 27(1): 10–32.

Wolfe, R.J. (1952) 'Wasage Beach: The divorce from the geographic environment', *Canadian Geographer*, 1(2): 57–65.

Wolfe, R.J. (1964) 'Perspectives on outdoor recreation: A bibliographical survey', *The Geographical Review*, 54(2): 203–38.

Wolfe, R.J. (1967) 'Recreational travel: The new migration', *Geographical Bulletin*, 9: 73–9.

Wolfe, R.J. (1970) 'Discussion of vacation homes, environmental preferences and spatial behaviour', *Journal of Leisure Research*, 2(1): 85–7.

Women's Equality Unit (1993) *Women and Safety Project*, Leicester: Leicester City Council.

Wong, P. (1986) 'Tourism development and resorts on the east coast of Peninsula Malaysia'. *Singapore Journal of Tropical Geography*, 7(2): 152–62.

Wong, P. (1990) 'Recreation in the coastal areas of Singapore', in P. Fabbri (ed.) *Recreational Use of Coastal Areas*, Dordrecht: Kluwer Academic, pp. 53–62.

Wong, P. (1993a) 'Island tourism development in Peninsula Malaysia: Environmental perspective', in P. Wong (ed.) *Tourism vs Environment: The Case for Coastal Areas*, Dordrecht: Kluwer Academic, pp. 83–98.

Wong, P. (ed.) (1993b) *Tourism vs Environment: The Case for Coastal Areas*, Dordrecht: Kluwer Academic.

Woo, Kyung-Sik (1996) *Korean Tourists' Urban Activity Patterns in New Zealand*, unpublished research report, Auckland: Master of Business Studies, Massey University at Albany.

Wood, R.E. (2000) 'Caribbean cruise tourism: Globalization at sea', *Annals of Tourism Research*, 27(2): 345–70.

World Tourism Organisation (WTO) (1981) *Guidelines for the Collection and Presentation of Domestic and International Tourism Statistics*, Madrid: World Tourism Organisation.

World Tourism Organisation (WTO) (1983) *Definitions Concerning Tourism Statistics*, Madrid: World Tourism Organisation.

World Tourism Organisation (WTO) (1985) *The Role of Transnational Tourism Enterprises in the Development of Tourism*, Madrid: World Tourism Organisation.

World Tourism Organisation (WTO) (1991a) *Guidelines for the Collection and Presentation of Domestic and International Tourism Statistics*, Madrid: World Tourism Organisation.

World Tourism Organisation (WTO) (1991b) *Resolutions of International Conference on Travel and Tourism, Ottawa, Canada*, Madrid: World Tourism Organisation.

World Tourism Organisation (WTO) (1996) *International Tourism Statistics*, Madrid: World Tourism Organisation.

World Tourism Organisation (WTO) (1998) *WTO Revises Forecasts for Asian Tourism*, Press Release, 27 January, Madrid: World Tourism Organisation.

World Tourism Organisation (WTO) (2001) *Millennium Tourism Boom in 2001*, Press Release, 31 January, Madrid: World Tourism Organisation.

World Travel and Tourism Council (WTTC) (2000) *Tourism Satellite Accounting Confirms Travel and Tourism As World's Foremost Economic Activity*, WTTC Press Release, 11 May.

World Travel and Tourism Council (WTTC) (2001a) *World Travel and Tourism Council Forecast Places Tourism among Leading Economic and Employment Generators*, WTTC Press Release, 8 May.

World Travel and Tourism Council (WTTC) (2001b) *Demographic Trends and Economic Research Lead International Tourism Conferences*, WTTC Press Release, 7 May.

Worster, D. (1977) *Nature's Economy: A History of Ecological Ideas*, Cambridge: Cambridge University Press.

Wrathall, J.E. (1980) 'Farm-based holidays', *Town and Country Planning*, 49(6): 194–5.

Wright, D. (trans.) (1957) *Beowulf*, Harmondsworth: Penguin.

Wright, J. (1980) 'Wilderness, Waste and history', *Habitat*, 8(1): 27–31.

Wu, C-T. (1982) 'Issues of tourism and socioeconomic development', *Annals of Tourism Research*, 9: 317–30.

Yoon, H-K. and Bedford, R. (1999) 'Korean visitors to New Zealand: A case of unsustainable tourism', *New Zealand Journal of Geography*, 108: 7–11.

Young, G. (1973) *Tourism: Blessing or Blight*, Harmondsworth: Penguin.

Young, T. (1996) 'Modern urban parks', *The Geographical Review*, 85(4): 535–51.

Young, M. and Wilmott, P. (1973) *The Symmetrical Family*, London: Routledge & Kegan Paul.

Zetter, F. (1971) *The Evolution of Country Park Policy*, Cheltenham: Countryside Commission.

Zurick, D.N. (1992) 'Adventure travel and sustainable tourism in the peripheral economy of Nepal', *Annals of the Association of American Geographers*, 82: 608–28.

Zuzanek, J., Beckers, T. and Peters, P. (1998) 'The "harried leisure class" revisited: Dutch and Canadian trends in the use of time from the 1970s to the 1990s', *Leisure Studies*, 17(1): 1–20.

INDEX